The Astro Twins
2025
Horoscope

Authors: Tali Edut, Ophira Edut
Managing Editor: Lisa M. Sundry
Copy Editor: Amy Anthony
Contributing Editors: Felicia Bender, Matthew Swann,
James Kerti, Jennifer Karnik, Stevie Goldstein
Research Editor: Stephanie Gailing

Cover Illustration © 2024 by Bodil Jane
Book Design: Yvette L. Robinson
Interior Illustrations: Will Dudley, Yvette L. Robinson
Cover Photo: Brittany Ambridge

TABLE OF CONTENTS

TREND REPORT
THE ASTROTWINS' GLOBAL PREDICTIONS FOR THE YEAR AHEAD

WELCOME TO 2025
the *Year* of
The Divine Pendulum

WHAT'S IN THE STARS FOR ALL OF US?

Back and forth we go! The planetary pendulum swings into wildly unscripted terrain in 2025, producing a brand-new story arc for humans to grapple with. We're not just talking about a garden-variety Mercury retrograde or supermoon here. The slow-moving outer planets, which shape society and larger trends, are the key players in the consciousness-shifting trajectory of 2025.

Evolutionary Pluto has reached cruising altitude in Aquarius, spending its first full year in this high-minded air sign, its zodiac home until 2044. The Age of Aquarius is officially underway, disrupting every industry and bringing rapid advancements in fields like science, technology, finance, fashion, space travel and medicine. Is there an AI chatbot for that? Bet your Bitcoin there is.

In 2025, three momentous planets—Saturn, Uranus and Neptune—will follow in icy Pluto's wake. Each one swings forward into a new zodiac sign for a portion of the year, giving us a glimpse of what's in store for the second half of the decade. And whoa! The next phase of the game is gonna hit different. Both Saturn and Neptune depart the watery well of Pisces and launch into fiery Aries' field—a big deal for Neptune especially, which has been in its home sign of Pisces since 2011. In between these two heavenly bodies, Uranus zips into ingenious Gemini, pulling out of the Taurean trench it's been stuck in since 2018.

When an outer planet changes signs, humanity takes a step in a new direction. It's been nearly 30 years since Saturn's footprint pressed into Aries from 1996 to 1998. In the case of Neptune and Uranus, many of us will experience these cosmic cycles for the first time in our lives. To wit, Neptune's last visit to Aries was from 1862 to 1875, and Uranus was in Gemini from 1941 to 1949.

But wait! Just as we begin to process these metamorphic transitions, all three planets oscillate back to the same zodiac positions that they started the year with. Record scratch! Was it all a dream? Not exactly. But it's definitely a sneak peek of what's to come. In 2026, Saturn and Neptune return for longer tours through Aries (two and 13 years, respectively) while Uranus buzzes back into Gemini for another seven years. Take notes! You'll need them next year.

If the pendulum swing of 2025 discombobulates us, here's where the "divine" part comes in. On January 11, the fateful lunar North Node slips into esoteric Pisces, opening the gateways to subconscious activity until July 26, 2026. Times of uncertainty can be catalysts for developments in the arts, spirituality and healing. This year, we are invited to reach beyond our day-to-day "3D" reality for a sense of meaning, as well as some emotional relief. It's also a 9 Universal Year, a year of sacred revelations and release as we prepare for a new nine-year numerological cycle to begin in 2026.

While we're all processing our feelings and spiritual downloads, the karmic South Node plants in sensual, pragmatic Virgo for this same 18-month period. There's no ignoring our connection to Mother Earth or the impact of the climate crisis on humanity. To borrow a lyric from Pisces Chappell Roan (who was born while the nodes were in Virgo and Pisces), we're "coming face-to-face with 'I told you so.'"

This Pisces/Virgo "earth magick" vibe explains how a mushroom made its way onto the cover of our 2025 Horoscope book, illustrated by artist Bodil Jane. (Although the amanita muscaria is a visual beauty, it's not one to ingest for, er, medicinal purposes.) These incredible organisms may hold the key to our survival. (Seriously!)

Renowned mycologist Paul Stamets lays out the true magic of mushrooms in his TED Talk, "6 Ways Mushrooms Can Save The World," which at this writing has been viewed over 8 million times. Spoiler alert: It's not about a psychedelic voyage. The mycelium network—the threadlike roots of mushrooms that go deep underground and branch out across the entire planet in a fascinating community of connection—is what Stamets calls "Earth's natural Internet."

Fun(gi) fact: Mushrooms hold soil together and break down nutrients that feed plants and trees, giving rise to the entire ecosystem of living things. They clean up industrial waste and eat polluted soil for lunch. They give us antibiotics to cure viral diseases.

That's not to dismiss their impact on another network, the neurological one. Psilocybin, the hallucinogenic chemical in certain mushroom strains, is being hailed as a groundbreaking treatment for depression, anxiety, ADHD, mood disorders. Microdoses of psilocybin have been touted as a way to increase sociability and creativity.

Mushrooms are also due to be hot with Big Pharma for 2025. Projections made by the Canadian drug company Optimi Health—which is licensed to produce GMP-grade psilocybin and functional mushrooms for the health and wellness markets—suggest that the legal psychedelics industry could generate over $10 billion annually by 2027. There's gold in this mold!

Will our connection to the divine all come down to 'dosing? Or maybe it's "dowsing," the metaphysical technique of using a pendulum to answer a probing question.

Jokes aside, we should not sleep on the magic of the simpler things, especially not in 2025. At first glance, a pendulum may appear to be little more than a weight on a string. In reality, this device packs a serious punch.

With gravity as their guide, pendulums have been used to measure time and distance since the era of the Mesopotamians five thousand years ago. Ancient Egyptians used a pendulum to measure and build the Great Pyramid of Giza. Galileo's discoveries about the arc of a pendulum's swing were fundamental to our ability to track hours, minutes and seconds on a clock. In 1851, French physicist Léon Foucault demonstrated the Earth's rotation using a pendulum that is now named after him.

Even as we make our way into outer space, humans are still universally bound by gravity. In the Age of Aquarius, discovering what connects us is more important than splintering ourselves with artificial divisions. During the Year of the Divine Pendulum, our survival may depend on (finally) surrendering the myth of "rugged individualism" and embracing a new, networked way of life.

In other words, what if we become more like the living, breathing branches of mycelium sharing resources, energy and instinctive wisdom? After all, these fantastic fungi have survived for 1.3 billion years, while humans have only been around for roughly 300,000.

Could the new arc of humanity be, "as below, so above"? That certainly sounds like a swing in the right direction, even if it comes with a string attached.

GROUNDED IN LOVE,
TALI & OPHI

2025 Highlights

THE FATEFUL LUNAR NODES SWITCH INTO PISCES (NORTH) AND VIRGO (SOUTH) ON JANUARY 11

The ethereal meets the material this January 11, as the destiny-directing lunar nodes launch a new 18-month journey through dreamy Pisces and practical Virgo. This spiritual cycle, which last took place from Jun 23, 2006 – Dec 18, 2007, puts a focus on healing in every way, from our energetic and emotional bodies to our physical ones. Artificial boundaries dissolve under the North Node in Pisces' spell, inviting us to discover new dimensions of the human experience. Meanwhile, the South Node in Virgo challenges us to live in greater attunement with Mother Earth. Goodbye micromanagement, hello mindfulness. It's time to embrace a holistic, heart-centered way of living. This pull toward a spiritual, compassionate and intuitive path will feel like a relief after the warmongering, ideologically divided Aries-Libra nodal cycle that began July 17, 2023 and finally wraps on January 11, 2025. Take stock of the relationship shifts and progress on personal initiatives that you've made since then. We're betting you've grown mightily!

MOTIVATOR MARS KICKS OFF 2025 IN RETROGRADE

Don't rush those resolutions! Go-getter Mars begins 2025 in full retrograde mode, continuing a reverse commute that began December 6, 2024, in passionate, regal Leo. The feisty red planet remains in reverse until February 23, 2025, backing into domestic Cancer on January 6. While Mars in Leo typically fires us up for bold moves and dramatic action, the retrograde cools that energy, asking us to hold back on launching any major initiatives. Instead of pushing for the spotlight, begin the year by reflecting on your personal power and motivations. Have you been seeking attention for the right reasons? Knowing the difference between fame and notoriety is important now. Keep hotheaded instincts in check. Once Mars slips into emo Cancer on January 6, it could be hard to tear yourself out of your hibernation station. Cozy up, but try not to isolate. With this rabble-rousing energy focused on home and family life, you may need to sort out some post-holiday feelings and set firmer boundaries with your inner circle.

JUPITER BEGINS THE YEAR IN GEMINI

Curiosity is piquing AND peaking this year as boundless Jupiter continues its yearlong trek through inquisitive, variety-loving Gemini. This cycle, which began on May 25, 2024 and lasts until June 9, 2025, powers up platonic partnerships and peer relationships with excitable, expansive energy. Mingle and network but take your time with formalizing agreements until Jupiter turns direct this February 4. New developments in education, transportation and media can surge in the first half of 2025, but since Jupiter is in a tough "detriment" position here—opposite its home sign of Sagittarius—it might take a while to get these innovations in motion. (Cue the electric vehicle market.) Lead with intellectual curiosity while this cycle lasts through June 9. Consider multiple perspectives rather than rushing to conclusions. With Jupiter's big-talking tendencies and Gemini's double-talking ones, fact-checking will be essential, especially in the age of AI and deepfakes.

MERCURY TURNS RETROGRADE THREE TIMES

Mark your calendar for these celestial speed bumps! Messenger Mercury spins retrograde three times this year, a signal-scrambling cycle which can skew information, screw with schedules and bring back people from the past. The first retrograde, from March 15 to April 7, straddles combative Aries and compassionate Pisces, pushing us to slow down and rethink impulsive choices while diving into our emotional depths. Beware a tendency to slip into denial or romanticize. Rose-colored glasses are NOT the accessory to rock this spring. Round two, from July 18 to August 11, crackles in fiery Leo, creating drama in creativity, leadership and dating. Deploy those ego checks! The final retrograde, November 9 to 29, kicks off in Sagittarius before shifting into intense Scorpio on the 18th, revealing hidden truths.

Retrogrades call for reflection, course-correction and lots of patience. Use these forced timeouts to focus on "re" activities: revising, reuniting, reviewing, rethinking.

ONE ECLIPSE SERIES ENDS (ARIES-LIBRA) AND ANOTHER KEEPS ROLLING ALONG (VIRGO-PISCES)

The eclipses, which move in the same cadence as the lunar nodes, will also say goodbye to Aries and Libra this year and shift into Virgo and Pisces. March 29 marks the final Aries solar (new moon) eclipse, bringing profound personal epiphanies. Where have you been trudging forward on an independent path since April 2023 and what changes need to be implemented in certain partnerships? This eclipse invites you to wrap it up with a bow and a bang. Two weeks later, the first Virgo eclipse since 2016 arrives with the March 14 full moon—a total lunar eclipse. Take inventory of your health and habits: How can you hack your routines to make life flow more seamlessly? The fall eclipse season starts with the September 7 total lunar eclipse in Pisces, throwing life into a surreal two-week crucible. Every belief and boundary may be up for examination until the sensible solar eclipse in Virgo brings back certainty with the September 21 new moon—the second in a rare back-to-back pair in Virgo this year! With this eclipse series waging on until February 2027, balancing fantasy with reality will be a delicate dance.

VENUS TURNS RETROGRADE THIS SPRING

Starting March 1, you'll need to get real about your love goals or your overall relationship patterns. Ardent Venus flips into a six-week retrograde, which could create

a temporary power outage for all things romantic. This cycle happens every 18 months as Venus shifts from being an evening star (visible in the sky at dusk) to a morning star (rising just before dawn). Metaphorically, we have a chance to put old love stories to bed and rewrite a fresh chapter. During this tense period compassion and compromise may go AWOL. To make matters more complicated, 2025's Venus retrograde in self-centered Aries (March 1 to 27) and gullible Pisces (March 27 to April 12) could mean that your prince or princess may revert into a wretched frog right before your eyes. Don't slip into denial. This is a time to take an unblinking look at reality while also reviewing your past patterns. If you're planning a wedding between March 1 and April 12, we recommend doing a City Hall ceremony beforehand or waiting to sign the marriage license until after April 12. Another option? Renew your vows on your one-year anniversary.

JUPITER IN CANCER TAKES HOME ON THE ROAD

On June 9, Jupiter heads into cozy Cancer for the first time since 2013-14. Talk about a planetary paradox! Worldly, nomadic Jupiter drops anchor in home-loving Cancer for a year this June 9. If that's not weird enough, Jupiter is actually "exalted" in Cancer, meaning the Crab's castle is its most potent place in the zodiac. After spending a year in "detriment" in Gemini, this transit is quite a code switch for the red-spotted titan. Between now and July 30, 2026, the buzzy energy subsides and our capacity for intimacy and emotional intelligence expands. Jupiter-in-Cancer cycles can bring developments in social protection and care for children and families. Housing, food security and domestic stability can also become key issues to resolve, especially as climate change impacts geographically livable zones. Who are the people in your innermost circle? Whether you're blood related or "chosen family," Jupiter in Cancer can bring a joyful sense of connection. And since this globe-trotting planet rules travel, the second half of 2025 could be an optimal time to visit your ancestral homeland and connect to your roots.

SATURN SWINGS BETWEEN PISCES AND ARIES

Among the planets having a "divine pendulum" swing in 2025 is stoic, structured Saturn, who divides the year between spiritual Pisces and aggressive Aries. The ringed taskmaster first parked in Pisces on March 7, 2023. Ever since, it's been challenging us to organize the most chaotic, unscripted parts of our lives, like mental health, spiritual beliefs and artistic expression. While Saturn is a boundary hound, Pisces is a boundary dissolver. Talk about a head trip! Literally, this cycle has dovetailed with developments in psychedelic legalization as treatments for everything from depression to creative blocks. This push-pull continues until May 24, when Saturn darts forward into Aries until September 1. The energy shifts dramatically then, as we flip from introspection to daring initiative. Personal responsibility (rather than Piscean victimhood) becomes the new flex, as Saturn in Aries pushes us to take ownership for our actions and evolve accordingly. We haven't experienced this cycle for nearly three decades, as the ringed planet's last visit to the Ram's realm was from April 1996 to October 1998.

While Saturn in Aries encourages bold action and self-reliance, it also warns against impulsive risks. As it serves lessons in conflict management, it reveals the detrimental impact of warmongering, gun violence and use of weapons of mass destruction. Got some original ideas brewing? You're invited to architect a new, self-directed path, as you lay the groundwork for personal (and societal!) reinvention. But advance slowly with new initiatives under cautious Saturn's watch. This surge of novel, enterprising energy kicks up again when Saturn settles into Aries from February 13, 2026 to April 12, 2028.

URANUS DOES A PENDULUM PIVOT BETWEEN TACTILE TAURUS AND INTELLECTUAL GEMINI

Also on the celestial swing set in 2025 is innovative, sci-fi Uranus, who does a back and forth between tenacious Taurus and gregarious Gemini. From July 7 to November 7, the planet of progress will briefly dip into Gemini, cracking the seal on a new set of possibilities. In the first half of 2025, however, Uranus is busy finishing its seven-year tour through earthy, sensible Taurus, where it's been revolutionizing finance, agriculture and labor since May 2018. Uranus in Taurus has transformed our material lives, producing a near-cashless society ("Venmo me!") along with fluctuating interest rates and cryptocurrency's slow but real adoption. In Gemini, the techie planet's focus shifts to the intellectual and interpersonal. Historically, Uranus in Gemini has brought metamorphic shifts in communication technologies, such as the rise of the telegraph and commercial television during its last tour through Gemini from 1941-49. And the telescope! Uranus was discovered by William and Caroline Herschel when it was transiting through Gemini in 1781.

Get ready for rapid developments and total disruptions to Gemini-ruled industries: telecommunications, data security, transportation, education and the media. In a flash, Uranus can break us free from outdated systems and incite us to embrace futuristic replacements. Keep up if you can! Everything from the cars we drive (or fly!) to the way we educate our children is up for grabs. Flexible, hybrid and fractional roles may become the new normal for employees. It's worth noting that past Uranus-in-Gemini transits have dovetailed with many wars—the War of Independence, the Civil War, WW2, the Arab-Israeli War and the Indo-Pakistani War to name a few. As we enter 2025, battles are raging across many continents, indicating that these trends may continue well into the second half of the decade.

NEPTUNE STEPS INTO ARIES FOR THE FIRST TIME SINCE 1862-75

Here's one for the history books! On March 30, numinous Neptune leaves its home sign of dreamy Pisces for the first time since April 2011 and makes a landmark (in our lifetime) trek into action-oriented Aries. For the past fourteen years Neptune has been on a mindfulness pilgrimage and a deep dive through the human psyche. We have the yoga studios, trauma-informed programs, plant medicine ceremonies and worldwide embrace of the "woo" to show for it. As Neptune surfs into Aries from March 30 to October 22, the shift may feel jarring. Neptune is compassionate, dreamy, fluid and soft. Aries is aggressive, daring, entitled and strong. What happens when the twain meet? We need to look all the way back to 1862-75 for clues. Historically, Neptune in Aries has coincided with periods of radical spiritual and ideological change. We saw this in the 1860s when causes like abolitionism drove the American Civil War. Visionary advances have also exploded, like the first printing press and camera obscura in 1544. Or the opening of the New York Stock Exchange in 1865 and the first "tube," London's Tower Subway, in 1872.

Autocrat alert! There may be a rise in cult-like leaders during Neptune in Aries. Martyr movements motivated by lofty ideals could draw zealots who are willing to fight to the death. On a personal level, this cycle provides the courage to build your dream. Watch out for a veiled thirst for power as you ascend along your path. Although Neptune swings back into Pisces on October 22, take notes! This is a preview of a longer, thirteen-year cycle that begins again when Neptune returns to Aries from January 26, 2026 to March 23, 2039.

PLUTO SPENDS ITS FIRST FULL YEAR IN AQUARIUS

The Age of Aquarius is officially on! Alchemical Pluto, the planet of transformation, power and rebirth, continues the unbroken leg of its journey through Aquarius, which began on November 19, 2024. Pluto first rolled into Aquarius for a brief spell on March 23, 2023. The entire transit lasts until January 19, 2044. This radical transit, which last occurred from 1778-98 during the end of the American Revolution—and for the whole of the French and Haitian Revolutions—signals profound societal shifts. How do we approach power, wealth and community, especially in this time of space travel, AI, quantum technology and deepfakes? In Aquarius, Pluto burns down our limited ways of thinking. With a push toward collective empowerment, old systems that serve only a few (rather than many) could break down. Over the next nineteen years, "power to the people" could look like radical transformations in all the collective structures that democratic Aquarius rules. It's no secret that climate change has become a crisis. With Pluto in sci-fi Aquarius, there may be groundbreaking developments that reverse the damage as well as a move toward new sources of energy (including nuclear). But will it happen fast enough? And will the entrenched monarchies and oligarchies (governed by Aquarius' opposite sign of Leo) release their stranglehold on the world? We have nearly two decades to find out. Get ready for intense clashes along the way—over everything from airspace to human rights to the ethical use of technology.

BLACK MOON LILITH BRINGS HER INTENSE WAKEUP CALLS TO THREE ZODIAC SIGNS

Shadow-dancer Lilith, a point in the sky associated with the female journey through scorn, rage, empowerment and sexual liberation, is moving through three zodiac signs in 2025. Until March 27, Lilith tours justice-oriented Libra, challenging us to redefine power within partnerships and to fight oppressive laws. Since this cycle began on June 29, 2024, women's rights became a key issue in the U.S. Presidential Election. On March 27, 2025, Lilith plunges into sultry Scorpio, taking us deeper into the heart of emotional truth and taboo topics. Scorpio's intensity stirs raw conversations about sexuality, control, and power, bringing hidden issues to light, especially in areas like reproductive rights and emotional intimacy. The year wraps with Lilith blazing into truth-seeking Sagittarius on December 20, sparking a desire for freedom, exploration, and unfiltered authenticity. Repressive religious regimes—especially those that restrict women's fundamental rights—could be met with a fiery global resistance as we move into 2026.

THE YEAR OF THE WOOD SNAKE BEGINS JANUARY 29

The Lunar New Year on January 29 ushers in the Year of the Wood Snake, a time for slow, steady growth and transformation. Like the serpent shedding its skin, we're called to release what no longer serves us, making space for evolution. Like the Western sign of Taurus, which the Snake is associated with, this year favors strategy, patience and precision—encouraging us to plan carefully and strike only when the timing is ideal. While the pace may feel subdued, if you play the long game, you can build something solid. With the Wood element promoting growth, thoughtful, subtle movements lead to lasting change. Trust the process and let the Snake's strategic wisdom guide you. This is the first Year of the Wood Snake since 1965. That year was marked by intensified warfare in Vietnam and Civil Rights action, such as MLK's four-day march from Selma to Montgomery.

2025 IS A 9 UNIVERSAL YEAR

Get ready for a sacred year of closure and completion. In numerology, 2025 is a 9 Universal Year (2+0+2+5=9) rounding out the full cycle before we reset with a 1 Universal Year in 2026. Globally, we're tasked with letting go of outdated systems and beliefs that no longer serve the collective good. This year will push us to shift from ego-driven actions to a more compassionate, humanitarian approach. The energy of 9 is a lot like Pisces, the final zodiac sign, encouraging surrender, spiritual growth and embracing flow instead of forcing progress. This is a time for healing, forgiveness and creating space for new beginnings as we lead with our hearts and contribute to building a more connected, compassionate world.

ZODIAC SIGNS

♈	ARIES
♉	TAURUS
♊	GEMINI
♋	CANCER
♌	LEO
♍	VIRGO
♎	LIBRA
♏	SCORPIO
♐	SAGITTARIUS
♑	CAPRICORN
♒	AQUARIUS
♓	PISCES

PLANETS

☉	SUN
☽	MOON
♂	MARS
☿	MERCURY
♀	VENUS
♄	SATURN
♃	JUPITER
♆	NEPTUNE
♅	URANUS
♇	PLUTO

MOONS

FM	FULL MOON
NM	NEW MOON
LE	LUNAR ECLIPSE
SE	SOLAR ECLIPSE

TAROT CARD OF THE YEAR

THE HIGH PRIESTESS

THE HIGH PRIESTESS
INTUITION, MYSTERY, INNER WISDOM

In 2025, the mysterious High Priestess emerges as the Tarot card of the year, inviting us to peer within and trust our deepest wisdom. Her presence signals a year of heightened intuition, spiritual awakening, and secrets waiting to be revealed. As the veil between the conscious and unconscious thins, the High Priestess urges us to tune in to the quiet, guiding voice of the soul. Mystical insights and deep self-discovery are on the horizon and in the hidden realms of your psyche.

CRYSTAL OF THE YEAR

LEPIDOLITE
CALM, BALANCE, TRANQUILITY

As Saturn, Neptune, and Uranus pivot between zodiac signs in 2025, Lepidolite's balancing properties provide a steadying force. Known for its high lithium content, this stone is a powerful mood stabilizer, often called upon for calming anxiety and emotional turbulence. While the outer world fluctuates wildly in 2025, Lepidolite (which means "scale" in Greek) supports with balanced clarity and resilience. Its gentle vibrations promote deep relaxation and sleep— fabulous for a year when the enchanting Pisces North Node brings messages through our dreams.

THE SUN IN
2025

The Zodiac Seasons

Break out the cake and candles! On the third week of every month, the Sun changes signs and initiates a brand-new zodiac "season." These four-week cycles show where opportunities are brightest and where your efforts will yield the sparkliest results. Think of each solar season like a costume party. What is it like to live like a Gemini or a Pisces for a month? Try it on for size!

season	focus
CAPRICORN **DEC 21, 2024** **4:21 AM** Winter Solstice	Earthy Capricorn's ambitious nature makes this the time to aim higher, and then put in a consistent and persistent effort to reach that goal. Network with the VIPs during Capricorn season; mentor someone younger or newer to the game.
AQUARIUS **JAN 19** **3:00PM**	Weird is wonderful during eccentric Aquarius season. Allow yourself to stand out in the crowd while also embracing the spirit of community. You can be different and belong when this air sign rules the skies.
PISCES **FEB 18** **5:07AM**	Compassionate, creative Pisces season is a time to feel and heal. Allow yourself to sit with uncomfortable emotions during this awakening water sign cycle. Dissect triggers and turn them into art. Your empathy will expand in the process.
ARIES **MAR 20** **5:01AM** Spring Equinox	Fiery Aries is the first sign in the zodiac, making this season all about blazing trails and starting fresh. Get to know what makes you tick by daring to do more things independently.
TAURUS **APR 19** **3:56PM**	Rooted earth sign Taurus reminds us of the importance of comfort and security. Review your finances, update your accounts, create a budget—both for practical necessities and life-enhancing luxuries. Inspect your personal goods—clothing, furniture, dwelling, accessories—and ensure everything is in good working order.

season	focus
GEMINI MAY 20 2:55PM	How well do you play with others? Gemini is the air sign of cooperation and communication. Stop making assumptions (or assertions) and start asking questions. That's how you'll master the art of creating win-wins.
CANCER JUN 20 10:42PM Summer Solstice	Home sweet sanctuary! Nurturing Cancer is the water sign that rules family and domestic matters. Get back in touch with relatives and spend quality time with closer friends. Make your space feel cozy, welcoming and supportive of your current lifestyle.
LEO JUL 22 9:29AM	We all have a special light to shine, as fire sign Leo reminds us. Lift the curtain during this zodiac season and show the world what you're made of. Let your wilder romantic nature come out to play and wear your heart on your sleeve! Put passion into action.
VIRGO AUG 22 4:34PM	Earthy Virgo is the sign of service. Where would a random act of generosity make a difference for someone else? Be humble and helpful. The simplest approach is the best during this season.
LIBRA SEP 22 2:19PM Fall Equinox	Peace, love and harmony! Great ideals, but ones that are seldom lived by. When air sign Libra blows through town, we get a chance to practice being kind, considerate and collaborative. Opposites attract so stay open to different types.
SCORPIO OCT 22 11:51PM	Sultry, transformational Scorpio isn't afraid of life's mysteries—or our animal instincts. This intuitive water sign season challenges us to bring sexy back by allowing ourselves to dive into our deepest desires and longings.
SAGITTARIUS NOV 21 8:36PM	What's happening on the other side of the globe, fence or aisle? Fire sign Sagittarius is the zodiac's ambassador. Reach across so-called boundaries to learn what makes others tick during this season. Travel or start to plan your next amazing journey.
CAPRICORN DEC 21 10:03AM Winter Solstice	The Sun swings back around into Capricorn at the end of every year putting the focus on the traditional side of this sign. Get to know a family custom and look for special ways you can provide support and happiness to your inner circle.

THE MOON IN
2025

MOTIVATE & MANIFEST WITH THE
New & Full Moons

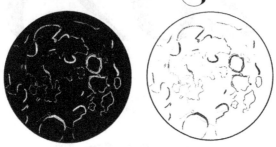

NEW MOONS mark beginnings and are the optimal time to kick off any new projects or plans. Lay the groundwork for what you want to manifest in the coming six months. Set intentions or initiate action while you have this lunar lift creating momentum.

FULL MOONS are ideal manifestation moments to show off and celebrate your hard work of the past six months. Full moons dial up feelings and can provoke emotional outpourings. It's time to cash in or cash out if you're ready for something new.

SUPERMOONS are new or full moons that arrive at the closest distance possible between the moon and Earth. The full supermoon will appear brighter. Both new and full supermoons deliver strong feels and potent manifestation energy.

PLAN YOUR SHORT-TERM GOALS BY THE MOON

Each month, there are four moon phases, spaced one week apart. Set intentions at the new moon, then, do a progress check at the waxing quarter moon. Celebrate results at the full moon. At the waning quarter moon, curate what to keep and what to set aside.

PLAN YOUR LONG-TERM GOALS BY THE MOON

Each new moon falls in a specific zodiac sign. Six months later, a full moon occurs in the very same sign, completing the half-year cycle.

phase	date	focus/celebrate
FULL MOON **CANCER** (24°00')	**JAN 13** 5:27PM	**Celebrate:** Bonds with your family and inner circle of friends, the places where you feel at home, nostalgic memories, creative alone time.
NEW MOON **AQUARIUS** (9°51')	**JAN 29** 7:36AM	**Focus:** Experiment with new technology and techniques, break out of the box with style and social expression, connect to community, activism and humanitarian work.
FULL MOON **LEO** (24°06')	**FEB 12** 8:53AM	**Celebrate:** The unique way that you shine, the people who make your heart sing, your romantic nature, fashion sense, childlike wonder, the places where you feel like a natural leader, your fiercely competitive streak that won't let you quit.
NEW MOON **PISCES** (9°41')	**FEB 27** 7:45PM	**Focus:** Connect to your dreams, spiritual exploration, find creative outlets, give back, inspire others, form supportive alliances, express empathy so people feel seen and understood.
FULL MOON **VIRGO** (23°57')	**MAR 14** 2:55AM	**TOTAL LUNAR ECLIPSE** **Celebrate:** The serenity of a freshly cleaned space, streamlined systems, your helpful spirit, being of service to those in need, taking great care of your body by eating clean and exercising, the magic of nature and natural beauty.
NEW MOON **ARIES** (9°00')	**MAR 29** 6:58AM	**SUPERMOON + PARTIAL SOLAR ECLIPSE** **Focus:** Sharpen your competitive edge, blaze your own trail, take the initiative with people and activities that matter to you, try new things.

phase	date	focus/celebrate
FULL MOON **LIBRA** (23°20′)	**APR 12** 8:22PM	**Celebrate:** The power of partnerships and synergistic connections, dressing up and socializing, transcendent music and the arts, peaceful moments of serenity, the parts of your life that are in beautiful balance.
NEW MOON **TAURUS** (7°47′)	**APR 27** 3:31PM	**SUPERMOON** **Focus:** Define your values, set up healthy and rewarding routines, enjoy arts and culture, simplify complexities, budget, get out in nature.
FULL MOON **SCORPIO** (22°13′)	**MAY 12** 12:56PM	**Celebrate:** Your loyal and caring spirit, intense exchanges, the sexiest parts of yourself, the ways you've transformed your struggles into gold, true friendship, resourcefulness and raw creative expression, your seductive powers.
NEW MOON **GEMINI** (6°06′)	**MAY 26** 11:02PM	**SUPERMOON** **Focus:** Sharpen your communication style, write and make media, pair up on short-term collaborations, socialize with new people, become active in your local community, flirt and joke!
FULL MOON **SAGITTARIUS** (20°39′)	**JUN 11** 3:44AM	**Celebrate:** The spirit of wanderlust, your unvarnished truths, people you love who live far away, the passport stamps you've collected or hope to one day, visionary ideas that you're bringing to life, the beauty of diversity and cross-cultural connections.
NEW MOON **CANCER** (4°08′)	**JUN 25** 6:32AM	**Focus:** Nourish yourself with good food and close friends, spruce up your spaces so you feel at home everywhere, connect to family, spend time near water, get in touch with your emotions.

phase	date	focus/celebrate
FULL MOON **CAPRICORN** (18°50′)	JUL 10 4:37PM	**Celebrate:** People you admire—heroes and mentors, family legacies, customs that you want to carry on, enduring friendships and business relationships, your most ambitious ideas, institutions or organizations that you believe in and support.
NEW MOON **LEO** (2°08′)	JUL 24 3:11PM	**Focus:** Express yourself through art and style, enjoy romance and playtime, spend time with kids, take a leadership role, host and attend glamorous parties, find your place to shine.
FULL MOON **AQUARIUS** (17°00′)	AUG 9 3:55AM	**Celebrate:** Your weirdest ideas, teams and communities where you feel seen and embraced, your sharing and accepting spirit, technology that keeps you connected, hopes and dreams for the future, your idealistic nature that refuses to give up on humanity.
NEW MOON **VIRGO #1** (0°23′)	AUG 23 2:07AM	**Focus:** Embrace healthy routines, work out and eat clean, implement efficient systems, hire service providers and assistants, break projects into actionable steps, be of service, adopt a pet.
FULL MOON **PISCES** (15°23′)	SEP 7 2:09PM	**TOTAL LUNAR ECLIPSE** **Celebrate:** Your secret fantasies, your creative spirit, messages from your dreams, people who inspire you to think beyond current limitations, compassion and empathy, blurry lines that don't need to be sharpened, the beauty in "ugly" things.
NEW MOON **VIRGO #2** (29°05′)	SEP 21 3:54PM	**PARTIAL SOLAR ECLIPSE** **Focus:** Organize your physical and digital spaces, refine your eating and workout routines, systematize workflow, volunteer, streamline your schedule to reduce stress.

phase	date	focus/celebrate
FULL MOON ARIES (14°08')	OCT 6 11:48PM	**Celebrate:** Your inner (and outer) bad bitch, new experiences you're brave enough to try, your competitive nature, every unique feature that makes you a rare individual, your fighting spirit that won't give up.
NEW MOON LIBRA (28°22')	OCT 21 8:25AM	**Focus:** Find synergies, network to build your contact list, nurture romantic relationships, enjoy art, music and fashion, and beautify everything.
FULL MOON TAURUS (13°23')	NOV 5 8:19AM	**SUPERMOON** **Celebrate:** The simple things that bring you joy, the beauty of nature, your favorite music and artists, finding holiday gifts that are sustainable and earth-friendly, creating a comfortable home environment, and food that you love.
NEW MOON SCORPIO (28°12')	NOV 20 1:47AM	**Focus:** Build trusted bonds, share secrets, join forces (and finances), form strategic partnerships, explore your erotic nature, give everything you do more sizzle and spice.
FULL MOON GEMINI (13°04')	DEC 4 6:14PM	**SUPERMOON** **Celebrate:** Build trusted bonds, share secrets, join forces (and finances), form strategic partnerships, explore your erotic nature, give everything you do more sizzle and spice.
NEW MOON SAGITTARIUS (28°25')	DEC 19 8:43PM	**Focus:** Turn each day into an adventure, broaden your social horizons, travel, study and self-development goals, make media, speak your truth.

ECLIPSES IN
2025

Eclipses

THESE YEARLY MOON MOMENTS SHAKE UP LIFE AS WE KNOW IT

Eclipses arrive four to six times each year, igniting unexpected changes and turning points. If you've been mired in indecision, an eclipse may force you to act, whether you're ready or not. Unanticipated events arise and demand a radical change of direction. Since eclipses reveal shadows, get ready for buried truths and secrets to explode into the open. Situations that are no longer "meant to be" are swept away without notice. Shocking though their delivery may be, eclipses help open up space for progress.

SOLAR VERSUS LUNAR ECLIPSES

A **solar eclipse** takes place when the new moon passes between the Sun and the Earth, temporarily blocking out the light of the Sun. The effect is like a spiritual power outage—you either feel wildly off center or your mind becomes crystal clear in the darkness.

Lunar eclipses arrive at full moons. The Earth passes directly between the Sun and the moon, cutting off their "communication" and casting a blood red shadow on the full moon. Situations could pivot abruptly or come to a sudden, unceremonious halt. There's no way around it. During a lunar eclipse, you have to deal with the stormy feelings that arise. Jolting information may come to light that redirects your journey.

MAR 14	MAR 29	SEP 7	SEP 21
Eclipse #1	Eclipse #2	Eclipse #3	Eclipse #4
2:55 AM	6:58AM	10:34PM	3:54PM
Total Lunar Eclipse in Virgo (23°57')	Partial Solar Eclipse in Aries (9°00')	Total Lunar Eclipse in Pisces (15°23')	Partial Solar Eclipse in Virgo (29°05')

Eclipse # 1

MAR 14 (2:55 AM) TOTAL LUNAR ECLIPSE IN VIRGO (23°57')

The first Virgo eclipse since 2016, this total lunar eclipse shines a spotlight on health, routines and service. It's a powerful moment to reassess how well your daily habits support your overall well-being. With Virgo's analytical energy, you can clean up the details of your life, from workflow to eating habits to your self-care practices. Emotional clarity around relationships and work-life balance may also surface, encouraging you to release perfectionism and embrace more sustainable ways of managing your responsibilities.

Eclipse #2

MAR 29 (6:58 AM) PARTIAL SOLAR ECLIPSE IN ARIES (9°00')

This partial solar eclipse in Aries marks the conclusion of a series on the Aries-Libra axis that began in April 2023, bringing closure to themes around self vs. relationships. Take bold, courageous action toward personal goals, especially those that align with your authentic desires. Aries energy is impulsive and pioneering, so this eclipse could propel you into a new chapter of independence, leadership, or self-discovery. Whether you're launching a new project or setting personal boundaries, the key is to prioritize yourself without sacrificing collaboration.

Eclipse # 3

SEP 7 (2:09 PM) TOTAL LUNAR ECLIPSE IN PISCES (15°23')

A dreamy and emotional total lunar eclipse in Pisces brings matters of intuition, spirituality, and creativity to the forefront. Let go of rigid structures and embrace flow and surrender. Here's your cue to release old emotional baggage or patterns that have been holding you back from experiencing peace or connection. Since Pisces rules imagination and compassion, this eclipse is perfect for healing wounds, exploring artistic projects and tapping into your intuitive side. Expect heightened sensitivity, but also a sense of relief as you let go of what's no longer serving your emotional and spiritual growth.

Eclipse # 4

SEP 21 (3:54 PM) PARTIAL SOLAR ECLIPSE IN VIRGO (29°05')

The second Virgo eclipse of the year, this partial solar eclipse at 29° Virgo brings a fresh start to how you manage your time, resources, and daily responsibilities. Since it's also the second in a rare pair of Virgo new moons (the first was on August 23), you could already be well on your way to handling these matters. Virgo's meticulous energy urges you to refine your plans and focus on practicality, efficiency, and self-care. This eclipse provides a push to set new intentions around your work habits, health routines, or even a project that requires detailed attention. It's a great time to create systems that support long-term growth and well-being, while also letting go of perfectionism.

INNER PLANETS IN
2025

Mercury

Messenger Mercury is the ruler of information, communication and our intellectual processes. The closest planet to the Sun, Mercury orbits through each zodiac sign for approximately three weeks. These cycles shape our cultural interests. From the topics we're buzzing about to the ways we communicate, whatever sign Mercury is occupying plays a role.

date	sign	what's going on
JAN 1	SAGITTARIUS	Blue-sky conversations are lit with excitement. Discuss expansion plans with a diverse pool of people, but make sure you research the details before you green-light them.
JAN 8	CAPRICORN	Conversations are serious, goal-oriented, and focused on results. Practicality prevails, but communication can feel rigid or overly formal.
JAN 27	AQUARIUS	Communication takes a visionary, innovative turn. Conversations are future-focused and idealistic, but emotions may be overlooked in favor of logic.
FEB 14	PISCES	Words become dreamy, poetic, and intuitive. Interactions are compassionate and imaginative, but clarity can drift and misunderstandings may occur.
MAR 3	ARIES	Communication is fast and direct. Attention spans are short, so speak in bullet points. Watch for impulsive words and fiery reactivity.
MAR 15	RETROGRADE IN ARIES	Tempers flare and harsh tones cause misunderstandings. Slow down before reacting, and double-check plans to avoid miscommunication or rushed decisions.

date	sign	what's going on
MAR 29	RETROGRADE IN PISCES	Communication gets foggy, and compulsions override logic. Daydreaming takes over, leading to confusion or missed details. Revisit plans with extra care.
APR 7	DIRECT IN PISCES	Clarity returns after a muddled period. Intuition and creativity flow smoothly again, making it easier to express emotions and connect with others on a deeper level.
APR 16	ARIES	Conversations are bold, direct, and action-driven. Expect fast-paced exchanges, but be mindful of bluntness or speaking without thinking.
MAY 10	TAURUS	Conversations slow down and become more thoughtful. People are practical and grounded. Stubbornness may creep in, but decisions are steady and deliberate.
MAY 25	GEMINI	The mind races with curiosity and multitasking rules. Ideas flow quickly, and conversations are lively, but focus can be scattered.
JUN 8	CANCER	Words are infused with emotion. Communication becomes nurturing and intuitive, but mood swings can cloud clarity. Speak from the heart.
JUN 26	LEO	Speak with flair and confidence! Conversations take on a dramatic tone, but watch out for self-centeredness. Creative expression thrives.
JUL 18	RETROGRADE IN LEO	Drama and ego clashes can derail conversations. Watch for overconfidence or misinterpretation. Revisit creative projects and be mindful of how you express yourself.
AUG 11	DIRECT IN LEO	Communication regains its bold, confident flair. Creative projects can move forward, and self-expression becomes clearer. Be mindful of ego trips.

date	sign	what's going on
SEP 2	VIRGO	Communication is detailed, analytical, and efficient. It's time to plan, organize, and solve problems, but don't get lost in perfectionism.
SEP 18	LIBRA	Diplomacy and balance rule conversations. It's all about finding harmony and weighing both sides, but decision-making won't be easy.
OCT 6	SCORPIO	Conversations go deep and reveal hidden truths. Words can be intense, investigative, and transformative—just avoid obsessiveness or secrecy.
OCT 29	SAGITTARIUS	Communication becomes bold, optimistic, and blunt. It's time to talk big ideas and philosophy, but be mindful of exaggeration or tactlessness.
NOV 9	RETROGRADE IN SAGITTARIUS	Plans go awry, and travel or grandiose ideas need revision. Enthusiasm is high, but avoid jumping to conclusions or making promises you can't keep.
NOV 18	RETROGRADE IN SCORPIO	Secrets come to light, and intense conversations resurface. Emotions run deep, so be cautious with power struggles and avoid obsessive thinking. Reflect before you react.
NOV 29	DIRECT IN SCORPIO	Conversations regain intensity but with more focus and control. Secrets that surfaced during the retrograde can now be addressed with clarity and depth.
DEC 11	SAGITTARIUS (until JAN 1, 2026)	Ideas flow freely, with a focus on big-picture thinking and optimism. You'll crave deep, philosophical conversations, but watch out for exaggeration or glossing over details.

Venus

Venus is the planet of love, beauty and luxury, lending its decadent energy to every zodiac sign for three to five weeks each year. Who will we fall for...and how? Venus sets the love language of the moment, determining the right romantic moves for pleasure and passion.

date	sign	what's going on
JAN 2	PISCES	Love becomes dreamy, compassionate, and romantic. Emotions are deep and poetic, but boundaries may blur. Idealism rules relationships and creativity.
FEB 4	ARIES	Passion ignites as love becomes bold and spontaneous. You're ready to take charge in romance, but impatience and impulsiveness can stir drama.
MAR 1	RETROGRADE IN ARIES	Old flames and unresolved issues resurface, urging you to reflect on your approach to love. Avoid impulsive decisions. Take time to reassess desires.
MAR 27	RETROGRADE IN PISCES	Emotions and past relationships come into focus, sparking nostalgia or confusion. Dreamy connections may cloud judgment, so reflect before committing.
APR 12	DIRECT IN PISCES	Clarity returns in love, and romantic dreams can now unfold with a sense of purpose. Compassion flows, but with stronger boundaries in place.
APR 30	ARIES	Love is fiery, spontaneous, and full of excitement. You're drawn to passionate connections, but impatience or a desire for instant gratification could spark drama in relationships..
JUN 6	TAURUS	Love is sensual, stable, and grounded. Relationships focus on pleasure, loyalty, and comfort, but possessiveness or stubbornness may also creep in.

date	sign	what's going on
JUL 4	**GEMINI**	Flirtation and curiosity dominate as love turns lighthearted, intellectual, and social. Keep conversations lively and fun, but beware of scattered or superficial interactions.
JUL 30	**CANCER**	Love becomes nurturing, emotional, and protective. You crave deeper connections and security, but watch out for moodiness or clinginess in relationships.
AUG 25	**LEO**	Romance is grand and dramatic. Self-expression and affection flow boldly, but be mindful of attention-seeking behavior or letting ego drive your love life.
SEP 19	**VIRGO**	Love takes a practical, devoted turn. You show affection through helpful acts and attention to detail, but watch for perfectionism or over-criticism.
OCT 13	**LIBRA**	Romance thrives on balance, harmony, and beauty. Relationships are diplomatic and fair, but indecision and people-pleasing could hinder deeper connections.
NOV 6	**SCORPIO**	Love is intense, passionate, and transformative. Deep bonds are formed, but emotional power struggles or jealousy can lead to turbulence.
NOV 30	**SAGITTARIUS**	Adventure beckons as love becomes free-spirited, bold, and open-minded. You seek excitement and growth in relationships, but commitment might feel restrictive
DEC 24	**CAPRICORN** Until JAN 18, 2026	Love turns serious, responsible, and goal-oriented. You're focused on building lasting commitments, but romance can feel practical and businesslike at times.

Mars

Mars is the planet of action, drive, and ambition, pushing you to take bold steps toward your goals. Mars brings a burst of energy when it transits through a sign for six to eight weeks on average and supports with tackling big projects or asserting yourself in key areas of life. Knowing when to harness Mars' dynamic influence helps you plan for periods of high motivation, but be mindful— Mars can also stir up conflict if not channeled wisely.

date	sign	what's going on
JAN 1	RETROGRADE IN LEO	Creative passions slow down, and you may second-guess bold actions. Old conflicts resurface, particularly around ego or pride. Reevaluate your desires before moving forward.
JAN 6	RETROGRADE IN CANCER	Energy turns inward, making emotional confrontations likely. You may feel less motivated or struggle with moodiness, as old family or home-related issues come to the surface for healing.
FEB 23	DIRECT IN CANCER	Emotional drive returns, and you feel protective and motivated to take care of home and family. Be mindful of passive-aggressive tendencies or emotional outbursts.
APR 18	LEO	Bold, confident, and dramatic, you're ready to take center stage and fight for what you want. Your energy is high, but watch out for overblown pride or over-the-top reactions.
JUN 17	VIRGO	Energy becomes focused and efficient. You'll want to tackle tasks with precision and productivity, but perfectionism or nitpicking could cause frustration.

date	sign	what's going on
AUG 6	**LIBRA**	Action takes a diplomatic turn as you seek balance in conflict. You'll focus on cooperation and harmony, but indecision or avoiding confrontation can heighten tension. Learn the power of negotiation.
SEP 22	**SCORPIO**	Passionate, intense, and fiercely driven, you're ready to pursue your goals with unshakable determination. Watch out for obsession or control issues in relationships or ambitions.
NOV 4	**SAGITTARIUS**	Energy is adventurous, bold, and optimistic. You'll feel motivated to take risks and explore new horizons, but be careful of impulsiveness or reckless behavior.
DEC 15	**CAPRICORN** Until JAN 23, 2026	Disciplined and determined, you're ready to tackle long-term goals with steady ambition. Productivity is high, but avoid becoming too rigid or overworking.

All dates and times in Eastern Time Zone

OUTER PLANETS IN
2025

Jupiter

Jupiter, the planet of expansion and abundance, blesses you with growth opportunities   during year-long tour through each zodiac sign. Whether it's luck in finances, learning, or personal growth, Jupiter helps you plan for periods of optimism and possibility. This is your time to dream big   and pursue goals that push your boundaries!

date	sign	what's going on
JAN 1	RETROGRADE IN GEMINI	Growth slows, and you may revisit old ideas or projects. It's a time to rethink big plans and fine-tune your communication skills. Be cautious of spreading yourself too thin.
FEB 4	DIRECT IN GEMINI	Expansion and learning speed up again. Conversations and opportunities for growth flourish, encouraging curiosity, travel, and exploring new collaborations.
JUN 9	CANCER	Emotional expansion and nurturing energy take the lead. You'll focus on deepening relationships and building a sense of security. This is a time for growth through family, home, and emotional fulfillment.
NOV 11	RETROGRADE IN CANCER (until MAR 10, 2026)	Reflect on how you seek emotional and domestic security. Reassess your connection to family, home, and inner growth, as this retrograde calls for revisiting and realigning emotional priorities.

Saturn

Saturn brings structure, discipline, and long-term success. The ringed taskmaster lends its sobering energy to a single zodiac sign for two to three years, helping you plan for serious commitments, hard work, and personal growth. Saturn asks you to build a strong foundation before reaching for success. Persistence pays off under its watchful eye.

date	sign	what's going on
JAN 1	PISCES	Discipline meets dreams as Saturn helps you structure your spiritual growth and creative pursuits. It's a time to turn fantasies into reality, but stay mindful of escapism or avoiding responsibilities.
MAY 24	ARIES	Time to take bold, decisive action toward your goals. Saturn's presence in Aries encourages leadership and initiative, but be cautious of impatience or a "my way or the highway" attitude.
JUL 13	RETROGRADE IN ARIES	Reflect on how you've been asserting yourself and pursuing your goals. This retrograde invites you to slow down, reassess your leadership style, and correct impulsive actions. It's a time to refine your strategies for long-term success.
SEP 1	RETROGRADE IN PISCES	Rethink your emotional and spiritual priorities. You're revisiting past dreams and reevaluating how to bring structure to your inner world. Watch out for feeling overwhelmed or ungrounded.
NOV 27	DIRECT IN PISCES	Solidify your dreams with a practical plan. Saturn's direct motion helps you get back on track with your creative and spiritual goals, with a renewed sense of discipline and clarity.

Uranus

Uranus is the planet of innovation, surprise, and rebellion, shaking things up during its seven-year cycles through each sign. Plan for unexpected changes, breakthroughs, and moments of liberation when Uranus transits. Embrace the opportunity to break free from old patterns and think outside the box.

date	sign	what's going on
JAN 1	**RETROGRADE IN TAURUS** (since SEP 1, 2024)	Unfinished business around stability, finances, and security is brought to the surface. Progress slows down, offering time to rethink how you approach material comfort and resources.
JAN 30	**DIRECT IN TAURUS**	Sudden shifts in finances, security, and personal values resume. You may experience breakthroughs in how you create stability and embrace change, especially around money and possessions.
JUL 7	**GEMINI**	Innovation takes flight in communication, learning, and adaptability. This is a time for experimental ideas and unconventional thinking—expect major shifts in how you connect with others and process information.
SEP 6	**RETROGRADE IN GEMINI**	Reassess how you communicate and adapt to changing circumstances. This period is about reflecting on new ideas or exciting collabs that require further refinement before moving forward.
NOV 7	**RETROGRADE IN TAURUS** (until FEB 3, 2026)	Here's another chance to reexamine your relationship with security, finances, and comfort. You're wrapping up unfinished lessons around stability before Uranus leaves Taurus for good in April 2026.

Neptune

Neptune, the planet of dreams and spirituality, brings each sign periods of heightened imagination, creativity, and intuition. Its lengthy 14-year stay in each sign allows you to plan for spiritual growth, artistic endeavors, and to draw from the deep well of your psyche. Be careful. Neptune's foggy influence can blur reality, so check those facts.

date	sign	what's going on
JAN 1	PISCES	Intuition and imagination are heightened. Spiritual growth and compassion flow easily, but be mindful of blurring boundaries or escaping into fantasy.
MAR 30	ARIES	Bold dreams and visionary action take the stage. Neptune in Aries pushes you to pursue your ideals with courage and creativity—just watch out for impulsive decisions or chasing unrealistic goals.
JUL 4	RETROGRADE IN ARIES	Revisit your dreams and ideals with a critical eye. This retrograde invites you to reflect on bold actions and fine-tune your approach to turning visions into reality.
OCT 22	RETROGRADE IN PISCES	Dive deeper into spiritual introspection. You'll reflect on your emotional and spiritual growth, reconsidering how well your ideals align with reality.
DEC 10	DIRECT IN PISCES	Clarity returns to your dreams and spiritual pursuits. You'll feel a renewed sense of inspiration, ready to pursue your creative and emotional goals with grounded vision.

Pluto

Pluto is the planet of transformation and power, driving deep inner change over its long transits. Each sign experiences Pluto's influence for over a decade, making it a time to plan for profound personal growth, shedding of old identities, and doing important shadow work that allows for emotional and spiritual evolution.

date	sign	what's going on
JAN 1	**AQUARIUS** Since NOV 18, 2024	Deep transformation arrives through technology, innovation, and social structures. You're called to embrace personal and collective change—expect radical shifts in how you relate to community and power.
MAY 4	**DIRECT IN AQUARIUS**	Time to revisit and reassess the transformations happening in your social life. This retrograde slows down the revolutionary changes, giving you space to reflect on personal growth and societal shifts.
OCT 13	**DIRECT IN AQUARIUS**	The pace of transformation accelerates once again. You'll feel empowered to embrace change, take control of your future, and contribute to the collective evolution with renewed determination.
SEP 6	**RETROGRADE IN GEMINI**	Reassess how you communicate and adapt to changing circumstances. This period is about reflecting on new ideas or exciting collabs that require further refinement before moving forward.
NOV 7	**RETROGRADE IN TAURUS** (until FEB 3, 2026)	Here's another chance to reexamine your relationship with security, finances, and comfort. You're wrapping up unfinished lessons around stability before Uranus leaves Taurus for good in April 2026.

The Lunar Nodes

The lunar nodes, with their 10-month cycles, show where destiny calls and where you must release outmoded ways. The North Node points to your growth path, while the South Node guides you in letting go of outdated habits. Plan for karmic shifts, major life changes, and alignment with your higher purpose.

date	sign	what's going on
JAN 1	**NORTH NODE IN ARIES** **SOUTH NODE IN LIBRA** Since JUL 17, 2023	Answer the call to embrace independence, courage, and fearless leadership. The North Node in Aries spurs bold action and personal empowerment, while the South Node in Libra asks you to release codependency and people-pleasing tendencies in order to balance relationships.
JAN 11	**NORTH NODE IN PISCES** **SOUTH NODE IN VIRGO** Until JUL 26, 2026	Put some steam behind your dreams. The North Node in Pisces encourages you to tap into your compassion and divine inspiration, while the South Node in Virgo helps you release the need to micromanage and over-analyze, opening up space for creativity and emotional connection.

Chiron

Chiron, the "wounded healer," asteroid helps you address deep emotional wounds and past traumas. As it moves through a sign, Chiron offers a time for reflection, healing, and personal growth. Plan for moments of vulnerability and the courage to transform pain into wisdom.

date	sign	what's going on
JAN 1	**ARIES**	Heal through courage and self-empowerment. You're confronting wounds around identity and independence. Embrace vulnerability to build inner strength. Get in touch with healthy anger.
JUL 30	**RETROGRADE IN ARIES** Until JAN 2, 2026	Reflect on past wounds related to self-worth and personal power. This retrograde encourages deep introspection, helping you uncover and heal old insecurities about asserting yourself.

RETROGRADES IN
2025

When planets go "backward," slowdowns and chaos can ensue

When a planet passes the Earth in its orbit around the Sun, it's said to be going retrograde. From our vantage point on Earth, the planet appears to be on a reverse commute, backing up through the zodiac instead of advancing ahead degree by degree. While these aren't optimal times to start anything new, they can be powerful periods to review our progress and enjoy nostalgia.

mercury	dates	retrograde in...
Communication style, social contacts, systems for workflow, short trips and travel plans, contracts and agreement.	MAR 15–29	ARIES (9°35'–00°00')
	MAR 29 – APR 7	PISCES (29°59'–26°49')
	JUL 18 – AUG 11	LEO (15°34'–4°14')
	NOV 9–18	SAGITTARIUS (6°51'–00°00')
	NOV 18–29	SCORPIO (29°59'–20°42')

venus	dates	retrograde in...
Relationships and love, personal values, self-worth, finances and spending habits, aesthetic and style choices.	MAR 1–27	ARIES (10°50'–00°00')
	MAR 27 – APR 12	PISCES (29°59'–24°37')

mars	dates	retrograde in...
Motivation and goals, energy levels, conflict resolution, anger management, physical fitness and health.	DEC 6, 2024 – JAN 6, 2025	LEO (06°10'–00°00')
	JAN 6-FEB 23	CANCER (29°59'–17°00')

jupiter	dates	retrograde in...
Long-term goals, beliefs and philosophy, expansion plans, travel and education, opportunities for growth.	OCT 9, 2024 – FEB 4, 2025	GEMINI (21°20'–11°17')
	NOV 11, 2025 – MAR 10, 2026	CANCER (25°09'–15°05')

saturn	2025 dates	retrograde in...
Responsibilities, long-term commitments, structures and foundations, career and ambitions, personal discipline.	JUL 13–SEP 1	ARIES (1°56'–00°00')
	SEP 1–NOV 27	PISCES (29°59'–25°09')

uranus	2025 dates	retrograde in...
Independence, innovation and change, technology use, social causes, freedom vs. stability.	SEP 1, 2024 – JAN 30, 2025	TAURUS (27°15'–23°15')
	SEP 6 – NOV 7, 2025	GEMINI (1°27'–00°00')
	NOV 7, 2025 – FEB 3, 2026	TAURUS (29°59'–27°27')

neptune	2025 dates	retrograde in...
Dreams and intuition, boundaries, spiritual practices, creative projects, escapism tendencies.	JUL 4–OCT 22	ARIES (2°10'–00°00')
	OCT 22–DEC 10	PISCES (29°59'–29°22')

pluto	2025 dates	retrograde in...
Power dynamics, transformation, control issues, deep-seated fears, emotional intensity.	MAY 4–OCT 13	AQUARIUS (3°49'–1°22')

chiron	2025 dates	retrograde in...
Emotional wounds, healing practices, personal vulnerabilities, old traumas, self-empowerment strategies.	JUL 30, 2025 – JAN 2, 2026	ARIES (27°09'–22°35')

All dates and times in Eastern Time Zone

2025
Year of the Wood Snake

Shed your skin and evolve! The Year of the Wood Snake slinks in on January 29, 2025, at the Aquarius new moon, bringing with it twelve months of renewal and growth. Known for its stealthiness and wisdom, the Snake wants you to move with purpose and precision. Relinquish what no longer serves you so you can evolve.

This serpentine energy guides us all until February 16, 2026 so embrace its slow, steady transformation. Changes might not happen overnight, but that's okay. The Snake is associated with pragmatic Taurus in the Western zodiac, an earth sign known for its grounded, deliberate approach to life. As you weave through the year, you can methodically align with your true path. The key lies in trusting the process.

While the pace of 2025 might feel more subdued compared to 2024's Dragon year, don't mistake this for a lack of action. A Snake year rewards those who think ahead, stay calm under pressure, and strike only when the timing is perfect. Summon your inner strategist. It's time to play the long game and build something solid from the ground up.

The Wood element, which governs all years ending in 4 or 5, brings its own unique flavor to the Snake's influence. Wood encourages growth, expansion, and renewal. Visualize a vine winding its way up a trellis, gaining strength with every twist. This is a year to rise strategically, rather than rushing to the top.

The last Wood Snake year was 1965, a time of profound cultural shifts. The world saw the rise of the counterculture movement, the birth of iconic fashion trends like the miniskirt, and a greater push for civil rights and equality. Sixty years later, we might find similar themes echoing back to us with the Wood Snake year, offering opportunities for transformation and renewal on a global scale.

As we usher in the Year of the Wood Snake, remember: Patience, precision, and strategy will be your greatest allies. Trust in the slow, steady growth that this year promises, and don't rush the process. In true Snake fashion, sometimes the best moves are the ones made quietly, when others least expect them.

HOW YOU CAN MAKE THE MOST OF THE YEAR OF THE WOOD SNAKE

MOVE STRATEGICALLY: Forget impulsive moves or leaping before you look. Slow down, observe and wait for the perfect moment to strike.

PLAY UP THE INTRIGUE: Snakes are masters of stealth, so don't be fooled by a calm surface. Major shifts are happening, both personally and globally, just beneath the radar. Be a bit more mysterious to draw people in.

INTEGRATE YOUR INSIGHTS: After the high-octane, action-packed energy of the Dragon year, the Snake offers a chance to integrate. Gather your insights and use them to carefully map out your next move.

REGENERATE AND EVOLVE: The regenerative Snake understands that you have to shed the old to evolve into the new. Growth may require you to release relationships and obligations that no longer serve you—even if there is grief involved.

ELEVATE YOUR TASTES: Quiet luxury and timeless elegance: This is what to invest in during a Snake year. Take time to curate the right option and savor the treasure hunting process.

DETOXIFY AND HEAL: In traditional Chinese medicine, the Wood element is linked to the liver, making it important to detoxify and nourish your body this year. Invite balance with a mindfulness practice, gentle daily exercise, clean eating and sleep sanctification.

SUBTLE MOVEMENTS, BIG RESULTS: Tone down the hype! In 2025, the bold, risky moves that caused a stir in the Dragon Year will fall flat. Focus on careful planning and thorough research. Work behind the scenes, laying the foundation for future success.

9
Universal Year
by Felicia Bender, the Practical Numerologist

2025 is an 9 Universal Year

$$2 + 0 + 2 + 5 = 9$$

themes
OF A
9 UNIVERSAL YEAR

Releasing
Flow
Completion
Compassion
Collectivism
Humanitarianism
Surrender

challenges
OF A
9 UNIVERSAL YEAR

Stagnation
Control
Resistance
Preservation
Fear
Ignorance

2024 gave us a crash course in power dynamics—how we empower and disempower; misuse and properly wield authority. The 8 Universal Year was all about money and value, as we saw global economies restructuring, AI taking off and worldwide wars escalating. Now, in 2025, we transition from the power-hungry 8 into the heart-driven 9. It's time to see where this new energy takes us.

As we enter 2025, we're stepping into a year of global closure and completion—a time to reflect on how we want to move forward as a collective. There's a lot on the line. We can either evolve into a new world rooted in compassion and humanity, or we can remain on our current course, risking self-destruction.

2026 will kick off a 1 Universal Year, marking the start of a fresh nine-year cycle. But first, we need to clear out what's no longer working. The 9 Universal Year is like a deep cosmic cleanse.

In numerology, the 9 is a sacred number. It's the number of the compassionate humanitarian, spiritual ascension, letting go and forgiveness. The 9 invites us to step back from materialism and lead with our hearts.

9 Universal Year

LET. IT. GO.

The big question for 2025: What do we need to release in order to make space for positive global change? The goal this year is to let go of what's outdated, so we can step into a new, transformative phase for our world. As spiritual teacher Eckhart Tolle suggests in A New Earth, the evolution of humanity requires us to dissolve the ego's grip and stop creating unnecessary suffering. Acute crises often precede great leaps in consciousness—and this year, we're being asked to take that leap.

This is a year of sorting, organizing and reevaluating. It's not about launching something brand new just yet. Instead, we're wrapping up the last nine years, preparing the soil for what's to come. Wherever we feel isolated, angry or defeated is exactly where we need to focus our collective healing energy.

A 9 Universal Year calls for forgiveness, selfless service and compassion. But it also exposes our deepest wounds, which can either inspire us to heal or push us toward anger and bitterness. It's a time when our collective heart can crack open. Will we use this to heal our world, or will we continue on a path of destruction?

DO WHAT'S BEST FOR THE COLLECTIVE

The 9 is one of the most evolved numbers in Numerology, carrying the energy of all the other numbers within it. It's often seen as sacred, representing loss, letting go and deep spiritual rewards. In a 9 cycle, the focus shifts from personal gain to the well-being of all. It's about aligning with the present, releasing the past and moving forward with curiosity and an open heart.

This year will challenge us to live by spiritual principles. As Brené Brown puts it, spirituality is the recognition that we are all connected by something greater than ourselves, rooted in love and compassion. The 9 Universal Year asks us to ground ourselves in these values and build a new world based on connection, not division.

ALLOW ENDING TO CREATE SPACE FOR NEW BEGINNINGS

The Lao Tzu said, "New beginnings are often disguised as painful endings." 2025 will be a year of raw emotions and hard truths. We'll be called to act with compassion and forgiveness on a grand scale, even as old paradigms crumble. It's easy to hold onto what's familiar, even when we know it's no longer viable. We must recognize if we're on a sinking ship instead of going into denial. Don't be disheartened by the heaviness of this year. It's also a time to celebrate the culmination of what we've worked toward over the past nine years. This is our chance to reset, to return to empathy and to realign ourselves with nature and each other.

HEAL FROM THE INSIDE OUT

The 9 Universal Year is like winter, a time to prune the dead growth, let the soil rest and prepare for spring. We're standing at a pivotal moment in history, both globally and personally. 2025 is a year for global healing—and individual healing, too. We can't build a new paradigm unless we've done our own inner work. That means dealing with our trauma, clearing out our emotional clutter and upgrading our personal operating systems. We're in a period of accelerated growth, when therapy, energy work and spiritual practices can help us level up.

ADD A SPOONFUL OF SUGAR

Astrology, numerology and esoteric wisdom all converge during this powerful transition. And you're already ahead of the curve because you're reading this now! Proponents of the new Earth speak of vibrational and dimensional shifts that are happening right now as well. Scientific research shows that electromagnetic fields are changing frequency, solar flares have initiated atmospheric changes and the Earth's tonal frequency has also shifted its harmonics.

If the 9 Universal Year were a character from a movie, it would be the enchanting-but-firm Mary Poppins. The enigmatic nanny (played by the iconic Julie Andrews) blew in with her umbrella in the midst of a storm to unify a family through her unconventional methods. Similarly, the 9 Universal Year swoops in with an esoteric agenda, helping us tidy up, put things to rest and open our hearts to love. As the song goes, "A spoonful of sugar helps the medicine go down." Find ways to sweeten the lessons of 2025 with self-care, relaxation and the support of kindred spirits.

The 9 Universal Year is a time for completion, reflection and healing. It's about facing the truth with compassion, releasing what no longer serves and preparing for a new cycle with a clear heart. We have the power to create harmony in our lives and the energy of this year urges us to do the same on a global scale—step by step. Let go of what's heavy, lighten your load and trust that by the year's end, you'll be ready for the fresh new beginnings that await when the 1 Universal Year resets the cycle in 2026.

A LITTLE ABOUT *Aries*

DATES March 19 - April 19

SYMBOL The Ram

ELEMENT Fire

QUALITY Cardinal

RULING PLANET Mars

BODY PART Head, face

BEST TRAITS
Energetic, encouraging, unstoppable, bold, devoted, heroic, caring, fierce

KEYWORDS
Willpower, initiative, determination, passion, beginnings, self-confidence, innocence

Read more about Aries

ARIES
IN 2025

ALL THE PLANETS IN ARIES IN 2025	YOUR 2025 HOROSCOPE	TOP 5 THEMES FOR ARIES IN 2025	LOVE HOROSCOPE + LUCKY DATES	MONEY HOROSCOPE + LUCKY DATES

Aries in 2025
YOUR YEARLY OVERVIEW

2025 is going to be a year of transition for Rams. You've known for a long time that you were ready to forge a new path and reshape your identity. This year, you begin making noticeable strides. Structured Saturn and imaginative Neptune both move into Aries for the first time since 1998 and 1875, respectively. While they'll only spend part of 2025 in your sign, you'll get a glimpse of longer cycles that begin again next year. In the meanwhile, roll up your sleeves and unleash your imagination. Your fearless brand of leadership could attract a wider audience! As new developments crystallize, there will be some baggage to deal with. The North Node's move into Pisces supports with spiritual growth and helps you process and heal age-old trauma. In love, intellectual connections are the hottest this year as Jupiter and Uranus spin through Gemini. But watch that fickle streak! Romance may hit a speedbump this March when both Mercury and Venus turn retrograde in your sign. Slow down and work on your communication style. On June 9, Jupiter settles into emo Cancer, turning your focus to home and family for the rest of the year. You'll be ready to put down roots—or pull them up and find a new place to plant them!

THE PLANETS IN *Aries*

♈

THE SUN
MAR 20–APR 19

It's birthday season for you, so step out and shine! Seek novelty and take extra initiative during this radiant monthlong phase.

NEW MOON, SUPERMOON & PARTIAL SOLAR ECLIPSE
MAR 29
6:58AM, 9°00'

Bonus New Year! This potent supermoon is also the final Aries eclipse in a two-year series. Celebrate your progress, set bold intentions and get ready to step out in a whole new way. The world is waiting for you!

FULL MOON
OCT 6
11:48PM, 14°08'

Ready, set, manifest! Your work of the past six months bears fruit and it's time to harvest the rewards.

MERCURY
MAR 3–29
APR 16–MAY 10
RETROGRADE IN ARIES:
MAR 15–29

Crown yourself monarch of social butterflies as popularity-boosting Mercury visits your sign twice this year. Circulate and get social. During the retrograde, don't make promises you can't keep or let energy vampires into your sphere.

VENUS
FEB 4–MAR 27
APR 30–JUN 6
RETROGRADE IN ARIES:
MAR 1-27

You've got the romantic It Factor when the galactic glamazon charges up your powers of seduction—and in 2025, you'll host Venus twice. You may revisit an old love issue or reconnect to an ex during the retrograde. Keep your boundaries firm. Willpower is weak in the face of beauty and luxury. Watch your spending!

SATURN
MAY 24–SEP 1
RETROGRADE IN ARIES:
JUL 13–SEP 1

Welcome to cosmic boot camp! For the first time since 1996-98, discipline and focus are demanded as you stabilize the foundation of your life over the coming three years. It ain't easy, but growth will be epic!

CHIRON
ALL YEAR
RETROGRADE IN ARIES:
JUL 30, 2025–JAN 2, 2026

The wounded-healer comet holds the key to turning pain into prescient gifts. And when it visits your sign (for eight years) every 50 years, you may journey through a dark night of the soul to emerge a sage.

NEPTUNE
MAR 30–OCT 22
RETROGRADE IN ARIES:
JUL 4–OCT 22

Welcome to a new cycle of shifting identity, spiritual self-discovery and enhanced connection to the ethereal realm. This sneak peek is the start of a 14-year cycle. Prioritize deep healing. Get involved in charitable work.

NORTH NODE IN ARIES
JAN 1-11

Celebrations are in order! The destiny-fueling North Node wraps up its 18-month tour through your sign that began on July 17, 2023. Here's hoping you feel purposeful and connected to your passions.

Aries in 2025
HIGHLIGHTS

THE NORTH NODE LEAVES ARIES ON JANUARY 11

The North Node, which has been directing the collective destiny in Aries since July 17, 2023, moves on to Pisces this January 11. For the past 18 months, this karmic point tested your mettle and showed you what a badass you are. Because wounded-healer Chiron was also in Aries (as it is from 2018 to 2027), this cycle put many Rams through their paces. As you worked through grief, anger, pain, or trauma, you strengthened yourself inside and out. New rules, new boundaries? You've got 'em set. You're on a mission, Aries, which could be launched into the world in a big way with the new moon solar eclipse in your sign on March 29. This is the final eclipse in a two-year series on the Aries-Libra axis, so look forward to less dramatic arcs after this. (Whew.)

MERCURY AND VENUS RETROGRADE IN ARIES

Mercury gives you the gift of gab as it weaves in and out of Aries from March 3 until May 10. Refine your messaging, polish up your brand, then present the "updated you" to the world. The adoring public awaits your leadership. Love is coming in hot early this year as Venus begins her tour through Aries on February 4. This Valentine's Day could be one for the records (send pics!). From March 1 to 27, Venus spins retrograde in Aries. Step back to reassess your goals—especially in love and relationships. When Venus turns direct in Pisces on April 12, you'll emerge with greater clarity. You may feel the need for a timeout or to somehow reconnect to your autonomy during this time. If anything veers off the rails, take heart. Venus takes a second, direct pass through Aries from April 30 to June 6, firing up your spring with sultry vibes.

NEPTUNE'S MAGICAL INFLUENCE AND PROFESSIONAL GROWTH

Fantasies will be flowing, thanks to Neptune's magical influence. The enchanting planet floats into Aries from March 30 to October 22—its first visit to your sign since 1862 to 1875! This is a sneak peek of a longer, 13-year cycle that begins again on January 26, 2026. Life could get seriously dreamy now, and you may shock yourself by how willing you suddenly feel to release things that you've been clinging to, hard. No need to make sudden changes, just pay attention to what is loosening up.

COLLABORATE AND INNOVATE FOR THE WIN

Professionally, the first half of the year is all about expansion and collaboration. With Jupiter in Gemini until June 9, your third house of communication and ideas will be buzzing with opportunities to network, learn, and share your vision. Expect exciting projects, new collaborations, and a boost to your social life. Then, on July 7, Uranus joins the Gemini party, shaking things up with innovation and unexpected twists that will push you to think outside the box and embrace bold changes in your career and daily life.

SATURN'S SUMMER BOOT CAMP

But Saturn has other plans starting on May 24, when the ringed taskmaster dips into Aries for a summer boot camp. You haven't hosted Saturn since 1996 to 1998, so this is a big deal. Saturn will bring structure and focus to your life, encouraging you to slow down and build solid foundations for your future. It's time to step into your leadership role with discipline and strategy.

While Saturn leaves on September 1, this is just a preview of what's to come when it returns on February 13, 2026, for a longer stay (until April 12, 2028), pushing you to develop resilience and long-term vision.

JUPITER'S INFLUENCE IN CANCER: HOME AND FAMILY IN THE SPOTLIGHT

Home and family take center stage starting June 9, when expansive Jupiter moves into Cancer, your domestic fourth house, for the first time since 2014. This is a golden opportunity to create more stability and comfort in your living situation, whether that means moving, renovating, or simply making your home life more nurturing. Family dynamics will also be a big theme, with lots of growth and healing possible—especially with female relatives or caretakers.

2025: A YEAR OF TRANSFORMATION

By year's end, you'll be wiser, stronger, and ready to manifest a future that aligns with both your ambition and your soul. With a blend of innovation, structure, and spiritual growth, 2025 is the year to break out of old patterns and blaze new trails!

TOP 5 THEMES FOR Aries in 2025

1	2	3	4	5
ACT LOCALLY	CONNECT TO YOUR ROOTS	PUT SOME STEAM BEHIND YOUR DREAMS	REIMAGINE YOUR LOVE GOALS	GO SLOW TO GO FAST

1 ACT LOCALLY

JUPITER AND URANUS IN GEMINI

JUPITER: MAY 25, 2024 – JUNE 9, 2025
URANUS: JULY 7 – NOVEMBER 7, 2025 • JANUARY 26, 2026 – MAY 22, 2033

This year's stars have all kinds of surprises in store for you, Aries, but the bottom line is this: Your solo acts could soon be upgraded to a party of two, three or twelve. As expansive Jupiter spends the first half of the year in Gemini and game-changing Uranus does a four-month lap through the sign of the Twins, your third house of communication and peers gets a giant burst of momentum. No more holding back! The world wants you to articulate your vision and shout an important message from the rooftops of your neighborhood and the digital sphere. This year, you'll find all sorts of ways to "platform" yourself, whether you're writing, speaking or using your courage to help others find their voice.

JUPITER IN GEMINI

MAY 25, 2024 – JUNE 9, 2025

So many projects, so little time! Not to worry, Aries, because everywhere you turn, people want to jump on your bandwagon and have a hand in supporting your efforts. For this you can thank lucky Jupiter, who continues its yearlong tour through partnership-powered Gemini that began back on May 25, 2024. Whatever you started last spring continues to get a turbocharged blast of accelerating energy while the expansive planet hangs out in the sign of the Twins until June 9, 2025.

Although Jupiter is the global jet setter, you won't have to log thousands of frequent flier miles to bring your quests to the finish line. Gemini rules your third house of local activities, which means you'll probably spend more time in your electric car than you will on an Airbus A320. That's not to say you won't take any trips; however, most journeys will be the long-weekend variety rather than three weeks abroad. You've got the first half of the year to make waves in your hometown and you don't want to squander this Jupiter cycle which only comes around every 10-12 years. Go ahead and claim your status as a local mover and shaker!

Commuting between a couple locations is another strong possibility. Jupiter in Gemini can make bi-city living both appealing and necessary. Some Aries could set up shop in a second city, whether you are doing business there regularly, dating someone fifty miles away or simply feeding your soul with cultural amenities not available in the zip code where you pay taxes.

Jupiter's energy is inherently independent, which may explain why it's not 100% comfortable in Gemini, the sign of cooperation. In fact, Jupiter is "in detriment" in Gemini, a weaker position because it sits directly opposite Jupiter's home base of Sagittarius. At times, you may feel like running away from all the social pressures, but do your best to curb those impulsive urges. Instead, take on the challenge of finding people who are worthy contenders for a tag-team effort. DIY-ing is fine, Ram, but your hands should not be the only ones in the clay. Hire an assistant or consider a joint venture with someone doing similar work.

With Jupiter's megaphone amplifying your voice and Gemini silvering your tongue, you no doubt have a lot to say this year. This Jupiter transit encourages you to learn new ways to express yourself. Let's face it, Ram: You can be blunt and impatient, making your point then forgetting to listen—or prematurely jumping to conclusions. This might be the time to sign up for some media training or hire a speaking coach to polish your presentation skills.

Jupiter rules publishing, so if you have an idea for a book, podcast or another media piece, pursue that passion while luck is on your side. Some Rams could be well into writing a manuscript or recording weekly podcasts by the time 2025 dawns. Keep on putting yourself out there. You could attract a global audience from the comfort of your own living room.

URANUS IN GEMINI

JULY 7 – NOVEMBER 7, 2025
JANUARY 26, 2026 – MAY 22, 2033

On July 7, 2025 revolutionary Uranus lands in Gemini, striking like a lightning bolt in your third house of friendship, siblings and communication. While the cosmic changemaker is only in Gemini for four months this year, until November 7, consider this electrifying surge a preview of what's to come. On April 25, 2026, Uranus will plug back into Gemini's grid until May 22, 2033.

If you've been feeling stuck or "lacking" in the social arena, you can look forward to a dramatic pivot soon. Intriguing new people could enter your sphere serendipitously, but you need to venture out of your bubble and meet them halfway. The transformative planet could draw you into the local culture, where you might discover a passionate new side to yourself.

Uranus is the planet of activism and while it inches into Gemini, it could push some Aries into local politics. No, you don't have to get on the ballot immediately, but you might start feeling the call for the next round of elections, sometime between 2026 and 2033. No ambitions to take office? You may be invited to the board of a non-profit, or even start one yourself. Pay attention to how you might make the biggest impact. You're a natural born leader and when you have actual resources to play with, you can effect change in ways that could literally make history.

While brief, this Uranus transit—which hasn't happened in Gemini since 1941-49— brings out the mad scientist in you. It can also jumpstart new initiatives, or at least Phase One. With your instincts and intellect connected, your genius just shines. Remember: Unleashing your creativity on the world is in itself a form of activism, which humanitarian Uranus rules. Look for ways to make your mark on your corner of the world using your rich imagination.

In a related way, your style of self-expression may shift in dramatic ways during this cycle. The third house rules communication, and mid-year, you may reconsider the way you present yourself to the world. Whether you push past a fear of public speaking or launch a podcast or other media project, your messaging may hit the mark using Gemini's duality. Can you be irreverent and impactful at the same time? Uranus challenges you to find that balance.

2

CONNECT TO YOUR ROOTS

JUPITER IN CANCER
JUNE 9, 2025 – JUNE 30, 2026

After a socially demanding first half of the year, Rams will be ready to slide on into home on June 9, 2025. For the first time since 2014, peripatetic Jupiter downshifts into Cancer where it will nestle in your domestic fourth house until June 30, 2026.

Hosting Jupiter the Traveler in this homebound part of your chart might feel like an oxymoron, or at the very least, a complex riddle to solve. Ask yourself this, Aries: How can I bring my adventurous spirit back to base camp? You might begin with a space audit. Is Chateau Aries—and everything associated with it—in good, working order? How about the people living under your roof? It may be time to rearrange rooms and make some new agreements about chores, quiet hours and other shared responsibilities. If adjustments are needed, optimistic Jupiter will help you spring into action, which might involve perusing the real estate listings. During this thirteen-month transit, Aries might take home on the road as a global nomad, or literally pack up for a long-distance move. If you don't change your mailing address, you may continue the Jupiter-in-Gemini trend of setting up a second home away from home.

Your nest egg could grow exponentially while abundant Jupiter blesses your security-minded fourth house. Look at ways to revamp both your savings plan and your investment strategy. Caution isn't necessarily an Aries trait, but you might need a reminder that Jupiter is the galactic gambler. If your portfolio is heavily stacked on the "safe but slow growing" funds, you may diversify with a few high-yield (albeit riskier) options. Conversely, the "more" of Jupiter could mean you put more into your savings or a diversified index fund.

Belt-tightening measures may be in order after June 9, at least when it comes to the impulse purchases an Aries finds hard to resist. Now's the time to save up for something bigger: a house, retirement, college funds, etc.

Interest rates will be what they will be; yet the second half of 2025 is an optimal time for purchasing property. If you're ready for your white picket fence fantasy, start talking to mortgage brokers, bankers and realtors. The stars are smiling on your search now, despite what is happening in the market. Keep the faith—and your Zillow alerts on!

Family (that other "home") also figures prominently, especially female relatives or anyone you consider a caretaker or nurturer. With worldly Jupiter playing tour guide, family vacation plans could include a multi-generational visit to your cultural homeland. Time to expand your horizons together, or maybe start a family business. Entrepreneurial Jupiter could turn your home into a test kitchen or lab for future products you'll bring to market. Your great grandmother's secret recipe could be the path to creating generational wealth with the fam.

If you've had babies on the brain, maximizer Jupiter beams bright promise in the parenting department, including the possibility of giving birth to multiples. Already have kids? Nothing will light up your life like having fun adventures with your brood, even if that means just tapping off the map app and going for a joyride through country roads. Jupiter also brings a nice shot of truth serum to your family relationships. If you've been hiding your true feelings from relatives, roomies and your inner circle, you won't be able to stay, um, mum after June 9, 2025. In the name of growth, start talking, but don't forget the compassion. These are folks you care about, after all.

Since the fourth house is associated with the archetypal feminine, women will be your lucky stars between now and June 30, 2026. Partner up with the powerbabes on projects, business ventures, and, well, pretty much anything. (The "yin" touch is by far the right touch in the second half of the year.) You might even start a business that serves the female population with Jupiter's venturesome vibes in the mix.

3 PUT SOME STEAM BEHIND YOUR DREAMS

SATURN AND NEPTUNE IN ARIES

NEPTUNE: MARCH 30 – OCTOBER 22, 2025 • JANUARY 26, 2026 – MARCH 23, 2039
SATURN: MAY 24 – SEPTEMBER 1, 2025 • FEBRUARY 13, 2026 – APRIL 12, 2028

Step right up! You may feel like the star of a three-ring circus, as two outer planets—Saturn and Neptune—surge into Aries and your first house of identity and self-sovereignty for a portion of the year. Saturn is the zodiac's taskmaster, dealing in empirical data and harsh realities. Neptune is the planet of dreams and illusions. This might sound like a conflict of interest, but in the right balance, Saturn and Neptune can help you bring your deeply held passions into a tangible reality.

Even more profound: Neither planet has visited Aries for a long time. Saturn's last tour through your sign was from 1996 to 1998. Neptune was last in Aries from 1862 to 1875!

While both planets only swing through your sign for part of this year, in 2026, they embark on longer passages through Aries—Saturn for another two years and Neptune for another thirteen! Here's what you can expect as they briefly warm your first house in 2025.

NEPTUNE IN ARIES
MARCH 30 – OCTOBER 22, 2025
JANUARY 26, 2026 – MARCH 23, 2039

Who do you think you are, Aries? That question could spawn a temporary identity crisis, when, for the first time in nearly two centuries, esoteric Neptune spins into your sign this March 30. Suspend judgment and lift all limitations you've placed upon yourself. You are capable of so much more than you've given yourself credit for, and Neptune loves to mine for your hidden gifts deep in your subconscious. Your artistic side could blossom under Neptune's watch, or you could unearth a passion for empowering people who weren't blessed with as much good fortune as you.

Neptune's mission is to help us transform pain into power, and during this transit, you may feel an intense pull to share your healing gifts with the world. But before—or even as—you do that, it's essential to focus on your inner work. If you're an Aries who grapples with anger, unhealthy competition (like comparing yourself to others on social media), or swinging between over-giving and defensive selfishness, this is your time to get to the root of your pain. Goal number one? Learning to express your upset feelings before they turn into rage or resentment.

Do you need to process a loss, Aries? Wrap yourself in support and consider finding a great therapist or coach who can guide you through your journey. Remember, suffering is optional: If you're ready to move forward, you will need to let go of pride and embrace your own humanity. Feeling your emotions is the first step to healing—they deserve to be honored! That truth will be amplified between March 30 and October 22.

This is just a preview of a longer journey that will shape your future. On January 26, 2026, Neptune returns to Aries for a long, dreamy spell that lasts until March 23, 2039. You may feel lost in the woods sometimes—or maybe it's an enchanted forest? Existential questions are bound to arise, some that you won't find fast or easy answers to. Find yourself a cathartic outlet and start some sort of meditation practice. Neptune in Aries will set your subconscious mind on fire, making you a powerful pipeline to the muse and the divine.

This is an ideal period to work with a therapist, mentor, or spiritual guide, especially if you struggle to articulate your vision, or your pain. If you've already done deep exploration in these areas, Neptune's transit could position you as a powerful force in the self-development world. Even the most reserved Rams will find it easy to step into the spotlight when you have something life-changing to share with others!

SATURN IN ARIES
MAY 24 – SEPTEMBER 1, 2025
FEBRUARY 13, 2026 – APRIL 12, 2028

"Safety first" isn't generally the motto for daredevil Aries, but when cautious, conservative Saturn drops into your sign from May 24 to September 1, it pulls the emergency brake on your riskier undertakings. Screeeeech!

It's been nearly three decades since the ringed taskmaster orbited through your zodiac sign. Its arrival isn't exactly cause for celebration; well, at least not in the traditional sense. Yet, if you consider the long game (which is the only game Saturn likes to play), rest assured that Saturn's three-year tour through Aries will make you stronger and more resilient than you've felt in forever. And for your strapping sign, that's saying something!

In 2025, Saturn will only spend three months in Aries, as it darts forward from Pisces on May 24 for a quick preview tour, then splashes back into the Fish's pond again on September 1. Life could take on a serious tone this summer, with adult responsibilities and weighty decisions landing in your lap. Aries born in March will feel this most intensely, but all Rams may simply have the feeling that some part of their life is ready to ripen and mature.

This realization can be bittersweet. An activity that once brought you full-bodied joy may start to feel ho-hum this spring. You may strain to find interesting subject matter to thread into conversations with your longtime friend group. Don't fight it, Aries, and don't force it. When Saturn comes to town, it won't let you rest on your laurels.

Saturn's longer tour through Aries begins next year, on February 13, 2026, an unbroken lap that wages on for two full years, until April 12, 2028. Good thing you love a challenge! Saturn in any sign will put you through the paces, like a boot camp instructor shouting in your face while your muscles strain to do one more pushup. But this intensity goes double in Aries, since Saturn is "in fall" here. Hasty, impulsive Aries is one the toughest signs for stalwart, sensible Saturn to forge through. One of the greatest lessons you will learn during the coming three years is how to pace yourself.

If you're not willing to pump the brakes, Saturn might just do the job for you. Sleep schedules can change dramatically under this regimented planet's watch. Aries night owls who could snack without impunity and stay "snatched" without a gym membership may suddenly feel like all the juice has drained from your batteries. Frustrating? One hundred percent. Try to remember that Saturn is here to make you healthy, wealthy and wise. That's hard to do on three hours of sleep, especially if your idea of a "quick dinner" is white wine and Takis.

Even Aries who take great care of their well being may find themselves making shifts this year. Since Saturn is the planet of authority and mastery, this transit can help you rise through the ranks and establish yourself as an even more powerful leader than you already are. Caveat: You'll have to follow protocol instead of railing against all the rules. For some Rams, this might herald a career pivot. If you're opposed to the way things are done at your company or cannot make peace with current industry standards, staying put is like attempting to swim upstream during the strongest current. Don't do that to yourself!

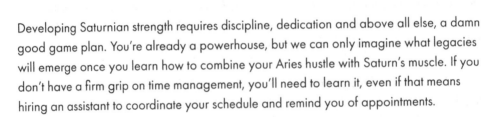

It might be time to enlist a coach, take a specialized training or return to school for a short-term program to make yourself eligible for the job that you DO want. Alas, there are no shortcuts under Saturn's watch. You might even decide to take a pay cut in order to learn a new field. Don't worry, you'll work your way back up through the ranks. Merit is what Saturn rewards, knowing that victory tastes sweetest when it's earned.

Developing Saturnian strength requires discipline, dedication and above all else, a damn good game plan. You're already a powerhouse, but we can only imagine what legacies will emerge once you learn how to combine your Aries hustle with Saturn's muscle. If you don't have a firm grip on time management, you'll need to learn it, even if that means hiring an assistant to coordinate your schedule and remind you of appointments.

While this might sound like a drag, remind yourself that you don't get the planetary Yoda in your corner every day. Saturn's last visit to Aries was from April 7, 1996 to October 25, 1998. Before that, Saturn was in Aries from March 3, 1967 to April 29, 1969. If you were born between those dates, you'll be experiencing your Saturn return, making this transit even more meaningful. While this will feel effortful at times, each time you get into action, you will feel the rewards. As Yoda advised Luke Skywalker, "Do or do not. There is no try!"

4 REIMAGINE YOUR LOVE GOALS

VENUS RETROGRADE IN ARIES AND PISCES

ARIES: MARCH 1 – 27
PISCES: MARCH 27 – APRIL 12

While other parts of your life heat up this spring, romance may simmer down temporarily. In fact, you may be more in the mood for an extended hibernation than an early romantic awakening. From March 1 to April 12, amorous, glamorous Venus slips into a six-week retrograde. There's no avoiding this cycle which happens every 18 months. Venus retrogrades can bring traffic jams on the romantic superhighway, which is never fun. But this year, you could find yourself proactively pulling over at a rest stop. The reason? Venus will spend part of the retrograde in YOUR sign (from March 1 to 27), which hasn't happened since March 2017.

Don't hit the panic button, Aries. This doesn't mean your love life is about to go to hell in a handbasket. But you may have some reckoning to do. Are you getting your needs met—and have you spelled them out clearly to dates or your mate? We teach people how to treat us and these four weeks could require some orientation sessions with the one(s) you adore. As it turns out, training season is never really over.

Single Aries might wish to hide their dating app profiles for the full six-week cycle, as you reconnect to your own needs and restore your confident core. When the retrograde ends on April 12, you could have some new ideas about how to refresh said profiles, in order to attract the type of person who is actually deserving of your precious time.

Attached Aries: Venus retrograding through your sign underscores the importance that autonomy has in maintaining chemistry. Give yourself the space you need to feel like a self-sovereign human, not a voluntary inmate in a couple bubble. Absence can make the heart grow fonder—as long as you don't remain "in absentia" for too long. Periodic check-ins, even by text, can go a long way to soothe the insecurities that Venus retrograde is infamous for rankling.

Since Venus is the cosmic creatrix, use this slower window to develop an artistic or musical project that keeps getting shuffled back on your priority list. And like we said, don't make yourself so busy that you fail to notice the needs of your partner or the smokeshow who's checking you out from across the room. Venus retrograde can help you plunge into more intimate places with people—and you'll have more patience than usual for these emotional investigations. But if you see red flags, don't ignore them. This Venus backspin can draw you towards dangerous liaisons and people with pasts so shadowy you couldn't locate their true souls with a stadium light! That's an especially loud warning between March 27 to April 12, when Venus paddles back through Pisces and your murky twelfth house.

If you're already committed elsewhere, beware the lure of an emotional affair, which, for you, can feel as erotically charged as "the act" itself. You'll know you're blurring lines if you can't stop thinking of ways to make a "friend's" problems better, or if you're counting down the minutes until you are together in the office/class/band practice, etc. Boundaries, Aries: They are a must now!

Hold off on any cosmetic updates like radically changing your hair or getting sleeve tats with Venus retrograde in your sign from March 1 to 27—and all the way through to April 12, for good measure. Radical changes now could lead to regrets with style queen Venus in reverse. If you see styles that you like, put them on a mood board and try them on in an AI app before you even remotely consider an impulse salon moment.

Same goes for any major purchases like mobile devices, cars, or trips abroad. With value-driven Venus in reverse, your fiscal decisions may be muddled, especially if you let your intense emotions dictate spending. (Retail therapy will be real during this retrograde, Aries.) Since retrogrades rev up the past, you might tap into a fresh income stream by reviving an old passion. Pull out that half-finished memoir or the ahead-of-the-curve app you almost beta-tested. The zeitgeist may soon be ready to embrace your visionary genius, especially if you do some research and sourcing during the retrograde.

5

GO SLOW TO GO FAST

LUNAR NODES IN VIRGO AND PISCES
NORTH NODE IN PISCES, SOUTH NODE IN VIRGO
JANUARY 11, 2025 – JULY 26, 2026

Slow down. Those are two words no Aries loves to hear, but starting January 11, the pace of your life could shift dramatically as the lunar nodes head into Virgo and Pisces until July 26, 2026. The South Node, which represents karmic cleanups, lands in Virgo and your sixth house of daily routines. Across the aisle, the destiny-driven North Node sets up its meditation mat in Pisces and your twelfth house of spirituality and surrender. New invitation for you, Ram: Let go of your over-scheduled, hyper-productive tendencies and open yourself up to a deeper, more intuitive way of living.

After 18 months of hosting the North Node in your sign, this upcoming shift into Virgo and Pisces will feel like a major turning point. With the North Node in Aries since July 17, 2023, you've been called to step into your power in a big way. This was a period of bold self-discovery and personal reinvention, and not necessarily an easy one. There was a strong push to reclaim your independence, redefine your goals, and set the firmest of boundaries. Decisive actions put you in the spotlight—a place where your showstopping sign doesn't mind hanging out. Whether you launched a passion project, redefined your identity, or made bold moves in your relationships, you've come a long way since this cycle began in the summer of 2023.

Now, as the North Node moves into Pisces until July 26, 2026, the energy downshifts. Take that pot of "me espresso" off the stove and get ready to serve up a relaxing cup of cosmic cava. You've spent 18 months cultivating your sense of self. In this upcoming cycle, you'll integrate what you've learned in a more internal, spiritual way. Rather than fixating on worldly achievements and personal milestones, inner growth is the path to deeper fulfillment. This can feel like a relief after such an action-packed cycle, but it can also be disorienting for someone so used to charging full speed ahead.

While you won't host the lunar North Node again for nearly two more decades, you'll be ready to say goodbye to the intense focus on personal growth. Change is exhilarating—but it can also be exhausting to do so much self-development all at once. Starting January 11, the North Node in Pisces weaves a soulful pathway through your twelfth house of dreams and spirituality, which sounds pretty idyllic. Peace may not come right away, however. When the North Node moves through your twelfth house every 18.5 years, it sends you on a healing and artistic journey. You may be ready to let go of some core activities that identified you for years, but now they feel like a weight on your shoulders.

Head's up: This transition could involve a bit of shadow work, as you mine the depths of your subconscious for its riches. This can be a profound cycle of transformation if you're willing to "do the work." Begin by examining past traumas (go deeper than you usually would), then connect the dots to current triggers. From there, practice bringing awareness to your unproductive reactions and responses—the ones that keep causing breakdowns in your personal and professional life.

One of the hardest parts of this process for you may be allowing certain emotions to arise. Fear and anxiety can be tough for even the most action-oriented Aries to sit with. Since the twelfth house rules the subconscious realm, consider hypnotherapy, EMDR, or breathwork. These can help you enter a relaxed state before tackling those tough emotional blocks. Starting a meditation practice during this time could also be incredibly effective. Besides healing fractured neural pathways, these practices will help divine downloads flow, turning your insights into actionable steps.

Need some guidance? Since Pisces rules your twelfth house of mentors, helpful people will miraculously appear between now and July 26, 2026. Whether it's a therapist, spiritual guide, or influencer who resonates with you, it might feel like you have an angel on your shoulder, guiding you through this exploration of your deepest self.

During this time, the muse will be a constant companion, and creativity your catharsis. If it's been years since you picked up a paintbrush, camera or musical instrument, no matter. These may become your tools of the trade again, at least in your off-duty hours.

This might sound like a tall order (and we're not gonna lie, it kind of is). Remember, however, that you don't have to achieve this newfound awareness overnight! Across the wheel from the Pisces North Node is the practical Virgo South Node in your process-driven sixth house. Lather, rinse, repeat? Suddenly that doesn't sound like such a bad idea. Repetition is what makes the lessons stick, after all. By doing, reading, or practicing the same thing repeatedly, you'll start discovering nuances within nuances. And that's when the epiphanies will arise!

With Virgo's influence from the South Node, ritualize your routines to make the process more meaningful. How can you make mundane moments feel more like special occasions? Play your favorite music while chopping ingredients for dinner, serve meals on your fancy plates, or listen to an inspiring podcast while motoring through household tasks. If you usually rush your morning routine, try waking up a little earlier to meditate, sip your coffee mindfully, and write in a journal to center yourself before the day begins.

This is also an excellent time for detoxifying your body and mind, perhaps by adopting a cleaner diet, reducing stress, and eliminating habits or relationships that no longer serve your highest good. Nurturing your overall wellbeing enhances your energy and gives your mind a sharp clarity that you haven't experienced for a while!

Consider your daily workflow, too. The sixth house rules healthy habits and efficient systems. With the South Node in Virgo, you'll be tempted to start micromanaging every detail of your life. As a capable cardinal sign, you like to get results. Time for reflection, Aries: Is your obsession with productivity truly fulfilling, or is it burning you out? The South Node in Virgo can make you overly critical, constantly striving for perfection and getting lost in the busyness of life. Step back and reassess if your routines are supporting your wellbeing or just keeping you in perpetual motion without true satisfaction. How can you work smarter, not harder? You might consider scaling back your hours or even taking a temporary pay cut to pursue a path that brings you fulfillment without the burnout.

Before you tender your resignation, however, would changing things like your workflow, time management, and scheduling systems make a difference? The sixth house is also the domain of service providers, and with the karmic South Node in Virgo, consider hiring a virtual assistant or outsourcing a few aspects of your work. This could make a world of difference, allowing you to focus on what really matters while avoiding unnecessary stress.

We all have healing gifts to offer the world, and yours will come to light during this nodal cycle. With your houses of service and healing activated, consider giving back through volunteer work, monthly donations, or even starting your own support circle for people dealing with similar challenges. If you're in a leadership position at work, how about starting an ERG (Employee Resource Group) to unify colleagues or create support for a segment of people who may have a specific focus. There's a humbling beauty in this, and you might find resonance in the expression: "Before enlightenment, chop wood and carry water. After enlightenment, chop wood and carry water."

Love

ARIES 2025 FORECAST

The frosty winter temps won't keep you from heating up every room you walk into this winter. Starting February 4, love planet Venus struts into your sign for an extended stay, lasting (on and off) until June 6. You've never been one to settle, Aries, and Venus here makes your boundaries crystal clear. If personal goals have slipped to the back burner, you may need to reconfigure your relationship roles so that you're getting the support you need with pursuing your independent interests. Autonomy (in the right amount) can make the heart grow fonder.

From March 1 to March 27, Venus spins retrograde in Aries, inviting you to take a step back and reassess your approach to love, how you present yourself, and your desires in relationships. You may stoke old flames or deal with unresolved romantic issues during this period. Not exactly fun, but a necessary step before you can forge ahead with a clear conscience. Do the work and when Venus takes her second lap through Aries from April 30 to June 6, you'll feel confident and crystal clear about what you want in love, making it a great time to start fresh or strengthen your current relationship.

Adding to the shifts, the South Node leaves Libra, your opposite sign, on January 11 after an 18-month stay, releasing you from old relationship patterns and karmic lessons around partnerships. During this cycle, you've been pushed to find balance between your fierce independence and desire for collaboration. Now that the South Node is moving on, you're free to step into more evolved dynamics in all your interactions. Expect to feel less weighed down by past relationship baggage and more ready to embrace healthier connections.

When your ruling planet, lusty Mars, moves into fellow fire sign Leo from April 18 to June 17, your fifth house of romance, creativity and pleasure lights up, boosting your love life with passion and playful energy. Mars already did a lap through Leo starting November 3, 2024, then turned retrograde from December 6 to January 6, 2025. You may be nursing a few battle scars from that period, like a lover's quarrel that never quite got settled.

As Mars circles back to Leo on April 18, your rizz returns with a roar. This transit makes you bold and assertive in pursuing romantic interests, helping you express your desires with confidence. Whether you're single or partnered, Mars in Leo brings a spark of excitement and adventure, making this a time for fun, flirtation, and heartfelt connection.

Mars enters Scorpio in Q4, setting off sparks in your eighth house of intimacy from September 22 to November 4. As your emotional connections intensify, dive deeper into your relationships, exploring vulnerability and trust. There's no halfway as 2025 winds down. Let go of superficial situationships and drop your guard where trust has been established. Give yourself free rein to max out on the passionate, sexy vibes this transit brings every other year. Hot!

ARIES: LUCKIEST *love* DAY

MAY 22

Cosmic lovebirds, Venus and Mars, connect the dots in fire signs, stoking the embers of passion and turning simmering attractions into red-hot romances. Venus in Aries enhances your charm and allure, while Mars in passionate, theatrical Leo elevates your confidence. Whether you're testing out chemistry or solidifying a bond, love flows effortlessly under this influence.

Money & Career

ARIES 2025 FORECAST

Aries, 2025 is a year for major professional breakthroughs and recalibration. You'll start the year fired up and ready to take on the world, thanks to Jupiter continuing its journey through Gemini, your third house of communication, collaboration and ideas, until June 9. This is prime time to share your vision far and wide, especially if you're working on writing, speaking, or media projects. Got a book idea or podcast dream? Jupiter in Gemini wants you to amplify your voice and get your message out there. And with everyone eager to jump on your bandwagon, teamwork will be your secret weapon—collaborations and group efforts will help you take things to the next level.

When Uranus enters Gemini on July 7, the pace picks up even more, bringing unexpected twists and turns in your career. Uranus, the planet of innovation and disruption, will electrify your professional sphere, inspiring you to break free from routine and explore bold, unconventional paths. This is the time to embrace change and think outside the box—whether that means switching industries, launching a side hustle, or taking your current role in a completely new direction. Uranus is all about experimentation, so don't be afraid to test out daring ideas or unorthodox strategies that could revolutionize your work.

But before you get too carried away with all that entrepreneurial energy, Saturn steps in to bring some structure. From May 24 to September 1, the ringed taskmaster will briefly visit Aries, your first house of identity and leadership, for the first time in nearly 30 years. Saturn's presence will demand discipline and focus, helping you lay the groundwork for long-term success. This isn't about shortcuts, Aries—Saturn will push you to set up sustainable systems, hone your skills, and take a more strategic approach to your career goals. The good news? Saturn rewards hard work and resilience, and this is the beginning of a powerful three-year cycle that will help you rise through the ranks, starting with a preview this summer.

When Saturn leaves on September 1, you'll feel the intensity lift, but you'll also have a stronger sense of where you're headed. Don't rest on your laurels. Saturn will be back in Aries from February 13, 2026 to April 12, 2028, so you're just getting started with this "build."

Neptune in Aries will weave its magic from March 30 to October 22, inspiring you to blend your dreams with practical action. Creative careers or roles that allow you to lead with compassion will flourish, as Neptune helps you turn visionary ideas into tangible results. By year's end, you'll have laid the foundation for career success that's aligned with both your purpose and your personal ambitions—making 2025 a year of growth, discovery, and serious momentum.

ARIES: LUCKIEST *career* DAY

APRIL 18

The very last full day of Aries season comes with an extra burst of magic as your ruler, make-it-happen Mars, joins the fire sign brigade and kicks off its 2025 tour through Leo. And with Mercury also in Aries, you'll feel inspired to take charge and manifest results for your career and finances. The icing on the cake? You'll be able to make this all happen in a way that feels authentic to your definition of success. Nice!

2025
ARIES

12*
MONTH
OVERVIEW

January MONTHLY HOROSCOPE

As 2025 kicks off, you're in full power mode, Aries! With the Sun blazing through Capricorn and your ambitious tenth house until January 19, you're ready to set epic goals and build a rock-solid foundation for success. But there's more: On January 11, the North Node wraps up its 18-month tour of your sign, a journey that's pushed you toward massive personal growth and set you on your life's true path since July 17, 2023. Now, with the lunar nodes shifting into Pisces and Virgo for 18 months, you're entering a whole new cycle that's all about spiritual growth, learning, and deeper connections. Your ruler, molten Mars, retrogrades back from Leo into Cancer this January 6. That could slow down your home and family plans until February 23, but use this time to fine-tune everything. When Aquarius season kicks in on January 19, your popularity soars. Come out of hibernation to network and spearhead group projects. (And maybe be the captain of an indoor sports team?) January 29 marks the arrival of The Year of the Wood Snake. Shed old skins and rise stronger, fiercer, and more determined than ever!

February MONTHLY HOROSCOPE

Charge ahead this February, Aries! The Sun in Aquarius lights up your eleventh house of friendships and long-term goals until the 18th, making this a prime time to collaborate, network and rally your squad around a big dream. But the real power move comes on February 4, when Jupiter turns direct in Gemini after a four-month retrograde, energizing your third house of communication. With Jupiter in this corner until June 9, your ideas are golden! Share them widely, start that podcast, or even dive into writing or teaching projects. Your message will resonate. Also on February 4, Venus embarks on a long tour through your sign, blessing you with extra charm and magnetism. Expect to turn heads and attract admirers, but with Venus going retrograde from March 1 to April 12, you may want to polish up your personal brand. The Sun slips into Pisces on the 18th, bringing focus to your twelfth house of healing and closure. This is your cue to rest and reflect before your solar return next month. Home will feel like a lively place to be once Mars turns direct in Cancer on February 23. Clear up friction under your roof and get household projects or moving plans in motion!

March MONTHLY HOROSCOPE

March drifts in with the Sun in Pisces, keeping you in a reflective, dreamy headspace until the 20th. But don't get too comfortable. This is just the calm before a cosmic storm of Aries energy! Venus retrogrades in your sign from March 1 to 27, pulling you inward to reflect on how you show up in love and relationships. Time to break old patterns and step into your true power. On March 14, the Virgo lunar eclipse brings an emotional release around health and work matters, helping you break some longstanding bad habits. As if that weren't enough, Mercury goes retrograde in Aries from March 15 to 29, calling you to hit pause on big plans and review how you're communicating and asserting yourself. As the Sun enters Aries on the 20th you'll feel the full force of your fiery nature, ready to charge ahead with confidence. But brace yourself for the March 29 Aries new moon, which happens to be the final solar eclipse in your sign after two world-rocking years. This could be the final push you need to get a personal project in motion. But wait, there's more! On March 30, Neptune moves into Aries for the first time since 1875, the beginning of a 14-year cycle of artistic visions and spiritual awakening. Make way for the divine downloads!

April MONTHLY HOROSCOPE

It's still your season, Aries, with the Sun shining in your sign until April 19! You're fired up and ready to take on the world, but don't rush into superproducer mode just yet. Mercury is retrograde in Pisces and your foggy twelfth house until April 7, with Venus retrograding there, too, until April 12. These backspins are pulling you inward—perfect for healing and deep introspection, but they can muddle your decision-making. Hit pause, do your research, and clear up any lingering uncertainties before racing ahead. Once Mercury goes direct on the 7th, your intuition will sharpen, and Venus straightens out on the 12th, bringing back your charm and untangling any love life confusion. Passion hits a new high when Mars, your ruling planet, struts into bold Leo on the 18th, firing up your fifth house of fame, romance and creative expression until June 17. You'll be brimming with confidence, passion, and that iconic Aries spark. Taurus season starts on April 19, shifting your focus from personal reinvention to locking in financial stability. Time to ground yourself, secure your foundation, and bring all those exciting ideas to life.

May MONTHLY HOROSCOPE

May kicks off with the Sun in Taurus until May 20, urging you to get serious about your finances and lock down some long-term security. Time to swap impulsive splurges for savvy investments—think high-quality wardrobe staples or a solid savings plan that'll have future-you feeling proud. On May 4, Pluto retrogrades in Aquarius until October 13, inviting a deep dive into your social scene. Have you outgrown certain friendships or group affiliations? It's time to reevaluate where your energy goes and who you align with. The big cosmic shift happens on May 24, when Saturn enters Aries for the first time since 1996-1998. This is your moment to step into leadership and structure your goals for the long haul. Saturn's no-nonsense vibes will have you leveling up, whether it's in your career, fitness, or personal growth. And just in time, Gemini season arrives on May 20, bringing playful, breezy energy that'll have you connecting with friends, exploring new ideas, and letting your curiosity lead the way. It's a perfect balance of work hard, play hard—just the way you like it!

June MONTHLY HOROSCOPE

June delivers a series of fast-paced shifts for you, Aries! With the Sun in Gemini until the 20th, your genius mind is buzzing. You'll be in your element connecting the dots, brainstorming and lining up exciting new projects. But the month's main headline comes on June 9 when bountiful Jupiter wraps its one-year tour of Gemini and downshifts into Cancer for the first time since 2014. For the next twelve months, Jupiter blesses your home, family, and fiscal foundations with its good fortune. If you've been itching to make changes in your personal life, you'll have the guts to go for it. Mid-month could be tricky as Jupiter squares off with both Saturn (June 15) and Neptune (June 18), challenging you to balance big dreams with practical responsibilities. Take a breath and adjust your course where needed. On June 17, Mars enters Virgo, helping you refine your routines and get organized. The Sun joins Jupiter in Cancer at the solstice on the 20th, then makes an exact conjunction on the 24th for the annual Day of Miracles. No more wasting energy chasing sparkly, but ultimately superficial, pursuits. Pour yourself into situations that truly sustain you and start laying a solid foundation that you can build on for years to come.

July MONTHLY HOROSCOPE

No apologies for hiding out in that hammock, Aries. While the Sun swings through Cancer until July 22, you'll enjoy getting lost in your cozy little corner of the world. But check your messages regularly! Your extracurricular life could surge simultaneously once convivial Venus lands in Gemini this July 4. It's going to be a balancing act, but make time to flirt, connect and join friends for summer activities in between naps. Unexpected changes in your social circle shake things up after the 7th when Uranus heads into Gemini and hurls a curveball into your cooperative, communicative third house. This is the side-spinning planet's first visit to this sign since 1949, which will demand that you stay alert, solution-focused and adaptable. Retrograde season hits hard with Neptune, Saturn and Chiron all shifting into reverse in Aries (on the 4th, 13th and 30th) and pushing you into deep self-reflection. Over the coming five months, you'll be forced to confront old patterns and reassess your approach to personal growth. Don't let these cosmic speedbumps throw you out of the game. Just slow down and recalibrate, Ram. With Mercury retrograde in Leo from July 18, creative projects may hit a temporary stall, but use this time to refine your strategy and test out new techniques. Once the Sun enters Leo on July 22, you'll feel more energized and ready to pursue your passions. Develop what you can behind the scenes until Mercury turns direct on August 11.

August MONTHLY HOROSCOPE

August is a month of both fiery momentum and thoughtful recalibration for you, Aries. With the Sun in Leo until August 22, you're ready to go "all in" on creative projects, summer fun, and any activities that swing the spotlight your way. This is your month to shine, but with Mercury retrograde in Leo until August 11, it's best to hold off on hard-launching anything until the second half of the month. Venus in Cancer until August 25 puts family and emotional connections in the spotlight, encouraging you to nurture close relationships and zhush up your home. In love, give the "nice guys" a chance to win your heart. Mars, your ruling planet, enters Libra on August 6, activating your partnership zone until September 22. Follow the urge to merge, but careful not to rush into anything before you've thoroughly vetted any so-called soulmates. The Sun moves into Virgo on August 22, shifting your energy towards health, routines, and getting organized. The first of two back-to-back new moons in Virgo arrives on August 23, making this a great time to set intentions around wellness, productivity, and getting your life in order. This one's laying the groundwork for an even bigger fresh start with next month's solar eclipse!

September MONTHLY HOROSCOPE

Ready, set, organize. The Sun is in efficiency-boosting Virgo until September 22, inspiring you to get back to the gym and streamline your workflow. While you're cleaning up your physical environment, also pay attention to your inner world. On the 1st, Saturn retrogrades out of Aries and back into Pisces and your transitional twelfth house. Then, on the 7th, a total lunar eclipse in Pisces activates this same arena, resurfacing buried emotions and forgotten baggage. Alas, you won't be able to sweep this stuff under the rug, Ram. Give yourself the gift of doing the healing work so you can lighten your psychic load. On the 6th, Uranus turns retrograde in Gemini, which will throw you a communication curveball or two. Stay flexible. People may be a bit less reliable over the next couple months, but this could pave the way for new partnerships to emerge. Romantically, you're in high season while Venus struts through Leo and your flamboyant fifth house until September 19. Once the love planet shifts into Virgo after that, you'll be more intentional about your love goals. A partial solar eclipse in Virgo on September 21 offers a powerful fresh start—perfect for setting new intentions around wellness, work, and daily habits, or building on ones you kicked off with the August 23 new moon. Sultry vibes seep into every area of your life after the 22nd, when your ruler, molten Mars, moves into Scorpio until November 4. Your vibe is "all or nothing" now, but careful not to flood people with too much intensity.

October MONTHLY HOROSCOPE

Every pot has a lid, Aries, and with the Sun in Libra until October 22, harmonious partnerships—both romantic and professional—are front and center. If you're casting for the role of "your other half," pass over the clones and scout out people who you'd consider a complementary force. You may have to orient them to your exacting processes or show them how you like it done. With diplomatic Venus in Virgo until the 13th you shouldn't have to dig TOO deep to find the necessary patience for that. By the time the planet of peace, love and beauty moves into her home sign of Libra (on October 13), you could have a fresh set of relationship goals that you feel confident achieving together. Single Rams will be especially magnetic in the second half of the month. And when Scorpio season begins on the 22nd? Fugeddaboudit! Your sultry embers could start a cosmic conflagration. (H-O-T-T-O-G-O!) Team efforts pick up steam once Pluto turns direct in Aquarius on October 13. Refresh social media profiles, shift into R&D mode on a team or tech project. On the 22nd, Neptune retrogrades back from Aries into Pisces, drawing you back into an imaginative flow. Get back into your meditation practice or pick up a creative project that you had set aside earlier this year.

November MONTHLY HOROSCOPE

You're rolling in the deep this November, as the Sun simmers in Scorpio until the 21st. Vixen Venus is also here from November 6 to 30, amplifying the sultry vibes. Even the most basic interactions may be filled with subtle hints and innuendoes; and your crush psychically texts you while you're daydreaming about your last date. Current relationships intensify while the Scorpio energy revs up the passion between you, but this month will reveal any hidden dynamics that need addressing. What—and who—you invest in could pay off for years to come if you play your cards right. On the 4th, your ruler Mars moves into Sagittarius lighting a fire under your ambitions and giving you the energy to explore, learn, and expand your horizons. You'll be craving adventure, but with Uranus retrograding back into Taurus on November 7, you'll need to get finances in order first. Mercury turns retrograde on November 9, first in Sagittarius until November 18 and then in Scorpio until the 29th. This is another cosmic cue to streamline your plans and make sure that you're representing yourself accurately in all your front-facing communications. Expansive Jupiter hits snooze on the 11th, turning retrograde in

Cancer. Use this four-month spell to iron out personal matters or any friction surrounding home and family. Radical optimism reigns supreme when the Sun joins feisty Mars in Sagittarius on the 21st. And once Saturn wraps up its five-month retrograde (in Aries and Pisces) on the 27th, you'll feel comfortable taking a few calculated risks to knock an EOY goal out of the park!

December MONTHLY HOROSCOPE

Lucky, lucky. Fortune favors the Ram this December with the Sun beaming in Sagittarius until December 21. With Venus and Mars traveling together through this sign for the first half of the month, you want nothing more than to explore, expand and do what excites you (right here and right now!). If you can squeeze in pre-holiday travel, slip off spontaneously—or crown yourself queen of the party scene closer to home. Got some goals left to crush before the year ends? Your ruler, driven Mars, sweeps in for the rescue on the 15th when it lunges into ambitious Capricorn for the rest of 2025. On December 10, Neptune turns direct in Pisces, bringing the spirit of forgiveness—plus some warm-fuzzy vibes—to your holiday season. On the 21st, the Winter Solstice and the Sun's move into Capricorn puts you back into a grounded groove and turns you into Santa Claus for the ones you love. When Venus joins her dance partner Mars in Capricorn on December 24, long-term love goals come into clearer view. With so much energy brewing in your tenth house of success, celebrate NYE in style. A black-tie event or VIP gathering could set the tone for a powerful 2026!

A LITTLE ABOUT *Taurus*

DATES April 19 - May 20

SYMBOL The Bull

ELEMENT Earth

QUALITY Fixed

RULING PLANET Venus

BODY PART Neck, throat

BEST TRAITS
Patient, organized, supportive, romantic,
careful, dedicated, reliable

KEYWORDS
Stability, security, elegance, sensuality, tenacity, artistry,
sophistication, luxury, comfort, ease

*Read more
about Taurus*

TAURUS
IN 2025

ALL THE PLANETS IN TAURUS IN 2025	YOUR 2025 HOROSCOPE	TOP 5 THEMES FOR TAURUS IN 2025	LOVE HOROSCOPE + LUCKY DATES	MONEY HOROSCOPE + LUCKY DATES

Taurus in 2025
YOUR YEARLY OVERVIEW

The wild and weird ride you've been on since 2018 is winding down, Taurus, but it's not quite over yet. In 2025, you'll at least get a glimpse of the grounded stability that your sign traditionally loves. Rebellious Uranus is almost done with its seven-year tour of Taurus, which has left you shaken, stirred and completely rewired. From July 7 to November 7, the side-spinning planet pops into Gemini, giving you a chance to digest this metamorphic period—one that won't come around for another 80-plus years after April 25, 2026. Financial growth is accelerated while Jupiter cruises through Gemini until June 9. Midyear, Uranus' move to the sign of the Twins can help you get innovative with your resource management. (One cold wallet, please!) Set up a savings and investment plan to avoid burning your earnings. Love may feel poetic and tinged with fantasy for much of 2025. Get ready for a spring of soulful reflections as your guardian Venus turns retrograde from March 1 to April 12. Some Bulls may need to release an old relationship (or relationship patterns) to clear space for the new this summer. With the North Node in Pisces after January 11 you'll have a chance to flex your team spirit, especially when in the company of artists, thought leaders and changemakers. Worldly Jupiter cruises into Cancer on June 9, which could turn you into a global nomad. From apartment swaps to vacation properties, you'll redefine home in the second half of the year!

THE PLANETS IN *Taurus*

THE SUN
APR 19–MAY 20

Bask in the spotlight—it's your birthday season! Dive into novel adventures and make audacious moves that put you front and center.

NEW MOON, SUPERMOON
APR 27
3:31 PM, 7°47'

Honorary New Year! Set personal intentions under this accelerating new supermoon, then dive into action!

FULL MOON, SUPERMOON
NOV 5
8:19 AM, 13°23'

Ready, set, manifest! Your work of the past six months bears fruit and it's time to harvest the rewards under the second supermoon in your sign in 2025

MERCURY
MAY 10–25

Crown yourself monarch of the social butterflies when popularity-boosting Mercury visits your sign once a year. Circulate, network and fill up your entertainment calendar.

VENUS
JUN 6–JUL 4

You've got the romantic It Factor when the galactic glamazon (your ruler!) charges up your powers of seduction each year. Willpower is weak in the face of beauty and luxury, so spend wisely.

URANUS
JAN 1–JUL 7
NOV 7, 2025–APR 25, 2026
RETROGRADE IN TAURUS:
SEP 1, 2024–JAN 30, 2025
NOV 7, 2025–FEB 3, 2026

Life feels like a sci-fi movie when Uranus visits your sign (for seven years) every 84 years. Ungrounding and chaotic as it's been, you've made incredible life changes since this cycle began in 2018. You're in the final stretch of this transit. Uranus pops out of your sign for half of the year, then leaves for good April 25, 2026.

Taurus in 2025
HIGHLIGHTS

STABILITY MEETS SURPRISE: URANUS IN TAURUS

Growth and innovation are reaching peak levels as Uranus takes the last lap of its seven-year transformative journey through your sign. Expect a few final cosmic curveballs, especially before July. Since 2018, you've navigated radical change. With Uranus leaving Taurus from July 7 to November 7 this year—and for good in April 2026—you'll feel more grounded in your newfound independence and personal reinvention. It's time to build on these shifts, creating a solid foundation for the next chapter of your life.

FINANCIAL GROWTH & INNOVATION: JUPITER AND URANUS IN GEMINI

Collaboration is your skeleton key to success this year, Taurus. Until June 9, lucky Jupiter in Gemini, the sign of the Twins, supercharges your second house of income and material wealth. Consider joint ventures or lucrative side gigs that align with your values. But don't get too carried away! Jupiter's expansive energy might tempt you to blow through your discretionary funds. Meanwhile, chaotic Uranus in Gemini could skew your normally shrewd spending habits from July to November. Enlist a bookkeeper and financial planner; build a budget that you can actually stick to. While you love indulgence, opt for treasures that qualify as "investment pieces" either because you'll use them often or they literally grow in value, like a collection of fine art.

UNEARTHING YOUR SOUL PURPOSE: PLUTO IN AQUARIUS

A seismic shift in your career and public life may be slowly underway, as Pluto in Aquarius squares your Sun until January 19, 2044. This is the first full year of Pluto's powerful presence in your tenth house of ambition, status and long-term goals. You're being called to alchemize the way you approach success, shedding any outdated structures that no longer align with your soul's true mission. While the road may have some unexpected speedbumps—especially when power dynamics arise at work—this is a

rare opportunity to reinvent yourself as a leader. Embrace your inner authority and trust that Pluto's deep-dive energy will help you emerge more influential than ever before.

SATURN AND NEPTUNE IN ARIES

In 2025, Saturn and Neptune both take up residence in Aries, activating your twelfth house of healing, closure and the subconscious. This cosmic duo encourages you to dive deep into your psyche, releasing old baggage and patterns that have been holding you back. Saturn's grounding influence will help you set up healthier boundaries while you shed what no longer serves you. Meanwhile, Neptune invites spiritual exploration and imagination, helping you tap into your dreams and inner guidance. The combo could feel like a tug-of-war between practicality and intuition, but it's all about finding balance as you prep for a major rebirth when Saturn moves into your sign on April 12, 2028.

SPRING SLINGS SOME INSIGHTS ABOUT YOUR LOVE LIFE AS VENUS TURNS RETROGRADE

Venus, your ruling planet, brings her magic to Taurus from June 6 to July 4, peak season for all things amour. But what's standing in the way of you deepening your emotional bonds? Some eye-opening insights stream in while Venus spins retrograde from March 1 to April 12. This could stir up past relationship drama or bring an old flame back into your life. This retrograde asks you to reassess what you truly want from love. Are you seeking soulful, lasting connections, or do you still have unresolved feelings to address? Use this time to gain clarity before diving into anything impulsive.

JUPITER IN CANCER: COMMUNICATION & LEARNING

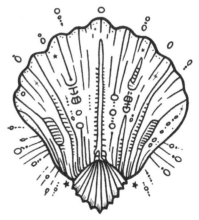

On June 9, Jupiter moves into Cancer, lighting up your communication zone for the next year. This shift helps you strengthen connections, both personally and professionally. Networking, short-term projects and new learning opportunities will bring joy and profitability. You don't need to travel far to feel stimulated. The local scene will be buzzing with one tantalizing offering after another in the second half of 2025. Whether it's diving into new hobbies, reconnecting with your community or embarking on an educational journey, this is the year to feed your curious mind. Bi-city living or a pied-à-terre may call. Consider finding a friend in that zip code who wants to do periodic home swaps.

TOP 5 THEMES FOR
Taurus in 2025

1	2	3	4	5
ELEVATE YOUR EARNING POWER	BECOME A LOCAL CELEBRITY	EMBRACE A SPIRITUAL PRACTICE	RELEASE ROMANTIC BLOCKS	ASSEMBLE YOUR DREAM TEAM

1 ELEVATE YOUR EARNING POWER

JUPITER AND URANUS IN GEMINI

JUPITER: MAY 25, 2024 – JUNE 9, 2025
URANUS: JULY 7 – NOVEMBER 7, 2025 • JANUARY 26, 2026 – MAY 22, 2033

Can stability and excitement co-exist? If free-spirits Jupiter and Uranus have anything to say about it, the answer is yes! Both planets do time in variety-loving Gemini this year, but they'll anchor in your rooted second house. Prepare to feel "in your element," but with a little extra burst of self-confidence and daring.

JUPITER IN GEMINI

MAY 25, 2024 – JUNE 9, 2025

Hustle culture may be passé, but given the choice, you'd rather be "working hard" than "hardly working." (Other than during siesta time, of course...) Bulls aren't afraid to break a sweat when it's time to push through and achieve your intended results. And thank goodness for that! The first half of 2025 will require equal parts "inspiration" and "perspiration" as enterprising Jupiter muscles through Gemini and your money-earning second house.

This cycle is well underway as 2025 dawns. Jupiter planted itself in Gemini in the middle of last year—on May 25, 2024, to be exact. Hopefully, the red-spotted titan has been blessing you—and your bank account—with its fortunate beams. If not, you can tap this energy until June 9 to get back to being the moneymaker you know yourself to be.

Partnership is the name of the game when Jupiter is in the sign of the Twins. Do you work for yourself? Seek out joint ventures and collaborations that still allow you to retain a sense of independence. For example, you and another contractor could team up for a project without merging your entire businesses—or maybe you create a separate, joint LLC that focuses solely on one service that you'll provide together.

If you, like many Bulls, prefer the security of a 9-5, look for more effective ways to collaborate with coworkers. Don't hide the fact that you're a "systems person," especially if your coworkers' capricious ways have been throwing your efficiency out of whack. Gently introduce new ideas that help the team work smarter, not harder. While you may have to bear some grumbling, trust that everyone will be thanking you soon enough when they can clink beer steins with you at happy hour instead of staying an extra hour to fix another avoidable glitch.

Warning: Your thirst for luxury has probably increased under this Jupiter phase, and impulsive Gemini energy could spark some impulse-buying. Practice restraint, letting your budget—and your willpower—be your beacon in all major decisions. This is a fine time to work with a financial planner or to familiarize yourself with budgeting software to get on track. If you have money to invest, you might dabble in collecting in the first half of 2025—anything from paintings by emerging artists to NFTs could be worth considering.

URANUS IN GEMINI
JULY 7 – NOVEMBER 7, 2025
JANUARY 26, 2026 – MAY 22, 2033

July 7, 2025 may dawn like any other day, but it marks the beginning of an important new era in your life, Taurus. Ground-shaking, game-changing Uranus exits your sign after an extended seven-year stay. Ever since the radical planet first knocked on your door—or came crashing through—on May 15, 2018, it's been a helluva ride, with more personal changes and reinvention tours than you can keep track of. Whew!

And it certainly hasn't been easy! Unconventional Uranus is in "fall" in process-driven Taurus, making it one of the side-spinning planet's most challenging spots in the zodiac. You've no doubt felt unmoored at times, due to all the random fits and starts in your life since 2018. We're betting you also feel like quite the survivor. Yes, Taurus, you deserve a medal for riding the disruptive cosmic currents a Uranus transit through your sign can bring.

Modern-day power outlets require a grounding wire to prevent a surge of electric energy from blowing out the system. For the last seven years, you've been running currents without that protection. So you'll be happy to hear that from July 7 to November 7 of 2025, chaotic Uranus heads into excitable Gemini. But—it will be running through your stabilizing and monetizing second house. At last! You can direct Uranus' flow of "mad genius" energy toward things that feed your bank account and bring lasting security.

While we wish we could say you're done with Uranus, the planet has one final hurrah in Taurus from November 7, 2025 to April 25, 2026. After that, Uranus is fully ensconced in Gemini, where it will be charging up your second house of money, security and foundations until May 22, 2033. During that time, any- and everything that falls into those categories will be up for review and inspection, from your career trajectory to your investment strategy.

Are you looking out for Numero Uno, or do you tend to get a little casual about things like insurance, taxes and savings? In Gemini, the wild child planet will bring ingenious solutions, but it will also settle down and take these matters a lot more seriously. While you don't have to do it all this year, use the four-month window of Uranus in Gemini to get as many ducks as you can in a row. Don't be afraid to use technology and modernized systems, which futurist Uranus rules. It's time to take all those brilliant ideas and find a way to monetize some of them!

2 BECOME A LOCAL CELEBRITY

JUPITER IN CANCER
JUNE 9, 2025 – JUNE 30, 2026

Quick, Taurus, pull together your OTG, camera-ready look. "Local celebrity" could be your new status starting June 9, when lucky Jupiter swings into Cancer and charges up your social and communicative third house until June 30, 2026. After an industrious first half of 2025, you'll be more than ready to lift your nose from the grindstone and open up spaces on your calendar for pure playtime.

Good news! You won't have to travel far to get your fix of fun. While affable Jupiter rolls through Cancer, new friends and project partners crop up everywhere from the school pickup line to the heated yoga studio. The hardest part will be exerting self-control. You don't need to volunteer for every steering committee or bake sale. Be rigorous about checking your calendar before saying "yes," even if the FOMO feels unbearable. Double-booking is a real threat while "more is more" Jupiter plays social director in your chart.

As an energy-efficient earth sign, you prefer to work smarter rather than harder. Adopt the buddy system after June 9. Since platonic partnerships fall under the third-house rule, your efforts could quadruple when you pair up with people who match your diligent work ethic. But here's how things are different when Jupiter's in Cancer: Instead of playing the long game, opt for short-term and one-off collabs. Life is more of a sprint than a marathon during this cycle and you may quickly outgrow partners after the first or second joint effort. Better to not box yourself in, even if it goes against your nature to be so free flowing.

Have you hit a wall in your personal growth? Philosophical Jupiter in the third house could shuttle you into a life-altering training or certification program. You might even enroll in a community college or online degree program with flexible, part-time hours. As change-resistant as you are, remember that the unknown is just another chance at discovery. This is the perfect time to learn a new and marketable skill, which could be anything from flower arranging to building an AI chatbot.

Thanks to enterprising Jupiter, some Bulls could open the doors to a brick-and-mortar business, offering new energy to your community. Or, jetsetter Jupiter could find you embracing the bi-city living model, commuting back and forth between two locales in the name of personal expansion.

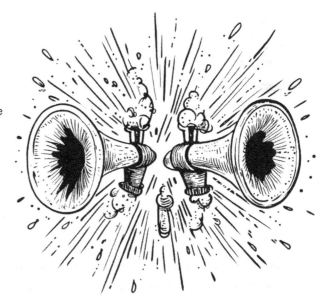

A sales job could also call your name under this 13-month Jupiter spell. Don't get stuck in that 9-5 groove if a more lucrative opportunity calls, perhaps one that lets you display your passion for a certain product.

Since the third house also rules communication, you could undergo some major growth here, too. If you're a writer or media-maker, this could be the year that you score a book or podcasting deal. Your name may become a recognizable byline at a prestigious publication.

Warning: Tell-it-like-it-is Jupiter can make you destructively direct in conversation, which is something that can happen when you suddenly go from sleeping bull to raging bull. On your self-improvement agenda? Learning to navigate conflict artfully. Deal with anger when it's at "yellow light" status, pausing and expressing yourself before you go into full-blown red mode. No more making like Yosemite Sam! You'll catch more flies with intentionally farmed honey than you will by charging like a toro after a waving red cape.

3

EMBRACE A SPIRITUAL PRACTICE

☉

SATURN AND NEPTUNE IN ARIES
NEPTUNE: MARCH 30 – OCTOBER 22, 2025 • JANUARY 26, 2026 – MARCH 23, 2039
SATURN: MAY 24 – SEPTEMBER 1, 2025 • FEBRUARY 13, 2026 – APRIL 12, 2028

Grab your scuba gear, Taurus, because you may not find yourself on the solid ground your earth sign prefers during the middle of 2025. Two planets—spiritual Neptune and sturdy Saturn—shift into Aries, activating your dreamy, subconscious twelfth house for part of the year.

There's not a ton you can do to prepare for this change; not in the practical sense, at least. Neither planet has visited Aries for a long time. Saturn's last tour through the Ram's realm was from 1996 to 1998. Nebulous Neptune was last in Aries from 1862 to 1875! The world is quite a different place now.

Fortunately, these planets make odd, but happy, bedfellows. Neptune supplies the imagination while Saturn brings the reality checks. Get ready to turn your dreams into something tangible—or start to. In 2026, Saturn plants in Aries for two full years and Neptune for thirteen. Surrender to the flow! The artsy side of your personality will thrive.

NEPTUNE IN ARIES
MARCH 30 – OCTOBER 22, 2025
JANUARY 26, 2026 – MARCH 23, 2039

Reality, what's that? Life could become as provocative as a Banksy installation starting this March 30 when hazy Neptune heads into Aries and your mystical twelfth house—its first visit to this zodiac sign since 1865 to 1875! Although Neptune's 2025 pass through the Ram's realm is brief this year, lasting only until October 22, consider it a warmup for what's to come. Neptune spins back into a thirteen-year cycle through Aries again from January 26, 2026, to March 23, 2039. Start preparing yourself for a soulful voyage. This dreamlike aura is set to become your "new normal" for the next decade-plus.

The prospect of softening, surrendering or releasing control may feel slightly destabilizing, especially for your earthy, grounded nature. Consider the wisdom in The

Pixies' classic track, "Where Is My Mind?" With "your head in the air and your feet on the ground," you can pull divine inspiration from the ether and weave it into your life here on Earth. It will take time before you can put your visionary downloads into words, much less a plan. Don't rush or force that process, Taurus, even if you, like most Bulls, love a good framework.

One thing you can be certain of: This Neptune cycle promises to be a fertile time for deep, soulful self-discovery. Where before you may have brushed off emotional exploration as "indulgent" or "unproductive," you could soon become obsessed with the workings of your own subconscious, like Taurus Sigmund Freud. If you don't already have a great therapist, spiritual counselor or artistic teacher, begin your search in earnest between March 30 and October 22.

Over the course of this longer cycle, you will transform ancient wounds into profound healing gifts. This Neptune transit might stir a calling within you, particularly if you've toyed with the idea of embracing a healing practitioner or an artist for change, like Bulls Bono, Melanie Martinez, Sam Smith and Ella Fitzgerald. No matter what, the pull towards integrating healing work into your life could grow irresistibly strong.

DO keep some boundaries in place, however. The slope could get slippery during this cycle, as both Neptune and the twelfth house are associated with codependence and addiction. Compassion could flood you in moments, making you feel like a psychic sponge soaking up everyone's pain and troubles. It will be important to remind yourself regularly that we are all souls on a journey and that you cannot do other people's healing work for them. If you are actively helping someone through their struggles, bolster yourself with support to avoid caretaker burnout and all the unhealthy offshoots of that from emotional eating to drinking or losing sleep out of worry and fear.

As Neptune weaves its magic through Aries, you'll find yourself at a powerful crossroads where personal transformation aligns with spiritual service. Whether it's through meditation, artistic expression, or therapeutic practices, this is your time to explore deeper realms of existence. The insights you glean could not only mend past hurts but also empower others on their own journeys to resolve generational trauma. Begin to visualize your role as a conduit of healing and wisdom, who bridges the divide between the seen and the unseen, the known and the mysterious. While this may seem like a distant dream, it could materialize faster than you expect, especially with Saturn co-piloting the mission for the next three years.

SATURN IN ARIES

MAY 24 – SEPTEMBER 1, 2025
FEBRUARY 13, 2026 – APRIL 12, 2028

You've always had a knack for turning lemons into lemonade Taurus, transforming what others see as setbacks into opportunities. It's one of the many reasons you command respect as a solid, stabilizing leader. And like the fabled tortoise who crushes the impetuous hare, you reach the finish line by setting microgoals and dusting them off one by one.

But come May 24, you're about to engage a different kind of skill set—one that focuses on attracting results rather than actively pursuing them. This shift comes courtesy of stalwart Saturn, as it enters Aries and your mystical twelfth house for a brief preview tour, from May 24 to September 1.

Although Saturn will retreat back into Pisces for one last round on September 1, it will set up camp again in Aries on February 13, 2026, hanging out there for a solid two years, until April 12, 2028. As pragmatic Saturn joins numinous Neptune in your twelfth house, finding the right emotional headspace will become just as crucial to your success as your famed tenacity. It's a good moment to pause and breathe deeply. Prepare to let go of some grueling tasks and allow yourself more downtime. You'll need a higher RDA of solitude, nature walks and ample self-care to navigate this transition effectively.

Some Bulls might feel the pull to step away from the hustle of urban life, perhaps finding a quiet beachside retreat to foster this deep introspection. And be prepared: As you do this inner work, there could be a shift in your professional life. You might find yourself considering a sabbatical or seeking less demanding roles, allowing you more time with loved ones rather than remaining married to your job. The twelfth house is the compassion corner of the zodiac, so any sort of "impact" work could also call your name, especially if it helps a disenfranchised group rise up and empower itself. Happy with your current career path? In your off time, look into volunteer work, charity efforts, or supporting friends through their own challenging phases.

This period is ripe for developing your intuitive abilities and remaining open to healing practices that help you overcome emotional barriers. If you've been too busy to address unresolved grief, toxic relationships, or clutter in your life—literal or metaphorical—those old excuses won't stand up anymore. Working with a therapist or coach might be necessary to help you gently let go of the burdens weighing on your psyche.

This isn't a quick process; this deep, steady work will set the stage for a powerful new beginning when Saturn enters Taurus on April 12, 2028. To ease any anxiety that comes with shifting away from your roll-up-your-sleeves instincts, consider starting a meditation practice or exploring techniques like tapping and breathwork to help smooth your path into this more reflective phase.

4 RELEASE ROMANTIC BLOCKS

VENUS RETROGRADE IN ARIES AND PISCES
ARIES: MARCH 1 – 27
PISCES: MARCH 27 – APRIL 12

The line between fantasy and "WTH is going on here?" could become extremely blurry from March 1 to April 12, when your ruler, love-goddess Venus, slips into a six-week retrograde. The planet of amour goes on these retreats every 18 months, but in 2025, she begins her backspin in Aries and your twelfth house of illusions, then slips into Pisces and your eleventh house of community from March 27 to April 12.

Did you recently weather a breakup, loss or a disappointing experience in life? Venus retrograde can be a powerful opportunity for heart healing. You may realize that it's time to bid a final farewell to someone who just won't commit to the level of relationship you want—or a friend who has stopped making efforts the way you both used to. Maybe you'll put up an uncrossable boundary in a relationship that keeps proving to be toxic for you. Whatever the case, swaddle yourself in support for this process, but get ready for a deluge of feelings. Your heart may take a little longer than your head to resolve this, so when it comes to your emotions, don't push yourself to "get over it" faster than is humanly possible.

If you feel utterly stuck, here's an unconventional idea: Create a mourning ritual for moving through the pain. What parts of this person or situation will you always love (and really miss for a while)? Set up a temporary altar with photos or objects, allowing yourself to feel the grief fully as you sit before it. By March 27, you might even be ready to build a fire and do a ceremonial burning of a few of those mementos—or else pack them away in storage. If visual evidence of the past is too triggering, as an alternative you could set aside a block of time each day to read healing books, journal about the loss, and give your emotions space to unleash. The fastest way to get over hurt is to go through it fully. Trust that you'll reclaim your access to joy once you allow yourself to plunge into the shadows.

Coupled Bulls won't be able to sweep issues under the rug—and thank goddness for that. This Venus retrograde may churn up buried issues that can, in turn, bring incredible insights for you both. If you're unable to host the conversation on your own, schedule a couples' therapy appointment or find another outlet where you can work together to heal issues and support one another through your self-discoveries.

Single? The colored lens trend might be huge, but keep the rose-colored glasses OFF your spring shopping list. Venus' backspin can skew your judgment and lure you towards the troubled types, even old hookups who seized your heart then ghosted because they weren't "ready" (or some other manufactured excuse). If there's any must-have accessory for the season, it's a levelheaded wingperson who can snap you back to reality before you race off trying to rescue another wounded bird from their self-inflicted demise.

Retrogrades can act as do-overs, too. If you ended a connection prematurely, you may get a second chance to reignite that flame, especially once Venus slips back into Pisces and your idealistic eleventh house from March 27 to April 12. Check in with yourself first: Is this "Let's make it work" urge coming from a true desire or a fear that you may never find anyone else? Some Bulls might be better off taking a little time out from dating until mid-April so you can get centered in your own power again.

In the meanwhile, fill yourself up with art, music and great friends. You could reconnect to an empowering community in April, which could cause your emotional cup to overflow with good vibes. That's the best antidote to being "thirsty," Taurus, which is never a good look in love. Should you find yourself feeling pangs of desperation during Venus retrograde, it may be a sign that you've neglected (or even abandoned) one of your own creative interests. Dig around in your archives and reignite your passion for watercolor painting, French cooking, playing guitar. Life's too short to let other people's actions control your happiness.

5

ASSEMBLE YOUR DREAM TEAM

LUNAR NODES IN VIRGO AND PISCES
NORTH NODE IN PISCES, SOUTH NODE IN VIRGO
JANUARY 11, 2025 – JULY 26, 2026

Pour yourself a giant mug of "me espresso." Like signmate Sabrina Carpenter, you could be the wakeup call the world didn't know it needed. Mark your calendars: On January 11, 2025, the lunar North Node sails into Pisces until July 26, 2026, energizing your eleventh house of popularity, teamwork and innovation. If you felt like a background player in 2024, prepare for a sudden surge in visibility. You're about to become a highly sought-after asset in any team, bringing your practical magic and grounded innovation to every project you touch.

The people you surround yourself with will play a critical role during this 18.5-month cycle. Be discerning with your social investments—this might mean setting boundaries or even cutting ties with those who drain your energy. Simultaneously, open up space to network and connect with people who don't just share your vibe but are also interested in creating the same world-changing things as you.

If there aren't many people like you in your zip code, find your kindred spirits online. Slide into DMs of people you admire, join international mastermind groups and put yourself out there on YouTube or Insta. That said, this is NOT the year to walk around in a tech trance instead of making eye contact with the people five feet in front of your face. Serendipitous encounters could spark unexpectedly, anywhere from a casual meetup to an after-work networking shindig. Don't miss the moment because you're too immersed in the latest flurry of trending TikTok memes.

Already part of a thriving dream team? Step on the accelerator after January 11. You're not one to shy away from improving and expanding the scope of your shared efforts. These initiatives are worthy of being pushed forward, perhaps with a practical twist only you can provide. If resistance pops up, remember it's just the usual fear of change. Your steadfast nature can help stabilize the group.

Since the eleventh house governs technology, the North Node in surreal Pisces might pull you into virtual realms. Got a groundbreaking idea for a digital platform or AI-based app? Start laying the groundwork. If it's viable, progress to the development phase, partnering with visionaries who can help turn your concept into reality.

Comfortably settled in a conventional job? That's not uncommon for your security-loving sign. The North Node in your futuristic eleventh house inspires you to be experimental. Start an ERG (employee resource group), spearhead an impact-driven initiative, like a product that donates a percentage of profits to cancer research. Back up your ideas with solid data, and you'll find others are more than willing to get on board with your plans.

While you want to be fair and democratic, there will be moments this year where you are called to take charge like the fearless Bull that you are. Across the zodiac wheel, the karmic South Node enters Virgo this January 11, revving up your fifth house of fame, leadership and romance. Public recognition is on the horizon, and you're ready to embrace it with surprising ease.

With the South Node in detail-oriented Virgo, you might worry about public perception. It's natural for your polished, polite sign to seek approval, but remember, you can't control people's opinions. Instead, focus on strengthening your self-assurance and confidence. Refresh your public profiles and materials to ensure that you're representing in a way that feels true to YOU.

Do you own a brand? Conduct a thorough review to ensure that your front-facing image is both stylish and cohesive. If public speaking isn't your forte, consider coaching to refine your presentation skills. Your role as a sought-after figure could accelerate. With some clear direction and a structure to lean into, your confidence will build.

On the romantic front, the Virgo South Node adds a fateful touch to your love life. Deep and enduring connections form during this period, ones that may have a simpler feeling of love and affinity. Nothing wrong will all the luxurious, high-key romantic experiences, of course—your Venus-ruled sign will always relish in these. But at the end of the day, you need someone who you love falling asleep with and who knows how you like your coffee when you wake up in the morning. Whether reigniting a past flame or elevating a current relationship, significant developments are likely. The trick, Taurus, is focusing on their enduring qualities rather than the adrenaline rush they give you.

For Bulls who are breaking up, this nodal cycle supports a respectful and thoughtful resolution, particularly in partnerships. Make Katherine Woodward Thomas' Conscious Uncoupling your manual for this separation, whether you do the work alone or together. The Virgo South Node's practical energy can facilitate an amicable breakup or a redefinition of relationships.

As you navigate this dynamic period, remember, Taurus, you're crafting a new social and public identity. Embrace the opportunities to stand out and to integrate your practical talents with your community and innovative projects. This is a time for growth, connection, and stepping confidently into a leadership role that showcases your unique strengths.

Love

TAURUS 2025 FORECAST

In love, you'd never settle for less than a soulmate, Taurus. But first, you may have some soul searching to do. Embrace it! This January 11, the karmic South Node lands in Virgo and your fifth house of passion, creativity, and romance; its first visit here in nearly twenty years. While this cycle unspools between now and July 26, 2026, it could pull you back to unfinished romantic business or help you create space in your heart for a deeper connection with your long-term love.

No matter your relationship status, 2025's starmap helps you refine your approach to love, bringing more discernment into matters of the heart. With the South Node's influence, you could release outdated patterns in romance, creating a future that resonates with your truest values.

Venus eases into spring with a retrograde from March 1 to April 12. The first half of this backspin takes place in Aries and your twelfth house of closure and reflection; then, on March 27, Venus slips back into obfuscating Pisces and your wishful eleventh house. During this hazy time, the future might feel unclear. Use this reflective period to heal old wounds and clear emotional clutter. Even happily coupled Bulls may feel like pulling back a bit in March and April.

But that all changes in early summer! From June 6 to July 4, your ardent ruler, Venus, sashays through your sign, amplifying your magnetism. This is the time each year where you feel like a total love magnet, drawing in admirers like moths to a flame.

Does it feel like life's been too kinetic for you to even THINK about relationships? Here's some heartening news. From July 7 to November 7, Uranus steps out of Taurus, giving you a breather from the unpredictable energy that's rocked your entire life since 2018. With this electric planet finally unplugged from your sign for a spell, you'll feel more stable, grounded and ready to build a lasting vision of love. Uranus leaves Taurus for good on April 25, 2026, so whatever sparks up during this six-month window could be prelude of what's to come next year.

As November 5 ushers in a powerful Taurus full moon (and supermoon), expect emotional clarity and romantic revelations. If you've been laying the groundwork in a relationship, this lunation marks a turning point where things begin to solidify. However, if a connection has reached its expiration date, this full moon may reveal that it's time to move on.

With Mars heating up Scorpio, your opposite sign and seventh house of partnerships, from September 22 to November 4, relationships will already be speeding toward a heightened level of intensity. This potent energy stirs up passion, but also calls for trust and vulnerability. Drop your defenses, Taurus—raw honesty will build the intimacy you crave.

Once Venus moves into Scorpio from November 6 to 30, the emotional depth continues, infusing your love life with transformation and deeper understanding. Prepare for a year-end surge of profound growth, where romance could turn into something life-changing.

TAURUS: LUCKIEST love DAY

JUNE 24

Not only do the passionate Sun and abundant Jupiter sync up in Cancer for the Day of Miracles this June 24, but they are uniting in parity in your flirtatious, communicative third house. This is the perfect day for discussing love goals or nudging a relationship to the next level. Better still? With your ruling planet, vivacious Venus, luxuriating in Taurus, you're already in your magnetic prime. Meanwhile, molten Mars in Virgo is stoking the flames in your romantic fifth house. Ask and you shall receive!

Money & Career

TAURUS 2025 FORECAST

Slow and steady is generally your best strategy for winning the race, Taurus, but this year, you may feel like you're riding both the gas and the brakes in your quest for success. Stay nimble and flex your patience along with your persistence. You've been learning how to be "both/and" in recent years instead of cleaving to one "right" way of doing things. This will come in handy now!

With Pluto spending its first full year in Aquarius and your tenth house of career and long-term goals, 2025 marks the early stages of a powerful transformation in your professional life. Pluto's influence is all about deep, lasting change. Since the metamorphic planet began weaving in and out of Aquarius in March 2023, it's possible that change has already begun to unspool for you.

Now you can prepare to shed old patterns and step into a new role of authority and influence. This could mean a complete overhaul of your career path or rising to the top in your current field. Alas, it won't come without a measure of hard work and intense self-reflection. Pluto's shifts demand an inside out evolution, but your power and magnetism will grow in the process.

Financially, Pluto in your tenth house demands that you play the long game. Invest in your future, even if it requires short-term sacrifices. If you've been holding onto outdated beliefs around money or success, Pluto will challenge you to rebuild those foundations from the ground up. Expect breakthroughs, but know they'll come through perseverance and strategic moves.

If it's fast cash you're after this year, you're in luck. Enterprising Jupiter continues its journey through Gemini, bringing its expansive energy to your second house of income and financial security until June 9. This time of accelerated opportunity can bring money in through both traditional and independent streams.

If you're up for a salary negotiation, schedule your review after February 4, once Jupiter ends its four-month retrograde. Maybe you want to launch a side hustle or learn a new monetizable skill. The red-spotted planet, which rules higher ed, can help with that, too. Focus on long-term financial stability and use that goal as your benchmark for whether or not to take a risk. If a certain "gamble" would threaten your baseline income, don't even think about it.

The push-pull prosperity dynamic continues when Uranus enters Gemini on July 7, electrifying your financial sector with unexpected opportunities and innovative ideas. Uranus brings change, so be prepared for sudden shifts in how you earn or manage your money. This could be a time of breakthroughs, where you explore unconventional ways to increase your net worth or make a career pivot that aligns with your true values.

Embrace flexibility and, possibly, flexible hours! You might be a 9-5er in some ways, but Uranus may push you out of your comfort zone to explore remote or hybrid work. Whether it's through technology, entrepreneurial ventures or a fresh approach to managing resources, experimenting with cutting-edge strategies could revolutionize your financial outlook before the year is through.

TAURUS: LUCKIEST *career* DAY

JANUARY 30

The Aquarius Sun is setting off sparks in your tenth house of career, pushing you toward a prominent professional position. As it trines lucky Jupiter in Gemini and your money corner for one day, get ready for a windfall! Pursue leads without hesitation, make a bold pitch. Opportunity could come knocking from a faraway location. Keep those WhatsApp notifications on!

2025
TAURUS

12 MONTH OVERVIEW

January MONTHLY HOROSCOPE

New year, new goal? Sure, but first, how about an extended holiday vacation? The Sun in ambitious Capricorn helps you broaden your horizons until the 19th. Since it's activating your worldly ninth house, you might literally do that by traveling or connecting with people overseas. Can't get away? Journey in the figurative sense by signing up for a class or a mastermind that's taught remotely to an international audience. Back at base, Mars retrogrades back through Cancer from January 6 to February 23, a time to iron out communication with your inner circle. (Watch your temper!) When the lunar nodes shift into Pisces and Virgo on January 11, they kick off an 18-month cycle packed with creative and collaborative opportunities. Your professional mojo returns on the 19th when the Sun moves into Aquarius. The Year of the Wood Snake starts on January 29, signaling transformation and adaptation as you build toward your 2025 goals, using your patient and practical approach.

February MONTHLY HOROSCOPE

Keep those lofty career goals in your crosshairs, Bull. With the Sun in Aquarius until February 18, you have the green light to think both inside and outside the box as you put your natural determination to work. In love, you may prefer fantasy to reality after your ruler, luxurious Venus, slips into Aries for an extended voyage starting February 4. Spin up romantic plans and float off on dream dates, but be careful not to idealize people instead of seeing them for who they really are. With lucky Jupiter snapping out of a four-month retrograde, also on the 4th, your enterprising spirit wakes up. Opportunities to increase your earnings and even sign your own paychecks will heat up between now and June 9. But wait, there's more! Collaborations take off at a gallop when Pisces season begins on February 18. This is the perfect time to strengthen existing friendships while generating new connections. Go-getter Mars corrects course and turns direct in your communicative, cooperative third house on February 23. Initiate coffee dates, pitch meetings and "chemistry tests" with all the new people you're considering for a role in the Taurus universe.

March MONTHLY HOROSCOPE

Your popularity is set to soar as the Pisces Sun enchants your communal eleventh house until the 20th. But don't overbook your schedule, Taurus! Your Aries-ruled twelfth house of solitude, spirituality and healing is getting rocked, making this one of the most introspective times of the year. If you need to tidy anything up, the March 14 Virgo full moon—an eye-opening lunar eclipse—delivers a loud wakeup call. Both Venus and Mercury will be retrograde in Aries—Venus from March 1 to 27 and Mercury from March 15 to 29—which could cause you to reassess the way you "do" relationships, friendships and romance in general. You're a giver, Taurus, and you expect a lot in return. Nothing wrong with that, but have your relationships grown too transactional? Release everyone from obligation and get back into a loving flow. Aries season begins on the 20th, helping you tie up loose ends before your birthday begins next month. The Aries solar eclipse on the 29th—the final one in a two-year series—could help you close a chapter for good. Stay open to divine downloads from the muse channel, which could come one day later, when numinous Neptune enters Aries for the first time since 1875!

April MONTHLY HOROSCOPE

Set your system to chill mode for the first part of April, with the Sun tucked away in your restful twelfth house until April 19. But don't go unconscious. There's still some internal work to be done. Mercury is retrograde in Pisces and your social eleventh house until April 7, and Venus, your ruler, follows suit, staying retrograde there until April 12. These cosmic backspins are pushing you to reassess your connections and collaborations. It's a great time to reflect on your friendships and team dynamics. Clear up any misunderstandings before moving forward with a supergroup (or prematurely breaking up the band). Once Mercury turns direct on the 7th, you'll feel more in sync with your squad, and when Venus gets back on track on the 12th, you'll have the charm to make new alliances or revive old ones. On April 18, Mars moves into Leo, firing up your fourth house of home and family until June 17. You'll feel energized to tackle any domestic projects or spruce up your living space. Birthday season begins when the Sun enters Taurus on April 19, bringing with it a surge of confidence and energy. With the new supermoon in Taurus on the 27th, set intentions so juicy that they scare you a little. You've got this, Taurus!

May MONTHLY HOROSCOPE

Taurus season wages on until the 20th, making this a month to shine like the Luxor Sky Beam. Don't be shy about sharing your visionary ideas, even if they're still technically "in progress." People will love cheering you on as you build your dream. Do you need to hone your leadership skills? Power broker Pluto slips into its annual five-month retrograde on May 4, backing up through Aquarius and your take-charge tenth house. There's always room to grow and improve, whether you're slowly ascending to a throne or living out your own version of Succession. Work with a coach, sign up for a management training or work alongside a seasoned exec who can give you insider tips for making it to the top. Relationship goals hit a milestone under the Scorpio full moon on the 12th. This "all or nothing" energy lays down the gauntlet: If you're not moving ahead together, you need to move in another direction. Life is too short to wait around! After May 20, Gemini season turns your focus to financial stability and security. With it comes a nudge to get out and build your professional network. Saturn joins Neptune in Aries on May 24—its first visit here since 1998! Strengthen your spiritual foundations by making time to reflect, meditate and heal old wounds. Your creative work could gain serious momentum while Saturn and Neptune team up in your twelfth house until September 1. Go forth and make art!

June MONTHLY HOROSCOPE

Finances are your primary focus while the Sun runs the numbers in Gemini until June 20. But no need to squint at an Excel spreadsheet. Now it's all about who you know! Become a regular at industry gatherings, set up power lunches and send out the pitch decks. On the 9th, worldly Jupiter swings into Cancer, where it will rev up your communicative, cooperative third house for an entire year. Joint ventures are the name of the game now, and you could find your ideal collaborators on any corner of the globe. Writing and broadcasting projects flourish with Jupiter in this live-out-loud zone. Get to work on that podcast, novel or workshop you want to lead. Summer love heats up early, as love planet Venus takes her annual strut through Taurus from June 6 to July 4. Romantically, you'll feel refreshed and renewed, so be proactive about pursuing those love goals. Mid-month may bring some challenges as Jupiter clashes with Saturn on June 15 and Neptune on June 18. In your desire to explore new opportunities, you could spin out in FOMO. Stay grounded, Taurus—focus on long-term plans rather than short-term fixes. On June 17, Mars enters Virgo, energizing your creative side and bringing a burst of productivity. When the Sun and Jupiter align on June 24, AKA the Day of Miracles, you could attract a kindred spirit or find an incredible outlet to let your voice be heard.

July MONTHLY HOROSCOPE

July 2025 brings a refreshing shift, Taurus, as Uranus finally moves out of your sign on July 7, bringing a sense of relief after its seven-year tour of shake-ups. With the planet of disruption settling into Gemini and your second house of income and stability until November 7, you'll spend the next six months focusing on innovative ways to boost your financial foundation. Venus spends most of the month in Gemini, too, easing this transition. Your social network—and possibly a romantic interest—can help light the way to financial opportunities. Until July 22, the Sun in Cancer keeps you grounded in your third house of communication and local connections, encouraging heart-to-hearts and getting back in touch with friends. But take note: Mercury turns retrograde in Leo on July 18, sending ripples through your fourth house of home and family. Expect some backtracking with renovations or family matters—double-check the fine print on any contracts or plans. Throughout the month, Neptune, Saturn and Chiron all turn retrograde in Aries (on the 4th, 13th and 30th, respectively). These five-month cycles could poke at old wounds or resurface some limiting beliefs. Don't get stuck in fear, Taurus! The challenge is to examine them and do some profound healing. When the Sun blazes into Leo on July 22, your focus shifts to creating a comfortable sanctuary. While retrograde delays might slow things down, you're in the mood to nest, so make sure your living space is your haven during this cosmic reset.

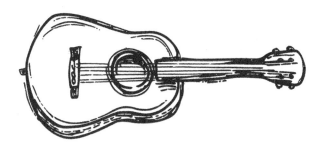

August MONTHLY HOROSCOPE

Security check! August is a month to get grounded and ensure that everything in your personal arena feels stable and snug. The Leo Sun beams into your domestic fourth house until August 22, pulling your attention back to base. Pour your energy into nurturing important family relationships and make sure your home feels like a sweet sanctuary. Caveat: Mercury will be retrograde until August 11, finishing up a backspin through Leo that began on July 18. Wait until mid-month to start any serious decor upgrades or renovations. Reunions can be heartwarming this month, but steer clear of relatives who may trigger (or straight-up traumatize) you. Lucky for you, peaceful, diplomatic Venus will be in Cancer and your communication zone until August 25. This can offset some of Mercury retrograde's sharp edges, while making dialogues flow with ease and warmth. Looking for love? Don't ignore a potential prospect who's been simmering in the friend zone. Coupled Bulls, bond through day trips, cultural activities and weekend getaways. On the 6th, energizer Mars lopes into Libra, activating your wellness zone until September 22. Pump up the power in your daily routines, but be careful not to overextend yourself running a half-marathon when you're only prepared for a sprint. Virgo season begins on August 22, shifting the energy to fun, romance and creative projects. When the first of two back-to-back new moons in Virgo arrives on August 23, expect a romantic (and artistic!) reboot. Whatever happens on this day will lay the foundation for an even bigger reset next month with the September 21 solar eclipse!

September MONTHLY HOROSCOPE

The only thing constant is change this month, Bull, which can be challenging for your stability-loving sign. The good news? As the Virgo Sun shines into your passionate fifth house until September 22, your romantic nature is in full force and people will appreciate your creative insights. Venus begins the month in Leo, harmonizing your home life and giving you the urge to nest. After the 19th, the love planet's move into Virgo lures you out for dress-up dates, red-carpet events and high-key romantic adventures. Who's on Team Toro? On September 1, retrograde Saturn slips back from Aries into Pisces, redirecting your attention to your social circle. Certain alliances could go through a stress test, revealing who you can and can't depend on. Uranus slips into its annual retrograde on the 6th, which could throw a wrench into a few initiatives before November 7. Stay flexible with your budget as you may need to allocate personal resources differently than expected this fall. That's not all! It's officially eclipse season on the 7th, when the total lunar (full moon) eclipse in Pisces reveals hidden dynamics within a group. Two weeks later, on the 21st, the solar (new moon) eclipse in Virgo blows fresh energy toward your creative projects—and may even reveal an unexpected romantic opportunity. Build on efforts you began with the first new moon in Virgo on August 23. You regain a bit of balance once Libra season starts with the equinox on the 22nd. Ground back into your healthy routines, like eating clean and getting sufficient sleep. But no rest for the Bulls this month! The very same day, sultry Mars enters Scorpio, intensifying your relationship zone. Partnerships could get passionate, but power dynamics may come into play.

October MONTHLY HOROSCOPE

Every Bull needs a pasture, and while the Sun nestles in Libra until October 22, implement routines that make your life flow. Whether that means a productivity overhaul or just increasing your self-care quota, "contagious ease" is the goal. If someone needs training in the way you like things done, take the lead, but with patience. Thanks to the Libra Sun, you'll be adept at handling any "teachable moments" that arise, both at work and in your love life. Sparks keep flying in your love life while Venus struts through Virgo and your glamorous fifth house until the 13th. Get your beauty rest during the workweek and fill your weekends with concerts, tastings and all the cultural activities a Taurus loves. Once Venus sashays into Libra on the 13th, your idea of a dream date could look more like a fall hike or a buddy workout at the gym. Career goals get back on track once Pluto turns direct in Aquarius, also on the 13th. Realign around a group goal or revamp a professional presentation. Budding attractions could blossom into full-on partnerships once Scorpio season begins on the 22nd. Pro tip: Look for a complement, not a clone. Existing relationships also get a boost from this four-week solar cycle. Make room in your schedule for "we time." Neptune retrogrades back from Aries into Pisces that same day. Dive into an altruistic project or pick up a group activity that sparks your imagination and fuels your sense of purpose.

November MONTHLY HOROSCOPE

Wanted: meaningful connections that are wired to go the distance. The Sun spends the month in your partnership houses—Scorpio and, after the 21st, Sagittarius—drawing you into the depths of intimacy. There's no settling for "casual" after November 4, when lusty Mars ignites a bonfire in Sagittarius and your eighth house of permabonding. And once Venus slips into Scorpiofrom November 6 to 30? It's all or nothing, baby. Think of your relationships as investments and give them the care and feeding they deserve. November 5, however, is all about you, when the year's only Taurus full moon (a supermoon) puts your desires front and center! Career-wise, you're fired up to merge assets or create a long-term partnership. That's great, Taurus, but take your time with negotiations! Mercury spins into its final retrograde of the year—in Sagittarius from November 9 to 18, then Scorpio until the 29th. Recalibrate shared ventures and double-check the details, from contracts to promises made. It might take you until December to iron out discrepancies. Adding to the uncertainty, disruptive Uranus retrogrades back into Taurus on the 7th for its final (in this lifetime!) lap through your sign. This seven-year cycle ends on April 25, 2026, but before then, you may need to set some of your visionary, innovative plans in stone—without any outside input. Expansive Jupiter turns retrograde in Cancer on November 11, giving you four months to work on your personal messaging and sort through relationships with your peers. By the time Saturn ends its five-month retrograde in your eleventh house of teamwork on November 27, you'll be ready to rally your soul squad and knock those year-end goals out of the park.

December MONTHLY HOROSCOPE

Lucky you, Taurus! This December, the Sun beams in Sagittarius until the 21st, highlighting your eighth house of shared resources, intimacy, and transformation. With Venus and Mars traveling together through this sign for the first half of the month, keep exploring ways to bond with the MVPs in your life, like merging finances or pursuing a strategic collaboration. Driven Mars moves into ambitious Capricorn on December 15, lighting up your ninth house of travel, expansion and higher learning. Wanderlust may strike pre-holidays. If so, try to slip off for a spontaneous escape, even if it's just for a weekend. On the 10th, Neptune turns direct in Pisces, lending a sweet, forgiving energy to friendships and your social circle. If there have been misunderstandings or emotional distance, now's the time to bridge those gaps. On December 21, the Winter Solstice and the Sun's move into Capricorn add more fuel to your ninth house of growth and adventure, inspiring you to take a leap of faith that broadens your worldview. The excitement continues once Venus joins Mars in Capricorn on December 24. If you weren't ready before, now you'll be compelled to dream about your visionary 2026 plans. Before the year is through, you may have your sights set on an epic goal, like applying to grad school, starting a business, writing a book or taking a bucket-list vacation. With all this ninth-house energy, New Year's Eve is poised to be anything but ordinary. Celebrate in a way that pushes your limits, whether it's a glamorous event or clinking glasses on another continent!

A LITTLE ABOUT Gemini

DATES May 20 - June 20

SYMBOL The Twins

ELEMENT Air

QUALITY Mutable

RULING PLANET Mercury

BODY PART Hands, arms

BEST TRAITS

Mesmerizing, original, resourceful, charming, friendly, adventurous, witty, unexpected

KEYWORDS

Communication, collaboration, synergy, intellect, ingenuity, versatility

*Read more
about Gemini*

GEMINI
IN 2025

Gemini in 2025

YOUR YEARLY OVERVIEW

Comfort zone? What's that? Lucky, expansive Jupiter continues its 12-month journey through your sign, energizing your trailblazing, self-sovereign first house until June 9. If it's novel, daring and out of the box, it's for you in 2025, Twin. And the hits keep on coming. From July 7 to November 7, renegade changemaker Uranus swings into Gemini, its first visit to your sign since 1941-49. This seven-year cycle—which picks up again April 2026—can radically reshape your identity. Ready to be Internet-famous or part of a buzzy supergroup? With serious Saturn and imaginative Neptune spending part of the year in Aries, your popularity is set to soar. But how to balance career aspirations and the demands at home base? Once the destiny-dusting lunar nodes decamp to Pisces (North Node) and Virgo (South Node) on January 11th, you'll have a solid year and a half to sort that out. You'll wave farewell to expansive Jupiter on June 9, as the red-spotted planet surfs on to Cancer and your zone of money and values. What will you do next to secure the bag? Professional growth is on the horizon, but you'll need to release old patterns to create space for your evolving dreams.

THE PLANETS IN *Gemini*

THE SUN
MAY 20–JUN 20

Bask in the spotlight—it's your birthday season! Dive into novel adventures and make audacious moves that put you front and center.

NEW MOON, SUPERMOON
MAY 26
11:02PM, 6°06'

Honorary New Year! Set personal intentions under this accelerating new supermoon, then shift into action mode.

FULL MOON, SUPERMOON
DEC 4
6:14PM, 13°04'

Ready, set, manifest! Your work of the past six months bears fruit and it's time to harvest the rewards. They'll be brighter and more bountiful than ever under this potent supermoon.

MERCURY
MAY 25–JUN 8

Crown yourself monarch of the social butterflies when popularity-boosting Mercury visits your sign once a year. Circulate and get social—but don't make promises you can't keep!

VENUS
JUL 4–30

You've got the romantic It Factor when the galactic glamazon charges up your powers of seduction each year. Willpower is weak in the face of beauty and luxury. Watch your spending!

JUPITER
MAY 25, 2024–JUN 9, 2025
RETROGRADE IN GEMINI:
OCT 9, 2024-FEB 4, 2025

How lucky can you get? Bountiful Jupiter visits your sign once every 10–12 years, blessing you with extra fortune. Everything's exciting...and extra! Take calculated risks but avoid gambles, particularly during the retrograde.

URANUS
JUL 7–NOV 7
RETROGRADE IN GEMINI:
SEP 6–NOV 7

Life feels like a sci-fi movie when Uranus visits your sign (for seven years) every 84 years. Ungrounding and chaotic as it is, you can make incredible life changes now—at lightning speed. The innovative planet will visit you for half a year, giving you a sneak peek of a longer cycle that begins again on April 25, 2026.

Gemini in 2025
HIGHLIGHTS

EXPANSION MEETS SELF-DISCOVERY: JUPITER IN GEMINI

2025 is a year of profound growth and self-discovery for you, Gemini. With Jupiter lighting up your sign until June 9, you're infused with a dynamic energy, ready to push pre-existing boundaries and bolt through new doors. The first half of the year could bring game-changing career moves, exhilarating travels or a revamp of your entire style and personal brand. You'll be inspired to say "yes" to anything that excites you, and that's just fine! Jupiter only visits your sign once every 12-13 years. There's no better time to stretch beyond your comfort zone and redefine what freedom truly means to you. As you realign with your authentic desires, allow yourself to prioritize personal growth without guilt.

REINVENTION ON THE HORIZON: URANUS ENTERS THE SCENE

If you were hoping to fit yourself neatly into a box, sorry, Gemini, that's just not gonna happen in 2025. Liberated, futuristic Uranus sweeps into Gemini from July 7 to November 7, basically turning everything you thought you knew about yourself on its ear. This planetary shift brings a sneak preview of a longer seven-year cycle that picks up again on April 25, 2026. Expect surprises, sudden changes and bursts of inspiration that urge you to break free from any lingering limitations. Uranus is the planet of disruption, but (mostly) in the best way possible. Embrace the unconventional as you step fully into your unique genius. Whether it's an overhaul of your lifestyle, a radical style makeover or a redirect of your personal goals, be open to surprises and release attachments to outdated ways of life.

LOVE & RELATIONSHIPS: VENUS IN GEMINI

Romance will also play a significant role in 2025, especially when Venus graces your sign from July 4 to 30. As summer begins, your natural magnetism will be off the charts, making it a perfect time to strengthen existing attractions or draw new love into your life. However, before this sweet spell, Venus spins retrograde from March 1 to April 12, which could bring unresolved relationship issues to the surface or rekindle past connections. Reassess what your heart truly desires before diving into any new romantic adventures. Don't shy away from having the "long-term plans" conversations you've been avoiding. You have TWO supermoons in your sign this year: The May 26 Gemini new moon and the December 4 Gemini full moon. Dream big in love and don't over-compromise!

FINANCIAL GROWTH: BUILDING STABILITY

With the Pisces North Node energizing your career house all year (as of January 11), your eye will be on a bigger, more profitable prize. Mingle with VIPs and you could lift yourself into a new income bracket in 2025. Meanwhile, the Virgo South Node underscores the importance of creating a security blanket, so tighten your belt, Twin. As Jupiter moves into Cancer on June 9, financial growth accelerates. Build on (and monetize!) the opportunities you explored earlier in the year. Whether through savvy investments, career advancements or a refined savings strategy, your hard work will begin to bear fruit. Stay focused on long-term rewards and avoid impulsive spending or anything that feels like a gamble. You could expand your earning power through studying, training or an entrepreneurial venture. Cast a wide net in your search for sustenance.

TEAMWORK MAKES THE DREAM "WERK"

With Saturn and Neptune spending part of 2025 in Aries and your eleventh house, you're in for a year that focuses on assembling your squad and establishing meaningful connections. Saturn encourages you to get serious about the people in your circle— quality over quantity is the name of the game. Become a key player in an existing group or take the lead in a new community venture. At the same time, Neptune's dreamy influence adds a creative, almost mystical dimension to your social life. You may find yourself drawn to artistic or spiritual collectives, where you can share your visionary ideas. Merge your ambitions with your ideals and connect with like-minded souls who inspire you to dream bigger while keeping your feet on the ground.

OWN THE ROOM: PLUTO IN AQUARIUS

With power broker Pluto in Aquarius forming a harmonious trine to your Sun for the first full year, you're radiating a quiet magnetism that others can't help but notice. This transformative energy fuels your desire for growth, pushing you to explore new philosophies and expand your worldview in profound ways. You're stepping into your leadership without having to shout about it. People will be drawn to your insights and ideas, recognizing your genius. Embrace your influence,  whether by teaching, sharing your story or taking a bold leap toward personal freedom. Expect deeper connections and a renewed sense of purpose to emerge as you reveal your most unapologetic self.

TOP 5 THEMES FOR
Gemini in 2025

1	2	3	4	5
UNVEIL THE TRUE YOU	INCREASE YOUR NET WORTH	REDEFINE SOCIAL BOUNDARIES	PLAN MEANINGFUL REUNIONS	CHASE BIG DREAMS

1 UNVEIL THE TRUE YOU

Ⅱ

JUPITER AND URANUS IN GEMINI

JUPITER: MAY 25, 2024 – JUNE 9, 2025
URANUS: JULY 7 – NOVEMBER 7, 2025 • JANUARY 26, 2026 – MAY 22, 2033

Who do you think you are, Gemini? That answer could fluctuate wildly in 2025 as two of the most radical, experimental and liberated planets, Jupiter and Uranus, do time in your sign. Jupiter spends the first half of the year in Gemini, freeing your nomadic soul. Then, radical Uranus plugs into Gemini from July 7 to November 7, giving you a preview of a seven-year, redefining cycle that begins in April 2026.

JUPITER IN GEMINI

MAY 25, 2024 – JUNE 9, 2025

Before the first champagne bottle hits the recycling bin, you may be off to the races on a personal quest this January! The reason for this momentum? Lucky, adventurous Jupiter reaches the halfway mark of its yearlong trek through Gemini, an accelerating cycle that kicked off on May 25, 2024. Since then, you've seldom had a chance to stop and catch your breath. Not that you've much longed for that sort of reflective down time. (You had far too much of it when Jupiter was in Taurus from May 16, 2023 to May 25, 2024. Heavy!)

You have, however, been fired up to take the initiative and direct your life in a more purposeful way. Novelty has always been the spice of Gemini's life. As you seek new people, places and experiences, be open to the possibility of creating something big and world-changing together. Although Jupiter is the planetary nomad, you and your prospective allies don't have to be two ships passing in the night. That said, you may operate out of two very distant ports from one another. Long-distance connections expand your reach!

Plus, Jupiter's tour through your sign has likely activated a very independent part of your spirit. "Joined at the hip" is not a desirable status for you in the first half of 2025, even if you're happily coupled. The red-spotted planet only visits your sign once every 10-12 years, a time that's meant for "selfishly" putting your desires first. It's not your job to be The Great Compromiser in 2025, Gemini, especially if that means deferring a long-held dream.

The need to regain your autonomy may become irresistible, and no matter what your relationship status, you are ready to pursue your individual interests. Absence can make the heart grow fonder, but if you've been unhappily partnered or married, now is the time to deal. In some cases, a temporary—or permanent—separation may be in order.

Before you do anything irreversible, however, look at the role you've played. Healthy boundaries may have been impossible to uphold. So quit playing "happy helper" or "martyr" in your relationship and pursue your passions without apology. You may be surprised at how supportive your partner can be. In some cases, it will be worth giving it one last shot before you call it quits. If you're single, enjoy your freedom. If you're being honest, you might realize you don't feel like being tied down right now.

If you haven't started tapping this game-changing energy, make haste! Jupiter will hang out in your sign until June 9, but after that, you won't host this lucky charm again for another 12 years. While you may have to roll the dice on an opportunity that doesn't have a certain outcome, your risk tolerance is higher than usual now.

Plus, you have places to go and people to see. Among them may be university professors, venture capitalists, world travelers and anyone you'd define as a trailblazing leader. Your days may be busier than they've been in a while, but you'll feed off the excitement. With this fuel in your tanks, get ready to grow in directions that are so off your radar that they never made it to your 2025 vision board. Yet, when you feel that wild surge of desire rise up, you owe it to yourself to follow that lead! Just make sure you drop a few pins along the route so you don't completely lose your way.

URANUS IN GEMINI
JULY 7 – NOVEMBER 7, 2025
JANUARY 26, 2026 – MAY 22, 2033

"Be the change you want to see in the world"? Careful what you wish for, Twin. On July 7, 2025 metamorphic Uranus blasts into your sign for the first time since 1941-49, electrifying your first house of self, identity and appearance.

You've already gone through quite the upgrade since Jupiter entered your sign from May 25, 2024 to June 9, 2025. Thought you could kick back and ride the wave of certainty? Guess again. While changemaker Uranus only spends four months in Gemini this year, until November 7, consider it a preview of an upcoming seven-year cycle. On April 25,

2026, Uranus will plant itself in Gemini until May 22, 2033, shaking up life as you know it once again.

For essentially the next eight years, Uranus sends jolts of transformative energy through your entire life. Uranus rules community activism, technology and inventions, so it feels right at home in your ingenious sign. Since May 15, 2018, Uranus has been stuck in the muck of Taurus and your spiritual, esoteric twelfth house. This has been a period of profound inner growth, marked by soulful lessons, grief, losses and divine inspiration. But getting your work into the world may have felt like a series of power surges and power outages. So. Damn. Frustrating.

Expansive Jupiter continues to lift you out of obscurity in the first half of the year, but then it will hunker down in Cancer and your stabilizing second house on June 9. However, starting July 7, Uranus picks up where Jupiter left off. This is your once-in-a-lifetime invitation to become the pop culture sensation you were born to be.

Don't stress about getting your name on any charts in 2025 (although it could certainly happen for the May-born Twins). Remember, you will have a solid seven years to harness Uranus' power starting April 25, 2026. You might, however, feel as if an alien abduction has taken place in your life. Space-cadet Uranus has a habit of throwing curveballs into every situation it touches. You may be speeding along one trajectory only to pivot onto a completely unexpected series of detours.

Thankfully, that's nothing new for you, Gemini. You live for the moment and thrill at the chance to change course when a better opportunity presents itself. Just make sure you do your due diligence before you race off willy-nilly. This disruptive cycle could also bring some false flags.

By the time Uranus moves on to Cancer in 2033, your identity, friend circle, career path and relationship status could be in a totally different place. We're not saying the same key players won't be there. But the way that you relate to them may go through more upgrades than the iOS on your phone. And that's due to your "internal operating system" upgrades. When Uranus comes to your sign every 84 years, it radically shifts your perspective, making you more open and free than you've possibly felt in your entire life. And for a Gemini, that's saying something. Buckle up!

2 INCREASE YOUR NET WORTH

JUPITER IN CANCER
JUNE 9, 2025 – JUNE 30, 2026

♊

Mid-year, you'll be ready to pull the e-brake and stop the wild ride. While slowing down might seem inconceivable before June 9, everything changes that day as speed demon Jupiter exits your sign and ambles into Cancer and your slow and steady second house until June 30, 2026. While this might give you temporary whiplash, it's officially time to get your bearings again, Twin. Embrace the opportunity to integrate all the incredible growth you've had since 2025 began.

And how about making some bank to fund the genius ideas you've cooked up while Jupiter toured your sign since May 25, 2024? As the abundant planet energizes your second house of finances and foundations it can turn you into a money magnet. Calculated risks pay off as long as they're anchored in some sort of strategic thinking. Cautious Cancer tempers some of Jupiter's gambling instincts, which could bring the "just right" balance of vision and common sense that will show up positively on your balance sheet. Whether you're building the ground floor of your future empire or moving and shaking in the corporate world, a moderate approach works best during these thirteen months.

Question: Are you getting paid what you deserve? If not, you might ferret out your own limiting beliefs in the salary department. Are there gaps in your skill set? Jupiter could send you back to campus to enroll in trainings, special seminars and perhaps a degree program.

Traveling for work is a strong possibility for Gems on the go. Make sure your passport is up-to-date so you can be first in line to volunteer for the opportunity to visit the London office or represent the company abroad at a sales conference. Regardless of where you log in every morning, you won't be getting a break from Zoom fatigue when Jupiter's in Cancer. The projects you're involved in may be so compelling, in fact, you might feel like you could work 24/7 and still not get it all done. The risk of burnout is as high as the potential for growth. For this reason, you'll need to be more protective of your personal time after June 9.

We're going to make a bold and unreasonable suggestion, Gemini. Carve out a few device-free hours each day and consider leaving your mobile devices out of reach when you're having family dinners, hanging out with friends or reading a paperback book. For your plugged-in sign, this might sound laughable; triggering, even. But pacing yourself is the key to staying productive while Jupiter's in Cancer, a cycle that's equal parts "tortoise" and "hare."

The second house is earthy, so bring on the open sky, lush forests and garden space! Adventurous Jupiter could make this your summer for wilderness adventures. If you don't have a yard to plant edibles in, get involved in a community garden. Farm-to-table delights await! Bonus: Getting dirt under your well-manicured fingernails reminds you of your connection to Mother Earth. Perhaps it's time to invest in that country house or move outside the big city for a year?

3 REDEFINE SOCIAL BOUNDARIES

SATURN AND NEPTUNE IN ARIES

NEPTUNE: MARCH 30 – OCTOBER 22, 2025 • JANUARY 26, 2026 – MARCH 23, 2039
SATURN: MAY 24 – SEPTEMBER 1, 2025 • FEBRUARY 13, 2026 – APRIL 12, 2028

You've never met a stranger, Gemini, but starting this year, you may revoke a few "all access" passes to your social circle. Two weighty planets—Saturn and Neptune—dart forward into Aries and your eleventh house of community and collaboration. Strict Saturn is a boundary hound while enchanting Neptune is desperately challenged at setting them. Contradictory as this sounds, these planets can work together to help you learn how to give, play and share without resentment.

Get ready to ad lib, Gemini. There's no recent template for how to interact with these transits. Saturn's last pass through Aries was from 1996 to 1998 while Neptune hasn't touched this zone since 1862 to 1875! People socialized and communed in very different ways during each of those periods. While Saturn and Neptune will only spend a portion of 2025 in Aries, both embark on longer, unbroken laps through the Ram's realm beginning in early 2026.

NEPTUNE IN ARIES

MARCH 30 – OCTOBER 22, 2025
JANUARY 26, 2026 – MARCH 23, 2039

Your renegade era is officially underway! It all begins on March 30 when, for the first time since 1875, imaginative Neptune floats into Aries and your innovative, game-changing eleventh house. With the compassionate planet awakening your activism, there will be no shortage of important causes to get involved with. But it's okay to be a little "selfish" here, devoting your attention to one (or two) that will impact a community that you hold dear.

Although Neptune's visit to Aries is brief in 2025, lasting until October 22, this is a preview of what's to come. On January 26, 2026, the numinous planet floats back into the Ram's realm for thirteen more years, until March 23, 2039. After fifteen long years of hosting the planet of illusions in Pisces and your career zone, this will be a welcome relief. Before 2025 is through, certain ambitions may come into sharper focus. If you're feeling burnt out from your current career path—or just ready to do something a little less draining—Neptune's exit from Pisces could steer you toward a job that involves technology or working in a more team-oriented way.

As Neptune drifts into dynamic Aries it begins a transformative journey through your eleventh house of friendships, networks, and social influence. While your natural curiosity drives you to explore new ideas and collaborations, this is a period for quality over quantity. From March 30 to October 22, 2025, you'll be called to reassess the people and communities you surround yourself with. Neptune, the planet of dreams and illusions, could blur the lines between true allies and mere acquaintances, urging you to tune into your intuition like never before.

Who are the people who truly uplift and inspire you? Prioritize those connections and let go of any relationships that drain your energy or no longer align with your evolving values. Focus on building genuine, meaningful connections rather than chasing every opportunity that comes your way.

This Neptune transit will also shine a spotlight on your digital presence. The eleventh house rules technology and online networks, making this prime time to refine your social media strategy or potentially launch a new online project. But Neptune's foggy influence means that not everything will be as it seems. Be cautious about who you partner with in the digital realm and, if you're selling online, protect customer data from breaches.

On a deeper level, Neptune in Aries could stir a powerful desire within you to engage in social causes or activism, particularly those that resonate with your core values. Whether it's advocating for environmental issues, human rights, or political change, you might feel an irresistible pull to use your voice for the greater good. Your gift for communication, combined with Neptune's visionary influence, can make you a compelling advocate for the causes you believe in.

As you navigate Neptune's swirling seas, the key is to stay true to your core values and long-term vision. Neptune in Aries is here to help you dream big, but it's also known to disorient you along the way. This is a period of profound growth and transformation, where the connections you forge and the causes you champion can have a lasting impact on your future. Embrace the journey, but keep your inner compass steady as you sail ahead.

SATURN IN ARIES
MAY 24 – SEPTEMBER 1, 2025
FEBRUARY 13, 2026 – APRIL 12, 2028

A significant life shift is on the horizon this May 24, and it's absolutely worth celebrating. Since March 7, 2023, you've weathered taskmaster Saturn in Pisces, challenging your house of career, ambition, and relentless efforts. And with Saturn forming a grueling square to your Gemini Sun, it's been a marathon of "Extreme Challenges." It's possible that you've been pushed to the limits, draining your reserves of confidence and forcing you to rebuild them under intense pressure.

But here comes the good news: Saturn darts forward into Aries from May 24 to September 1, landing in a much more favorable position that promises to bring not just relief but some rock-solid allies, too. Aries rules your eleventh house of community, collaboration and activism, sparking the call to assemble your Gemini dream team—a collective of change-makers ready to join you in your quest to better the world (or at least your corner of it). This brief cycle is a preview of a longer, two-year cycle that begins on February 13, 2026, when Saturn circles back into Aries until April 12, 2028.

Alas, it's not going to be all fun and games in the "people department." During this transit, you may feel the weight of responsibility in your group activities and collective endeavors. Saturn in Aries demands that you step up as a leader, but in a way that's both disciplined and strategic. Whether you're involved in a work project, a community organization, or a social cause, Saturn's presence will urge you to take your commitments seriously and ensure that your contributions are both meaningful and sustainable.

While you're no elitist, Gemini, your social circles during this period may resemble an insider's club. This isn't the time for superficial connections or fleeting collaborations—Saturn wants you to build something that lasts, something that truly matters. The realization may dawn that you've outgrown some of your longtime pals. No need to go on an unfriending spree. A gentle drifting apart is better than a dramatic ghosting under slow and steady Saturn's watch. Even if the cast of your innermost circle changes, you can never have too many allies.

Professionally, Saturn's transit through your eleventh house could bring a moment of truth regarding your career aspirations and the role your network plays in achieving them. If you've been cruising along, relying on your charm and adaptability, Saturn will insist that you get more intentional about who you collaborate with. This could mean tightening your circle to include only those who are genuinely supportive of your ambitions, or it might involve taking on more responsibilities within your professional networks. Saturn's lessons are rarely easy, but they're always valuable, pushing you to mature and solidify your path forward.

Have a groundbreaking idea for an invention, app, or profitable website? The eleventh house also governs technology, so with Saturn in Aries, your Silicon Valley aspirations could very well become a reality. Social responsibility also falls under the domain of the eleventh house. Dismiss any exploitative, get-rich-quick schemes and focus on launching an impact-driven venture, or find ways to bring the spirit of inclusivity into your current endeavors. Your quest to better the world (or at least your corner of it) might be idealistic, but tap into Saturn's planning powers and the path forward will soon become clear.

4

PLAN MEANINGFUL REUNIONS

Ⅱ

VENUS RETROGRADE IN ARIES AND PISCES
ARIES: MARCH 1 – 27
PISCES: MARCH 27 – APRIL 12

Scroll through your contact lists and scan old timeline posts. Charming, vivacious Venus turns retrograde for six weeks this spring, backing up through Aries and your eleventh house of community from March 1 to 27, then slipping back into Pisces and your career zone until April 12. Maybe it's time to reconnect to a beloved friend group from which you drifted...or get the band back together for a reunion tour.

Since Venus is the pleasure planet, the universe could send you a strong signal to level up your spring break plans. Think about doing something decadent in March, like reuniting in Paris for a long weekend of clubbing, exhibitions and boulangeries. Of course, this comes with a retrograde alert to book accommodations with care and avoid buying sketchy tickets on the secondary market. Even a staycation to a dear friend's home could bring enough warm-fuzzy vibes (and fun!) to speed you through the final weeks of winter.

When Venus backs into Pisces and your professional sector from March 27 to April 12, get ready to put more effort into generating leads and opportunities. Maybe you had an initial brainstorming meeting with someone that never quite materialized into anything tangible. Timing could now be on your side. Set up conference calls and coffee dates to see if the synergies are still there. Already got the wheels in motion? You could do some major behind-the-scenes development on an ambitious plan, one that could be ready for a big reveal near your birthday.

In love, Venus retrograde cautions against putting the cart before the horse. If you've only gone on a handful of dates, for example, stop tormenting yourself with questions like, "Is this person The One?" Until April 12, Venus will be tightening those reins, insisting that you follow due process. Slow down and, if you're still single, temper that urge to rush headlong into serial monogamy before you've sampled a few possibilities.

If you've had a prolonged—and unrequited crush—on someone who keeps flitting in and out of your heart, this is the time to be more hardcore with yourself. Don't take yourself off the market as you wait for them to upgrade you from "situationship status." Better still? Use Venus retrograde for the weaning process and limit the time you spend together. That way, you can open up space for someone who is actually ready to commit. Plus, you know what they say: Absence makes the heart grow fonder.

Coupled Twins may have some real negotiating to do about your shared future. Your big plans and dreams are generally a topic of everyday conversation; but when was the last time you asked your S.O. about THEIR five-year plan (or heck, even the next six months)? The retrograde creates a peaceful window to discuss "what's next" for each of you. But get ready, Gemini, because if you really probe, your partner might reveal some independent desires that don't easily dovetail with your own. You might even have some strong emotions about it, feeling blindsided, angry or upset. Try to remember that everything is a negotiation. Maybe your partner wants to move to Portugal for a yearlong design intensive and you just accepted a job at a firm in Manhattan; or suddenly one of you wants a baby, when last year, you were both sure that a Labradoodle was the next big move.

Whatever the case, there's a strong possibility that you're going to have a few things to work out. Life paths don't always line up perfectly, even when you love someone, and this Venus retrograde may reveal a fork in the road; but that's what "playing the long game" (your favorite game) looks like, right? Things like this don't have to be the END of the road, but perhaps the beginning of an adventurous new chapter. Get it all out into the open!

5

CHASE BIG DREAMS

LUNAR NODES IN VIRGO AND PISCES
NORTH NODE IN PISCES, SOUTH NODE IN VIRGO
JANUARY 11, 2025 – JULY 26, 2026

Money, power, success! You'll take all three, thanks, with a whole lotta heart thrown in. For this you can thank the lunar nodes, which change signs this January 11, 2025. As the North Node soars into Pisces, it sails to the top of your chart, charging up your tenth house of career and public image until July 26, 2026. Simultaneously, the karmic South Node anchors in Virgo at the bottom of your chart, your fourth house of home, security and roots. Balancing these two areas of life will become a huge theme of this 18-month cycle.

If you've been blending into the background, prepare for a surge in visibility and responsibility. Your witty, intellectual flair will draw attention, setting you apart in any professional setting. Think of yourself as a key player whose insights can propel projects and teams to success. You're the zodiac's communicator and connector. Take the reins and guide with your clever insights and innovative ideas.

While you love to "twin up," discernment is a must now. Set high standards for your collaborations and step away from people who drain your dynamism. This is your time to work with the pros, whether you're commanding their boardrooms or pouring their coffee as you get your Prada loafer in the door. If you're still building your contact list, invest in memberships that allow you to mingle with ambitious, successful people. Mastermind groups, weekend seminars, private clubs, retreats—these are where you'll find opportunity now.

Well-established Geminis, your long-range vision comes into sharper focus now, but not in a rigid way. With dreamy, creative Pisces ruling your career house, your imagination is one of your greatest professional assets. What's that "Wouldn't it be crazy if..." idea you've been contemplating? See if you can get a tangible project plan in place and you might just build it out over the coming 18 months.

If you're well-established at a company, you may play the role of the tide turner this year. Adaptation and improvement are second nature to your mutable sign. Use these strengths to spearhead developments, whether you're carving out new markets or connecting the dots between the company's long-term strategies and the modern operational tools of AI—and even spirituality. Innovate from within your organization. Understandably, there may be resistance to change, but your persuasive power and foresight could lead to significant advancements, earning you awards.

As the South Node enters Virgo and your fourth house of home and family, you're called to balance public achievements with personal life. When you're not out playing Shark Tank, nurture your roots. This is the year to solidify your base of operations. Does your living situation support your growth trajectory? Changes may be needed to get the proper work-life balance. This can range from a simple room reconfiguration to a total relocation.

Warning: The South Node in detail-oriented Virgo will throw family dynamics under the microscope. If you've been sweeping generational traumas under the rug for too long, this could be the year you finally break that chain. While it would be great if all your relatives got on board, begin the process yourself. Know that this may create some ripples of discomfort throughout the lineage and make sure you also bolster yourself with support from your "chosen family" of dear friends, therapists, healers and advisers. While estrangement doesn't have to be the outcome (although in some cases, you may realize it's best), you may need to redraw boundaries with certain family members.

On the plus side, the South Node's passage through your fourth house can deepen connections with loved ones or help you establish new family traditions like analog Sunday dinners, game nights or new bedtime rituals with the kiddos. This is your time to get creative. If you've been pondering parenthood, the nurturing energy of the fourth house could get the conception plans in motion.

For single Geminis, this could be a time when home-based gatherings, like a weekly book club, may lead to meaningful encounters. Let your friends—and maybe your mom—fix you up! Their "pickers" could be on point right now, radaring in on people who actually tick your boxes.

If you've been thinking about a more significant commitment or change in your living arrangements, the fertile energy of the South Node makes this an ideal time to act. Whether it's moving in with a partner, expanding your family, or simply revitalizing your living space, the foundations you lay now can bring security for years to come.

Love
GEMINI 2025 FORECAST

You may have earned an emotional PhD in partnership, Gemini, but unconventional advice for you: In 2025, you need to forget everything you've learned. The planets are conspiring to put you in touch with your self-sovereign desires this year. How else will you really understand what you need in a mate?

Your mission, should you choose to accept it? Form a fundamental connection to "me, myself and I." Let's up the ante a little. How about having a full-on love affair with yourself? We dare you! With two of the most liberated planets—Jupiter and Uranus—both sweeping through your sign for six months of the year, your independent desires will be screaming too loudly to be ignored.

We're not suggesting you break up your happy home or leave your long-term boo behind while you, say, travel to the jungle for a medicine ceremony or go on a summer tour with your band. (Unless, of course, that is something you deem to be the right next step for your roadmap of life.) But do make sure you relentlessly pursue your personal passions while Jupiter is in your sign until June 9.

Put energy into both the individual realm and the relational realm of your life. For many Twins, the latter takes precedence at the expense of the former, which can lead to frustration, submission and, as our therapist friend Terri Cole calls it in her book Too Much, "high-functioning codependence." Ugh!

Here's a novel concept for Geminis in relationships: What if you enlisted your partner as a source of support for YOUR dreams, too? There can be a lovely flow of give and take for Twins this year, if you're willing to ditch the resentment and start asking (lovingly) for what you need. Begin with small tasks. Give rewards when completed. Training season begins in 3, 2, 1!

Try to get this started early because Venus has a retrograde phase this year, from March 1 to April 12. Whatever hasn't been ironed out around your future dreams and love goals will be in your face to reckon with then. Some Gems could reconnect with "the one that got away." Timing might be on your side this go 'round, especially if you've both done the emotional work to move through past traumas. Ease in slowly and hold off on making any life-disrupting moves until AFTER April 12.

The new supermoon in Gemini on May 26 opens a powerful window for setting intentions around your love life. Whether you're looking for a partner or deepening an existing bond, this is your moment to ask for what you want in love. The influence of this new moon, combined with Jupiter wrapping up its time in your sign on June 9, will give you the cosmic push to take romantic risks and open your heart.

Venus sweeps through Gemini from July 4 to July 30, amplifying your goddess-given charm and laying out a banquet of romantic opportunities. You'll be magnetic and irresistible, whether you're meeting new people or spicing things up with a current partner.

That's not all! Experimental, liberated Uranus moves into Gemini from July 7 to November 7. You'll feel a strong desire for freedom and unconventional experiences in your relationships. Expect spontaneity and surprises. Your sign thrives on variety, and this period will bring plenty of it. Single Geminis could meet someone exciting through social connections, while committed Geminis may feel a renewed sense of passion and curiosity in their relationships.

The full moon in Gemini on December 4, also a supermoon, is a celebration of your personal growth in relationships over the year. Any lingering doubts or emotional confusion will come to light, offering a chance to resolve them and move forward with clarity and confidence. This lunation helps you make empowered romantic decisions and reflect on how far you've come in love.

With Venus in Sagittarius from November 30 to December 24, your love life will take on a more adventurous, expansive tone as the year winds down. Paired with Mars in Sagittarius from November 4 to December 15, this could be the most rewarding time of all! In the final month of 2025, love becomes a journey of excitement and discovery. Fill it with as many spontaneous adventures as you can squeeze in pre-holidays. Starting Christmas Eve, Venus and Mars canoodle in your loyal, intimate eighth house, putting a sultry bow on this year of exploration—and bringing you the gift of fulfilling mutuality that you've worked so hard to cultivate!

GEMINI: LUCKIEST *love* DAY

DECEMBER 4

The full supermoon in Gemini puts your desires front and center, making you impossibly irresistible. Meanwhile, love planets Venus and Mars are canoodling in Sagittarius, combining their romantic resources in your seventh house of committed relationships. Talk about a memorable day for love—no mistletoe required.

Money & Career

GEMINI 2025 FORECAST

Oh, the places you will grow, Gemini! Your professional trajectory is headed skyward in 2025, driven by the game-changing influence of Jupiter and Uranus in your sign. Ideas that sounded too impossible to achieve in the past could catch on like wildfire. Get those creative briefs, pitch decks and proposals ready. Funding may be a few conversations away.

Expansive, enterprising Jupiter first entered Gemini on May 25, 2024 and keeps buzzing through your sign until June 9. Once it snaps out of retrograde this February 4, big plans can take off at a supersonic rate. This is a prime time to take calculated risks, share your ideas widely, and showcase your unique talents. Just make sure you protect your IP! Have people sign NDAs and consult an attorney about anything that needs to be trademarked. Global Jupiter could help you attract income streams from every corner of the world. (Would you like to be paid in Bitcoin or Euros, Gemini?)

Be prepared for a pivot—or an out-of-the-box opportunity that's too good to pass on—when changemaker Uranus bursts into your sign from July 7 to November 7. This sneak peek of a longer spell (from April 25, 2026 to March 22, 2033) might only drop some hints about the innovative breakthroughs coming down the pike. Uranus thrives on experimentation and will encourage you to break free from old routines and traditional career paths. Embrace new technologies, explore unconventional work opportunities, reinvent your professional image.

Surprise! What initially seems like a detour could lead you to your next big opportunity. On January 11, the destiny-driven North Node ascends into Pisces and your tenth house of career and public life until July 26, 2026. Its mission? To align your professional path with your higher purpose.

Visionary career goals come to the fore as you add a spiritually fulfilling and impact-driven dimension to your work. The Pisces lunar (full moon) eclipse on September 7 pushes you to aim higher, helping you break free from limitations and step into your true potential.

Meanwhile, the South Node in Virgo, your fourth house of home and stability, supports you with creating financial security. Two eclipses here—on March 14 and September 21—can direct you toward stabilizing investments that set you up for retirement and keep you prepped for the inevitable rainy days. Whether a real estate purchase or a chunk of cash to put into an index fund, these play-it-safer paths can help balance out the more venturesome vibes of 2025.

GEMINI: LUKIEST *career* DAY

JUNE 24

Make it rain, Gemini, or just close your umbrella and let the abundance flow in. As the Sun and lucky Jupiter hold their once-a-year summit, they enjoy this "Day of Miracles" in Cancer and your second house of money and valuables. You could tap into a promising job lead, sell something for a profit or otherwise devise new ways to make your cash compound.

2025
GEMINI

12
MONTH
OVERVIEW

January MONTHLY HOROSCOPE

We, us, ours: a few of a Gemini's favorite words as the ball drops on a new year! The spotlight is on long-lasting partnerships until January 19, while the Sun shines in devoted Capricorn and your eighth house of resources, deep relationships and long-term financial strategies. Which emotional bonds will you nurture in 2025? What people will you invest in? Give that some solid consideration. This sultry season can make one or two special bonds airtight. Hibernating never felt so sexy. On January 11, the lunar nodes shift into Pisces and Virgo, kicking off an 18-month cycle that will bring unprecedented evolution to both your career and home life. Before July 26, 2026, you could make some seismic shifts in regard to your professional and domestic goals. Once Aquarius season begins on the 19th, you may start to feel claustrophobic. (Help...air!) Roll out of bed and let your travel dreams take flight. Use this visionary four-week phase to map out your expansion plans for 2025. The call for adventure might lead you to some unexplored corner of the globe—or possibly, the ivory tower. With spontaneous Jupiter in your sign until June 9, forget the endless lists and overthinking. Grab your passport and go! The Year of the Wood Snake begins on January 29, marking a period of shedding old skins and transforming into the next iteration of you!

February MONTHLY HOROSCOPE

You're off to the races this February, Gemini! The Aquarius Sun illuminates your ninth house of adventure and higher learning until the 18th, making the world feel like your oyster. But that's not all! On February 4, globetrotting Jupiter wakes up from a four-month retrograde and powers forward through your sign. You've got the abundant planet in your corner until June 9, so make the most of the days until then by broadening your horizons, exploring new terrain and jumping into every growth opportunity that you can. You'll feel a strong pull to connect with like-minded people, as Venus begins its long tour through Aries and your eleventh house of friendships and networking on the 4th. Slide into those DMs and let your friends play matchmaker for you. After February 18, when the Sun moves into Pisces and your tenth house of career, your focus shifts to your professional ambitions. Finally, Mars turns direct in Cancer on February 23, pouring rocket fuel into your second house of money and security. If finances have been in limbo, this shift helps you make smart moves to strengthen your foundation.

March MONTHLY HOROSCOPE

You're poised for success—no selling out required—as the imaginative Pisces Sun revs up your tenth house of career and reputation until the 20th. But don't spread yourself too thin. Your Aries-ruled eleventh house of friendships and group dynamics is getting rocked, demanding discernment in your social choices. Both Venus and Mercury will be retrograde in Aries this month—Venus from March 1 to 27 and Mercury from March 15 to 29. This duo could stir up some confusion in your social circle, calling you to reassess your friendships and romantic connections. Are you giving too much or not enough? Now's the time to balance those scales. Home and family matters demand attention during the March 14 Virgo lunar eclipse. No more sweeping issues under the rug, it's time to deal. As the Sun enters Aries on the 20th, you'll feel the urge to refine your approach to teamwork and collaboration. The solar eclipse on March 29 marks the final chapter of a two-year eclipse series in your eleventh house, offering a powerful moment to close the door on any lingering group drama or unhealthy dynamics. One day later, on March 30, Neptune enters Aries for the first time since 1875, kicking off a 14-year cycle of spiritual growth and visionary inspiration. Stay open to serendipitous encounters. You could literally manifest the perfect teammates between now and October 22.

April MONTHLY HOROSCOPE

Get ready to juggle, Gemini! With the Sun in your eleventh house of teamwork and social connections until April 19, you're in full-on networking mode. But hold off on hard-launching anything massive just yet. Mercury, your ruling planet, is retrograde in Pisces until April 7, along with Venus until April 12, both in your tenth house of career. Reassess your strategy and smooth over any work-related tensions before making your next move. After the retrograde air clears on the 12th, your goals come into sharp focus again. And with a Libra full moon happening that same day, some well-connected people may come out of the woodwork, ready to support your efforts. Feisty Mars charges into Leo on April 18, igniting your third house of communication and cooperative ventures. You'll be buzzing with genius ideas while this cycle lasts until June 17. Capture them all for consideration—and make sure to legally protect your IP. Today's napkin sketch could be tomorrow's billion-dollar viral sensation. Slip off to the "studio" to imagineer in private once Taurus season begins on the 19th. Or take a breather! As the Sun steals into your twelfth house, it's the perfect time to slow down, recharge, and tie up loose ends before your birthday season begins later next month.

May MONTHLY HOROSCOPE

Hit pause and recharge while the Taurus Sun nestles in your twelfth house of rest and reflection until May 20. Use this downtime to clear out anything that's been weighing you down—whether it's emotional baggage, energy-zapping habits or the cold-shouldered tops and skinny jeans in the back of your closet. On May 4, metamorphic Pluto spins into its annual retrograde, paddling back through Aquarius and your expansive ninth house until October 13. Some of your big picture plans could be up for reconsideration. As you think about evolving to the next level this year, this transit can lead you to powerful teachers, awakening courses and retreats. The best news of the month arrives on May 20, as the Sun soars into Gemini and hard-launches your birthday season! You'll feel the cosmic winds shift as you shake off sluggish energy and embrace fresh-start vibes. Disciplined Saturn changes signs on the 24th, heading into Aries for the first time since 1998. The taskmaster planet will do drills in your eleventh house of teamwork and tech (on and off) for the coming three years. Time to build a solid, supportive community that aligns with your goals. Got an idea for an online venture, an influencer account or a project that could benefit from AI? With Saturn joining imaginative Neptune in Aries for this longer cycle, your digital dreams could pay the bills! Take the first step toward a personal goal with the year's only new moon in Gemini on the 26th. And start a buzz about it while you're at it, since your ruler, messenger Mercury, cruises through Gemini from May 25 to June 8.

June MONTHLY HOROSCOPE

Don the cosmic crown! You're uncontested zodiac royalty while the Sun shines in Gemini until June 20. What's fresh and novel? Curiosity could lead you in all sorts of exhilarating directions this month while your fanbase expands wildly. But don't be surprised if some of that restless energy is tempered after June 9. As adventurous Jupiter leaves your sign it nestles into Cancer for a year, pouring Miracle-Gro into your second house of money and values. This year-long cycle can bring major growth opportunities for your financial life, from savvy investments to increased earnings at your 9-5 job. Once the Sun joins Jupiter in Cancer at the solstice, you might feel ready to settle down in ways you haven't for months. And when the two celestial bodies make an exact connection on the 24th, AKA the Day of Miracles, you could discover something (or someone) priceless right under your nose. Clashing values could rattle the ranks of a team or social group mid-month when Jupiter clashes with Saturn on June 15 and Neptune on June 18. Don't bolt out of frustration, but if you need to take a timeout to think things through, give yourself that grace. Motivator Mars sweeps into Virgo on June 17, giving you the drive to organize your home and tackle family matters head-on. The sweetest moment for relationships comes this June 11, when the year's only full moon in Sagittarius pours passion into your seventh house of relationships. Get ready for a soul-baring moment of truth.

July MONTHLY HOROSCOPE

July 2025 is a game-changer for you, Gemini, as Uranus finally makes its grand entrance into your sign on July 7 for a four-month tour. Breakthroughs and bold reinventions could be your daily practice starting now, and why not? The side-spinning planet only comes to your sign every 84 years and, when it does, it writes you a permission slip to wander as far from conventional conformity as you dare go. The Sun keeps shining in Cancer and your second house of money and security until the 22nd, helping you stabilize your resources and make grounded financial decisions. Be mindful with your mic drops after July 18! Mercury spins retrograde in Leo until August 11—a double-whammy, since it's backing up through your third house of communication. Take down controversial posts and block those frenemies and troublemaking exes. Neptune, Saturn, and Chiron all turn retrograde in Aries (on the 4th, 13th, and 30th, respectively), slowing things down in your eleventh house of teamwork and tech. These five-month cycles could rile up old issues around group dynamics or make you question the direction of your dreams. Don't shy away from these challenging assessments, Gemini. This is your opportunity to refresh your connections, heal past wounds with friends, and realign your shared vision for the future with Team Twin. On July 22, the Sun blazes into Leo, illuminating your communication zone, which is usually your comfort zone—but with Mercury retrograde in the mix, don't be surprised if things get a little tangled. Do your part to de-escalate drama by staying out of gossip and getting the facts before you react.

August MONTHLY HOROSCOPE

Your social life is ablaze with the Sun lighting up convivial Leo until August 22, and with your locally zoned third house alight, the fun may be a Lyft ride away from your front door. Mercury is retrograde until the 11th, bringing happy reunions with pals from back in the day. Warning: this may also stall a few of your plans and reveal a frenemy who needs to be blocked ASAP. Polish up projects and fine-tune your "marketing" so you can make all the big reveals after Mercury turns direct on the 11th. Meanwhile, Venus is in Cancer until August 25, helping you quietly evaluate whether your investments—emotional and financial—are giving you the returns you desire. If you're uncertain, it's smart to hold back. There's plenty of passion to be found this month, too! Red-hot Mars zips into Libra on August 6, activating your fierce fifth house of romance and creative expression until September 22. In the second half of the month, you can unleash that Gemini Wave on the world with colorful style and artistic expression. On August 22, the Sun enters Virgo, pulling some of your attention to home and family matters. With the first of two back-to-back new moons in Virgo arriving on August 23, set intentions for your domestic life and emotional well-being. Next month, a rare second Virgo new moon—also a solar eclipse—brings an opportunity for another reset that helps you plant even deeper roots.

September MONTHLY HOROSCOPE

Work-life balance: What does that look like for you? September brings a mix of home life and career shifts as retrogrades and eclipses push you to evaluate your path. The Sun in systematic Virgo until the 22nd helps you bring some order to your court and smooth out any family tension that sprang up during last month's Mercury retrograde. But no slipping on those career goals! As stern Saturn retrogrades back into Pisces on September 1, unfinished business demands your attention. Adding to that squeeze, Uranus turns retrograde in your sign on September 6, stirring up internal restlessness and the urge to break free from old patterns. Grant yourself grace and space to work through the feelings that arise, but don't numb out because it feels overwhelming. Venus moves between Leo and Virgo this month, meaning supportive people are all around you who can guide you through any transitions. Major career news could arrive around September 7, as the total lunar eclipse in Pisces rocks your tenth house of success. Your efforts since the spring could bring a flood of rewards—or you could arrive at a turning point that forces you to let go of an outdated role. The solar eclipse in Virgo on September 21—also a rare second new moon in Virgo—offers a powerful reset, perfect for new beginnings in your living situation or family dynamics. If this all feels "extra," fear not. Libra season begins with the equinox on the 22nd, bringing balance along with a high-octane boost of positive, passionate and playful energy. Mars enters Scorpio that same day, pushing you to focus on wellness and work. Bring some order to your court but have fun doing it! Think: dance classes, brainstorming over pizza, networking with thought-leaders and flirting like it was your second job.

October MONTHLY HOROSCOPE

Make love and art, Gemini! With the Sun blazing through Libra until October 22, your fifth house of creativity, romance and self-expression is electrified. This passionate solar spell could push you into the spotlight—and you're ready to command it like a celebrity. Been stashing a creative project in the wings? Whether it's a half-finished screenplay or a side hustle you've been too shy to share, pull it out and get to work. Venus in Virgo until October 13 brings warmth and harmony to Casa Twin, along with some cuffing season romance. Home is your haven, so set up your relaxation zones (for two!). Create a cozy nook for painting, writing, or recording podcasts. When Venus glides into Libra on October 13, get out and mingle! Sparks can ignite everywhere, from a friend's dinner party to the UPS store. Coupled Twins: Rekindle romance with sweet surprises like spontaneous date nights, love notes or a memorable getaway to a place that neither of you has ever explored. Pluto snaps out of its retrograde on the 13th, sounding a call for higher learning and adventure. Sign up for a fall course or a personal development retreat. Been dreaming of designing a workshop or writing a book? This is your nudge from the universe to get started. As the Sun moves into Scorpio on October 22, you'll have the discipline to knock out tasks one by one. With your efficiency-boosting sixth house alight, declutter, refine your routines and make choices that nourish your well-being—whether that's committing to a morning yoga practice or cooking healthy meals from scratch. Neptune retrogrades back into Pisces that same day, casting a mist over a few of your loftier goals until December 10. Don't stress. Treat it as a cosmic pause, a chance to reassess your game plan with clarity and intuition.

November MONTHLY HOROSCOPE

Do your daily routines feel like life-giving rituals, Gemini? Time to transform anything that's zapping your spirit! With the Scorpio Sun illuminating your work and wellness center until November 21—and luxe Venus joining the party from November 6 to 30—sensuous self-care is the name of the game. Delegate what you can, then, bundle tasks together. Prep meals in bulk while catching up on phone calls, meet a friend for coffee next door to the laundromat and chat between loads. If joining a more elevated gym will inspire you to actually work out, the investment could be worth it. Partnerships come under the microscope on November 4, when activator Mars storms into Sagittarius until December 15. You won't be able to sweep anyone's negligence under the rug. Time to hold people accountable! This dynamic transit can bring some spicy thrills to your love life and inspire you and a business ally to take on a challenging project together. But there IS a catch, or rather a few of them, as retrogrades rumble through the skies. On the 7th, Uranus slips back into Taurus after six months in your sign, taking its final (in our lifetime) lap through your twelfth house of introspection, solitude and healing until April 2026. Leave room in your schedule for quiet reflection. On the 9th, your galactic guardian Mercury turns retrograde—in Sagittarius until the 18th, then in Scorpio until the 29th. Getting a read on people could be challenging, so don't rush to set any relationship rules or make things official. On the 11th, Jupiter slips into a four-month retrograde through Cancer, insisting that you budget and even tighten your belt through the holiday season. Despite these curveballs, you'll have plenty of positive momentum for partnerships once Sagittarius season begins on the 21st. Saturn ends its retrograde on the 27th, powering forward through Pisces and bringing a powerful EOY push for your career goals. A little bit of hustle goes a long way!

December MONTHLY HOROSCOPE

Partnerships are in the spotlight this month—happy news for the zodiac's doppelganger! The Sun beams in worldly, adventurous Sagittarius until December 21, helping you diversify your "people portfolio." What will it be, Gemini: a lover in every port or maybe just the perfect plus-one to explore the globe alongside? With cosmic copilots Venus and Mars together in Sagittarius until the 15th, you could attract some rare hybrids who are both exciting and dependable. Don't settle for less! Mars moves on to Capricorn on December 15, activating your intimate, erotic and entwined eighth house. Venus follows suit on the 24th, deepening soul connections and securing long-term financial arrangements as the year winds down. On the 10th, Neptune turns direct in Pisces, clearing the fog around career aspirations. Allow your dreams to crystallize as you move closer to manifesting your long-held professional goals. As the Winter Solstice arrives on December 21, the Sun's entrance into Capricorn illuminates your eighth house even further, ushering in a season of introspection, empowerment and commitment. Love becomes a deep, transformative force in the final days of 2025. Long-term goals and the pursuit of lasting emotional bonds become crystal clear priorities. With all this mystical energy in the ether, New Year's Eve holds the promise of magic, whether you're attending an intimate celebration or a spiritual ceremony. Take a moment to appreciate the incredible ways you've evolved this year and set the tone for a profoundly rewarding 2026!

Read your extended monthly forecast for life, love, money and career! astrostyle.com

A LITTLE ABOUT Cancer

DATES June 20 - July 22

SYMBOL The Crab

ELEMENT Water

QUALITY Cardinal

RULING PLANET The Moon

BODY PART Chest, stomach

BEST TRAITS
Helpful, patient, compassionate, nurturing, romantic, creative, solitary, introspective

KEYWORDS
Empathy, sensitivity, emotional intelligence, family, home, creativity, intuition, comfort

Read more about Cancer

CANCER
IN 2025

| ALL THE PLANETS IN CANCER IN 2025 | YOUR 2025 HOROSCOPE | TOP 5 THEMES FOR CANCER IN 2025 | LOVE HOROSCOPE + LUCKY DATES | MONEY HOROSCOPE + LUCKY DATES |

Cancer in 2025
YOUR YEARLY OVERVIEW

Squeeze in as much solitude as your heart desires early this year, because you'll be a Crab in demand in the second half of 2025. Adventurous, philosophical Jupiter splits the year between Gemini and your dreamy, introspective twelfth house and your trailblazing, attention-getting first house. Circle June 9 in neon ink. That's the day that the red-spotted planet blasts into your sign for the first time since mid-2014, kicking off a once-in-12-years chapter of unabashed personal expansion. By the time this cycle ends on June 30, 2026, your outlook on life—or your life itself—will have changed exponentially. Adding to your exploratory spirit, on January 11, the destiny-driven North Node heads into Pisces and your ninth house of global adventures. This is a huge nudge to venture beyond familiar waters, whether you're taking a life-changing vacation or enrolling in a degree program. No doubt, you'll have some grand goals in your crosshairs as stabilizing Saturn and soothsayer Neptune spend part of the year in Aries and your ambition zone. And thanks to radical Uranus spending half the year in Gemini, you won't lose touch with your spiritual side as you pursue success in the material world.

THE PLANETS IN *Cancer*

THE SUN
JUN 20–JUL 22

It's birthday season for you, so step out and shine! Seek novelty and take extra initiative during this radiant monthlong phase.

NEW MOON
JUN 25
6:32AM, 4°08'

Bonus New Year! Set your intentions for the next six months and get into action.

FULL MOON
JAN 13
5:27PM, 24°00'

Ready, set, manifest! Your work of the past six months bears fruit and it's time to harvest the rewards.

MERCURY
JUN 8–26

Crown yourself monarch of the social butterflies when popularity-boosting Mercury visits your sign once a year. Circulate and get social—but careful not to make promises you can't keep or fall into people pleasing.

VENUS
JUL 30–AUG 25

You've got the romantic It Factor when the galactic glamazon charges up your powers of seduction each year. Willpower is weak in the face of beauty and luxury. Watch your spending!

MARS
JAN 6–APR 18

RETROGRADE IN CANCER:
JAN 6–FEB 23

Motivation is high when energetic Mars visits your sign every couple years—but check your combative streak and try not to come on too strong, especially during the retrograde portion of this programming.

JUPITER
JUN 9, 2025-JUN 30, 2026

RETROGRADE:
NOV 11, 2025–
MAR 10, 2026

How lucky can you get? Bountiful Jupiter visits your sign once every 10–12 years, blessing you with extra fortune. Everything's exciting...and extra! Take calculated risks but avoid gambles, particularly during the retrograde.

Cancer in 2025

HIGHLIGHTS

THE FIRST FULL MOON OF THE YEAR IS IN CANCER

The first full moon of 2025 lands in Cancer this January 13, starting the year off with a major manifestation moment for Crabs. This also sets a nurturing tone for the world that's right in sync with your softer style. Lean into your personable style to pitch, promote and present. This is one of the best moments of the year to get yourself and your work in front of the VIPs. If you've been waiting for a breakthrough, this could be the time you see your efforts bear fruit—whether that's in relationships, health or a creative endeavor. Let this lunar spotlight help you release anything that no longer aligns with who you are becoming.

JUPITER AND URANUS IN GEMINI: SURRENDER TO THE SURREAL

Cancer, 2025 starts off with Jupiter and Uranus journeying through Gemini, lighting up your twelfth house of closure, solitude, and dreams. Think of the first half of the year as a celestial sabbatical—an opportunity to lean into introspection, solitude, and healing. With Jupiter in this placement until June 9, life may feel dreamlike, as if boundaries are a little blurry and reality is fluid. As you tie up loose ends, surrender what no longer serves you. Uranus, the planet of surprises, picks up the baton, streaming through Gemini from July 7 to November 7—its first visit here since 1949! Your subconscious realm will be actively bringing an innovative wave to your creative and spiritual work. Take notes! This is the preview of a longer, seven-year cycle of Uranus in Gemini that starts April 25, 2026.

JUPITER IN CANCER: YOUR COSMIC COMEBACK

Let the Renaissance Tour begin! Bountiful, exploratory Jupiter soars into Cancer on June 9, setting you off on a twelve-month cycle of personal expansion. You haven't hosted the red-spotted miracle maker since 2013- 14. As the universe rolls out the red carpet, you might not be sure whether to sashay down it like a Met Gala superstar or dust it with Aladdin's magic and set off on a ride. Whatever the case, set your GPS to "anywhere but home." This expansive cycle boosts your confidence and revs you up to explore new opportunities—whether in love, career or personal projects. Independent ventures can take off quickly. No one's clipping your wings now! Remember to take calculated risks and avoid unnecessary gambles, especially during Jupiter's retrograde from November 11, 2025, to March 10, 2026. This is your "cosmic comeback" year, so focus on self-care and don't be afraid to aim high.

BYE-BYE COMFORT ZONE: LUNAR NODES IN PISCES AND VIRGO

Thought you could hide out in the crab shell? Guess again! On January 11, the destiny-driven North Node moves into Pisces and your adventurous ninth house, nudging you out of your comfort zone and pushing you toward new horizons. Whether it's a literal journey or a metaphorical leap of faith, the energy of the nodes will make the unfamiliar feel necessary and appealing between now and July 26, 2026. The South Node in Virgo, meanwhile, brings past-life karma to the forefront in your third house of communication, encouraging you to release old mental habits and ways of thinking that no longer serve you. Enough small talk and superficial "bonding." During this eighteenmonth cycle, you'll be nourished by expansive conversations that feed your soul.

SATURN AND NEPTUNE IN ARIES: DREAMS WITH A DEADLINE

Two more outer planets do a pendulum swing into a new sign for part of 2025: liquid Neptune and solid Saturn. With both of them visiting Aries and your tenth house of career (Neptune from March 30 to October 22 and Saturn from May 24 to September 1), you'll have an interesting blend of energy to funnel toward your ambitions. Saturn will bring the discipline and structure needed to achieve long-term goals, while Neptune adds a colorful burst of idealism and creativity. You may feel inspired to pursue a dream job or passion project that aligns with your values. However, this mix also means balancing practicality with vision. Make sure that your dreams have a strong foundation under them, especially as Neptune's influence can sometimes blur practical details .

TOP 5 THEMES FOR
Cancer in 2025

1	2	3	4	5
CLAIM YOUR SAGE STATUS	RESET YOUR COMPASS	ELEVATE YOUR PROFESSIONAL PROFILE	RIGHT-SIZE YOUR LOVE GOALS	PACK YOUR BAGS

1

CLAIM YOUR SAGE STATUS

JUPITER AND URANUS IN GEMINI

JUPITER: MAY 25, 2024 – JUNE 9, 2025

URANUS: JULY 7 – NOVEMBER 7, 2025 • JANUARY 26, 2026 – MAY 22, 2033

Might as well add some caftans and flowing robes to your wardrobe, Cancer. In 2025, philosophical Jupiter and high-minded Uranus ascend to the most ethereal zone, your Gemini-ruled twelfth house. If you haven't already earned "sage" status, that's a likely fate this year. Dreams and your creative visions will be otherworldly. Unleash your inner artiste!

JUPITER IN GEMINI

MAY 25, 2024 – JUNE 9, 2025

Float into 2025, Cancer. You're halfway through a dreamy, and possibly surreal, odyssey as the year begins with nomadic Jupiter sailing through Gemini and your fantasy-fueled twelfth house. The red-spotted adventurer began its tour through the sign of the Twins mid-2024, on May 25. We're betting life has been pretty trippy ever since. Things you once considered solid became fluid, shapeshifting (and possibly evaporating) before your own two eyes.

What's a Crab to do? Stop, drop and surrender. "Ha!" you may reply. That's a tall order for a sign that craves certainty as much as you do. Accept that some things are simply beyond your control? Sounds great in theory, but the practice of it can bring both agony and ecstasy.

Keep working that muscle until June 9, 2025 and you may undergo profound transformation. Jupiter in the twelfth house invites you to let life carry you along on a fantastic voyage. Like Cancer Elizabeth Gilbert, you could "Eat, Pray, Love" your way to some pretty remote places on a quest for true connection, the pursuit of a creative passion, even on a spiritual pilgrimage. If there were ever a time to take a sabbatical, this is it.

Your creative, poetic nature will blossom during this Jupiter phase. If you have something (or someone) to mourn, working with a therapist or grief counselor can help immensely. There's no better time than now to start or return to a meditation or yoga practice. While Jupiter in Gemini can be an undeniably heavy time, there's a light at the end of the tunnel. On June 9, Jupiter will blast into Cancer for the first time in over a decade, reshaping life in exciting ways.

Until then, however, you may feel like you're walking through marshmallow taffy. Tasks that once came easily to you may take ten times as long to complete. It's not that you mean to procrastinate, Cancer. It's just that the Muse channel is turned up so loud that it will drive you to distraction. One minute, you're sitting down to bang out the weekly expense report, the next, WTH?! You're composing an entire playlist of vibey music on Spotify, unsure how you drifted onto this sonic quest.

If you're feeling exhausted, take it as a sign that you need to lighten your load. Begging the question, are you ready to let go of a job, relationship or other situation that you've outgrown? Like a powerful life coach, optimistic Jupiter will hold your hand every step of the way, cheering you on and helping you segue into a far more fulfilling direction. Of course, you might also want to hire a human coach, mentor or other guide who can talk and walk you through any changes you're making.

Jupiter in Gemini might make you of two minds when it comes to some things, but here's one place to be singular in focus: Showering yourself with unapologetic self-care. No more settling for less than what you deserve, Cancer, or sacrificing your dreams to serve a codependent relationship. Free-spirited Jupiter writes you a permission slip to stop playing the martyr. Make sure you're untethered from excessive responsibility by June 9, so that when the planet of possibilities rolls into your sign, you'll be ready to soar!

URANUS IN GEMINI
JULY 7 – NOVEMBER 7, 2025
JANUARY 26, 2026 – MAY 22, 2033

Just as lucky Jupiter is sweeping you back into the public eye, another planet gives you the "excuse" you secretly wanted to set up an Away message again. (Well, at least for a few carved-out time slots every week.) On July 7, 2025, metamorphic Uranus slips into Gemini, shooting delta waves into your twelfth house of introspection, dreams and deep soul work. It's probably not news to your flowy sign that some of the best work can be done when you're not actually "working," but rather whilst in deep (and quiet!) contemplation.

Set up your meditation cave, Cancer! Or reconstruct the one you built while Jupiter was in Gemini from May 25, 2024 to June 9. Uranus hangs out in Gemini for four months this year, until November 7, then returns to Taurus and your communal eleventh house for a final hurrah. But this is hardly the end of an era. On April 25, 2026, the side-spinning planet whirls back into Gemini for seven years, until May 22, 2033. We're not sure whether to say, "whoosh" or "woo-sah," but with Uranus in dualistic Gemini, you're sure to feel both on a regular basis.

The last time Uranus toured Gemini was from 1941 to 1949, so this truly is a once-in-a-lifetime cycle. Over the eight years that the radical rebel will spin through this subconscious realm, you'll start to see things from a very different perspective. Your inner life may become more real (and at times more surreal) than the day-to-day. Uranus here can ignite your imagination and hone your intuition in ways you've never experienced.

And here's something that you, as a Cancer, may relish: Opportunities will present themselves to heal childhood wounds and release people and behaviors that don't support your highest mission. If you've been thinking of working with a holistic healer, shamanic practitioner or cognitive behavioral therapist, now is the time. With futurist Uranus here, anything that gives you access to your subconscious—and even your unconscious—will make you feel a sense of increased wholeness. You may be up for trying everything from plant medicine to hypnosis to a wearable device that sends vibrating waves to support your sleep, focus and relationships.

Even as you're working on your own issues, don't forget your karmic responsibility to the rest of humanity. Uranus rules activism and social crusades, and in this empathetic placement, it can inspire you to use your gifts to heal the world. Technology may figure in, another tool of Uranus' trade. There are many ways this could play out, from seeing clients for Zoom appointments to building a website or social media feed to share your insights. As long as it has heart and meaning, you won't feel shy about showing your face.

2 RESET YOUR COMPASS

JUPITER IN CANCER
JUNE 9, 2025 – JUNE 30, 2026

On the off chance that you've forgotten how much of a badass you are, listen up, Crab! A loud reminder from the stars reverberates through your psyche this June 9. For the first time in over a decade, jovial, auspicious Jupiter swings into Cancer, widening your viewfinder to take in a breathtaking, panorama.

Jupiter only visits your sign once every 12-13 years, so this is a huge deal. While it tours your self-authorized first house until June 30, 2026, it pours cosmic Miracle Gro on your personal universe. Flip back in your calendar for clues of what's to come. The last time Jupiter visited Cancer was June 25, 2013 to July 16, 2014. Did any significant life events happen then? While this transit won't be an exact 2.0 replica, similar themes could arise.

And allow us to add some icing on this already-sweet cake: Jupiter is exalted in Cancer, which means your sign is the red-spotted titan's happiest place in the zodiac. Are you popping the bubbly yet? Jupiter sure is. Your pesky habit of being over-involved in other people's dramas is coming to a swift end. Concentrate on Numero Uno again. Invest in your own self-development. Don't worry that lavishing yourself with love will be detrimental to your relationships. Au contraire! You'll have more energy for others and you'll be an inspiring role model instead of the resentful Best Supporting Castmate.

As the ruler of higher education, Jupiter could lead you back to a degree program. If you're more of a master than a student, this could be your cue to develop your very own curriculum. Don't be shy about charging a premium rate if you know you have something no one else can offer. With the abundant planet in your court, people will find it weirder if you undercharge rather than extend a VIP package.

If you've been stuck in the vague, grey area of life, you can kiss that tired old phase goodbye. Jupiter, the galactic gambler, helps you aim high. You won't have to break a giant sweat to attract attention. Just open yourself up energetically to being found and people may come a-knocking for you. Of course, should you choose to prime the pump with a little shameless PR, get ready. You'll be opening the floodgates for a tsunami of opportunity to come your way. With Jupiter's worldly influence, you might even relocate for a job or relationship or connect to a second home base in another city.

Sounds exciting but also maybe a little scary? Private Cancers notoriously struggle with leaving your nest, especially once you have everything set up to your comfy standards. With spiritually activating Jupiter in your sign, you simply can't stay in a place that doesn't resonate with your soul. Get moving and shaking—not hiding away in your crabshell!

With your independent spirit fired up, some Cancers could go into business for yourselves during this 13-month cycle, or perhaps take on a more sovereign leadership role within an existing company. While you'll cherish your independence, try to remember that this doesn't boil down to you doing everything by your lonesome. The freedom Jupiter grants you may come from sharpening your leadership skills. This isn't just about delegating or micromanaging. How about using your nurturing gifts to empower the people around you? Hold up the mirror to reveal their greatness and you'll be amazed by how willing they are to step into that reflection. That's the kind of win-win your caring sign can get behind.

3 ELEVATE YOUR PROFESSIONAL PROFILE

SATURN AND NEPTUNE IN ARIES
NEPTUNE: MARCH 30 – OCTOBER 22, 2025 • JANUARY 26, 2026 – MARCH 23, 2039
SATURN: MAY 24 – SEPTEMBER 1, 2025 • FEBRUARY 13, 2026 – APRIL 12, 2028

Passion and purpose unite for Cancer, as two powerful outer planets rise into your tenth house (Aries) of career success. For a brief time in 2025, stalwart Saturn and imaginative Neptune change signs, heading out of watery Pisces and into fiery Aries.

Talk about a sea change! Saturn has been paddling through the sign of the Fish since March 2023 and Neptune's been there since 2011. Moreover, it's been three decades since Saturn charged through Aries (1996 to 1998) and literally centuries for Neptune (1865 to 1875). Buckle up because your dreams could take off at a gallop midyear. Brief as these spells are, they're a prelude of what's to come. In 2026, Saturn races back through Aries for two full years and Neptune for thirteen. Ain't no stopping you now!

NEPTUNE IN ARIES

MARCH 30 – OCTOBER 22, 2025
JANUARY 26, 2026 – MARCH 23, 2039

Cancer, get ready to infuse your professional life with a deeper sense of purpose. On March 30, compassionate, spiritual Neptune moves into Aries for the first time since 1875. Translation? Your career will be guided by the dreamy planet until October 22, and then again from January 26, 2026, to March 23, 2039. No matter what industry you're in, this transit will bring your creativity, empathy and healing gifts to the forefront of your life and, soon enough, your work.

As a cardinal sign, leadership comes naturally to you, Cancer, often propelling you into executive roles, sometimes even unexpectedly. While being at the helm has its perks, if your ascent to the top has compromised your well-being, Neptune's journey through Aries invites a significant recalibration. Over the coming decade-plus, shift your focus from mere professional achievements to cultivating a life marked by inner peace and balance.

As the zodiac's Most Maternal, you can slip into caretaker mode, and soon enough, you're shouldering the work for the perfectly capable adults around you. Warning: Sacrificial Neptune's tour through your tenth house could pull you down into the vortex of codependence, enabling and burnout if you don't set healthy boundaries. Used correctly, this period will teach you the art of delegation and the importance of surrounding yourself with a team that supports rather than drains you. No more picking up the slack at work. Instead, hold people accountable and train them until they learn how to do things to your elevated standards.

If you're on the job hunt, start by looking for companies whose vision and values resonate with your soul. Even if it means adjusting your salary expectations temporarily, the fulfillment from doing work that truly matters might be enough to make up for a pay cut. That said, be mindful not to fall into the trap of spiritual bypass when it comes to money. You deserve to be paid fairly for your efforts, Cancer—and "office martyr" is a good look for absolutely no one.

Ultimately, Neptune's tour of Aries is not just about growth but also can help you make your work environment a reflection of your highest ideals. Dive into this transformative phase with an open heart, Cancer, and your career can blossom into a source of both success and soul satisfaction.

SATURN IN ARIES

MAY 24 – SEPTEMBER 1, 2025
FEBRUARY 13, 2026 – APRIL 12, 2028

"On your mark, get set, goal! May 24 marks a major turning point in your professional life, as structured Saturn joins flowy Neptune in Aries until September 1. The ringed taskmaster planet hasn't set up shop in your tenth house of career success and public prestige in nearly three decades. If you were in the workforce between 1996 and 1998, you may see similar themes arise.

Although Saturn is only in Aries for a brief three months, the cycle begins again on February 13, 2026—and for an unbroken, two-year lap which lasts through April 12, 2028. This isn't just another phase, Cancer; it's the grand opening of your most ambitious period yet. It's time to chase those monumental dreams—the ones that not only give your life deeper meaning but could also position you as a go-to expert in your field. With soulful Neptune co-piloting this mission, the timing couldn't be better to craft a career that resonates deeply with your passions.

Saturn demands perseverance and dedication, so while you won't build your empire overnight, this cosmic coach knows just when to push you and when to reward your efforts to maintain your drive. If you've already started paving your dream career path, Saturn's influence will be crucial in helping you devise strategies to make your business or personal brand enduring and profitable. Embrace this cycle, even though it may come with a steep learning curve.

When everything feels "effortful," remind yourself that Saturn only circles through your tenth house every 29.5 years. However, during these crucial cycles, you can make significant achievements—ones that draw public recognition.

The journey to the summit won't be a cake walk. Saturn in Aries forms a tense 90-degree square with your Cancer Sun, presenting some additional challenges. There may be moments when you feel frustrated enough to throw in the towel, but if you believe in your mission, stay humble and stay the course. A new tier of leadership, self-reliance and expertise awaits.

Crabs who have enjoyed flexible work arrangements might find yourselves drawn to more traditional, 9-5 roles that offer stability, benefits, and clear-cut responsibilities (albeit the possibility of a demanding boss). Well worth it, if it gives you your ticket to learning the ins and outs of an exciting field and cementing valuable connections.

Self-employed Cancerians may soon be ready to increase your rates, even if it means losing some clients and feeling anxious as you await more lucrative fits. Stand firm in your worth and the value of your offerings, and the market (with a bump from Saturn!) will eventually reflect your value back to you.

4 RIGHT-SIZE YOUR LOVE GOALS

VENUS RETROGRADE IN ARIES AND PISCES
ARIES: MARCH 1 – 27
PISCES: MARCH 27 – APRIL 12

Amorous plans could hit a speed bump this March 1, as romance junkie Venus spins into a six-week retrograde. Like it or not, this cosmic event happens every 18 months. In 2025, the retrograde takes place in two signs: Aries and Pisces. Starting March 1, Venus reverse commutes through the Ram's realm and your mission-driven tenth house. On March 27, the love planet backs into Pisces and your ninth house, making truth slippery (at best) until April 12.

Before Venus turns retrograde, it will power forward through Aries from February 4 to March 1. During that time, you could find yourself fixating on the future of your love life—perhaps gaining significant ground. But once the retrograde begins, it's like Cupid is slamming on the brakes, forcing you to slow your roll. As frustrating as this may initially feel, try to see it as a blessing in disguise. You have six weeks to make sure your relationship goals are truly aligned with one another's souls. While you believe in being unwaveringly supportive, you and your other half may define "support" in very different ways. It's time to get real about what you're willing to offer and what is a no fly zone.

A word to the wise, take these discussions in smaller bytes. Setting up systems to stay on the same page as your sweetie would be smart. Create a shared calendar that syncs with your smartphones, and pick one or two nights a week that are sacred "just the two of us" time. You may also discover that certain larger life objectives don't exactly mesh with your mate's. Before you bail, TRY to work out compromises. Consider a few couple's therapy sessions to help you hash out a better plan. Remember: You don't have to be attached at the hip to have a successful union; in fact, when Venus moves back into Pisces and your independent, worldly ninth house from March 27 to April 12, you might have to arrange your relationship around each other's travel schedules. A little absence can make the heart grow fonder between these dates. Set off on a solo journey or trip with one of your besties.

Single? Venus retrograde could leave you ruminating, obsessing about the one that got away. It's easy to glorify the past, but don't delude yourself about the reason you broke things off. If it was merely bad timing that messed things up, Venus' backspin could provide a do-over. Take things slowly because you won't get a clear read until after April 12. If an ex keeps interfering with your dating goals, you may need to put any friendship-building efforts on hold for a while so you can actually heal and move on with your life.

Don't drop your guard around the office, Cancer. During Venus' backspin in Aries (March 1 to 27), you'll have to navigate professional relationships with greater care. Make a point of building stronger bonds with your boss or key clients—and using greater diplomacy in your interactions. You don't have to treat them with kid gloves but check those eye rolls when you disagree with their policies. (Oh, you thought they didn't see that?) Now, more than ever, you need to position yourself as a team player.

Cancer business owners might have to dig deeper—both for client leads and creative inspiration. Take on the challenge! Sign up for networking events or just go out to places where you can mingle with people who you'd consider your ideal customers or collaborators. What starts as friendly chit chat could evolve into a promising (and profitable!) partnership before your next birthday rolls around.

5 PACK YOUR BAGS

LUNAR NODES IN VIRGO AND PISCES
NORTH NODE IN PISCES, SOUTH NODE IN VIRGO
JANUARY 11, 2025 – JULY 26, 2026

Cancer on the go! This January 11, the lunar North Node sails into Pisces and your adventurous ninth house, turning you into a veritable Dora the Explorer until July 26, 2026. The invitation to expand beyond your comfort zone is one that may feel both exciting and a tiny bit terrifying for your sign. Deep breaths, Cancer. Your world is about to get a whole lot bigger!

The lunar nodes are cosmic destiny points, not actual celestial bodies, but they play a crucial role in your spiritual growth. They cycle through the zodiac every 18-20 years, marking periods of significant personal and collective evolution.

From July 17, 2023 to January 11, 2025, the North Node was in Aries, emphasizing your tenth house of career and long-term goals, while the South Node activated your domestic fourth house. This period likely asked you to balance worldly aspirations with the needs of family and your own private life.

But as the nodes shift into Pisces and Virgo, your focus pivots dramatically from public endeavors to personal expansion. The Pisces North Node invites you to embrace new experiences with an open heart and mind. Whether it's through travel, higher education, or personal growth experiences (with a spiritual twist), this is a time to explore what lies beyond your familiar shores.

Begin planning now, Cancer, because once peripatetic Jupiter zooms into your sign on June 9, there's no holding you back. While trips "back home" are always balm for your soul, dream up destinations that spark your soul's curiosity. Don't just think about the food, shopping and historical monuments. Envision who you want to become through these experiences. While you're plotting your adventures, look into courses and workshops you might take that allow you to immerse with the local traditions.

The ninth house also governs intellectual and spiritual exploration, so a suitcase and passport aren't required for you to tap this rich vein of adventure. A semester-long course at the local or online college could blast open the doors to a whole new passion. Where are the thought leaders convening? Expand your philosophical horizons by connecting with people who challenge and inspire your thinking. You could meet them in a virtual mastermind group or at a weekly gathering in your area.

Pondering a change of address? The North Node in Pisces supports you in casting a wide net. This could be the year you relocate to pursue your dreams. A job opportunity could arise that requires travel, or you decide to work with overseas clients or collaborators. Embrace the chance to integrate into new communities and networks.

The entrepreneurial spirit will also be strong with the North Node in Pisces. If you've been nurturing a business idea, this is the time to bring it to life, especially if it aligns with your personal beliefs and passions. Publishing and mediamaking fall under the ninth house domain. Cancer writers could celebrate a juicy book deal or optioning during this cycle. Shop around or find an agent to do it for you.

Across the wheel, the South Node will spend the next 18 months in Virgo and your third house of peers, communication and local activity. Everyday interactions are tinged with karma after January 11, so don't sleep on your own zip code. You might lead local initiatives or connect to broader global organizations through your neighborhood activities.

With Virgo's influence, pay attention to the details—effective communication can help you bridge the gap between your lofty ideals and practical reality. However, take care not to overextend yourself. The South Node in your third house warns against getting lost in the weeds of daily interactions or letting petty disputes cloud your broader vision. Maintain a balance: Allow yourself to dream big, but stay grounded in your immediate environment.

Partnerships could also be highlighted during this cycle. Collaborative projects, especially those that combine your visionary ideas with practical applications, can be particularly fruitful. Be clear about what you expect from others and be willing to listen to their needs and ideas as well.

Finally, ensure all agreements are clear and formalized to avoid misunderstandings. That goes triple if you're working with friends, neighbors or siblings. Even if it feels awkward, setting clear boundaries and expectations will protect your relationships and ensure that everyone is on the same page. There's no reason you shouldn't have at least some sort of written agreement (if not a full-on contract) to keep all lines clear.

Ultimately, this nodal cycle brings an exciting paradox. How can you spread your wings while also making sure to enjoy your time back at the nest? Embrace the adventures that await, knowing that your base is secure and your communications clear. The world is wide, and your heart is ready to explore it!

Love
CANCER 2025 FORECAST

In 2025, Cancer, your love life kicks off with a period of scintillating introspection as lusty Mars retrogrades in your sign from January 6 to February 23. This fiery backspin encourages you to slow down and reassess your romantic needs, including those you may have been too shy or uncertain to express. Think of it as a cosmic pit stop—a chance to lift the hood on your love life and fine-tune your emotional engine.

You can also use this opportunity to confront any unresolved issues from the past and to get crystal clear about what you truly desire—from your relationship "must haves" to your erotic requirements. During this reflective phase, you'll learn how to become more assertive about communicating your needs, breaking free from any fears of being too "demanding" or vulnerable.

When the passionate red planet course corrects and spins direct on February 23, you have the green light to pursue your desires with renewed energy and clarity. Mars pulses forward through your sign until April 18, giving you six scorching-hot weeks to tap into its molten magic. Assertiveness? Check! This is the time to take charge of your well-deserved pleasure—both in and out of the bedroom. (Just know that Mars might make you so forthright that you come off as pressure-y. Not a good look for anyone!)

But how close is "too close" for you, Cancer? You may need to adjust the intimacy dials on June 9, once free-spirited Jupiter enters, igniting a year-long journey of independence and personal growth. This is a time when you'll feel confident in your own skin, willing to stand on your own two feet, and insanely curious about discovering who YOU are inside.

If you were plagued by possessiveness earlier this year, shake it off! Jupiter's influence will help you shed old dependencies, inspiring a sense of freedom and autonomy that will impact all areas of your life—including love. For single Cancers, this newfound self-assurance could draw someone into your life who truly respects and values your autonomy, giving you the breathing room you need while also supplying emotional security. Coupled Crabs: Your goal is to strike a balance between togetherness and individuality. No suffocating in the couple bubble, thanks! The new moon in Cancer on June 25 will further amplify this sense of renewal, offering the perfect opportunity to set intentions around creating a love life that nurtures both emotional well-being and personal freedom.

That said, 2025 brings plenty of opportunities to swoon. Late-summer love will be as flavorful as a full-bodied Cabernet once vivacious Venus, the planet of love and beauty, enters your sign from July 30 to August 25. You'll happily enjoy a stream of affection and ardent gestures. That defensive shell of yours will be lowered, too, allowing you to exude the warmth and nurturing you usually reserve for familiars. Don't freak out if "strangers" see your shine. How else will you attract a compatible partner unless you actually show them who you are?

Heat-seeking Mars brings another wave of passion during its tour of Scorpio from September 22 to November 4, adding intensity and passion to your love life. This transit stirs powerful emotions and pushes you to dive deeper into your romantic connections. Whether you're single or partnered, you'll crave profound emotional intimacy, and your relationships will take on a more transformative tone. This is a time to explore the depths of love and commitment, as Mars in Scorpio encourages you to be fearless in your pursuit of deep, meaningful relationships.

Cosmic canoodlers Venus and Mars come together in Capricorn on Christmas Eve, lighting a fire in your seventh house of partnerships that burns into 2026. The cosmic mistletoe hangs over your relationships, Cancer, inviting you to heat things up and seal it with a kiss. Venus, the goddess of love, brings harmony, sweetness and a touch of romance, while lusty Mars lights a spark of passion, making this a season where love feels both tender and thrilling. For single Crabs, this dynamic duo could bring someone captivating into your life, someone who appreciates your nurturing nature but also gets your heart racing. With Mars adding assertiveness and Venus softening the edges, you'll find the courage to express what you want in love, whether it's a commitment, a fresh start or simply more passion.

CANCER: LUCKIEST *love* DAY

AUGUST 12

Open your heart wide. Now, wider still. Passion is flowing with a strong current as ardent Venus unites with expansive Jupiter in Cancer. The truth tumbles out in a romantic rush, whether you're professing feelings or sharing a long-held desire with your partner. Get exciting plans underway, like a baecation or ceremony.

Money & Career

CANCER 2025 FORECAST

Mars in Cancer is a game-changer for your career in the first quarter of 2025, but it all starts with a bit of recalibration. From January 6 to February 23, the high-key motivation planet takes a retrograde spin, offering you the chance to reflect on your ambitions and reassess your professional goals. What's been holding you back, Cancer? The answer may be a grab bag of limiting beliefs and fears, along with some polishing up of your skillset that can support forward momentum. Use the early part of the year to strategize and refine your plans without rushing ahead.

One exception? The January 13 full moon in Cancer is a ribbon-cutting ceremony for any hard work you've done since your 2024 birthday season. Seize any opportunity that arises to pitch your visionary ideas or, at the very least, get yourself in the same room as the movers and shakers in your industry. A winter conference or a guest pass to a social club—whatever you can cleverly finagle will do!

Do that behind-the-scenes work and you'll be prepared for lift-off once Mars course corrects on February 23, then powers through Cancer until April 18. Competitive Mars doesn't do "subtle," and neither should you during this transit. Swing out of your comfort zone and step into a leadership role. As one of the zodiac's trailblazing cardinal signs, you are more of an Alpha than you care to admit.

Just be mindful of veering into cutthroat terrain. Balance aggressive instincts with some of that classic Cancerian empathy and you'll sail to the top without losing essential allies along the way. With Mars' drive backing you up, you'll be unstoppable. Grab the wheel and steer your career exactly where you want it to go in 2025.

Professional aspirations could take off at a gallop once enterprising Jupiter enters your sign on June 9. This year-long cycle of expansion could bring anything from a game-changing opportunity to a total pivot in a new direction. Relocate to the London office for a year? Enroll in grad school for a hybrid program? Shop your screenplay with an agent? Start a kitchen table empire making sustainable merch? Well, why not?

Jupiter in Cancer is waving the checkered flag, giving you the drive to pursue your goals with renewed vigor. You'll feel more optimistic and ready to embrace new opportunities that align with your values and emotional well-being. Take advantage of this solid-gold celestial support to manifest your ambitions.

There's plenty more planetary action raising your professional profile this year. On March 29, a powerful solar eclipse in Aries activates your tenth house of career and public life. This is the final eclipse in a two-year series that's been catalyzing your professional journey since April 2023. Eclipses often bring sudden shifts. Be prepared for opportunities that could shake up your current work situation, propelling you toward something more aligned with your calling. If you're truly "on path," the action may accelerate, so buckle up and ride the ride!

Two outer planets are also teasing your tenth house, spending part of the year in Aries before beginning longer cycles through this sign starting in 2026. Dreamy, imaginative Neptune rolls into Aries (for the first time since 1875!) from March 30 to October 22. Then, on May 24, Saturn darts into the Ram's realm until September 1.

While Saturn encourages hard work and strategic thinking, Neptune adds a creative, visionary element to your career. Neptune invites you to dream big, blending your practical efforts with a sense of purpose and imagination. Saturn's focus is on concrete, long-lasting achievements. With the emphasis on long-term planning and sustainable success, you could be at the starting gate of massive growth that unfolds over the next few years. Be patient but persistent with the process.

CANCER: LUCKIEST *career* DAY

JUNE 24

The Day of Miracles has your name written all over it as the Sun and abundant Jupiter make an exact connection, combining forces in YOUR sign for the first time in over a decade! Swing for the fences with your ambitions and share your visionary ideas with people who might put dollars behind those dreams. Lean into the high-visibility energy of the day and your talents could be discovered by people near and far!

2025
CANCER

12
MONTH
OVERVIEW

January MONTHLY HOROSCOPE

The Sun shimmers in Capricorn, drawing your attention to partnerships and your closest connections until January 19. Your nurturing nature shines here, as you focus on how to create balance and support within these bonds. On January 11, the lunar nodes shift into Pisces and Virgo, marking the start of an 18-month cycle of travel, learning and enhanced communication. Forget about hiding in your comfort zone, Crab—your world is about to expand in untold ways. Mars retrograde slips back into Cancer on January 6, which could stall a few of your personal goals until February 23. Embrace this period to refine and reflect before hitting the accelerator next month. One exception to that rule is on the 13th, when the full moon in Cancer brings your hard work and achievements right into the spotlight. Promote yourself without apology! Even a humble brag could hit the mark. You never know who might see your offerings, so take the "risk" to put yourself out there. Aquarius season begins on the 19th, shifting your focus to shared resources and long-term investments, both key for building the security you crave. This sizzling cycle may bring you closer to a romantic partner, so make room in your hibernation station for a "winter warmer." Get ready to shed old skins on the 29th, when The Year of the Wood Snake begins—it's time to release beliefs and habits that aren't serving your growth.

February MONTHLY HOROSCOPE

What's happening behind the curtain, Cancer? (And who's there with you?) The Aquarius Sun simmers in your eighth house of mysteries, transformation and shared resources until the 18th, drawing you into more intimate connections and financial arrangements. But the big news arrives on February 4, when Jupiter powers forward in Gemini after a four-month retrograde, waking up your twelfth house of healing and closure. You've got the expansive planet in your corner until June 9 (then it goes into YOUR sign, hooray!). Use this period to release old baggage, work through emotional blocks and tap into your inner wisdom. Also on the 4th, Venus begins a long tour through Aries and your tenth house of career. It's time to show off your leadership skills and make strategic moves professionally. Aim high with your love goals, too. No settling! After February 18, the Sun moves into Pisces, energizing your ninth house of travel and higher learning. This is your moment to explore new horizons and embrace adventure. Finally, Mars turns direct in your sign on February 23, putting you back in the driver's seat with your personal plans and aspirations. With all this fiery energy, you'll feel unstoppable. Charge ahead with confidence!

March MONTHLY HOROSCOPE

Wanderlust hits you hard as the Sun continues soaring through Pisces and your peripatetic ninth house until the 20th. Travel as often as you can, but don't go too far off the grid, Cancer. Your Aries-ruled tenth house of career is getting major action this month and those "OOO" notifications could derail some major momentum. Venus retrogrades in Aries from March 1 to 27 and Mercury follows suit, spinning back through the Ram's realm from March 15 to 29. Are you chasing your true passions or just going through the motions? You could find yourself reassessing your path. If you need to polish up your professional presentation, start working on that this month. On March 14, the Virgo full moon and lunar eclipse brings helpful associates out of the woodwork. No, Cancer, you don't have to do it all alone! When the Sun moves into Aries on March 20, you'll be fully available to focus on those ambitious goals. Then, on March 29, the Aries new moon (a solar eclipse) closes out a powerful two-year eclipse series that brought excitement and instability to your professional life. A major career breakthrough or shift could be on the horizon. That's not all! Neptune enters Aries on March 30 for the first time since 1875. This kicks off a 14-year cycle of visionary inspiration that may add a spiritual dimension to your most important goals.

April MONTHLY HOROSCOPE

Show and prove, Cancer! As the Sun blazes through your prestigious, ambitious tenth house until April 19, you're a fearless contender. But don't even think about faking it 'til you make it. Mercury is retrograde in Pisces and your expansive ninth house until April 7, and Venus is also retrograde there until April 12. Use the first part of the month to check facts and educate yourself so that you have a bulletproof presentation mid-month. Travel plans may stall due to the retrogrades, but use this hiccup as an opportunity to strengthen ties close to home. After revving you up with both motivation and anxiety since January 6, feisty Mars leaves your sign on April 18. As the red planet plows into Leo, it fires up your second house of money and security until June 17. You'll be pumped to get your financial kingdom in order and create new income streams. Taurus season arrives on April 19, reminding you that it's all about who you know. Connect with your community, collaborate with like-minded people and enjoy the support of your network. You've laid the groundwork—now let others help you build on it

May MONTHLY HOROSCOPE

It's officially your turn to play entertainment director while the Taurus Sun buzzes through your eleventh house of friendships and collaborations until May 20. Rally your crew for a fundraiser, spearhead a group vacation or convince everyone to put on a Derby hat and sip mint juleps with you. When Pluto turns retrograde in Aquarius on May 4, you may have some stormy vibes to contend with in a close relationship (or two), especially if one of you has been burying feelings or sweeping a power imbalance under the rug. Sorting this out won't be comfortable, but the naked honesty could bring you closer. Close your tab on the 20th when the Sun drifts into Gemini and your twelfth house of closure, healing and reflection. You've got four weeks before Cancer season to deal with emotional baggage and tie up loose ends. But forget about disappearing from the public eye. On May 24, prestige-boosting Saturn rises into Aries for the first time since 1998, beginning a three-year (on and off) passage through your tenth house of career success. Saturn's disciplined energy will bring structure to your ambitions, encouraging you to step into leadership roles and start (or keep) building your legacy. Time to lay the groundwork for long-term success!

June MONTHLY HOROSCOPE

Get ready for some magic that's been over a decade in the making! On June 9, abundant, expansive Jupiter sweeps into your sign, charging up your trailblazing, self-sovereign first house with its adventurous energy. This isn't just wind in your sails, Crab, it's a turbine-engine whipping your dreams into an exciting frenzy. This yearlong cycle, which lasts until June 30, 2026, opens doors to opportunities that could transform your life. Whether you're pursuing an artistic passion, living abroad or reinventing your career, lean into what truly matters to you. When the Sun joins Jupiter in Cancer at the solstice on June 20, you'll feel a surge of confidence. Instead of setting goals, experiment wildly. Get out and try as many new things as your heart, soul and imagination desire. Soon enough, those journeys will inspire your next big move. Mid-month brings a few challenges with "authority figures" as Jupiter squares Saturn on June 15 and Neptune on June 18. Pay attention to power dynamics and make sure you aren't veering too far out of your lane in your zeal to get a plan in motion. Put on your entertainment director's hat on the 17th, as excitable Mars enters Virgo and revs up your social life until August 6. Organize barbecues, festival road trips and rooftop drinks. Curate guest lists carefully, however, as Mars can stir up tension between incompatible friends. On June 24, the Day of Miracles, the Sun and Jupiter align in your sign for the first time since 2014! You've got the cosmic green light to do something daring. Trust your instincts and roll the dice. Then, do it again on the 25th, when the year's only new moon in Cancer gives your dreams another liftoff.

July MONTHLY HOROSCOPE

With the Sun and growth-agent Jupiter copiloting through Cancer until the 22nd, birthday season 2025 could bring sweeping developments. Pour energy into personal projects. Try as many new activities as your curious mind desires. These inquiries could lead you down an artistic and spiritual rabbit hole beginning this July 7! For the first time since 1949, renegade Uranus sidespins into Gemini and your dreamy twelfth house of transitions. This six-month transit is a sneak peek of a seven-year cycle that begins again in April 2026. Change, and possibly closure of a major chapter, are already in the ether, but don't rush to upend your life—just take notes. On July 18, Mercury flips into a three-week retrograde, backing up through Leo and your second house of money. Keep a careful watch on your spending, review your budget and hold off whatever major purchases you can. Throughout the month, Neptune, Saturn, and Chiron all turn retrograde in Aries (on the 4th, 13th, and 30th, respectively), which could add some complexity to your career. These five-month retrogrades may stir up old doubts around your professional path or resurface issues with authority figures. Reexamine your ambitions and do any necessary training to get your skills up to snuff. Once the Sun moves into Leo on July 22, your focus turns to building security and self-worth, but with Mercury retrograde in this arena until August 11, you may need to revisit old financial plans or reassess your approach to abundance. Stay flexible and patient—this cosmic reset is setting the stage for a stronger foundation!

August MONTHLY HOROSCOPE

Money's on your mind as August opens up. With the Sun in Leo until August 22 and Mercury retrograde in the lion's den through the 11th, continue to fine-tune financial plans as you streamline and simplify your life. Increased earnings could come through a past colleague. If it's time to raise your rates or refresh your offerings, get all your ducks in a row for a mid-month reveal. Sultry love planet Venus struts through your sign from July 30 to August 25, blessing you with irresistible, It-sign status. Start by romancing yourself. Book massages, head to the salon, create more spaciousness in your schedule so you can luxuriate instead of rushing. Relaxing helps you be more receptive to a partner. Don't be afraid to show some edge in relationships now by playfully asking for exactly what you want. Go-getter Mars lands in peaceful, aesthetic Libra on August 6, harmonizing your home and family life until September 22. How can you make the Crab Castle feel like a sanctuary? Decorate and set up zones for relaxing, working and entertaining. Your mind is hungry for new data once Virgo season begins on August 22. One day later, the first of two back-to-back new moons in Virgo arrives, which could lead you to a fall workshop or kick off a media project like writing a screenplay or recording a podcast. Random socializing has never been your style. Look for intentional gatherings like book clubs, salons and mastermind groups where you can share ideas and feed your intellect.

September MONTHLY HOROSCOPE

This tide-turning month of retrogrades and eclipses brings a chance to reset and reflect. But forget about slipping out of social commitments. Until the 22nd, the Virgo Sun keeps your life buzzy and interactive. With Venus moving from Leo into Virgo on the 19th, your communication skills are both sharp and compelling. Get ready! You may be invited to speak on a panel, guest on a podcast or catch a wave of inspiration to begin a Substack. But that's not all! On the 21st, the second in a rare pair of Virgo new moons arrives—and it's also a galvanizing solar eclipse! Cooperative ventures get a burst of momentum from these moonbeams. New collaborators could emerge in the most obvious, everyday places. Who knew? Start slowly and test the waters with a one-off project to see if your styles truly mesh. Earlier in the month, there are waves of uncertainty to contend with. On the 1st, Saturn retrogrades back into Pisces, which could force you to reconsider some of your personal beliefs or academic goals. When changemaker Uranus starts its yearly retrograde on the 6th, buried issues could bubble to the surface. Consider deeper forms of healing to process these memories: hypnotherapy, energy work, EMDR, even plant medicine. A total lunar eclipse in Pisces on September 7 brings a major breakthrough related to your worldview. Travel plans could materialize quickly or you could connect to an important person living halfway around the globe. Lusty Mars enters Scorpio on September 22, intensifying your focus on creativity and romance. Your passions will be running high between now and November 4, so beam that heat selectively.

October MONTHLY HOROSCOPE

How cozy is your cove? While the Sun nestles in Libra and your domestic zone until September 22, implement routines that make your home life flow. Declutter and up the comfort factor, making "contagious calm" the goal. Make time for lively gatherings under your roof, too! With convivial Venus spinning through Virgo and your social third house until the 13th—then into your family-focused fourth (Libra) after that—your place could be ground zero for movie nights, elegant dinner parties and family gatherings. Romantically, Venus stacks the first half of the month with meet-cutes and cultural activities. Bring date nights home mid-month when the love planet slinks into Libra on October 13, setting the stage for key exchanges, cohabitation plans or updates to your love nest. Wealth-agent Pluto wraps up its retrograde also on the 13th, powering forward through your eighth house of investments. You could radar in on a high-yield opportunity or find clever ways to make your money compound. Realign around a financial goal or revamp your shared resources with a partner to make sure everything feels fair and on the level. Scorpio season begins on the 22nd, swinging the spotlight into your fifth house of fame, fertility and creative expression. This four-week cycle is high-season for passion, so dress up and paint the town red! Travel plans could lead you to a nostalgic location as soulful Neptune retrogrades back into Pisces and your worldly ninth house that very same day.

November MONTHLY HOROSCOPE

November goal: Weave as much pleasure as you can into your everyday activities. Until the 21st, the Scorpio Sun is casting a seductive spell in your fifth house of romance, fame and creative expression. For a change, you'll enjoy feeling eyes on you, especially when you're skillfully directing the action with curated plans (and a runway-worthy outfit to match). On the 4th, energetic Mars lunges into Sagittarius, pouring fuel into your sixth house of work and wellness until December 15. Talk about finishing the year strong! You'll have both the hustle and the muscle to get your Q4 goals to a stunning finish. In love, there's no settling for casual once Venus sashays into sultry Scorpio from November 6 to 30. Make romance and sensuality part of your everyday life. Remember, if no worthy contenders are on the scene, you can buy yourself flowers! With Mercury spinning through its final retrograde run from November 9 to 29—in Sagittarius, then Scorpio after the 18th—it will be easy to let self-care commitments slip if you don't let your loved ones know what you're devoted to accomplishing. Mix up the mocktails and invite them to join you for that dance class. On November 7, unpredictable Uranus retrogrades back into Taurus for its final lap through your friendship sector. This seven-year cycle ends on April 25, 2026, but you may need to solidify some visionary community plans before then. Expansive Jupiter also turns retrograde in Cancer on November 11, giving you four months to reassess personal growth goals and key relationships. By November 27, when Saturn ends its five-month retrograde in your ninth house of expansion, you'll be ready to set new learning or travel goals for the upcoming year.

December MONTHLY HOROSCOPE

Healthy, wealthy and wise—that's how you're wrapping up 2025, Cancer. The Sagittarius Sun is shining its life-giving rays into your work and wellness zone until the 21st, keeping your eye on the ball. But that's not all! Motivator Mars is also in Sagittarius until the 15th, joined by Venus until the 24th. Eating clean and moving your body will keep you thriving and energized for holiday networking and wrapping up EOY projects. This power-posse of planets makes you an excellent leader who not only harmonizes team and family but keeps everyone lovingly connected and focused on what REALLY matters. Compassionate Neptune turns direct in Pisces as it ends a five-month retrograde on the 10th. Here's more momentum to get travel plans locked down, which may be part of your 2026 career expansion! Who are the MVPs in your world? You'll be ready to reap the rewards of one-on-one relationships once fervent Mars heads into Capricorn on December 15. When the Sun joins on the 21st (which is also winter solstice), then Venus on the 24th, you'll get a string of green lights to move ahead with people who are the right fit for you. As the year winds down, set your sights on an important "couple goal," which could mean anything from taking the next important step with your S.O. to working with a love coach who can help you identify what you actually need in a partner. Business contracts are also blessed by this cosmic trifecta, so get those deal memos signed before 2025 ends! You might feel like spending NYE (or part of it) with one special soul. No apologies if three feels like a crowd!

Read your extended monthly forecast for life, love, money and career! astrostyle.com

A LITTLE ABOUT *Leo*

DATES July 22 - August 22

SYMBOL The Lion

ELEMENT Fire

QUALITY Fixed

RULING PLANET The Sun

BODY PART Heart, upper back, spine

BEST TRAITS

Courageous, generous, loyal, protective, nakedly honest, entertaining, romantic, heart-centered

KEYWORDS

Passion, self-expression, fun, energy, devotion, nobility, leadership, decadence, creativity

Read more about Leo

LEO
IN 2025

| ALL THE PLANETS IN LEO IN 2025 | YOUR 2025 HOROSCOPE | TOP 5 THEMES FOR LEO IN 2025 | LOVE HOROSCOPE + LUCKY DATES | MONEY HOROSCOPE + LUCKY DATES |

Leo in 2025

YOUR YEARLY OVERVIEW

Posse up with your pride, Leo! Community is your path to freedom in 2025 as two of the most liberated planets, Jupiter and Uranus, each do a six-month lap through Gemini and your collaborative eleventh house. Choose your allies wisely as they will shape and influence the way this year goes for you. With the destiny-dusted North Node dropping into Pisces and your intimate eighth house, pursuing one soulful (and sexy!) relationship could also be high on your priority list. As you follow that urge to merge, the South Node in Virgo nudges you to work on self-love, too, and balance the intensity of these relationships with self-care practices. When Jupiter slips into Cancer on June 9, it beams its expansive energy into your twelfth house of rest, healing and subconscious growth. This year-long cycle could send you on a meditative journey within. Rather than pushing for external accolades, go on a healing journey and restore your energy for when Jupiter takes its once-every-12-year lap through Leo starting June 30, 2026. Not that you'll go on a total sabbatical. Structured Saturn and imaginative Neptune spend a little time in Aries this year, putting some steam behind your dreams. That might look like grad school, publishing a book or moving to a far-flung corner of the world. Entrepreneurial Leos could start work on a profitable project—or pass the torch as you cash out on your efforts.

THE PLANETS IN *Leo*

THE SUN
JUL 22–AUG 22

It's birthday season for you, so step out and shine! Seek novelty and take extra initiative during this radiant monthlong phase.

NEW MOON
JUL 24
3:11PM; 2°08′

Bonus New Year! Set your intentions for the next six months and get into action.

FULL MOON
FEB 12
8:53AM, 24°06′

Ready, set, manifest! Your work of the past six months bears fruit and it's time to harvest the rewards.

MERCURY
JUN 26–SEP 2
RETROGRADE IN LEO:
JUL 18–AUG 11

Crown yourself monarch of the social butterflies when popularity-boosting Mercury visits your sign once a year. Circulate and get social—but careful not to make promises you can't keep or fall into people pleasing.

VENUS
AUG 25–SEP 19

You've got the romantic It Factor when the galactic glamazon charges up your powers of seduction each year. Willpower is weak in the face of beauty and luxury. Watch your spending!

MARS
RETROGRADE IN LEO:
JAN 1–6
DIRECT IN LEO:
APR 18–JUN 17

Motivation is high when energetic Mars visits your sign every couple years—but check your combative streak and try not to come on too strong, especially during the retrograde portion of this programming.

$\mathscr{L}$eo in 2025
HIGHLIGHTS

𝔑

EMOTIONAL DEPTH AND TRANSFORMATION: NORTH NODE IN PISCES

What's your attachment style? You'll get an up-close-and-personal look starting January 11, 2025, as the North Node moves into Pisces, alchemizing your eighth house of intimacy, power and shared resources. Sensuality becomes a spiritual experience. Connections crop up that feel fated, as if the universe strategically placed these people in your path. Meanwhile, the South Node in Virgo and your second house of finances pushes you to release control issues around money. Instead of clinging to old habits, trust in the power of merging your resources with others. This is your moment to reconfigure your approach to spending and saving. Investing in the right relationships can yield new levels of abundance—both financially and emotionally.

POPULARITY HITS NEW PEAKS WITH JUPITER AND URANUS IN GEMINI

The Leo supergroup is assembling! As expansive Jupiter and unconventional Uranus both spend a chunk of the year in Gemini, your popularity skyrockets, but not necessarily in predictable ways. Live-out-loud Jupiter continues its twelve-month journey through your eleventh house until June 9, which could turn everything you touch into a viral sensation. The eleventh house is offbeat and radical, so forget about selling out. It's your refreshing (and rebellious) authenticity that attracts superfans in 2025. Want to make a truly meaningful impact? Share the limelight, Leo, with people who bring their own sharply unique talents to the mix. When game-changing Uranus sidespins through Gemini from July 7 to November 7, it brings some wildcards into the mix—sudden friendships, surprising allies, and even out-of-the-blue group projects that take off like wildfire. These enterprising planets could bring good fortune with tech-based and impact-driven projects. Analog Leos, get the intentional community together. Sharing is caring!

PLUTO PLUMBS THE DEPTHS OF YOUR PARTNERSHIPS

Relationships become a profound area of growth for you, as metamorphic Pluto settles into its long, underground tour through Aquarius, opposing your Sun until 2044. While you already experienced waves of this energy in 2023 and 2024, this year begins the unbroken, nineteen-year lap that can radically shift your approach to partnerships. Pluto is the "projector" planet, revealing where you go unconscious and point the finger—until you surrender to seeing your own shadows. Your mission now? To confront power dynamics, control issues and the deeper truths about your one-on-one bonds.

Any relationship built on a weak foundation may crumble, while those that survive will emerge stronger and more authentic. This is a long, slow process, so give yourself lots of grace, space and self-love as you learn.

JUNE SHIFT: FROM CENTER OF THE ACTION TO CELESTIAL SABBATICAL

Vibe shift! Lions will need a quiet den to retreat to starting June 9, when nomadic Jupiter slips into a yearlong retreat through Cancer and your twelfth house of spirituality and restorative healing. After the whirlwind energy of the first half of the year, you may be feeling a bit spent and eager to dive into some solitary creative work and reflection. If you're grieving a loss or breakup, or just preparing for a transition once Jupiter springs into Leo on June 30, 2026, this can be a profound cycle of inner evolution. The catch? You might not see immediate results on the surface. Growth during this Jupiter cycle is an inside job. Start a meditation practice, work with therapists, shamans, holistic healers. It's okay to hit pause for a bit, Leo; in fact, it's necessary.

EXPLORING NEW TERRAIN: SATURN AND NEPTUNE IN ARIES

Pack your bags—or find another way to broaden your horizons—when Saturn and Neptune enter Aries, your ninth house of travel, higher learning and big ideas this spring. This odd-couple pairing will only visit the Ram's realm for part of the year, previewing longer tours that both planets will begin in 2026. Big ideas come flooding in. Take note of them all, even if you're not ready to pull the trigger yet. Structured Saturn helps you map out project plans and detailed itineraries. Neptune adds a dose of magic, making the journey feel inspired and mystical. Want to start a travel blog, go back to school or launch an online venture? The universe is nudging you forward, but balance the inspiration with a solid plan. Your ideas have serious potential to take off in 2025, Leo, as long as you're willing to put in the work to make them soar.

Leo ♌

TOP 5 THEMES FOR
Leo in 2025

1	2	3	4	5
SPARK UP SYNERGIES	TAKE A CELESTIAL SABBATICAL	JOURNEY WITH PURPOSE	REVISIT LOVE LESSONS	GROW YOUR WEALTH

1 SPARK UP SYNERGIES

JUPITER AND URANUS IN GEMINI

JUPITER: MAY 25, 2024 – JUNE 9, 2025
URANUS: JULY 7 – NOVEMBER 7, 2025 • JANUARY 26, 2026 – MAY 22, 2033

Many hands make light work in 2025, and they can ease up your intensive schedule exponentially! Liberated Jupiter and innovative Uranus both do time in your eleventh house of teamwork and technology. Pay close attention to the company you keep. It's time to ditch the energy vampires and hangers-on and open up space for meaningful connections—with people who give as good as they take.

JUPITER IN GEMINI

MAY 25, 2024 – JUNE 9, 2025

Keep on collaborating, Leo! A popularity spike that began in mid-2024 keeps on going for the first half of 2025, as expansive Jupiter continues its yearlong festival through Gemini and your eleventh house of community. During this phase, which began on May 25, 2024, your social life is poised to shoot through the roof. Manage your time carefully if you want to "do it all" and not get burnt out.

While you're busy widening your social circle, you might also need to refine it. Everyone loves a Leo who's shining brilliantly, like the Sun that rules your sign. But who among them can give you doses of tough love to shore you up after you plummet into a dark spell? Jupiter demands authenticity from everything it touches. With your interpersonal life in its crosshairs until this June 9, genuine connections are the only ones that will make the cut.

If you've found your true crew, early 2025 is peak season for teamwork. Some of your most meaningful wins will be group efforts. Need to cast some new members for your supergroup? With worldly Jupiter at the helm, step into the role of the cultural ambassador. If you draw people together from a wide range of backgrounds, diversity doesn't have to divide. Tap into your magnanimous leadership style to focus everyone on a higher mission as well as their common humanity.

Your humanitarian nature is aroused, and you could feel called to volunteer or work for an activist group in your community. Visionary Leos might start their own nonprofit or foundation. Your esprit de corps can also be applied to lighter activities, like group travel. Nomadic Jupiter can guide you to some far-flung places. Perhaps that tour of the Egyptian pyramids, a cooking intensive at a Tuscan villa or walking the Camino Santiago.

If you're doing something newsworthy, alert the media, but don't center your pitch around yourself. While Jupiter is in Gemini, star powered Leos will capture the limelight with an ensemble cast. Is your life fodder for a fascinating reality show; could you go on-camera as an expert or a live reporter? For Leos who have the theater gene (and that's a LOT of you!), these genres could be your jam. Spotlighting other people's talents will also position you as the noble Lion you are. Pay it forward and backward and keep the supportive love flowing through your networks.

URANUS IN GEMINI
JULY 7 – NOVEMBER 7, 2025
JANUARY 26, 2026 – MAY 22, 2033

We interrupt your hammock nap to give you this important announcement. Shortly after Jupiter in Cancer lures you into a meditative groove starting June 9, get ready for a summer popularity spike that begins this July 7.

The reason for this social surge? For the first time since 1941-49, communal Uranus sidespins into Gemini, where it will send energizing currents through your eleventh house of teamwork and technology until November 7. Stop leaving those texts on Read and start responding "Yes" to the invites piling up!

This is simply a prelude of what's to come. On April 25, 2026, Uranus plugs back into Gemini for seven years, until May 22, 2033. That's sure to be happy news for festive Leos who love nothing more than an excuse to gather your favorite people together for a party, adventure or humanitarian cause—sometimes all rolled into one.

With the eccentric planet here, your social life could start to look even more like a circus, filled with fascinating characters, radical disrupters, fearless activists and thought leaders. No, they won't all be appropriate to invite to the family barbecue, so get used to having more of a silo'd social life—and maybe some people who you hang with one-on-one because they're too strong a brew for the rest of your crew. As long as you feel a kindred connection, you don't have to listen to the comments section.

Disruptive Uranus inspires you to share your most outré ideas—and it gives you the confidence to bring others onboard with them. The eleventh house rules humanitarianism and activism, and under this spell of do-good radicalization, you could find your calling, along with a squad of like minded idealists.

But this doesn't happen by you shapeshifting to accommodate others' ideas or game plan. This is a jet-powered blast of self-assurance and liberation that comes from thinking, speaking and living your most authentic truths.

Collaboration is a key to your success, but you're going to have to do it differently, o' royal one. Descend from the throne and get in the trenches with "the people." Yes, you may be the most capable leader in the bunch, but this is not the time to do your de facto "take-charge" schtick.

Instead, Uranus in Gemini serves lessons in empowering another leader to rise—especially if you're more than ready to pass the baton. True, you may witness a few cringey moments as they fumble through their enhanced responsibilities. Cheer them on, guide them, but don't (we repeat, don't) start doing their job for them. What a relief this will be! Now, back to that hammock you go.

2 TAKE A CELESTIAL SABBATICAL

JUPITER IN CANCER
JUNE 9, 2025 – JUNE 30, 2026

Toss your raffia sandals into a backpack and hop on that Vespa scooter! This June 9, 2025, nomadic Jupiter decamps to Cancer, your flowy, nomadic twelfth house, signaling the start of a thirteen-month sabbatical. Even the most polished Leo will long to feel the breeze in your mane—professional blowouts, be damned!

After a buzzy, interactive start to the year, this transit can feel like a sudden record scratch. You were flying high, and now all you want to do is come in for a landing and maybe a weeklong nap in a beach hammock. Figuring out how to go with the flow is one of the huge lessons for you during this thirteen-month stretch.

That's hardly an easy challenge for a superstar multi-tasker like you, but enjoy the lull while you can. Next summer Jupiter lunges into your sign for a year, which will send you off to the races once again. Cherish any opportunity you have to rest, recalibrate, and process your emotions.

While you might wish results would hurry up and materialize, you'll have to be patient. Like seeds germinating under the soil, your growth might happen in the invisible realm of emotions and the subconscious while Jupiter works its quiet magic in Cancer.

Here's an idea for an energy conservation plan: Give up the need to micromanage every detail and turn the wheel over to your spiritual side. Life may feel a bit surreal, like a lucid dream at times. Once you surrender to this, you may realize something utterly unexpected. In the space that opens up, you begin to see possibilities—miraculous ones—that you failed to notice when you were busy playing Executive Producer of Everything.

The trick of Jupiter in Cancer is to keep life breezy and open-ended rather than commit to anything stressful, time-consuming, or, you know, permanent. Indeed, this Jupiter phase, which lasts until June 30, 2026, will feel like a long, sweet escape. Since, as a fixed sign, you like to be grounded, this ebbing and flowing can churn up anxiety. We recommend starting (or ramping up) a yoga and/or meditation practice now, even getting into a more soulful form of dance.

The twelfth house is transitional, so try not to get too attached to any outcome. Just when you think you've radared onto the thing, it could slip out of your grasp like a handful of flowing water. If you're ready to close a chapter of your life, like a relationship you've outgrown or saying goodbye to a job or a neighborhood that no longer delights in your 2025 era, Jupiter gives you the courage to forge a new path.

While this could happen quickly, you may also choose to ease through the transition slowly. That's especially true if you're still figuring out what the next phase of your life will look like. Envisioning will be easier once Jupiter sambas into your sign from June 30, 2026 until July 25, 2027.

Before then, be prepared for unresolved emotions to bubble to the surface. You may feel a bit raw after June 9, but you'll also feel really alive, even amidst the tears, fury or bursts of laughter. In addition to perfecting that drop-to-your-knees surrender prayer, you might want to work with a spiritual advisor, therapist, coach or support group to help you glean the golden lessons of your feelings.

While your creativity is this heightened, open the doors for your magnum opus to emerge. Let the muse guide you to your deepest expression and give you the green light to turn your pain or grief or personal blocks into a true work of art. Hello, catharsis!

3 JOURNEY WITH PURPOSE

♌

SATURN AND NEPTUNE IN ARIES

NEPTUNE: MARCH 30 – OCTOBER 22, 2025 • JANUARY 26, 2026 – MARCH 23, 2039
SATURN: MAY 24 – SEPTEMBER 1, 2025 • FEBRUARY 13, 2026 – APRIL 12, 2028

All the world is your oyster in 2025, but one place you won't want to be very often is hiding out in your lion's den. Two important planets are weaving out of Pisces and your mysterious eighth house and making their first of two passes into Aries and your ninth house of global adventures. You're ready to step out and shine again, Leo, in ways that perhaps you haven't allowed yourself to do for years. And even if you have, you may find yourself drawn to a totally different "stage" or playground where you can share even more of your gifts.

The planets involved here are quite the odd couple: boundary-hound Saturn and boundary-dissolver Neptune. While this might sound like a conflict of interest, it actually isn't. Saturn's realism can help support Neptune's enchanted ideas (which often have a slippery grasp on reality). Together, they become "imagineers" who can help you turn your fanciful visions into a meaningful product or offering. Yes, Leo, it's time to put your name on the map in a brand new way!

NEPTUNE IN ARIES

MARCH 30 – OCTOBER 22, 2025
JANUARY 26, 2026 – MARCH 23, 2039

A visionary voyage begins for Leos this March 30, when, for the first time since 1875, enchanted Neptune sets sail in Aries and your worldly, philosophical and adventurous ninth house. This can awaken a deep yearning for experiences that expand your mind and spirit—whether that means hiking the Camino Santiago, enrolling in grad school or starting an entrepreneurial venture that helps people tap into their fullest human potential.

While Neptune's visit to Aries is brief in 2025, lasting only until October 22, it's a prelude of what's to come. On January 26, 2026, the numinous planet circles back to the Ram's realm for a solid thirteen years, until March 23, 2039. Pay attention to the broader horizons that begin to call you in 2025. Over the next decade-plus, your dreams could lead you to far-flung corners of the globe to explore, study and possibly relocate to join an expat community abroad.

No matter your GPS coordinates, Neptune's long tour through Aries will broaden your spiritual and intellectual horizons. Be mindful, however, of the hazy planet's penchant for creating mirages. Much of what you encounter during this cycle will not be what it seems. Approach new ideas, trends and the latest gurus with extra discernment and take it upon yourself to verify data that seems a little too good to be true. It's fine to dabble and play, Leo, just know that not everything you explore is meant to stick around for the long haul. Enjoy the experiences, even if they're just a one-time thing.

As selfless Neptune encourages you to serve and heal others, consider how you can use your natural leadership in writing, media, education, or bridging cultural gaps—all areas of life that fall into the ninth house. You might find yourself stepping into roles that require you to teach, inspire, and connect people from all walks of life, turning your knowledge and experiences into tools for collective healing and growth. Your imagination could be put to wonderful use writing memoirs, children's books or making any sort of media that is "edutaining" (educational and entertaining).

If fear has kept you playing it safe in recent years, that phase of resistance to risk will soon melt away. Neptune in Aries dares you to be authentic as it pushes you to express your truths boldly and openly. As you do, you may be drawn into a more public, influential role, like Leo Melinda French Gates, who, in the aftermath of her divorce from Bill and her exit from The Gates Foundation, is devoting her resources to supporting women's rights.

No matter where you are on the goddess' green earth, you're poised to become an ambassador of sorts, not only in your local community but also across digital platforms, where your influence can extend globally. This period is ripe for you to craft a message that resonates deeply with others, one that speaks to the soul of who you are and invites others to explore new perspectives. Keep your heart open and your mind clear, and you'll emerge from this transit with a richer, more expansive understanding of the world and your place in it.

SATURN IN ARIES

MAY 24 – SEPTEMBER 1, 2025
FEBRUARY 13, 2026 – APRIL 12, 2028

If it's felt like you couldn't catch a break for the past few years, that unlucky streak is coming to an end, Leo. On May 24, taskmaster Saturn makes its first exit out of Pisces and your intense, mysterious and transformational eighth house, where it's been teaching you harsh lessons since March 7, 2023. Now on deck? Saturn's move into Aries and your bright, optimistic ninth house.

While this cycle is brief in 2025, lasting only from May 24 to September 1, it's a preview of what's to come. Saturn returns to the Ram's realm from February 13, 2026 to April 12, 2028, picking up on whatever good times you get rolling this year.

Wherever Saturn goes, it brings a measure of challenge. Like Yoda, it wants you to learn how to "use the force" and gain the strength of a Jedi. But when it tours your ninth house, it delivers a ray of hope; a measured sense of optimism. While you may not be able to hit the gas as hard as you'd prefer, you're set to grow steadily and significantly over the coming three years.

With Saturn in Aries, your reach will extend in both predictable and surprising ways—be it through travel, relocation, enhancing your existing skills, or diving into entirely new areas of learning. Entrepreneurial Leos might feel inspired to draft detailed business plans and seek out discussions with potential partners. However, it's unwise to quit your day job without a solid safety net—and ideally, another income source—locked and loaded. Gradually build up your new venture at a pace that ensures sustainability. That way, you can smoothly transition into whatever role awaits, be it as a respected employee or the full-time leader of Leo, Inc.

Since the ninth house also rules publishing, part of your success during this cycle could involve writing a book, launching a blog, or creating instructional videos. And with Saturn forming a supportive trine to your Leo Sun, you'll find the backing you need to maintain this new, more measured pace. The biggest challenge? Keeping your focus tight without veering off into too many directions. If you discover you're lacking a critical skill to fulfill your dreams, consider enrolling in a degree or certification program, even one that you can do while maintaining your current job.

You might even find it beneficial to work as an understudy or apprentice in order to gain valuable experience. This can position you to venture out on your own later with greater confidence. With Saturn finally moving out of your eighth house of bonding, you're also due for some relief in your personal life. Finding "the One" or simply enjoying the partner you have will become much easier. The lessons of the past few years have finally solidified, and now you're ready to apply them to craft a more joyful and fulfilling love life. This is your time to expand, learn, and transform at a deliberate pace, Leo—embrace it!

REVISIT LOVE LESSONS

VENUS RETROGRADE IN ARIES AND PISCES

ARIES: MARCH 1 – 27
PISCES: MARCH 27 – APRIL 12

You're in love with love, Leo, but starting March 1, flip your love light inwards. Amorous Venus embarks on a six-week retrograde, backing up through your philosophical ninth house (Aries) and your eighth house of eroticism and unbreakable bonds (Pisces). Your psyche is a beautifully complex place, Leo. When Venus shifts into reverse every 18 months, you have a golden opportunity to excavate all the buried emotions, beliefs and patterns that are informing your love life.

While this can churn up a whole host of feelings, this won't be as intense as the last time Venus was retrograde, which took place in Leo from July 22 to September 3, 2023. Thankfully, you're in the clear this go 'round. From March 1 to 27, Venus slips back through Aries and your ninth house of truth, travel and optimism. Then, the planet of love sinks into Pisces and your mysterious, seductive eighth house from March 27 to April 12, which is sure to bring you anything but a clear answer about your romantic life.

Check in with yourself: Have you been using positive thinking to try to sidestep a conflict in a relationship? You can't pep-talk yourself out of your honest feelings or put off speaking up because you don't want to rock the boat! While Venus backs up through forthright fire sign Aries (March 1 to 27), stop painting sunshine over a legit issue. Diplomatic Venus can help you start addressing problem areas directly without wounding anyone's pride. The gift of Venus retrograde is that it brings a golden opportunity to revisit the past and see where

you can make things better. While broaching certain topics will be uncomfortable, once you open the floodgates, you'll feel so relieved!

In all your closest connections, it's time to put long-range goals on the table and see how they align. Though discussions may reveal that you want different things, that doesn't have to signal the end of the line. Use these six weeks to cleverly brainstorm ways you can support each other's dreams. That might mean living in different cities for part of each year or reconfiguring finances temporarily so one of you can afford to go back to school. Put it all on the table and discuss! Need help reviving the magic? Before March 27, revisit a location that makes you feel like your most beautiful and magical self. You can journey solo or with a plus-one. The point of the exercise is to connect to YOUR power, and the sensual parts of yourself that haven't gotten enough attention for a while.

Spoiler alert—or shall we say, advance preparation warning! When Venus slips back into Pisces and your shadowy eighth house from March 27 to April 12, you may be susceptible to a toxic player's charms, perhaps one who has ghosted on prior occasions. Old habits die hard, especially when there's ultra-strong sexual chemistry between you. But since you know this can happen, it's wise to block a few numbers just to keep that door from accidentally-on-purpose swinging open.

Another risk during Venus' backspin through Pisces, after March 27? You could fall under the spell of an enchanting raconteur who woos you with promises but fails to follow up. Fortify your willpower in March so you can make it to April 12 without getting swept into a dangerous liaison. Sexual energy will be extremely potent during these two weeks, but it can bring up a host of unexpected feelings. While you may find it scintillating to play cat and mouse games, failing to suss out key details can leave you lost in a maze of ruminating and obsession. Do your very best to avoid that sort of "catnip," Leo, and opt for the more direct styles of communication that your sign favors.

Are you still misty-eyed over "the one that got away"? Venus' pivot could bring an old flame back into the picture who actually has soulmate potential. If the connection is still strong, it could be worth exploring, but don't expect to get a clear read on the situation until the end of April. Pace yourself and, this time around, put all truths on the table. The conditions don't have to be "perfect," but they should be something that you can live with.

5

GROW YOUR WEALTH

LUNAR NODES IN VIRGO AND PISCES
NORTH NODE IN PISCES, SOUTH NODE IN VIRGO
JANUARY 11, 2025 – JULY 26, 2026

Leo Unleashed! As a vibrant fire sign, your spirit thrives on exploration and grandeur. Mark your calendars for January 11 when the lunar North Node shifts into Pisces and your eighth house of transformation and deep, soulful bonding. This transition invites you into the mysteries of intimate relationships and shared resources until July 26, 2026—significant change from your previous adventures.

Since July 17, 2023, the North Node has been gallivanting across your worldly ninth house in Aries. You've been soaking up diverse cultures and broadening your horizons. But the January 11 pivot plunges you into the depths of closeness and complexity. This cycle, last experienced nearly two decades ago (2006 to 2007), promises a profound exploration of intimacy and mutual empowerment.

As the North Node snakes through esoteric Pisces, expect to dive deep into the realms of emotional and financial entwinements. Explore the uncharted territories of your psyche, your passions, and your power dynamics with others. This cycle helps you discover a new kind of magic, one that's woven through the most private parts of your life.

You may find yourself more involved in joint financial ventures or navigating the intricacies of emotional and sexual intimacy. To make the most of this nodal cycle, you'll need to embrace vulnerability and trust. Self-awareness is key, but so is honesty. If people aren't willing to be forthcoming, you may drop them cold—or at least put the relationship in temporary deep freeze while you go to your corners and work through your issues.

Across the aisle, the karmic South Node in Virgo and your second house of possessions and values acts as a grounding force. As you face intense transformations, it's easy to spin out. The South Node helps you maintain a sense of stability and security. The trick? Balance the give-and-take in relationships to ensure that your needs aren't overshadowed by the desires of others.

During this nodal cycle, integrity is everything. Be extremely mindful of the commitments you make—and the secrets you share. Clear intentions will be crucial as you navigate the complexities of deeper bonds. You may need to put people through a loyalty test or two. But it goes both ways, Leo. Be ready to prove your own fidelity. Keep confidential information in the vault and respect people's boundaries.

Leos in relationships could face challenging (but necessary) conversations about your shared resources and future plans. Are you aligned and supporting each other? Take an unflinching inventory. Some adjustments may be necessary to make sure that you're both thriving. In some cases, you may need to bring in a third party to help mitigate some fractures. Couples' therapy facilitators, house cleaners, accountants and babysitters can all be part of that equation.

Do your dreams overlap enough to make staying together make sense? If your attachment issues are in constant fight-or-flight mode, this nodal cycle could find you at the breaking point. Maybe you truly love one another but are moving in vastly different directions. Tough talks could arise during this 18-month cycle, which may result in letting each other go.

That doesn't have to be the case, though! The soulful energy of the Pisces North Node can cast a powerful spell over lovers. Fantasies (of all varieties) can come to life during this boundary-blurring phase. Choose a safe word and get the costumes ready.

Concurrently, the Virgo South Node helps you put structures in place that support your day-to-day existence. Simplifying aspects of your life can have a profound effect on your key relationships. When you're not running here, there and everywhere, Leo, you might actually have the space to relax and get yourself in the mood for some spicy playtime with bae.

Joint finances could pave the path to profitability now. The eighth house rules "other people's money" so if you're looking for investors for a project, get your pitch deck ready and go start a bidding war. Getting your own retirement plan in place is also a wise idea. It's never too soon or too late to start, Leo. Open up an index fund account or a Roth IRA (or both) or increase your monthly contributions to accelerate your compounding growth. Be proactive about addressing debts, too. You could pay them off in creative ways over the coming 18 months.

Professionally, this could be a period of significant empowerment. You might find yourself drawn to roles that involve managing others' resources or providing emotional support and counseling. Your natural leadership will shine in situations that require empathy and discretion.

As you embrace the intense energy of the North Node in Pisces, keep in mind that your strength lies in your ability to lead from the heart. This cycle challenges you to integrate your charismatic presence with a deeper, more introspective approach to life and relationships.

Remember, Leo, while this period demands much from you in terms of emotional and financial engagement, it also offers profound growth and transformation. By the end of this nodal cycle, you'll have a richer understanding of what it means to truly share your life with others—both in the material and emotional realms.

$\mathcal{L}$ove

LEO 2025 FORECAST

Love in 2025 is anything but ordinary for you, Leo. You're stepping into a year when relationships will grow more intense, mystical and profoundly connected. Thankfully, that's just the way your whole-hearted sign likes it. (And if not, you'll definitely learn to!)

Intimacy is the name of the game starting on January 11, as the destiny-dusted lunar North Node climbs into Pisces and your erotic eighth house—its first visit here since 2007. This cycle, which lasts until July 26, 2026, is NOT about surface-level attraction; it's about going all-in. The eighth house rules sex, shared resources and deep emotional transformation. Nothing light and fluffy here, folks. Tear down the walls that have kept you "safe," and you'll experience the magic that comes from genuine emotional risk.

Simultaneously, you could come face to face with a few of your control issues. If you've been expecting relationships to operate according to a script (one that you write, produce and direct), you've got another thing coming, Leo. The Pisces total lunar eclipse on September 7 could bring tensions to a head, forcing you to look some of your demons in the eye.

Please don't slip into denial! Owning your $#!% is the way to transform it. Adding to this push for partnership is shadow-worker Pluto, who is now on a solid nineteen-year tour through Aquarius and your committed relationship zone. Dig deep and transform the dynamics of your closest relationships in the name of soul evolution. Partnered Leos: Get ready to face power struggles head-on. If your relationship is worth its salt, you'll weather these storms together and grow more united in the process. Note that you might need some outside support, like a couples' therapist, for the heavier emotional lifts. Jealousy, possessiveness, secrecy, taboos: Pluto brings it all up for examination.

Venus, the planet of love, will also be on a journey of its own, spinning into a spring retrograde from March 1 to April 12. The backspin begins in Aries and your ninth house of independence and truth, then carries on in Pisces and your intimate, erotic eighth house from March 27 to April 12.

How much "me time" do you need in relationships and what seductive forces draw you into the depths? You may find yourself asking what adventure means in a relationship or even contemplating love's higher purpose. A person from a different cultural or spiritual background could come into your life, opening your heart and mind in surprising ways.

Between the thrill-seeking energy of Aries and the dreamy idealism of Pisces, you may find yourself revisiting an old flame or even rekindling a long-lost romance that once felt unfinished. Warning: The perils of denial and illusion (with a dose of destructiveness) could hit hard during this retrograde. Don't go sabotaging your hard-won progress—or a solid relationship that's hit a little plateau—just because you're craving "excitement."

Lusty, passionate Mars rolls into Leo on April 18, amping up your sex appeal with its raw intensity through June 17. Pursue what you want unapologetically, since you'll have the courage to express your desires boldly and passionately. Caveat: With Mars' aggressive influence, you'll need to keep that legendary Leo pride in check to avoid coming off as too overbearing.

The summer ends on a sweepingly romantic note as Venus struts through Leo from August 25 to September 19. Expect to feel playful, flirtatious and eager to indulge in all the luxuries that love has to offer. You'll be in the mood for romantic extravagance—think grand dates, meaningful gifts and being adored and admired. And after weathering Mercury retrograde in your sign from July 18 to August 11, Venus' arrival could not come a moment too soon. Single Lions will burn up the dating apps Attached? Bring more warmth and passion into an existing relationship.

December brings another high-key surge as Venus and Mars team up for half the month in Sagittarius and your fifth house of fairy-tale romance. No mistletoe required to convince a Leo to pucker up. Try to slip off for a pre-holiday baecation. Single Lions could meet someone while out and about, and with Sagittarius' worldly influence, they could come in a very different package than your own.

LEO: LUCKIEST *love* DAY

AUGUST 30

As the pulse-quickening vibes of Venus in Leo rev up your love life, passion is oozing out of your pores. On August 30, the quarter moon in Sagittarius shines its balancing beams into your fifth house of romance, helping you think through your romantic trajectory with both an open heart and a level head. Amorous adventures await your careful and thoughtful planning!

Money & Career

LEO 2025 FORECAST

Abundance attunement time! How you manage your money matters mightily in 2025. Starting January 11, the destiny-driven North Node shifts into Pisces, activating your eighth house of shared resources, investments and transformation. Across the galactic game board, the karmic South Node moves into Virgo and your second house of earned income and personal finances. This nodal cycle, which last happened from 2006-07, is like an abundance attunement.

A job that once seemed like a "safe bet" is now draining you, or perhaps you've outgrown the habits that have kept you stuck in a financial rut. This nodal cycle, which lasts until July 26, 2026, inspires you to explore new and possibly unconventional ways to generate wealth. This could mean building an investment portfolio, partnering on a business venture or refreshing your skill set so that you can command higher pay. The Pisces and Virgo eclipses in 2025—on March 14, September 7 and September 21—will add fuel to this transformative fire.

Fiery Mars starts the year retrograde, cooling its jets in Leo until January 6, then slipping back into Cancer and your transitional twelfth house for the remainder of the backspin, until February 23. If you have a personal venture cooking, you might shift it to the backburner until spring. By the time the passionate planet returns to Leo on April 18, you'll be ready to hit the accelerator. Step into a leadership role, pitch your start-up to funders or start Leo LLC. With Mars powering you up until June 17, you'll feel unstoppable. Caveat: Mars can make you a bit impatient or even combative if things don't go your way. Channel that fiery energy into your ambitions and you'll be able to move mountains.

And then there's unpredictable Uranus, stirring the pot in Taurus and your tenth house of career until July 7 before making a monumental move into Gemini until November 7. Disruptive Uranus has been posted up in your professional zone since 2018, keeping you on your toes. If you've felt like your job has been in constant flux, or if you've switched directions entirely, thank (or blame) this freedom-loving planet.

The good news? The end of this seven-year cycle is in sight, and 2025 brings the final bursts of chaotic—but ultimately liberating—energy. Expect a few surprises in the first half of the year: sudden promotions, changes in leadership or an out-of-the-blue opportunity to pivot in an exciting way. On November 7, Uranus spins back into Taurus for the final leg of its journey before moving on to Gemini for a solid seven years on April 25, 2026. Phew!

If you need to refresh your front-facing profile, you'll have plenty of creative inspiration once Venus—the planet of attraction and abundance—moves into Leo from August 25 to September 19. Network, network, network! You'll charm effortlessly and draw fascinating, well-connected people into your orbit. With this glamorous energy comes the temptation to indulge. Keep an eye on those big purchases or lavish outings that could eat into your hard-earned income.

How about ending 2025 with a plume of feathers in your crown? As of Christmas Eve, both Venus and Mars will be in Capricorn and your systematic sixth house of work and service. This all but ensures that your diligence of the year will be roundly recognized. Bring on the humble brags and make sure the VIPs know of your contributions to the success of the team. And yes, you CAN write it into those holiday cards.

LEO: LUCKIEST career DAY

JUNE 1

Knock it out of the park, Leo! The moon is in your sign June 1 and it teams up with go-getter Mars who's been pulsing through your sign since April 18. Abundance-attractor Venus (in Aries) trines the moon now, too, making you a total money magnet. Today could bring solo gains along with a team victory as Jupiter wraps up its yearlong cycle through Gemini. Focus on the best way forward, then hurry up and make your move.

2025
LEO

12
MONTH
OVERVIEW

January MONTHLY HOROSCOPE

Start the year strong, Leo! With the Sun in Capricorn until January 19, it's time to focus on your daily routines, health and overall wellness. Mars, which has been retrograde in your sign since December 6, slips back into Cancer on January 6, taking the heat off you. While this will free up some energy, make sure you also have time to pause and recharge in between lifting weights and attempting to prove that you're the real office MVP. On January 11, the lunar nodes shift into Pisces and Virgo, beginning an 18-month cycle that highlights shared resources, intimacy, and financial stability. You're ready to raise your fiscal IQ and set yourself up for long-term gains. Relationships become your primary focus once Aquarius season begins on the 19th. This monthlong cycle could bring some attractive "opposites" into your orbit, so stay open to people who can complement you with their own brand of shine. The Year of the Wood Snake kicks off on January 29, bringing transformative changes that will require your famous courage and leadership.

February MONTHLY HOROSCOPE

The allure of your purr is absolutely magnetic this month, as the Aquarius Sun sparkles in your relationship zone until the 18th. Focus on deepening those one-on-one connections, but hold onto your crown when the year's only full moon in Leo puts your name in lights on the 12th! On February 4, Jupiter wakes up from a four-month retrograde and powers forward in Gemini, activating your eleventh house of friendships and networking. With the planet of abundance enchanting this sphere until June 9, collaborative projects and group endeavors could catapult you to a new level of success. Romantic Venus starts a long tour through Aries and your ninth house of adventure and expansion also on February 4, pulling you toward exciting, far-flung experiences—some that might even have an educational or entrepreneurial component. Get those plans dialed in before Venus turns retrograde on March 1. Pisces season begins on the 18th, plunging you into the depths of your eighth house of intimacy and transformation. Connections get spicier and more enmeshed as you find people and projects worth investing in. Finally, Mars turns direct in Cancer on February 23, reigniting your twelfth house of healing and closure. Any emotional blocks that have been holding you back? Work on metabolizing the feelings so you can blast ahead when Mars returns to Leo on April 18.

March MONTHLY HOROSCOPE

Nothing superficial for you this month, thanks. As the Pisces Sun shimmers in your esoteric, erotic eighth house, part of you just wants to focus on the closest, most "meant to be" connections and nothing else. But good luck ignoring the rest of the world! All month long, your global ninth house is getting activated by a spate of activity in Aries. Convivial Venus retrogrades through Aries from March 1 to 27, bringing some serious moments of truth about your love life. As Mercury retrogrades in Aries from March 15 to 29, you may find yourself rethinking travel plans, educational pursuits or spiritual practices. Slow down and reassess before making any big moves, especially after Venus and Mercury retrograde back into Pisces and your internal eighth house on the 27th and 29th, respectively. On March 14, a Virgo full moon and lunar eclipse rocks your second house of money and values. If you've been unclear about your resources or priorities, this eclipse will help you course-correct and put things in order. Nonetheless, you'll feel the fire of inspiration returning when the Sun bursts into Aries on the 20th. The March 29 Aries new moon and solar eclipse closes a two-year chapter of eclipses that reconfigured your entire outlook on life. A major opportunity for travel, education or personal growth could arrive, marking the start of an exciting new journey. But there's more! On March 30, Neptune enters Aries for the first time since 1875, kicking off a 14-year cycle of spiritual expansion and visionary thinking. Stay open to profound insights and life-altering discoveries—your world is about to get a whole lot bigger in 2025!

April MONTHLY HOROSCOPE

It's go time, Leo! Well, for the most part. The Aries Sun is blazing through your adventurous ninth house until April 19, making this the perfect month to broaden your horizons—whether it's jetting off to a dream location, diving into personal growth studies or working under a master coach. Before you go full throttle, know this: Mercury is retrograde in Pisces and your intense eighth house until April 7, with Venus retrograde there until April 12. Relationship and financial friction could follow you on your journeys, which is not the kind of baggage you need to check. Try to get it sorted in the first half of the month. Once Mercury goes direct on the 7th and Venus follows on the 12th, you'll be able to roam the world with a clear conscience. Major momentum pours in starting this April 18 when red-hot Mars rolls into your sign and supercharges your confidence. With Mars in your first house until June 17, you're unstoppable—time to take courageous action on your goals and, once again, show the world why you are so legendary.

Taurus season kicks off on April 19, as the life-giving Sun streams into your tenth house of career. Get serious about your ambitions and make those power moves. All eyes are on you, so claim your throne, Leo!

May MONTHLY HOROSCOPE

May is a power month as the Taurus Sun illuminates your ambitious tenth house until May 20. Remain laser-focused on career moves as you solidify your long-term goals. Relationships could hit a reckoning moment as power-tripping Pluto turns retrograde in Aquarius on May 4. You may need to push back on a domineering person in your life or rebalance the way you share resources (emotional, physical and financial) in key partnerships between now and October 13. Some Leos may have second thoughts about a close connection, which should not be ignored. By the same token, don't rush into reactivity. Pluto wants you to plumb the depths. Along with legitimate complaints, you could be projecting childhood wounds and forgotten traumas on people. Lift your nose from the grindstone this May 20, when the Sun shifts into garrulous Gemini and your eleventh house of teamwork and technology. Collaborate, network and rally the troops—both online and IRL. Just four days later, disciplined Saturn returns to Aries for the first time since 1996-1998, firing up your ninth house of expansion, travel and big-picture dreams. Saturn's steady energy is here to help you lay the groundwork for a bold new vision, which may involve traveling, studying or making media over the next three years.

June MONTHLY HOROSCOPE

Get out and mingle like it was your second job! With the Sun blazing in Gemini and your eleventh house until the 20th, warm leads could turn into red-hot collabs after a single conversation. Tired of struggling as a solo act? Scout out people who can fill in the blanks for you. This is your month to form and succeed as a supergroup, if you're willing to pass a few batons. June's biggest news comes on the 9th, as magnanimous Jupiter slips into Cancer and your twelfth house of spirituality, transitions and healing until June 30, 2026. Like a celestial sabbatical, this yearlong cycle helps you slow down and enjoy life behind the curtain and away from the pressures of the mainstage. What does that look like for you, Leo? Maybe it's a gap year, a mindfulness practice, a plant-medicine retreat or weekly sessions with a somatic therapist. When the Sun joins Jupiter in Cancer at the solstice on the 20th, you may feel ready to release something that you've honestly outgrown. Letting go can be such a relief! Mid-month could bring a reality check as Jupiter squares Saturn on June 15 and Neptune on June 18, stirring up tensions between your adventurous spirit and a deeper need for rest. Don't rush a plan, Leo—this month is about pacing yourself, even if that means rescheduling travel. Motivator Mars leaves your sign on the 17th, bringing more restful energy. As it revs its engines in Virgo until August 6, the excitement comes from getting your budget, self-care and daily routines into a manageable groove. As the Sun and Jupiter align for The Day of Miracles this June 24, you could tap into a teaching (or a Yoda-like teacher!) that guides you to a deeper dimension of spiritual and emotional discovery.

July MONTHLY HOROSCOPE

Countdown to birthday season! Rest, recharge and tie up loose ends while the Sun lingers in Cancer until your solar return on July 22nd. But don't fall out of touch with your network. On July 7, communal Uranus makes a monumental move into Gemini. This sneak peek of a longer cycle (that begins April 25, 2026) will already electrify your team-spirited, collaborative eleventh house until this November 7. Fresh connections, innovative collaborations and unprecedented social shifts are on the horizon. But take note: Messenger Mercury spins retrograde in Leo (womp womp) from July 18 to August 11, which could scramble communications and throw some curveballs into your personal plans. When the Sun returns to Leo on July 22, it's time to celebrate your royal fierceness! Although Mercury retrograde may slow down your big birthday plans until August 11, you can always go with a nostalgic theme. (Y2K soiree, let's go!) Throughout the month, Neptune, Saturn and Chiron all slip into their annual, five-month retrogrades (on the 4th, 13th and 30th, respectively). The backspins begin in Aries and your ninth house of travel, media and higher learning. Seek out your personal Yodas and bring on the teachable moments. Circle July 24 for intention-setting when the year's only new moon in Leo creates a potent launch pad for your visionary ideas!

August MONTHLY HOROSCOPE

With the radiant Sun blazing through your sign until August 22, your cosmic call to action is clear: Embody your most vibrant, creative self. Reach back into your archives for inspiration while messenger Mercury spins back through Leo until August 11. Use the first part of the month to polish plans behind the scenes, then, unveil them to the world once Mercury corrects course on the 11th. Feelings may be tender while affectionate Venus nestles in Cancer until August 25. Tighten up the radius of your social circle so you can nourish your closest connections. Single Leos, stay open to the "mom-approved" types. Attached Lions could benefit from more private time together. Feather your love nest or get conversations going about cohabitation, meeting each other's families and all those cozy things. The mic drops roll in once assertive Mars strides into harmonious Libra on the 6th, activating your communication sector until September 22. Plug in the mic and get started on a podcast or EP. Let your copious thoughts flow into a novel, screenplay or Substack. Short-term projects can bring long-gain wins and you might even pair up with a BFF, sibling or neighbor to accomplish these. As the Sun shifts into practical Virgo on August 22, the focus turns to finances, stability and getting your house in order. The first of two back-to-back Virgo new moons arrives on August 23 and could bring a wave of money motivation—one that will accelerate with the September 21 solar (new moon) eclipse. It won't be hard to visualize what you want—in romance, finance or any area of life—when glamorous Venus parades through Leo from August 25 to September 19. Talk about ending the summer on a sweet (and sultry!) note.

September MONTHLY HOROSCOPE ♌

Where is the sweet spot between practical magic and passionate momentum? The Sun hangs out in Virgo until September 22, turning your focus to mundane matters like budgets, schedules and household projects. Meanwhile glamorous Venus is strutting through Leo until the 19th, keeping you out circulating with the cultural cognoscenti. (Send a pic!) This is peak season for romance, so hang on to those summer lovin' vibes until the season's bitter end. You won't wriggle out of any "emotional work" that needs to be done, alas. On September 1, Saturn retrogrades back into Pisces and your deep-feeling eighth house for the remainder of its backspin, until November 27. Don't be surprised if old issues bubble up around jealousy or how to fairly distribute shared resources. With a total lunar eclipse in Pisces on September 7, these situations could reach a boiling point. No more sweeping things under the rug! Uranus does its own retrograde shuffle in Gemini on September 6, throwing a little unpredictability into your social life and group dynamics between now and November 7. There could be some casting changes on Team Leo before the fall is through. Make sure you align with people who share your values because on the 21st, the second in a rare pair of back-to-back Virgo new moons arrives, underscoring the importance of sticking to what you consider ethical. Since it's also a game-changing solar eclipse, news about a money-making opportunity could arrive. If you've been saving up for a necessary item, you could radar in on something that's as aesthetically pleasing as it is practical. Home is where the heat is when fiery Mars dives into intense Scorpio on September 22. Family dynamics or deep-rooted emotions might rise to the surface between now and November 4, making this a powerful moment to address any lingering feelings and strengthen those foundations.

October MONTHLY HOROSCOPE

Every Lion needs a pride, and while the Sun nestles in Libra until September 22, set up routines that keep your connections thriving. Whether that means catching up with old friends or exploring your creative side, "contagious warmth" is the goal. If someone needs guidance on how to bask in your sunny energy, take the lead, but with patience. Thanks to the Libra Sun, you'll shine at handling any "teachable moments" that arise, both in friendships and in romantic connections. Sparks keep flying in your social circle while Venus struts through Virgo and your luxurious second house until the 13th. Get your beauty sleep during the workweek and spend weekends indulging in self-care, shopping or treating yourself to life's finer pleasures. Once Venus sashays into Libra on the 13th, your idea of a dream date could include a sunset picnic or visiting an art gallery. Career goals get back on track once Pluto turns direct in Aquarius, also on the 13th. Realign with a collaborative project or refine your approach to teamwork. Budding attractions could blossom into more committed partnerships once Scorpio season begins on the 22nd. Pro tip: Seek someone who complements your grandeur, not just another shining star. Existing relationships also get a boost from this four-week solar cycle. Make room in your schedule for nurturing those closest to you. Neptune retrogrades back from Aries into Pisces that same day. Dive into an introspective activity or explore a creative endeavor that brings you deeper emotional fulfillment.

November MONTHLY HOROSCOPE

Feather your nest and foster meaningful connections this month while the Scorpio Sun gets cozy in your fourth house of home, family and foundations. And once Venus sashays into sultry Scorpio from November 6 to 30, the Leo lair could turn into dinner party central, a love den or both! It won't take much convincing to get people to gather around your hearth. Just know that they might be too comfortable to leave. This COULD potentially become a problem since your festive side kicks up on the 4th. That day, energetic Mars lunges into Sagittarius, firing up your fifth house of romance, creativity and fun until December 15. Half of you is the opposite of a homebody, ready to turn up the heat with your compelling charisma, theatrical flair and gram worthy OOTDs. The one hiccup of November? Mercury takes its final retrograde spin from November 9 to 29. The "fun" starts in Sagittarius, creating mixed signals in your romantic life and warning you to keep your ego in check. On the 18th, Mercury slips back into Scorpio, which could cause some pre-holiday upsets with triggering family members (deescalate or avoid them as much as you can). Unpredictable Uranus retrogrades back into Taurus from November 7 until February 3, 2026, wrapping up a shake-up in your tenth house of career. There's still time to stabilize any chaotic career issues before the cycle ends in April 2026, so reflect on your goals and figure out what's missing from the equation. Expansive Jupiter also turns retrograde in Cancer on November 11, giving you four months of inward exploration and healing that may require more solitude and time. Saturn ENDS its retrograde on November 27, course-correcting in your seductive, alchemical eighth house. Just in time for the mistletoe to hang, you're ready to create lasting structures for love in your life.

December MONTHLY HOROSCOPE

Close the year on a high note! The Sagittarius Sun is beaming its vibrant rays into your fifth house of romance, creativity, and self-expression until the 21st. With motivator Mars also in Sagittarius until the 15th, joined by Venus until the 24th, you're practically oozing charm and passion. Dance and romance your way through the holiday circuit, Leo. You're shining brighter than the tree at Rockefeller Center. This planetary power trio also makes you a magnetic leader—one who inspires joy and creativity in others. When Neptune ends its five-month retrograde in Pisces on December 10, the energy in your eighth house of intimacy and joint resources gets an extra boost, helping you solidify deeper bonds and even get your EOY financial plans back on track. Think about who really has your back and who you want to take along for the ride in 2026. Those deserving souls are the ones to focus on as fervent Mars heads into Capricorn on December 15, energizing your sixth house of work and wellness. When the Sun joins Capricorn on December 21, followed by Venus on the 24th, it's all about building solid routines and finding the right people to form a support circle with. Healthy living resolutions are blessed under this cosmic trifecta, so even while you're munching and sipping on gingerbread everything, keep your body moving and think about how you'll start 2026 with a plan that says, "Healthy, wealthy and wise." This NYE might find you in service-oriented spirits. Perhaps you do a shift at a shelter before heading out with friends. A candlelight yoga class or spiritual circle could also feel meaningful as you wave 2025 goodbye.

*Read your extended monthly forecast for
life, love, money and career! astrostyle.com*

A LITTLE ABOUT *Virgo*

DATES August 22 - September 22

SYMBOL The Virgin

ELEMENT Earth

QUALITY Mutable

RULING PLANET Mercury

BODY PART Stomach, waist

BEST TRAITS
Dedicated, resourceful, helpful, hardworking, witty, practical, analytical, disciplined, inspiring

KEYWORDS
Health, sustainability, systems, efficiency, innocence, cleanliness, nature, wisdom, perfectionism

Read more about Virgo

VIRGO
IN 2025

ALL THE PLANETS IN VIRGO IN 2025	YOUR 2025 HOROSCOPE	TOP 5 THEMES FOR VIRGO IN 2025	LOVE HOROSCOPE + LUCKY DATES	MONEY HOROSCOPE + LUCKY DATES

Virgo in 2025
YOUR YEARLY OVERVIEW

Swing for the fences, Virgo! In 2025, no-limits Jupiter and innovative Uranus each do a six-month tour through Gemini, firing up your ambitious tenth house and putting your career in the spotlight. This is your moment to step up, set big goals and make strategic moves. Choose your partners and projects wisely. This year, the right collaborations could catapult you to new heights. As the North Node moves into Pisces and your partnership zone on January 11th, you'll be drawn toward soul-quenching connections in every area of life, from business to romance to joint creative ventures. Just don't lose yourself in the mix during this 18-month cycle, which lasts until July 26, 2026. The karmic South Node will simultaneously trail through Virgo and your sovereign first house, bringing a strong reminder to maintain ample independence and keep a solid commitment to your self-care. Networking is your superpower once Jupiter shifts into Cancer on June 9. This year-long cycle urges you to find your people—the ones who inspire, support and elevate you. Meanwhile, structured Saturn and dreamy Neptune spend time in Aries and your eighth house of shared resources and transformation. What—and who!— you invest in could bring rewards for years to come. Choose wisely!

THE PLANETS IN *Virgo*

THE SUN
AUG 22–SEP 22

It's birthday season for you, so step out and shine! Seek novelty and take extra initiative during this radiant monthlong phase.

NEW MOON #1
AUG 23
2:07AM, 0°23'

Bonus New Year! Set your intentions for the next six months and get into action. Set 30-day goals, too, because 2025 brings a second new moon in Virgo on September 21.

NEW MOON #2
PARTIAL SOLAR ECLIPSE
SEP 21
3:54PM, 29°05'

Sweet sequel! You have two new moons in your sign this year, giving you a second chance to plant seeds and prioritize your passions. Since this new moon is also a solar eclipse, be intentional to avoid wasting time.

FULL MOON
TOTAL LUNAR ECLIPSE
MAR 14
2:55AM, 23°57'

Ready, set, manifest! Your work of the past six months bears fruit and it's time to harvest the rewards. Since this supercharged full moon is also a total lunar eclipse, don't be afraid to look in the shadows or explore hidden possibilities. Your efforts could bring a surprise bounty, but be discerning about what you share and with whom.

MERCURY
SEP 2–18

Crown yourself monarch of the social butterflies when popularity-boosting Mercury visits your sign once a year. Circulate and get social—but don't make promises you can't keep!

VENUS
SEP 19–OCT 13

You've got the romantic It Factor when the galactic glamazon charges up your powers of seduction each year. Willpower is weak in the face of beauty and luxury. Watch your spending!

MARS
JUN 17–AUG 6

Motivation is high when energetic Mars visits your sign every couple years—but check your combative streak and try not to come on too strong.

SOUTH NODE
JAN 11, 2025–
JUL 26, 2026

Life feels both surreal and karmic when the lunar South Node backs up through your sign (for 18 months) every 18.5 years. Surrender to the vision quest and prepare to let go of unworkable habits. This will all make sense when the cycle ends.

Virgo in 2025
HIGHLIGHTS

KARMIC LESSONS: THE SOUTH NODE IN VIRGO

Your phoenix rising moment is here, Virgo! On January 11, the lunar South Node circles back into Virgo for eighteen months, its first return to your sign since 2006-07. While this karmic cycle wages on until July 26, 2026, you shed old patterns and embrace a new chapter of personal growth. Where have you veered away from your core values or gripped so tightly to control that you've become stuck in a rut? The invitation of the South Node is to gain a profound awareness of your automatic functions so that you can give yourself a choice to either continue them or start reprogramming yourself to make different decisions—ones that serve your higher purpose and evolution. With two Virgo eclipses on March 14 (lunar, full moon) and September 21 (solar, new moon), plus a bonus new moon in Virgo on August 23, you have even more momentum to release unworkable patterns and reinvent parts of your life. This shadow work isn't technically "easy," but it's integral for your growth. Push through with self-love and lots of support and you will end the year feeling aligned with your truest, most spiritual self.

NEW LOVE LANGUAGES: THE NORTH NODE'S MOVE INTO PISCES

As the destiny-driven North Node moves through Pisces, opposite your sign, from January 11, 2025 to July 26, 2026, relationships become your classroom. Surprise! You may need to try out a new love language—ideally one besides "Acts of Service." The total lunar eclipse in Pisces this September 7 can bring soulful recalibrations in love and partnerships. While your anxious tendencies are part of being a Virgo, see if you can talk through these fears in order to allow room for the magic of soulmates and connections that transcend the material plane. For some Virgos, this could be the year you get engaged, married or coupled/uncoupled in a way that feels in alignment with your most authentic self. Trust the process, even if it feels like a roller coaster—it's leading you to a higher love.

VENUS RETROGRADE: REFLECT AND REALIGN IN LOVE

Venus will be in retrograde from March 1 to April 12, casting a reflective glow over your relationships. Pause and reassess how you're giving and receiving love. As Venus sweeps back through Aries and your intimate eighth house until March 27, secrets may come to light. If you can deal with them transparently, there's a chance a bond could deepen. In some cases, this could create an unworkable breach of trust. Whatever the case, remember to be loyal to yourself first, Virgo. As Venus slips back into Pisces on March 27, it plunges into the seas of your seventh house of committed relationships, helping you rebalance dynamics that have grown lopsided. Beware the temptation of an old flame, who may pull you back into a potentially toxic tie. Even if it was just "bad timing" that broke you up, don't rush to reconcile. This is a time for recalibration, not impulsive decisions. By the end of the retrograde, you'll have a clearer understanding of what your heart truly desires.

JUPITER AND URANUS SUPERCHARGE YOUR CAREER

Abundant Jupiter spends the first half of 2025 in Gemini, charging up your ambitious career house until June 9. This cycle, which began on May 25, 2024, can feel like an express-elevator ride to the top. Don't lose your nerve, Virgo, you are there for a reason! Do make sure that you cast a wide net. Global Jupiter could bring opportunities from every corner of the globe by June, along with opportunities to travel for work. Expect the unexpected between July 7 and November 7, as Uranus moves into Gemini for the first time since 1949 and electrifies your career path with bold, innovative energy. Like a lightning bolt of inspiration, this transit shakes loose stagnant routines and sparks fresh, unconventional ideas. This six-month sneak preview will pick up again in April 2026, when Uranus heads back into Gemini for another seven years. Over the course of this full cycle, you could pivot in a new direction or reinvent your professional life in exciting and futuristic ways. Don't be surprised if you find yourself drawn toward cutting-edge industries or pioneering a path that feels completely outside the box. The key is to remain flexible — allow Uranus to guide you toward opportunities you never saw coming. Meanwhile, Pluto's deep dive into Aquarius and your work and wellness zone (which lasts until 2044) reminds you to stay balanced. Success is sweeter when you're thriving on all levels. Set up systems to support both wealth AND health.

THE SHIFT: FROM SOLO SUCCESS TO COLLECTIVE MAGIC

As magnanimous Jupiter moves into Cancer on June 9, some of your focus shifts from personal achievement to the power of collaboration. Start passing out some of those feathers that you've collected in your cap. This transition into your eleventh house of teamwork and community encourages you to step away from your natural inclination to take on the burden of responsibility alone. During this yearlong cycle, which lasts until June 30, 2026, you'll discover what can be manifested through shared visions and collective magic. Surround yourself with kindred spirits who inspire and uplift you—whether it's for a major group project or a social cause close to your heart. With empathic, family-oriented Cancer energy directing you, get ready to weave a powerful support network around your grandest dreams. Together, you can achieve more than you ever could on your own.

SATURN AND NEPTUNE: FORTIFYING DEEP, LASTING BONDS

Love, intimacy and shared resources take on a profound new meaning this year, and here's yet another reason why! Stable Saturn and dreamy Neptune both dart forward from Pisces into Aries, spending part of 2025 in your eighth house of emotional depth and transformation. Neptune's ethereal influence from March 30 to October 22 adds a touch of magic and mystery to your relationships, allowing you to connect on a deeper, spiritual level. It's officially soul bonding time. Whether in love or in business partnerships, you'll be drawn to relationships that have a fateful quality. Saturn, the cosmic architect, steps in from May 24 to September 1, ensuring that these connections are built on a solid foundation. Whether you're merging finances with a partner, investing in joint ventures or deepening emotional ties, this planetary duo urges you to be both vulnerable and practical. Lay the groundwork in 2025.

Once these cycles pick up again in early 2026—Saturn for two more years and Neptune for another thirteen—you'll be ready to co-create something real, enduring and transformative.

TOP 5 THEMES FOR
Virgo in 2025

1	2	3	4	5
TURBO CHARGE YOUR CAREER GOALS	BECOME A VIRAL SENSATION	MAGNETIZE THE POWER PLAYERS	BARE YOUR SOUL SELECTIVELY	SHED AN OLD IDENTITY

1 TURBO CHARGE YOUR CAREER GOALS

JUPITER AND URANUS IN GEMINI

JUPITER: MAY 25, 2024 – JUNE 9, 2025
URANUS: JULY 7 – NOVEMBER 7, 2025 • JANUARY 26, 2026 – MAY 22, 2033

Are you ready for the big leagues, Virgo? Batting practice is over, and it's time to take your rightful place in the starting lineup! Goals get turbo-charged with rocket fuel, thanks to supersizer Jupiter and inventive Uranus, who are both taking laps through your tenth house of prestige, status and success.

JUPITER IN GEMINI

MAY 25, 2024 – JUNE 9, 2025

The sweet smell of success is your signature scent in 2025! Thank lucky Jupiter, who's been cruising through Gemini and your professional tenth house since May 25, 2024. This reputation-boosting cycle only comes around every twelve years and when it does, you're unstoppable! Set aside your modesty, Virgo. While the planetary titan is in Gemini until June 9, it can thrust your work into the public eye and turn you into an industry heavy-hitter; a household name.

Nevertheless, you do need to meet the universe partway, moving the needle and signaling your desire for its bounty. What's a Virgo to do? Network, leverage, call in the favors from the VIPs and "media friendlies." Jupiter stampedes through your tenth house until June 9, giving you almost half a year to tap its career-catapulting magic.

Because Gemini is the sign of the twins, strategic partnerships will be an essential ingredient of your ascent. Who would you like to call in as your plus-one on a project? Have you been thinking "official joint venture" about someone whose offerings are the perfect complement to your own? Although Jupiter begins the year retrograde, once it pivots forward on February 4, you could be ready to bring in the lawyers to officialize a deal.

Since Jupiter is the digital nomad of the zodiac, your kindred-spirit collaborators—and customers—may be living in all corners of the world. Whether you're literally flying international or meeting on Zoom, you're sure to find opportunities far beyond your current sphere. Widen your search radius between now and June 9; get out of that WFH office as much as possible.

You'll synergistically feed off the energy of other movers and shakers. Make a point of attending industry conferences, elite gatherings and even joining a social club where the VIPs sip cocktails with clients and drop in for a day of coworking. Entrepreneurial Virgos may finally become their own bosses this year. There's no doubt about it, your leadership skills are ready to be flexed. Your keen, strategic mind will make it easy for others to root for and rally around you. Which begs the question, Virgo: What would you like to be the CEO of in 2025? Aim high!

URANUS IN GEMINI
JULY 7 – NOVEMBER 7, 2025
JANUARY 26, 2026 – MAY 22, 2033

How lit up do you feel about your current path? If the answer isn't, "Like the stadium at a Taylor Swift concert" (or anything to that degree), we suggest you start putting out some feelers. Beginning July 7, electrifying Uranus heads into Gemini, where it will send a supersonic surge through your goal-getting tenth house.

You've already been riding an enterprising wave in 2025, thanks to Jupiter spending the first half of the year in Gemini. But since Jupiter shifted into Cancer on June 9, you may have felt less ambitious. Welp, Virgo, hope you enjoyed that sabbatical, because from July 7 to November 7, you'll have innovative Uranus charging up Gemini and your tenth house. Considering the fact that the side-spinning planet hasn't traveled through this sign in, oh, eighty years, it's truly a huge deal. This four-month cycle is a preview of a seven-year Uranus-in-Gemini cycle that will pick up again on April 25, 2026 and last until May 22, 2033.

While the tenth house indicates success in the traditional sense, neither Gemini nor Uranus play by conventional rules. No, Virgo, you probably won't be fading into the grey industrial fabric lining the rows of corporate cubicles. The next eight years could see you disrupting entire industries, reinventing wheels so hard that it makes the whole idea of a wheel seem irrelevant.

Surprise twist: People who might normally be too strait-laced to get behind your vision could become your biggest champions. Don't be afraid to punch above your weight, professionally speaking. Popularity-boosting Uranus can bring friends from "on high" who want to finance your genius.

If you truly love what you spend most of your time doing, see how you can take it to the next level. Lean into Uranus' geekery with AI, apps, gadgets and other scientific developments. If you know in your gut that change is coming, pave the way now. Get advanced training, become a savvier networker, research companies and their mission statements. Take small practical steps on a regular basis, and seamlessly—and painlessly—you can redirect your entire career trajectory! And if you're still lacking for inspiration, don't worry. This year is just a warmup for the seven-year cycle that begins again in spring 2026.

2 BECOME A VIRAL SENSATION

JUPITER IN CANCER
JUNE 9, 2025 – JUNE 30, 2026

Beginning June 9, you can stop hustling and start rustling up contenders to be part of the Virgo supersquad. For the first time since July 2014, larger-than-life Jupiter beams its lucky charms into Cancer and your collaborative eleventh house. Get ready for thirteen months of teamwork that is certain to make your most grandiose dreams soar.

While it's never easy for a Virgo to cede control, it's time to loosen your grip on the reins. You could hit a plateau if you keep trying to be the CEO of Everything. Start inviting creative input and radaring in on people who share your impeccable work ethic. You may have Mensa-level skills at managing moving parts, but what are you trying to prove? No one's handing out awards for playing martyr. How about medaling in the Efficiency Expert category instead?

Stop, drop and take a look at your systems. There's one overriding question to ask yourself: "Is there an app for that?" And if not, how about an AI assistant? While freedom-loving Jupiter flows through your eleventh house, AKA, the tech sector, it's time to liberate yourself from mundane tasks that are draining precious hours from your ability to focus on high-impact efforts. Fight the voice in your head that tells you no one can do it like you or that it's too hard to explain your process. A little orientation period will go a long way.

If your online presence could use a refresh, you're in luck! Jupiter is the publishing planet. Its presence in Cancer supports you with building a close-knit community of followers via social media. (Picture Virgo Beyoncé's BeyHive as you create...) Rather than spreading yourself too thin (a risk with "more is more" Jupiter), pick one or two platforms where you'll make your impact. Trying to strategize a rollout on YouTube, TikTok and Instagram all at once is just...a lot.

Did you build or produce something meaningful while Jupiter in Gemini charged up your career zone from May 25, 2024 to June 9, 2025? Bring it to market now or start test-piloting it with friends and family. Need capital for your venture? Don't rule out crowdfunding or putting together your own group of angel investors who want to get in on the ground floor of your genius.

On a personal level, Jupiter's exit from your prestigious tenth house signals the return of something you hold dear: Your social life! Obsessively focused as you can be on a goal, you're also ruled by buzzy, loquacious Mercury. Without your RDA of interactivity, you can get kinda anxious. "Tending and befriending" is a proven stress-soother, thanks to the flow of the calming hormone oxytocin that is released when humans commune and care for each other.

Yes, that means you have scientific proof that "having fun for fun's sake" has known health benefits. So, Virgo, begin to implement this practice at once. (And make sure it's guilt-free!) If you feel like flexing your planning powers, organize besties for a food tour of southern Italy or a long weekend at a boutique resort and spa.

Stay open to being a "joiner" as well. Jupiter's happy dance through Cancer can bring you in touch with a chosen family of friends who share your common interests. You could meet them at a weekly dance class, wine club or mom-and-me group. Just get out and mingle. You'll know pretty quickly if there's a vibe there or not. (And if there isn't, move along!)

Jupiter is the cosmic entrepreneur. In the humanitarian eleventh house, the generous planet inspires you to add a social impact element to your work. Whether you're applying for a grant or doing a weekly shift at a community organization, you'll be a powerful mouthpiece for the cause. And you'll be absolutely magnetic as a recruiter of volunteers or raiser of funds.

This could also be your cue to build an app of your own or find a way to get paid for your skillful wordsmithing. A book deal, influencer deal or ad sponsorship could pad your pockets in the second half of 2025. Get to work on those proposals!

3 MAGNETIZE POWER PLAYERS

SATURN AND NEPTUNE IN ARIES

NEPTUNE: MARCH 30 – OCTOBER 22, 2025 • JANUARY 26, 2026 – MARCH 23, 2039
SATURN: MAY 24 – SEPTEMBER 1, 2025 • FEBRUARY 13, 2026 – APRIL 12, 2028

Lust, trust and a not-so-demure dose of passion await you in 2025 as two prominent outer planets make landfall in Aries and your seductive eighth house. First up is fantasy-agent Neptune, who briefly lunges out of Pisces for the first time since 2011. Spring fever could keep burning hot into summer and fall while Neptune is in Aries from March 30 to October 22—a preview of a longer, thirteen-year cycle that begins in January 2026.

Second to bat is no-nonsense Saturn, who will briefly visit Aries (May 24 to September 1) and lend some gravitas to all your intimate encounters. Next February 13, Saturn will head back into Aries for two more years, giving you a chance to play "mergers and acquisitions" in romance and finance. One thing's for certain: This oddball mashup of Neptune and Saturn can have a strong effect on your partnerships. As you magnetize people of influence, power couple fantasies come to life!

NEPTUNE IN ARIES

MARCH 30 – OCTOBER 22, 2025
JANUARY 26, 2026 – MARCH 23, 2039

Starting this March 30, you could plunge so far into your feelings that you make Jacques Cousteau look like a basic snorkeler. The reason for this deep dive? For the first time since 1875, fantasy-agent Neptune is sailing into Aries and your eighth house of intensity, seduction and permanent bonds.

In 2025, Neptune only hangs out in the Ram's realm until October 22, but take notes! On January 26, 2026, the numinous planet embarks on a thirteen-year mission through Aries, which won't end until March 23, 2039.

The past fourteen years with Neptune in Pisces have felt like a crucible, refining your understanding of relationships and your desired role within them. You've navigated intense emotional waters and have likely emerged with essential insights about your attachment style, patterns and core needs. As spiritual Neptune logs in to Aries, it's not just about teaming up with a complementary force. You want to blend lives, combine assets and lock into a permanent arrangement that you can devote your whole self to.

With your erotic eighth house under Neptune's spell, sex takes on a mystical, transcendent quality. This is a time when intimacy can feel almost otherworldly, as if you're connecting with your partner on a soul-deep level. Neptune invites you to explore the spiritual side of sex, merging not just bodies but also energies and emotions. However, this transit can also blur boundaries, leading to confusion or idealization in your sexual relationships. Sure, it would be great if every encounter felt like a divinely tantric cosmic union, but sometimes, a cozy quickie can get the job done.

As much as you SAY you want a fairy tale, reality check, Virgo: Are you actually ready to get THAT up close and personal? With Neptune in self-sovereign Aries, you could butt up against your own intimacy barriers. Rather than pushing yourself to overcome these blocks—or running as fast as you can in the opposite direction—surrender and let Neptune shine a light on the deeper aspects of your psyche.

With your sensitivity heightened, it's actually crucial to protect your energetic boundaries. The deep emotional and psychic work this cycle demands can leave you vulnerable to taking on others' energies. Incorporate practices like salt baths, using protective crystals, or cultivating a supportive network of friends who understand and respect your spiritual journey. These measures will help you retain a healthy level of autonomy.

Shared finances and investments fall under the eighth house domain. Under Neptune's watch, money matters take on a dreamy, almost surreal quality. This transit can blur the lines between what's yours, what's shared, and what you truly value. It's a time to be extra vigilant with joint finances, loans, and investments. There will be plenty of opportunities to merge resources with others, but don't enter these agreements lightly. To avoid confusion or deception, spell all agreements out to the letter, even with people in your personal life.

On a deeper level, this transit invites you to explore your relationship with money— are you using it to create the security you need, or is it slipping through your fingers in pursuit of an illusion? Investing can feel like navigating through a fog—exciting yet uncertain. Tune into your intuition, but guard against getting swept up in unrealistic dreams or schemes.

You might be drawn to more spiritual or altruistic investments, like supporting causes that align with your higher ideals. However, Neptune's influence can also obscure the true value of what you're putting your money into, so it's crucial to stay grounded and do your research. While the potential for gains exists, the real lesson here is about learning to discern fantasy from reality in your financial decisions.

While you may feel in over your head in moments, embrace this transformational phase, Virgo. It's a time to harness your inner strength and redefine your relationship with power and intimacy. Over the next decade-plus, you could cement some of the most mutually beneficial bonds of your lifetime, through marriage, business partnerships and other fruitful alliances.

SATURN IN ARIES
MAY 24 – SEPTEMBER 1, 2025
FEBRUARY 13, 2026 – APRIL 12, 2028

"Is it casual now?" is a question NO Virgo is likely to be asking between May 24 and September 1. As solemn Saturn returns to Aries for the first time in nearly three decades, your desire for deeper, more meaningful connections intensifies. Similarly to Neptune, Saturn is only visiting Aries for part of 2025. But on February 13, 2026, the hazy planet swings back into the sign of the Ram for two solid years, until April 12, 2028.

When it comes to love and sex, you'll find yourself either completely captivated or totally uninterested—there's no middle ground with Saturn's definitive energy. That goes triple when it's plodding ahead through Aries, a sign that knows exactly what it wants.

Don't fret over the potential for monotony or, heaven forbid, dullness. The eighth house isn't just about deep commitments; it's also the realm of seduction and eroticism. Don't look for instant fireworks OR fleeting encounters. Saturn in Aries is all about the slow burn. For some Virgos, a profound romantic connection—or perhaps a business partnership—could evolve from a longstanding, trust-filled friendship. And the best part? With Saturn here, you're in it for the long haul.

Dynamics in your existing relationships become clearer with help from no-nonsense Saturn. Over the course of the next few years, you will learn to balance power more effectively, even when finances or emotions occasionally tip the scales. That said, the eighth house isn't about dividing everything 50/50. In all manner of partnership, the key to success is playing to your individual strengths and talents. What matters most is that you are both putting in a solid effort, even if you're handling completely different aspects of the project. TBH, it's probably best that you and anyone you collab with have well-defined, individual lanes.

Speaking of finances, Saturn in your eighth house of shared resources is here to bolster your efforts in building sustainable wealth, particularly with a partner. You may lean towards fiscal conservatism, but don't shy away from calculated risks. This is an ideal period for laying down the foundations for long-term security, whether that's learning about retirement planning or dipping your toes into the world of crypto. With Saturn's guidance, you're building slowly but surely, aiming for a future where stability and satisfaction go hand in hand.

4 BARE YOUR SOUL SELECTIVELY

VENUS RETROGRADE IN ARIES AND PISCES
ARIES: MARCH 1 – 27
PISCES: MARCH 27 – APRIL 12

Spring arrives with a complex and spicy flavor this year. On March 1, amorous Venus turns retrograde, backing up through Aries and your erotic eighth house, then paddling back through Pisces and your relationship house from March 27 to April 12. Brace yourself: This six-week pivot might scramble signals in your love life or cause some friction in other types of partnerships.

When Venus flips in reverse every 18 months, we learn why people say that relationships take work. There could be bumps in the road, yes, even with people with whom you've had the smoothest of connections.

You're a savvy judge of character, Virgo, but between March 1 and April 12, you won't be able to rely on your intuitive senses to get a clear read of people. What they're signaling—with body language, unspoken cues or distance—may have nothing to do with your suspicions. You may worry that perhaps you've pushed them away or fear they are taking you for granted.

Make no assumptions, Virgo, yet don't ignore the changing dynamics. If something has shifted, you don't want to spend your waking hours ruminating about what might be. Instead, lean into your journalistic curiosity and ask open-ended questions. That's certain to go down smoother than any subtle hinting or attempts at mind-reading. Once Venus backs into compassionate Pisces (March 27 to April 12), pile on some extra empathy and do your very best to get into other people's worlds.

The good thing about Venus retrograde is that it can help you deepen intimacy. If you rushed into a relationship without reviewing practical considerations (like, say, incompatible life paths or totally different financial values) you may have to tap the brakes. Retrogrades stir up the past and things could heat up with an old flame again. But if you hear from a toxic ex, don't kid yourself about developing a "friendship." It might be best to block them as a preventative measure.

In the first part of the retrograde (March 1 to 27), guide your erotic life down a scintillating tantric trail. With the right partner, you'll see a string of green lights for any such activities, as long as you create enough space for the exploration. Design a few relaxation rituals before you try to get yourself in the mood. What helps you unwind and connect to your own inner peace? As the sign of service, your knee-jerk reaction is to give and give and give some more. If you bring that energy to the bedroom it can create a lopsided dynamic and leave you both feeling resentful and unsatisfied. No thanks!

What can draw you closer to the one you adore? Prying open your own chamber of secrets. Maybe you've been hiding something that's really important to you, but you're afraid to say it for fear of coming on too strong. Venus retrograde can pave the way for serious soul baring, which might be the best way forward. You don't want to sell a false bill of goods, right? Eventually, anyone you date or do business with will find out the truth. That's the beauty of relationships: being loved for ALL of who you are.

Perfectionism can be an Achilles heel for your sign, which, in turn, can block people from getting to know (and love) the true you. Venus retrograde invites you to wipe away some of the polish that's concealing your authentic self. Miracles transpire when you show a little (or a lot) more of your hand. Not just with any rando, of course. But if you've hit a plateau in the getting-to-know-you phase, it may be a symptom of both people being overly guarded. Sure it may feel initially terrifying to share a weak spot, but that's how you'll create a safe space that invites others to do the same.

On the flip side, it might be your "other half" who has the deep, dark secret to share. Without interrogating like an FBI agent, don your Nancy Drew cap and create a safe space for real talk. Ask questions in a relaxed tone, without expecting a "right answer." If you hear something jarring, you don't have to freak out; but definitely don't sweep it under the rug. Do the investigative work to figure out if you can establish enough trust to accompany the lust. By the time April 12 rolls around, make it your mission to dig deep enough to discover whether or not your styles truly mesh.

5 SHED AN OLD IDENTITY

LUNAR NODES IN VIRGO AND PISCES
NORTH NODE IN PISCES, SOUTH NODE IN VIRGO
JANUARY 11, 2025 – JULY 26, 2026

Karma is calling, Virgo, don't ignore those texts! On January 11, the lunar South Node settles into your sign, spinning you into a deep inquiry around identity, personal passions, and self-expression. This cycle hasn't come around for nearly two decades, so yes, it's a really big deal. The last time the South Node toured Virgo was from June 23, 2006 to December 18, 2007. Significant themes around individual growth, identity, and service may recur this year. You might even pick up where you left off or resume a path that you thought you'd finished for good. Surprise, surprise!

Even if you're too young to remember the last time the South Node paddled through your sign, this promises to be an interesting moment in your personal development! While the South Node occupies your sign from January 11, 2025 to July 26, 2026, it helps you "true up" with your innate skills, the ones you've had for as long as you can remember. (And probably before then, too!) Get ready to (re)discover your superpowers, Virgo. You may have packed them away, hiding these talents for fear of being ridiculed or misunderstood. Perhaps you even forgot that these parts of yourself existed!

As the South Node pings your sign this January 11, you might feel like Sleeping Beauty awakening to your own precision and practical magic. Like a calling that can't be ignored, you're invited to unveil the real you to the world—in a way that inspires others to live out loud.

Transparency? Authenticity? You're here for it! But don't expect this transit to be a walk in the park. As willing as you are to bare your soul, you hate the idea of not looking perfect when you do. This process could get a little messy, causing people to question you. Take heart, Virgo! With a little courage and conviction, you can help them understand the message behind your "madness."

So, Virgo, who do you think you are? That exploration could take you on a fascinating voyage between January 11, 2025 and July 26, 2026. You may feel a call to "rebrand" yourself—not as the person who has it all together, but rather, as someone relatable who can own their mistakes and is figuring it out along the way.

Have faith! While the karmic correction of a South Node transit can be unsettling, there's a reason its tests are pushing you past the edge of reason. Breaking up stagnant energy is the path to this next round of transformation. Even if you've done twenty plant medicine ceremonies, decades of therapy, and dismantled your ego structure, the "work" is never done.

If you've outgrown certain situations, there's no need to start pulling plugs. But gently begin untangling yourself from these bonds. Messy goodbyes can be rough for meticulous Virgos. You prefer when they're done as neatly as possible. And you never know! The universe may bring you back together again in the future after you've both evolved.

Plus, there's another half to this equation. The lunar North Node will concurrently travel through the opposite pole of the zodiac in Pisces and your seventh house of partnerships. Until July 26, 2026, you'll have repeated opportunities to find, develop, or improve on a special dynamic duo. You'll already enter the year feeling a strong urge to merge, thanks to the North Node's trek through Aries and your "all or nothing," erotically-charged eighth house. That cycle began on July 17, 2023 and no doubt made for some intense ups and downs in your closest partnerships last year.

Thankfully, when the North Node shifts into Pisces this January 11, you're entering a more romantic, playful stage of partnership. You'll feel far less hesitant to take the plunge into collaboration with a romantic interest, a writing or performing partner, or a professional associate. But whoever it is, there's some weight behind the connection—that feeling that fate brought the two of you together.

For many Virgos, the Pisces North Node may bring a milestone moment for relationships. If you're ready to tie the knot, there couldn't be a more beautiful time for it. (Just mind the Venus retrograde cycle from March 1 to April 12, a less-than-ideal astrological time for nuptials.) Maybe marriage isn't your thing, and you want to openly embrace ethical non-monogamy or date several people seriously. Whatever way you define "relationship bliss," the Pisces North Node gives you permission to soften your rigid stance and go pursue your love goals.

But forget about living for other people's approval ratings! To manifest great relationships, you need to remain deeply in touch with yourself. Pleasing your partner is one thing—and Virgos are skilled lovers and helpers. But if you feel like you're coming out of your own skin to make someone happy (or that you crash when they aren't able to meet your needs for a night), let that be a sign that you need to actually pull back and focus on your own independent goals.

Counterintuitive as it sounds, nothing creates a more magnetic field for relationships than self-love and healthy boundaries. Sure, you'll dip into the couple bubble aplenty in 2025. But with sacrificial Pisces guiding this operative, you have to take extra care to not "lose yourself" in the process.

Advance warning: When the inner work feels too hard, you might want to go for your favorite fixes—tapping the apps for a spicy date or getting wrapped up in solving other people's problems. But don't! That's just an unconscious avoidance technique. Creating drama in existing relationships is another sneaky distraction technique you'll want to avoid.

For Virgos in relationships, there may be temporary turmoil as everyone adjusts to new roles. But ultimately, there's no greater aphrodisiac than a little bit of space—yes, even when every cell in your body is screaming, "I want more!"

Figuring out what makes you happy is a process. Set up a sanctuary, chill space, meditation room, whatever, so you can slip off for reflective alone time. The sooner you start thinking about these quiet spells as "personal growth and development sessions," the faster you'll evolve toward your true north. Until then, keep bravely looking into the shadows—with as many coaches, healers, therapists, shamans, and guides as you need to help you relax and learn to receive.

Love

VIRGO 2025 FORECAST

Thought you'd dodge Cupid's arrows this year? Guess again, sweet Virgo. With so much action going down in your solar seventh and eighth houses (Pisces and Aries), relationships are on a fast-moving trajectory this year.

No doubt, you're already feeling this pull toward partnerships for a while. Serious Saturn has been streaming alongside fantasy-fueled Neptune in Pisces and your committed seventh house since July 17, 2023. The urge to merge gets stronger starting January 11, when the fateful North Node swings into Pisces for the first time in nearly twenty years! For eighteen months, there's a strong "meant to be" energy around commitments that's calling your name.

Turn on your love light so your soulmate can see you in their "search results." That might mean putting yourself out there on the apps again, hiring a matchmaker or getting involved in groups where you can organically meet attractive people who share your interests. Expect a balancing act: Saturn demands you build your relationship on solid ground, while Neptune wants you to dissolve your boundaries and embrace unconditional love. And with the North Node cruising through Pisces, your relationships will feel more karmic, almost destined— taking you into deeper waters and guiding you to truly let go of control. Soulmate vibes? 100 percent.

Remember, Virgo: You get to "do love" by your own design. Whether you're role-playing the tradwife, coupling, throupling, living apart together or enjoying someone's occasional companionship is up to you. Just know that the lessons in chemistry will be exothermic now.

That becomes even more obvious by spring when Neptune, then Saturn, sashays into Aries and your erotically charged eighth house. These "sneak peeks" are a preview of longer cycles. While Neptune will be in Aries from March 30 to October 22 this year, it will rejoin the Ram's realm for thirteen solid years on January 26, 2026. Saturn will set a sexy foundation in Aries this year from May 24 to September 1, then pick up this cycle again for two years on February 13, 2026. Whatever seductive seeds you sow this year could bring a boot-knocking bumper crop next year. Meow, Virgo!

But watch where that love jones leads you from March 1 to April 12! That's when Venus, the goddess of love, hits a retrograde speedbump. To make things more intense, this backspin goes down in Aries (until March 27) and Pisces, resurfacing old flames and unresolved dynamics. Past lovers could pop back up, or you could find yourself questioning someone's loyalties—or your own! The flame is getting higher, but generally speaking, retrogrades are for rethinking, not necessarily restarting. This is the perfect time to review your boundaries and make sure your actions are moving you toward the RIGHT romantic conditions. Pace yourself, even if you don't hit the brakes.

Summer love promises to be passionate as lusty Mars thrusts its way through Virgo from June 17 to August 6, turning you into a magnet for attention and desire. Play the role of pursuer now, initiating erotic adventures or laying an obvious breadcrumb trail for your amour du jour.

On September 7, a total lunar eclipse in Pisces may whip up a hurricane in your love life, revealing truths you can't ignore. Whether it's time to commit or release, this potent lunar event will push you toward your next 76 chapter. Single Virgos could have a fateful encounter with a potential soulmate, while coupled Virgos might reach a breakthrough in how you relate to each other. Under this dreamy but raw energy, lean into the vulnerability—embrace the imperfect but perfect-for-you love story that's unfolding.

Seductive Venus glides into Virgo from September 19 to October 13, bringing a softer, more enchanted energy. Negotiating the terms of relationships will be easier with the peaceful planet here. That's a huge relief, especially after the sharp and cutting energy the eclipse may have stirred up.

Starting on Christmas Eve, Venus and Mars have a cuddle party in Capricorn and your fifth house of true love, creativity and romance. Just in time for the holidays, this delicious duo helps you seal the emotional bonds you've built throughout the year. It's a "serious fun" vibe—yes, you can be swept away, but Capricorn's grounded energy keeps your eye on the long game. Snuggle up by the fireplace to talk about shared dreams for 2026. Single Virgos could meet a solid prospect during your holiday celebrations. That New Year's snog might not be "just a kiss" after all!

VIRGO: LUCKIEST *love* DAY

FEBRUARY 1

Ardent Venus dances a dreamy pas de deux with fantasy-fueling Neptune today, giving everything a fairy-tale quality. As these celestial romantics spin through Pisces, they activate your seventh house of relationships. Drop your guard a little, Virgo, and you could usher in a tidal wave of loving feelings that flow both ways between you and the object of your affection.

Money & Career

VIRGO 2025 FORECAST

How big of an impact do you want to make, Virgo? Multiply that by five (or more) because 2025 could be one of the most heavy-hitting years you've had in a while. Bountiful, worldly Jupiter is halfway through its yearlong trek through Gemini and your tenth house of public recognition and success. Harness this once-every-twelve-years energy while it lasts until June 9. This is the time to launch a start-up, spearhead an "intrapreneurial" project within a company or make your timely ascent into the C-Suite. If you've been craving recognition, grab the mic—your work could get major visibility, and doors you never expected to open might suddenly swing wide.

Innovative Uranus picks up the baton on July 7, taking a six-month lap through Gemini. Forget about staying stuck in the same old routines between now and November 7. This out-of-the-box cycle can pull you toward cutting-edge projects. They might feel ahead of their time now, Virgo, but once Uranus begins a longer cycle through Gemini from April 25, 2026 to May 22, 2033, you could benefit handsomely from getting in on the ground floor of this industry-disrupting venture.

Purpose meets passion when activator Mars makes its biennial visit to Virgo from June 17 to August 6. You'll get a fiery shot of motivation to tackle ambitious projects and assert your ideas with full confidence. Mars doesn't do halfway, and neither should you. Advocate for that promotion, campaign for a leadership role or get to work on your side hustle. Don't be ashamed of your competitive streak. As long as you're playing fair, it's your ace in the hole.

Certain aspects of your career may get a karmic shakeup starting on January 11. The lunar South Node slips into your sign, coaxing you to redefine your professional identity between now and July 26, 2026. This isn't just about changing jobs or updating your resume—it's a deeper transformation that involves letting go of outdated roles that no longer resonate with who you are. Perhaps you've outgrown your current post or are longing for a work environment that aligns with your values. Peel away layers that feel heavy or limiting and make space for the next iteration of your journey.

With stable Saturn and psychic Neptune parked in Aries and your eighth house of investments for part of the year, there's an emphasis on strategic planning and long-term financial growth. Now's the time to raise your fiscal IQ and prepare for both Saturn and Neptune's longer cycles through Aries that begin in early 2026. Merging your practical skills with your visionary aspirations could be the key to unlocking new opportunities. Follow your intuition when it nudges you to go explore a potential investment opportunity, especially this spring and summer.

How you do your daily work could evolve in subtle-but-powerful ways in 2025, as metamorphic Pluto settles into Aquarius, now fully entrenched in your sixth house of routines, wellness and service, until 2044. You're slowly revolutionizing how you approach your work—and it's not just about efficiency. Pluto wants you to dig deep and uncover the core of what motivates you, bringing a sense of power and purpose to your daily grind.

You might find yourself drawn to roles that require deep problem-solving or help you become a transformative leader in your field. Whatever direction you choose, your day-to-day will never be the same. Old habits are up for a complete overhaul as you tap into a more innovative, cutting-edge approach to productivity and well-being.

VIRGO: LUCKIEST *career* DAY

JUNE 8

Lucky Jupiter's final day of a yearlong tour through Gemini and your career house comes with a sweet bonus: an exact connection to your ruler, savvy Mercury. You have wind in your sails and the gift of gab making this the perfect day to close a deal, pitch a new venture or become besties with the industry VIPs.

2025
VIRGO

12

MONTH
OVERVIEW

January MONTHLY HOROSCOPE

As the Sun makes magic in Capricorn until January 19, you could find yourself stealing the spotlight with your creativity and style. You're feeling productive and ready to take charge of projects close to your heart. No dragging slackers along for the ride! When Mars retrogrades in Cancer from January 6 to February 23, you'll clear the decks for a dream team to assemble next month. Huge news for 2025! On January 11, the lunar nodes shift into Pisces and Virgo, beginning an 18-month cycle that will encourage both personal and professional growth. With the karmic South Node in your sign until July 26, 2026, you're entering a phase of profound empowerment that simply will not allow you to play small! This can be daunting, but tap into your analytical side to map out the journey ahead. Then, embrace the power of partnership to bring the dream to life. The Sun enters Aquarius on the 19th, helping you fine-tune your daily routines and focus on wellness—music to a Virgo's ears. With the Year of the Wood Snake beginning on January 29, you'll be ready to shed bad habits like an old skin.

February MONTHLY HOROSCOPE

Salud, Virgo! With the Aquarius Sun energizing your sixth house of wellness until February 18, self-care and organization are your focus. Give your fitness pass a proper workout and start pinning healthy spins on your favorite comfort foods. This efficiency-boosting cycle can help you streamline your schedule. Working smarter not harder? That's Virgo goals! This glow up brings secondary benefits: On February 4, Venus begins a long tour through Aries, heating up your eighth house of seduction, binding relationships and shared investments. Head's up: With Venus going retrograde from March 1 to April 12, it's wise to review how you handle those close bonds NOW. February 4 also sees Jupiter turning direct in Gemini, awakening your tenth house of career and long-term goals. Stalled engines turn over and you could make major professional strides between now and June 9. Partnerships take the spotlight once the Sun moves into Pisces on February 18, so make time for one or two VIPs in your life. But leave a few spaces on the calendar for group hangs, too. Motivating Mars turns direct in Cancer on February 23, which sends you on a networking spree! You may feel inspired to take the lead in a community project or pump up your participation on a team endeavor.

March MONTHLY HOROSCOPE

Bring back the balance, Virgo! As the Sun beams in Pisces until the 20th, you can restore a healthy give and take in your relationships, personal and professional. But the real action is happening in your Aries-ruled eighth house of intimacy, transformation and shared resources. Venus retrogrades in Aries from March 1 to 27, then back into Pisces until April 12. Mercury also spins back through Aries from March 15 to 29, then Pisces until April 7. There could be friction, jealousy and added intensity to contend with as you reassess all the commitments in your life. What's best for YOU, Virgo? You could get some surprising epiphanies during the March 14 full moon lunar eclipse in your sign! A project you've been working on since fall 2024 may be blessed with some angelic support. When the Sun moves into Aries on March 20, your focus will shift to transformation and emotional renewal, making it a great time to clear out what no longer serves you. On March 29, a new moon and solar eclipse in Aries mark the final chapter of a two-year cycle of transformation in your eighth house. A significant shift in your financial life or a deep emotional release could be on the horizon. But wait—there's more! Neptune enters Aries for the first time since 1875 on March 30, kicking off a 14-year wave of spiritual and emotional awakening. Prepare for profound shifts that will transform how you approach intimacy, healing and shared resources! Yes, it IS a very big deal.

April MONTHLY HOROSCOPE

Until the 19th, the Aries Sun is rolling in the deep of your mysterious eighth house, adding an intensity to all that you say and do. Relationships feel fated, for better and for worse, and you might come face to face with your own possessive streak. Before you tag anyone as your soulmate, you might want to pump the brakes. Mercury is retrograde in Pisces and your partnership zone until April 7, and Venus is retrograding there, too, until April 12. This could skew your "picker" as much as it causes misunderstandings to erupt. You'll have a chance to smooth over ruffled feathers and, ideally, create a new consensus that feels like a win-win once these backspins both end on the 12th. Create some whitespace in your schedule starting April 18, as Mars decamps to luxurious Leo, nestling in your twelfth house of rest and reflection until June 17. This is your cue to hit pause, recharge and focus on behind-the-scenes projects. As Taurus season begins on April 19, your ninth house of expansion, travel and learning lights up, shifting your attention to new adventures and growth opportunities. Whether it's a long-distance trip, signing up for a course or diving into a personal passion, this is the perfect time to broaden your horizons and explore new possibilities.

May MONTHLY HOROSCOPE

Spread your wings, Virgo! The Taurus Sun beams in your worldly ninth house until May 20, turning you into a global citizen. How can you broaden your perspective—no matter your GPS coordinates? Sign up for a personal growth seminar or maybe a retreat in the jungle. Pluto spins retrograde in Aquarius starting May 4, making it essential to stay committed to healthy routines. With the regenerative planet in snooze mode until October 13, you could burn out if you don't manage your time and energy with care. Find clever lifehacks for self-care on the go, like traveling with green powder, supplements and exercise bands. On May 20, the Sun shifts into Gemini and your tenth house of career and ambition. You'll be in the professional spotlight, ready to showcase your skills and make a name for yourself. Whether you're aiming for a promotion or a new project, let the VIPs know what you're capable of. Life could feel like a mystery novel starting May 24 when Saturn slips into Aries and sets up camp in your erotic, esoteric eighth house. Saturn's steady, disciplined energy can guide you toward savvy investment strategies over the next few years. (What's your "number," Virgo?) Joint ventures could emerge that help you build your way to wealth. Protect your IP with contracts, trademarks and other legal coverage.

June MONTHLY HOROSCOPE

You're kicking butt and taking names this June, as the Gemini Sun swirls through your tenth house of success until the 20th. With all those career goals in your crosshairs, you're bound to attract interested parties who want to join in. Good news! On the 9th, lucky, enterprising Jupiter swings into Cancer, kicking off a yearlong tour through your collaborative, innovative eleventh house. Teamwork will absolutely make the Virgo dream work between now and June 30, 2026, but don't rush to assemble your supergroup. Indie-spirited Jupiter likes to aim far and wide. You need collaborators who won't cramp your style—and with this worldly influence, they could be dotted all over the globe. As Jupiter squares Saturn on June 15 and Neptune on June 18, make sure you give a couple VIPs in your life your undivided attention so those key relationships don't suffer. The tech sector will call your name. Get trained on AI or industry software, learn about crypto, get angel funding for the app you want to develop or build a subscription product. If you're more of an analog type, pooling resources can be a pathway to abundance. This energy really takes off on the 20th, when the Sun joins Jupiter in Cancer at the solstice. And when the two heavenly bodies make their annual connection on the 24th (AKA The Day of Miracles) you could be introduced to a game-changing group of people. There's even MORE momentum starting on the 17th, as energizer Mars charges into your sign for the first time in two years. Prioritize one or two personal desires you want to fulfill before this cycle ends on August 6.

July MONTHLY HOROSCOPE

Who are the people in your network, Virgo? As the Sun vibes alongside lucky Jupiter in Cancer until the 22nd, you're a veritable superconnector. Save some of that momentum for your own top-tier dreams (and try not to get scattered!). Game-changing Uranus kicks off a four-month tour through Gemini and your career on the 7th, which could bring a fleet of unanticipated projects and opportunities that put your name on the map. Vet them all carefully before signing on, because Mercury spins into a signal-skewing retrograde on July 18, backing up through your twelfth house of illusions until August 11. Things may not be what they seem during this cycle so let people show their hands. You'll have plenty of forward momentum, however, thanks to go-getter Mars powering through Virgo all month. Channel it toward a passion project or set off on an adventurous odyssey. Just mind the Mercury retrograde warnings to leave early for planes and trains and book with reputable travel companies only. Throughout the month, Neptune, Saturn and Chiron all turn retrograde in Aries (on the 4th, 13th and 30th, respectively), activating your eighth house of intimacy, shared resources and transformation. These five-month backspins may poke at emotional wounds, particularly around trust, vulnerability or shared financial matters. Rather than avoiding these feelings, Virgo, use this time for deep emotional healing and transformation. When the Sun joins Mercury retrograde in Leo on July 22, you may need to hit the brakes on situations that feel stuck or unsatisfying. Pull back and give yourself time to reflect on the best way forward. Focus on restoring your energy levels so you can zoom ahead again once your birthday season rolls around in late August.

August MONTHLY HOROSCOPE

August begins as a month of reflection and preparation for you, Virgo. With the Sun in Leo until the 22nd, your energy stores are a bit depleted. Instead of pushing ahead, grab your sunglasses and beach umbrella and go rest, heal and tie up loose ends. Convivial Venus in cozy Cancer until August 25 sets the stage for sweet reunions and casual gatherings with your favorite people. If you organize anything, keep it simple: potlucks in the park after work or an open house hang at your place. With Mercury retrograde in Leo until the 11th, you may have the momentum for a deep cleaning and decluttering mission. Release objects that have a negative charge and lovingly send off clothes, furniture and "sentimental" trinkets that would be more useful in someone else's closet. Money is one area of life where you'll feel fired up! Make-it-happen Mars pulses into Libra from August 6 to September 22, helping you sort out your financial plans and set yourself up for strategic advancements at work. Get your ducks in a row so you can make a case for yourself once Virgo season begins (yay!) on August 22. This fresh-start energy comes with a major bonus in 2025: the first of two rare, back-to-back Virgo new moons this August 23. The intentions you set around personal goals, fulfillment and growth will get a booster shot of momentum again with the solar (new moon) eclipse on September 21!

September MONTHLY HOROSCOPE

♍

Personal growth accelerates in beautiful ways while the Sun shines in your sign until September 22. Sign up for as many experiential things as your heart desires: retreats, workshops, sessions with coaches and healers. It's all about connecting to your core essence at the deepest level possible now. Relationships may move to the back burner temporarily as structured Saturn retrogrades back from Aries into Pisces on the 1st for the remainder of its backspin (until November 27). One partnership in particular could be up for review this September 7, thanks to the total lunar eclipse in Pisces. If you need clarity or closure, you might not get it immediately. Don't stress. Instead, take some of the heat off yourself to please or serve others. By making yourself happy, everyone wins. On September 6, unpredictable Uranus turns retrograde in Gemini, which could shift aspects of your career or public image. Use these disruptions as opportunities to discover innovative ways to progress. (Technology and AI are your friends, Virgo.) And fear not, Cupid won't abandon you. Ardent Venus kicks off her annual tour through Virgo on September 19, blessing you with an attractive glow-up and bringing peace to your romantic realm. Ahhh. Just days later, on September 21, the second new moon in Virgo—a galvanizing solar eclipse—brings a potent burst of momentum for your personal projects. Resources could materialize unexpectedly and decision-makers could green-light your initiatives. Be ready to dive into the action! Fortunately, you'll have plenty of eager collaborators for the mission once Mars whizzes into Scorpio and your cooperative third house from September 22 to November 4. Many hands make light work.

October MONTHLY HOROSCOPE

Back to basics, Virgo! (But not necessarily in a "basic" way.) The Sun beams into aesthetic Libra until the 22nd, dosing your life with practical magic. Time to set up new systems and prettify the ones you already have in place. This money-making cycle can bring new ideas for how to save and earn. Keep your ears peeled for profitable opportunities, which could come through your network of friends. Sparks keep flying in your love life while Venus struts through Virgo until the 13th. Single Virgos won't be in any hurry to settle down, but don't let a good one slip away in the process. Attached? Autonomy AND adventure make the heart grow fonder, so plan more exciting activities with your amour. When Venus sashays into Libra on the 13th, you'll be ready to sink into a slow-jamming groove or tend to the more mundane matters of your love life. Career goals get back on track once Pluto turns direct in Aquarius, also on the 13th. Reboot your commitment to your healthy living routines or sprinkle in some variety with a new cardio class or eating plan. Budding attractions could evolve into more meaningful connections once Scorpio season begins on the 22nd. With lusty Mars riding shotgun to the Sun for a couple weeks, flirtations could heat up fast! Love could emerge from the friend zone or you could meet someone through the intro of mutual pals. Also on the 22nd, boundary-blurring Neptune retrogrades back from Aries into Pisces for the final month and a half of its backspin. Revisit a creative or spiritual partnership, but set clear expectations this time.

November MONTHLY HOROSCOPE

So many people, so little time! Scorpio season has you in full social swing until the 21st. And as vivacious Venus sashays into Scorpio from November 6 to 30, you'll be everyone's favorite plus-one. This COULD become a challenge, since your domestic side kicks into high gear on the 4th, when energetic Mars hunkers down in Sagittarius, firing up your fourth house of home, family and foundations until December 15. Half of you will be haunted by FOMO, wanting to be at every show, opening and after-house event. But with Mars in the mix, you might feel the urge to make some bold moves at home—whether it's a renovation project or addressing long-standing family matters. Don't go swinging those hammers, Virgo, because Mercury takes its final retrograde spin from November 9 to 29. The "fun" starts in Sagittarius, which could send renovation projects off the rails or turn a simple discussion into a family feud. On the 18th, Mercury slips back into Scorpio, which could stir some confusion in your communications more broadly—whether it's with neighbors, coworkers or within your friend circle. Take the high road and avoid potentially tense topics altogether when possible. Adding to the intensity, unpredictable Uranus retrogrades back into Taurus from November 7 until February 3, 2026, causing you to reassess a few of your broader aspirations, like travel plans, school, even your political worldview. Expansive Jupiter also turns retrograde in Cancer on November 11, which may slow the progress of a team effort over the coming four months. Use these timeouts to fortify relationships and do the requisite research to ensure you're on the right path. Fortunately, taskmaster Saturn ENDS its five-month retrograde on the 27th, pivoting forward in your partnership house. Just in time for the mistletoe season, Virgo, you're ready to create strong foundations for long-lasting love and deeper commitments in your life.

December MONTHLY HOROSCOPE

Gather 'round the hearth! The Sagittarius Sun is beaming its vibrant rays into your fourth house of home, family and emotional roots until the 21st, putting you in a domestic state of mind. With motivator Mars also in Sagittarius until the 15th, joined by Venus until the 24th, you're the hub of the holiday season, upping the comfort and joy for everyone who comes into your orbit. You may feel like Sleeping Beauty waking up from her nap once dreamy Neptune snaps out of its five-month retrograde on the 10th. The rest of the month could feel like a fairy-tale, whether you're snuggling up to someone special or keeping an eye out for hot prospects while you're working the seasonal soiree circuit. That fervent energy only gets hotter once passionate Mars heads into Capricorn on December 15, energizing your fifth house of creativity, romance and playfulness. As the Sun moves into Capricorn on December 21, followed by Venus on the 24th, you're the unapologetic life of the party! Love will be exciting and accelerated, no mistletoe required. Elevate your celebrations with sparkly decor, danceable music, icebreaker games, even a costume theme. (Why not?) Set some financial limits though! It's easy to blow through your funds if you don't have a clear-cut budget. Eating, drinking and making merry doesn't have to break the bank, Virgo. Save up a little coin for a glitzy NYE party. You'll want to ring in 2026 at the heart of the action. Is there a rooftop bar in Miami or a live show in the closest downtown that's calling your name? What happens on NYE doesn't have to stay on NYE as this amorous energy rolls right into the New Year for you!

Read your extended monthly forecast for life, love, money and career! astrostyle.com

A LITTLE ABOUT *Libra*

DATES September 22 - October 22

SYMBOL The Scales

ELEMENT Air

QUALITY Cardinal

RULING PLANET Venus

BODY PART Lower back

BEST TRAITS
Charming, lovable, fair, sincere, sharing, hopelessly romantic, compassionate, wise

KEYWORDS
Commitment, partnership, equality, balance, mutuality, fairness, luxury, justice, decadence

Read more about Libra

LIBRA
IN 2025

ALL THE PLANETS IN LIBRA IN 2025	YOUR 2025 HOROSCOPE	TOP 5 THEMES FOR LIBRA IN 2025	LOVE HOROSCOPE + LUCKY DATES	MONEY HOROSCOPE + LUCKY DATES

Libra in 2025

YOUR YEARLY OVERVIEW

The world is your oyster in 2025, Libra, so go scoop up some pearls! Celestial seekers Jupiter and Uranus are each doing time in Gemini, sending waves of wanderlust through your worldly ninth house. You could broaden your horizons in profound ways, like taking a once-in-a-lifetime trip, diving into an advanced degree program or publishing a book. The key is to leave your comfort zone. Go embrace the vast unknown, and trust that the right people and experiences will appear. If it's time to relocate, you could be packing up the U-Haul (or shipping container!) before the year is through. Plus, with the karmic South Node leaving your sign on January 11 (after 18 months there), you'll feel as if you've been untethered from a huge weight. But don't run off leash without SOME semblance of a routine. The lunar nodes are now heading into Pisces and Virgo until July 2026, where they'll push you to prioritize self-care and discover a soulful connection to your work. Release old behaviors that no longer serve your highest self, especially in areas where perfectionism has been holding you back. Career goals gather steam after June 9, when abundant Jupiter shifts into Cancer, bringing its generous energy to your tenth house of professional prestige. This yearlong cycle could see you stepping into a major leadership role or boosting your reputation significantly. Dreamy Neptune and solid Saturn spend part of the year in Aries, stirring up a new energy in your partnerships. Pairing up can be life-changing, but make sure you unite with people who are aligned with your long-term vision.

THE PLANETS IN *Libra*

THE SUN
SEP 22–OCT 22

It's birthday season for you, so step out and shine! Seek novelty and take extra initiative during this radiant monthlong phase.

NEW MOON
OCT 21
8:25AM, 28°22'

Bonus New Year! Set your intentions for the next six months and get into action.

FULL MOON
APR 12
8:22PM, 23°20'

Ready, set, manifest! Your work of the past six months bears fruit and it's time to harvest the rewards.

MERCURY
SEP 18–OCT 6

Crown yourself monarch of the social butterflies when popularity-boosting Mercury visits your sign once a year. Circulate and get social—but don't make promises you can't keep!

VENUS
OCT 13–NOV 6

You've got the romantic It Factor when the galactic glamazon charges up your powers of seduction each year. Willpower is weak in the face of beauty and luxury. Watch your spending!

MARS
AUG 6–SEP 22

Motivation is high when energetic Mars visits your sign every couple years—but check your combative streak and try not to come on too strong.

SOUTH NODE
JUL 17, 2023–
JAN 11, 2025

Life feels both surreal and karmic when the lunar South Node backs up through your sign (for 18 months) every 18.5 years. Surrender to the vision quest and prepare to let go of unworkable habits. This will all make sense when the cycle ends.

Libra in 2025

HIGHLIGHTS

NOVEL EXPERIENCES: JUPITER AND URANUS IN GEMINI

Take that leap of faith, Libra! Until June 9, lucky Jupiter continues expanding your horizons in Gemini, your ninth house of travel, learning and growth. This is your cosmic green light to break free from routine and dive into new experiences. Whether you're booking a trip abroad or exploring a long-distance relationship, the first half of 2025 is all about pushing boundaries. Then, from July 7 to November 7, game-changer Uranus joins the mix, surfing into Gemini for the first time since 1949! This is a glimpse of a longer, thirteen-year cycle that kicks up again in April 2026. Get ready for a midyear shift toward an even more adventurous global perspective. Some Libras could relocate for school or work. You could take a life-changing trip to study with a master teacher or shaman. Stay open to whatever exciting paths unfold, even if that means recalibrating your entire worldview.

KARMIC RELIEF: SOUTH NODE IN VIRGO

Say ahhh, Libra. After eighteen agonizing months, the karmic South Node leaves your sign this January 11, freeing you up from an intense period of shadow work that may have rattled your sense of identity to the core. As it drifts into Virgo from January 11, 2025 to July 26, 2026, it provides a period of integration. What did you learn about yourself and your approach to relationships? And what are you ready to release? Across the wheel, the fateful Node in Pisces helps you simplify and streamline your life and achieve some work-life balance. Give your body lots of love with clean eating, ample sleep and regular exercise that clears your physical AND psychic fields.

GOAL-GETTER TIME: JUPITER RISES TO YOUR TENTH HOUSE

Your professional life gets a leveling up starting June 9, once enterprising Jupiter soars into Cancer and activates your high-achieving tenth house for an entire year. Promotions, leadership opportunities or complete career pivots could be in store. Don't throw out the baby with the bathwater just because something new intrigues you. All that you've mastered over the past nine years (since Jupiter was last in YOUR sign) could come to a profitable climax now. Cha-ching! Strategic moves, coupled with your natural charm and diplomacy, will set you up for long-term success.

SATURN AND NEPTUNE IN ARIES RESTRUCTURE RELATIONSHIPS

Relationships are ripe grounds for evolution this year, as two outer planets head into Aries and your partnership zone for the first time in, literally, ages. Dreamy Neptune takes a pass through the Ram's realm from March 30 to October 22; traditional Saturn from May 24 to September 1. These sneak peeks give you glimpses into longer cycles that begin at the start of 2026. Serious shifts could already begin this year as you find yourself longing for both deep connection AND a stable structure. With Neptune activating these desires until 2039 and Saturn until 2028, you could feel the push to put a clear label on your connections or formalize a business agreement. Overall, you're stepping into a time that's all about creating solid, meaningful partnerships that stand the test of time.

VENUS RETROGRADE: REFLECT AND REALIGN

Your cosmic ruler Venus has a retrograde this year, a period that comes around every 584 days. From March 1 to April 12, the planet of love, beauty and harmony drifts back through Aries (until March 27) and Pisces. During this reflective reversal, you have a chance to reassess relationship dynamics. Are you giving too much or sacrificing your needs for others? As hard as it can be to admit, this is an opportunity to restore balance and address any unresolved emotional or financial issues. Take this time to fine-tune your approach to love and money—patience will pay off.

TOP 5 THEMES FOR
Libra in 2025

1	2	3	4	5
WIDEN YOUR SEARCH PARAMETERS	SHIFT INTO MOGUL MODE	CALL IN POWERFUL PARTNERSHIPS	RECONFIGURE RELATIONSHIP DYNAMICS	HEAL FROM THE INSIDE OUT

1 WIDEN YOUR SEARCH PARAMETERS

JUPITER AND URANUS IN GEMINI

JUPITER: MAY 25, 2024 – JUNE 9, 2025
URANUS: JULY 7 – NOVEMBER 7, 2025 • JANUARY 26, 2026 – MAY 22, 2033

The world is your oyster in 2025, Libra, as two intrepid planets—Jupiter and Uranus—string you along an exciting journey. Pearls of wisdom that you glean along your voyages will be the hottest commodity this year. Expect to find them in the rarest of places, from your travels to your studies.

JUPITER IN GEMINI

MAY 25, 2024 – JUNE 9, 2025

Time for a new suitcase, Libra, or maybe some stylish wilderness gear? Your global expansion efforts may already be underway in 2025 as limitless Jupiter continues its fortuitous yearlong cruise through Gemini and your worldly ninth house. Since the adventurous planet began this quest on May 25, 2024, you've been propelled out of your comfort zone and into the vast unknown.

Your World Clock app could get quite the workout while Jupiter ziplines through Gemini until June 9. During this time, geographic distance can't hold you back from much, if anything. Some Libras will relocate to new cities under this Jupiter phase while others may choose to live or study abroad for an extended stay.

Travel-plus is the theme of your year, so forget about holing up at a resort. You'll feel far too restless. Want to attend (or lead!) a yoga retreat in Costa Rica? Study Renaissance painting techniques in Positano? Mastermind with a group of entrepreneurs from every part of the world at a global summit? Now we're talking.

Your circle of friends becomes vastly diverse now, too, and for single Libras, all sorts of romances smolder with possibility. You may be attracted to an unconventional arrangement or someone from a completely different "flavor profile" than you've tasted in the past. Attached? Stoke the embers with an epic vacation together. Even if you don't set sail on this fantastic voyage until later in the year, the planning and research can be like foreplay.

If you're an entrepreneur, writer, blogger or media maker, you'll be extra blessed by this Jupiter phase, especially if you're engaged in socially responsible work, which idealistic Jupiter approves of. The free flying ninth house is abundant Jupiter's happiest place, so you owe it to yourself to take a gamble* on your dreams.

Yes, we added that asterisk* for a reason, Libra. Jupiter is indeed the galactic gambler, known to make you leap with little consideration for a net. Try not to rush ahead without some semblance of a plan—even if said plan only calculates your first five steps along the journey.

There's a risk of overdoing everything in the first half of the year: spending, indulging, eating, romancing. And while we're all for you having some well-deserved moments of hedonism, you will struggle to find your saturation point and your "off" switch. We don't mean to kill the thrills. Just read the safety precautions before you jump out of any planes, okay? With a little project management and your goddess-given charms, you won't just land on your feet, you'll launch your life into the stratosphere. And away you go!

URANUS IN GEMINI
JULY 7 – NOVEMBER 7, 2025
JANUARY 26, 2026 – MAY 22, 2033

This July 7 you may start seeing things through a VERY wide-angled lens as you turn your microscope into a telescope. That day marks an extremely rare and potentially ground-breaking transit in your life. Revolutionary Uranus sidespins into curious Gemini and your ninth house of travel, adventure and expanded horizons, its first visit to this sign since 1941-49.

While this circuit only lasts for four months in 2025 (until November 7), you're just getting warmed up, Libra. On April 25, 2026 Uranus will surge back into Gemini for seven years, until May 22, 2033.

Oh, the places you will go, literally and figuratively. Heady Uranus in intellectual Gemini could send you on some profound philosophical voyages, no plant medicine required. Your genius knows no limits under this spell. Plus, you'll find all kinds of applications for your brilliant ideas. Jupiter's tour through Gemini earlier in 2025 may have already gotten the ball rolling on entrepreneurial or publishing ventures. As Uranus picks up the baton, you could invent a ground-breaking product or "method" that changes the landscape of an industry. And if you're not quite that ambitious, well, Libra, you'll still enjoy finding more innovative ways to do your work. Any sort of writing or composing could be a worthwhile pursuit. You could wind up setting trends while simply making media for media's sake.

Where have you been holding yourself back in a misbegotten belief that you weren't ready/capable/good enough? Limiting thoughts can vanish under this eye-opening cycle! Of course, if you do need further education or training or desire personal gratification, you might find it outside of the conventional campus quads, like think tanks, incubators, even ceremonies deep in the woods.

This expansive transit will inspire you to grow and develop exponentially. (But for your own sake, Libra, leave the self-criticism and judgments at the door.) You might finally plan, and take, a gap year (or month) or challenge yourself to a half-marathon or bike-a-thon. Anything that pushes your limits in a positive way is encouraged. Since this realm rules publishing and entrepreneurial enterprises, this is a good time to grow a sideline business or spend all your free hours writing a memoir. Get the professional advice you can and aim high!

2 SHIFT INTO MOGUL MODE

JUPITER IN CANCER
JUNE 9, 2025 – JUNE 30, 2026

Be careful what you touch beginning this June 9, Libra, because it could instantly turn to gold. For the first time since 2014, lucky Jupiter soars to the very peak of your chart, making "Midas" your official moniker. As the planet of abundance bids Gemini farewell, it moves into its absolute favorite (exalted) sign, Cancer, and charges up your tenth house of professional prestige until June 30, 2026.

Ultimately, this is fabulous news for Libras. Yet, as the saying goes, with great power comes great responsibility. After spending the first half of 2025 with nomadic Jupiter in your "free as a bird" ninth house (Gemini), this cosmic call of duty might feel like the school bell clanging at the end of recess. Nevertheless, adulting is unavoidable after June 9. Pack up your festival gear and slip into something a little more...corporate.

Fortunately, once you switch back to focus mode, you'll be off to the races like a Formula One Ferrari. If you aren't already on a mission, you soon will be. Pro tip: Set your sights on the upper echelons. When Jupiter rolls through your tenth house every twelve years or so, you belong in the presidential suite, the VIP arena box, and on the privileged side of every red velvet rope.

Do you enjoy being your own boss? The digital nomad lifestyle that lured you earlier this year will be hard to pull off once Jupiter arrives in Cancer. That said, you could travel often between now and June 30, 2026—for sales conferences, client meetings, retreats (led by you!) or to check out potential distribution partners.

This thirteen-month period could be one of the most professionally liberating and profitable phases you've had in over a decade. While Jupiter puts the "free" in "freelance," don't be surprised if you crave more security after June 9. Upgrade one-off assignments to six-month engagements, professional residencies or yearlong contracts with a handful of premier clients.

Have you developed expertise in your field? The podium calls! Get yourself booked as a keynote speaker at summits, seminars and industry conventions. With your goddess-given charm, this could turn into a lucrative gig, but even if a fee is not part of the package, think: exposure. Play your cards right and these opportunities become a chance to get your name circulating among the VIPs. Like we said, Jupiter in Cancer will pull you into elite circles and bless you with insider access. It's all about who you know! And with your smooth social skills, expanding your professional network is a piece of gold-leaf-dusted chocolate ganache cake.

The tenth house also rules the archetypal masculine realm. Fathers, brothers, sons and all male-identified people could play a more prominent role in your life now. If you're hoping to develop a more honest relationship, seize the day. Jupiter is nothing if not authentic. Your relationships with these men will grow in direct proportion to your ability to share your truth, but it doesn't stop there. Your challenge will be to listen to theirs in return, whether or not you see eye to eye on political, spiritual or other life matters.

Jupiter is also the liberator, so some Libras may feel that it's time to cut ties with a guy in your life. But don't be rash! You should think very carefully before going for full estrangement, especially if you are relatives or tied in a significant way. Declarations like these can be irrevocable and have their own set of consequences. And Jupiter can be impulsive and hotheaded in its influence. Start with "taking space," if you haven't done so before, or setting up firmer boundaries. Absence might have the effect of making the heart grow fonder—or at least healed in a significant way.

3 CALL IN POWERFUL PARTNERSHIPS

SATURN AND NEPTUNE IN ARIES

NEPTUNE: MARCH 30 – OCTOBER 22, 2025 • JANUARY 26, 2026 – MARCH 23, 2039
SATURN: MAY 24 – SEPTEMBER 1, 2025 • FEBRUARY 13, 2026 – APRIL 12, 2028

Power to your partnerships, Libra! We're talking about the ones that already exist and those that have yet to be actualized. This year brings a special emphasis on twosomes, which sounds like music to your collaborative sign's ears.

For part of 2025, two notable outer planets, Saturn and Neptune, will pass through Aries and your seventh house of relationships. It's been a very long time since either planet visited this part of the sky—nearly three decades for Saturn and over a century for Neptune! Their combined energy can help you actualize some of your relationship goals, whether for business, pleasure or a heady mix of both.

NEPTUNE IN ARIES

MARCH 30 – OCTOBER 22, 2025
JANUARY 26, 2026 – MARCH 23, 2039

Starting March 30, Libras begin writing a new chapter in relationships, which could mean embarking on the next step with your longtime love or pivoting in a wholly new direction. For the first time since 1872, numinous Neptune drifts into Aries, where it casts a spell in your seventh house of partnerships. Neptune's visit to Aries is brief this year, lasting only until October 22. But pay attention to what (and who!) shows up. On January 26, 2026, the cosmic dreamweaver will circle back into Aries for a longer, thirteen-year tour.

There's plenty for a Libra to enjoy about this transit! The fearless pursuit of love that it engenders. The way it helps you declare your feelings with full throated confidence. After fourteen years of hosting the hazy planet in your sixth house of work and wellness (Pisces), this will be a welcome sea change. You're one of the zodiac's most hopeful romantics and any time a planet nudges you toward partnerships, you are in your element.

Consider this a gilded invitation to explore the deeper, more spiritual aspects of your one-on-one connections. That goes for romantic relationships, creative collaborations and even the bonds that you share with colleagues and dear friends. With dreamy Neptune in action-oriented Aries, you may find yourself reimagining what commitment, love, and partnership mean to you.

During this idealistic cycle you'll crave soul-stirring connections that transcend the mundane. Single Libras could be on the hunt for a bond that feels otherworldly, almost destined. And we wouldn't be surprised if you manifested more than one person who at least SEEMS to fit that bill between March 30 and October 22.

But Neptune's foggy influence can also blur the lines between reality and fantasy. While you might be tempted to idealize the concept of a relationship, keep expectations grounded in reality. Even your "perfect spouse" needs days off from tossing rose petals at your pedicured feet. (Sorry.)

Compassionate, charitable Neptune in Aries may inspire you to be more giving in a relationship. This, too, comes with a red flag. Guilt, sacrifice and codependence are this planet's shadow side. To keep things from going sour, ensure that the flow of give and take remains equal in any partnerships.

Since Aries is your opposite sign, this Neptune cycle provides objective distance about the role you play in relationships. Your mate is your mirror now, reflecting back parts of yourself that may have been buried in your subconscious. Make room for a few meltdowns as well as some eye-opening discoveries about areas where you could afford to evolve. Some growth can't happen alone, Libra. You have to drop your guard, get vulnerable and onto the playground with the other kids.

With that in mind, Neptune in Aries promises to be an incredibly healing time for existing relationships. Compassionate energy might inspire you to forgive past grievances, soften your heart, and approach your partnerships with a renewed sense of empathy. If you've been holding onto old wounds, this transit encourages you to release them and move forward with grace.

You might feel a magnetic pull towards people who challenge your usual approach to relationships. Aries' fiery influence can inspire you to take bold steps, like breaking up with someone who refuses to put a ring on your finger after five years or, conversely, deciding that you prefer to hold on to elements of your single life like keeping your own apartment and NOT spending every night together with your S.O.

You may find yourself attracted to individuals who embody the Aries spirit—independent, assertive, and unapologetically themselves. This could be a period of awakening where you realize that love doesn't have to fit the traditional mold you once envisioned. Instead, it can be a thrilling adventure that pushes you out of your comfort zone.

However, with illusory Neptune's influence, there's always a potential for confusion. You might meet people who seem perfect at first glance but later reveal themselves to be less than what they appeared. It's important to watch out for the Neptunian tendency to see what you want to see rather than what's actually there. This transit might bring situations where you're tempted to overlook flaws, hoping that love will somehow transform them. Remember, Libra, while Neptune encourages unconditional love, it's also vital to maintain healthy boundaries and protect your heart.

SATURN IN ARIES
MAY 24 – SEPTEMBER 1, 2025
FEBRUARY 13, 2026 – APRIL 12, 2028

Two months after fluid Neptune darts into Aries, its odd-couple counterpart, stable Saturn, does the same. This May 24, the cosmic architect begins a three-year build in your seventh house of committed relationship. Saturn hasn't visited Aries since 1996 to 1998, making this transit largely unscripted for you. But you only get three months to work on the blueprint this year. On September 1, Saturn dunks back into Pisces for its final introspective dance. The foundation you pour this spring and summer could be a solid launch pad for partnerships when Saturn returns to Aries from February 13, 2026 to April 12, 2028.

No pressure, Libra! Saturn won't hurry you through this process; however, it doesn't reward fence sitting either. Promising relationships that haven't gotten past the spark phase could ignite with newfound intensity between May 24 and September 1. Brace yourself for a little adjustment. As a Libra, choosing "just one thing" has been known to stir up anxiety. You like to weigh out every option, always wondering if something "better" might be waiting around the next corner. Saturn in Aries is here to show you the beauty that can come from building a relationship one brick at a time. A perfect partnership is as much a co-creation as it is a fated destiny.

Saturn will be opposing your Libra Sun during this cycle, which can also bring some rude awakenings. It's time to master the art of seeing through others' eyes, even if their view on life is diametrically opposed to yours. These lessons in empathy and compromise might be challenging, but they're also the secret ingredients to enduring partnerships. Think of this as tough love that's meant to enrich—not restrict—your life.

With a partner worth their salt, you'll be able to let go of control and trust them to take the reins when you need a rest.

Be super selective about who gets a second or third date. Quality over quantity is already your mantra, but that goes triple with Saturn in Aries. For coupled Libras, wise, maturing Saturn can propel your relationship into more "adult" territory. Time to shop for that love nest, get engaged, merge assets or take out insurance policies together. Each step forward will cement your connection and enhance your emotional security.

Professionally, ambitious Saturn could lead you to your ideal business partner, someone whose strengths are a natural complement to your own. Don't rush into this or move forward with a handshake and verbal "understanding." Saturn likes everything done by the books, Libra, and the seventh house rules legal affairs. The last thing you need is to find yourself in arbitration next year because your so-called business partner is trying to stake claim to the original IP that you forgot to protect by law.

Saturn's departure from your work and wellness zone signals a shift away from burning the candle at both ends. If you've been consistent and hardworking, the middle of 2025 may usher in significant career milestones like a well-deserved promotion. Balance the scales of your professional and personal life, making room for relationships that truly reflect and respect your worth. Welcome to a period of growing and glowing, Libra!

4 RECONFIGURE RELATIONSHIP GOALS

VENUS RETROGRADE IN ARIES AND PISCES
ARIES: MARCH 1 – 27
PISCES: MARCH 27 – APRIL 12

Everyone has baggage, Libra, some of it buried in storage and some that you trot out like an enviable Louis Vuitton luggage set. But there comes a time when you can't move another inch forward without unpacking what is cluttering up your life. You may hit that very wall this March 1, as your ruling planet Venus pivots into retrograde mode until April 12. The demand is clear: take an unflinching look at how you're handling romance and finance, the areas of life that Venus governs.

This U-turn happens every 18 months, but in 2025, Venus splits the reverse-commute between two signs, complexifying the cycle. From March 1 to 27, the planet of love and beauty backs up through Aries and your relationship zone, putting key partnerships in her crosshairs. Then, from March 27 to April 12, your galactic guardian drifts back into Pisces and your sixth house of work and wellness, sending up an S.O.S. for self-care and a healthy work-life balance.

Does that sound like an overwhelming way to "ease into" spring, Libra? Take a breath and break it into phases. While Venus retreats through Aries from March 1 to 27, focus on restoring equilibrium to your relationships. There's nothing wrong with forming dependencies, but have you become so reliant on another person that you'd spiral without their input? Challenge yourself to reclaim some self-sufficiency. You're an excellent problem solver when you take a breath and think things through, Libra. Learn some calming techniques (breathwork, yoga, meditation) that can help you access your prefrontal cortex when the fight-flight-freeze part of your brain is activated.

This advice goes both ways. Should a loved-one be leaning too heavily on you for pep talks, tech support or emergency Cash App contributions, well, Libra, you may have to put down your satin mule for once and for all. (Yes, even quiet luxury can make a loud statement when a Libra decides to be firm.)

If you've been quietly fuming about "the little things," don't keep stuffing them down, not even with your favorite French truffles. With the heavenly harmonizer in snooze mode, conversations about doing the dishes and paying the mortgage could devolve into power struggles. Choose your battles carefully this March. For instance, if you got cropped out of an Instagram shot, don't fly into the assumption that your S.O. is hiding your relationship.

We're not suggesting you ignore something that bothers you. Just know that you will be prone to overblowing things and taking minor oversights as personal offenses. If you have buried issues to excavate, you might do best hashing them out with the support of a third party, like a couple's therapist.

Single and dating? Be ultra-discerning so as not to gloss over red flags. Venus retrograde is no time to quietly wonder about things that don't quite sit right with you, like a date who gets squirrelly when you ask about their "roommate." (Which could turn out to be their mother...or spouse.) If you feel unsettled, make like a Libra: Be diplomatically direct and inquire further into the subject until you get clear intel.

An ex could return with unfinished business—even the second chance you've been hoping for. But be careful about opening those doors, since Venus' backspin can muddle your better judgment. Timing might be on your side this time around, but you may not get a clear read on that until Venus turns direct on April 12. It's not just about a strong connection, Libra. Are your lifestyles even compatible? No matter how much you love each other, you need to get real about whether or not a relationship would work on the day to day...or if it continues to feel like jamming a square peg into a round hole. There's always a chance that Venus retrograde can help you unearth a juicy creative compromise, too.

From March 27 to April 12, Venus drifts back into Pisces and your sixth house of work and wellness. If you abandoned your self-care rituals, weave them back into your schedule. Managing professional relationships—and your time—will be essential to this process. No, Libra, you won't make it to evening spin if you don't set boundaries with coworkers about when meetings should begin and end, or keep WhatsApp notifications on while you're trying to get through your assignments! Monotask instead of multitasking, and be crystal clear with colleagues that you need to reserve personal talks for happy hour.

Venus retrograde can plunge you back into a passion project or get you inspired to start a fitness routine (or full-on yoga practice). Trouble is, you may feel so mired in day-to-day duties that you can't find the time you desire to devote to it. The sixth house rules service and service providers. Outsourcing time-sucking tasks like housecleaning or answering client emails might cost you some coin, but if it opens up space for you to focus on higher-dollar tasks, it's absolutely a worthy investment. Vet any candidates carefully though, especially if you're trusting them with your personal data, passwords and credit card numbers.

5 HEAL FROM THE INSIDE OUT

LUNAR NODES IN VIRGO AND PISCES
NORTH NODE IN PISCES, SOUTH NODE IN VIRGO
JANUARY 11, 2025 – JULY 26, 2026

Can we get a "woosah," Libra? A well-deserved break from intensity comes this January 11, when the moon's karmic South Node leaves your sign, not to return for another 18 years! You've hosted this soul-stirring, shadowy point in your sign since July 17, 2023, which has been no cakewalk. You may, in fact, feel as if you're emerging from a dark night of the soul. Painful though this has been at times, it's also been a beautiful process of "true-ing up" to your genuine self. This heavy round of internal searching won't come again for nearly two decades. Whew.

Not that you're completely out of those deep, reflective woods. On January 11, the lunar nodes reposition themselves across your axis of health and healing—Pisces and Virgo—and help you integrate your insights into your self-care routines until July 26, 2026. Reducing stress will be an especially important mission for Libras in 2025. Burnout could hit you hard if you've been pushing through long hours or making sacrifices for the ones you love. The remedy? Simplify your life, then systematize your workflow.

Fortunately, the lunar North Node in Pisces begins a cleanup mission in your salubrious, systematic sixth house this January 11. Time to get every area of your life shipshape. Tempting as it will be to tackle all of these with your balanced determination, take a holistic approach. Take stock of your present circumstances. What's working well and what do you wish was working better?

Then, dig deeper. What got you here in the first place? With the lunar South Node in analytical Virgo slowly moving across your twelfth house of subconscious healing, you have an opportunity to root out some of the hidden patterns in your life that might be holding you back. Start by observing how you move through your daily routines. Pay attention to your mindless habits, which keep you numb or checked out. These may be masking things like limiting beliefs and defensive moves that were birthed in childhood trauma like people-pleasing or rushing in as the "fixer."

Trigger alert: The South Node in Virgo, your twelfth house, can poke at old wounds, attachment issues and unmetabolized grief. Don't resist the feelings, Libra. The sooner you unblock emotional dams, the faster you'll get back to your happy place. Watch sad movies, soak in the tub, do what you can to get things flowing. Bottled-up feelings lead to all kinds of unwanted things, from literal weight on your body to chronic disease. This healing nodal cycle helps you shed whatever you've been holding in. Let go and let yourself be liberated!

Now for a friendly PSA from the North Node in Pisces and your sixth house of self-care: Your body is your soul's address here on Earth. Start incorporating healthy eating, resistance training and regular movement into your daily repertoire. If you've been ignoring aches and pains, you'll need to deal. Vitality is the goal, so make sure you're also loading up on preventative medicine. Sleep, supplements, and bodywork can go a long way to keep you humming.

Since Pisces rules the subconscious, the North Node's journey through this sign can turn your attention to neuroplasticity. While many neural pathways are formed during childhood, they aren't all hard-wired. Because of the brain's plasticity, new pathways can be formed, often through repetitive activities such as breathing exercises or learning a new word every day. Exploring new things, like travel, reading fiction and even making crafts have proven to boost brain activity.

As the fluid Pisces North Node activates your sixth house of daily routines and work, it may be time to upgrade your workflow. If you find yourself scattered in a million directions, you might try bundling tasks so that you are doing similar things at once — for example, answering phone calls while walking to the post office or shutting off all devices to write and crunch numbers.

With this destiny-driver pointing you toward professional growth, you could find a new job or perhaps create one for yourself at the company you already work for. Don't rush a resignation if you're unhappy in your current role. If you're a valued employee with a solid track record, at least try to have a conversation about carving out a more suitable, fulfilling position for yourself. You may be pleasantly surprised!

No matter what, before July 26, 2026, make it your mission to add more meaning to your work. Already there? Now's the time to do a health check. Have you slipped into "office martyr" mode, working around the clock or without clear boundaries? Burning out is never a good look, Libra, so let the Pisces North Node help you reclaim personal limits—and systematize your workflow so you have time to prepare a healthy dinner, hit the gym for an evening cardio class, and enjoy weekend trips.

The last time the nodes were in this position was from June 23, 2006 to December 18, 2007. Significant themes around health, spirituality, and work could arise again between January 11, 2025, and July 26, 2026. Revisit parts of your life that fed your soul back then. Nostalgia aside, you may discover that they nourish 2025 you!

Love

LIBRA 2025 FORECAST

Oh, the power of two! A fresh crop of planets is moving into Aries and your seventh house of committed partnerships this year. While you've been known to slot neatly into the "serial dater" category, there are only so many cups of coffee you can down with right-swiping strangers before you want something REAL. This year, you may close the Starbucks app and brew up a pot of "Me espresso" to serve to someone who deserves it.

News alert: The inner journey is equally important to the discovery process now. And transformational Pluto is here to help you carve out space in your own universe to allow someone to penetrate your (so graceful, you might miss it) shield. Since November 19, 2024, Pluto began its solid, two-decade journey through your fifth house of true love. Peace, love, beauty, harmony—those are a Libra's stock in trade. But shadow dancer Pluto demands that you show your full hand, or at least a couple more fingers.

If you, like Libra Oscar Wilde, have clung to the belief that "uncertainty" is "the very essence of romance," you could change your tune under Pluto's new rules. Lift the veil bit by bit and you may discover a radical new dimension in relationships. Fears of the romance dying if you reveal your less-than-coiffed self are generally unfounded. Because, let's be honest, a bad hair day for a Libra is #salongoals for the rest of us style plebes out here.

Your ruler, lovebug Venus, makes a grand entrance into Aries on February 4, lighting a sexy bonfire in your seventh house of relationships. This will warm you to the idea of closeness, attracting a keeper or helping you deepen an existing bond.

But there IS a twist. From March 1 to April 12, Venus slips through a retrograde—which takes place in Aries until March 27. This could poke the bear of a relationship issue or bring back a lover with unfinished business. Mercury will also turn retrograde from March 15 to April 7, skewering attempts to discuss any issues. That's especially true while the messenger planet spins back through Aries until March 29.

Adding to the intensity, on March 29, a (new moon) solar eclipse in Aries rattles your relationship cage. This final eclipse in a two-year series on the Aries-Libra axis CAN bring closure. Near this date, it will be impossible to ignore anything that's been simmering beneath the surface. This grand finale eclipse could bring the courage to lock down a commitment (rings, titles, co-signed leases) or draw the line in the sand with a situationship that has dragged on for far too long. While some developments will be immediate and obvious, others could plunge you into deeper indecision. We recommend waiting until the Mercury-Venus retrograde smoke clears after April 12 (and a couple weeks more from there!) to do anything binding.

That's not all! On March 30, dreamweaving Neptune spins into Aries—its first visit here since 1875! The fantasy planet sprinkles fairy dust into your seventh house until October 22, then returns for a longer cycle from January 26, 2026 to March 23, 2039. It's easy to get swept up in romantic idealism now. And hey, there's nothing wrong with a little escapism! Just make sure to keep one Louboutin in the reality zone, too. If you're getting those "too good to be true" vibes, pace yourself. Even attached Libras could get a little lost in the couple bubble during these six months, so don't let those mundane responsibilities slide.

If early spring was rocky, fear not. Venus circles back into Aries from April 30 to June 6, providing a second chance to smooth over any lingering relationship bumps. Initiate open-hearted, "state of the union" conversations.

Stabilizing Saturn will also do a short lap through Aries, from May 24 to September 1, providing a sneak peek of a longer cycle that goes from February 13, 2026 to April 12, 2028. The planet of adulting helps you take a mature approach to love. This might mean having those "What are we building together?" talks or setting some joint financial goals. If you're single, Saturn's influence can help you get super clear about what you're looking for. Saturn will weed out any wishy-washy pipe dreams.

While there will be lots of compromising and co-creating in the first half of the year, you'll get to guide the ship a bit more from late summer into fall. Molten Mars makes its biennial passage through Libra from August 6 to September 22, amping up your charisma and erotic appeal. The thrill of the hunt will be exciting for single Libras. Coupled? Load up the shared calendar with adventurous dates, from skydiving to a weeklong vacation in the jungle.

Venus caps off Q4 with a tour through Libra from October 13 to November 6. You're at your sultriest when your galactic guardian visits your self-directed first house every year. Autonomy (but not absence!) makes the heart grow fonder. Dive back into activities you love, then invite the object of your affection to enjoy SOME of the fun along with you.

LIBRA: LUCKIEST *love* DAY

MAY 22

Venus is rolling through her second wave in Aries, making you absolutely magnetic. Today, she sambas into a free-flowing trine with dance partner Mars, who's shimmying through Leo and your open-minded, experimental eleventh house. Love could appear in the most unexpected places, including a group hangout or an event you drop into "just for the heck of it." Coupled Libras could make big, exciting plans today that shift your relationship into an enviable status.

Money & Career

LIBRA 2025 FORECAST

In 2025 it's not just what you're doing for work, but how you're doing it. On January 11, the lunar North Node shifts into Pisces, cutting the ribbon on an eighteen-month tour through your administrative sixth house. It's time to get organized! This efficiency-boosting cycle can streamline your workflow in ways you haven't experienced for years. If you're already starting to yawn, don't! Pisces energy is dreamy and creative. Soulful. Aesthetic. Picture the beauty of a bookshelf arranged by color or stacked intermittently with "objet" like hunks of crystal, small sculptures or treasures gathered from your travels. A sparse desktop and home screen of neatly categorized folders and subfolders can also do the trick.

As the karmic South Node leaves Libra that very same day, January 11, you'll be more than ready to sort through the rubble of self-excavation that began on July 17, 2023. Some of this deep and profound inner work could begin to inform your career between now and July 26, 2026. A push toward your soul-purpose. A desire to find deeper meaning from your everyday work. Joy in sixth house service—work that might not be seen or recognized, but fills you with a profound connection to humanity. This may not make up the entirety of your professional life, but in 2025, devoting a portion of your path to impact work just feels right.

Simultaneously, you're calling in savvy service providers. Partnerships are your jam, Libra, so find ways to fill in the blanks where you may be struggling. If funds allow, you could hire a professional organizer or monthly housecleaning service. Maybe you barter your photography skills with a graphic designer or create a clear-cut delegation chain with your colleagues.

There's plenty of focus on your high-profile goals, too. Driven Mars basically spends the first four months of the year in Cancer and your ambitious tenth house. Research visionary plans behind the scenes while the red planet is retrograde here from January 6 to February 23. Put ideas through stress tests to see where they break down. When Mars zooms ahead from February 23 to April 18, plans shift into high gear. This is even MORE reason to get your systems in place. When you're trying to crush a top-tier goal, you won't have time to go searching for a boilerplate document or a freakin' stapler!

The momentum crescendos further starting June 9, when enterprising Jupiter soars into Cancer, setting the stage for twelve months of accelerated professional growth. This cycle, which lasts until June 30, 2026, could put you on an express elevator to the top of your game. Experienced Libras could position yourselves as experts, filming TED Talks or speaking at conferences. You could be tenured or tapped for a leadership role. (C-Suite, calling!)

New to the game or ready for a pivot? Jupiter is the zodiac's risk-taker, so this could be the year that you go back to school—especially while Jupiter rounds out its tour of Gemini and your academic ninth house in the first half of 2025. The worldly planet could set the stage for a relocation or regular travel in conjunction with your career. Figure out what broader horizons are calling out to you, Libra, then, spread your wings!

With momentum-builder Mars swinging through Libra from August 6 to September 22, you have a powerful window to pitch any bold ideas or push forward on an initiative. Refine your talking points and make sure you tell people what's in it for THEM. A string of green lights will keep you moving from there.

LIBRA: LUCKIEST *career* DAY

JUNE 24

Modesty is SO overrated—and should be shucked completely this June 24, as the attention-getting Sun unites with larger-than-life Jupiter in Cancer and your tenth house of success. This "Day of Miracles" could get you in good graces with the gatekeepers and VIPs. Make it your mission to impress!

2025
LIBRA

12
MONTH
OVERVIEW

January MONTHLY HOROSCOPE

Home sweet home will be your focus as the Sun shimmers in Capricorn and your domestic fourth house until the 19th. Whether you're putting down roots or pulling up the stakes, you need your space to feel like a sanctuary. On January 11, the lunar South Node leaves your sign. Ahhh. After 18 months of intense karmic growth, you'll be glad to bid this transit farewell. Life feels sweeter and more soulful now as the nodes head into Pisces and Virgo until July 26, 2026. This healing cycle will tune up your body, mind and spirit and help you create a disciplined approach to things that bring you joy and purpose. Career goals may slow temporarily as Mars retrogrades through Cancer from January 6 to February 23. Don't panic! This is a perfect window to finesse your personal brand. The Sun moves into Aquarius on the 19th, rolling out the red carpet in your fifth house of fame and romance. With the Year of the Wood Snake starting on January 29, your tastes could elevate to a new level—who knew that was even possible, Libra?

February MONTHLY HOROSCOPE

You're the breakout star of February, as the Sun shines in your fifth house of fame, fashion and fearless flamboyance until the 18th. Forge ahead with a passion project. Pursue a love interest. Let your playful side take the wheel. While there's no rush to commit, you might find an option that's too good to pass up after February 4. That's when Venus, your ruling planet, embarks on a long tour through Aries, igniting your seventh house of relationships. Partnerships, both romantic and business, heat up! But know this: From March 1 to April 12, Venus will be retrograde. Get ahead of any hiccups by ironing out clear agreements and getting contracts set in stone. Also on February 4, Jupiter turns direct in Gemini, activating your ninth house of expansion and adventure. Travel plans or educational pursuits that have been on hold get the green light now. Your focus shifts to work and wellness after February 18, when the Pisces Sun brings its dreamy-but-detoxifying influence to your sixth house. Refine your routines and streamline your workflow. Your inner mogul takes the wheel after the 23rd, when Mars turns direct in Cancer and powers forward through your ambitious tenth house. Polish up your presentation and go network with the VIPs!

March MONTHLY HOROSCOPE

You're poised for success—no need to compromise—as the imaginative Pisces Sun energizes your sixth house of daily work and wellness until March 20. But don't get lost in the grind, Libra! Your Aries-ruled seventh house of relationships is being stirred up, demanding some careful consideration in your partnerships. With both Venus and Mercury retrograde in Aries this month—Venus from March 1 to 27 and Mercury from March 15 to 29—you could face some confusion in your closest relationships. It's time to reassess the balance in your connections. Are you giving too much, or not enough? This month is your cosmic call to restore equilibrium. Home and family matters come into sharp focus during the March 14 Virgo lunar eclipse. No more sweeping things under the rug—it's time to confront what's been brewing. As the Sun enters Aries on the 20th, you'll feel the pull to fine-tune your approach to partnerships, whether romantic or professional. The Aries solar eclipse on March 29 marks the final chapter of a two-year eclipse cycle in your seventh house, offering a powerful moment to let go of any lingering relationship drama or toxic dynamics. Then, on March 30, Neptune enters Aries for the first time since 1875, kicking off a 14-year cycle of spiritual growth and deepened connections. Stay open to unexpected, serendipitous encounters. This could be the moment you manifest the perfect partner or collaboration to spring forth between now and October 22.

April MONTHLY HOROSCOPE

The Sun is powering through your seventh house of relationships until April 19, putting your partnerships in the spotlight. Simultaneously there's some self-care work to do, so save a little space on the calendar for "me, myself and I." Mercury is retrograde in Pisces and your sixth house of health and routines until April 7, with Venus retrograde there until April 12. Reassess how you're balancing your day-to-day life. Are you setting clear boundaries between your work time and rest time? Eating clean and moving your body? Try not to take on any huge assignments until those retrogrades clear, but if you have to, take extra pains to map out your accountabilities to the letter. April 12 will be an epic day. Your ruler, Venus, snaps out of retrograde AND the year's only full moon in Libra brings a huge burst of attention your way. Be ready for a big reveal or just put yourself out there with people who will appreciate what you have to offer. Mars roars into Leo on April 18, heating up your eleventh house of social connections and teamwork until June 17. Rally a supergroup for a world-changing project and network like a boss. As Taurus season begins on April 19, your eighth house of intimacy and shared resources takes over, shifting your focus toward deeper connections and financial matters. This sultry cycle could draw in a soulmate or an investor who wants to fund one of your business ideas. Private time will be inspiring, sexy and insanely creative. Put your phone in airplane mode and do your thing!

May MONTHLY HOROSCOPE

The Taurus Sun beams in your intimate eighth house until May 20, inviting you to deepen emotional connections and strengthen your financial foundations. This annual phase is prime time to explore joint ventures, investments and trust-building with those closest to you. But as Pluto spins retrograde in Aquarius starting May 4, you'll need to stay on top of your creative flow. With the regenerative planet in snooze mode in your fifth house of passion and self-expression until October 13, don't let burnout stifle your imagination. Find clever ways to spark your creativity, like traveling with a journal or experimenting with new art mediums. On May 20, the Sun shifts into Gemini and your expansive ninth house of travel and learning. You'll be eager to broaden your horizons—whether that means booking an adventure, signing up for a course or diving into an exciting new project. Life could take a serious turn starting May 24, when Saturn slips into Aries and sets up camp in your partnership-focused seventh house for four months. Saturn's steady, disciplined energy will push you to commit to relationships and collaborations that can go the distance. Whether in love or business, it's time to build something lasting and make long-term plans.

June MONTHLY HOROSCOPE

Your adventurous spirit is on fire until June 20th as the Gemini Sun beams into your nomadic, expansive ninth house. Traveling is your jam this month, so detour away from the familiar any chance you get. Casual conversations quickly spin into deep, philosophical explorations, which can happen anywhere from an airport lounge to a buzzy public marketplace. Wherever wanderlust leads you, don't stray from your Wi-Fi signal for too long. On the 9th, enterprising Jupiter leaps to the top of your chart, moving into Cancer and your career zone for the first time since 2014. This momentous yearlong cycle could bring epic opportunities for professional growth, recognition and success. Partners may get threatened by your ambitions when Jupiter squares Saturn, then Neptune, on the 15th and 18th, respectively. Try not to bring shop talk into EVERY conversation, especially when you're off duty. On the 20th, summer solstice, the Sun joins Jupiter in Cancer, setting you up for four weeks of poolside power lunches and elite invitations. A golden opportunity to elevate your status could land in your lap on the 24th, when the Sun and Jupiter unite for The Day of Miracles. Staying balanced is always the goal, and these external pressures can be a lot for your sensitive sign. Fortunately, wired Mars settles into Virgo from June 17 to August 6, powering down in your twelfth house of healing restoration. Spa days, massages, daily meditation—set blocks in your schedule for essential self-care. This Mars cycle is also prime time to refine some of your plans behind the scenes. Pace yourself. Not everything has to be debuted right away!

July MONTHLY HOROSCOPE

Keep your eye on the target, Libra. Career goals zoom ahead at a fast and furious pace while the Sun sails alongside lucky Jupiter in Cancer until the 22nd. With your tenth house of ambition and public recognition getting lit, don't allow yourself to be distracted from YOUR top-tier goals. We'd never suggest you stop supporting others, but you may need to dial back that ratio a bit, in the name of not squandering this key time for personal advancement. On July 7th, side-spinning Uranus moves into Gemini for a six-month preview tour through your worldly, wisdom-seeking ninth house. This philosophical cycle, which picks up again from April 2026 to May 2033, is bound to be an expansive one in every sense of the word. Get ready to break free from old beliefs and claim a new worldview through travel, higher education or a philosophical shift. (And like many Libra authors from bell hooks to Truman Capote, your unique perspective could make it to print.) Don't expect everyone to agree with your perspective; in fact, a few relationships could grow rocky as Neptune, Saturn and Chiron all turn retrograde in Aries (on the 4th, 13th and 30th, respectively), provoking idealistic differences for the next five months. Alas, "agreeing to disagree" may be too thin of a solution. Friendships both new and old are in the spotlight in the latter part of the month. When the Sun swings into Leo on July 22, invitations pour in and you'll be ready to bond with the changemakers, thought leaders and activists. Don't leave your standby squad in the lurch though, Libra! With Mercury spinning retrograde through Leo from July 18 to August 11, your crew may need to come together for midsummer love and support. Since the eleventh house is the tech sector, strengthen your passwords and be extra mindful of what you post to avoid getting misunderstood and canceled.

August MONTHLY HOROSCOPE

You're in full-on social butterfly mode as August kicks off. With the Sun in Leo shining through your eleventh house of community and networking until August 22, you'll be on everyone's invite list. Circulate widely, but remember that Mercury will still be retrograde until August 11 (also in Leo), which could bring friction within existing teams. On the plus side, this period paves the way for fulfilling reconnections. Time to get the band back together for one more reunion tour? While you're out working the beach barbecue circuit, don't shy away from shop talk. With convivial Venus in Cancer and your career zone until August 25, a casual conversation could pave the way toward a professional victory. It's all about who you know! Reserve a little whitespace for spontaneous, unscripted adventure. Thrill seeking Mars bursts into Libra from August 6 to September 22, making its biennial lap through your first house of self-discovery. This charismatic cycle pegs you as a passionate leader. People will follow you, so make sure you know where you're guiding them if you take the helm! When Virgo season begins on August 22, the energy shifts to your inner world. While the Sun streams through your twelfth house of rest, closure and healing for four weeks, give yourself time to process all the developments in your life before your birthday season begins on September 22. The following day, August 23, brings the first of two rare, back-to-back new moons in Virgo. What do you need to gently release, Libra? Whether it's an outdated belief, an emotional block or a chapter that's run its course, use this fresh-start energy to prepare yourself for an even bigger reset with the solar (new moon) eclipse in Virgo on September 21.

September MONTHLY HOROSCOPE

Your quest for truth could lead you down the rabbit hole while the Virgo Sun tunnels through your subterranean twelfth house until September 22. Befuddling? Yes, but embrace the process! Adventurous Mars is in your sign until the 22nd, which makes you game to explore every facet of your personality. How about a retreat or personal growth workshop? With Venus in Leo until the 19th, you'll thrive in a group setting devoted to discovery. While you're at it, do sessions with coaches and healers to help bring those buried parts of your soul to illumination. Two eclipses support this mission. The first one, a total lunar eclipse with the September 7 full moon in Pisces, highlights the mind-body connection. How you eat, sleep and care for yourself on a daily basis could be affecting you more than you realize. Tweaking even one of these things can have a seismic effect, especially since Saturn retrogrades back into Pisces on September 1. The second eclipse, with the new moon in Virgo, on the 21st, helps you shed limiting beliefs and get a handle on addictive patterns that are blocking joy. You may decide to cut ties with an energy vampire or a situation that's officially toxic. On September 6, renegade Uranus turns retrograde in Gemini, which could throw a wrench into a few of your expansion plans. You may need to reschedule a trip or event for some time after November 7, when the side-spinning planet tucks into Taurus. Roll with it, because trying to force things will only bring chaos. Libra season kicks off on the 22nd with the autumn equinox, putting you back on the level ground your sign prefers. With feisty Mars exiting your sign the same day, you'll be happy to have some of the heat off of you. Focus on setting up comfortable routines that bring a sense of peace and security. That's anything BUT boring now!

October MONTHLY HOROSCOPE

Birthday season is in full swing while the Sun beams into Libra until October 22. This is the time to experiment wildly, explore novel activities and pamper yourself in the apologetic manner that you richly deserve. By the time the new moon in Libra arrives on October 21, you'll know just what intentions to set in order to kick off an exciting six-month cycle of personal development. Your ruler, ardent Venus, also sweeps into your sign on the 13th, turning you into a viral romantic sensation. If you were feeling neglected, invisible or passed over in any way earlier this month, that all changes now. And when magnetic Pluto turns direct in Aquarius and your fifth house of fame and fierce expression (also on the 13th), you'll get your "revenge" by simply stepping out of the shadows and sharing your brilliant vision, style and personality. Scorpio season begins on the 22nd, helping you turn all your birthday season findings into something tangible—and profitable. This money-motivated four-week cycle can get you back onto a smart budget, while also supporting you with attracting new income streams. Some of this work may be less glamorous than you'd prefer, but if it puts food on the table (and plumps up your entertainment fund), it will be well worth the hustle. Also on the 22nd, Neptune retrogrades back into Pisces for the remainder of its backspin, until December 10. Holistic healing modalities and preventative medicine (sleep, exercise, vitamins) will keep you humming like a well-oiled machine. Give your body some love!

November MONTHLY HOROSCOPE

Security and stability? Yes, please. Prioritize the practical as the Scorpio Sun weaves through your second house of finances, values and material resources until the 21st. Sort out your schedule, wrangle spending into a budget and simplify areas of life that have grown too complex. Not that you can't enjoy a taste of luxury. Your covetous cosmic ruler, Venus, nestles into Scorpio from November 6 to 30, sanctioning a splurge or two. Opt for treasures that you could justify as "investment pieces." As a Libra, the best things in life are also people and places, ones that hold a sentimental value. The "cheap thrill" of a conversation or an afternoon at the library can keep you in good spirits while energetic Mars sweeps into Sagittarius and your social, intellectual third house for six weeks on the 4th. Writing, podcasting, designing workshops—these are all things that get a burst of speed from Mars between now and December 15. One communication caveat: Mercury pivots into a retrograde from November 9 to 29th, scrambling signals in Sagittarius and your vocal third house until the 18th, then causing money mixups in Scorpio after that. This is not the time to overcommit yourself, especially when it comes to work or social obligations. Be patient, curb impulsive texting, and save those receipts! Adding to the cosmic shifts, unpredictable Uranus retrogrades back from Gemini into Taurus on November 7. There could be a curveball to contend with around joint ventures, investments or deep emotional connections, so stay flexible. On November 11, expansive Jupiter turns retrograde in Cancer for four months, which may slow a professional initiative. Use this period to fortify connections with the VIPs and refine your ambitious project plans. Fortunately, structured Saturn ends its five-month retrograde in Pisces on November 27, powering forward in your sixth house of work and wellness. Sure, it might be holiday season, but you'll feel inspired to reinstate some healthy routines and structures so that you can wrap up the year on a productive note!

December MONTHLY HOROSCOPE

'Tis the season to be a superconnector! The Sagittarius Sun beams vibrant energy into your third house of communication, peers and local activities until December 21, but that's not all! Excitable Mars and Venus are also zinging through the Archer's domain, until the 15th and 24th, respectively. Gatherings will be as cheer-filled as you make them, Libra. Bring people together for Secret Santa swaps, charity food drives and general revelry. Mistletoe moments can catch you by surprise as a friend could cop to a crush. (Swoon!) Coupled Libras will enjoy socializing together with a calendar full of cultural activities.

On the 10th, hazy Neptune snaps out of retrograde and forges ahead in Pisces, your administrative sixth house. Get a handle on outstanding tasks that are taking up real estate in your head and delegate what you can. Healthy habits feel easier to embrace (yes, even during the holidays), and you'll be more inspired to take care of your mind, body and spirit. Cozy, loving energy takes hold once passionate Mars heads into Capricorn on December 15, energizing your fourth house of home, family and emotional roots. With the Sun joining Mars in Capricorn on the winter solstice this December 21, followed by Venus on the 24th, you're all about creating warmth and comfort for the people you love most. You'll be the heart and soul of any gathering, so bring on the nostalgic decor, intergenerational playlists and toasts that won't leave a dry eye in the house. As New Year's Eve approaches, consider swapping the glitzy party scene for something more intimate. This year, an intimate dinner party or reflective ceremony could feel more like your jam. Live music, a Libra favorite, could also be the perfect way to step into 2026 with your heart open and your soul singing!

Read your extended monthly forecast for life, love, money and career! astrostyle.com

A LITTLE ABOUT Scorpio

DATES October 22 - November 21

SYMBOL The Scorpion

ELEMENT Water

QUALITY Fixed

RULING PLANET Pluto, Mars

BODY PART Reproductive system

BEST TRAITS
Magnetic, passionate, loyal, protective, trendsetting, intuitive, observant, mysterious, introspective, savvy, resourceful

KEYWORDS
Intimacy, secrecy, power, intensity, seduction, spirituality, transformation, wealth

Read more about Scorpio

SCORPIO
IN 2025

ALL THE PLANETS IN SCORPIO IN 2025	YOUR 2025 HOROSCOPE	TOP 5 THEMES FOR SCORPIO IN 2025	LOVE HOROSCOPE + LUCKY DATES	MONEY HOROSCOPE + LUCKY DATES

Scorpio in 2025

YOUR YEARLY OVERVIEW

You're in your sultry, mysterious element this year, Scorpio. Werk! Two of the most adventurous, experimental planets—Jupiter and Uranus— each take a six-month plunge into Gemini, sending ripples through your eighth house of transformation, intimacy and shared resources. From passionate relationships to joint investments, you're ready (eager, even) to explore new ways to combine forces. As intense as this can be, you don't have to worry about drowning in melancholy. Starting January 11, the destiny-fueling North Node drifts into Pisces, revving your starpower and setting you up for eighteen months of fun, flirtation and fame. This could be the year you get signed to a label or your art gets hung in a prestigious gallery. Romantically, expect plenty of highs as you make room for joy and unapologetic self-expression. Meanwhile, the South Node in Virgo nudges you to step back from overwhelming group commitments. Let go of social obligations that drain your energy and cultivate connections that feed your soul. If a far-flung corner of the world starts calling after June 9, thank Jupiter. For the first time since 2014, the red-spotted planet boards a flight through Cancer, jetting through your worldly ninth house until June 30, 2026. Say yes to experiences that broaden your horizons, like doing a few months as a digital nomad or signing up for a semester of school. A life-changing trip could also be in the cards so start researching and learning the language!

THE PLANETS IN Scorpio

THE SUN
OCT 22–NOV 21

It's birthday season for you, so step out and shine! Seek novelty and take extra initiative during this radiant monthlong phase.

NEW MOON
NOV 20
1:47AM, 28°12'

Bonus New Year! Set your intentions for the next six months and get into action.

FULL MOON
MAY 12
12:56PM, 22°13'

Ready, set, manifest! Your work of the past six months bears fruit and it's time to harvest the rewards.

MERCURY
OCT 6–29
NOV 18–DEC 11
RETROGRADE IN SCORPIO:
NOV 18–29

Crown yourself monarch of the social butterflies when popularity-boosting Mercury visits your sign once a year. Circulate and get social. During the retrograde, be careful not to make promises you can't keep or allow energy vampires into your sphere.

VENUS
NOV 6–30

You've got the romantic It Factor when the galactic glamazon charges up your powers of seduction each year. Willpower is weak in the face of beauty and luxury. Watch your spending!

MARS
SEP 22–NOV 4

Motivation is high when energetic Mars visits your sign every couple years—but check your combative streak and try not to come on too strong.

Scorpio in 2025

HIGHLIGHTS

JUPITER AND URANUS IN GEMINI SPARK A REVOLUTION FROM WITHIN

Your spiritual landscape has always been rich, Scorpio. Peer inward. Two of the most intrepid planets, Jupiter and Uranus, spend nearly half the year in Gemini and your alchemical eighth house. Their invitation? Mine your potent internal assets and you're sure to discover pure, shimmering gold. Feelings that may have stopped you in your tracks before are now welcome guests at the table: trust issues, vulnerability, power struggles, abandonment fears, control. Like an archaeologist, you can put on the nitrile gloves, dust them off with an ultrafine brush and examine them for historical context. In so doing, you have the power to free yourself from the grips of intergenerational trauma and lore.

MONEY, POWER, SEX: A NEW APPROACH TO THIS TRIFECTA

The eighth house, which is a lot like Scorpio, the eighth sign, is concerned with money, sex, power and the way joint resources are invested and allocated. This is comfortable terrain for you! But with free-spirits Jupiter and Uranus both spending time here (Jupiter until June 9 and Uranus from July 7 to November 7), there's an experimental element in the mix. If, like megastar Chappell Roan, "your kink is karma," you may need to change your tune. Dissecting the past in order to move forward is one thing. Dwelling on it and staying stuck? Not under these forward-thinking planets' watch. A new attitude is emerging. Before the year is through, you could be climbing into bed with a new type of partner—literally, financially or metaphorically. Hint: They may be more of an equal partner than someone who worships you or who you hoist onto a pedestal.

GLOBAL ADVENTURES CALL: JUPITER IN CANCER

If all this sounds intense and heavy, even for you, Scorpio, here's some news you'll love hearing. Starting June 9, Jupiter sails into Cancer and your uplifting, expansive ninth house. The world becomes your oyster and those treasure-hunting instincts of yours are back in the rarest form they've been in for over a decade. Pearls of wisdom can be collected anywhere from a plant medicine retreat in the jungle to the ivy-covered halls of a university quad. Independent quests will be as essential to your happiness as shared ones, so make sure you're feeding your autonomous spirit, too. Take a solo trip abroad,

Your spiritual landscape has always been rich, Scorpio. Peer inward. Two of the most intrepid planets, Jupiter and Uranus, spend nearly half the year in Gemini and your alchemical eighth house. Their invitation? Mine your potent internal assets and you're sure to discover pure, shimmering gold. Feelings that may have stopped you in your tracks before are now welcome guests at the table: trust issues, vulnerability, power struggles, abandonment fears, control. Like an archaeologist,

you can put on the nitrile gloves, dust them off with an ultrafine brush and examine them for historical context. In so doing, you have the power to free yourself from the grips of intergenerational trauma and lore. rent a studio to develop your art or music, write a memoir or start your side hustle in earnest. The doors of opportunity are open wide!

JOY RISING: THE LUNAR NODES IN PISCES AND VIRGO

Starting January 11, the fateful North Node heads into Pisces and your fifth house of fame and creative expression where it will push you out of the shadows until July 26, 2026. Consider this your permission slip to dive headfirst into your passions. The universe wants you to prioritize what makes your heart sing, Scorpio, and it's not about perfection or practicality right now. It's about raw, unapologetic expression. Across the aisle, the karmic South Node in Virgo urges you to loosen your grip around social expectations and group obligations. If you've been too wrapped up in organizational politics, or playing fixer in your social circles, it's time to release that weight. You're not here to please everyone or be the glue that holds everything together. This year, it's about focusing on your individual desires, even if that means saying no to people who expect too much from you.

DREAM BIG, WORK HARD: SATURN AND NEPTUNE IN ARIES

Two outer planets dart forward from Pisces into Aries for part of this year, moving their energy out of your playful fifth house and into your disciplined sixth. From March 30 to October 22, dreamy Neptune makes its first pass through Aries, previewing a longer journey that will go from January 26, 2026 to March 23, 2039. Stable Saturn will zoom through Aries from May 24 to September 1, a cycle that picks up again for two years starting February 13, 2026. As they combine their energies (even for a glimpse of time), you'll be pumped to streamline your daily routines—and in a way that also makes room for a magical, even spiritual, flow. This cosmic duo might feel like a push-pull, but really, they're asking you to integrate both. How can you create daily habits that not only get the job done but also nourish your soul? Begin to master the art of turning your everyday life into something meaningful and aligned with your higher purpose.

TOP 5 THEMES FOR Scorpio in 2025

1	2	3	4	5
GET CURIOUS (AND CURIOUSER)	SOAR OUT OF YOUR COMFORT ZONE	ADD SOUL TO YOUR GOALS	LOVE YOUR BODY	REVITALIZE YOUR ROMANTIC STREAK

1 GET CURIOUS (AND CURIOUSER)

JUPITER AND URANUS IN GEMINI

JUPITER: MAY 25, 2024 – JUNE 9, 2025
URANUS: JULY 7 – NOVEMBER 7, 2025 • JANUARY 26, 2026 – MAY 22, 2033

You might want to upgrade your snorkel gear to scuba, Scorpio. Two of the most adventurous, experimental planets lure you deeper than even you might normally go— and that's saying something. Until June 9, intrepid Jupiter sends you on a journey 20,000 leagues below the sea as it continues its trek through Gemini and your mysterious, seductive eighth house. On July 7, rebellious Uranus follows suit for four months, taking a quick preview lap into Gemini for the first time in, oh, 76 years. This exciting plunge will teach you so many things about how to be both free and connected at once, a paradox that any Scorpio is sure to understand.

JUPITER IN GEMINI

MAY 25, 2024 – JUNE 9, 2025

There's no limit to your mystical, seductive powers as 2025 opens up. Wield them with care and enjoy the #^$% outta them. Abundant Jupiter is midway through its 13-month trek through Gemini and your sultry eighth house (AKA "the Scorpio house"). You're in your element, Scorpio, which means you can turn up the volume on traits you might have felt the need to dial down in the past. Your intensity. Your thirst for extremes. Your obsessive curiosity. Your desire for deep and powerful bonding. All of it.

There's a solid chance you're already tapping this rich vein of alchemical energy. Bountiful Jupiter has been cruising through inquisitive Gemini since May 25, 2024—and it's solidly there until this coming June 9. Since you're at the halfway mark of the transit, use the early part of 2025 to "sort the crops."

What and who have you magnetized since mid-2024? Are these situations adding to your quality of life? Our friend and literary agent Jackie has a great metric: Is it a fountain or a drain? In other words, if it's not causing you to bubble over with excitement, it might be sucking on your valuable time, resources and energy. Jupiter is retrograde until February 4, which is the perfect period of time for this assessment. You might be traveling with a lighter pack (and pack of friends) when Jupiter resumes forward motion in early February, and what a relief that will be.

Love and sex? Make that a double. We'd be remiss if we didn't underscore how potent this Jupiter cycle can be for your erotic life. Add Jupiter's philosophical, exploratory energy to Gemini's insatiable curiosity and pour it all into your soul-merging eighth house. That's a recipe for some truly mind-blowing encounters. Whether you share them with a monogamous partner, explore them through workshops, study tantra or simply find a way to experience this on your own is fully up to you. Whatever the case, make sure you give your erotic identity some airplay this year. Despite your reputation as the zodiac's sex sign, you can have long drought periods. Sex can be so all-consuming for you, Scorpio. When the demands of life pull you in different directions, you often feel like you "can't afford" to give it your full focus so, instead, you give it none. Try letting go of the idea that sex has to be such an extreme experience, Scorpio. With fast-moving Jupiter in the frame, you might master the art of the mind-blowing quickie!

If you've been keeping your creative talents under wraps, it's time to "out" yourself. Worldly, expressive Jupiter beckons you to share your magic with a wide public. Even if the locals don't get your magic, you could become huge in South America, Europe or down under. Scorpios who prefer to remain BTS should tap influencers and friends with the hookup to spread the word of your offerings. A global guerrilla marketing team can turn your quietly developed, underground ideas into a cult classic.

Since the eighth house rules joint ventures, entrepreneurial Jupiter could attract funders who want to invest in your dreams. It might be time to combine resources (including finances) with like-minded people for a major win-win. Another possibility? You could invest your savings in a startup that you truly believe in, and help bankroll someone else's success, and by extension, your own.

Romantic partners may be ready to take their first significant "merging" steps by sharing assets, opening a joint bank account or co-signing legal documents, like a lease or mortgage. It's a better time to pay off debt than accumulate more. But if you are under water, with lucky Jupiter in this position, you could negotiate a settlement or a repayment plan and redeem your credit rating. On the plus side, you could receive an inheritance, commission check or other lump sum of cash. What NOT to do? Blow it on something frivolous. A crypto token saved is a crypto token earned.

URANUS IN GEMINI

JULY 7 – NOVEMBER 7, 2025
JANUARY 26, 2026 – MAY 22, 2033

Can you sync your higher mind with your lower regions? Sounds like #ScorpioGoals to us. And you might hit that target in your direct sight line, starting this July 7. That day, experimental Uranus sidespins into Gemini and activates your mystical, metaphysical, erotic eighth house.

Life gets soulfully sexy during this four-month cycle, which lasts until November 7, 2025. Don't worry, Scorpio: This is just the beginning. Next year, on April 25, 2026, the radical planet plugs back into the Gemini grid for seven full years, until May 22, 2033. It's safe to assume that this next phase of life will be full of emotional, sexual and alchemical experiences that will shape you in ways you can't even begin to predict.

Uranus hasn't been in Gemini since the 1940s, so this is a rare opportunity to call in people and situations that can keep you transfixed for more than a couple interactions. True passion can't be faked, and scenarios may arise to show you how meaningless inauthentic behavior is. Regardless of your current partnership status, stay open to experimentation and be willing to "go there" under the right circumstances. Starting or amping up a spiritual practice will keep you grounded and give you clarity when things get hard to fathom. Tantra, kundalini meditations and any sort of energetic practice will do wonders for your sexual identity, no partner required.

There's a paradox to contend with here. Gemini energy is curious, distractible and loves variety. Meanwhile the eighth house—AKA "the Scorpio house" since it shares many similar qualities to the eighth zodiac sign (yours!)—wants you to plunge in deep, set up a spiritual outpost and get to know every nuance of a situation. Your job during this Uranus cycle is to learn to balance levity with commitment. Dare we say it, Scorpio, you need to lighten up about relationships!

Stay aware, and you will be treated to plenty of priceless life lessons. One of them may involve breaking your Scorpio habit of trying to quietly intuit other people's needs instead of coming out and asking direct questions. How many hours have you wasted privately analyzing people's motives, only to discover later that they had no agenda, no preconceived notions. They were just clueless about your needs.

Uranus in loquacious Gemini will pique your journalistic curiosity and give you the courage to say what's on your mind. The words might even slip out unintended, so get ready to blush a few times. No one suffers a worse vulnerability hangover than you. But Uranus in Gemini is laying down the law: It's time to build some inner resilience to perceived "fails." Your world won't fall apart because of a hopelessly awkward or embarrassing moment. Nor are you doomed if you bare your soul to a plebe who can't match your emotional depth. Or you pitch your passion project to a boardroom full of blank stares.

Far more painful is your habit of putting yourself into emotional purgatory after you said "the wrong thing" or "pushed someone away" or "blew an opportunity." We've known Scorpios who suffer for years from their own self-flagellation, even swearing off relationships, because of one gut-wrenching experience. And while we do understand (we have a four-planet Scorpio stellium), we also wish we could pull our incredible Scorpio friends out of their suffering and place them back onto the field to find the deep connections they deserve.

And here's where lightning-quick, edgy Uranus in Gemini can lend a hand! While the heady planet spins through cheeky Gemini, you may finally gain the ability to laugh at your own humanity. (And not just snark about other people's missteps in moments of gleeful schadenfreude—although Uranus in Gemini will serve plenty of those, too.)

The good news is, you have eight years to work this out, meaning it's a marathon, not a sprint. So start here in 2025: Pick one relationship habit that you're ready to break and see if you can bring a little humor to it. Name that part of you who takes the wheel, "Desperate Darcy" or "Thirsty Thurston" or "Grade-Grubbing Gretchen." Since Gemini is the sign that rules our besties, score extra credit points by getting a few of your friends in on this game. Along with some deep belly laughs, you might just gain deep compassion for the sides of your personality you once tried to push away. Ah, progress!

2 SOAR OUT OF YOUR COMFORT ZONE

JUPITER IN CANCER
JUNE 9, 2025 – JUNE 30, 2026

Flying under the radar won't be an option after June 9. In fact, you might be flying the friendly skies as jetsetting Jupiter emerges from the hidden depths of your eighth house and soars into the blue skies of your optimistic, adventurous Cancer-ruled ninth.

Get ready to gain some serious altitude in every area of your life during this yearlong cycle. The red-spotted titan hasn't toured this realm since June 25, 2013 to July 16, 2014, so flip back to that era for clues about what may lie ahead. Jupiter is exalted in Cancer, meaning it's most powerful in this zodiac position. And since the Crab is a fellow water sign, you're bound to feel in your element once you get your "sea legs" for this journey. But that's not all. The ninth house is Jupiter's favorite place to hang out, since both are associated with travel, philosophy, entrepreneurship and publishing.

Yes, Scorpio, you could be the breakout star of the second half of 2025 and well into the next year. Jupiter flows through Cancer until June 30, 2026, giving you nearly thirteen months to soak up the positive vibes.

Introverted Scorpios, here's a tip: Don't resist the pull from private to public that may come from this shift. Instead, devise a few coping strategies, like setting shorter appointments, bringing a wingperson along to parties and meeting people in familiar spaces whenever possible. The social discomfort will pass quickly. A more likely scenario is that you'll be far too busy vibing with all the new opportunities and networks to be self-conscious for long.

Make sure your passport is up to date and consider getting approved for TSA pre-check. With worldly Jupiter in your nomadic ninth house, you could be attending global conferences and drumming up business on all corners of the Earth. If you're a creator, your work could be informed by ancient philosophies or traditions from your cultural heritage.

Teachable moments ahead! And we mean that in so many ways. For one thing, higher education falls under the domain of both philosophical Jupiter and the ninth house. The ivy tower of academia could call you back to a degree program or podium to pass on your hard-won wisdom. If you've ever thought of producing a TED talk, carpe diem. Any topic relating to international relations will be especially well-received. Same goes for media. This is prime time to score a book deal, pitch a pilot or get a media literacy grant to support people in an underserved community.

You could also be on the receiving end of a few key lessons yourself. Jupiter in the ninth house pours liberal shots of truth serum, making it hard for you to bite your tongue—or retract your notorious stinger. But with Jupiter in sensitive Cancer, most people won't be down for that sort of tough (make that, brutal) love. Learning to get your point across without doing collateral damage could be one of the most important lessons of this cycle.

For the most part, Jupiter in Cancer could feel like one of the luckiest eras you've had in a while. During this freeing transit, it's almost impossible to be anything but your truest self. While yes, that may cause a few vulnerability hangovers here and there, your relationships become richer as a result of your openness. Authenticity may become a bigger aphrodisiac than mystery, at least for these thirteen months. Enjoy this shift!

♏

3

ADD SOUL TO YOUR GOALS

SATURN AND NEPTUNE IN ARIES

NEPTUNE: MARCH 30 – OCTOBER 22, 2025 • JANUARY 26, 2026 – MARCH 23, 2039
SATURN: MAY 24 – SEPTEMBER 1, 2025 • FEBRUARY 13, 2026 – APRIL 12, 2028

Your body is a wonderland, Scorpio, and no one's arguing with that. (Oh hello, you sexy beast!) But starting this spring, the planets have an updated memo. Your body is also your temple and your soul's address here on planet Earth. This planetary PSA comes courtesy of two slow-moving outer titans: structured Saturn and spiritual Neptune. For a brief period this year, both will plunge forward from Pisces into Aries, then back into Pisces again for one final lap.

First up is Neptune, who dips into Aries and your sixth house of daily routines from March 30 to October 22. Talk about a sea change! Since this is Neptune's first visit to the

Ram's realm since 1862 to 1875, we've never experienced this energy in our lifetimes. Following suit is taskmaster Saturn, who does a shorter, three-month marathon through Aries from May 24 to September 1. We haven't experienced Saturn in Aries in nearly three decades, so this is also going to feel quite new.

Whatever gets charged up this year is a preview of what's ahead. In 2026, both Neptune and Saturn embark on longer treks through Aries, for thirteen and two more years, respectively. As these planets move out of the familiar watery vibes of Pisces and into the forward-thrusting fire of Aries, it could take your sensitive sign a moment to regain your bearings. Keep the pressure off of yourself to nail this new groove in 2025. Instead, take notes and embrace the process of exploring fresh ways to move through your day-to-day life.

NEPTUNE IN ARIES
MARCH 30 – OCTOBER 22, 2025
JANUARY 26, 2026 – MARCH 23, 2039

Get ready to add more "flow" into your "workflow," starting March 30, when fluid Neptune switches signs for a brief, six-month spell. For the first time since 1875 (yes!), the dreamweaving planet darts into Aries, activating your sixth house of health, wellness, and daily routines until October 22.

When Neptune's ethereal energy meets the fiery drive of Aries in the part of your chart that governs your day-to-day life, so much can change! You're entering a period where you're called to reimagine your approach to self-care, work, and how you structure your daily grind. This is a significant shift for you, Scorpio, one that you'll only get a brief taste of in 2025. Take notes of what occurs between March 30 and October 22. On January 26, 2026, Neptune will plant itself in Aries for an unbroken thirteen-year lap, which drifts on until March 23, 2039!

As a lifelong seeker, you've never been one to just go through the motions. That said, you tend to channel your intense focus toward one or two key areas of life. While Neptune's been paddling through Pisces since 2011, much of its imagination-boosting energy spilled into your romantic and artistic life. Now, the focus moves to a different space: work and wellness.

If your professional life has been ho-hum in recent years, Neptune's trek through Aries can reignite the spark. You don't necessarily have to change jobs (although you might), but you WILL crave a deeper sense of purpose from your vocation. Slowly but surely,

Neptune can help you uncover meaningful and creative ways to contribute to your daily tasks.

Ready to pursue a new path? The sixth house is the "service sector" of the zodiac, which could draw you toward humble work that aligns with your spiritual values. Jobs that fall in the essential worker category—teaching, elder care, infrastructure work—may appeal to some Scorpios. Others among you may be intrigued by the healing arts, working as wellness practitioners, medics, massage therapists, nutritionists and the like. In the professional sector? Neptune in Aries could call you toward impact-driven work or inspire you to add a socially responsible spin to your current offerings.

A fat paycheck is always a plus, but it might not be the primary pull between now and 2039. That's not to say you can't get paid for doing what you love. Neptune is the planet of sacrifices and when it tours the sixth house, it can cause you to undervalue what you do. (Watch out for that!) Fortunately, Aries is a sign with a healthy amount of entitlement. Neptune's placement here can balance out any self-worth issues that may arise when you hit the negotiating table.

If money is no object in your life, you might even consider taking six months off to do a skills-building apprenticeship. Even if the hands-on experience is your only payment, consider the long-term gains of kneeling at the feet of a master who passes down generations of wisdom to you.

Or...keep your corporate job if that's what puts food on the table. Then, consider filling your off-duty time with volunteer work, perhaps starting your own charity, non-profit or industry networking group. As long as you keep a healthy amount of time for recharging, this will fill your cup.

Be mindful of Neptune's tendency to cast a fog over reality. In the sixth house, this can manifest as disorganization or a lack of focus on the details. It's crucial to stay vigilant about maintaining your routines, even as you explore more creative and spiritual approaches to your work and health. Implementing systems that help you stay on track, like to-do lists or regular check-ins, can be incredibly helpful during this time. These small, structured steps will keep you anchored as you navigate Neptune's dreamy waters.

Another Neptune-in-Aries pitfall? Idealism that leads to perfectionism. Nothing wrong with wanting to build a viral, indie brand like the world has never seen, Scorpio. Equally crucial? Balancing your inspired visions with practical steps to avoid burnout or frustration when reality doesn't match your dreams.

Speaking of burnout, Neptune in Aries is a time where stress-management is critical. Any planet in Aries can fire up your ambition but the competitive vibes can cause you to push yourself too hard and tax your adrenals. Reassess your relationship with productivity. You may find that your usual go-getter approach needs a more intuitive, go-with-the-flow adjustment. Instead of pushing through fatigue or stress, listen to your body's signals and prioritize self-care routines that nurture both your physical and spiritual health.

While Neptune's influence can sometimes bring confusion or a lack of clarity, it can also open you up to spiritual ways of taking care of your body and mind. Pay attention to subtle signals from your body, and don't ignore the messages from your subconscious—they could lead you to a breakthrough in how you manage stress or maintain balance.

While there's no replacing Western MDs for some ailments, Neptune in Aries could lead you to explore alternative healing methods, such as energy work, meditation, or holistic therapies. Think of them as preventative medicine, tuning and toning your system.

If you do nothing else with Neptune's six-month plunge out of Pisces and into Aries, rethink your daily rituals. Mindfulness is key with Neptune in Aries. Whether it's your exercise regimen or how you prepare your meals, bake in creativity and imagination. Daily life can be as magical and meaningful as you choose to make it, Scorpio, so start creating practices that truly resonate with your soul.

SATURN IN ARIES
MAY 24 – SEPTEMBER 1, 2025
FEBRUARY 13, 2026 – APRIL 12, 2028

How far will you go to get the gold, Scorpio? Whether you wear it like a badge of pride or wield it like a secret weapon, your competitive spirit is indomitable! Now for some news that could switch up your whole game: How you score the metaphoric metal is set to change starting May 24, when drill sergeant Saturn returns to Aries and your disciplined sixth house, its first visit here since 1996 to 1998.

Saturn will only pre-game in Aries for a few months this year, from May 24 until September 1. If nothing else, this gives you a glimpse of what lies ahead when the planet of rigor returns to the Ram's realm from February 13, 2026 to April 12, 2028. This two-and-a-half-year transit wants you to treat your body as a temple and elevate your efficiency to new heights. But you'll do it Saturn's way: slow, steady and systematic, moving one step at a time.

As someone ruled by the transformative power of Pluto, you're no stranger to deep, internal changes. However, the constant emotional ebbs and flows that come with being one of the zodiac's water signs can make it challenging for Scorpios to stick to a day-in-day-out routine. Yes, you ARE a mood, Scorpio, and a fluctuating one, at that. Saturn in Aries is here to teach you the value of a consistent effort.

Endurance and resilience are your new M.O., even (especially!) when progress has plateaued. Get creative: Infuse your routines with variety to keep them from becoming monotonous. Instead of hitting the same old Spin class three days a week, mix it up with Pilates and resistance training, trying out different teachers and working a variety of muscle groups. On more introspective days, a calming yoga session or a long walk could be just what you need to stay balanced. One thing's for sure: With Saturn in your wellness-focused sixth house, you need to make self-care a priority. No more skipping meals and blowing off workouts—not unless you want to experience a cascade of crashing energy levels throughout your life.

Saturn isn't completely finished with its time in Pisces and your fifth house of romance and creativity. But you'll be happy to know that the end is in sight. Tough lessons in these arenas have been the norm since this cycle began on March 7, 2023. As Saturn moves on to Aries, even for the three months in 2025, you may feel a reinfusion of vitality in your personal life.

This spring and summer, you can rekindle a passion that's been on the back burner. Spend time with a lover or revive an artistic project that's been lying dormant for a couple good years. As Saturn hunkers down in Aries and your regimented sixth house, reintroduce healthy habits in every area of life, including your personal interactions.

Saturn in Aries won't be a walk in the park, however. The cosmic curmudgeon is said to be "in fall" in this sign, since its controlling energy is a mismatch for the Ram's wild impulsivity. And it doesn't help that escape-artist Neptune will be traveling alongside Saturn in Aries, driving you to distraction at every turn.

The trick for you, Scorpio, may be to work in sprints instead of marathons. For every hour devoted to focused productivity, you may need fifteen minutes to meditate, breathe or take a walk around the block. Or maybe you'll hustle through two hours on and take an hour off—or vice versa! The time away from your desk, laptop or phone could become part of your workflow, moments where your resting brain becomes an open channel for divine inspiration.

Since the sixth house is the service sector of the zodiac, you could ramp up your output by working with qualified, capable associates. Forget about being the office martyr, attempting to juggle your colleagues' responsibilities alongside your own. Streamline your workload by hiring an assistant or forming strategic partnerships with people who specialize in the areas you're not interested in handling. Wherever possible, delegate tasks that don't require your unique skills. It will free you up to concentrate on what truly matters.

Above all, don't try to get this all handled in 2025. Saturn's developments don't happen overnight and pressuring yourself could backfire, causing performance anxiety to creep in. (Same with comparing and despairing, so stay off your nemesis' socials!) If nothing else, use May 24 to September 1 to streamline, simplify and scale back anything that's turned into a logistical nightmare. Less is absolutely more when pared-down Saturn visits your efficient sixth house every thirty years, so consider this the start of a new, Clean and Green Era!

4 LOVE YOUR BODY

VENUS RETROGRADE IN ARIES AND PISCES
ARIES: MARCH 1 – 27
PISCES: MARCH 27 – APRIL 12

Beginning March 1, you could find yourself in a reflective mood about all things "love and romance." That's not altogether unusual for you, Scorpio. As a deep feeling water sign, you're happy to paddle past the shallow plunge pool when it comes to your emotions.

Nevertheless, you may find yourself in unfamiliar seas once Venus slips into a six-week retrograde this spring. There's no avoiding a Venus retrograde, which happens every 18 months. This year, the planet of amour spirals back through two signs. From March 1 to 27, she beats a retreat through Aries and your logical, systematic sixth house. Then, on March 27, Venus slips back into Pisces and your passionate, creative fifth house for the remainder of the retrograde, until April 12. With two very different energies to navigate, you'll need to work hard to keep your bearings.

While Venus drifts through Aries and your sixth house, she encourages you to slow down and take a more measured approach to your feelings. Rule of thumb: More self-care, less caretaking. The sixth house is the wellness zone, and with beauty queen Venus retreating here until March 27, nourish your body with clean, green food and make sure that you're eating at regular intervals to keep your energy from spiking and crashing. Consider having a doctor do a blood panel to see if you're low on any vitamins or sensitive to any foods. Getting your gut health up to snuff will boost your immunity, helping you ward off change-of-season sniffles, even allergies.

If you're single and dating, extend the "getting to know you" phase even longer than you normally might. When Venus retrogrades back into Pisces from March 27 to April 12, you'll be in the mood for love, but not exactly eager to hand out loyalty points to just anyone. Just make sure your suspicious mind doesn't spiral out, pushing people away for the smallest infraction. Pace yourself appropriately while remaining open-hearted and you might find the rare soul who can match your intellect and wit. There's nothing quite so scintillating to your alchemical sign as a full-body connection that starts with the mind and travels south.

Even for coupled Scorpios, learning the art of restraint can be a game-changer. Instead of fuming within two seconds of getting triggered, step back and calm down first. What if you hit the gym, did a fifteen-minute meditation, or scrawled in your journal BEFORE you responded to the perceived injury? Don't let your lizard brain hijack your rational mind.

Speaking of the gym...there are times when you love to break a sweat with a high-intensity workout, but during Venus' backspin, gentler exercise will do the trick. Single? Pay attention to who's getting their heart rate up on the adjacent elliptical. Your eyes might lock and lead to a flirty, après-workout conversation at the smoothie bar. If you're happily hooked up, how about turning your bae into your workout buddy?

Regardless, all that effort will put you in fine form for the second half of Venus' retrograde (March 27 to April 12), which takes place in Pisces and your flamboyant fifth house. Dressing up and enjoying more time OUT will be a must then. Before March is through, make sure you have enough space cleared on your calendar for a weekly date night, or a weekly hang with your wingpeople who can help you search for love while refining your romantic criteria. No settling please.

Avoid handing out second chances for unreliable exes—even if they still hold the esteemed title of "the best sex I ever had." Venus retrograde has a habit of awakening ghosts of lovers past, all while skewing your better judgment. So should someone arrive for an Act II, keep 'em waiting in the wings until Venus resumes direct motion on April 12.

5 REVITALIZE YOUR ROMANTIC STREAK

LUNAR NODES IN VIRGO AND PISCES

NORTH NODE IN PISCES, SOUTH NODE IN VIRGO
JANUARY 11, 2025 – JULY 26, 2026

Summon the glam squad! As the destiny-driven North Node shifts into Pisces on January 11, the lowkey vibes of the last 18 months will soon be a thing of the past. Instead of dodging the spotlight, you're ready to step right into it, like a Hollywood A-lister walking the red carpet at the Met Gala.

Pisces rules your fifth house of fame, romance and creative expression. As the North Node swoops into this sign for the first time since 2006-2007, you may feel friskier and more playful than you have in a while. Between now and July 26, 2026, even the most understated Scorpio is invited to serve main character energy.

This is sure to be a welcome relief! Since July 17, 2023 the North Node in Aries put you to task as it fired up your disciplined, hardworking sixth house. You've been deep in the grind, fine-tuning your wellness, focusing on your goals. But as the Node shifts into Pisces, it's time to trade your toolbox for something a little more glamorous. Your transformation from behind-the-scenes power player to front-and-center star is about to begin.

Embrace your creative prowess and turn up the heat. Whether you're pouring your energy into a passion project, building your personal brand, or hiring a PR agent to get your work out into the world, this is your time to shine. Scorpio performers could land a plum, on-camera assignment, but no need to wait for the auditions to roll around. Share your insights on TikTok Live or YouTube and you might become internet-famous first.

Call your inner minx out of hibernation. The North Node in fantasy-fueled Pisces can make your love life steamier than a Bridgerton episode. Single Scorpios might find themselves in a whirlwind affair (or five) where you're wined and dined like royalty. If that sounds daunting to you, now's the time to work on your "receptivity issues." We get it, Scorpio, allowing others to shower you with adoration can make you feel out of control. During this year-and-a-half long nodal cycle, you could start getting comfortable with being worshiped every now and again.

Of course, it's always a give and take with you, so it's perfectly fine if you want to spoil your S.O. to ridiculous proportions. Date nights, baecations and grand gestures of love are all on the menu. Plus, with the fifth house ruling fertility, some Scorpios could be hearing the pitter-patter of little feet before July 2026. Time to start thinking about your own "mini me"!

On the opposite side of the zodiac, the South Node slides into Virgo, activating your eleventh house of teamwork, friendships, and technology. This is your karmic comfort zone, but instead of hiding out in your usual Scorpio solitude, it's time to surround yourself with a supportive squad who lifts you up and helps you achieve your goals. The South Node will help you filter out those who've overstayed their welcome. Time to unfollow stale connections and embrace collaborations that are truly aligned with your current vision.

If you've given too many chances to the wrong people in the past, forgive yourself, Scorpio. Your heart is huge and when you're hurt, you get guarded and may feel like surrounding it with barbed wire. With the South Node in Virgo, you can ease back into community with a newfound discernment. Whether in work, friendship or an organization, this cycle will free you up to "people" again. After January 11, you'll be readier than ever to get strategic with who's on your team. You are poised to attract people who can help you level up and lead in a bigger way. Let's go, Scorpio—it's your year to be iconic!

Love

SCORPIO 2025 FORECAST

Let's start with the sultriest news: 2025 could be a year of sexual liberation for you. First, untethered Jupiter, then, experimental Uranus, swing through Gemini and your erotic eighth house, inviting you to unabashedly explore the realm of desire. While Scorpio may have a rep as the zodiac's "sex sign," your carnal urges can be so complex that some days, you just don't want to deal.

Not this year, Scorpio. Whether privately or with a partner, you're invited to tap the rich vein of fantasy that courses through your scene-spinning imagination. You don't have to DO anything with these visions. Simply giving yourself permission to let them roam through your head could be more than enough. Try not to judge yourself if a few of those veer into taboo territory. The Freudian complexity might reveal some old psychic knots that need untangling.

By the same token, you have a hall pass to play in a wider amorous arena. As philosophical Jupiter coaxes you out of your comfort zone between January 1 and June 9, you could find yourself curious about everything from tantra to BDSM. This could be the year that you bravely attend a workshop or retreat that explores sexuality and desire. High-minded Uranus brings another tidal wave of curiosity from July 7 to November 7, which is a preview of its seven-year transit through Gemini that begins on April 25, 2026.

But, plot twist: The anatomy of your desires may not fit conveniently into the lifestyle you've laid out for yourself. What's a Scorpio to do? That question could push you toward some profound reflections this year, and possibly some structural changes to your relationships or roles within them.

The destiny-driven lunar North Node shifts into Pisces on January 11, refreshing your approach to love and romance. Ditch the cynicism. During this eighteen-month cycle, you could literally be swept away. You might cross paths with a past-life lover or rediscover the creative spark within an existing partnership. Love pulses with magic this year with key players involved who are part of a grander cosmic plan.

From March 1 to April 12, Venus takes a retrograde spin, inviting you to revisit your romantic history. Are there unresolved feelings for an ex still floating around? This is a time to tie up loose ends, whether through a face-to-face conversation or a ritual release complete with a bonfire. Tread carefully. It's a potent time for closure, but not necessarily for new beginnings—unless you're absolutely sure the past is worth rekindling.

Uranus continues to keep things unpredictable in Taurus, your relationship house, until July 7 and then again after November 7 for its final four-and-half months in this lifetime. Whether it's a sudden breakup, an unexpected proposal or a surprising twist in an existing relationship, Uranus isn't interested in stability—it's here to shake things up for your highest growth.

Love doesn't come with guarantees this year, but it does bring excitement. Like the North Node, Saturn and Neptune spend a good part of the year hand-in-hand in Pisces, combining forces in your fifth house of love and creativity. Since March 7, 2023, traditional Saturn has been pushing for serious commitments and amplifying your desire to build something lasting in love. Boundary-blurring Neptune, however, wants to keep things dreamy and magical. This is the blue planet's final year in Pisces—a cycle that has been infusing romance with fairytale energy since it began in 2011.

Can fantasy and reality coexist? Make it your mission to figure that out this year. You could discover it during 2025's emotional high tide: the total lunar eclipse in Pisces on September 7. Eclipses bring revelations, and this one may unveil your deepest desires, fears or even a hidden romantic truth.

Fantasies keep flowing into fall as lusty Mars makes its biennial visit to Scorpio from September 22 to November 4. This courage-boosting time could bring erotic adventures and the hottest pursuits you've had in a while. Demure, seductive Venus parades through Scorpio from November 6 to 30, helping you attract the depth and mystery you crave.

With Mercury retrograde in your sign from November 18 to 29, you could tap back into a few buried desires that are ready to come out and play! Vulnerability is your superpower here, so drop the mask and watch something truly transformative emerge.

SCORPIO: LUCKIEST *love* DAY

FEBRUARY 1

Getting swept away isn't your cool-and-in-command sign's style, but as love planet Venus meets Neptune's rushing romantic river, you're in for a treat. Surrender your cynicism, Scorpio, and this could be a fantasy-fueled day for the books—and possibly your locked diary.

Money & Career

SCORPIO 2025 FORECAST

Get ready to put the "flow" in "workflow," Scorpio. While professional stability tops one of this year's professional goals, you can anchor into your creativity and spirituality to achieve that end. No more grinding through the motions. This is the year you turn your "lather, rinse, repeat" routines into joyful rituals. Hint: It's as much about attitude and mindset as anything else.

Beginning January 11, the destiny-driven lunar North Node heads into Pisces, taking center stage in your fifth house of passion, fame and playful expression until July 26, 2026. This is an invitation to swing out of the safety zone with your work and allow your emotional intelligence to shine.

For Scorpios who are talented in the arts, there will be an obvious upleveling. Your work may become riskier and unbound in ways that attract fans and media attention. Polish up your personal branding and don't shy away from self-promotion. If that's too hard for you, enlist an agent or even your friends to start a buzz on your behalf. This isn't narcissistic! You have something incredible to share and it's time to step into the light.

Artistic genes are not required to maximize this cycle. Bringing a more playful, joyful attitude—or dialing it up by a few mere percentage points—can have a seismic effect on your workplace. Your intuition and ability to read people will be your ace in the hole this year. Take it upon yourself to make the office a place where everyone feels a lot more at home, whether that's a casual Friday or monthly mingling over a shared lunch.

In 2025, two outer planets—numinous Neptune and disciplined Saturn—begin tours through Aries and your sixth house of work and wellness. Soulful Neptune streams into Aries from March 30 to October 22—its first visit to this sign since 1875! Timekeeper Saturn spins through Aries from May 24 to September 1, its first time here in nearly thirty years. As they team up together in the Ram's realm, the magic is in the methodology.

How can you work smarter, rather than harder? Lean into the cutting-edge vibes of Aries to solve this riddle. The goal is a healthier work-life balance. More time for family, yoga, sleep and other restorative practices can boost productivity while you ARE on the job.

Are you ready to leave an old work habit or unfulfilling job behind? The solar eclipse in Aries on March 29 is the final eclipse in a two-year cycle, and could catalyze the change. You might find yourself stepping into a new role, taking on a project that feels more aligned with your values or restructuring your work environment. Focus on the details and ensure that your daily efforts are contributing to your long-term goals.

Entrepreneurial dreams get a burst of momentum after June 9, as venturesome Jupiter wanders into Cancer for a yearlong trek through your ninth house. Cast a wide net because work opportunities could lead you to far-flung locales. A trip to the London office might turn into a full-on relocation, for example, or maybe you take a job that involves monthly cross-continental treks or Zoom meetings with people in a dizzying array of time zones. If you've honed your gifts, you could write a book, teach a course or make money as part of the expert industry.

With go-getter Mars sweeping through Scorpio from September 22 to November 4, you'll have a busy Q4! Grab the wheel on a team project or dive into a solo mission that requires a deep emotional investment.

Speaking of investments, both Jupiter and Uranus could free up funds this year that you can funnel toward a savvy purchase; one that increases your net worth. From real estate to cryptocurrency to index funds, you may need to take a little more of a risk in order to grow your wealth faster. Avoid anything that feels like too much of a gamble and don't plunk it all down in one place!

SCORPIO: LUCKIEST *career* DAY

MAY 24

Stability and security with a soulful twist: That's the Scorpio dream. The Gemini Sun is beaming into your eighth house of investments and wealth, accompanied (for another week) by lucky Jupiter. On May 24, el Sol makes an auspicious trine with your ruler, savvy Pluto, in Aquarius and your fourth house of financial foundations. Today, you could get word of an asset, like a house or stock, that becomes a valuable part of your portfolio. Scorpios on the hunt for work could find steady employment or a dream client through the recommendation of family or a close friend. Put your feelers out there!

2025
SCORPIO

12
MONTH
OVERVIEW

January MONTHLY HOROSCOPE

Your strategic mind is in razor-sharp form as 2025 begins with the Sun in Capricorn and your communicative, cooperative third house until the 19th. Connect to kindred spirits, digitally and close to home. Finesse your messaging and your personal brand. On January 11, the fateful lunar North Node heads into Pisces where it will charge up your fifth house of fame, romance and creative expression for eighteen months. Forget about flying under the radar or hiding out in a group. Your work and talents vault you into the public eye and peg you as a leader. Feisty Mars will be retrograde all month, slipping back from Leo into Cancer from January 6 to February 23. Go easy on the truth serum. What you consider "honest feedback" could sound like fighting words to someone else. Tension with a faraway friend, relative or businessy ally could boil, so take a breather to let tempers cool. Once the Sun hunkers down in Aquarius on the 19th, home is where the action is. Reconnect to your inner circle and start transforming your space once the luxuriating Year of the Wood Snake begins on January 29.

February MONTHLY HOROSCOPE

You're in hygge heaven until February 18, as the Aquarius Sun serves "Nate and Jeremiah" vibes in your domestic fourth house. No apologies for hiding out in hibernation mode and giving your undivided attention to a few close friends and relatives. Radiant Venus begins a long tour through Aries and your wellness zone on the 4th, inspiring a galactic glow-up through cleaner eating and regular exercise. At work, make your daily routines feel more like rituals by adding beauty and creative flourishes. Take time to connect to coworkers and strengthen team spirit. Also on the 4th, Jupiter snaps out of a four-month retrograde in Gemini and powers up your eighth house of seduction, investments and shared resources. Simmering attractions could heat up like a boiler room. Surround yourself with wealthy influencers. You could get a lucky tip about a stock or real estate listing before June 9. Your playful, outgoing side returns big time once the Sun moves into Pisces on February 18. Bundle up for concerts, dinner dates and winter fun—and don't be surprised if you find yourself at the center of many people's attention. Travel plans pick up speed once Mars turns direct in Cancer on February 23. Spin the globe and find a new place to explore! Can't get away? Jump into an online group with an international cohort.

March MONTHLY HOROSCOPE

Your imagination's in overdrive as the Pisces Sun lights up your fifth house of romance and self-expression until March 20. Whether you're diving into a passion project or revving up your romantic life, you're going in with your whole heart. But stay grounded, Scorpio—your Aries-ruled sixth house of work and wellness is about to take center stage. Both Venus and Mercury will be retrograde in Aries this month—Venus from March 1 to 27 and Mercury from March 15 to 29—causing you to reflect on your daily habits, health routines and work dynamics. Are you overextending yourself? Reassess your boundaries and find balance between work and self-care. The Virgo lunar eclipse on March 14 will bring clarity to your social circle and long-term goals. Address any issues with friends or group projects that have been lingering. When the Sun shifts into Aries on March 20, your focus will sharpen on refining your work and wellness routines. The Aries solar eclipse on March 29 marks the end of a two-year cycle in your sixth house, offering a powerful moment to close the chapter on unhealthy habits or work dynamics. On March 30, Neptune enters Aries for the first time since 1875, beginning a 14-year cycle that will bring spiritual growth and visionary insight into your daily life and wellness. Stay open to new self-care strategies. You could discover a more holistic, inspired way to live and work between now and October 22.

April MONTHLY HOROSCOPE

Order in the Scorpio court! With the Sun in your sixth house of healthy routines until April 19, fine-tune your habits and streamline your schedule. But don't move too fast just yet. Mercury is retrograde in Pisces and your fifth house of romance and creativity until April 7, while Venus is retrograde in Pisces until April 12. Whether you're pouring your genius into a creative project or focusing on a legendary love affair, your judgment may be slightly off. Exes could come out of the woodwork early this month or you may find yourself steeped in a drama that you THOUGHT was over and done with. Try not to escalate the situation. After the 12th, some new information may come to light that helps you clear up the tension. Career goals accelerate after April 18, once Mars zooms into Leo and fires up your tenth house of career and ambitions. If you're ready for a professional pivot, Mars can help you blaze new trails. For other Scorpios, the C suite may be calling. As long as you're focusing up, you're looking in the right direction between now and June 17. When Taurus season kicks off on April 19, your attention shifts to your seventh house of partnerships. Strengthen personal and professional relationships, seal deals and build solid connections that will go the distance.

May MONTHLY HOROSCOPE

Two is your magic number this May. While the Taurus Sun shines in your seventh house until the 20th, you could attract a complementary force in every area of your life. Strengthen your existing bonds by carving out more moments for quality, one-on-one time. Spoil yourself ridiculously on May 12, when the year's only full moon in Scorpio sanctions a splurge. On May 4, your ruler, mystical, metamorphic Pluto, turns retrograde. Between now and October 13, your personal life could go through essential shifts. Make sure your home feels supportive of your deepest goals. Turn a spare bedroom into your artist's studio, downsize to a smaller space or call a house meeting to craft rules that work for everyone. Deep emotional ties with family members could be the subject of more than one therapy session this month. You're in your magnetic element once the Sun heads into Gemini on the 20th. People will flock to you, so beam your charms selectively to attract the people you WANT in your orbit. On May 24, Saturn struts into Aries for the first time since 1998, turning its disciplined, structured energy on daily routines. From your workflow to your workouts, start putting savvy, stress-busting systems in place for sustainable success. The groundwork you lay now will pay off for years to come!

June MONTHLY HOROSCOPE

Beachside meditations, yoga in the park, starlight ceremonies—you're in your soulful Scorpionic element this June, and your sultry one, too! Until the 20th, the Sun simmers in Gemini and your intimate, introspective eighth house (AKA "the Scorpio house"). Chemistry could bubble into a real-deal relationship while other flatlining connections could finally hit their breaking point. While you're craving closeness, get ready for a tidal wave of independent energy to wash over you on June 9, when Jupiter moves into Cancer for the first time since 2014. With your ninth house of travel, entrepreneurship and higher learning getting an excitable rush from Jupiter until June 30, 2026, it's time to soar out of your comfort zone and grow! The odyssey may already begin on the 20th as the Sun joins Jupiter in Cancer at the solstice, then syncs up on the 24th for The Day of Miracles. Go ahead, Scorpio, branch out! Say yes to that invitation to a friend's wedding in Buenos Aires. Go on tour in Tokyo or take a semester-long class at the Sorbonne. On June 15 and 18, Jupiter squares Saturn, then Neptune—two days this month when you might have to deal with administrative tasks. Pay attention to details and don't underestimate the importance of the little things. And remember: Independent doesn't necessarily mean alone. When thrillseeker Mars moves into Virgo on June 17, it buzzes through your communal eleventh house until August 6. Start scouting for your dream team or get out and mingle with the movers and shakers who share your timelessly savvy outlook on life.

July MONTHLY HOROSCOPE

The wider world is calling you, Scorpio, and with the Sun and Jupiter synced up in Cancer until the 22nd, you could radar in on a few places that feel like a "home away from home." If you're indeed in the market for a move, relocation or pied-à-terre, set up those Zillow alerts, STAT! Your private world could go through some shifts starting July 7, when changemaker Uranus heads into Gemini and your mysterious, spiritual and sexual eighth house. This four-month cycle, which lasts until November 7, is a preview of a longer Uranus-in-Gemini transit from April 2026 to May 2033. Breakthroughs around finances, investments or intimate relationships could come when you least expect them. Embrace innovation instead of clinging to the past and you'll sail into a new dimension of exploration—one that could keep your life fresh and interesting for decades to come. Throughout the month, Neptune, Saturn and Chiron all turn retrograde in Aries (on the 4th, 13th and 30th, respectively) and your sixth house of work, wellness and daily routines. These five-month retrogrades may bring old habits or health concerns to the surface, urging you to rethink how you're managing your everyday life. Don't get overwhelmed, Scorpio! This is a chance to recalibrate your routines and heal any patterns that aren't serving your highest good. Your professional life takes center stage when the Sun moves into Leo for a month on July 22, so bring on the rooftop networking and golf-course goal setting. The only catch? Pesky Mercury will be retrograde in Leo from July 18 to August 11 which could slow down deal-making and bring some competitors out of the woodwork. Be discreet about sharing your big ideas, since it's hard to know who to trust during the retrograde—not that we have to tell YOU that, Scorpio!

August MONTHLY HOROSCOPE

Power up and go play ball, Scorpio! The Leo Sun sets off fireworks in your tenth house of achievements and ambition, putting you front and center until August 22. It's your time to rise—but you'll need to be as strategic as Bobby Fischer before the 11th, while Mercury plays a game of retrograde chess. Revisit unfinished projects and revive opportunities that were left on the table. Pleasure-planet Venus keeps you in adventurous spirits, touring Cancer and your worldly ninth house until August 25. Need a vacation? As long as you plan it properly (because, Mercury) and keep a strong Wi-Fi signal for work emails, the change of scenery can do wonders. With the love planet at the helm, a baecation (or fun fling with a local) splashes juicy color into your summer. DO leave time for inward reflection. Agitator Mars settles into Libra and your restorative twelfth house from August 6 to September 22. This soul-searching cycle can help you get in touch with feelings that you pushed down—ones that need to be processed in order for you to move forward with clarity. Don't be afraid of anger, which is Mars' touchstone emotion. Virgo season begins on the 22nd, getting you excited about cutting edge ideas, community connections and collaborations. Find your people, Scorpio! With the techie influence of this transit, a virtual group could be your ticket to togetherness. The following day, August 23, brings the first of two rare, back-to-back new moons in Virgo. Use this fresh-start energy to align yourself with people who inspire and support your growth. And keep your eyes on the bigger picture because the upcoming solar (new moon) eclipse in Virgo on September 21 will supercharge your network-building efforts.

September MONTHLY HOROSCOPE

You're as popular as you want to be this September, as the Virgo Sun shines the spotlight into your eleventh house of teamwork and technology. From your social circle to social media, everyone wants a piece of your time. You, on the other hand, may feel a bit more selective, thanks to Mars simmering in your soulful twelfth house until the 22nd—then beaming its lusty vibes into Scorpio and your magnetic first house until November 4 (H-O-T-T-O-G-O!). Save those VIP slots on your calendar for artists, thought leaders and people who push you farther than you'd go on your own. On September 1st, structured Saturn, who's already been retrograde since July 13, slips back into Pisces for the rest of its backspin, until November 27. Get to work on your personal brand and any front-facing materials, ensuring that they reflect your present-day vibe. Creative and romantic epiphanies stream in during the September 7 total lunar eclipse in Pisces. There could be some milestone developments for your love life during this fertile full moon. On September 21, a rare second Virgo new moon of the year—a potent solar eclipse—could reorganize your social life, helping you figure out what company to keep and the kind of community you want to build. On September 22, Libra season begins, shifting the energy to your twelfth house of endings and introspection. This is a four-week period for rest and reflection before your birthday season. Wrap up loose ends, give yourself space to recharge and let go of anything not serving you. But don't slip too far off the radar. That very same day, your driven co-ruler, fierce Mars, moves into Scorpio for the first time in two years, supercharging your first house of identity until November 4. This instant surge of motivation flashes a string of cosmic green lights. Off you go, Scorpio, in hot pursuit of whatever (and whoever!) you're passionate about.

October MONTHLY HOROSCOPE

October is a work hard, chill hard month for you. While the Libra Sun nestles in your twelfth house of rest, closure and introspection until October 22, you'll need time to process all the feelings and maybe spin them into one of your genius creative works. Simultaneously, driven Mars is storming through Scorpio all month, charging you up with enthusiasm and making you a force of nature. When you're not disco-napping or meditating in savasana, you'll be pumped and productive, especially when it comes to a passion project. Taking the lead comes naturally to you now. Grab the reins! Romance could take a backseat to time with friends for the first part of the month, but once Venus sweeps into Libra and your fantasy-fueled twelfth house on October 13, you'll be ready to spin up some fairy-tale moments that feel like a sweet escape from your everyday life. The very same day, your ruler, magnetic Pluto, turns direct in Aquarius and your rooted fourth house. Real estate deals, home renovation projects, even a move to a new city—i.e. matters related to home and family—move to the front burner now. When the life-giving Sun joins Mars in Scorpio (birthday season!) this October 22, your ferociously unstoppable energy returns with a vengeance. Take command of any situation that's spiraling off track—and step back from anything that's draining your energy. Permission to prioritize yourself: Granted! Also on October 22, soulful Neptune retrogrades back into Pisces, where it will remain for the rest of its backspin until December 10. Dig through your archives for creative inspiration—which may literally weave its way into your fashion choices. Romantically, this is a time for healing, forgiveness and selectively sharing your softer side.

November MONTHLY HOROSCOPE

Scorpio season is in full swing this November, with the Sun in your self-sovereign first house ablaze until the 21st. Audacious moves and authentic self-expression? Bring. It. On. You might just turn this into an art form as glamorous Venus joins the Scorpio party from November 6 to 30. By the time the Scorpio new moon arrives on the 20th, you could be ready to launch an exciting venture or take a bold new step toward a dream. Aggressive Mars waves Scorpio goodbye on the 4th. As the red planet hunkers down in your sensible, sensual second house (Sagittarius) until December 15, you'll be pumped to monetize some of your genius ideas. That goes double once the Sun lands in the

Archer's domain for a month on the 21st. But there IS a catch: Mercury spins retrograde from November 9 to 29. As it backs up through Sagittarius until the 18th, it may create confusion with your cashflow. Then, from November 18 to 29, Mercury retreats through Scorpio and creates communication chaos. Prep your pitches and back up all ideas and assertions with solid data—or wait until December to seal any deals. On the 7th, unpredictable Uranus retrogrades back into Taurus, and you might need to rethink how you approach any shared ventures. Expansive Jupiter turns retrograde in Cancer on November 11, a four-month cycle that could send you back to school (or some form of training) to sharpen your skills. Fortunately, one planet is ending its retrograde in November! On the 27th, structured Saturn corrects course and moves ahead for its final two-and-a-half months in Pisces. Creatively and romantically, you'll feel back on solid ground and your efforts in these arenas will pay off again. Take the initiative!

December MONTHLY HOROSCOPE

Practical matters dominate your schedule in the first half of the month as the Sun, Venus and Mars all swirl through Sagittarius and your grounded second house. (Until the 21st, 24th and 15th, respectively.) As you wind down to the holidays, you may be laser-focused on enhancing your stability. Use this last month of 2025 to organize your budget, boost your income and treat yourself and your loved ones to meaningful gifts that stand the test of time. (Think: quiet luxury.) Mistletoe moments take a turn for the dreamy after the 10th, when fantasy-agent Neptune snaps out of its retrograde in poetic Pisces. Add a signature splash of magic to everything you do, from your holiday outfits to your gift-wrapping and festive playlists. Once Mars heads into Capricorn on December 15, you'll be ready to deck the halls—a social energy that continues to build when the Sun joins Mars in this social sector on the 21st, followed by Venus on the 24th. Appoint yourself entertainment chair and keep everyone connected with interactive fun: game nights, karaoke, shopping local and doing good in the neighborhood. This could be the "excuse" you need to nurture a budding friendship or play superconnector for your favorite people. With all this buzzy energy flowing, you might even take it upon yourself to organize NYE. Hosting at Casa Scorpio could be a blast if you're up for it, but so could a staycation to a driveable spot. Get an Airbnb within walking distance of a club, theater or concert venue or a cabin with a fireplace and hot tub to ring in 2026 with your besties.

Read your extended monthly forecast for life, love, money and career! astrostyle.com

A LITTLE ABOUT Sagittarius

DATES November 21 - December 21

SYMBOL The Archer

ELEMENT Fire

QUALITY Mutable

RULING PLANET Jupiter

BODY PART Hips, thighs

BEST TRAITS
Honest, adventurous, inspiring, optimistic, enthusiastic, encouraging, open-minded

KEYWORDS
Exploration, travel, expansion, wisdom, outspokenness, diversity, study, independence, decadence, spirituality

Read more about Sagittarius

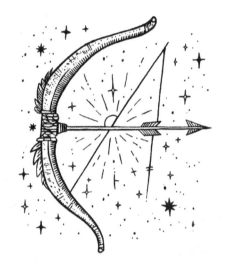

SAGITTARIUS
IN 2025

ALL THE PLANETS IN SAGITTARIUS IN 2025	YOUR 2025 HOROSCOPE	TOP 5 THEMES FOR SAGITTARIUS IN 2025	LOVE HOROSCOPE + LUCKY DATES	MONEY HOROSCOPE + LUCKY DATES

Sagittarius in 2025

YOUR YEARLY OVERVIEW

Upgrade alert! Trade some of your famous independence for the power and magic of interdependence. Your cosmic ruler Jupiter splits the year between Gemini and Cancer, activating your seventh house of commitments and your eighth house of permabonding. The new flex? Finding freedom within relationships. (Hot!) You'll do that by spelling out boundaries and learning to set clear expectations from the get-go, which might require a legal contract in some cases. On January 11, the lunar nodes shift into Pisces and Virgo, recalibrating your work-life balance. Family bonds could suffer if you keep putting them at a distant second to your career goals. Set up smarter structures for productivity so you can joyfully immerse yourself in both cherished areas of life. By the same token, you may need to rearrange some household structures so that everyone in your world pulls their proper weight. This same measured approach can do wonders for your romantic life as well as your artistic gifts. Disciplined Saturn and dreamy Neptune both do laps through Aries for part of 2025, combining their disparate energies in your fifth house of fame. Let your imagination soar, then back it up with a solid action plan. There's nothing you can't pull off this year when you combine your visionary gifts with a sound strategy.

THE PLANETS IN *Sagittarius*

THE SUN
NOV 21–DEC 21

It's birthday season for you, so step out and shine! Seek novelty and take extra initiative during this radiant monthlong phase.

NEW MOON
DEC 19
8:43PM, 28°25'

Bonus New Year! Set your intentions for the next six months and get into action.

FULL MOON
JUN 11
3:44AM, 20°39'

Ready, set, manifest! Your work of the past six months bears fruit and it's time to harvest the rewards.

MERCURY
NOV 2, 2024–JAN 8, 2025
OCT 29–NOV 18, 2025
DEC 11, 2025– JAN 1, 2026
RETROGRADE IN SAGITTARIUS:
NOV 9–18

Crown yourself monarch of the social butterflies when popularity-boosting Mercury visits your sign three times this year! Circulate and get social. During the retrograde, be careful not to make promises you can't keep or allow energy vampires into your sphere.

VENUS
NOV 30–DEC 24

You've got the romantic It Factor when the galactic glamazon charges up your powers of seduction each year. Willpower is weak in the face of beauty and luxury. Watch your spending!

MARS
NOV 4–DEC 15

Motivation is high when energetic Mars visits your sign every couple years—but check your combative streak and try not to come on too strong.

Sagittarius in 2025

HIGHLIGHTS

SECURITY CHECK: THE PISCES NORTH NODE RESHAPES YOUR HOME LIFE

Security and safety aren't usually at the top of the "hierarchy of needs" for an adventurous (and sometimes risk-loving) Sagittarius. But that all changes starting January 11. As the fateful North Node ebbs into Pisces for the first time since 2007, it fills the tidepool of your fourth house of home, family and comfort. Your mission during this eighteen-month cycle is to define what "a happy home" and "emotional intelligence" mean to 2025 you. This year, you design the ideal space for yourself, whether that means bi-city living, downsizing or finding more time to recharge in your already-cozy abode.

CAREER SHIFTS INTO A STEADY GEAR WITH THE VIRGO SOUTH NODE

Across the board, the karmic South Node lands in Virgo, releasing the pressure valve of your tenth house of career. If you've been running on fumes chasing success, now's the time to design a sustainable career plan that supports a flourishing personal life. Design lasting systems and structures that allow your professional world to function smoothly without constant hustle. By the time this cycle ends on July 26, 2026, your day-to-day lifestyle could be moving at a very different beat.

JUPITER AND URANUS IN GEMINI POWER UP YOUR PARTNERSHIPS

Partnerships are the path to expansion and excitement for you in 2025 as your ruler, limitless Jupiter, and innovative Uranus both spend a chunk of the year in Gemini and your seventh house of dynamic duos. A profitable business proposal could be on the table, or you might finally find the person who matches your energy and vision for the future. When Uranus swoops into Gemini from July 7 to November 7, the rules of the game could shift! This rebellious planet thrives on surprises, so prepare for the unexpected. Your usual "type" might fly out the window as you attract unconventional people and experiences that challenge your idea of what a relationship should look like.

SPRING'S VENUS RETROGRADE HITS PAUSE ON PASSION

Too hot for even you to handle? You may need to turn down that flame of desire on March 1, as love planet Venus spins into her every-584-days retrograde. Until March

27, the reverse commute takes place in Aries and your fifth house of romance, which could poke the bear of an old drama or even bring an ex back into the picture for consideration. (Take. Your. Time.) The final half of the backspin, from March 27 to April 12, will be in Pisces, which may bring some changes to your home situation while schooling you on what healthy boundary-setting really looks like. The emotional roller coaster may be dizzying some days. This is a time for recalibration, not rushing!

DEEPENING BONDS: JUPITER IN CANCER AND THE 8TH HOUSE

The urge to merge—with someone who tantalizes your mind, body and soul—could strike once your ruler, exploratory Jupiter, heads into Cancer for a year, starting June 9. Your ruling planet is exalted in Cancer and loves being here—but that doesn't mean you can dash in and out of relationships now. During this "money, power, sex" cycle, you could meet a crop of interested parties who see you as an ally and an asset that they want in their "portfolios" for, like, ever. The eighth house rules investments, so if you're the enterprising sort of Sagittarius, you could be shopping an idea for VC or putting together your own angel investor group. Cancer is classically associated with women, so you could have success with the circle of ladies in your life who believe in your dreams. Purchasing real estate could also put money in the bank, leveling up the push from the Pisces North Node to create that dream home.

CREATIVE RENAISSANCE: SATURN AND NEPTUNE IN ARIES

While much of 2025's energy is happening behind the scenes, forget about disappearing from the public eye. This year, two outer planets weave into Aries and your flamboyant fifth house of fame for a spell. First up is imaginative Neptune, from March 30 to October 22, joined by stabilizing Saturn from May 24 to September 1. A disciplined and business-savvy approach to your artistic pursuits could put money in the bank. Both planets kick off longer cycles through Aries at the beginning of next year, so 2025 may simply bring a preview of what's to come. Romantically, Saturn and Neptune make you want to be serious AND swept away. Coupled Archers need to be less spontaneous and more structured about planning dates, baecations and the like. Block out time for romance, then let things flow within that container.

TOP 5 THEMES FOR Sagittarius in 2025

1	2	3	4	5
EMBRACE INTER-DEPENDENCE	INVEST WITH INTENTION	CLAIM YOUR FAME	SURRENDER TO SENTIMENTALITY	BALANCE CAREER AND HOME

1 EMBRACE INTERDEPENDENCE

JUPITER AND URANUS IN GEMINI

JUPITER: MAY 25, 2024 – JUNE 9, 2025
URANUS: JULY 7 – NOVEMBER 7, 2025 • JANUARY 26, 2026 – MAY 22, 2033

Ready for a relationship revolution, Sagittarius? How about a soulful sexual revival? One thing you can take to the bank: Things in those departments are not going to stay the same in 2025. Two of the most intrepid, unconventional planets are hitting switches in your seventh house of partnerships and one of them happens to be your ruler, adventurous Jupiter. The other is ingenious Uranus, who's touching through Gemini for a brief preview tour for the first time since the 1940s.

JUPITER IN GEMINI

MAY 25, 2024 – JUNE 9, 2025

So many partnerships, so many ways to expand. As 2025 opens, you're halfway through abundant Jupiter's trek through Gemini and your seventh house of dynamic duos. Wherever your ruling planet goes, it brings more. (And sometimes more than you think you need.) Since it landed in Twin Town on May 25, 2024, you may have your hands full with people who want to pair up with you. While this transit wages on until June 9, 2025, you could enjoy a raft of new collaborations, from romantic to strictly professional.

Thanks to peripatetic Jupiter, you may find yourself traveling back and forth between two places to pursue a partnership. Lucky for you, long-distance relationships are blessed while Jupiter hangs out in Gemini until June 9. Don't let geography prevent you from exploring a promising connection. As long as you stay in regular communication, you may find that the distance increases your desire. Gemini is the zodiac's communicator and with Jupiter here, the texting (and sexting) could be full-tilt, giving you a chance to explore the most sapiosexual parts of your personality, ones you didn't realize you had.

While relationships are blessed under this Jupiter spell, they are also huge mirrors, reflecting back the good, the bad and the ugly. Jupiter is "in detriment" in Gemini, a somewhat uncomfortable position, since it's opposite your ruler's home base of Sagittarius. Prepare to do a little work to make things stick with a partner. Certain unsavory truths that you haven't wanted to look at may get revealed. Tap your

Sagittarian optimism and consider couple's therapy or workshops that teach you about healthy communication and relating. If you're willing to put in the effort, Jupiter will reward you with an improved love life and revived affection for your partner.

If it's time to end things, you'll have the easiest time possible breaking free. There's no avoiding the grief that comes from breaking up. Still, Jupiter's wisdom and optimism increase the odds of a "conscious uncoupling."

Jupiter will be retrograde until February 4, giving you a prime opportunity in the early part of 2025 to do some sorting. Since last May, you've eagerly given any promising person or enterprise a chance to be your ally. Now you need to think long-range: Which of these hold the promise of becoming something even bigger? When Jupiter moves on to Cancer on June 9, it shines its magnanimous beams into your eighth house of investments. You may attract funding for a venture, "marry into money" or otherwise tap a source of revenue that keeps you liquid for a long time to come.

Do you like the sound of that, Archer? Then think of the first half of 2025 as priming the pump. If certain unions are delivering less-than-stellar results (no matter how much you attempt to finesse them), you may decide to cut bait. In other cases, you may feel like you're only scratching the surface of what's possible. Clear room in your schedule to maximize more of the potential with these folks. Growth is the name of Jupiter's game, but you need to plant seeds in fertile soil.

If you do go into business with someone, don't take the legal aspects for granted, especially if YOUR money or intellectual property is involved. If you don't have a good contract lawyer, ask around for a recommendation. The same holds true for any Sagittarius who is thinking about moving in with a partner or tying the knot. It's easy to be glib about the "business" aspects of love relationships, especially when you're in the optimistic crush of new love. But there's a reason divorce lawyers make the big bucks.

We aren't trying to rain on your romantic parade, Sagittarius. We're warning you against Jupiter's gambling instincts which can make you rush into (and out of!) relationships. Create your personal parachute and you'll set yourself up for success. Ironically, knowing where the exit is makes it safer for your commitment-shy sign to stay in place. It's time to take a new kind of gamble: Taking the risk to lay out what you want from a relationship before you're deep in it. You don't have to build the partnership plane while it's already in the air. Figure out the terms from a grounded place and you'll see who's fit to soar as your co-pilot..

URANUS IN GEMINI

JULY 7 – NOVEMBER 7, 2025
JANUARY 26, 2026 – MAY 22, 2033

Ready to update your sensual system software? Sagittarius 5.0 could emerge beginning this July 7, 2025, attracting a whole new crop of admirers. That day, electrifying Uranus zips into Gemini, shooting currents of kundalini energy through your seventh house of partnerships. This is the radical planet's first visit here since 1949, sending you on an unconventional voyage to get in touch with what your heart truly desires, what you're no longer willing to put up with, and to envision and draw in the perfect partner in crime.

While Uranus only sidespins through Gemini for four months this year, until November 7, take notes! The full, seven-year cycle picks up again next year and spans from April 25, 2026 to May 22, 2033. That means you don't have to do anything radical in 2025, although you might. Just know that change is in the air.

If you've been (unhappily) doing things the same way while Uranus slogged through Taurus and your pedantic sixth house since May 2018, you're in for a major shift. It's time to mix up your dating strategies and communication style. Uranus is "in fall" in Taurus, making that one of its least favorite signs of the zodiac. You've been working harder than ever since 2018—and frustratingly, seeing more modest results than your supersizer sign prefers. You might feel weary of experimenting and ready to just find a work routine that you can stick to. Not because you want to "lather, rinse, repeat" your way through your days, of course. But honestly, you're ready to bring Uranus' edgy, metaphysical energy into something besides your job. Like, say, your interpersonal relationships.

Well, Sagittarius, buckle up. The people who come into your life over the coming eight years could truly blow your mind—and that's saying something. You might even feel a tad out of your depth at first, as if you're meeting folks who run on a totally different operating system. What not to do? Ditch all your hard-won lessons to adapt to their current. Gemini is your opposite sign and with quirky Uranus here, these "alien beings" are likely to cherish the things that make you different than them. How can you plug yourself into their world without losing your authenticity?

It goes both ways. You may be carving out space for a partner—business, romantic, artistic—who doesn't fit neatly into your current social structure. The types of people you attract will start to shift in fascinating ways between this July 7 and May 22, 2033. Another rule of thumb: Ignore the comments! Tongues may wag when you shake up the status quo in your circle by introducing someone who marches to a different beat. Thankfully, you're the zodiac's ambassador. If anyone can build new bridges, it's you, Sagittarius. But first, just focus on getting to know people one by one. You can merge them into your friend group later—or not, because you may be leaving a few small-minded folks in the dust once Uranus sparks it up in Gemini on July 7.

Coupled Archers, Uranus in Gemini invites you to shun convention and play only by rules you set for yourselves. You may need more freedom in your living arrangement or even the relationship itself. There are no rights or wrongs here: As long as you're upfront—and kind—following your heart will lead to quantum personal growth.

This realm also rules professional partnerships, and you might find a dream business or creative associate. If money or intellectual property is involved, get everything in writing—in a contract when appropriate. Since Uranus rules technology, you might merge forces with a company that can A.I.-ify your offerings or help you reach a mass market through their vast online networks. For more analog Archers, teaming up with a social-impact organization can give you a renewed purpose between now and 2033.

2 INVEST WITH INTENTION

JUPITER IN CANCER
JUNE 9, 2025 – JUNE 30, 2026

Here today, gone tomorrow? That might be your mutable sign's M.O. in the first part of 2025, but prepare for a major sea change starting June 9. As your ruling planet, abundant Jupiter, downshifts into Cancer, it sets off a thirteen-month journey through your eighth house of investments and permanent bonds. Suddenly, you're willing to forgo FOMO for the delayed gratification of long-term gains.

Every Sagittarius loves a chase, so how about chasing the bag, as they say? During this thirteen-month cycle, "money, power, respect" could replace "eat, drink and make merry" as your new trinity. Play your cards right and by the time Jupiter moves on to regal Leo on June 30, 2026, you could be in a whole new income bracket.

Sagittarians are naturally lucky, so many of you have seen five and six figures before. With Jupiter in water sign Cancer, you may have more liquid assets than you have in a while. The trick is to not evaporate them as quickly as they stream in. By all means, make an entertainment budget. Deprivation is not a good look for your fun-loving sign and often leads to binge-spending. But the smart Sag will flow the lion's share of the funds you earn into things that compound instead of depreciate.

That could be anything from real estate to crypto to a good old-fashioned index fund. As the sign that loves diversification, make sure your portfolio includes a broad mix of stocks. Yes, we have to underscore that to you since you're also the zodiac's gambler, prone to putting every egg in a single basket. Nevertheless, you could radar in on worthwhile places to make a larger investment, such as a business that you're funding for yourself or a project that you feel passionately will yield high returns. (Again, watch out for blithe optimism.)

Got a venture that you need funded? Lucky Jupiter is exalted in Cancer, meaning this is its favorite sign to tour. Security-minded Cancer loves a safe bet while Jupiter's not afraid to roll the dice. This combo may provide the perfect balance for you to make sound financial decisions. You could attract people to one of your business ideas, and if you're willing to give up some ownership, their dollars could help you scale or build an empire.

Another way this Jupiter cycle could play out? You might find yourself drawn into the extreme makeover camp, ready to seriously transform your life. One caveat: Jupiter can be hasty and overarching at times, so avoid taking shortcuts. Your hard work is what will bring rapid results—the kinds that last!

The eighth house is also the erotic zone and with lusty Jupiter here, your sexual palate could expand to include a few new menu items. Experimentation comes with a warning flag, however. In sensitive Cancer and the possessive eighth house, Jupiter won't be as much of a free-love advocate as it normally is. What starts out as a "fun little fling" could snowball into a full-on obsession pretty quickly. Make sure your lust is matched by trust, which, need we remind you, Sagittarius, takes time to earn. You've never been a fan of going slow, but try to temper your pursuit to avoid projecting qualities onto people that may not be there.

A relationship that's been growing—perhaps since Jupiter moved into Gemini on May 25, 2024—could become official during Jupiter's trek through Cancer. This merger may involve joining assets in some way. For example, you could buy a home with your fiancée or open up a shared checking account for household expenses. Documentation may be drawn up, such as marriage licenses, wills or prenups. If you're ready to call it quits, Jupiter in Cancer can accelerate the process. No matter where you are on the partnership spectrum, during the second half of the year, things could feel formal and need to be formalized.

3 CLAIM YOUR FAME

SATURN AND NEPTUNE IN ARIES

NEPTUNE: MARCH 30 – OCTOBER 22, 2025 • JANUARY 26, 2026 – MARCH 23, 2039
SATURN: MAY 24 – SEPTEMBER 1, 2025 • FEBRUARY 13, 2026 – APRIL 12, 2028

A star is born! Get ready to meet your own fame monster this spring, Sagittarius, as two heavy-hitting outer planets sashay into Aries and your passionate, romantic head-turning fifth house. First up is glamorous fantasy agent Neptune, who moves through this sign from March 30 to October 22—it's first spin through Aries since 1862 to 1875! Then, from May 24 to September 1, serious Saturn throws its weight behind your reputation when it swings into Aries for the first time since 1996 to 1998.

These transits, while brief in 2025, are a preview of what lies ahead for you. In early 2026, both Neptune and Saturn will swing back into Aries for longer spells—thirteen and two more years, respectively. It's been such a long time since either planet visited the Ram's realm that both cycles are bound to feel ultra-new.

That goes double since Neptune and Saturn are also darting forward from Pisces (the last sign of the zodiac) and your introverted fourth house and into Aries (the first sign of the zodiac) and your flamboyant fifth house. No more flying under the radar or putting your love or your art on the backburner. Get ready to live passionately and live out loud, with both Neptune's wild fantasies and Saturn's harsher realities informing your journey.

NEPTUNE IN ARIES

MARCH 30 – OCTOBER 22, 2025
JANUARY 26, 2026 – MARCH 23, 2039

Dive into a sea of inspiration, Sagittarius, as Neptune sails into Aries for the first time in nearly two centuries! From March 30 to October 22, the planetary flowmaster charges up your fifth house of creativity, romance, and self-expression. Don't be surprised if your life feels like a fairy tale this spring and summer. And while your "Disney princess moment" only lasts for six months of 2025, there's no need to write "The End." On January 26, 2026, Neptune returns to the magic kingdom of your fifth house for an unbroken thirteen-year chapter.

The invitation, should you choose to accept it, is to infuse more imagination and wonder into your life. For your starry-eyed, optimistic sign, saying yes is a no brainer! But don't go racing around the planet for your fix of joy. While you're naturally inclined to widen your vistas through travel and socializing, Neptune in Aries wants you to source the depths of your subconscious to unlock creative inspiration. Whether it's through writing, music, or visual art, mystical and abstract themes may inform your work. Release your typical need for broad strokes and big pictures. Then, delve into the finer details of your creative process. Subtleties and nuances are where it's at!

Once you've honed your craft, get ready for your close up. Since Aries rules your fifth house of fame, the next fourteen years will serve amazing opportunities for you to share your work, scoop up awards and grow an audience. Publicity and marketing? That's where you CAN cast the widest net and find fans on every continent.

All this DOES come with a yellow flag. Neptune is the planet of illusion, which can cause you to misread signals, especially when it comes to fame, romance and creative expression. With Neptune's slippery grasp on reality, you run the risk of getting swept away in your enthusiasm. That goes triple with the oft-delulu planet puffing up in the entitled sign of Aries. To avoid falling prey to a scam, balance your gift for making things "bigger, stronger, faster" with regular reality checks.

Here's how to sidestep the tendency to overshoot the mark that comes from Neptune in Aries and your fifth house. When you find yourself attached to an idea, pushing against all odds, do a risk assessment. Do you actually know what you're getting yourself into here, Archer, like down to the dollar figures and daily schedules? Drowning in stress—or worse, debt—is probably not worth the price of bringing a dream to the mainstage. Good news! Sensible Saturn's parallel move into Aries will come in handy (more on that in the next section). Bolster your manifestation powers with hardcore logistics such as a timeline, financial projections and a realistic understanding of the production process. Like Sagittarius Taylor Swift's Eras Tour, you could put on (and star in!) the greatest show on Earth.

Romantically, get ready for heightened pleasure and elevated experiences with dating and relating. Fantasy-spinning Neptune in Aries makes you utterly magnetic—and oh, the places your libido will go! Better still? Because Neptune is a "sub" and Aries is a "dom," this transit helps you strike the perfect balance between "pursuer" and "pursued." Lay down your crossbow, Archer, and allow someone to chase YOU for a change. Remember that you are a treasure; a prize. Even if you have to fake it till you make it, hold back from serving every gallant gesture and opening gambit. Now's the time to work on being confidently receptive and highly selective about who gets to be close to you.

That could feel like a big shift for some Archers. Since Neptune paddled into sacrificial Pisces way back in 2011, you may have slipped into overfunctioning, especially at home. Caretaking energy was amplified, which has undoubtedly brought on moments of resentment and exhaustion over the past decade and a half. Slowly untie yourself from those codependent apron strings, retraining your inner circle to be more dependent on themselves. Neptune in Aries rolls out the red carpet for vivid color, unapologetic glamour and unfiltered artistic expression. These are all things that require you to spend more well-deserved moments pampering yourself.

While boundaries aren't this hazy planet's strong suit, carve out specific times for fun and pleasure. If you'd like to enjoy the company of a special soul, avoid filling every single second of your calendar with activities that drain your energy or tax your output. Say yes to brunches, concerts, cultural activities and vacations with friends. Do remain aware of Neptune's tendency to blur the lines between healthy escapism and avoidance. If tequila tastings and after-hours clubs don't align with your wellness goals, spearhead a move toward mocktails and daytime dance parties.

Nocturnal Neptune here could definitely turn you into a festive night owl, but no matter when you catch your Zs, make sure there's ample whitespace on your calendar for rest. Without proper downtime, you may be too tired to be "bothered" by the dating apps or your partner's sensual advances. And what a loss that would be, Sagittarius! Neptune in Aries is a cycle that only happens every 150-ish years, and it's peak season for proposals, weddings, pregnancies and other epic milestones for your love life.

Sagittarius parents could adopt a more playful approach to interacting with your kids between March 30 and October 22. For the past fourteen years, Neptune in Pisces tested your ability to set boundaries (and stick to them) with your little ones. In Aries, you'll have an easier time laying down the law with compassion in tow. Get more invested in helping them develop their creative talents. Make time to explore spiritual and imaginative activities together. In the process you'll reconnect to your own childlike wonder. That's the ultimate secondary benefit to spending time with the children in your world.

SATURN IN ARIES

MAY 24 – SEPTEMBER 1, 2025
FEBRUARY 13, 2026 – APRIL 12, 2028

Just as you're ready to float off on a pink cloud, gravity comes along and brings you back down to Earth. For the first time in nearly three decades, grounded, no-nonsense

Saturn strides into Aries. From May 24 to September 1, the heavy planet joins Neptune in that same fifth house of romance, creativity and fame. Womp-womp.

No, this doesn't have to interrupt your previously scheduled romantic high, but it may tone down the plot a little. As future-minder Saturn grinds its way through Aries for three months, it's going to be harder to keep your love life free-flowing and undefined. While earlier this spring, everything was just rolling along without a hitch, suddenly, you find yourself having serious conversations about the Future with a capital F. For some Sagittarians, "will we or won't we?" anxiety could pervade interactions making it impossible to stay present in each other's company.

Before you heave a disappointed sigh, remember that a mature, grounded approach to love could lead you to the kind of lasting partnership that REAL happily-ever-after's are made of. Saturn in competitive Aries can put your romantic life through endurance tests. The ringed taskmaster is "in fall" in Aries, one of its most challenging places on the zodiac wheel due to the fundamental mismatch of energies. Cautious Saturn rides the brake while impulsive Aries hits the gas. You may feel caught in a cycle of stops and starts between May 24 and September 1.

If you're willing to grit your teeth and work through the hiccups, you might wind up with a grand prize on the other end of this three-year cycle, which picks up again from February 13, 2026 to April 12, 2028. True love requires effort and commitment, but it's not just about tying the knot. Finding healthy ways to work through the tangles and kinks as a couple is what builds strength and cements your bond. This means embracing your person for better or worse. Caveat: If "worse" means toxic, Saturn advises you to let that not-so-charming character ride off into the sunset alone.

Before you can lower the drawbridge to your heart, you may need to embrace your own so-called flaws. For the record, Sagittarius, these are the authentic gifts that make you special and unique. Praise and people-pleasing can be pitfalls for your sign, but it's exhausting being "on" all the time. Even YOU can't keep up the performative bit forever. If you've built bonds on false expectations, unraveling these could cause breakdowns and possibly breakups. Know this: People worth keeping around have probably already seen, loved and accepted the full spectrum of who you are, even if you've been trying to conceal certain aspects of your humanity. Time to find out, one way or another!

For Sagittarians who've put romance on the back burner—or those who've been lounging a little too long in Archer-off-duty mode—it's time to revive your inner Sleeping Beauty. This isn't about waiting for someone else's kiss to awaken you; it's about rekindling your zest for life and self-care, which in turn will make you glow. Reconnect with your own allure through rituals and routines (Saturn's favorite words) that ignite your glow. This could be anything from a nightly skin-care routine to a weekly dance or art class that gives you an outlet for creative expression. Hello, joy!

If you're single, know this: Embracing your authentic, effortlessly attractive self is what will magnetically draw the right person to you. It's not about magic, Sagittarius; it's about letting your true beauty shine through. Long-term relationships also benefit from your self-love. When you fill your own cup, your love interest gets to experience your wholeness and has space to tend to their own personal growth alongside yours.

With Saturn forming a supportive trine to your Sagittarius Sun, efforts to deepen connections will feel rewarding and fulfilling—just give it time. This is also a powerful opportunity to polish up your personal brand, making sure that you stand out in your industry and among your peers. Work with the pros, from an elevated glam squad to a professional photographer (or videographer) who can help you polish your image to a brilliant, five-star shine. Saturn's three-month cycle may be brief, but put your best foot forward. Whether you're wearing a glass slipper or a Prada loafer, you could strut right into the VIP room once Saturn returns to Aries in February of 2026.

4 SURRENDER TO SENTIMENTALITY

VENUS RETROGRADE IN ARIES AND PISCES

ARIES: MARCH 1 – 27
PISCES: MARCH 27 – APRIL 12

Retro romance is on the agenda this March 1, as Venus spins into a nostalgic six-week retrograde. If you suddenly can't stop obsessing about "the one that got away" or wish you could access that old, familiar tug on your heartstrings with your live-in partner, get ready. Cupid's arrows could lead you back through a time warp while this cycle wages on until April 12.

While Venus turns retrograde every 18 months, this year's backspin could deepen your longings in ways you haven't felt for quite a while. The retrograde begins in Aries and your passionate fifth house from March 1 to 27, which is sure to set off some dormant fireworks or give you the urge to go ignite them your damn self. Then, on March 27, Venus dips back into Pisces and your sensitive, domestic fourth, which brings the focus closer to home. Is it time to cohabitate, exchange keys or move somewhere that you'll have better luck in love? Questions like these could consume you while Venus retreats through this zone until April 12.

Before you make any radical moves, consider this: Maybe you've been looking for love in all the wrong places, or not looking at all because you didn't want to deal with the constraints of a relationship on your precious free time. Your indie-spirited sign can get quite comfortable being a party of one; too comfortable, maybe. With Venus backing up through self-authorized Aries, you could meet someone who understands the delicate balance between "together time" and giving each other space to pursue individual interests.

Attached Archers may find themselves revisiting old drama or even being tempted by an outside attraction. Even if nothing physical is happening, be honest with yourself: Are you spilling more personal intel and sexual fantasies with your work BFF than you are with the person who shares your bed? Maybe it seems easier to open up to them because you don't have a history, but they don't call it an emotional affair for nothing. This faux intimacy can be exhilarating at first (baring souls with no strings attached, woohoo!), but it's like filling up on low-grade fuel.

Our recommendation? Take the Venus retrograde challenge and lovingly confront the issues in your relationship(s). With some gentle excavation, you'll figure out where chemistry started to fall off. Did you become too accommodating and wind up resenting your boo? Have finances and responsibilities become lopsided, throwing you into an unsexy parent-child dynamic?

While you can never replace the dopamine-fueled buzz of "new relationship energy," you might discover an equally delightful (and far more intimate) way to bond with your tried-and-true boo. Hint: It may involve doing things that the two of you have never tried before. While Venus is reversing through Aries, dabble with dressing in sexier ways, which you probably have the wardrobe for already. Splurge a little on pampering: that weekly blowout and massage, the monthly facial; when you treat yourself like a million bucks, your confidence soars. When it comes to more dramatic style shifts, like a new hair color or tattoo, it's honestly best to hold off until beauty queen Venus is back to her senses on April 12.

If you're still nursing a wound, use these six weeks to process the pain and fully heal. You could be back on the dating scene before May. When Venus backs into Pisces from March 27 to April 12, you'll be especially tapped in to your emotions and, if you devote the time, you can really use this window to process them and begin to move them through your body.

During this time, home and family matters could demand extra attention. No blowing off spring gatherings, like Easter, Passover or a family vacation this year, Sagittarius. Well, not without paying a hefty emotional price for making your inner circle feel like second thoughts. Don't forget where your bread is buttered in the first half of April and you won't wind up with a higher-than-usual "churn rate" when it comes to your loyal supporters.

Got designs on any home improvements? While Venus backs up through Pisces (March 27 to April 12) hold off on changes, even the cosmetic ones. Your tastes could fluctuate wildly, but the plum velvet Chesterfield that you snagged at a weekend antique market might cramp your living room—if you can even get it through the front door! Have fun researching different styles and also measuring the space, gathering swatches and giving yourself ample time to see what's out there before settling on any changes. After April 12, you'll have a clearer idea if "Regency" or "California Coastal" is a better look to lean into.

5 BALANCE CAREER AND HOME

LUNAR NODES IN VIRGO AND PISCES
NORTH NODE IN PISCES, SOUTH NODE IN VIRGO
JANUARY 11, 2025 – JULY 26, 2026

Thrill seeking Sagittarians are always chasing the next big adventure, but what's going on back at the ranch? Starting January 11, the destiny-driven North Node drifts into Pisces, anchoring itself in your fourth house of home, family, and roots. Don't worry—we're not telling you to hit pause on your wild expeditions (never!), but even the most free-spirited archer needs a cozy basecamp. This transit only rolls around every 18-19 years, Sagittarius, so think of it as your cosmic call to find balance between your wanderlust and your foundation.

While this may not herald the Eat, Pray, Love journey you were hoping for in 2025, it's a necessary cycle to fortify your roots for the next chapter. But here's the exciting part! Between now and July 26, 2026, you've got a golden opportunity to (re)design your version of "domestic bliss." With your eclectic tastes, this could be the start of your very own Nomadland-inspired adventure or maybe a makeover of your space that looks like it's straight out of Architectural Digest. Whether you're turning your home into a sanctuary or setting up the ultimate travel launchpad, it's time to create a space that feels as expansive as your dreams.

Don't wait to make changes. Your environment affects your vibe more than you might realize. If your place still has that "backpack and hostel" vibe, maybe it's time for an upgrade. Start with easy swaps: some globally inspired decor, fresh plants, or a paint color that sparks joy. Need some flow? Try Feng Shui or rearrange your space to reflect your ever-evolving energy. Boost the positive energy in your environment by removing clutter.

Thinking of a bigger move? Well, buckle up! After January 11, those plans could shift into high gear. Whether you're dreaming of a tiny house that lets you travel more freely or a chichi apartment with Emily in Paris vibes, the North Node in Pisces will support you. Just don't let your Sagittarius enthusiasm run wild—avoid committing to any huge renovations unless you can genuinely create the time and budget for them.

There's no rush to make changes. You have until July 2026 to move through this state. Whether you're swapping roommates, moving in with a partner, or buying your first home, begin by visualizing your dream scenario. Picture it in vivid detail—what does your ideal home look like, feel like, even smell like? The clearer your vision, the closer you'll be to making it a reality.

Heads up: Who you share your space with will matter more than ever during this North Node transit. After January 11, your sensitivity to other people's moods will be on high alert. Emotional energy is contagious, and living with a human tornado could make you feel like you're stuck in a reality show you didn't sign up for.

Let's talk about your ultimate "home," AKA your body. With the North Node weaving through your fourth house—in detoxifying Pisces—you're ready to break some unhealthy habits. While moderation is key, you may try cutting out certain foods from your diet to reset your system. Look into anti-inflammatory (even anti-histamine) eating plans. Work with a doctor or nutritionist if this is a struggle for you. Your sign doesn't do well with deprivation, so it may work to slowly crowd out some of the starchy, sugary foods with fiber-rich veggies and lean proteins.

The fourth house sits at the base of your chart and is associated with secure foundations. While the North Node moves through Pisces, thoughts may turn to life passages that are inevitable for us all. It may be time to draw up a will, especially if you have kids or own property that you want to make sure goes into the right hands after you leave this plane. A life insurance policy can be a smart investment, too, helping to cover costs in your elder years or distribute to your family as an inheritance. On a less somber note, it's never too soon to have a retirement fund in place. If you don't have a Roth (or SEP) IRA, an index fund or anything that pays a higher-yielding interest, this is your time to raise your financial IQ and start making contributions.

Worried about your career momentum slowing down while you focus on nesting? Fear not! Across the zodiac, the South Node moves into Virgo and your tenth house of career from January 11, 2025, to July 26, 2026. This is the perfect time to streamline your professional goals and sharpen your focus—without losing your Sagittarius aim at the highest target. You'll still have plenty of opportunities to spread your wings, but Virgo's influence will help you get organized for the next phase.

In discerning Virgo, the South Node helps you attract professional partners who match your work ethic and pace. This is a time to "work smarter, not harder" by really concentrating on things like your value proposition, core offerings and overall strategy.

Ready for a pivot? This could be a stellar time to explore new career paths, start a side hustle, or dive deeper into a project you're passionate about. Consider work that allows you to inspire others, whether through travel, coaching, or something that plays into your wellness goals.

As you align your home and career, this is your chance to find harmony between your Sagittarius thirst for adventure and the need for a solid foundation. Your wanderlust will never fade, not even with the North Node in Pisces. But creating a strong base will only empower you to reach even greater heights in your next great adventure.

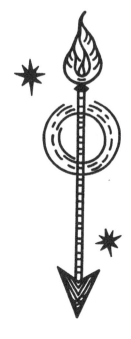

Love

SAGITTARIUS 2025 FORECAST

Partnerships are your playground AND your classroom in 2025, as a spate of planets ping your seventh house of relationships and your fifth house of high romance. Wild experimentation and liberation? Sure, but not without a measure of boundaries and some sort of game plan for how you want your future to roll out.

As the year opens up, free-spirited Jupiter is already halfway through a twelve-month tour through Gemini and your seventh house of relationships. (Throw your hands in the air! And wave 'em like you just don't care!) Your red-spotted ruler has been laying the groundwork here since May 25, 2024, helping you break free from outdated relationship patterns and inviting you to author the kind of coupling that works for YOU.

Once Jupiter's retrograde ends on February 4, you'll have until June 9 to really make the most of this expansive energy. You may be inspired to take a "life partnership" leap, maybe with someone from a different background or even long-distance. On the flip side, if a relationship is feeling more like a ball-and-chain, Jupiter's liberating vibe could have you planning a fabulous "divorce partyyyyyy!"

When Uranus swoops into Gemini from July 7 to November 7, the rulebook flies out the window. This planet of surprises could evoke an attraction to someone completely unlike your usual "type." Coupled Archers, get ready for a love revolution as you're inspired to do something edgy with your partner, like living abroad for a year (both of you—or one of you). This is just a preview of what's to come on April 25, 2026 when Uranus fully settles into your seventh house until 2033.

Careful not to make any rash moves while ardent Venus spins into her every-584-days retrograde from March 1 to April 12. As she backtracks through Aries (until March 27) and Pisces, you could find yourself questioning everything—especially if a hotter-than-a-furnace ex pops up for round two. But you put that love story to bed for a reason, right? Even if you DO rekindle that flame, make sure you can REALLY get to the other side of your prior sticking points. Attached? Careful not to kick up the dust of old dramas, just to keep things "interesting."

The final solar eclipse in Aries on March 29 is like a love reset button, closing a two-year chapter of romantic shifts. If you've been stuck in a loop of "will they or won't they" or "should I or shouldn't I?" this eclipse can bring much needed closure. Move ahead together or let go and move on to a more fulfilling plan.

And that's not all the push-pull going on. Odd-couple Neptune and Saturn are both doing a pass through Aries. This cycle can help you get serious about what you really want in love, while still leaving room for a little magic and fantasy. You'll be craving a connection that feels solid but also feeds your soul. Dreamy Neptune dissolves boundaries and oft-dreary Saturn lays them down like cement bricks. Yes, here's where the classroom part comes in. Tap the courageous instincts of self-authorized Aries to talk through your fears and architect a structure that works for you. With Neptune in Aries from March 30 to October 22 and Saturn joining from May 24 to September 1, you have a chance to practice this "not a people-pleaser anymore" energy—with love, of course. Don't worry about acing this overnight. Next year, Neptune rolls back into Aries for thirteen years starting January 26, 2026. Saturn kicks off a longer, two-year cycle on February 13, 2026. Practice makes perfect.

On June 9, your ruler, daring Jupiter, heads into Cancer and your intimate, erotic eighth house. While Uranus in Gemini takes you on a wild ride, Jupiter is now inviting you to get seriously invested. Can you find liberation through devotion? Challenge! Major commitments are on the table during this yearlong cycle, which lasts until June 30, 2026: Moving in together, marriage, or even signing a prenup to protect your assets. Whether you're merging lives or investment portfolios, establish clear financial rules to ensure that both love and money flow smoothly.

The spiciest time of year comes in Q4. Not only will Jupiter in your seductive eighth house expand your sensual palette, but lusty Mars takes a lap through Sagittarius from November 4 to December 15.

Head-turning confidence? Check! Just make sure you beam those charms selectively to attract a focused pool of contenders. You like a high-low mix in your lovers, but 'tis the season to elevate your standards. And just in time for the holidays, Venus sweeps through your sign from November 30 to December 24, gift-wrapping the year in romance, pleasure and plenty of passion.

SAGITTARIUS: LUCKIEST *love* DAY

MAY 22

Get ready to put the "lust" in "wanderlust" as Venus and Mars dance into a titillating fire trine today. Seductive Venus is in Aries and your fifth house of true love, putting you in passionate spirits. As Mars chimes in from Leo and your worldly ninth house, sparks could fly with someone from any corner of the globe. Travel is your love language, so coupled Archers could slip off for a sexy, one-night staycation or get a longer vacation on the books.

Money & Career

SAGITTARIUS 2025 FORECAST

Career takes on a laser-sharp focus as the purpose-driven South Node settles into Virgo and your professional tenth house. This karmic transit, which lasts from January 11, 2025 until July 26, 2026, encourages you to simplify, structure and streamline your approach to career.

First order of business: Strip away the distractions and zero in on what truly matters. No more juggling endless projects or saying yes to everything. This is your year to create lasting income streams and cement your financial security by focusing on the long game. Think steady growth, not quick wins.

With this shift in mindset, you'll be more attuned to the structures that create sustainability. Thanks to your ruler, abundant Jupiter, rolling through your Gemini- and Cancer-ruled partnership zones all year, you won't have to do that alone. Sign on with savvy collaborators, assemble a team or redesign your front-facing materials to ensure that you attract clients who value your expertise.

Are you a seasoned pro? Step into your role as an expert and position yourself as a trailblazing leader in your field. Think (and act) more like a boss and less like a doer, Sagittarius. No more getting buried in the day-to-day grind. In 2025, you need to keep your eye on the big picture, create systems, and above all, delegate. Lasting success is the goal!

By the end of this transit, you'll feel more in control of your professional destiny, with systems in place to create long-term income streams that don't rely on constant hustle. Speaking of systems, chaotic Uranus has been in Taurus since May 2018, shaking things up in your administrative sixth house—and creating plenty of instability along the way. Whether it's job changes, exhaustive schedules or unpredictable revenue streams, Uranus has kept you on your toes. So you'll feel a huge burden lift when, from July 7 to

November 7, Uranus darts into Gemini, offering a preview of the fresh energy to come. The disruptions to your workflow begin to abate as you regain control of your daily grind. But don't get too comfortable just yet. Uranus will return to your 6th house for one final round from November 7, 2025 to April 25, 2026, demanding a few end-of-year pivots and innovative strategizing.

Two magic words to use like a spell in 2025: compounding interest. Starting June 9, your ruler, bountiful Jupiter, powers into Cancer and your eighth house of investments and big money, the kind earned from royalties, commissions, inheritances, property sales or classic Wall Street earnings. What NOT to do? Gamble it all in one place—a real risk with Jupiter here. But a savvy, diversified portfolio could set you up for long-term wealth and the kind of money you can have fun with. (The best kind, as far as a Sagittarius is concerned.)

Joint ventures could pay off handsomely now. You might find yourself working closely with partners or pooling resources with trusted family and friends. If you've been thinking about buying or selling real estate, Jupiter may flash the cosmic green light. Enterprising Sagittarians: Get that business plan ready! People will want to put dollars behind your dreams.

Before the year is through, you could be pitching to VCs or putting together your own group of angel investors to build your dream.

You'll finish the year strong with make-it-happen Mars powering through your sign from November 4 to December 15. Take the helm and surge on through to the holidays! You'll whip up excitement and support at every turn, making this one of the best times of 2025 to boldly forge ahead. And...action!

SAGITTARIUS: LUCKIEST *career* DAY

JUNE 24

The Day of Miracles is always a boon for you, when your ruler, bountiful Jupiter, syncs up with the magnanimous Sun. As the two heavenly bodies unite in Cancer this June 24, they'll team up in your eighth house of "big money" for the first time in over a decade. An investment could pay off or you could tap into a lucrative opportunity that brings in a large lump sum of cash. Don't shy away from shop talk!

2025
SAGITTARIUS

12
MONTH
OVERVIEW

January MONTHLY HOROSCOPE

Money is on your mind until January 19, as the Capricorn Sun shines into your second house of resources and value. While you might be itching for a splurge, skip the instant gratification fixes. This is an optimal time to evaluate spending habits and set financial goals that support your long-range dreams. On January 11, the lunar nodes shift into soulful Pisces and pragmatic Virgo, sparking a transformative 18-month cycle that will impact your home life and career. Expect seismic shifts in your work-life balance that align with your desire for growth and freedom in both areas. Your social life will be abuzz starting January 19, when the Sun moves into free-spirited, experimental Aquarius and your communication sector. This four-week cycle is all about networking, sharing ideas and test driving innovative plans. On the 29th, The Year of the Wood Snake begins, which could metamorphosize your relationship to money and add richness to your daily routines.

February MONTHLY HOROSCOPE

February's off to a buzzworthy start for you! With the Sun beaming into Aquarius and your uber-social third house, everyone wants to partner with you and enjoy a piece of your time. This is peak season for networking, coworking and pairing up on short-term ventures. Writing and media projects will also get a rush of energy. Even more happy news! On February 4, Jupiter, your ruling planet, turns direct in Gemini, reigniting your seventh house of partnerships. Relationships that have felt stalled could see a burst of forward momentum, opening up exciting new possibilities. Also on the 4th, Venus embarks on a long tour through Aries, heating up your fifth house of romance and creativity well into the spring. But here's a slight plot twist. From March 1 to April 12, Venus will be retrograde, so whatever kicks up now might hit a speedbump next month. (Don't panic!) Your rarely seen nesting instincts take hold once Pisces season begins on the 18th. Take a breather from socializing and traveling to deal with matters back at home base. Molten Mars turns direct in Cancer on February 23, sending sultry waves into your eighth house of permanent bonding. Whether you're ready for breakthroughs or breakups, you're ready to take command of the action again.

March MONTHLY HOROSCOPE

Casa Archer is a buzzing hive of creativity as the Pisces Sun illuminates your fourth house of home, family and emotional foundations until March 20. Pour your energy into a decorating project. Host movie nights, dinner parties and out-of-town guests. But don't get too comfortable! Your Aries-ruled fifth house of romance, creativity and self-expression is about to take the stage. Both Venus and Mercury will be retrograde in Aries this month—Venus from March 1 to 27 and Mercury from March 15 to 29—which could stir up some buried longings. Find balance between giving to others and nurturing your own passions. An ex could return with tantalizing promises. You're not the same person you were when you first met so be careful not to romanticize this "second chance." The Virgo lunar eclipse on March 14 brings clarity to your career and long-term goals, helping you realign with your true path. When Aries season begins on the 20th, unleash your creative energy and let yourself be seen. The Aries solar eclipse on March 29 marks the end of a two-year cycle in your fifth house. Your hard work since 2023 could bring fame and recognition—at last! That goes triple after March 30 when Neptune enters Aries for the first time since 1875, starting an iconic 14-year cycle that will put your name on the map.

April MONTHLY HOROSCOPE

Blaze new trails, Sagittarius! With the Sun lighting up your fifth house of creativity, romance and pure, unadulterated fun until April 19, you're ready to run off leash. But before you dive headfirst into all the excitement, take a pause. Mercury is retrograde in Pisces and your emotional fourth house until April 7, and Venus is spinning in reverse until April 12. This cosmic slowdown gives you a chance to resolve a few home and family matters that are weighing heavily on your conscience. If you're in the market for a move or simply want to get out and play more, you'll have the green light after April 12. That goes triple after the 18th, as thrillseeking Mars soars into Leo and your ninth house of travel, adventure and personal growth until June 17. This expansive cycle only comes around every other year, and when it does, it's anyone's guess what corner of the globe you'll find yourself on. Entrepreneurial ventures, publishing projects and educational pursuits all get a high-octane blast from Mars in Leo. But, ground control to Major Sag! Taurus season begins on the 19th, as the Sun anchors into your sixth house of work and wellness. While you're zooming into the stratosphere, make sure you have healthy habits in place. Work-life balance is not an oxymoron, Archer, it's your new benchmark for success.

May MONTHLY HOROSCOPE

Get organized, Sagittarius! As the Taurus Sun blows the whistle in your sixth house of health, work and daily routines until May 20, it's your annual call to bring more structure to your life. Clean up your overbooked schedule, streamline your tasks and refresh your wellness habits by designing a workout and eating plan you can actually pull off. (Think: 30-minute HIIT workouts and premade grain bowls.) On May 4, Pluto flips retrograde in Aquarius, backing through your third house of communication and community until October 13. Take a step back to refine your message. Are you being heard, or are your ideas getting lost in translation? Small changes can bring big results. People are your passion again once the Sun moves into Gemini and your seventh house of relationships this May 20. Some exciting collaborations are in store during this four-week cycle, so take the initiative to get those underway. But the real game-changer arrives on May 24, when Saturn enters Aries for the first time since 1998, activating your fifth house of creativity, romance and self-expression. Saturn's steady influence will help you get serious about your passions, pushing you to commit to creative projects or romantic relationships with long-term potential. It's time to lay the foundation for lasting joy!

June MONTHLY HOROSCOPE

Shift from wide-angled lens to focus mode, Sagittarius. This June 9, your roaming ruling planet Jupiter radars in on a new position as it moves into Cancer and your sharp, sexy (and dare we say, obsessive) eighth house. This fresh, yearlong cycle wraps up twelve months of Jupiter in Gemini, which has brought a fleet of partnership opportunities from every corner of your universe. But as every Archer knows, "more" isn't always actually "more." Now it's time for a deep curation. Energy flows where your attention goes, and between now and June 30, 2026, you need to pick the sources that will bring the healthiest, wealthiest ROI. And that goes from the bedroom to the boardroom during this "money, power, sex" cycle. But easy does it. The Sun is still in Gemini until June 20, keeping you in a jovial, "the more, the merrier" mood. Mid-month might bring a bit of friction as Jupiter hits some complex squares with Saturn on the 15th and Neptune on the 18th. Competitors and critics could have some opinions to share. Are they just jealous or should you respond to SOME of their feedback? A subtle pivot may be in order to get yourself back in everyone's good graces—the place where an optimistic-yet-principled Sagittarius belongs. Momentum-builder Mars moves into Virgo on June 17, energizing your career sector and pushing you to get organized about long-term goals. Cancer season begins with the solstice on the 20th, shifting you into full power-player mode. Poolside strategy meetings? Let's go! By June 24, the Day of Miracles, when the Sun and Jupiter align, you'll have a golden opportunity to manifest breakthroughs in intimacy, finances or personal transformation. Jupiter's got mogul-sized plans for you now, Sag—embrace the journey!

July MONTHLY HOROSCOPE

You're on a roll this July, making impactful moves, attracting funding, living your erotic truth. While the Sun copilots alongside Jupiter in Cancer until the 22nd, some of your best work will be done behind the scenes or at a private table at the most exclusive restaurant or club. Circulate the NDAs and protect your IP. Your ideas will be worth their weight in platinum so don't underestimate their current value. Who will co-sign on your genius? Make zero assumptions, Archer. On July 7, disruptive Uranus shakes things up as it moves into Gemini and your seventh house of partnerships for six months, sparking unexpected shifts in your relationships. New alliances could form, or existing ones might take surprising turns. Since this is a preview of a longer, seven-year cycle of Uranus in Gemini that begins in April 2026, you may merely feel the rumblings of change that kick in next year. Pro tip: Forget about what the so-called neighbors think. Innovative solutions for how you "do" relationships can save you from tumbling down a fearful rabbit hole of abandonment issues and insecurity. Adding to this inquiry, Neptune, Saturn and Chiron all turn retrograde in Aries (on the 4th, 13th and 30th, respectively), spotlighting your fifth house of romance, fame and self-expression. Creativity will be cathartic during these five-month cycles. Keep your still-developing ideas—and your relationship goals—private. When the Sun moves into Leo on July 22, your thirst for adventure kicks into high gear, but there IS a catch. Just a few days earlier, on the 18th, Mercury slips into a three-week, signal-scrambling retrograde. Plan all travel with care between now and August 11, double-confirming reservations and bringing along plenty of things to entertain yourself in the event of possible delays.

August MONTHLY HOROSCOPE

Let curiosity be your guide! While the Leo Sun treks through your nomadic, entrepreneurial ninth house until the 22nd, you're in full-on seeker mode. Travel, study, explore new entrepreneurial possibilities. Caveat: You may want to wait until Mercury wraps its retrograde on August 11 to pull the trigger on plans. Stay flexible if you hit delays and remember that detours often lead to better destinations. When it comes to love, familiarity might just breed the sexiest encounters you've had in a while! Thank love planet Venus, who is burrowed in Cancer and your intimate, erotic eighth house until the 25th. Vulnerable conversations bring you closer now. If you need to align around shared resources, diplomatic Venus can help with negotiations. Give the VIPs up-close-and-personal levels of attention during this cycle. As for everyone else? Make it a group hang! Collaborations will be lively as spark plug Mars bursts into Libra on August 6. With the red planet powering up your eleventh house of teamwork and tech until September 22, you could join forces with fellow innovators to create something the world has never seen. Just make sure everyone's roles are spelled out clearly (and respect those agreements!) to avoid friction. Your career profile shoots to the sky once Virgo season begins on August 22. With the Sun beaming into your tenth house of public achievements and success, you won't mind bringing your projects to the poolside to work out in the sunshine. On August 23, the first of two rare, back-to-back new moons in Virgo arrives, getting you pumped about your achievements. This powerful new moon provides the spark for a fresh start, one that will get an even bigger boost with the solar (new moon) eclipse in Virgo on September 21. Suit up, Sagittarius! What you put into motion now could be a game-changer for your future!

September MONTHLY HOROSCOPE

Boss up, Sagittarius, because the life-giving Sun is shining into Virgo and your tenth house of career ambitions until the 22nd. You'll make significant strides as a leader, especially if you stay focused on a few key goals instead of scattering far and wide. On the 21st, the second in a rare pair of Virgo new moons arrives as a galvanizing solar eclipse. This powerful catalyst helps you launch a new initiative (or one you began with the August 23 Virgo new moon) or push forward to a major milestone. Unexpected opportunities could arise that propel you into the spotlight. Brava! Meanwhile, Mars keeps building steam in Libra and your eleventh house of teamwork and community until September 22. Rally the thought leaders and go-getters and collaborate on shared goals. The only catch? You may have to manage all the strong personalities to mitigate conflicts before they combust. Personal life developments could reach a fever pitch on September 7, when a total lunar eclipse in Pisces illuminates your fourth house of home, family and foundations. Saturn also retrogrades back into Pisces on September 1, reversing through this sign until November 27. You can run, but you can't hide from unresolved family matters or domestic situations that need closure. This could mean making important decisions about where you live or addressing complex dynamics with a relative. Romantically, you have Venus in Leo until the 19th, which gives you the perfect excuse to slip off for a long weekend baecation. Single and looking? Someone who falls outside your usual array of types could sweep you off your statement sneakers. On September 22, the Sun shifts into Libra, highlighting your social life and eleventh house of friendships. You're in the mood to connect, but aggro Mars downshifts into Scorpio the same day, activating your twelfth house of rest and closure until November 4. Balance the social buzz with solitary moments to meditate and recharge. Unless you want to get a reputation for last-minute cancellations, try not to overbook yourself!

October MONTHLY HOROSCOPE

What's good for the gander, Sagittarius? You'll be in an "all for one and one for all" frame of mind as the Sun beams into Libra and lights up your eleventh house of community and long-term goals until October 22. You're in the mood to make a social impact, organize events for your community and network with people who inspire you. By the time the new moon in Libra arrives on October 21, you'll have gathered a fleet of prospective collaborators and may already have a vision for a project you can kick off together this fall. With love planet Venus also heading into Libra on October 13, romance could bubble up from one of your community affiliations. Coupled Archers: Get out and mingle together as a pair. Also on the 13th, magnetic Pluto turns direct in Aquarius and your third house of communication, giving you the power to amplify your voice and influence. Step out of the shadows and share your ideas with conviction. Your mic drops will make a major impact. Dial back some of the socializing on the 22nd, when the Sun slips into Scorpio and your twelfth house of restorative healing and closure. Tie up loose ends and integrate important lessons learned before your birthday season begins on November 21. This four-week period is ideal for wrapping up unfinished projects, letting go of old habits and focusing on rest and reflection. While the work you're doing now may be more behind-the-scenes and less glamorous, it's essential for your growth and will set you up for success. Also on the 22nd, Neptune retrogrades back into Pisces for the rest of its backspin (until December 10), making you crave a bit more time at home. Work on forgiveness, especially with family members and close friends with whom you're ready to do some healing work.

November MONTHLY HOROSCOPE

Sweet, sweet fantasies! The Sun slow-jams in Scorpio and your dreamy, soulful twelfth house until the 21st which could make life feel as surreal as a Salvador Dali painting. With vivacious Venus slipping into Scorpio from November 6 to 30, your imagination will be on fire, whether you're painting a series of nudes or dancing a sultry striptease for your amour du jour. Either way, your boundaries could be softer this month. Not that you'll be in a complete fog! On the 4th, go-getter Mars launches into Sagittarius for the first time in two years snapping your ambitious side to attention. This cycle, which fires up your personal passions until December 15, will really kick into high gear on November 21, when the Sun marches into Sagittarius and lights up your trailblazing first house for four weeks. Before then, you'd do well to sort through what initiatives are actually paying off—and which ones might be leading you astray from your higher goals. On the 9th, Mercury spins retrograde, starting off the signal-scrambling circuit in YOUR sign, then slipping back through Scorpio and your befuddling twelfth house from November 18 to 29. Consider this a caution flag, Sagittarius, warning against your impulsive habit of racing off on a spontaneous mission and "building the plane in the air." As Uranus retrogrades back into Taurus and your systematic sixth house from November 7 until February 3, 2026, follow protocol! Your ruler, enterprising Jupiter, is also slipping into its annual four month retrograde on the 11th, this year in Cancer and your eighth house of joint ventures. Every move you make impacts other people on the game board. Be strategic—and considerate! A bright spot of news for the month's end: Stabilizing Saturn turns direct and powers forward through Pisces and your foundational fourth house on the 27th. With all these moving parts, this grounding influence will feel like a huge relief. Home and family matters may straighten out miraculously, just in time for the holidays!

December MONTHLY HOROSCOPE

Birthday season rages on until the 21st, and with brilliant Mars and glamorous Venus also in your sign (until the 15th and 24, respectively), you'll have a shine that could put the Trafalgar Square tree to shame. This trifecta makes you magnetic, adventurous and eager to take the lead. Launch those bold EOY plans and say "yes" to any opportunity that lets the world see your magic. Dreamy Neptune ends its five-month retrograde on December 10. Now, it shifts into drive in Pisces and your fourth house of home, family and emotional roots. Confusion around your living situation or family matters begins to lift, making way for peace—and space to set healthy boundaries with the people closest to you. Passionate Mars waves farewell on the 15th and moves into Capricorn, energizing your second house of finances, values and material resources until January 23, 2026. With the Sun following suit on the 21st (solstice) and Venus heading into Capricorn on the 24th, you wind down the year on a more grounded, practical note. Financial fluctuations could stabilize. You don't have to stuff every stocking, Sagittarius. Streamline your spending and wow people with one thoughtfully chosen gift that they'll love. Work opportunities may already flow in before 2026, setting you up for a prosperous time. With this lowkey vibe in the air, ring in the New Year with a celebration that's both intimate and luxe, such as a fancy, five-course dinner with friends or a starlit soak in a hot tub at a cabin in the woods. If you can score tickets to an amazing show, that could pull you out into the crowds, but you'll be eager to cuddle up in bed for a luxurious sleep shortly after the calendar turns.

Read your extended monthly forecast for
life, love, money and career! astrostyle.com

A LITTLE ABOUT *Capricorn*

DATES December 21 - January 19

SYMBOL The Sea Goat

ELEMENT Earth

QUALITY Cardinal

RULING PLANET Saturn

BODY PART Knees, skin, bones, teeth

BEST TRAITS
Loyal, family-oriented, hardworking, devoted, honest, resourceful, wise, protective

KEYWORDS
Ambition, structure, goals, long-term plans, prestige, status, achievement, abundance

*Read more
about Capricorn*

CAPRICORN
IN 2025

ALL THE PLANETS IN CAPRICORN IN 2025	YOUR 2025 HOROSCOPE	TOP 5 THEMES FOR CAPRICORN IN 2025	LOVE HOROSCOPE + LUCKY DATES	MONEY HOROSCOPE + LUCKY DATES

Capricorn in 2025

YOUR YEARLY OVERVIEW

So many people, so little time! If you thought your popularity peaked before, guess again. On January 11, the fateful North Node glides into Pisces, energizing your curious, social third house for eighteen months. Across the board, the karmic South Node treks through Virgo, which can stir up restlessness and turn you into a bit of a nomad. You'll want to do, see and enjoy it all, which means managing your schedule is a must. Lucky for you, expansive Jupiter and innovative Uranus will both spend six months of the year in Gemini and your efficiency-boosting sixth house. Lifehacking is your new superpower (and your lifestyle), whether you're streamlining your work habits, adopting new tech to simplify daily tasks or finally finding the fitness routine that keeps you motivated. This year, think of structure not as a restriction, but as a pathway to more freedom and better health. Partnerships get a burst of momentum on June 9, when growth-agent Jupiter heads into Cancer and your seventh house of relationships for a year. But here's the rub: You won't take kindly to anyone clipping your wings. Can you be more of yourself rather than less? For business, pleasure or mind-blowing romance, create solid alliances that feel expansive. Flowy Neptune and your ruler, structured Saturn, dart into Aries for part of the year, giving your home and family zone a creative but grounded shakeup. Whether it's a move, renovation or establishing firmer roots, blend imagination with practicality and craft a home base that supports your aspirations.

THE PLANETS IN *Capricorn*

THE SUN
DEC 21, 2024–
JAN 19, 2025

DEC 21, 2025–
JAN 20, 2026

It's birthday season for you, so step out and shine! Seek novelty and take extra initiative during this radiant monthlong phase.

NEW MOON

None in Capricorn this year—your work is underway so keep building on what you started at the end of 2024.

FULL MOON
JUL 10
4:37PM, 18°50'

Ready, set, manifest! Your work of the past six months bears fruit and it's time to harvest the rewards.

MERCURY
JAN 8–27

Crown yourself monarch of the social butterflies when popularity-boosting Mercury visits your sign once a year. Circulate and get social—but don't make promises you can't keep!

VENUS
DEC 24, 2025–
JAN 17, 2026

You've got the romantic It Factor when the galactic glamazon charges up your powers of seduction each year. Willpower is weak in the face of beauty and luxury. Watch your spending!

MARS
DEC 15, 2025–
JAN 23, 2026

Motivation is high when energetic Mars visits your sign every couple years—but check your combative streak and try not to come on too strong.

Capricorn in 2025
HIGHLIGHTS

REFINE YOUR ROUTINES WITH JUPITER AND URANUS IN GEMINI

Work and wellness are two areas of life that will NOT be "business as usual" in 2025. Liberated Jupiter and rebellious Uranus are both spending half the year in Gemini and your sixth house of daily routines. Jupiter, which is halfway through this transit (May 25, 2024 to June 9, 2025), has you longing for more fluidity in your schedule. Want freedom? Curb your complexifying tendencies and simplify instead. When disruptive Uranus pops into Gemini from July 7 to November 7, you'll get a glimpse of a seven-year cycle that begins in earnest on April 25, 2026. Stay flexible and ready for change because this cycle could bring shifts in colleagues, project timelines, even the entire way that you do your job! Implement healthy habits and prioritize self-care—it may be the best way to stay grounded during all these fluctuations.

COMMUNICATE AND CIRCULATE: THE LUNAR NODES IN PISCES AND VIRGO

Is it all about who you know or all about what you say? This year, the answer might be, both. On January 11, the fateful lunar North Node begins an eighteen-month trek through Pisces and your articulate third house, encouraging you to share your story. Whether you're recording a podcast, writing a book or just getting out to socialize on a regular basis, you have a lot to say this year. Collaborate, build networks and pass along your knowledge. Across the zodiac wheel, the karmic South Node takes flight in Virgo and your worldly ninth house, helping you reach a wider audience. Traveling could open up important connections, which might even lead you to relocate or become a regular visitor of a second location. From university campuses to YouTube home studios, teaching could become a new (or renewed) passion.

VENUS RETROGRADE: REFLECT, RESET AND REALIGN

What's your love language, Capricorn? And how fluent are you when it comes to speaking other people's dialects? Romantic Venus drops into her every-584-day-retrograde from March 1 to April 12, giving you a chance to refresh your skills. What's worked for you in the past may be falling flat or drawing in people who just aren't your type anymore. But what ARE you transmitting? These eye-opening six weeks might just teach you to flirt, seduce and even search for love in a new and improved way. Put pride aside and ask friends and family to weigh in with honest feedback. Where might your communication style be sending out the wrong signals—not just in love, but with friends and business associates? A little fine-tuning goes a long way.

HOME BASE MAKEOVER: SATURN AND NEPTUNE IN ARIES

The spotlight swings to your domestic life this spring as two outer planets decamp to Aries, giving you a sneak-peek of longer cycles that pick up again in early 2026. From March 30 to October 22, soulful Neptune sweeps through the Ram's realm making you crave a peaceful oasis. Then, from May 24 to September 1, your ruler, stabilizing Saturn, joins Neptune in this fire sign. If you don't love where you live, start looking around. (And watch the tendency to make sacrifices around this area of your life.) Already in your dream home? The activating Aries energy could inspire some decor updates or give you the motivation to entertain regularly. You may need to set new boundaries with family members this year, especially if they've become a little too reliant on you being their rock and provider at your own expense!

JUPITER IN CANCER: EXPANSIVE RELATIONSHIPS

On June 9, abundant Jupiter shifts gears, heading into Cancer, where it will activate your seventh house of relationships until June 30, 2026. You need partnerships to feel limitless and freeing now. Anyone who tries to control you or hold you back? Uh, good luck, babe. Emerge from the couple bubble and go mingle—both independently and as a pair. Single Capricorns could meet their match while traveling, studying or doing personal development work. You may feel inspired to co-create with your partner. During this yearlong cycle, you could launch a joint venture from your love nest, buy property together or take a life-changing baecation. If there are unresolved issues brewing, Jupiter's truth-seeking energy can help you clear the air and reach a new level of authenticity with one another.

TOP 5 THEMES FOR
Capricorn in 2025

1	2	3	4	5
RITUALIZE YOUR ROUTINES	EXPAND YOUR ROMANTIC PALETTE	TURN HOME INTO A SANCTUARY	SET BOUNDARIES WITH YOUR INNER CIRCLE	BROADCAST YOUR BELIEFS

1 RITUALIZE YOUR ROUTINES

JUPITER AND URANUS IN GEMINI

JUPITER: MAY 25, 2024 – JUNE 9, 2025

URANUS: JULY 7 – NOVEMBER 7, 2025 • JANUARY 26, 2026 – MAY 22, 2033

Quick, Capricorn! Grab your copy of James Clear's Atomic Habits and learn all that you can about "temptation bundling" or "reducing friction" around your daily routines. While you're at it, start turning some of those rote tasks into rituals. Two of the most inventive planets, Jupiter and Uranus, are doing laps through Gemini and your systematic sixth house this year. Structure (your sign's favorite word) creates a clear pathway to freedom. Bonus: You might get into the best shape you've been in for years.

JUPITER IN GEMINI

MAY 25, 2024 – JUNE 9, 2025

Yoga retreat in Bali? Bikini boot camp in So-Cal? Travel and wellness go hand-in-hand in 2025, thanks to intrepid Jupiter. The vitality-boosting planet is halfway through a yearlong journey through Gemini and your salubrious sixth house. Healthy living has been in the spotlight since May 25, 2024, so you may already have made your mark on the Peloton leaderboard or found the perfect Pilates studio for stretching and strengthening.

Still stuck in couch potato mode? No more! Good-news Jupiter is buzzing through Gemini until June 9, 2025, bringing supersized momentum for your fitness goals. Capitalize on a New Year's membership sale and score yourself a birthday present at a fitness studio that has the elegant vibes a Capricorn needs to stay inspired.

Those workouts will help zap stress, which can ratchet up this year. Projects may have ballooned with expansive Jupiter in your industrious sixth house, which is exciting but also brings another set of challenges. Before you wind up with an administrative nightmare on your hand,s put proper workflows, systems and apps in place to keep you organized. If you want to grow, you have to make sure you are ready to handle the crush of new clients, expenses and other details.

Fortunately, the expansive and hopeful planet can bring a sense of purpose to all your efforts. How can you make them feel less dutiful and more self-empowering? You may need to tap a coach or mastermind group who can help you prioritize and stay accountable. Whenever possible, find ways to turn dull-as-dishwater routines into "sacred rituals"; make momentous tasks "challenges."

Jupiter is the traveler of the zodiac, so your job this year may afford you enough frequent flyer points to earn priority status with your airline of choice. If you're on the hunt for fresh work opportunities, expand your search radius or follow enterprising Jupiter's lead. Starting your own business might be in the cards for many Caps this year. Already the CEO of your own venture? Stake out new markets for your offerings, perhaps in a totally different area code (or country code!).

Liberated Jupiter also reminds you of the importance of personal freedom: both the day-to-day, vacations and flex time. You might be able to renegotiate the terms of your employment and work remotely at least occasionally. This alone will give you the time to prepare healthy meals and get regular movement into your life.

Just one (not too tiny) heads-up: Jovial Jupiter is the god of the feast, and it warns that there really IS such a thing as too much of a good thing. Jupiter in the sixth house can inspire overeating if you aren't mindful since your appetite for everything is growing. This is a great time to work with a nutrition coach and learn how to cook more delicious plant-based and protein-rich dishes. In addition to cardio and weight training, add in exercises that ground you and put you in a meditative mindset. Pull that yoga mat out of the closet and let the Vinyasa flow.

URANUS IN GEMINI
JULY 7 – NOVEMBER 7, 2025
JANUARY 26, 2026 – MAY 22, 2033

If your motivation—or momentum—starts to flag by the June solstice, just hang on till July 7. That day, high-voltage Uranus lands in Gemini for the first time since 1949, inaugurating what's sure to be a dynamic eight-year journey through your sixth house of work, service, wellness and self-care.

The way you move through your days is about to shift dramatically. The new focus is on simplifying steps and increasing ease. How can you do more with less? That's a puzzle you'll be eager to solve. And once you do, feel free to monetize it as your "proprietary method" or make it accessible through an app.

But let's not get ahead of ourselves. In 2025, Uranus only hangs out in Gemini for a brief, four-month stint, until November 7. Nevertheless, that should be enough of a wave to alert you that a seismic lifestyle shift is heading your way. Next year, on April 25, 2026, Uranus plants itself back in Gemini for seven more years, until May 22, 2033. And yes, this will be a game-changer, particularly when it comes to the way you structure your days.

Since May 2018, Uranus has been in Taurus and your glamorous fifth house, where it's been helping you to add more pleasure to your life. Doing so may have felt like an act of revolution for your hard-driving sign. Incorporating play into work? Prioritizing fun over work some days? That's been a radical concept for you to swallow over the past seven years, Capricorn. Here's hoping that you're among the Sea Goats who allowed yourselves to experience joy, even during the hardest hours (like say, a pandemic), while Uranus toured Taurus.

Starting this July 7, your desires shift in a more streamlined direction. The excessive energy of the past seven years will start to feel burdensome; like something that you're "so over." Overdoing it could take a toll on your health, especially if you're running on a cocktail of stress, adrenaline and caffeine. As futuristic, metaphysical Uranus plugs into curious Gemini and your work and wellness sector, it's time to stop silo-ing those two categories. How can you accomplish more and stress less? Get ready to explore. With edgy Uranus in inquisitive Gemini, you'll be as open to holistic healing and naturopathic medicine as you will be to treatments involving lasers, AI and psychedelics.

Don't worry about being bored! Under this innovative cosmic energy, your workaday routines could become charged with excitement in a different way. While your focus may always be on the final result, you'll become at least as interested in the journey as you are the destination.

Still, we must warn you that there's a paradox to contend with here. Rebellious Uranus goes against the grain, while the sixth house follows processes and procedures. From July 7 to November 7, you may feel constrained by "authority figures" and frustrated by people who insist about playing by the rules. Isn't it ironic, Capricorn, since you're essentially railing against the role that you, as the zodiac's CEO, so often play.

During Uranus in Gemini, embrace the metaphoric role of Chief People Officer instead of Chief Executive Officer. Collaborate with innovators, thought leaders and colleagues you consider to be ahead of the curve. Who you work with determines everything, so set yourself up for success by aligning with a team that values your contributions and demands excellence from every person on board.

While this might sound like a tall order, you don't have to charge in with your usual go-getter zeal. Small tweaks can add up to an entire lifestyle shift with minimal inconvenience or discomfort. Start with: Do your routines support your work life or make things more complicated? Could your systems be more organized or streamlined? In savvy Gemini, technologist Uranus can help you hack your way to a more efficient flow. Ditto for any adjustments you've been wanting to make to your nutritional or exercise regimen.

You may already know what would be ideal, Capricorn. Yet, it's that giant leap from knowing to doing that always trips us up. So rather than put undue pressure on yourself, add one or two tiny new things (weekly yoga, cooking at home) at a time as you phase out unhelpful stuff (boozy brunches, working after hours)...or people. Come up with a game plan and a few specific pivots you can make this year. Stay the course, and you'll realize noticeable progress before Uranus spins back into Gemini at the end of April 2026!

2 EXPAND YOUR ROMANTIC PALETTE

JUPITER IN CANCER
JUNE 9, 2025 – JUNE 30, 2026

Ready to add a plus-one to your roster? When Jupiter swings into Cancer on June 9, it lends its exploratory, broad-minded energy to your seventh house of relationships. Two becomes your magic number in the second half of the year, especially if you're willing to stretch beyond the confines of what (and who) you've traditionally pursued. Opposites attract now—and how! Prepare to have your eyes opened and your mind blown during this cycle, which lasts until June 30, 2026.

Pack your bags, Capricorn. Since Jupiter is the cosmic jetsetter, your preferences may meander into new, unexplored terrain. Stay open to people from diverse cultural backgrounds, as well as the hottie who lives long-distance. Put your suburban, four-bedroom Tudor fantasies on ice for a moment, and open your mind to commuting for monthly visits to a lover in another ZIP code. Absence can make the loins grow hotter.

For coupled Capricorns, this thirteen-month cycle provides bountiful opportunities for co-creation. Jupiter's entrepreneurial influence could see you mixing business and pleasure, teaming up with your sweetie on a professional venture, which is a dream come true for work-hard Capricorn. Start saving up for an epic baecation. Nothing seals a bond quite like a pilgrimage with your partner. How about a cruise on the Caspian Sea or visiting the sacred pyramids in Cairo?

If trouble's been brewing in your closest partnerships, look out! Honest-to-a-fault Jupiter rips off the mask and forces you to stop pretending that everything is (clenched teeth) "fine." But stay aware of your own intensity, Capricorn. Whatever you've held in could rush out like a torrent, completely overwhelming your other half. While you don't want to deny or suppress your feelings, try to keep your focus on the long-term objectives that you want to reach together. If you need help processing anger, perhaps sort through your feelings with a neutral third party before broaching these tender topics.

The last time Jupiter visited Cancer was from June 25, 2013 to July 16, 2014. Flip back in your timeline to see what was happening for you then. Similar themes may arise for you in partnerships or you may be completing a cycle that began nearly twelve years ago. This doesn't necessarily portend a breakup, but it could point to a breakthrough. As the zodiac sign that ages in reverse, you become lighter and freer with every year that passes. You may feel ready to shed some heaviness or undue responsibility that you've carried for others. That's nothing to feel guilty about, Capricorn. Jupiter is here to lift excess burdens so you can be fully present (read: not seething with resentment) in your relationships.

That said, free-spirited Jupiter may indeed be here to liberate you from a connection that you've outgrown. That's a hard concept for you as a devoted Capricorn to swallow. You hate to give up once you've invested. If you've tried everything from tantric retreats to couples' therapy to tandem skydiving and satisfaction is still eluding you, then you may want to face the music. Grief will be unavoidable, but the sooner you feel, the faster you'll heal.

Professional and creative partnerships are also blessed by Jupiter's beams. Since Cancer is your opposite sign, you may find yourself drawn to people who are basically your opposite. You'll do best with a complementary force now, the yang to your yin, rather than a kindred spirit. Plus, it's good sense to ally with people who know how to pick up where you leave off. Jupiter happens to be "exalted" in Cancer, which is its most potent position in the zodiac. Power couple fantasies—which every Capricorn has—could come to life after June 9. Keep your standards high, but not so impossibly rigid that no one gets past the first checkpoint.

3 TURN HOME INTO A SANCTUARY

SATURN AND NEPTUNE IN ARIES

NEPTUNE: MARCH 30 – OCTOBER 22, 2025 • JANUARY 26, 2026 – MARCH 23, 2039
SATURN: MAY 24 – SEPTEMBER 1, 2025 • FEBRUARY 13, 2026 – APRIL 12, 2028

Whether you're putting down roots or pulling them up, get ready for some shifts in your home life this year. Two significant planets—stable Saturn and fluid Neptune—will spend a portion of 2025 in Aries and your domestic fourth house. It's been a very long time since either one visited the sign of the Ram. Saturn last trekked through Aries from 1996 to 1998. Neptune hasn't been here since 1862 to 1875!

The energy of Aries is fiery, independent and active, which is an interesting vibe to have ruling all things "home and family." While Saturn is only in Aries for three months this year, and Neptune for six, things could get lively under your roof. If you've been pondering a change of address, renovations or a new family plan, 2025 could elicit exciting developments. No need to rush, however. In 2026, both planets spin back into Aries for longer cycles—Saturn for two more years and Neptune for another thirteen.

NEPTUNE IN ARIES

MARCH 30 – OCTOBER 22, 2025
JANUARY 26, 2026 – MARCH 23, 2039

Home sweet sanctuary? Neptune drifts into Aries from March 30 to October 22, casting a spell in your fourth house of family, domesticity and emotional roots. Your concept of personal space and security begins to go through a transformation, one that will be fourteen years in the making. Although Neptune only visits Aries for six months in 2025, the effects will be eye-opening. And once the numinous planet settles back into the Ram's realm for a longer stay, from January 26, 2026 to March 23, 2039, changes can REALLY get underway. Don't resist the call to explore the more subtle, spiritual aspects of your personal life this year, even if all you hear is a whisper.

As someone who values structure and stability, fluid Neptune in this foundational part of your chart can feel destabilizing. It's a definite departure from your pragmatic approach to life! Over the next decade-plus, you will get a master class in relying on intuition as much as logic when it comes to making personal decisions. We're not saying you should ignore statistics or the numbers on your precious spreadsheets. The thing is, they may not align with your deeper instincts—the ones that are calling you to do something "impractical," like selling off an asset, buying a fixer-upper or making a cross-country (or out-of-country!) move.

Spiritual Neptune in self-sovereign Aries turns up the volume on your core desires and could shift your compass in an unexpected direction after March 30. Heck, you might just be entering your "Eat, Pray, Love" era. Pay attention to what (and who!) makes you feel like your truest, most sacred self. This is where you want to be, Capricorn, and also who you should keep around.

During this cycle, your connection to home and family may take on a more mystical or spiritual dimension. You're typically focused on creating a solid, reliable environment, but Neptune's influence will encourage you to infuse your space with a sense of peace, creativity, and emotional warmth. Personal tastes matter mightily when it comes to your home. This spring, you could begin customizing Casa Capricorn or turning an area of your house into a music studio or meditation room.

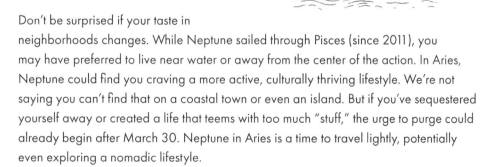

Where before you only noticed the dust bunnies, don't be surprised if you start to pick up on energy strands and vibes in every room. Soulful Neptune here could inspire you to try metaphysical modalities. Use feng shui to get the chi flowing in the right direction. Enlist a shamanic practitioner to do a house blessing or space clearing.

Don't be surprised if your taste in neighborhoods changes. While Neptune sailed through Pisces (since 2011), you may have preferred to live near water or away from the center of the action. In Aries, Neptune could find you craving a more active, culturally thriving lifestyle. We're not saying you can't find that on a coastal town or even an island. But if you've sequestered yourself away or created a life that teems with too much "stuff," the urge to purge could already begin after March 30. Neptune in Aries is a time to travel lightly, potentially even exploring a nomadic lifestyle.

Some Capricorns could ponder a move closer to family, especially if a relative is in need of support. Note: Neptune is the planet of compassion and sacrifice. Stay aware of how much you're giving on a day-to-day basis. Caretaker burnout is a real concern. You would do anything to provide for your loved ones, but gentle reminder: Draining your reserves (no matter how mighty), will render you incapable of giving anyone a hand.

Have you been estranged from a relative? Forgiveness is Neptune's domain. You may finally have a chance to bury the hatchet with someone in your family. Be cautious of unspoken expectations that could lead to disappointment. This is a time to communicate openly and honestly, ensuring that everyone is on the same page and that you're not carrying the weight of unresolved issues. Conversely, you may realize that it's time to put a hardcore boundary in place with someone whose very presence continually triggers a trauma response in you.

In that vein, Neptune in Aries is a powerful time to process old pain around your childhood. Generational patterns have a way of repeating themselves and now's the time to break free of anything from your lineage that feels unhealthy. Therapeutic Neptune can help you access buried memories and shed light on family dynamics that are ready for a 2025 upgrade. Be mindful of Neptune's tendency to blur reality. Try to stay grounded and avoid idealizing the past or getting lost in nostalgia.

As you ease into this longer Neptune cycle, you may notice yourself softening some of your hardcore judgments. That's especially true when it comes to the judgments that you cast on your own emotions. Some feelings won't fit easily into a behavioral model or be explained in a scientific study. And that's okay, Capricorn! Allow yourself to get a little messy. It might just be the healthiest thing you do this year. The trick is to focus on naming and claiming your feelings instead of falling into Neptune's other trap of denial, avoidance and escapism.

Equally important? Keeping healthy boundaries around food, drink and any addictive substances. Avoid anything resembling a slippery slope when you're going through an issue. In daredevil Aries, Neptune could lead you toward destructive behaviors that may temporarily distract you from your pain. Fortunately, your sensible sign understands the concept of taking on a challenge!

SATURN IN ARIES
MAY 24 – SEPTEMBER 1, 2025
FEBRUARY 13, 2026 – APRIL 12, 2028

It's not all incense and crystals in Chez Chèvre in 2025. On May 24, your ruler, structure-hound Saturn, joins Neptune in Aries for three months. Until September 1, it's shining its trusty inspector's headlamp into that very same fourth house of home, family and emotional foundations. Similarly to Neptune, Saturn's tour through Aries is a preview of a longer cycle that begins again on February 13, 2026 and lasts for two more years, until April 12, 2028.

When your galactic guardian changes signs, it can profoundly redirect the focus of your life. Since March 7, 2023, Saturn's been stirring up sediment in Pisces and your third house of peers, communication and local activity. The past couple years may have brought significant changes in your social circles. Old friends that you've outgrown may have faded away while other, newer connections have slowly been getting off the ground. Saturn's restraining energy hasn't made it easy for you to express yourself, but when you did, you made every word count.

As Saturn darts forward into Aries for three months, you may feel more playful and free to speak your mind than you have for a while. Home and family matters will now be under traditional Saturn's watch, and there's added gravitas there. So what's a Sea Goat to do? Tuck into your shearling slippers and put a cast-iron pot on the stove. With disciplined Saturn moving through Aries from May 24 to September 1, you may become more of a homebody than you've cared to be for a while.

Top of the agenda? Making your space truly feel like home. If you're already nodding in agreement, wondering why it's taken so long, Saturn is here to get things moving. Remember, Saturn is the zodiac's legendary taskmaster, demanding commitment and diligence. So if you're truly ready to create your dream dwelling, it's time to roll up your sleeves and get strategic.

Being the process-driven soul that you are, it's best to start with a plan. What are the most pressing changes that you'd like to make to your space? If you're contemplating a move, make a list of preferences in order of importance: natural light to keep your moods up, ample square footage so you have privacy but not SO much that cleaning becomes a never-ending chore. What amenities do you want (need!) in your neighborhood: indie businesses, healthy grocery stores, good public schools? Saturn abhors ambiguity (and so do you, as a Saturn-ruled sign). Write lists, make mood boards, get a picture in your mind before you even start the search. The same holds true for any redecoration or renovation you're contemplating. Between now and April 12, 2028, you can methodically work toward these domestic dreams.

Saturn's trek through Aries can also stir up some reflection (and even regrets) around your relationship with a few key relatives. Do you wish you had a better connection to a parent? You might find yourself navigating difficult, but long-overdue, conversations. Whether it's about setting healthy boundaries or strengthening your connection, this period is ripe for working through these issues. And if you have children, Saturn challenges you to establish clear boundaries in your parenting style. Enforcing rules consistently will be vital. (Sorry kids, no more phones at the dinner table!)

With Saturn in self-sovereign Aries, it's equally important to maintain your own identity and not lose yourself in helicopter parenting. This isn't selfish, Capricorn, it's about modeling an important virtue: Living life with a growth mindset rather than stubbornly refusing to evolve after a certain age. Carve out necessary "me time" and make sure everyone else under your roof is pulling their weight. With Saturn in Aries forming a challenging square to your Capricorn Sun, be prepared for some tough compromises. Family life can be both a source of joy and stress, and without firm boundaries, you may feel taken advantage of due to your protective nature and instincts to provide.

Your social circle may shrink during this time, but that's not necessarily a bad thing. You need supportive, reciprocal relationships now more than ever, Capricorn—friends who truly support and uplift you. Saturn values longevity and people who you meet between May 24 and September 1 could be keepers who become part of your inner circle. No need to rush to become besties—that's not Saturn's style. Be aware of a tendency to judge people on status. Elitism is a pitfall that your sign occasionally struggles with. While Saturn's in Aries, some of the cool kids you hang out with could fade away for the more heartfelt, enduring types you normally might look right past.

4 SET BOUNDARIES WITH YOUR INNER CIRCLE

VENUS RETROGRADE IN ARIES AND PISCES
ARIES: MARCH 1 – 27
PISCES: MARCH 27 – APRIL 12

Spring break reunion, anyone? Starting this March 1, you may feel the urge to reconnect with your innermost circle. The reason for this? Convivial Venus slips into her biennial retrograde, backing up through Aries and your family-oriented fourth house until March 27, then rounding out the retreat in Pisces and your social third house until April 12.

Relatives that you haven't talked to in ages could start pinging you on WhatsApp. And while you're scrolling through Insta between appointments, you could go down a rabbit hole of posts that inspire you to reach out to your college besties. Follow those urges, Capricorn, because these reconnections can be extra sweet during Venus retrograde.

Need to get away for an end-of-winter reprieve? If you're in the mood for a change of scenery, you MIGHT opt for a chic resort with spa amenities. But also think about renting an Airbnb with an open-plan kitchen and heated pool. Domestic vibes follow you wherever you go during the first half of the retrograde, which could be unfortunate if you find yourself surrounded by piña-colada-swilling tourists sharing drunken exchanges at a swim-up pool. (Can't they see that you're trying to read?) Enjoying healthy meals and easy downtime in a private space could be more in alignment with the low-key vibes of this cycle.

Home sweet home could be your favorite location during this cycle. Set up the spare bedroom or couch and invite guests to Casa Capricorn, where you can give them the grand tour of your favorite cultural hotspots. If you want to bury the hatchet with a frenemy or difficult relative, skip the trip and take the process in much smaller bites. With peacekeeping Venus off her game, you might rush to "make nice" only to find the unresolved issue rearing up ten times stronger. Start with a phone call and maybe a lunch date on neutral territory after that.

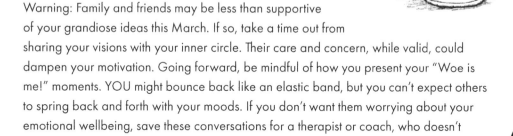

Warning: Family and friends may be less than supportive of your grandiose ideas this March. If so, take a time out from sharing your visions with your inner circle. Their care and concern, while valid, could dampen your motivation. Going forward, be mindful of how you present your "Woe is me!" moments. YOU might bounce back like an elastic band, but you can't expect others to spring back and forth with your moods. If you don't want them worrying about your emotional wellbeing, save these conversations for a therapist or coach, who doesn't have so much skin in the game.

Venus is the planet of love and romance, and this retrograde reminds you that like attracts like. To draw in an emotionally aware partner, you have to be tuned in to your own inner workings. Take time to honor your sentient self, even if that means more alone time or a few extra therapy sessions. You'll find that, as you do, your existing relationships will also improve. Bottom line: It's not frivolous to feel!

With this romantic retrograde going down in your domestic zone until March 27, you may have to negotiate new rules if you share a home with your partner. Do you have adequate space for relaxing in privacy and doing your creative work? If not, you could be quite the cranky member of the lair. Of course, elbowing out your S.O. or family won't work. Look into renting an outside space for your memoir writing or drum practice. If your home and workspaces just don't feel cozy enough, make a few cosmetic upgrades now. But hold off on any massive renovation until Venus is back on track mid-April. Otherwise, you could spend a fortune making your bedroom look like an upscale boutique hotel only to wake up in six weeks to realize it's totally the wrong look.

5 BROADCAST YOUR BELIEFS

LUNAR NODES IN VIRGO AND PISCES
NORTH NODE IN PISCES, SOUTH NODE IN VIRGO
JANUARY 11, 2025 – JULY 26, 2026

Whatever you're selling, Capricorn, we'll take it in bulk! Your strategic genius is about to hit new levels starting January 11, as the fate-fueled North Node returns to Pisces for the first time in nearly 20 years. Until July 26, 2026, it sprinkles some serious cosmic fairy dust into your communicative third house, setting the stage for a major popularity spike. Get ready to start a buzz!

While you're usually heads and tails above most people, this cycle could connect you to peers who can match your standards and work ethic. Surprise twist? Someone you thought was a competitor could actually be the missing link in your success strategy. Fortunately, your practical Capricorn nature isn't one to hold grudges—you're too focused on results to let pettiness get in the way. The third house rules your siblings, friends, coworkers, and neighbors, so don't be surprised if these folks start playing essential roles in your projects. Just make sure you've got everything in writing. Ambiguity? No thanks. In your world, every contract is ironclad, because unclear expectations breed discontent.

Got a message to broadcast? This is your moment to elevate your voice. Start a blog, podcast, or a series of viral social campaigns. As a Capricorn, you are full of actionable insights that improve systems and get things done. With the North Node in Pisces, you'll find the perfect platforms to share your expertise, perhaps within an industry group or a community organization. Publish those white papers, or become the go-to expert in your field. Either way, 2025 is the year to make your mark as a thought leader.

During this 18-month nodal cycle, you could step into roles ranging from spokesperson to brand ambassador. Of course, being the conscientious Capricorn you are, you'll make sure every endorsement reflects your values—sustainably sourced, ethically produced, and, yes, profitable. Your personal brand will be on point, and everything you touch could turn to gold.

While the fate-fueling North Node is giving you the local spotlight, the karmic South Node will simultaneously travel through Virgo and your nomadic ninth house, reminding you that the world is your oyster. Are you casting a wide enough net? While the North Node showers you with nearby opportunities, the South Node encourages you to think big. Did a 23andMe test reveal some far-flung relatives? Maybe it's time to explore your roots with a meaningful trip. After January 11, these kinds of journeys could be life-altering. Make sure your passport is up-to-date.

For many Capricorns, multi-city living could become the new norm. Maybe you're negotiating to go "permanently remote" or setting yourself up as a digital nomad, hopping between locations without skipping a beat at work. Even if globetrotting isn't in the cards for you long-term, spending a few weeks as a "touring resident" in different cities could add some adventure to your year.

Not ready to pack your bags? No worries—the South Node in Virgo could spark your inner scholar. If higher education has been on your radar, now might be the time to apply for that MBA program or take up a new certification. The ninth house also rules spirituality, so you might find yourself revisiting a practice or philosophy that once brought you peace. Whether you're diving into ancient teachings, developing a new workshop, or writing your memoir (Eat, Pray, Capricorn?), this is the year to go deep and share your wisdom with the world.

2025 is setting you up for a whole new level of success, Capricorn—both locally and globally. Whether you're building powerful partnerships, expanding your knowledge, or becoming the voice of authority in your field, the world is ready to hear from you!

Love

CAPRICORN 2025 FORECAST

The love rollercoaster is still serving some ups and downs in the first part of the year, so buckle up, Capricorn. Renegade Uranus has trekked through Taurus since May 2018, shaking things up in your fifth house of love. Whether single or attached, this cycle has kept you on your toes, encouraging you to experiment and break free from convention. Relationships may be one area of life that has felt very un-Capricorn since 2018—and frankly, you're probably ready for a bit more of a steady pace.

Fortunately for you, that's coming soon. From July 7 to November 7, Uranus will dart into Gemini and your sensible sixth house, clearing your love life from its chaotic influence. As the year wraps up, Uranus will do one final lap through your Taurus-ruled romance realm (from November 7, 2025 to April 25, 2026) then won't be back for another eighty years. Whew!

This destabilizing energy hasn't been ALL bad; in fact, it may have felt liberating for many Sea Goats out there. No more trying to keep up with the "Love Joneses." Your romantic trajectory has been yours to author and that may have led to some exciting discoveries that you'll carry into this next season of your life. Perhaps you learned to really, REALLY enjoy your own company. Maybe you discovered your edges in partnership or experimented with a different pace in dating.

If you're still not quite certain what turns you on, carpe diem, Capricorn. And if you are? Carpe diem to you, too. While Uranus twerks through Taurus until July 7, you have a hall pass to explore, experiment and let your body do the talking. This can be a high-minded pursuit, even an intellectual one.

You'll get a tantalizing boost from lusty Mars, who is spending half of 2025 in Cancer and Leo—the rulers of your seventh house of partnerships and erotic eighth house, respectively. Caveat: The feisty red planet will be retrograde until February 23, which could turn up the flame a little too high. Anger and frustration could heat up easily or you may rebel against anyone trying to "pin you down."

Once Mars turns direct on February 23, you're ready to get proactive about love again. While Mars moves through Cancer until April 18, pleasure is your priority. Make a point of getting out more often, dressing up and enjoying cultural activity dates. When Mars heads into Leo from April 18 to June 17, your seductive purr could lure one special soul into your lair, where you're sure to break out some showstopping moves.

This passionate period is anything BUT casual, so say goodbye to the neverending situationships and clear the decks for a relationship that feels like a mutual investment.

The biggest news for your love life this year comes on June 9, when lucky, expansive Jupiter bursts into Cancer, showering your seventh house of relationships with its abundant energy for an entire year. The red-spotted titan hasn't blessed this part of your chart since 2013 to 2014, and its impact could spark a major renaissance in your love life. Turn on that soulmate search light and expand your reach. Worldly Jupiter could serve up a compatible match from an incompatible location. However, this is not the year to rule out a long-distance relationship; well, not if you've FINALLY found someone who ticks all your boxes. (A Herculean effort, if you're being honest.)

Existing relationships may expand in fascinating ways under Jupiter's influence. Perhaps you'll pair up on an entrepreneurial venture, move across the country or get plans in motion for a bucket-list trip to Portugal or Peru. Another possibility? Jupiter's indie-spirited influence can nudge you out of the couple bubble and give you the space to explore separate interests. The right amount of autonomy CAN make the heart grow fonder.

Another wave of magnetism sweeps through your love life at the end of the year, as love planets Mars and Venus copilot through Capricorn in December. Red-hot Mars powers into Capricorn from December 15 until January 23, 2026, giving you the confidence to go after what (or who) you want. And just in time for the holidays, Venus joins the party, sweeping into Capricorn on Christmas Eve and riding alongside Mars until January 17.

This charmed energy could bring more than a mistletoe moment or a NYE kiss, if, that is, you want it that way. Single Sea Goats might be perfectly happy to retain that status through the holidays and enjoy the buffet of romantic options. Even the happily coupled Capricorns could find themselves longing for a little variety, which could lead to some steamy fantasies that you can play out with your partner in real time.

CAPRICORN: LUCKIEST *love* DAY

JUNE 24

The Day of Miracles could bring sweeping surprises for your love life as the shining Sun and lucky Jupiter roll the dice in Cancer and your seventh house of relationships today. Be open to the attractive force of an "opposite" or a situation that expands your view of what love and relationships can look like.

Money & Career

CAPRICORN 2025 FORECAST

Capricorn, 2025 is your year to break free from the grind and discover innovative ways to work smarter, not harder. With both Jupiter and Uranus doing laps through Gemini and your sixth house of work, routines and wellness, you're craving liberation from the daily hustle. And, dare we say, it's about damn time!

Jupiter has been transiting through the sign of the Twins since May 25, 2024, showing you the freedom that can come from streamlining, systematizing and outsourcing certain aspects of your work to experts. If that level of efficiency already comes naturally to you, consider memorializing your methodology. From an orientation manual for employees to a published book or a series of online classes, your lifehacks light the way for others to level up.

If work has grown too complex, you may feel like downsizing certain elements of your job—or even let them go completely. While that might require you to tighten up your belt a bit, think of it as a temporary measure. The gift of time will allow you to think through a new financial strategy that allows you to actually work smarter, not harder.

From July 7 to November 7, game-changing Uranus swoops into Gemini, giving you a sneak preview of a longer seven-year cycle that kicks off in April 2026. Uranus thrives on disruption, cueing you to embrace unconventional methods. Could AI be used to speed up your outflow? Would working as a fractional executive instead of a full-time one open up room for you to finally produce that documentary? You don't have to shake everything up overnight, but don't be surprised if outdated work habits start fading away in the second half of the year, allowing you to experiment with a more liberated, innovative approach to your career.

PS: Capricorn, these changes CAN feel exciting! Starting January 11, the karmic South Node shifts into Virgo and your worldly, entrepreneurial ninth house. During this cycle, which lasts until July 26, 2026, travel or remote work could play a significant role in your career. If ever there were a time to be a digital nomad, tour with your band or expand your business internationally—this could be it.

Your entire approach to money is also going through a profound metamorphosis. Wealth-agent Pluto—who wrapped up a sixteen-year tour of Capricorn on November 19, 2024—is now in its first full year in Aquarius and your second house of financial security and values. While this cycle lasts for a protracted era, until 2044, your eye may already be on some new balls, ones that will create lasting security. (Music to your ears!)

Here's yet another cue to trim back excess and stabilize a few of the pricier moving parts of your life. Pluto's changes are a slow-burn process, but by the end of 2025, you'll start to feel the benefits of a more focused and sustainable approach to your income and spending. Moves you make now can set the foundation for lasting wealth and financial freedom.

Could that involve purchasing a home sweet home? Quite possibly! On March 29, the final solar eclipse in a two-year series lands in Aries and your rooted, domestic fourth house. With your ruler, serious Saturn, also parking in Aries from May 24 to September 1, you could warm to the idea of putting down roots or creating rental income through an investment property.

Business collaborations heat up after June 9, when lucky Jupiter moves on to Cancer and your partnership zone for an entire year. You won't even have to turn on the searchlight to find allies who want to team up to achieve a common vision. Lawyer up, because you could be formalizing a flurry of deals in the second half of the year.

A final burst of motivation comes on December 15, as go-getter Mars revs into Capricorn—its first visit to your sign in two years. While other people are winding down for the year, you could be rolling up your sleeves. Progress is imminent and you'll have the grit to finish 2025 with some impressive accolades. Take the lead and end the year with a windfall.

CAPRICORN: LUCKIEST *career* DAY

AUGUST 10

Go-getter Mars in partnership-powered Libra is at the apex of your chart, helping you lock in VIP collaborators. As it makes an exact trine to wealth-agent Pluto in Aquarius and your money house, you could tap into revenue streams that were previously hidden from your view. Mercury is on its final day of a retrograde, so you'll need to vet whatever you discover today. Look through your past contacts, as you could discover a promising investment partner or the gatekeeper of an opportunity who's already in your database!

2025
CAPRICORN

12
MONTH
OVERVIEW

January MONTHLY HOROSCOPE

Happy birthday, Capricorn! The year kicks off with the radiant Sun in your sign, which is a good reason to keep the celebrations going. This extra solar power lasts until January 19, giving you the energy, discipline and confidence to move the needle on your personal goals. Make room to dabble and try new things before you settle on any major plans. Following the spirit of curiosity can lead you on an exciting new path. On January 11, the lunar nodes shift into Pisces and Virgo, marking the start of an 18-month cycle of personal growth through communication, global travel and education. As one of the zodiac's seekers, you'll revel in this transformative period. After January 19, the Sun drifts on to airy Aquarius, giving you a cosmic tailwind in the area of finances and material security. You could whip up new income streams or breeze right into a brand new job during this four-week cycle. Make a budget for luxury and entertainment, because when the Year of the Wood Snake begins on January 29, your appetite for life's finer things will be huge.

February MONTHLY HOROSCOPE

Tighten up that belt a bit, Capricorn. With the Aquarius Sun activating your second house of money and values until the 18th, you're ready to be wiser—and more collaborative—about the way you manage your resources. Get your family (chosen or blood-related) involved! With value-driven Venus anchoring down in Aries on the 4th, you could inspire everyone around you to create a more secure life. This Venus cycle also brings out your desire to beautify your space and, if necessary, bring it up to "Capricorn code." Family relationships get a dose of peaceful energy from this harmonizing transit. Smooth over ruffled feathers before Venus turns retrograde from March 1 to April 12. Jupiter turns direct in Gemini on the 4th, bringing a much-needed mindset shift about your work and wellness goals. If you've been feeling sluggish or uninspired, the broad-minded planet pushes you to explore new processes. The Sun sails into Pisces on the 18th, activating your third house of communication. This is a great time for networking, learning and sharing ideas with your community. Finally, Mars turns direct in Cancer on February 23, spicing up your relationships and getting you motivated to take more initiative with the people you love.

March MONTHLY HOROSCOPE

You're sending out more signals than a satellite tower this March, as the Pisces Sun charges up your third house of communication, learning and community until the 20th. While you're busy networking, info-gathering and swapping ideas, don't neglect your personal life. Both Venus and Mercury will be retrograde in Aries and your home and family zone this month—Venus from March 1 to 27 and Mercury from March 15 to 29. You may need to temporarily distance yourself from a relative or set some boundaries by declaring certain hot-button topics "off-limits." If you've been planning a move or home renovation, expect delays and try to postpone those projects until April. In the meantime, shift your focus to more exciting horizons: The Virgo lunar eclipse on March 14 could bring a serendipitous opportunity for travel or a chance to study with a master teacher. When the Sun enters Aries on March 20, it's time to get serious about making your home life a true reflection of your inner peace. The Aries solar eclipse on March 29 wraps up a two-year cycle in your fourth house, offering a powerful moment to reset your emotional foundations and begin a new chapter in your personal life. Just as you're settling into this shift, Neptune enters Aries on March 30 for the first time since 1875, beginning a 14-year cycle of spiritual growth and transformation in your home and family dynamics. Time to set up your sanctuary!

April MONTHLY HOROSCOPE

How secure is your foundation? With the Sun hunkered in your fourth house of home and family until April 19, you're focused on your roots, creating a solid base of operations. But before you start laying bricks, slow down. Mercury is retrograde in Pisces and your communication zone until April 7, and Venus is retrograde there until April 12. You may need to refine your communication strategy and clear up any misunderstandings with your partners-in-crime before you can move ahead with ease. Your social charm returns with the Libra full moon on the 12th, which could also bring a peak moment for your career. On April 18, Mars enters bold Leo, firing up your eighth house of seduction, permanent bonds and shared resources. Between now and June 17, you'll feel motivated to fortify relationships and take control of financial matters. Longevity and stability are the goal, so think of each person (or situation) that presents itself as if it were an investment. Taurus season kicks off on April 19, lighting up your fifth house of creativity, romance and self-expression. As the Sun moves into this playful sector, it's time to loosen up, tap into your passions and enjoy life's most decadent pleasures.

May MONTHLY HOROSCOPE

Creative inspiration streams in this May as the Taurus Sun continues shining in your fifth house of art, romance and self-expression until the 20th. Forget about following trends! This month, you'll lead the way with your inspired fashion sense and visionary ideas. This playful period casts you in the role of cultural activities director for your crew. Bring on the concerts, gallery openings, operas and more! On May 4, Pluto spins retrograde in Aquarius, backing through your second house of money and values until October 13. (Celebratory note: This is the first year since 2008 that stormy, triggering Pluto is NOT in your sign!) Review your financial strategy. Are your resources supporting the life you want to build? It may be time to rethink your approach to earning, saving and investing, or at least an aspect of it. Spring training, spring cleaning—you're ready for all of it starting May 20 when the Sun enters Gemini and your orderly sixth house. On May 24, your galactic guardian Saturn switches signs, temporarily moving into Aries and your fourth house of home and family. Saturn's disciplined energy can help you feel more rooted even if that means planting yourself in a new place over the course of this three-year cycle. Your new job? To lay a foundation that supports your long-term security and emotional well-being.

June MONTHLY HOROSCOPE

June 2025 is a pivotal month for you, Capricorn, as the cosmos shift focus from career to connection. With the Sun in Gemini until June 20, you're all about efficiency and productivity, perfect for streamlining your day-to-day tasks and tackling those lingering projects. But the real headline arrives on June 9, when Jupiter moves into Cancer for the first time since 2014. This is huge—Jupiter will spend the next year in your relationship zone, expanding your partnerships and helping you form deeper, more meaningful, connections. Whether it's in business or love, expect opportunities to grow and strengthen key relationships. When the Sun joins Jupiter in Cancer at the solstice, it's time to prioritize collaboration over going it alone—lean on others and let teamwork take you further. Mid-month could bring some tension as Jupiter squares Saturn on June 15 and Neptune on June 18, highlighting the need to balance personal connections with your big-picture goals. Don't stress—just take a step back and reassess your priorities. Mars enters Virgo on June 17, giving you the motivation to focus on long-term growth and explore new ideas. By June 24, the Day of Miracles, the Sun and Jupiter align, offering a powerful moment to manifest relationship goals or seal a deal. Jupiter's here to help you build partnerships that last, Capricorn—don't be afraid to let others in!

July MONTHLY HOROSCOPE

Make it a double! While the Sun copilots alongside expansive Jupiter in Cancer until the 22nd, some of your most meaningful progress will happen through close, one-on-one interactions. Seek out powerful allies from the boardroom to the bedroom. You're building something that needs a strong foundation, and collaboration will be key. On July 7, unpredictable Uranus shifts into Gemini and your sixth house of work, wellness, and daily routines, where it will remain until November 7. Prepare for some shake-ups in your day-to-day life. This six-month preview is just a taste of the larger cycle of change that Uranus will bring starting in April 2026. During this innovative cycle, you may find yourself drawn to completely new methods of working or adopting unconventional approaches to health and wellness. A little chaos can create the space for radical improvements. Adding to the introspective energy of the month, Neptune, Saturn and Chiron all turn retrograde in Aries—on the 4th, 13th, and 30th, respectively—focusing their energy in your fourth house of home, family and emotional security. Over these next five months, you could reconnect to your roots while also navigating some complex dynamics with your inner circle. Set clear boundaries while also remaining compassionate. That will be the key to healing any generational trauma and childhood wounds. You're on the prowl for soulful, sexy exchanges once Leo Season begins on the 22nd. But with Mercury retrograde, also in Leo, from July 18 to August 11, your eighth house of secrets, power plays and erotic energy is getting a bit of a shakeup. Wires may cross around shared finances or deeply personal matters. Double-check the fine print and even lawyer up if you need to sign anything. Mercury retrograde is also notorious for bringing back old flames. Careful not to rekindle anything that was once toxic. The "excitement" isn't worth the price.

August MONTHLY HOROSCOPE

Your urge to merge may be verging on insatiable as August kicks off with the Leo Sun prowling through your seductive, mysterious eighth house until August 22. Whether you're signing a business deal or coordinating a rendezvous with a lover (or something equally scintillating), revel in the power of your allure. But don't be TOO hard to get. Mercury remains in a signal-jamming retrograde through the 11th, which could throw the right person off your trail if you don't give a few direct hints. Fortunately, gracious Venus is sweetening the deal, hanging out in Cancer and your seventh house of parity and partnership until August 25. Cultivate relationships that bring out the best in you and make sure to give the people who have already earned your trust plenty of acknowledgement. Career goals (your favorite!) get a giant tailwind starting August 6 as momentous Mars blazes into Libra and your tenth house of success and recognition for six weeks. A leadership role is calling your name, so take charge without apology. It's the Capricorn way! Once Virgo season kicks off on August 22, you'll be ready for a vacation—the further from home the better. With your globetrotting ninth house lit up, you might even tie this trip to a secondary purpose, like a personal growth seminar or business meeting. The very next day, August 23, brings the first of two rare, back-to-back new moons in Virgo, providing another push outside your comfort zone. Use this fresh-start energy to pave the way for an even bigger leap when the solar (new moon) eclipse in Virgo arrives on September 21. The world is your oyster, filled with pearls of wisdom that you're ready to discover and incorporate into your view of life.

September MONTHLY HOROSCOPE

How wide can you cast your net? With the Sun in Virgo lighting up your ninth house of exploration, travel and higher learning until September 22, there's no limiting your wingspan. But don't sleep on the neighborhood scene. On the 1st, your ruler, structured Saturn, retrogrades back into Pisces and your third house of hometown happenings. You could make a solid name for yourself by simply taking on a local initiative. That goes triple on the 7th, when the Pisces lunar (full moon) eclipse brings surprising opportunities to network, study or stir up excitement in your own backyard. If there's been a miscommunication or lingering tension with a sibling, coworker or neighbor, this eclipse can bring it to a head. Push for resolution, whether that means walking away or hashing out a win-win. On September 21, the closing solar eclipse arrives with the new moon in Virgo—which is also the second in a rare, back-to-back pair to hit this sign. News could come from afar or you could get the nudge you need to take a big risk like enrolling in a degree program, moving to a new city or starting your own business. Capricorn media makers could get a surprising offer near this date. Not that you need to wait around for it. Take-charge Mars continues to ignite your tenth house of career (Libra) until September 22, pushing you to be proactive about professional matters. You're ready to lead, but keep your secret autocrat in check. You need allies, even when you're at the top! The 22nd is the equinox and the start of Libra season, as the Sun picks up the baton from Mars and keeps your ambitious energy flowing. Don't try to shoulder it all alone. Teamwork makes a few of those dreams work once Mars heads into Scorpio and your communal eleventh house from September 22 to November 4. You'll feel a surge of energy for collaborative projects and social causes, making this the perfect time to rally your network and work together for a greater goal. Geek is chic, so don't shy away from AI or other tech tools that can make your life easier.

October MONTHLY HOROSCOPE

October is peak season for your professional life as the Libra Sun directs its rays straight into your tenth house of ambition and success. Push ahead on those goals, whether you're angling for a promotion, launching one of your impressive projects or stepping out as a leader in your field. Important people will take note, so find a way to get on their radar, even if that means joining an elite club or volunteering for a charity that they support. Love goals will also be in your crosshairs once Venus shifts into Libra on the 13th. Prior to that, you may be too distracted by all the eye candy to notice someone's enduring traits. With magnetic, intimate Pluto turning direct, also on the 13th, you may suddenly change your tune, remembering how sweet it can feel to "settle down." Pluto's about-face can help you gain command of your resources and make some strategic moves that have a lasting impact on your financial landscape. Lift your nose from the grindstone on the 22nd! The Sun streams into Scorpio, bringing a seductively fun energy to your communal, collaborative eleventh house. If you've been lonely at the top, that ends now. Join forces with innovative people who aren't afraid to disrupt the status quo in the name of progress. You may find it difficult to put all your thoughts into words, however. That same day, hazy Neptune retrogrades back into Pisces, finishing its retreat (until December 10) in your communication house. Listen, observe and let those ideas marinate. Those napkin sketches and 3AM doodles will come in handy by the end of the year!

November MONTHLY HOROSCOPE

Summon your supergroup! The Sun swirls through Scorpio and your community-oriented eleventh house until the 21st, inviting you to deepen connections within your network. With Venus gliding through Scorpio from November 6 to 30, creative brainstorms could turn into mental monsoons. Capture all those "wouldn't it be crazy if" ideas, even if you don't take action on them until early next year. Your subconscious mind is working overtime as busy, buzzy Mars catapults into Sagittarius on November 4 and activates your imagination until December 15. While your visionary plans could be epic, also use this time to clean house—physically and energetically—and to let go of what no longer serves you. With Mercury turning retrograde in Sagittarius from the 9th, and slipping back into Scorpio from the 18th to the 29th, some old collaborations or group dynamics may need review. This is your cue to reassess which relationships are pulling their weight—and which ones are draining you. Meanwhile, Uranus retrogrades back into Taurus and your fifth house of creative self-expression on November 7, encouraging you to push the envelope until February 3. Romantic experimentation could also lead to new levels of pleasure and fulfillment. Just make sure you choose a safe word and safe playmates. The month's end offers relief when stabilizing Saturn turns direct in Pisces and your third house of communication on the 27th. You'll finally feel like you're speaking a language that others understand, and that your words are carrying weight.

December MONTHLY HOROSCOPE

As December kicks off, you feel like winding down, reflecting and setting the stage for your next big chapter. With the Sun, high-octane Mars and glamorous Venus are swirling through your twelfth house of rest and release until the 21st, 15th and 24th, respectively, you're in a phase of deep contemplation and strategic plotting. Use this introspective energy to tie up loose ends, close any lingering chapters and prepare for a powerful new beginning when birthday season begins at the winter solstice this December 21st. Dreamy Neptune ends its five-month retrograde on December 10, shifting into forward motion in Pisces and your communicative third house. Suddenly, conversations flow more easily and any misunderstandings—especially with siblings or neighbors—begin to clear up, giving you the green light to express your thoughts with compassion and clarity. On the 15th, get ready for a surge of vitality as passionate Mars charges into Capricorn for the first time in two years, energizing you with motivation and drive. This momentum only intensifies as the Sun enters your sign on the solstice (December 21), and Venus follows on the 24th, adding a touch of glam to your assertive edge. You're stepping into your power, Capricorn, ready to wow the world as you close out 2025. With the planetary energy moving from your twelfth house into your first, it's time to put yourself front and center. Your ambitions are calling, and the universe is giving you a megaphone—don't be shy about letting your presence be known! When it comes to wrapping up the year, go for a celebration that truly honors you. Whether that's hosting an intimate but upscale birthday-slash-NYE gathering or heading out for an unforgettable night of club-hopping, ring in 2026 in a way that feels like a fresh start. Dance until dawn, fiercely declare your resolutions and step confidently into the new year knowing that it's yours to conquer!

A LITTLE ABOUT Aquarius

DATES January 19 - February 18

SYMBOL The Water Bearer

ELEMENT Air

QUALITY Fixed

RULING PLANET Uranus, Saturn

BODY PART Ankles, calves

BEST TRAITS
Communicative, original, visionary, fair, logical, friendly, humanitarian, futuristic, quirky

KEYWORDS
Community, originality, teamwork, progress, technology, intellect, science, spirit

Read more about Aquarius

AQUARIUS
IN 2025

| ALL THE PLANETS IN AQUARIUS IN 2025 | YOUR 2025 HOROSCOPE | TOP 5 THEMES FOR AQUARIUS IN 2025 | LOVE HOROSCOPE + LUCKY DATES | MONEY HOROSCOPE + LUCKY DATES |

Aquarius in 2025

YOUR YEARLY OVERVIEW

There's no dodging the spotlight in 2025, Aquarius, not even with mysterious Pluto spending its first full year (of the next 19!) in your sign. The reason? Live-out-loud Jupiter and your ruler, kinetic Uranus, are each doing a six-month lap through Gemini and your fifth house of fame, romance and creative expression, giving you superstar status. Showcase your talents and lean into your eclectic ideas without fear; the right people will appreciate your unique brilliance. On January 11, the lunar North Node heads into Pisces putting the focus on your finances, personal values and helping you fortify a secure foundation. Set up smarter savings or invest in assets that bring long-term comfort. Meanwhile, the South Node in Virgo helps you work through control issues around money, power and sex. This journey could be intense at times, but it will set you up for fulfilling partnerships in the long run. Saturn and Neptune trek through Aries for part of the year stoking your third house of communication and giving your words extra weight. You could find your way to a brand new neighborhood or make a noteworthy impact on the local scene. Once Jupiter settles into Cancer for a year on June 9, your daily routines could evolve as you design a lifestyle that nourishes both body and mind. It's all about crafting a sustainable rhythm that fuels your productivity while keeping you healthy, wealthy and wise!

THE PLANETS IN *Aquarius*

THE SUN
JAN 19–FEB 18

It's birthday season for you, so step out and shine! Seek novelty and take extra initiative during this radiant monthlong phase.

NEW MOON
JAN 29
7:36AM, 9°51′

Bonus New Year! Set your intentions for the next six months and get into action.

FULL MOON
AUG 9
3:55AM, 17°00′

Ready, set, manifest! Your work of the past six months bears fruit and it's time to harvest the rewards.

MERCURY
JAN 27–FEB 14

Crown yourself monarch of the social butterflies when popularity-boosting Mercury visits your sign once a year. Circulate and get social—but don't make promises you can't keep!

PLUTO
ALL YEAR

Evolve! Your soul undergoes a profound metamorphosis when intense, edgy Pluto visits your sign—a rare occurrence since this only happens about every 248 years. Certain parts of your identity may burn away as you rise like a phoenix from the ashes of anything you've lost or are leaving behind.

Aquarius in 2025

HIGHLIGHTS

FINANCIAL RESET: NORTH NODE IN PISCES AND SOUTH NODE IN VIRGO

Your financial future takes a turn in a fresh direction starting January 11, as the fateful lunar nodes shift into your money houses. Ready or not, this eighteen-month cycle recalibrates both your mindset and your total approach to wealth. The Pisces North Node is directing your destiny in your second house of earnings, which could lead you toward a dream job or give you the ability to finally save up for a purchase that's been on your wish list for the longest time. Across the board, the karmic South Node in Virgo orchestrates long-overdue changes in your eighth house of assets. Lump sums of cash may come in from a property sale, inheritance, commission or settlement. Invest wisely—which you may do with a partner, since joint finances fall under the rule of the eighth house.

SENSUALITY MEETS SPIRITUALITY

The lunar Nodes activate more than just your money moves—they're all stirring up some soulful sensuality. The North Node in Pisces enriches your fantasy life and helps you bring a few of those body-loving desires to life. With the service-oriented Virgo South Node in your erotic eighth house, you'll get plenty of joy from giving, too. Expand your sexual palette in meaningful ways between January 11, 2025 and July 26, 2026, while honoring your own limits and boundaries.

CREATIVE SPARKS: JUPITER AND URANUS FIRE UP YOUR PASSIONS

A creative and romantic renaissance may already be underway for you as the year begins. No-limits Jupiter, who's been trekking through Gemini and your passionate fifth house since May 25, 2024, keeps sashaying through this zone until June 9, making you feel like "THAT girl." Have fun turning heads with your inimitable style, shameless PDA and other shock-value-inducing moves that are simply your authentic self-expression. Your artistic and intellectual works could peg you as an influencer or a thought leader. Fame is a genuine possibility this year. The sparks keep flying on July 7, when your revolutionary ruler, Uranus, sweeps into Gemini until November 7. This is a mere glimpse of a seven-year cycle that begins again in April 2026 and helps you solidify your status as an avant-garde disruptor. Whether it's an unconventional romance or a groundbreaking public project, you're ready to break molds, shake up old patterns and experiment with radical methodologies.

JUPITER IN CANCER PUTS THE "FLOW" IN YOUR WORKFLOW

Health is wealth starting June 9, as philosophical Jupiter moves on to Cancer. As the red-spotted planet elevates your sixth house of self-care, systems and daily routines, you need your work to nurture your spirit. Some Water Bearers will go back to school, as either a student or a professor. If you've been sporadically employed, you'll want something steady now, but not at the price of your freedom. Consider a hybrid or fractional role or remote work—always a plus with Jupiter, the global nomad, at the helm. Traveling and interfacing with international clients may figure into your duties. Just make sure that you also have space for self-care! With the vitality-boosting planet here, you could change your eating habits and incorporate a new form of fitness into your life.

PHOENIX RISING: PLUTO IN AQUARIUS

You say you want an evolution? Pluto spends its first full year in your sign after teasing this transit for part of 2023 and 2024. The planet of alchemy, destruction and rebirth, Pluto only visits your sign every 250 years—so yes, this is a HUGE deal. This slow, steady transit, which lasts until January 19, 2044, will reveal the deep inner shifts that have been brewing beneath the surface. Simultaneously, you're moving through a total life overhaul, one that can radically shift your career, identity or even your public image. Shadow work is part of the process, and that isn't always easy. But this inside-out metamorphosis will connect you to your core values and power like never before.

MASTERING YOUR MIND: SATURN AND NEPTUNE IN ARIES

Mental discipline meets imagination as Saturn and Neptune take turns traveling through Aries and your third house of communication and learning. Saturn's visit from May 25 to September 1 helps you structure your thoughts and refine your communication skills, making this an ideal time for serious study or important conversations. Meanwhile, from March 30 to October 22, soothsayer Neptune sprinkles some magic into your mindset, encouraging you to explore your spiritual and creative sides. Life feels like a moving meditation and this slow, surreal pace can inspire the sorts of ideas that inform a book, workshop, podcast or other methodology that you share with the world. Both planets will revisit Aries for longer periods starting in early 2026.

TOP 5 THEMES FOR
Aquarius in 2025

1	2	3	4	5
GO FOR THE GLAM	GET HEALTHY AND WEALTHY	COMMUNE WITH KINDRED SPIRITS	REFINE YOURLOVE LANGUAGE	RAISE THE FINANCIAL STAKES

1 GO FOR THE GLAM

JUPITER AND URANUS IN GEMINI

JUPITER: MAY 25, 2024 – JUNE 9, 2025
URANUS: JULY 7 – NOVEMBER 7, 2025 • JANUARY 26, 2026 – MAY 22, 2033

Lights, camera, Aquarius! While you're not a showboater by nature, center stage is where you belong in 2025. Not only is live-out-loud Jupiter spending the first half of the year in Gemini and your fifth house of fame, romance and creative expression, but from July 7 to November 7, your ruling planet Uranus pulls into Twin Town. Their liberating message? Stop worrying what others will think about you and focus on sharing your divine gifts with the world. Don't be surprised if the media, or an enthusiastic fanbase, comes a-knocking.

JUPITER IN GEMINI

MAY 25, 2024 – JUNE 9, 2025

Stock the tour bus with your favorite refreshments and send the hotel your rider. (Six dozen flame-orange roses, CBD gummies and a Theragun massager, please.) The Aquarius Show could be going on the road in the first half of 2025 as nomadic Jupiter takes the stage in Gemini and your star powered fifth house.

Before this VIP cycle ends on June 9, you could take the stage as a speaker, performer or presenter. Your art could hang in a gallery or your literary works may get published, even self-published. Bottom line: Stop waiting to be discovered and get proactive instead. Fortune favors the bold when risk-taker Jupiter is in town.

Already swinging for the fences? Jupiter has been in Gemini since May 25, 2024, where it's been spotlighting your talents ever since. Perhaps you've already had your proverbial close-up, but why settle for five mere minutes of fame? Look for ways to build upon whatever buzz you got started in the second half of 2024.

In this passionate position, Jupiter blesses your romantic life until June 9 (and hopefully far beyond!). While touring cool, sapiosexual Gemini, the cosmic titan helps you attract someone who matches your intellect and can roll with your eclectic ideas. Red-hot vacation romance, anyone? You might just meet your soulmate while traveling or decide to relocate in the name of love. You could just as easily enjoy a memorable hookup that gives you a lifetime of fantasies to tap into. Jupiter's free-spirited like that, so why not?

Attached? Bring the glamour back to your union. Host parties together, enjoy (at least) one official date night each week, and surprise each other with cultural activities. Fly to Vegas for a weekend to see your favorite megaperformer in concert. Slip off to Kauai for a weeklong couples' intimacy workshop. (That's "Into-me-I-see," Aquarius, in case you were wondering...)

Working with children is another hallmark of this Jupiter cycle—especially in an educational capacity. If you've entertained the idea of getting a teaching certificate, Jupiter may send you back to school. Or, since the fifth house is your fertility zone, you might catch baby fever and wind up with a bun in the oven. If you're dealing with fertility challenges, Jupiter can bring more than just a ray of hope for conception or a divinely delivered adoption.

No matter what, your imagination will be fertile. Make love, make art and make heads turn with your outré fashion sense. This is no time to fade into the background. Unless, of course, said background is eye-popping, retro-patterned wallpaper, which you might just peel and stick to every corner of your home before June 9.

URANUS IN GEMINI
JULY 7 – NOVEMBER 7, 2025
JANUARY 26, 2026 – MAY 22, 2033

Come out, come out, wherever you are! Life is about to get a whole lot more glamorous, romantic and fulfilling for you again starting this July 7. That's when your cosmic custodian, high-vibe Uranus, pulls itself out of languid Taurus and zips into buzzy, social Gemini for the first time since 1949!

To be clear, Aquarius, any time your ruling planet changes signs, it's a big deal. But this shift is sure to be epic. Since May 2018, Uranus has been "in fall" in traditional Taurus, a deeply uncomfortable place on the zodiac for the edgy planet. Moreover, Uranus was parked in your domestic fourth house, destabilizing home and family life and making it hard for you to feel rooted in any way.

While the Uranus in Taurus cycle isn't totally over, it's winding down. The side-spinning planet buzzes through Gemini this year for only four months, from July 7 to November 7.

Take notes, Aquarius, because next year, Uranus returns to Gemini for seven years from April 25, 2026 to May 22, 2033.

Gemini is a fellow air sign, so immediately, you're going to feel more at ease when your ruler slips into this zone. Better still? Gemini rules your fifth house of creativity, romance and fame. It's a safe bet that one, if not all, of these areas will get a radical makeover. But things won't happen in a linear or predictable fashion, since Uranus is the great disruptor of the universe. Opportunities come out of the blue under this planet's watch, whether you meet the love of your life while you're on a silent meditation or a talent you never dreamed of monetizing makes you millions.

You can gain some control over things by playing to your own strengths and staying tuned in to energetic currents. Consciously choose the skills and talents you want to showcase after July 7, while also being selective about your audience. Rebellious Uranus is not known for being subtle, but the last thing you need, Aquarius, is to give the small-minded critics a chance to pan your efforts before you've built up your solid, indie fanbase. In other words, don't rush to bring a genius idea to the masses or even worry about marketing yourself this year. Start testing the waters with people who are ahead of the curve; the ones who set trends rather than follow them.

Should your fifteen (or more!) minutes of celebrity come knocking, you want to make sure there are no closet skeletons or embarrassing episodes that could be revealed. If you have amends to make or messes to clean up, make it your mission to handle things in 2025.

Your romantic life will get an electrifying jolt of excitement and experimentation with Uranus in Gemini—and it probably won't follow every conventional rule in the book. If you're in a happy, stable union, shock jock Uranus will detour you away from that premature fate of turning into "old marrieds" who rarely leave the rocking chairs. But choose a safe word and take baby steps if you start "loosening up boundaries" in the name of keeping it fresh. Uranus here can make you feel like a teenager, living for the moment but not always contemplating regrets. But this planet is also a high-minded one: You might take things to a way deeper level with practices from tantra or the affirming technique of mirroring one another (which is so Gemini!).

Uranus is as indie-spirited as Jupiter, so here's your second prompt of the year to find innovative ways to support each other's dreams. You and your beloved may wind up on different corners of the planet for swaths of time between now and 2033. How can you embrace this as an adventure and create ways to become closer through cheering each other on?

Single Water Bearers can look forward to a change in the status quo, though Uranus may throw in a few surprises along the way. Where do you want to make changes? Start there, and you should see powerful progress by November 7. Since Uranus is the planet of technology, don't turn your nose up at the apps, even if you've been burned on Bumble or become un-Hinged from past experiences. It only takes one right swipe to make magic and with Uranus in playful Gemini, the "why the heck not" chance you take could be a fateful one.

2 GET HEALTHY AND WEALTHY

JUPITER IN CANCER
JUNE 9, 2025 – JUNE 30, 2026

After spending the first half of the year in the limelight, you may be ready for a saner pace of life. You're in luck, Water Bearer, because on June 9, maximizer Jupiter settles into Cancer, activating your systematic sixth house until June 30, 2026. Suddenly you're more interested in reducing stress than adding more projects to your plate. Even if you can't stem the tide of your in-demand status, you can deploy some efficiency tactics that help you to work smarter, not harder.

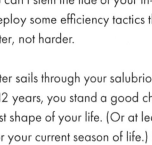

When Jupiter sails through your salubrious sixth house every 10-12 years, you stand a good chance of getting into the best shape of your life. (Or at least the best shape possible for your current season of life.) No deprivation allowed! Cancer is the sign of comfort and nourishment, so put the focus on living clean and green. Flip the 80/20 rule on your plate to be 80% fresh produce. Stave off boredom by eating the rainbow: juicy red berries, luscious peaches, green kale, purple cabbage. Your nutritional habits could go through a major transformation as you use food as fuel for the body, not just fodder for the taste buds.

If you, like many Aquarians, are already a disciplined eater, you may be inspired to learn more about your body's unique chemistry. Schedule a food allergy test or a hormone panel to discover where you might be sensitive or just plain out of balance. If you're dealing with a health issue, there couldn't be a more beneficent planet to have on your team than joyful, robust Jupiter! You might explore a mix of Western and Eastern medicine, too, mixing MDs with naturopaths and holistic practitioners to restore your wellness.

Harness Jupiter's get-up-and-go energy and give your fitness routine a burst of novelty. As it tours water-sign Cancer, you could spend the summer on a stand-up paddleboard or doing laps in a salt-water pool. Since Cancer is the zodiac's homebody, make sure Chez Aqua has a dedicated workout area—or a space where you can roll out a mat for some floor exercises when you're too busy to get to the gym. Over the next thirteen months, you may be inspired to take on a marathon fitness challenge or even enroll in teacher training.

All this self-care is sure to offset the fact that, like it or not, work will not slow down with Jupiter in this zone of your chart. You may feel deluged by administrative tasks that are not your favorite thing to deal with at all. It also happens that the sixth house is the "service sector" of the chart, which includes services providers. Freeing up time for meaningful tasks might require you to finally delegate some of the grind work to an assistant or intern.

New responsibilities may land in your lap, and with Jupiter's global influence, you could be traveling or working with people from a new corner of the Earth. Independence is the hallmark of Jupiter, too, so some Aquarians might leave a desk job to pursue the freelancer's lifestyle. As projects roll in, take extra care to schedule your time, set clear boundaries with clients and intentionally not stay in your PJs 'til 1PM as you WFH. Aquarians thrive in community so if you start to feel isolated, rent a desk at a coworking space. Even one or two days a week can fill your tanks and bring bonus opportunities to build your professional network.

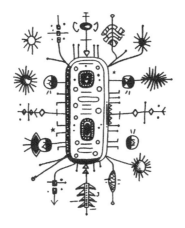

3

COMMUNE WITH KINDRED SPIRITS

SATURN AND NEPTUNE IN ARIES

NEPTUNE: MARCH 30 – OCTOBER 22, 2025 • JANUARY 26, 2026 – MARCH 23, 2039
SATURN: MAY 24 – SEPTEMBER 1, 2025 • FEBRUARY 13, 2026 – APRIL 12, 2028

Big ideas are brewing as two outer planets return to Aries and for the first time in literally ages! Imaginative Neptune and ambitious Saturn both cycle through this sign for part of 2025—Neptune from March 30 to October 22 and Saturn from May 24 to September 1. As they do, they energize your third house of communication, local activities and cooperative ventures. Neptune and Saturn are quite the odd couple, but their combined powers can help you blend fantasy with reality.

Neptune's last spin through Aries was from 1862 to 1875. Saturn hasn't visited the Ram's realm since 1996 to 1998. The world has changed immensely since, especially the way we connect and communicate—which is the domain of the third house. Who knows, Aquarius? You may lead the charge on both AI and analog interactions in the years ahead.

You might find yourself streamlining your social life, gravitating toward people and projects that truly resonate with your soul. This planetary pairing is perfect for testing new ventures—whether it's a side hustle, a writing project, or even deepening your ties to your local community. Neptune's dreaminess combined with Saturn's structure? That's the winning formula for turning your vision into something tangible!

NEPTUNE IN ARIES

MARCH 30 – OCTOBER 22, 2025
JANUARY 26, 2026 – MARCH 23, 2039

From March 30 to October 22, 2025, Neptune drifts into Aries, casting its ethereal influence over your third house of communication, cooperation and local connections. While you thrive on intellectual stimulation, this transit offers you a unique opportunity to explore fluid dimensions of thought and expression. Logic? Highly overrated during these six months. (Though not to be dismissed altogether!) From March 30 to October 22, you're more interested in tapping your intuition and letting it guide you on a soulful quest.

Although Neptune's visit to Aries is brief in 2025, this flight of fancy will resume again for thirteen whole years, starting January 26, 2026. Record your observations. Do your best to adjust to this new and numinous vibe. It's going to be your new normal by and large until March 23, 2039.

Get ready for some shifts in your social style. You have 1,001 friends, most of whom you keep at a "close distance" (Read: Near enough to form a bond, far enough to preserve your extreme autonomy). Neptune's boundary-dissolving influence could change your approach. You could find yourself yearning for deeper emotional connections. In conversations, you'll be attuned to subtle nuances, picking up on what's unsaid as much as what's spoken.

Imagination and empathy reign supreme while Neptune is in your third house. Since the third house rules media, this a great time to explore creative writing, poetry or any form of expression that allows you to convey deeper feelings and abstract ideas. As an Aquarius, you're known for your sharp, analytical mind that also tends to see the world through a scientific lens. You might find yourself intrigued by esoteric topics now, such as astrology (hello!), shamanic breathwork and dream interpretation. Let your curiosity guide you into new territories that challenge conventional ways of thinking. Caveat: Neptune has a slippery grasp on reality. Make sure to balance your mystical explorations with critical thinking to avoid getting lost in illusions or wishful thinking.

Peer relationships with neighbors, siblings or close friends may also undergo a subtle transformation. Neptune's energy can make you more sensitive to their needs and emotions. With the compassionate planet in this zone, you might feel a stronger urge to be of service within your community, perhaps through volunteer work or simply offering a listening ear to those who need it. Be mindful of Neptune's tendency to make sacrifices. Your generosity might not have an "off" switch now. Make sure to set realistic expectations and clear boundaries (for yourself and others!) to avoid disappointment.

The third house rules short journeys, so get ready to pack your out-of-office time with spiritual mini-pilgrimages. A yoga studio in the woods two hours from home base might be offering a weekend posture clinic or sound bath. And yes, you should go, Aquarius, even if you don't know a soul in attendance. It's all but guaranteed that you'll connect to some new friends who can meet you at this high vibe.

Music and dance are also Neptune's domain. Join a local choir or sign up for lessons at a ballet studio. Learn how to play guitar or pack your summer schedule with festivals. Since the third house also rules transportation, this might be the excuse you've been waiting for to start saving up for the Volkswagen ID. Buzz—an electric bus that has "Aquarius" written all over it.

With Neptune leaving Pisces and your second house of money and values, you're bound to experience some economic relief in the years ahead. Don't loosen your belt quite yet. The elusive planet is still spinning through Pisces for half of 2025, which could necessitate a few day-to-day expenses—household repairs, vet bills, car notes—that cut into your entertainment budget.

You haven't exactly been a stranger to making these sorts of sacrifices since Neptune began this 14-year cycle in 2011 and hey, it's built character. You can look forward to greater ease in this realm starting in 2026, even if you decide to simplify and scale back your lifestyle in order to get there. It's worth meditating on, Aquarius. Your intuition may have some clear messages about what's next for you—not just how you move through your days, but with who and where. Stay open to all possibilities.

SATURN IN ARIES
MAY 24 – SEPTEMBER 1, 2025
FEBRUARY 13, 2026 – APRIL 12, 2028

Your budget gets a bit of breathing room this May 24. Frugal Saturn darts out of Pisces and your second house of money and joins Neptune in Aries until September 1. The taskmaster planet has kept a tight grip on your finances since it plunged into the Fish's pond on March 7, 2023. And while it's not completely out of those waters until February 13, 2026, you'll get a brief, three-month reprieve this year. (Sounds like sweet music to your ears, right?)

Over the past couple years, circumstances may have forced you to master the art of hard work and meticulous money management. Even if you've always been "good with money," Saturn's tour through Pisces may have directed you to a new source of income—or smarter habits around saving and investing. And while you're ready to sprinkle a bit more luxury into your life, don't rush to splurge. Once Saturn moves into Aries for a longer period (February 13, 2026 to April 12, 2028), you'll have more wiggle room for a long-overdue indulgence.

Fortunately, as an Aquarius, you know that the best things in life aren't actually things. Your people-centric sign relishes experiences with intentional communities of mindful, conscious types. As Saturn makes its grand entrance into Aries and your third house of communication and cooperation this May 24, you could see an uptick in your bank balance through freelance work or a short-term project. As the zodiac's quintessential collaborator, you thrive in joint efforts rather than solo ventures. Start reaching out and you might be amazed at the pool of talent that's ready to join forces.

Discerning Saturn could bring some noteworthy changes to your social life as it sweeps through Aries and your outgoing third house. While you've never met a stranger, your tolerance for superficial connections could rapidly decrease. Purposeful interactions, on the other hand, will keep your soul fed. You don't have to outright unfriend anyone, Aquarius. Just tighten up the radius of your inner circle. Quality over quantity is the new rule. Get ready. Over the next few years, your network might transform dramatically, proving that success often hinges on who you know rather than what you know.

Dreamed of writing a memoir, launching a blog or curating a collection of essays? Start this year while Saturn and visionary Neptune are together. While traditional Saturn might nudge you towards a literary agent and a publishing deal, don't overlook the powerful self-publishing platforms available. Develop a robust marketing strategy and explore tools like Amazon's suite of publishing services.

Like Neptune, Saturn's preview tour through Aries is a glimpse into what's to come starting in 2026. You may simply get the feeling that you've outgrown aspects of your life but feel unsure about what the future holds. Rather than locking down something that feels "good enough," give yourself room to explore and experiment. The third house is all about variety and even serious Saturn understands the benefits of a try-before-you-buy mindset.

If you're thinking of relocating, for example, rent an Airbnb and live like a local for a few weeks. Could you see yourself being happy in this neighborhood for more than six months or a year? Pondering a pivot in your career? Start with a community college course or a weekend workshop to vibe out whether or not this idea is as exciting in real time as it is in your imagination. Saturn does not rush, nor should you, Aquarius. Allow yourself to experiment—that's always the best part, right?

4 REFINE YOUR LOVE LANGUAGE

VENUS RETROGRADE IN ARIES AND PISCES
ARIES: MARCH 1 – 27
PISCES: MARCH 27 – APRIL 12

Stop! Don't send that audio note! Loose lips might sink ships, but this spring, they could create a Titanic-sized wreck on the Sea of Love. For this you can blame normally diplomatic Venus. From March 1 to April 12, the planet of beauty and harmony slips into a six-week retrograde, an event that happens every 18 months. This time around the U-turn takes place in two signs, first in Aries and your third house of communication (March 1 to 27), then in Pisces and your sensual second house (March 27 to April 12).

For most of March, you'll be tasked with improving your communication style, particularly with the people closest to you. Are you saying what you REALLY mean, Aquarius? Or are you using jokes and sarcasm to get your point across? From March 1 to 27, it's all but assured that you'll need to strengthen your sensitivity filters. While you're at it, send your raw humor on a sabbatical. During this sensitive cycle, what's "just a joke" to you could be a grievous offense to someone you love, potentially jeopardizing your whole relationship.

On the flip side, some Water Bearers could be a little TOO democratic in moments when you need to take charge. We're not advocating for a tyrannical tear, Aquarius, just a tweak. Venus retrograde can help you finesse your requests so no one has to read your mind or dance around being polite when it's time to get down to business.

The third house (Aries, in your chart) also governs platonic love. If you're feeling nonplussed about your current romantic situation, try not to panic. The spring fever vibes will return after March 27, once Venus retreats back into Pisces and your second house of TLC. Before then, focus on strengthening the camaraderie in your connection. As a sapiosexual Aquarius, you need to connect intellectually, but you also need someone who can be your BFF. A few chill bonding activities—pub trivia, weekend campouts with mutual friends—can take your relationship from "buddy call" to "booty call" again.

Single Water Bearers may feel the sparks with someone from the friend zone. Advance carefully because feelings will run hot and cold during Venus retrograde. This could all get SO much more complicated than you bargained for. If you're not sure anything may come of it, file feelings in the "secret crush" category for now. With Venus in reverse, double check ring fingers and ask the obvious questions like, "Are you in a relationship?" You could attract people who are charismatic but not exactly available. P.S. That may be a mirror for your own indecision about being tied down. Stay off that slippery slope. It's all fun and games until the idealistic Aquarius gets hurt.

When Venus inches back into Pisces and your sensual second house from March 27 to April 12, you may find yourself in a touchy-feely mode once again. If you were pushing a romantic interest away, suddenly you won't be able to pull them close enough. DO give people a chance to adjust to your sudden change of heart. You may have some amends to make for being a little cool and distant in March—and some massages to give to help them with their emotional whiplash.

Are you due for a financial clean-up? If you've been splurging without restraint, there will be bills to take care of, but you also want to do something that sings with your soul. While Venus backs up through Pisces from March 27 to April 12, surf through your LinkedIn contacts. One of your old colleagues could be working for your dream company. A former creative collaborator might also appear with an offer worth considering. Take time to crunch the numbers before agreeing to a sequel. Time is money and you need to make sure that the hours you spend will pay off!

5 RAISE THE FINANCIAL STAKES

LUNAR NODES IN VIRGO AND PISCES
NORTH NODE IN PISCES, SOUTH NODE IN VIRGO
JANUARY 11, 2025 – JULY 26, 2026

Your "secure the bag" era begins this January 11 as the North Node flows into Pisces and activates your house of money and values until July 26, 2026. Steady work and a smart approach to spending are your new M.O. even if that means tightening your belt a bit more than you've had to in recent years. Rethink a few indulgences, not as a sacrifice, but to make your money work harder for you through savings and investments.
Beyond just covering rent and bills, how can you maximize your earning power? Across the zodiac, the South Node moves into Virgo and your eighth house of shared resources, nudging you to look at collaborations and pooling assets. This could be the year you

apply for a mortgage, seek venture capital, or explore small business loans to turn a side hustle into something bigger.

The good news? If the last 18 months of the Aries-Libra nodal cycle (July 17, 2023 to January 11, 2025) helped you build up your network, you're sitting on a goldmine of connections. Those relationships could pay dividends in the form of job offers and strategic partnerships now. You'll need to speak up, though, and make clear asks. The squeaky wheel gets the oil!

With the South Node in Virgo, it's time to lean into your analytical side. Whether it's investing in real estate, mutual funds or dipping your toe into crypto, now's your chance to diversify and make smart choices. The more you educate yourself about financial systems, the more you'll be able to secure long-term stability.

Been in the same job for a while? Use your experience to level up. This year you could negotiate a sizable raise, move up the corporate ladder or make a strategic leap to another company. Self-employed Aquarians could raise your rates or launch a subscription service that ensures steady income. It's all about creating long-term stability, and honestly, who knew adulting could feel this empowering?

Your mindset matters, too. As you navigate this nodal cycle, remember that money is a tool—not something to avoid or obsess over. With the North Node in dreamy Pisces and the South Node in practical Virgo, this is your chance to get aligned with your financial goals. What's worth saving for this year? Maybe it's that dream vacation you've been planning or launching a passion project. Instead of swiping the credit card, start a savings plan to make it happen.

Here's the plot twist: Financial stability can actually enhance your freedom, Aquarius. With fewer money worries, you'll have more space to dive into your creative projects and big ideas. Whether you're merging finances, planning for the future or adjusting your budget, the less you stress about money, the more you can focus on the visionary stuff that makes you you. And let's be real, Aquarius—when you're free to think outside the box, the world benefits. Now's your chance to build the foundation that will help you take your brilliance to the next level!

Love

AQUARIUS 2025 FORECAST

Love is your playground in many ways this year, Aquarius, but ride that merry-go-round mindfully to avoid spinning out. As 2025 kicks off, adventure-seeking Jupiter is halfway through its tour of Gemini and your fifth house of giddy, starstruck love—a cycle that began on May 25, 2024, and runs until June 9, 2025. Your romantic horizons are expanding, as are your preferences for pleasure.

Whether you're deepening an existing relationship or hooking up with wild abandon, Jupiter's spontaneous influence can make this a fun and memorable era. The only issue? This hot-to-go cycle can make you a hard one to pin down. Intimacy requires consistency, but the variable energy of Jupiter in Gemini won't necessarily leave you craving commitment. As Aquarius Janis Joplin sang, "Freedom's just another word for nothing left to lose." So if you actually DO have something (namely someone) to lose, swill Jupiter's love potion carefully until June 9.

On July 7, your ruler, experimental Uranus, picks up where Jupiter left off, taking its first side-spin through Gemini until November 7. This will bring another wave of thrilling unconventionality to your love life. Uranus loves to break the rules; an urge that will only get stronger when the planet parks in Gemini for seven more years from April 25, 2026 to May 22, 2033. Whether you're meeting someone who challenges your romantic boundaries or taking a lover who lights up your wild side, you'll feel the need to be fully, unapologetically yourself in love. And let's be honest, Aquarius, that's a lot for one person to handle!

You might even feel drawn to a more flexible dating arrangement, one that allows you to embrace all the dimensions of your ever-evolving self. Coupled Water Bearers could slip off for a baecation that turns into an elopement. It's your life!

If you have kids—or are thinking about starting a family—you may feel torn between the responsibilities of parenthood and your need for independence. A pregnancy could be on the horizon, bringing both excitement and the weight of new commitments.

That said, you might start 2025 on a little bit of a tense note. Lusty Mars turned retrograde in Leo and your seventh house of relationships on December 6, 2024, a cycle that can create friction for you and your beloved—or potentially turn a "beloved" into an ex. But there's no telling if that plot is going to stick. Mars returns to Leo from April 18 to June 17, which could create an opportunity for a passionate reunion.

Even before then, love planet Venus has a spring retrograde from March 1 to April 12, which might give you and your ex-bae a chance to talk through your differences. At the very least, this six-week window can help you get some closure. Coupled Water Bearers may have some negotiating to do around values and the way you handle finances. There's nothing wrong with separating bank accounts or opening up a third, shared fund while keeping your own private investments.

So ready to move on? Don't worry. New love blossoms once Mars resumes direct motion in Leo from April 18 to June 17. You could meet someone who challenges your mind and body, keeping you fully engaged. When Mars sweeps into Virgo and your eighth house of erotic desire from June 17 to August 6, you may be ready to go "all in." Warning: With Mercury retrograde in Leo from July 18 to August 11, don't be surprised if an old flame resurfaces, offering a second shot at love or closure on a past relationship.

What's really making everything so complicated for your love life this year is this: Deep-diving Pluto is spending its first full year in Aquarius. Since the metamorphic dwarf planet began weaving in and out of your sign in March 2023, you've been undergoing a powerful transformation.

As you evolve from the inside out, it can be tricky to figure out who is even compatible. If you're in a relationship, there may be moments where you send mixed signals, torn between craving solitude and soothing. Be mindful of Pluto's intensity and don't let its ruthless energy creep into your relationships. If you're feeling cold or detached, make sure you communicate clearly with your partner instead of icily pushing them away.

Interestingly, love planet Venus won't visit Aquarius in 2025—a rare occurrence that could make love feel a bit less of a priority this year. And while Mars won't be visiting Aquarius either, don't worry: You'll be rewarded for all your inner (and outer) work mid-January 2026, as the cosmic lovebirds team up in Aquarius and deliver a sultry surge of kundalini energy. Until then, make way for a year of unscripted romantic possibilities that could find you breaking every mold you ever set for yourself.

AQUARIUS: LUCKIEST love DAY

JULY 7

Amorous Venus is flirting with abandon in Gemini and your playful, passionate fifth house. Today, she'll connect the dots to sultry, magnetic Pluto in your sign. Sing your siren's song selectively to draw the right "sailors" to your shores.

Money & Career

AQUARIUS 2025 FORECAST

What's your number, Aquarius? No, we're not asking for the digits to your phone. We're talking about the ideal figure you'd like to have in your financial accounts. Whether retirement is a few decades or a couple years away, money is on your mind starting January 11. The fateful lunar nodes are shifting into Pisces (North) and Virgo (South) where they will activate your second house of values and earnings and your eighth house of investments, respectively, until July 26, 2026.

The Pisces North Node can help you attract work that resonates with your soul. If you're the type who gets foggy about budgets, bring in support ASAP. This watery cycle could reveal all the ways that money slips between your fingers. Boundary-setting becomes essential now, which might be best handled by having parts of your paycheck auto-deposited into an IRA or index fund before you spend it. Make sure you also set up a vacation fund and entertainment fund, Aquarius. Small deposits add up, ensuring that you'll be motivated to keep on hustling!

It's not just about making money, however; it's about making your money work hard for you. The sensible Virgo South Node inspires you to amass assets or grow existing ones through investments in the market, joint ventures or real estate. Wealthy people may be interested in backing your business plans, too. Lawyer up and go through all the appropriate channels to ensure that your intellectual property (and your piece of the pie!) is protected.

Two powerful eclipses in Virgo—on March 14 and September 21—could push you to release old habits around money and reshape your financial strategy. And on September 7, the total lunar eclipse in Pisces will bring a chance to reset your financial goals, potentially sealing a big deal or job offer that propels you forward.

How you move through your daily grind could shift starting June 9. That's the day that bountiful Jupiter settles into Cancer sending its abundant beams into your steady, systematic sixth house until June 30, 2026. Work becomes an exciting challenge now, one that offers opportunities to climb the ladder, travel or even orient yourself to an entirely new role. Since Jupiter rules higher ed, you might enroll in a fall semester of training or apply to a graduate program. (Perhaps out of state or even out of country!)

We have to talk about Pluto, which has been burning down parts of your life that were ready to evolve ever since March 2023, when it began weaving in and out of your sign. In 2025, the metamorphic dwarf planet settles in Aquarius for nineteen solid years, altering your thinking around personal power. You could find yourself drawn to a leadership role, one that brings a measure of clout. Because of Pluto's underground influence, a good deal of this work may be done behind the scenes or in a private boardroom—or on private jets! Get ready for a lot more attention from the VIPs, whether you were seeking it or not. Joining members-only clubs and elite organizations could pave the way to prosperity for you during this two-decade cycle, a definite departure from your "for the people" ways of the past.

But forget about flying under the radar completely! With live-out-loud Jupiter in your fifth house of fame until June 9, your efforts could draw quite the fanbase. Best of all, you can be "so Julia" about it. (A nod to iconoclastic Water Bearer Julia Fox from Charli XCX's 2024 banger, "360.")

From September 22 to November 4, go-getter Mars makes a powerful pass through Scorpio and your tenth house of prestige. Get ready for a surge of energy to tackle those Q4 goals with confidence and strategic vision. Whether you're pushing for a promotion, launching an impressive project or taking command of the ship, Mars' bold, assertive energy can help you make serious strides. By the time 2025 draws to a close, you'll have laid the groundwork for long-term success, with new opportunities on the horizon and a deeper sense of control over your financial future.

AQUARIUS: LUCKIEST career DAY

OCTOBER 28

Red-hot Mars is making moves in Scorpio and your tenth house of career, sending you on an express elevator ride to the top of your game. As the excitable planet teams up with abundant Jupiter in Cancer and your sixth house of hustle, give those projects an extra push. Victory!

2025
AQUARIUS

12
MONTH
OVERVIEW

January MONTHLY HOROSCOPE

Ease your way into 2025 in a space of rest and reflection. (Those resolutions can wait until your birthday, right?) With the Sun grounding in Capricorn and your twelfth house of divine inspiration, your visionary nature will benefit from a few weeks of quiet introspection. But don't ignore your inbox entirely. On the 6th, stressful Mars retrogrades back into Cancer and your industrious sixth house, which could bring some big demands and potential chaos at work that requires immediate attention—and your knack for creative problem solving. With the red planet in reverse here until February 23, go easy on your winter exercise routine. Skip the bootcamps and opt for something sustainable, like a weight-training routine that builds strength incrementally. Once Aquarius season begins on the 19th, you'll get a burst of renewed energy, confidence and the zeal to go after your personal goals. Better yet? The Year of the Wood Snake begins on January 29—the day of the year's only new moon in Aquarius—helping you lay down a solid structure for whatever you want to build in 2025.

February MONTHLY HOROSCOPE

Birthday season wages on until the 18th, making February a month of fierce independence and personal reinvention. Don't wait to be discovered. Scout out opportunities where you can showcase your brilliance. Take the lead when you feel the call, steering teams with your originality and collaborative approach. Your charisma goes full blast on the 4th when convivial Venus begins a long tour through Aries and your third house of communication. Careful not to make promises that may be too lofty to keep, however. When Venus spins retrograde from March 1 to April 12, you may need to revisit old conversations or rethink your approach to certain collaborations. Also on the 4th, Jupiter turns direct in Gemini, reawakening your fifth house of romance, creativity and passion. Enough stagnation! You're ready for growth and excitement that puts your name on the map between now and June 9. Get your ducks in a row—and your bank account back in the black—when the Sun moves into Pisces on February 18. You'll get some help from Mars who turns direct in Cancer on February 23 and sparks momentum in your sixth house of health and daily routines. Efficiency, at last!

March MONTHLY HOROSCOPE

March kicks off with your practical side in high gear, as the Pisces Sun hunkers down in your second house of money, values and financial security until the 20th. Assess your resources and plan for a secure future. But don't get too wrapped up in the material world. Both Venus and Mercury will be retrograde in Aries, highlighting your communication and community zone—Venus from March 1 to 27 and Mercury from March 15 to 29. Take this time to reevaluate your social style and refresh your messaging. You might need to revisit old conversations or resolve lingering issues within your friend circle. Meanwhile, the Virgo lunar eclipse on March 14 brings some clarity around shared finances or emotional entanglements. Is it time to move forward together or just move on? Epiphanies about the right next steps are coming. When the Sun moves into Aries on March 20, you'll be back to your experimental self. With all the new people coming your way (and old friends, too, thanks to the retrogrades), test drive some potential joint ventures. The Aries solar eclipse on March 29 wraps up a two-year cycle in your third house, bringing clarity around who belongs in your circle—and who needs to be evicted. And just as things are shifting, Neptune enters Aries on March 30, kicking off a 14-year cycle of visionary insights and spiritual growth in communication. Writing, teaching and podcasting projects will flourish now. Get your message out there!

April MONTHLY HOROSCOPE

Welcome to the innovation station! With the Sun parked in your mentally agile third house until April 19, your mind is buzzing with ideas, connections and projects. But before you broadcast anything, pause. Mercury is retrograde in Pisces and your money zone until April 7, while Venus is retrograde there until April 12. You may need to revisit your budget, refine financial strategies or clear up any money misunderstandings. Once Venus and Mercury are both direct (after the 12th), you'll be ready to present your big ideas with confidence and clarity. Lusty Mars swoops into Leo on April 18, sending a blast of sexy heat into your seventh house of partnerships. You're a people magnet during this cycle, which lasts until June 17. The only warning? Careful not to come on so strong that you push away your fans. When Taurus season kicks off on April 19, your focus shifts to home and family. Get your space set up for springtime entertainment. If you're ready to move, buy or sell, the stars are on your side.

May MONTHLY HOROSCOPE

Drop anchor, Aquarius! With the Taurus Sun cozied up in your fourth house of roots until May 20, you'll be happiest under your own roof. Have you created a stable, nurturing environment? Whether you're sprucing up your space, deepening family bonds or figuring out where your next address will be, give domestic affairs top billing. On May 4, transformative Pluto turns retrograde in your sign until October 13. This could stir up a bit of discontent—a nagging feeling that there's more you want to do, be and have. Figuring out WHAT that is, exactly, is not going to be an overnight discovery. With Pluto in Aquarius until 2044, your entire existence is reshaping itself. So how about signing up for one personal-growth experience like a retreat or workshop, then taking the next step after that? On May 20, the Sun zips into Gemini, lighting up your creative, romantic fifth house. As your playful side takes the stage, you'll feel more comfortable cutting loose and enjoying the lighter side of life. Saturn makes a major move on May 24, entering Aries for the first time since 1998 and settling into your third house of communication, learning and community. If you've dreamed of writing a book, starting a podcast or designing a curriculum, Saturn's disciplined energy helps you structure your thoughts. Socially, get serious about building a network that supports your goals.

June MONTHLY HOROSCOPE

June 2025 brings a wave of productivity and focus for you, Aquarius! While the Sun in Gemini until June 20 keeps your social calendar buzzing, the real shift comes on June 9 when Jupiter moves into Cancer for the first time since 2014. This is huge—for the next year, Jupiter will occupy your sixth house of work, health and daily routines, pushing you to streamline your life, improve your well-being and tackle long-term projects. Whether it's revamping your fitness routine, organizing your schedule or diving into a work project, Jupiter's expansive energy will help you thrive in the details. When the Sun joins Jupiter in Cancer at the solstice on June 20, you'll feel the urge to really get things in order—think healthy habits, solid routines and a renewed focus on wellness. Mid-month could bring a few bumps as Jupiter clashes with Saturn on June 15 and Neptune on June 18, stirring up tension between your big ambitions and practical limitations. Stay grounded, Aquarius— slow progress is still progress. Mars enters Virgo on June 17, supercharging your efforts in tackling financial or shared resource matters. By June 24, the Day of Miracles, when the Sun and Jupiter align, you'll have a prime opportunity to manifest a healthier, more productive lifestyle. Jupiter's setting you up for long-term success, so lean into the small wins, Aquarius!

July MONTHLY HOROSCOPE

Stand-up paddleboarding or down-dogs in the park? Whatever your poison, just get moving! You're in your vibrant element this July as the lifegiving Sun and vital Jupiter stream together through Cancer, your sixth house of wellness and daily routines. Some of your most fulfilling moves will be ones you might normally consider "mundane," like developing a savvy workflow so you can slip off for a mid-day cardio class. This is the zone of service providers. Aquarians on the hunt for an assistant could radar in on the perfect support staff. Maybe it's YOU who's looking for new work. Circulate your resume or LinkedIn profile during this lucky cycle. On July 7, electrifying Uranus (your ruling planet) makes a radical move into Gemini, its first visit here since 1941-49. Your fifth house of creativity, romance and self-expression will be charged up until November 7, which offers a glimpse of the joy, rebellion and public recognition the full Uranus cycle from April 2026 to May 2033 will bring. Let your daring side lead the way and take note of what opens up. Negotiations are in order as Neptune, Saturn and Chiron all go retrograde in Aries this month—on the 4th, 13th, and 30th, respectively. Over the next five months, you may need to revisit old conversations, reassess agreements or deal with lingering sibling dynamics. Partnerships get a solar-powered surge when Leo season kicks off on July 22. You'll be eager to team up for all sorts of collaborations, but be mindful. Social Mercury pivots retrograde in Leo from July 18 to August 11 making it hard to get the clearest read on people. As unresolved relationship issues bubble to the surface, slow down, clarify expectations and don't be afraid to revisit old ground if it means establishing a stronger, more honest connection.

August MONTHLY HOROSCOPE

Forget about holding anyone at arm's length this August. With your relationship houses (Leo and Virgo) getting blasted by sunbeams all month, you're ready to pull your people close. While the Sun shines in Leo until the 22nd, you may need to right-size a few relationships that have spun into undefined territory. Need to rebalance communication dynamics? Wait until Mercury turns direct on the 11th before broaching touchier topics. You'll get less friction then. In the meanwhile, keep your focus on beautifying your workspace and giving yourself a glow-up with clean eating and exercise. With radiant Venus in Cancer until the 25th, you can cultivate harmony in your daily routines—all with an aesthetic touch! Wanderlust strikes on August 6 as thrill seeking Mars zips into Libra and charges up your ninth house of expansion, travel and higher learning. With the red planet propelling you toward adventure, let your curiosity lead you to horizon-broadening experiences. Relationships take on a more serious tone once Virgo season begins on August 22. One day later, the first of two rare, back-to-back new moons in Virgo arrives, bringing fresh-start energy to your eighth house of intimacy and investments. From sex to money, you want to have a say in how you share yourself and your resources. Get back into the driver's seat without steamrolling other people in the process. An even deeper reset comes when the solar (new moon) eclipse in Virgo on September 21 brings transformative momentum. Radar in on the area that's crying out for empowerment and start making changes that lead you in that direction.

September MONTHLY HOROSCOPE

Slip on the scuba gear, Aquarius, because it's time to plunge into the depths. As Virgo season wages on through to the 22nd, your mystical, seductive and alchemical eighth house is lit. Venus splits the month between Leo (until the 19th) and Virgo, your partnership and intimacy zones, raising the romantic stakes even higher. If you don't see a future, you won't want to waste your time. Plus, you have zero tolerance for superficial exchanges, especially since you may be parsing through some heavier feelings surrounding loss or transformation. The sooner you feel, the faster you'll heal, emerging with a new layer of wisdom to share with the world. Your quest for answers could lead you far from home while adventurous Mars sails through Libra and your nomadic ninth house until the 22nd. Work with a master teacher or dive into a cutting-edge workshop that helps you move through your process. Two eclipses put the focus on both romance and finance this month. On the 7th, the total lunar (full moon) eclipse in Pisces reveals where you've been burning through cash. Simultaneously you could see a new strategy for simplifying that allows you to create a buffer for yourself, and also incorporate better self-care into your routines. On the 21st, the Virgo solar eclipse—which is also the second in a back-to-back pair of Virgo new moons that began on August 23—highlights intimacy and investments. Pull back from relationships that are more of a drain than a fountain. This is the month to start or add more to your retirement account. Bring on the index funds and Roth IRAs! Life feels significantly lighter once Libra season begins on the 22nd. This monthlong cycle turns your focus to travel and higher learning. Sign up for a fall-semester course or work with a coach. With go-getter Mars leaping into Scorpio and your driven tenth house the very same day, anything that bolsters your business skills or putsyou in line for a pay increase would be a worthwhile use of time.

October MONTHLY HOROSCOPE

Comfort zone? What's that? You're stretching way beyond your familiar horizons as the Sun shines brightly in Libra and illuminates your ninth house of travel, expansion and entrepreneurship until the 22nd. Get in on those "shoulder season" rates and book an overseas trip. Can't get away? Sign up for a mind-blowing fall course in anything from a personal-development workshop to Tarot 101 to The History of Colonialism. With love planet Venus also entering Libra on October 13, romance could arise while you're off exploring new places or mingling with people who inspire you. Coupled Aquarians, try to slip off for a baecation in the second half of the month. Even one night away can recharge your bond. Your magnetism returns to full strength after the 13th, too, as alchemical Pluto wakes up from its five-month retrograde in Aquarius. With the planet of power and wealth in your sign until 2044, you're on a steady journey of evolution that can position you as a leader. But first, you're diving deeper into your own psyche to find out what turns you on. That momentum picks up now with Pluto direct. Career goals are set to soar starting October 22, when the Sun enters Scorpio and your ambitious tenth house. Take all the inspiration you've gathered and put it to work. Stay focused like a laserbeam on your most impactful goal. While you're doing that, don't let money slip through your fingers. Also on October 22, Neptune retrogrades back into Pisces and your second house of finances, where it will stay for the remainder of its backspin, until December 10. Money mindfulness is a must! Bring more clarity to your spending habits, rethink your material priorities and make sure your investments align with your true values.

November MONTHLY HOROSCOPE

Shift into baller mode while the Scorpio Sun powers up your goal-getting tenth house until the 21st. Go hard on those Q4 missions and network like it was your second job. With charming, personable Venus also in Scorpio from November 6 to 30, you'll easily attract the MVPs in your field. Treat yourself to an investment piece that'll elevate your professional presence, like a chic blazer or a new tablet. On November 4, energetic Mars enters Sagittarius and your eleventh house of community, friends and long-term aspirations, where it will stay until December 15. Hivemind discussions will be epic as you bring people together around a shared vision. Your influence can help a group project gain momentum, but keep an eye on team dynamics. Mars here can also rile up conflicts if people aren't seeing eye-to-eye. Another reason to remain alert: On November 9, Mercury spins into its final retrograde of the year, backing up through Sagittarius until the 18th, then Scorpio until the 29th. You may need to step back and review certain strategies, rather than pushing ahead aggressively. On the plus side, Mercury's retreat can reconnect you to powerful allies and colleagues from your past. More retrograde news: On November 7, your ruler, radical Uranus, slips back from Gemini into Taurus, reversing through your domestic fourth house until February 3, 2026. Family dynamics and household issues could be shaken and stirred. Lean into your experimental side to smooth things out. Practical magic helps here, too, as Jupiter flips into a four-month retrograde in Cancer and your administrative sixth house on November 11. What can you simplify, streamline and systematize, Aquarius, in the name of serenity? Grounding energy arrives just as the month wraps! On the 27th, stable Saturn finally ends its five-month retrograde. As it does its final lap through Pisces and your money zone (until February 13, 2026), you won't mind tightening your belt a little so you can save up for something that brings you lasting joy.

December MONTHLY HOROSCOPE

Let the reindeer games begin! You're at the center of the action until the 21st, and the Sagittarius Sun has appointed you entertainment director for your crew. But no 101 movie nights happening here. With excitement junkie Mars and glamorous Venus also in Sagittarius, until the 15th and 24th, respectively, you might get everyone out for a weekend on the slopes or to see an off-Broadway production that's on tour in a nearby city. If money matters have been muddled, take heart. On the 10th, hazy Neptune wakes up from its retrograde and shifts into drive in your fiscally savvy second house. Not only will this help you get your budget back on track, but you'll get a soul-deep reminder about what is truly important to YOU—no matter what the "Joneses" think. Downshift a bit on December 15 as Mars decamps to Capricorn and activates your twelfth house of rest, reflection and closure. With the Sun following suit on December 21 (the winter solstice) and Venus joining the Capricorn camp on the 24th, you'll wrap up the year feeling reflective. In between family celebrations, create space to meditate, rest and tie up loose ends. This restorative cycle is getting you ready for Aquarius season, which begins late January. With so much twelfth house action, you may prefer to spend NYE doing something quiet or spiritual. Think: candlelight meditations, vision-boarding, even a release ceremony if you made any major transitions in 2025.

Read your extended monthly forecast for life, love, money and career! astrostyle.com

A LITTLE ABOUT Pisces

DATES February 18 - March 20

SYMBOL The Fish

ELEMENT Water

QUALITY Mutable

RULING PLANET Neptune, Jupiter

BODY PART Feet

BEST TRAITS
Romantic, helpful, wise, caring, imaginative, free-flowing, magnanimous, empathic, soulful, tuned-in

KEYWORDS
Dreams, fantasy, healing, compassion, creativity, escape, intuition, magic

Read more about Pisces

PISCES
IN 2025

ALL THE PLANETS IN PISCES IN 2025	YOUR 2025 HOROSCOPE	TOP 5 THEMES FOR PISCES IN 2025	LOVE HOROSCOPE + LUCKY DATES	MONEY HOROSCOPE + LUCKY DATES

Pisces in 2025

YOUR YEARLY OVERVIEW

Destiny is calling, Pisces, and it has your name written all over it. 2025 is an extremely special year for you as the lunar North Node arrives in your sign on January 11, kicking off an 18-month journey that will guide you to your highest purpose. This cycle hasn't come around since 2006-07, so if you can remember what was happening then, similar themes may echo. Two outer planets—serious Saturn and numinous Neptune—will pop out of your sign for part of the year, moving into Aries and activating your second house of money and values for a short time. Neptune's dreaminess and Saturn's discipline make an unusual but potent combo. This year, they'll help you lay the groundwork for long-term wealth while ensuring that your ventures resonate deeply with your soul's purpose. Home and family matters could go through some restructuring as two free-spirited planets— Jupiter and Uranus—move through Gemini and your fourth house of roots. Stability may be hard to come by, but you're also learning that home (in the truest sense) lives within YOU. Keep on building internal resilience and you'll be the calm in the storm. Life takes a playful, passionate turn mid-year, which is happy news for Fish! On June 9, abundant Jupiter moves into Cancer, starting a romantic and artistic renaissance that washes over your entire life. The muse will be your constant companion during this fertile phase, which could bring anything from babies to a breakthrough in your creativity that leads to a body of work. Unleash!

THE PLANETS IN *Pisces*

THE SUN
FEB 18–MAR 20

It's birthday season for you, so step out and shine! Seek novelty and take extra initiative during this radiant monthlong phase.

NEW MOON
FEB 27
7:45PM, 9°41'

Bonus New Year! Set your intentions for the next six months and get into action.

FULL MOON
TOTAL LUNAR ECLIPSE
SEP 7
2:09PM, 15°23'

Ready, set, manifest! Your work of the past six months bears fruit and it's time to harvest the rewards. Since this full moon is a total lunar eclipse, opportunities may come from unexpected sources, changing the course of your destiny!

MERCURY
FEB 14–MAR 3
MAR 29–APR 16

RETROGRADE IN PISCES:
MAR 29–APR 7

Crown yourself monarch of social butterflies as popularity-boosting Mercury visits your sign twice this year. Circulate and get social. During the retrograde, don't make promises you can't keep or let energy vampires into your sphere.

VENUS
JAN 2–FEB 4
MAR 27–APR 30

RETROGRADE IN PISCES:
MAR 27–APR 12

You've got the romantic It Factor when the galactic glamazon charges up your powers of seduction—and in 2025, you'll host Venus twice. You may revisit an old love issue or reconnect to an ex during the retrograde. Keep your boundaries firm. Willpower is weak in the face of beauty and luxury. Watch your spending!

SATURN
MAR 7, 2023–MAY 24, 2025
SEP 1, 2025–
FEB 13, 2026

RETROGRADE IN PISCES:
SEP 1–NOV 27

Welcome to cosmic boot camp! Discipline and focus is demanded as you stabilize the foundation of your life. Saturn visits your sign every 29.5 years for a 3-year visit. It ain't easy, but growth will be epic!

NEPTUNE
JAN 1–MAR 30
OCT 22, 2025–
JAN 26, 2026

RETROGRADE IN PISCES:
OCT 22–DEC 10

You're winding down a 15-year cycle of shifting identity, spiritual self-discovery and enhanced connection to the ethereal realm, which began back in 2011. Continue to prioritize healing and internal work while also celebrating the profound progress you've made.

NORTH NODE
JAN 11, 2025–
JUL 26, 2026

The destiny-fueling North Node begins an 18-month tour through your sign, connecting you to your passion and purpose. This cycle, which only happens every 18.5 years, may put you through your paces but helps to true you up with your authentic self.

Pisces in 2025
HIGHLIGHTS

IDENTITY OVERHAUL: NORTH NODE IN PISCES

Who do you think you are, Pisces? By the time this year is through, you will be able to answer that in a refreshingly new way. On January 11, 2025, the transformative North Node moves into your sign for an eighteen-month odyssey through your first house of identity. Welcome to a fresh chapter of self-discovery and personal empowerment—one that aligns with your higher purpose. Expect to shed old roles, habits and expectations that no longer resonate with 2025 Pisces. This nodal cycle, which only comes around every 18.5 years, will evolve you in ways that might feel challenging at times. Hey, it can be confronting to own your power to express yourself with vulnerable authenticity. Trust the process and honor your journey! The total lunar eclipse in Pisces will reveal important "next steps" on September 7.

RELATIONSHIP RECONSTRUCTION: SOUTH NODE IN VIRGO

While the destiny-driven North Node is busy reconstructing the Pisces "personal brand," across the zodiac wheel, the lunar South Node in Virgo will work its karmic magic in your seventh house of relationships. From January 11, 2025 to July 26, 2026, this phase supports you with healing old wounds and releasing toxic dynamics. Examine everything from your generational patterns to your attachment style. The South Node invites you to let go of codependency, people-pleasing and any patterns that have kept you stuck in unfulfilling ruts. It's time to balance your needs with the needs of others and embrace healthier, more empowering connections. Two Virgo eclipses—the total lunar eclipse on March 14 and the partial solar eclipse on September 21—will expedite this process.

GIVE ME SPACE! JUPITER AND URANUS BRING LIBERATION TO YOUR FRONT DOOR

Home sweet...anywhere? Two of the most liberated planets, Jupiter and Uranus, travel through Gemini and your fourth house of family and roots. This year, you may find yourself redefining what "home" and "family" mean to you—whether that's through moving, downsizing or finally working to heal toxic generational patterns. If you want to expand your family or purchase a dream home, lucky Jupiter's on your side until June 9. From July 7 to November 7, Uranus, the planet of freedom and innovation, brings a free-spirited, experimental vibe to your personal life. Whether you're embracing a nomadic lifestyle or renovating your space, 2025 is about creating a home that aligns with your freest self.

SATURN AND NEPTUNE WEAVE BETWEEN PISCES AND ARIES

In 2025, two powerful planets—Saturn and Neptune—dart out of your sign for part of the year. As they head out of Pisces and your identity-focused first house, they give you a preview of longer cycles through Aries and your second house of money and values that begin again in early 2026. These shifts can feel disorienting, since Saturn has been in your sign since March 7, 2023, and Neptune since wayyyy back on April 4, 2011. While they'll be back in Pisces by fall (Saturn on September 1 and Neptune on October 22), take notes! At the beginning of 2026, both planets will embark on longer journeys through Aries which could reshape the way you earn, spend and save money. Fortunately, you'll be armed with the wisdom and strength of two potent planets who have gifted you with their presence over the past decade-plus. This year, call forth your discipline and commitment to solidify personal goals—and determine what is worth investing your energy in.

VENUS RETROGRADE: REVISITING LOVE AND SELF-WORTH

Do you know how valuable you are? Loving Venus wants to make sure that you do, when she spins into her every-18-month retrograde from March 1 to April 12. The first part of the backspin begins in Aries and your second house of self-worth and personal values. If you've been hiding your truth to please others, that won't cut it this spring. And once Venus backs up into Pisces, from March 27 to April 12, you could have some eye-opening revelations about your heart's true desires. While these six weeks might bring some turbulence, they will set the stage for greater personal fulfillment in all of your relationships.

JUPITER IN CANCER PUTS YOU CENTER STAGE

Lights, camera, Pisces! On June 9, 2025, live-out-loud Jupiter catapults into Cancer where it will activate your fifth house of fame, romance and creative expression for the first time since 2014. If you haven't been embracing life with open arms, this passionate cycle is sure to change that. But forget about flying under the radar. This yearlong cycle vaults you into the public eye, which could mean stepping onto the throne of a leadership position or literally into the spotlight as a performer, presenter or the face of a movement. Romantically, Jupiter in Cancer can bring a heady mix of adventure and high-key moments. But know this, Fish: Your need for freedom will be as strong as your carnal desires, which might mean negotiating some new boundaries in love.

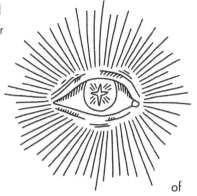

TOP 5 THEMES FOR
Pisces in 2025

1	2	3	4	5
TAKE HOME ON THE ROAD	TURN LIFE INTO A COSTUME PARTY	STABILIZE YOUR FINANCES	RECLAIM YOUR WORTH	ILLUMINATE YOUR HIGHER PURPOSE

1 TAKE HOME ON THE ROAD

JUPITER AND URANUS IN GEMINI

JUPITER: MAY 25, 2024 – JUNE 9, 2025
URANUS: JULY 7 – NOVEMBER 7, 2025 • JANUARY 26, 2026 – MAY 22, 2033

Should you put down roots or pull them up? Your domestic plans may be up for a total makeover in 2025, Pisces. (Yes, this may feel a tad unmooring.) Two of the most experimental and free-spirited planets—Jupiter and Uranus—roll through Gemini and your domestic fourth house throughout the year. Even if you don't move to a new space, you could shuttle regularly between your base camp and a "home away from home." Settling down is not an option.

JUPITER IN GEMINI

MAY 25, 2024 – JUNE 9, 2025

Home may be a moving target in the first half of 2025, thanks to peripatetic Jupiter. Last year, on May 25, 2024, the nomadic planet trekked into Gemini for the first time in twelve years. Bouts of claustrophobia have undoubtedly been a frequently occurring issue since then. Well, Pisces, you can forget about holing up for hygge season in early 2025. Jupiter continues its adventurous spin through Gemini until June 9, calling you into the wide world to find places that feel like a "home away from home."

Jupiter is the galactic gambler so you might be ready to throw caution to the wind, take a gap year and go live in your BFF's Parisian apartment while she's on assignment in another part of the world. While all this stimulation might be a bit much for some people, you actually love the idea of flowing from place to place. If you have kids or are caring for a parent, there will be more considerations, but be honest with yourself: Would your family be happier in a different environment? If the answer is yes, be the catalyst for change. They will thank you later.

Bear in mind that things happen fast with Jupiter in the picture. Mull your options carefully before you do anything drastic. Putting your stuff in storage is one thing. Putting your house on the market when interest rates are high could come with steeper consequences. But then again, Pisces, it's really your call. If you feel stuck in a golden fish tank, it may indeed be time to cash out on your real estate investment, downsize and paddle out into the ocean of life.

If your love interest lives elsewhere or a job opens up in another time zone, that can make your decision easier. But if you're just feeling antsy and like you need a hard reset, start playing out scenarios in your head while also checking in with the wise counsel of advisers in your life. Jupiter is retrograde until February 4, so if possible, wait until after then before making any irreversible decisions.

Jupiter is the planetary entrepreneur, and you may get a brilliant idea for a home-based business—on your own or with a like-minded friend or family member. Start small and reach out to social contacts who'd make an ideal client or can lead you to new avenues of income. But making money isn't the whole point. Wise Jupiter in Gemini can teach you to manage your assets like a pro. With the red-spotted planet grounded at the bottom of your chart, you're primed to build your nest egg.

No matter how restless you feel, keep at least one eye open for a miraculous real estate deal, which could be an investment that you use as a rental property. Abundant Jupiter here also advises that you increase the amount that you're tucking away into an index fund or 401K. Compounding interest is your friend in the end, Pisces, even if that means delaying a bit of gratification now.

URANUS IN GEMINI
JULY 7 – NOVEMBER 7, 2025
JANUARY 26, 2026 – MAY 22, 2033

If you thought you could drop anchor and settle down after Jupiter leaves Gemini, guess again. Home could literally look like anything for Pisces in 2025, with multiple locations or impermanent arrangements. The reason for this? On July 7, eclectic, unpredictable Uranus sidespins into Gemini for four months, previewing a longer, seven-year cycle that picks up again next year (April 25, 2026 to May 22, 2033).

Both Jupiter and Uranus are free spirits, the great liberators of the sky. Wherever you hang your hat, Pisces, you'll need to feel a sense of limitlessness and inspiration. You could wake up in a surf shack, an ashram or a family home, that doesn't matter. But you need to customize the space so that you feel untethered in your self-expression.

This may necessitate a change of inhabitants—or at the very least some hard boundaries. If you're rooming with someone who piles dishes in the sink or, conversely, demands that you clean up when you're immersed in a project, there's a chance you're simply incompatible as roommates. If you don't have the luxury of changing your residence, how can you reconfigure the square footage so that you both feel free? Maybe you don't turn the kitchen into your painting studio or maybe you do. It's all about negotiation, which is a specialty of high-minded Uranus in communicative Gemini. Discuss!

Don't sacrifice your need for sovereignty in your private life. Uranus hasn't been in Gemini since the 1940s, so this is your once-in-a-lifetime opportunity to richly explore what a "sacred space" looks like to you. If you're coupled or caring for kids or elders, perhaps you rent a studio or get a tiny home or RV as a second space that's all your own. There's no need to rush this process. Just start imagineering while Uranus is in Gemini from July 7 to November 7 this year. You might surprise your own capricious self by some of your choices and decisions during this game-changing cycle, Pisces. The city mouse might become a country mouse, or vice versa.

This Uranus cycle can trigger seismic shifts with relatives or close friends. You might decide to "have a word" with someone who's grown a little too dependent on you—or who meddles in your affairs. Ultimately, Pisces, you teach others how to treat you, and if you're not happy with a certain dynamic, it's on you to initiate a revision.

Watch your temper though! Spontaneous Uranus in loose-lipped Gemini—and in your moody fourth house, at that—could bring some emotional downpours you'll wish to the gods you had unleashed in therapy instead of around the dinner table. Know that you may be more easily triggered by close friends and family during this cycle. Unfortunately, any impulsive expression of upset feelings could send shock waves through your circle that will be hard to come back from.

If you treat people with kindness, then speaking your truth can only be a good thing. Make this your new M.O. and wait until you are fully connected to the high-vibe side of Uranus in Gemini before attempting to hash out differences with the people you love the most.

2 TURN LIFE INTO A COSTUME PARTY

JUPITER IN CANCER
JUNE 9, 2025 – JUNE 30, 2026

The landscape of your life becomes insanely fertile beginning June 9, as bountiful Jupiter cruises into Cancer, a compatible water sign. Get ready for the abundant planet to hydrate your spotlight-stealing fifth house until June 30, 2026. The second half of the year could herald a creative and romantic renaissance like you haven't seen in over a decade!

Give yourself a couple days—or weeks—to adjust to this dialed-up energy. There's a good chance you spent the first half of 2025 in a bubble as Jupiter paddled through your cozy, security-loving fourth house. Hopefully, you got a solid RDA of alone time and family moments because you're about to be thrust into the public eye for thirteen months.

Manifestation experts recommend "dressing for the role that you want to play." As Jupiter tools around in the fifth house's costume closet, might we recommend bright colors, shimmering beadwork, maximalist patterns and even jaw-dropping cutouts if you dare. (Not getting the picture? Just search for photos of Pisces Chappel Roan.) Don't forgo comfort. Jupiter is still in flowy Cancer, after all. Fortunately, Pisces, boho-chic never goes out of style for your sign. Opt for tunics, caftans, maxidresses and palazzo pants that look more glamorous than off-duty.

The point is that you want to be ready for a photo-op at any moment. The fifth house rules fame and with high-visibility Jupiter in this zone, public acclaim could come your way in the year ahead. By the second half of 2025 you could be hanging your art in a gallery, making a keynote speech at a conference or signing a record deal. Whatever it is you want to be known for, Jupiter brings the kind of momentum that can thrust you into the limelight and make you a sought-after name in your industry.

This is slightly complicated by the fact that shy, reserved Cancer rules this part of your life. Make sure you don't sabotage your well-deserved recognition in a moment of panic. Most Pisces love to share your art but you don't relish feeling exposed. If you built a supportive bubble while Jupiter was in Gemini, keep that inner circle close! You might add an agent or other sort of rep to that roster, especially if you, like many sacrificial Fish, struggle to state your value.

Romantically, Jupiter's yearlong circuit through Cancer could spur a straight up renaissance. The last time the red-spotted planet pulsed through this part of your chart was from June 25, 2013 to July 16, 2014. What was going on in your love life then and who were the key players? Similar themes could repeat or, in some cases, you might even pick up where you left off with someone a decade ago.

Regardless of your status, get ready for a surge of va-va-voom energy to sweep through your life. Jetsetting Jupiter draws spicy prospects from far-flung ports of call. (Oui, oui!) Long-distance romances should not be ruled out, even with a partner with whom you've cohabitated for years. One (or both) of you may need to relocate to pursue an opportunity, challenging you to support each other's personal growth even if it means seeing one another less frequently. Think of all the fun you'll have exploring a new region together. Some Pisces might actually move to start a life with a romantic interest.

Honesty is the only policy wherever Jupiter goes, and it's time to pour that same truth serum onto your love life. If you're already in a relationship, you may need to address the most triggering aspects of your union without flinching. Working through the kinks could be the most exciting chapter you've had to date. Scholarly Jupiter could send you to a couple's workshop to learn about love, like The Gottman Institute. Peeling back the layers of intimacy can be confronting, but your bond stands a chance of deepening in untold ways.

Make sure to adopt this maxim, too: The couple that plays together, stays together. World travel is Jupiter's terrain, making this an optimal window for planning that epic baecation or finally taking the (second or third) honeymoon you're long overdue to enjoy. Cultural activities dates will keep you excited, especially if you're enjoying the arts from incredible seats, strutting down red carpets and basically being the most eye-catching pair in the room.

Pisces on the pregnancy track are in luck since Jupiter in family-friendly Cancer is also charging up your fertile fifth house. If you're not quite ready, you may think about freezing eggs. And if you are hot to go, but you're struggling, IVF could be a promising option. Babies the last thing on your brain? Protect with added measure because multiplier Jupiter wants more of you in any way possible now.

3 STABILIZE YOUR FINANCES

SATURN AND NEPTUNE IN ARIES

NEPTUNE: MARCH 30 – OCTOBER 22, 2025 • JANUARY 26, 2026 – MARCH 23, 2039

SATURN: MAY 24 – SEPTEMBER 1, 2025 • FEBRUARY 13, 2026 – APRIL 12, 2028

Did you just lose your bearings, Pisces? We wouldn't be surprised because this year brings some seismic shifts that are hitting your sign more than any other. Two impactful outer planets are swinging out of Pisces and into Aries for part of 2025, shifting your entire outlook on life.

First up is your ruler, Neptune, who takes its first step out of your sign since 2011! As it drifts into assertive Aries from March 30 to October 22, it activates your second house of money, values and self-worth. For the past fourteen years, you've explored the outer bounds of your own identity and self-expression. Now, the focus turns to grounding your dreams into reality. Neptune's influence will encourage you to reimagine your relationship with material possessions, helping you overcome any limiting beliefs or insecurities around abundance. While you only get a sneak peek of Neptune in Aries this year, this cycle begins again next January 26, lasting for thirteen years.

Adding to this cosmic shift, Saturn will join Neptune in Aries from May 24 to September 1, offering structure and discipline to your financial planning. You've hosted Saturn since March 7, 2023, which has put you through your ⟶ paces. While Neptune inspires dreams, Saturn ensures that those dreams come with a realistic strategy. During these three months, you'll get a preview of Saturn's longer stay in your second house (February 13, 2026 to April 12, 2028) which will help you establish lasting financial security. With Saturn's stabilizing influence, you'll have the opportunity to apply the lessons you've learned over the past few years to boost your income and build a solid foundation for your future.

NEPTUNE IN ARIES
MARCH 30 – OCTOBER 22, 2025
JANUARY 26, 2026 – MARCH 23, 2039

Call it an identity crisis or just a profoundly new vision for how you want to live your life. Either way, Pisces, things could begin to look very different for you beginning this March 30. For the first time in fourteen years, your ruling planet Neptune is heading into a new sign. That alone is earth-shaking news, but it's only half of it. Since April 5, 2011, Neptune has been on a homecoming tour through Pisces and your trailblazing, self-authorized first house. In many ways, you've been in your element ever since—embracing the boundless fluidity and ethereal magic that comes with being a mutable water sign.

Neptune only visits your sign once every 165 years or so, which has made this passage a profound one for you, Pisces. As this cycle began, the world mourned the loss of visionary Pisces Steve Jobs (October 2011). Justin Bieber, a Fish, was ranked No. 2 in Forbes' best-paid celebrities in 2011. As Neptune reached its 29th degree of Pisces in 2024, we watched the meteoric rise of Chappell Roan, born February 19, 1998. Drew Barrymore, Olivia Rodrigo, Lupita Nyong'o, Stephen Curry, Olivia Wilde, Rihanna—all are Pisces who have touched the zeitgeist's emotions since 2011.

Whether the seas were smooth or choppy, you've been quite the wave-rider for the past decade-and-a-half. And we'd wager that you wouldn't mind taking a timeout to get yourself on stable ground. You're in luck. On March 30, Neptune treads into Aries, its first visit to the Ram's realm since 1862 to 1875. While the celestial soothsayer only spends six months here (until October 22), you get a sneak preview of what's ahead. Neptune circles back into Aries on January 26, 2026 where it will flow through your second house of money, values and security for thirteen full years, until March 23, 2039.

As Neptune leaves your first house, a sense of clarity begins to emerge, allowing you to focus on grounding your dreams into reality. Visionary Pisces are never at a loss for ingenious ideas. It's turning them into tangible assets that can be a struggle. As your ruling planet heads into assertive Aries and your tenacious second house, you'll be ready to put a stake in the ground and start building something that you can touch, taste and feel.

Material and financial stability are not things you like to stress about, but you know that without them, you feel unmoored. As Neptune casts its mystical glow over your second house, your relationship with money and possessions undergoes a profound transformation. Are you holding onto limiting beliefs about money—even feeling guilty about having more than a certain figure in your bank account? Or maybe you find that money slips between your fingers, a sneaky way of disowning your earnings because you don't feel that you "deserve" them. That sacrificial side of being a Pisces is a tough one to overcome. As subconscious Neptune heads into your second house of self-worth, you can do the deep work on your psyche and begin to take those guardrails off.

As a Pisces, you're naturally attuned to the spiritual and emotional aspects of life. Your new challenge? Figuring out how to integrate these qualities into your plan for creating material security. Neptune's transit through your second house may inspire you to explore more creative and intuitive ways to generate a paycheck. With your rich imagination and strong connection to the arts, this period could see you monetizing talents that you never thought to charge for in the past. Whether you're composing music, playing crystal bowls at a retreat center or coaching couples in tantric breathwork, there's really no limit to what you can do. Even left-brained Pisces may tap into their creativity and apply it to science and tech.

Be mindful of Neptune's tendency to idealize, but also create illusions. While Neptune's in Aries from March 30 to October 22, make sure your financial decisions are grounded in reality. Remember, this is a long cycle. There's no need to rush. Simply allowing yourself to explore new ways of earning and managing money can be a game-changer.

On the emotional front, you may notice a shift in your sense of self-worth and confidence as Neptune moves into courageous (and entitled) Aries. This will be a welcome change! For the past decade-plus, Neptune in Pisces may have left you stewing in periods of self-doubt, uncertain where you fit in. Now, you're encouraged to build a more solid foundation for your self-esteem, one that's based in giving yourself permission to be YOU.

Start by taking great care of yourself. Update your daily routines to support this. Healthy eating, ample rest, luxuriating in beauty routines and regular workouts—these not-so-little things can do wonders to make you feel great in your own skin. Transformation via the second house is about taking things one step at a time. Daily affirmations like, "I deserve happiness," or, "I can create safety and security for myself," are not just lip service; they're the beginning of a powerful mindset shift. And as Neptune, which rules the psyche, knows, our thoughts create our reality.

SATURN IN ARIES
MAY 24 – SEPTEMBER 1, 2025
FEBRUARY 13, 2026 – APRIL 12, 2028

Dream big, Pisces, but don't forget to set an alarm! Timekeeper Saturn spends most of 2025 in your sign as it continues winding through a cycle that began on March 7, 2023. For a brief, three-month spell, you get a break! This May 24, Saturn dashes into Aries lending its stabilizing influence to your second house of money and values until September 1.

Hosting Saturn is no picnic. The "personal trainer planet" puts you through paces, throwing challenges in your path that force you to grow. Wisdom and maturity are Saturn's domain, but no one rides for free. You've been earning your merit badges for the past two years under the rigorous schooling of taskmaster Saturn. So you'll be grateful for even this slight reprieve from May 24 to September 1. Saturn has been a strict teacher, delivering one challenging lesson after another. You've undoubtedly felt the pressure, perhaps even felt pushed to your limits. But you also can't deny that you've grown immensely in the process.

For three months this year, Saturn will lend its discipline and structure to your second house of stability, finances, and practical planning. Take notes of what developments arise in these areas. This is a prelude of what's to come again when Saturn runs its unbroken lap through Aries from February 13, 2026 to April 12, 2028.

Now comes the pivotal question: How can you begin turning the lessons of the past two years into financial gain? With the right strategies, savvy planning, and elbow grease, you can jump into a new income bracket over the next few years. Be prepared for a learning curve—this is Saturn, after all—and expect some inevitable growing pains along the way. If you find yourself feeling unprepared or needing to master the nuances of a new field, it's the perfect time to study up or seek guidance from a mentor, consultant, or coach.

And get ready for a masterclass in patience. With Saturn, the lord of long-term planning, settling into Aries, you'll have to balance some tricky energies. Saturn is slow and steady while Aries is impulsive and "go, go, go." Saturn is "in fall" in Aries, considered to be one of the most challenging spots in the zodiac for the ringed planet to express its natural energy. Remind yourself regularly that Rome wasn't retrofitted in a day! The next few years are about pouring the concrete foundation so you have solid ground under your feet. That might take a minute, Pisces, so don't rush the process.

Discerning Saturn can elevate your tastes while in Aries. You may lean toward "quiet luxury" between May 24 and September 1. Yes, the Chappell Roan "miniskirts and go-go boots" might look more like "pencil skirts and Chelsea boots" for this upcoming era.

What not to do? Splurge on extravagant items like Louis Vuitton luggage or a Hermes scarf—unless they're comfortably within your budget, of course. Instead, consider investing in one impeccably designed accessory. Focus on quality and thoughtful design. That alone can elevate your personal style, making you feel like a vibrational match for high-end (and high paying!) opportunities.

When Saturn swings 'round to Pisces again from September 1 to February 13, 2026, you'll have a fresh perspective about yourself and your worth. Friends have no doubt begged you to see yourself through their eyes—if only you were able to get the full breadth of your magic, Pisces! While in proud, confident Aries, Saturn holds up a mirror, giving you a glimpse of your strength. Carry this empowering energy with you through the last quarter of the year. Know that you are worthy, Pisces, and that it's not your lot in life to be the martyr.

4 RECLAIM YOUR WORTH

VENUS RETROGRADE IN ARIES AND PISCES
ARIES: MARCH 1 – 27
PISCES: MARCH 27 – APRIL 12

You're ever the hopeful romantic, Pisces, but from March 1 to April 12, raise your discernment filters to their strongest settings. Amorous Venus pivots into a six-week retrograde, an event that happens every 18 months. From March 1 to 27, the reverse commute begins in Aries and your second house of sensuality, quiet luxury, money and values. Then, from March 27 to April 12, Venus slips back through Pisces, churning up the still waters of your first house of identity and basically making you question everything (and everyone) that you claim "completes" you.

Because part of the retrograde takes place in your sign, the effects could hit you harder. This is the first time since 2017 that the planet of love and beauty has reversed through your sign for part of her backspin. Between March 27 and April 12, while the harmonizing planet is in Pisces, you could get an extra serving of Venus retrograde's "Don't put the cart before the horse" lessons. Consider yourself fairly warned.

But let's start with March 1 to 27 when Venus is retrograde in Aries. During this time, a few abandonment issues could flare up. Be careful not to clutch too tightly to your love interest or the vibes could get suffocating. Should the "You're going to leave me!" fears strike, call up a level-headed friend or book an extra therapy appointment. This will be far more productive than making teary demands for reassurance.

If anger and frustration have built up, don't just spew on the ones you love. Find a healthy outlet to release those feelings first, like, say, your own art. Some of the greatest works of history have emerged from the "tortured poets department" of a Pisces' mind. (Cue Rihanna, E.E. Cummings, Alexander McQueen, Kehinde Wiley.)

While you may feel like powering up your fins and racing away until there's oceans between you and your troubles, that might not be the best solution during Venus retrograde either. Avoidance has a funny way of causing problems to repeat themselves. So, Pisces, here's an idea. How about dropping anchor—even if a small, safe distance away—and using this six-week cycle for an open-eyed (and open-minded) examination of these recurring issues?

Take time to nurse your inner child's hurt feelings or allow yourself to be thoroughly annoyed. Then, add some adulting into the equation. How might you have (perhaps unconsciously) played a part in setting up these dynamics? Did you suppress your truth in an attempt to create harmony or be "professional"? Fail to set boundaries? Try to fit yourself into someone else's value system, even though doing so chafed like a pair of too-tight festival jorts? Uh-oh.

Rather than going into victim mode, make it your mission to unearth the behavior pattern within yourself that's responsible for co-creating the dissonance. You don't have to cut people out of your life when simply setting clear boundaries—and vocalizing your needs—can do the trick. That can be hard for your sacrificial sign, since you must unlearn certain ingrained beliefs. You were not put on this earth to be a martyr, Pisces, even if it feels that way sometimes.

Warning: Your trademark compassion might go on hiatus during the final two weeks of this cycle, when Venus backs into Pisces and your first house of self-sovereignty. In some ways, this could be a positive, especially if you've been beating around the bush instead of saying what you feel. You don't have to back down from a fight if it's one that you know is worth having. People-pleasing Pisces, turn your fish scales into a spine and use this retrograde to practice diplomatically pushing back against any "strong personalities."

Above all, remember this: While you can't control what other people say and do, you CAN take command of your own life. Do the 101s to get yourself grounded. Eat clean, get eight hours of beauty (and sanity) sleep nightly, drink more water than you do coffee, and move your body daily. If other people want to act the fool, well, that's their business. Buffer yourself against their clowning by taking excellent care of yourself.

5 ILLUMINATE YOUR HIGHER PURPOSE

LUNAR NODES IN VIRGO AND PISCES
NORTH NODE IN PISCES, SOUTH NODE IN VIRGO
JANUARY 11, 2025 – JULY 26, 2026

Calling all purpose-driven Pisces! 2025 is the year to fully embrace your mystical nature and step into your power. On January 11, the fate-fueling North Node returns to your sign for the first time in nearly two decades, marking the beginning of an 18-month cycle that will push you toward profound personal and spiritual transformation. This isn't just another chapter. It's a cosmic call to action to lean into your intuition and pursue your soul's true path.

The lunar nodes aren't planets, but powerful points in the sky tied to your spiritual evolution. Every 18.5 years, the North Node moves into Pisces, igniting a period of self-discovery and emotional growth. Think back to June 23, 2006 to December 18, 2007, the last time this cycle happened. Whatever was unfolding in your life back then could come full circle now, offering closure or a fresh start.

Starting this January, expect significant developments to come your way. Magical new opportunities will arise, but this period will also challenge you to step far outside your comfort zone. You'll be called to explore deeper spiritual or creative depths, which could feel like navigating uncharted waters. Old passions may fade as new ones spark, and relationships might need some renegotiating. It's all part of the journey to figure out what you're truly capable of. Embrace the process, even if it's messy at times.

If ever there was a time to invest in personal growth, it's now. Workshops, retreats, or private coaching could be game changers for your sensitive sign, especially when group settings feel overwhelming. And when those inevitable waves of self-doubt hit, having a supportive mentor or guide could be invaluable, reminding you that you have the strength to keep moving forward.

Got gaps in your skills or knowledge? You might prefer to go it alone, but this nodal cycle encourages collaboration. By teaming up with others or delegating tasks, you'll free yourself to focus on the bigger picture and the deeper spiritual explorations you crave. Let others help you, Pisces. You don't have to carry it all alone.

Meanwhile, the South Node will be hanging out in Virgo and your relationship sector from January 11, 2024, to July 26, 2026, causing a bit of a shake-up in your closest connections. The South Node deals with past karma and old habits, so if any of your relationships have been holding you back, you might feel compelled to reassess—or even release—what's no longer serving you.

As you evolve, your relationships will naturally shift. This can be unsettling at first, but it's all part of the process. Open communication is key. Loop your loved ones into your personal journey so they can understand and support the changes you're going through. This way, you can avoid feelings of alienation or sudden disruption.

But remember, Pisces, while relationships are important, your personal growth comes first during this cycle. Too much oversight or interference can stifle your development. Establish boundaries that allow you the space to grow and encourage those around you to pursue their own evolution as well. It's all about mutual respect for the journey you're each on.

This nodal cycle might even bring a karmic reunion. Someone from your past may re-enter your life to challenge or inspire you in a major way. Whether this connection lasts or not, it'll spark powerful insights that help you grow on your path.

Keep your focus on your spiritual and creative pursuits, and don't let relationship dynamics pull you off course. The North Node in Pisces is highlighting your natural gifts, making this an ideal time to showcase your talents and embrace your personal truth. This is your period of extraordinary growth. By the end of July 2026, you'll be passing the torch, deeply enriched by the journey and ready to inspire others to follow their own bliss.

Love

PISCES 2025 FORECAST

Romantic resolutions are percolating, Pisces. Amorous Venus sweeps into your soulful sign from January 2 to February 4, infusing your New Year with enchanted vibes. What love story would you like to write for yourself in the year ahead? The universe hands you an ostrich-feather quill and invites you to script your very own version of a fairy tale.

But here's the deal: You might not be turning to a totally fresh page in this book. From March 1 to April 12, Venus pivots into her every-584-day retrograde, which partially takes place in your sign. Yep, after beginning the reverse commute in Aries and your sensual second house of values, Venus steals back through Pisces from March 27 to April 12. No need to panic! This could bring a chance to set new depth records with the person you j'adore. Love could blossom with someone you never thought of "that way" before.

If, like Pisces Chappel Roan, your kink is karma, you will have plenty of fodder to work with. Venus retrograde may reveal unfinished business left to resolve, either with an ex or a recurring dynamic that keeps showing up with one lover after another. If you keep hitting the same wall in a relationship, embrace this profound period of introspection. Rather than rushing headlong towards "the next level," reconnect with your core values, and reassess how you show up in love.

Once Venus turns direct and powers ahead through Pisces from April 12 to 30, you really get a chance to put old fables to bed, like those negative thoughts about yourself or a defeatist attitude toward dating. This may feel like a fresh start for many Fish, especially if you've worked through past blocks in the first quarter of the year.

But that's not the only transformational influence happening in 2025. On January 11, the South Node moves into Virgo and your seventh house of committed partnerships, offering you an eighteen-month window to correct unworkable relationship patterns and clear out some lingering karmic baggage. If you've been stuck in cycles of codependency, over-giving or pain, get proactive about healing. Between now and July 26, 2026, you have a chance to dress relationship wounds and nurture healthy, reciprocal dynamics.

Two powerful eclipses in Virgo amplify this process: the total lunar eclipse on March 14 and a partial solar eclipse during a rare, second new moon on September 21. These eclipses could trigger dramatic shifts in your partnerships, unveiling hidden truths or accelerating a meant-to-be connection. You may decide to go "all in" (ring shopping!) or close the books (divorce party!) for good.

The second half of the year is when the fun truly begins. Happy-go-lucky Jupiter kickstarts a romantic renaissance when it enters Cancer on June 9, lighting up your fifth house of love, passion and fertility for the first time since 2014. This expansive energy frees your spirit and makes you more experimental than you've been in a while. Forget about the "old marrieds" vibe. While Jupiter sails through this playful, passionate zone until June 30, 2026, your shared calendar will fill with adventure dates, baecations or whirlwind romances if you're feeling more like a bon vivant than a bride-to-be.

A little more autonomy can make the heart grow fonder during this Jupiter cycle. Slip out of the couple bubble or take a break from the apps for a spell. As you nurture your own interests, especially the artistic ones, you not only become more attractive but also selective. If you could have more fun by your damn self, why would you let a dull or problematic person mess THAT up? No thanks.

Live-out-loud Jupiter here inspires greater freedom of expression, both in and out of the bedroom. You could start dressing in ways that make you feel attractive and show your flair—hello, head turner. Get real about what turns you on, or, if you're not 100 percent sure, open yourself up to a sultry exploration.

Since the fifth house rules pregnancies and children, you may feel a surge of excitement about starting or growing your family. With the expansive planet's influence you might even give birth to multiples or have an unexpected + to celebrate. Wedding, vow renewals and all sorts of celebrations could be in the offing. Spending more time with the kids you have will also reconnect you to your joy.

One thing's for sure: By the time Jupiter finishes its tour in mid-2026, you'll have redefined what love means to you, embracing a more expansive, liberated version of romance. That's good news for the slippery Fish in you, but don't forget the side of you that also wants to get "caught" in the net. Finding a way to satisfy both parts of your nature is an exciting challenge to take on this year!

PISCES: LUCKIEST *love* DAY

JUNE 24

The Day of Miracles is always exciting each year, as the sparkling Sun unites with lucky Jupiter for their annual heart-to-heart. In 2025, they connect in Cancer and your fifth house of passionate, playful romance. Let your hair down and let the games begin!

Money & Career

PISCES 2025 FORECAST

What's that ringing we hear? Oh, just your higher calling, Pisces. This year, the skies open up to guide you along a purposeful path—one that taps right into the heart of your passions. It all begins on January 11, when the fateful lunar North Node arrives in Pisces and activates your trailblazing, self-directed first house for eighteen whole months. The last time this cycle came around was from 2006-07, so this is indeed a rare moment. While you've surely changed a lot over the past two decades, echoes of that distant past could inform your current money moves.

The time has come to blend your goddess-given creativity, intuition and compassion into your work. Between now and July 26, 2026, the North Node's game-changing influence could shift your career compass in an unscripted direction. Spiritual and artistic pursuits, or your healing gifts, may figure in. No matter where you land on the power pyramid, this is your time to lead with empathy and make an impact that feels deeply meaningful.

Going first could also mean stepping out solo in the beginning. There's a reason people say it's lonely at the top, but this doesn't have to be your fate. Think "independent" rather than "isolated" and make it your mission to connect to peers. Whether you're setting up a desk at a shared office or coworking space, serving on boards or joining networking groups, make sure you're out mingling with savvy, supportive types.

This independent path is not altogether unfamiliar. Since "adulting" planet Saturn hunkered down in your sign (a transit that happens every 29.5 years) on March 7, 2023, many of you grew serious about turning a personal venture into your bread and butter. The only catch? Saturn teaches from the school of hard knocks, and you might have some bumps and bruises from the journey.

Here's some news you'll probably like hearing: From May 24 to September 1, Saturn gives you a bit of reprieve, heading into Aries and your second house of income. Time to take all these lessons of the past couple years straight to the bank. "Can I monetize that?" isn't always the first question your spiritual sign asks, but starting this spring, it's a key consideration. Take notes because the ringed planet will head out of Pisces for good on February 13, 2026, giving you two solid years in Aries that will discipline your entire approach to money.

But that's not all. Your ruler, imaginative Neptune, is also spending part of the year in Aries, from March 30 to October 22, which is a huge shift. Neptune has been lodged in Pisces since 2011, where it's been slowly shifting your subconscious beliefs and reshaping your identity. Neptune will also move on to Aries early next year, kicking off a solid, thirteen-year odyssey through your second house of money on January 26, 2026.

As Saturn and Neptune traverse the Aries terrain together, they deliver a blend of practicality and inspiration to your financial life. Saturn's influence helps you build long-term stability and set up solid structures for sustainable income growth. Meanwhile, dreamy Neptune in Aries encourages you to get creative with how you earn money. Visionary ventures can take flight if you tap Saturn's discipline to make sure your dreams have a solid foundation.

This isn't a free ride though. You may need to tighten up your budget, but don't worry, Pisces, it's not all about restrictions. Neptune in Aries can attract luxury experiences your way, ones that might even be bartered for or gifted to you. Pay attention to what opportunities show up near March 29! That's the day that the final solar eclipse in Aries wraps up a two-year series that has been teaching you all about money management. The ups and downs of your financial life could be attributed to the shadow influence of these "moon moments" on the Aries-Libra axis, but like Saturn, they've been teaching you SO much about balancing your books and staying out of debt.

Play your cards right and by Q4 you could land right in the VIP room, C Suite or another limited-access area. From November 4 to December 15, go-getter Mars ascends to Sagittarius and the top of your chart, boosting your career mojo skyward. Money-magnet Venus will also be in this zone from November 30 to December 24 sharpening your acumen. If you have a chance to give someone younger and greener a hand up the ladder, be their "Christmas miracle." What goes around comes around!

PISCES: LUCKIEST *career* DAY

JANUARY 18

When money-magnet Venus syncs up with stabilizer Saturn in Pisces and your self-sovereign first house on January 18, you get a chance to feel your worth—and charge what you deserve. These two planets will unite again on April 7 (during Venus retrograde) and again on April 24, so what you kick off in January could ripple out in waves of prosperity through the spring.

2025
PISCES

12
MONTH
OVERVIEW

January MONTHLY HOROSCOPE

So many people, so little time! Start the year with a round of strategic socializing as the Sun in status-driven Capricorn activates your eleventh house of community until the 19th. Your compassionate and empathetic nature shines when you're involved in group efforts. Make sure you're putting your energy into organizations that fulfill your sense of purpose. On January 11, the destiny-driven North Node ascends to Pisces, starting an 18-month cycle that will call you into your highest self. Get ready to stretch during this period of accelerated growth! Across the wheel, the Virgo South Node helps you recalibrate your expectations in relationships. Right-size your vision of what love can provide, so you're holding people accountable without falling into codependent patterns. Slip into solitude to reflect and recharge when Aquarius season begins on the 19th. The rejuvenating cycle of self-care will get you ready for your Pisces season, which begins February 18. Tie up loose ends and work with healers, therapists and spiritual guides to support you with identifying (and releasing) old patterns that are not serving you. On the 29th, The Year of the Wood Snake begins, marking twelve powerful months when even subtle movements can bring big wins.

February MONTHLY HOROSCOPE

Hibernate away until the 18th, Pisces, as the Aquarius Sun shines its ambient rays into your twelfth house of healing, closure and reflection. This pre-birthday season wants you to slow down, process your feelings and tie up loose ends. This is an inside job, Pisces. Work with therapists and healers; journal and get a meditation practice underway. On February 4, Venus embarks on a long tour through Aries, activating your second house of money and values. You'll be motivated to improve your financial stability, but with Venus retrograde from March 1 to April 12, you may need to reassess your spending habits or rethink how you invest your time and energy. Also on the 4th, Jupiter turns direct in Gemini, reigniting your fourth house of home and family. If there have been delays or confusion in your living situation or family dynamics, you can finally clear the air. Get the candles and cake ready for February 18 when Pisces season begins! This celebratory month brings renewed energy for your personal passions. The new moon in Pisces on the 27th brings a bonus New Year, so set an audacious goal that's all about making yourself happy! Here's something just as hot: Mars turns direct in Cancer on the 23rd, turning up the temperature in your fifth house of romance and self-expression. Get ready for an inspiring boost in your love life and creative pursuits!

March MONTHLY HOROSCOPE

Your Main Character energy is undeniable this March, as the Sun beams into your sign until the 20th. This is your birthday season, so step into the light and forge ahead on your personal goals. But DO pace yourself with any major changes. Both Venus and Mercury will be retrograde in Aries, then Pisces, which could cause you to underestimate your self-worth or attempt to shape-shift to please other people. Until both planets turn direct in your sign, on April 12 and 7, respectively, it's best to treat life like a costume party where you can try on different "characters" and see what suits you best. On March 14, the Virgo lunar eclipse illuminates your partnership zone, which could bring an out-of-left-field development in your love life. Address glaring imbalances in existing relationships and strengthen those bonds. When the Sun moves into Aries on March 20, your focus shifts to financial stability, making this a great time to lay the groundwork for long-term success. The Aries solar eclipse on March 29 marks the final chapter of a two-year cycle in your second house, offering you a powerful moment to realign your values and reset your approach to money. Then, on March 30, your ruler, Neptune, moves into Aries for the first time since 1875. While Neptune will dip back into Pisces again from October 22 to January 26, 2026, this is a warm-up of a 14-year Neptune-in-Aries cycle. Stay open to new insights that merge the mystical with the material—you're entering a profound phase of growth and abundance!

April MONTHLY HOROSCOPE

How are you showing up in the world, Pisces? With the Sun shining in your second house of money and values until April 19, you're focused on building financial security and boosting your self-worth. But before you make any binding decisions, press pause. Mercury is retrograde in your sign until April 7, along with Venus until April 12, asking you to reflect on your front-facing presentation. This is a great time to ponder your personal goals and take a timeout from nurturing everyone around you. Once these retrogrades clear after the 12th, you can hit go on a brand refresh or start shopping around one of your big ideas. Mars enters Leo on April 18, sparking your sixth house of work and wellness until June 17. You'll feel energized to overhaul your routines—whether it's hitting the gym harder, cleaning up your diet or tackling a backlog of work projects. Productivity is your superpower now! Taurus season kicks off on April 19, lighting up your third house of communication. Use this time to share your ideas, start that passion project, or dive into learning something new. It's your season to connect, express and grow.

May MONTHLY HOROSCOPE

Let your voice be heard, Pisces! With Taurus Sun circulating in your third house of expression until May 20, everyone from your curious colleagues to the random stranger in the coffee shop will listen eagerly to your visionary ideas. This could inspire you to take things further. Record a podcast episode or start a mastermind group. Be the center of intentional gatherings with friends. On May 4, transformative Pluto turns retrograde in Aquarius, backing through your twelfth house of healing and closure until October 13. If you've been toting around some emotional baggage, this reflective period helps you deal with the claim checks. Work with a therapist, healer or intuitive (or all of these) to root out whatever's holding you back. When the Sun slips into Gemini and your domestic zone on the 20th, reconnect with family and cherished friends. If you're in the market for a move, this solar powered cycle can shine a light on some lucky listings. After two grueling years in Pisces, Saturn leaps into Aries from May 24 to September 1, giving you temporary reprieve from its strict intensity. In your Aries-ruled second house of money and values, Saturn gets you serious about your long-term security. Open your mind: Over the next few years, you could become a pro at budgeting, investing and creating generational wealth.

June MONTHLY HOROSCOPE

A deeply creative and heart-centered shift is ahead for you this June, Pisces. With the Sun in Gemini until June 20, you'll happily tuck away at home, surrounded by family and inner circle friends. But don't get TOO comfortable behind closed doors. The mainstage is calling you this June 9, when live-out-loud Jupiter soars into Cancer and showers your fifth house of fame, romance and self-expression with its magnanimous beams for an entire year. This is the red-spotted planet's first time back to Cancer since 2013-14, marking one of 2025's major transition points. The Sun heads into Cancer for a month at the solstice on June 20, then meets up with Jupiter on the 24th for "The Day of Miracles." Both events provide a golden window of opportunity to manifest your creative or romantic dreams. Mid-month may bring some challenges, though, as Jupiter squares Saturn on June 15 and Neptune on June 18, stirring up conflicts between your dreams and practical responsibilities. Don't let the obstacles throw you off. Adjust your approach and stay flexible, as only a mutable water sign can. Mars blazes into Virgo on June 17, amping up your aura and augmenting your magnetic attraction until August 6. Whatever you're selling, Pisces, we're buying in bulk!

July MONTHLY HOROSCOPE

Your creative cup runneth over this July, Pisces, so open your mind, heart and soul to all the divine inspiration pouring in. The Sun and expansive Jupiter have a playdate in Cancer until the 22nd, inviting you to experiment wildly. Whether you're working on large-scale paintings or free-range dating, this is peak season for anything that ignites your passion. Take bold risks in the name of adventure. Does that mean liberating yourself from a few obligations? If you've saddled yourself with OPP (Other People's Problems), the shackles come off on July 7, as change-agent Uranus buzzes into Gemini and your fourth house of kith and kin. There could be changes to your living situation, surprising family developments or a new way of understanding your emotional roots. While this disruptive cycle only lasts until November 7, it's paving the way for a seven-year chapter (from April 2026 to May 2033) that could reshape your approach to home and roots. Money moves may lead you back to old sources of income as Neptune, Saturn and Chiron all turn retrograde in Aries this month—on the 4th, 13th and 30th, respectively. Saturn will slip back into Pisces for a final lap on September 1 and Neptune on October 22. Before then, reassess your financial landscape, rethink your budget and evaluate what you value most. Getting life into a well-ordered groove will be your obsession once Leo season begins on the 22nd. After all, a Pisces needs to balance work and play. Mix up the mocktails and hit the pickleball courts, bike trails and aqua aerobics classes. Schedule wellness appointments and get to sleep at a decent hour. With Mercury spinning retrograde through Leo from July 18 to August 11, reconnecting to past colleagues could bring client referrals or word of a work opportunity that has "Pisces" written all over it.

August MONTHLY HOROSCOPE

Bring it back to an uncomplicated basis this August, as the Leo Sun shows you the beauty of simplicity until the 22nd. With Mercury still retrograde in Leo until August 11, you may have to deal with disruptions to your workflow and time-management challenges. Seize the opportunity to set up better systems, ones that leave you feeling supported rather than drained. Hint: This may involve a bit of much-needed delegating and outsourcing. Romantically, August is high season, while ardent Venus shimmers in Cancer and your fifth house of passion and pleasure. Hand your playful side the wheel because no one plans a dream date quite like you, Pisces. This fame-fueling cycle can draw attention to your beauty, style and artistry. Werk! Adding to the seductive equation, lusty Mars slips into Libra from August 6 to September 22, stirring the pot in your eighth house of intimacy, transformation and shared resources. Intensity heats up with the people closest to you. Confront what lies beneath the surface, whether it's in your finances, relationships or personal fears. When Virgo season kicks off on August 22, the Sun spotlights your partnerships for a month, helping you harmonize any union that's fallen out of balance. Another bond-strengthening boost comes on August 23, as the first of two rare, back-to-back new moons in Virgo arrives. Set those relationship goals. Are you ready to deepen your commitment, form a new partnership or release something that's been blocking true connection? This fresh-start energy will get a second boost with the solar (new moon) eclipse in Virgo on September 21, helping you move forward with clarity and purpose.

September MONTHLY HOROSCOPE

Power to your partnerships! The Virgo Sun sends nurturing beams to your relationship realm until the 22nd, drawing a few VIPs close. You've been known to lose sight of where you begin and they end, but retain some autonomy! On the 1st, boundary-hound Saturn retrogrades back into Pisces (until November 27), kicking off its final lap through your sign in a three-year cycle that began March 7, 2023. This cosmic boot camp has not been easy for you, but you're emerging stronger, wiser and resilient AF. The cherry on top of the self-awareness sundae could arrive on September 7, the day of the annual Pisces full moon, which is also a total lunar eclipse this year. Don't be afraid to peer into your own beautiful shadows. You'll have a kaleidoscopic view into your own brilliance, which could inform your artistic or spiritual work for years to come. With make-it-happen Mars in your mystical and erotic eighth house until the 22nd, there's no telling who you'll attract. People want to invest in you now, whether they're purchasing your art or giving you the lion's share of their time and affections. A new chapter for relationships opens up with the closing eclipse on September 21—a solar eclipse and the second in a pair of back-to-back new moons in Virgo that echoes whatever kicked up on August 23. Libra season begins on September 22, turning the focus inward as the Sun enters your eighth house of transformation and intimacy. Stop holding people at arm's length, Pisces. You'll never know what's possible until you drop the mask. Just as the Sun shifts, Mars moves into Scorpio and your ninth house of expansion until November 4. You'll feel a surge of energy to explore, learn and embark on new adventures. Use this motivating force to chase down an opportunity that excites you—whether it's an actual journey or a deep dive into a subject you've always wanted to learn more about.

October MONTHLY HOROSCOPE

Serenity now! While the Sun nestles in Libra until September 22, your number one goal may be rebalancing interpersonal dynamics to restore a harmonious flow. With your erotic eighth house getting this solar-powered boost, you can bring that parity to the bedroom or into your dating style. You don't need a perfect complement, but rather, someone whose energy calls forth the most spiritual and sexy dimensions of your own personality. Are you expecting your love interest to be a mind reader? Stop dropping hints. Class is in session while Venus struts through instructional Virgo until the 13th. (Please be more playful than stern, Pisces.) Your sultry student could become the master once Venus sashays into Libra on the 13th. Don't be surprised if talks about the future get serious this month, too. Try not to fence yourself into something that isn't right, however! Once Pluto turns direct in Aquarius on the 13th, you'll be in no mood to force a fit. That goes double once Scorpio season starts on the 22nd. Synergies need to feel freeing and expansive for you, Fish! Otherwise, you'll just want to swim away from that "net." On the 22nd, your ruler, numinous Neptune, retrogrades back into your sign, starting its final (in our lifetime!) lap through Pisces. Make the most of this closing ceremony, which lasts until January 26, 2026. You've hosted your ruling planet since 2011, and it's reshaped your psyche and identity in profound ways ever since. You're in touch with your true essence and starting next year, it may guide you toward opportunities to create lasting security for yourself and the ones you love.

November MONTHLY HOROSCOPE

"Anywhere but home" is your favorite place to be this November, while the Scorpio Sun ignites your wanderlust until the 21st. Sate your urges with weekend road trips to air travel—or a figurative journey through spiritual studies and self-development workshops. With pleasure-planet Venus sweeping into Scorpio from November 6 to 30, love could lift off with someone from a different culture or who lives a considerable distance from the place you currently call home. Creative opportunities could also cast you out to wider seas. Keep an open mind, Pisces. This could be the start of a beautiful adventure. Professional matters demand attention after the 4th, once hard-driving Mars moves into Sagittarius and fires up your career zone until December 15. If you want to finish the year strong, Mars will support you with hustling, networking and locking down solid opportunities that you can take to the bank. Don't leap without a net! Mercury will be retrograde from November 9 to 29, in Sagittarius until the 18th, then Scorpio. Read the fine print and stay focused on the mission. Even a minor detour can derail the whole game plan this month if you decide to go rogue. Adding to the mix, unpredictable Uranus retrogrades back into Taurus on November 7, shaking up your third house of communication, peers and local activity until February 4, 2026. Expect some surprises in your daily interactions or changes within your community. Rethink how you express yourself or embrace a new way of learning and sharing information. Next to backflip is Jupiter, who moves into its annual, four-month retrograde on November 11. This year, the expansive planet is in Cancer and your fifth house of romance, fame, fertility and creativity. You may have second thoughts about one of your love goals. This is a good time to develop ideas BTS. As you ride these waves, know that you'll finish the month strong. On the 27th, sensei Saturn turns direct in Pisces. Take your ambitions seriously and get to work! Saturn is only in your sign until February 13, bringing discipline and sense of purpose to all your efforts.

December MONTHLY HOROSCOPE

Network, circulate, slide into those DMs. With the Sagittarius Sun lighting up your tenth house of career and public recognition until December 21, the halls are decked for your success. Add to the equation go-getter Mars in Sagittarius until the 15th, plus charming Venus there through the 24th, and you have quite the supportive trifecta to tap into. Efforts you make now could launch you into a leadership role early next year. Before 2025 wraps, you could get an important initiative green-lit. While it might feel like a gamble to "pressure" people, gracious Venus can make you hard to resist. On the 10th, your ruler, enchanted Neptune, wraps up its retrograde and powers forward through Pisces for its very last lap in this lifetime. On January 26, the beguiling blue planet will move on to Aries for thirteen years. You've hosted Neptune since 2011, a period that has shifted your identity and honed your intuitive gifts. With less than two months left in this cycle, tune in to one of your long-held dreams. What can you do to move the needle on that starting NOW? There will be plenty of people lining up to support your initiative, especially after the 15th, when passionate Mars moves into Capricorn, energizing your eleventh house of friendships, community and long-term dreams until January 23. With the Sun joining Mars in Capricorn on December 21, followed by Venus on the 24th, the focus turns to your network and your vision for the future. You're ready to connect with like-minded souls and form a supergroup or an ongoing support network. Your social calendar could fill up quickly as you become the driving force behind community projects or rallying your friends for a good cause. New Year's Eve 2025 will find you craving connection, laughter and a sense of hope about what's ahead. Start the night out with intention-setting or make vision boards. When the clock strikes midnight, make sure you're surrounded by your chosen family, celebrating the friendships that keep you inspired and the dreams that unite you all.

Read your extended monthly forecast for life, love, money and career! astrostyle.com

January

JANUARY
Moon Phase Calendar

SUN	MON	TUE	WED	THU	FRI	SAT
			1 ♑ ♒ 5:50AM	**2** ♒	**3** ♒ ♓ 10:21AM	**4** ♓
5 ♓ ♈ 2:01PM	**6** ♈ 2nd Quarter	**7** ♈ ♉ 5:11PM	**8** ♉	**9** ♉ ♊ 8:07PM	**10** ♊	**11** ♊ ♋ 11:24PM
12 ♋	**13** ♋ Full Moon 5:27PM	**14** ♋ ♌ 4:12AM	**15** ♌	**16** ♌ ♍ 11:46AM	**17** ♍	**18** ♍ ♎ 10:33PM
19 ♎	**20** ♎	**21** ♎ → ♏ 11:20AM ♏ 4th Quarter	**22** ♏	**23** ♏ ♐ 11:29PM	**24** ♐	**25** ♐
26 ♐ ♑ 8:43AM	**27** ♑	**28** ♑ ♒ 2:31PM	**29** ♒ New Moon 7:36AM	**30** ♒ ♓ 5:52PM	**31** ♓	

Times listed are Eastern US Time Zone

KEY

♈	ARIES	♌	LEO	♐	SAGITTARIUS	**FM** FULL MOON
♉	TAURUS	♍	VIRGO	♑	CAPRICORN	**NM** NEW MOON
♊	GEMINI	♎	LIBRA	♒	AQUARIUS	**LE** LUNAR ECLIPSE
♋	CANCER	♏	SCORPIO	♓	PISCES	**SE** SOLAR ECLIPSE

JAN 13 5:27PM
full moon in Cancer (24°00')

CANCER FULL MOON CRYSTAL

SELENITE

This calm and soothing gemstone forms in long bands and has a high, clear and pure vibration. Named after Selene, the goddess of the Cancer-ruled moon, this crystal is believed to help the flow of bodily fluids and support fertility. Since selenite does not hold negative charges, it is fantastic to use to neutralize your own energy. Like a "crystal crab shell," selenite is often used to make a protective energetic "grid" around your house or workspace.

CANCER FULL MOON = CELEBRATE!

Your divine emotional intelligence

The importance of creating safe spaces

The power of family—blood-related or chosen

Intuitive hits that guide you toward your dreams

The healing power of water

Mother figures and your own maternal instincts

JAN 29 7:36AM

new moon in
Aquarius (9°51')

AQUARIUS NEW MOON CRYSTAL

APOPHYLLITE

High vibes: incoming! This spirit-elevating stone enhances Aquarian-ruled hope for the future. As a clear-hued cluster, the light apophyllite emits encourages self-reflection and gratitude while energizing the soul.

AQUARIUS NEW MOON = FOCUS

Experiment with new technology and techniques

Break out of the box with style and social expression

Connect to community, activism and humanitarian work

Explore cooperative models for life, living, finances

Gather your people together for fun times

January 2025

Longitude & Retrograde Ephemeris [00:00 UT]

Day	Sid.time	☉	☽	+12h☽	☿	♀	♂	♃	♄	♅	♆	♇	☊	☊	⚸	⚷	Day
1 We	06:43:36	♑10°48'49	♑23°54'55	♒00°39'41	D♑19°52	♒27°42	℞ 01°55	℞ 13°12	♓14°31	℞ 23°38	♓27°17	♒01°03	℞ 01°29	℞ 00°52	♎20°33	♈19°00	**1** We
2 Th	06:47:32	♑11°50'00	♒07°27'28	♒14°17'31	♐21°10	♒28°47	♌01°35	♊13°06	♓14°36	♉23°36	♓27°18	♒01°05	♈01°26	♈00°41	♎20°40	♈19°00	**2** Th
3 Fr	06:51:29	♑12°51'10	♒21°09'56	♒28°03'59	♐22°29	♒29°50	♌01°14	♊13°00	♓14°40	♉23°35	♓27°19	♒01°07	♈01°23	♈00°33	♎20°47	♈19°00	**3** Fr
4 Sa	06:55:26	♑13°52'21	♓04°59'50	♓11°56'49	D 23°50	♓00°54	♌00°53	♊12°54	♓14°45	♉23°33	♓27°20	♒01°09	♈01°20	♈00°28	♎20°53	♈19°00	**4** Sa
5 Su	06:59:22	♑14°53'31	♓18°55'12	♓25°54'25	♐25°11	♓01°57	♌00°31	♊12°48	♓14°50	♉23°32	♓27°21	♒01°11	♈01°17	♈00°26	♎21°00	♈19°01	**5** Su
6 Mo	07:03:19	♑15°54'40	♈02°54'48	♈09°55'52	♐26°34	♓03°00	♌00°09	♊12°42	♓14°55	♉23°31	♓27°22	♒01°13	♈01°13	D 00°26	♎21°07	♈19°01	**6** Mo
7 Tu	07:07:15	♑16°55'50	♈16°57'57	♈24°00'35	♐27°58	♓04°03	♋29°47	♊12°37	♓15°00	♉23°30	♓27°23	♒01°15	♈01°10	℞ 00°26	♎21°13	♈19°01	**7** Tu
8 We	07:11:12	♑17°56'58	♉01°04'06	♉08°07'55	♐29°22	♓05°05	♋29°24	♊12°31	♓15°05	♉23°28	♓27°24	♒01°16	♈01°07	♈00°25	♎21°20	♈19°02	**8** We
9 Th	07:15:08	♑18°58'07	♉15°12'19	♉22°16'35	♑00°48	♓06°07	♋29°01	♊12°26	♓15°10	♉23°27	♓27°25	♒01°18	♈01°04	♈00°23	♎21°26	♈19°02	**9** Th
10 Fr	07:19:05	♑19°59'15	♉29°20'53	♊06°24'22	♑02°14	♓07°09	♋28°38	♊12°21	♓15°15	♉23°26	♓27°26	♒01°20	♈01°01	♈00°17	♎21°33	♈19°03	**10** Fr
11 Sa	07:23:01	♑21°00'22	♊13°27'02	♊20°27'58	♑03°41	♓08°10	♋28°14	♊12°16	♓15°20	♉23°25	♓27°27	♒01°22	♈00°58	♈00°09	♎21°40	♈19°04	**11** Sa
12 Su	07:26:58	♑22°01'30	♊27°27'04	♋04°23'22	♑05°08	♓09°10	♋27°51	♊12°12	♓15°25	♉23°24	♓27°28	♒01°24	♈00°54	♓29°59	♎21°46	♈19°04	**12** Su
13 Mo	07:30:55	♑23°02'36	♋11°16'46	♋18°06'20	♑06°36	♓10°11	♋27°27	♊12°07	♓15°31	♉23°23	♓27°30	♒01°26	♈00°51	♓29°48	♎21°53	♈19°05	**13** Mo
14 Tu	07:34:51	♑24°03'42	♋24°52'04	♌01°33'10	♑08°05	♓11°10	♋27°03	♊12°03	♓15°36	♉23°22	♓27°31	♒01°28	♈00°48	♓29°36	♎22°00	♈19°06	**14** Tu
15 We	07:38:48	♑25°04'48	♌08°09'46	♌14°41'18	♑09°34	♓12°10	♋26°39	♊11°58	♓15°42	♉23°22	♓27°32	♒01°30	♈00°45	♓29°26	♎22°06	♈19°07	**15** We
16 Th	07:42:44	♑26°05'53	♌21°08'06	♌27°29'48	♑11°04	♓13°08	♋26°15	♊11°55	♓15°47	♉23°21	♓27°33	♒01°32	♈00°42	♓29°17	♎22°13	♈19°08	**16** Th
17 Fr	07:46:41	♑27°06'58	♍03°46'56	♍09°59'22	♑12°35	♓14°07	♋25°51	♊11°51	♓15°53	♉23°20	♓27°35	♒01°34	♈00°39	♓29°11	♎22°20	♈19°09	**17** Fr
18 Sa	07:50:37	♑28°08'02	♍16°07'50	♍22°12'20	♑14°06	♓15°04	♋25°27	♊11°47	♓15°59	♉23°19	♓27°36	♒01°36	♈00°35	♓29°08	♎22°26	♈19°10	**18** Sa
19 Su	07:54:34	♑29°09'07	♍28°13'46	♎04°12'18	♑15°37	♓16°02	♋25°03	♊11°44	♓16°05	♉23°19	♓27°37	♒01°38	♈00°32	♓29°07	♎22°33	♈19°11	**19** Su
20 Mo	07:58:31	♒00°10'10	♎10°08'53	♎16°03'47	♑17°09	♓16°58	♋24°40	♊11°40	♓16°10	♉23°18	♓27°39	♒01°40	♈00°29	D 29°08	♎22°40	♈19°12	**20** Mo
21 Tu	08:02:27	♒01°11'14	♎21°58'03	♎27°51'59	♑18°42	♓17°54	♋24°16	♊11°37	♓16°16	♉23°18	♓27°40	♒01°41	♈00°26	♓29°09	♎22°46	♈19°13	**21** Tu
22 We	08:06:24	♒02°12'17	♏03°46'37	♏09°42'18	♑20°15	♓18°50	♋23°53	♊11°35	♓16°22	♉23°17	♓27°42	♒01°43	♈00°23	℞ 29°09	♎22°53	♈19°14	**22** We
23 Th	08:10:20	♒03°13'19	♏15°40'03	♏21°40'08	♑21°49	♓19°45	♋23°31	♊11°32	♓16°28	♉23°17	♓27°43	♒01°45	♈00°19	♓29°08	♎23°00	♈19°16	**23** Th
24 Fr	08:14:17	♒04°14'22	♏27°43'33	♐03°50'29	♑23°24	♓20°39	♋23°08	♊11°30	♓16°34	♉23°16	♓27°45	♒01°47	♈00°16	♓29°05	♎23°06	♈19°17	**24** Fr
25 Sa	08:18:13	♒05°15'23	♐10°01'49	♐16°17'36	♑24°59	♓21°32	♋22°46	♊11°27	♓16°41	♉23°16	♓27°46	♒01°49	♈00°13	♓29°00	♎23°13	♈19°18	**25** Sa
26 Su	08:22:10	♒06°16'24	♐22°38'33	♐29°04'32	♑26°35	♓22°25	♋22°25	♊11°25	♓16°47	♉23°16	♓27°48	♒01°51	♈00°10	♓28°52	♎23°20	♈19°20	**26** Su
27 Mo	08:26:06	♒07°17'25	♑05°36'05	♑12°12'50	♑28°11	♓23°17	♋22°04	♊11°23	♓16°53	♉23°16	♓27°49	♒01°53	♈00°07	♓28°43	♎23°26	♈19°21	**27** Mo
28 Tu	08:30:03	♒08°18'25	♑18°55'05	♑25°42'12	♑29°48	♓24°09	♋21°43	♊11°22	♓16°59	♉23°15	♓27°51	♒01°55	♈00°04	♓28°34	♎23°33	♈19°23	**28** Tu
29 We	08:33:60	♒09°19'24	♒02°34'17	♒09°30'30	♒01°25	♓24°59	♋21°23	♊11°20	♓17°06	♉23°15	♓27°53	♒01°57	♈00°00	♓28°25	♎23°40	♈19°25	**29** We
30 Th	08:37:56	♒10°20'22	♒16°30'46	♒23°34'03	♒03°04	♓25°49	♋21°04	♊11°19	♓17°12	♉23°15	♓27°54	♒01°59	♓29°57	♓28°18	♎23°46	♈19°26	**30** Th
31 Fr	08:41:53	♒11°21'19	♓00°40'12	♓07°48'07	♒04°43	♓26°38	♋20°45	♊11°18	♓17°18	D 23°15	♓27°56	♒02°01	♓29°54	♓28°13	♎23°53	♈19°28	**31** Fr
Δ Delta	01:58:16	30°32'30"	396°45'16"	397°08'26"	44°50'	28°55'	-11°09'	-1°54'	2°47'	-0°22'	0°38'	0°57'	1°35'	2°39'	3°19'	0°28'	**Delta**

Ephemeris tables and data provided by **Astro-Seek.com.** All times in UTC.

1

JAN 1 (NEW YEAR'S DAY) WAXING CRESCENT MOON IN CAPRICORN UNTIL 5:50AM; THEN, AQUARIUS

If you break dawn on NYE, you might wind up holding an impromptu brainstorming session (or board meeting!) over bubbles. The moon holds court in Capricorn until 5:50AM EST, igniting everyone's ambitions as 2025 dawns. Capture those ideas in a voice memo, then set them aside. In the early hours of the day, la luna shifts into social, idealistic Aquarius, turning the black tie vibes into a casual athleisure affair. Spend the day sending friendly texts to the people who matter most and meeting as many of them as you can for a hair-of-the-dog hangout or an inspired vision-boarding session.

JAN 2–FEB 4 VENUS IN PISCES

How perfectly poetic! On the second day of 2025, ardent Venus glides into romantic Pisces, bringing artists and romantics a cure for the impending winter blahs. Pisces is the love planet's favorite (exalted) position in the zodiac, which is sure to turn anything "mundane" into pure magic between now and February 4. Rethink any punishing or hardcore resolutions you were about to adopt. Instead, how about transforming them into pleasure-enhancing rituals that feed your mind, body and spirit? Turn your living room into a club for cardio dance routines. Trade massages with your partner and set up a smoothie bar in your kitchen. While this boundary-blurring transit works well for cuddling by the fireplace, it can make business dealings dodgy. Don't drop your guard completely with people you've just met. Before you sign a contract or send out your top-secret pitch deck, run the background checks to make sure they're "as advertised."

JAN 3 MARS-PLUTO OPPOSITION

Clash of the titans! Ferocious Mars is retrograde in fiery Leo, which has already set everyone's teeth on edge. Today, the feisty red planet locks into the second of two exact oppositions to powermonger Pluto in Aquarius. Whether you're wearing a crown, leading a rebellion or trying to wrangle your family back to a non-holiday schedule, check your authoritative style. Today comes with a strong warning to not abuse your power. Entitlement and egos can masquerade as "doing the right thing," but if you wind up polarizing the people you need in your corner, you'll only shoot yourself in the foot.

JAN 6

MARS RETROGRADE ENTERS CANCER (JAN 6–FEB 23)

Don't say the quiet part out loud. Firecracker Mars has been retrograding through ferocious Leo since December 6, 2024, making everyone's roar a little (or a lot) more intense. Today, the red planet goes into "silent simmer" mode, as it retreats into Cancer for the rest of its backspin, until February 23. Sensitivities are heightened and you may feel like you're wading through a minefield of mixed messages. Cut stressful people a wide berth and bring awareness to the emotional energy you bring into a room. Moods are especially contagious now, and it's easy to get passive aggressive instead of being direct. Strong emotions could surge up around family, especially if you're processing generational trauma or navigating complex dynamics that reared up over the holidays. If you're planning to move or renovate, try to wait until Mars is direct in Cancer after February 23. Not an option? Do everything you can to eliminate stress from the process.

MERCURY-NEPTUNE SQUARE

Mercury in adventurous Sagittarius is eager to gallop out of the starting gate, but not so fast! That could spell wasted energy, thanks to a befuddling beam from hazy Neptune who's fogging up the picture in Pisces. What looks like a "next step" could be a wrong turn into quicksand. And with both planets in mutable signs, every option may seem as enticing as the next. Hold off on decision-making and, instead, do some whiteboarding, mind mapping or "wouldn't it be crazy if...?" visioning. Ponder all the possibilities, from both the left and right hemispheres of your brain.

WAXING QUARTER MOON IN ARIES (6:56PM)

CEO, MVP, Queen of (fill in the blank). As you set your sights on your 2025 goals, today's quarter moon in competitive Aries brings a burst of excitement to your imagineering process. Visualize yourself at the top of your game and start thinking about what it will take to get there. Is there something you want to be known for this year? Since this is a moderating quarter moon, don't set the bar so high that it becomes impossible to reach. Beware of shiny object syndrome, too. As exciting as the new and trendy option may be, there's a chance it's not worth its weight in glitter.

JAN 8–27 MERCURY IN CAPRICORN

Strategic socializing is the name of the game as Mercury buzzes through Capricorn, the sign of the mogul, until January 27. Over the next few weeks, go rub shoulders with well-connected people who might help you get ahead. Join mastermind groups and online courses; apply to be part of a club where people with similar aspirations gather. Got a business idea brewing? Stop the guesswork and seek expert guidance. This can save you costly mistakes and help you map out a path to lasting success. Speedy Mercury can feel constrained when buzzing through cautious, conservative Capricorn, but don't put the pedal to the metal. Slowing down will bring results that are worth the wait.

JAN 11–JUL 26, 2026 NORTH NODE IN PISCES, SOUTH NODE IN VIRGO

Calling all sirens, narwhals and merfolk! Life on Earth may soon feel like a chapter in your favorite fantasy lit novel. (And maybe an underwater dive to the lost city of Atlantis.) For the first time since December 2007, the destiny-driven lunar North Node sets sail on a fantastic voyage through Pisces. The veil will be thin during this 18-month transit, which could bring a global spiritual awakening. Across the zodiac wheel, the lunar South Node hunkers down in analytical Virgo, bringing common sense into the equation. As magical as the tidal wave of Pisces energy can be, we will need periodic reality checks. In comes the Virgo South Node to remind us that the Wizard of Oz was really just a "man behind the curtain." Fittingly, this is a powerful time to tune up both the front end and the back end of your life. Virgo's systems and routines support the free-flowing enchantment of Pisces. What levers must be pulled in order to achieve the Fish's elevated state? Both Virgo and Pisces are associated with healing, which could stretch across all modalities—and both the 3D material plane and 5D ethereal realm—during this 19-month transit. Give your body AND your soul some love.

JAN 12 MARS-NEPTUNE TRINE

Flashes of feelings will be too strong to ignore today as insistent Mars dances into a powerful water trine with psychic Neptune. Serendipities, coincidences and "signs" are everywhere you turn, practically announcing themselves in bold neon lights. Conversations could feel so connected that you and the other person keep finishing each other's sentences. Don't dismiss these directives from the universe, but don't take them at face value, either. Since Mars is retrograde, emotional biases may cloud your ability to view your findings objectively. Follow up with a fact-check before you continue to pursue any intriguing leads. Couples could find the perfect balance of lust and trust, as compassionate Neptune softens the red planet's raw intensity. Single? A sultry person with a strong spiritual side will be more appealing than the sparkly unicorn with sheer animal magnetism.

JAN 13

SUN-URANUS TRINE

Hot damn! Ingenious ideas emerge at every turn as the unstoppable Capricorn Sun syncs up with innovative Uranus in Taurus. Energy is electric and people will be eager to jump into action around world-changing projects and revolutionary ideas. Put your surge protector in place! Uranus is still retrograde until January

30, which could send you on a wild goose chase as you pursue what seems like the next viral hit. Get excited, then, take a deep breath and run the background checks. With a little due diligence dynamic dreams can come to life.

CANCER FULL MOON (5:27PM; 24°00')

It's peak cozy season today as the first full moon of 2025 glows in warm-fuzzy Cancer. Emotions that have been simmering below the surface may spill out under these stirring moonbeams. And thanks to luna's flowing trine to compassionate Neptune, your sentimental side could be caught in 4K. Naked vulnerability is 100 percent acceptable when you're having lunch with your work wife or gushing to besties in a group thread. Try to keep it professional when the situation requires. Just because you can turn a client into a confidante doesn't necessarily mean that you should. The full moon cuts a close connection to retrograde Mars, dialing up the intensity level of your exchanges. Be gentle when delivering feedback to avoid bruised egos or ruffled feathers. Under Cancer's domestic influence, home life is equally top of mind. First major project of the New Year? Redoing your closets, updating your bedroom furniture—or changing your address entirely!

JAN 14 VENUS-JUPITER SQUARE

How green is the grass beneath your feet? As Venus in quixotic Pisces butts heads with "more is more" Jupiter in variety-loving Gemini, you'll be hard-pressed to find satisfaction. Comparing is despairing: under this biannual transit, which can make you feel like everyone else has the better deal. Venus and Jupiter are considered the two "benefic" planets because of their primarily positive qualities; yet today's square may prove that it's possible to have too much of a good thing. In romance, people will be fickle, rocking the rose-colored glasses one minute, then suddenly losing interest the next. Hold off on making any irreversible decisions, especially when it comes to your dating life or a pricey purchase that is final sale only.

JAN 15 SUN-MARS OPPOSITION

You could feel pulled in two directions with equal force under today's headstrong tug of war between the Sun and Mars. Instigator Mars is retrograde in domestic Cancer, driving up family drama. Meanwhile, the Capricorn Sun is fixated on your career goals. Distractions from home will be impossible to screen out, no matter how desperate you are to give a professional initiative your undivided attention. While it's never wise to leave your loved ones in a lurch, do your best to set boundaries around your time—especially with people who play the helpless role to get attention. Jumping in and making sacrifices won't do either of you any good.

JAN 18 VENUS-SATURN MEETUP #1 OF 3

Matters of the heart feel heavy and serious as Venus bumps into stern Saturn for the first of three conjunctions in Pisces this year. This odd-couple mashup can put a reality check on fantasies that have spun wildly out of control. No more riding on assumptions. Couples should sit down to talk through agreements, like how you budget and divide up household duties. While you may be wholeheartedly enjoying a situationship, this eye-opening transit could reveal long-term disparities, such as different political views. Saturn rules experts, so if you're at an impasse, a coach or couple's therapist could help you navigate your way through it. Ready to cut someone off who's draining your resources? Make a smooth and steely exit now—no explanations required.

JAN 19–FEB 18 SUN IN AQUARIUS (3:00PM)

Group hug! The Sun beams into communal Aquarius, the sign of collective and humanitarian efforts. This is peak season for activism, and there's no shortage of important causes to rally behind in 2025. How can you make your corner of the world a safer, more egalitarian place for all? The Sun in "one love" Aquarius shines a light on innovative solutions. Crowdfunding, crowdsourcing or any pooling of resources gets a thumbs up now. Aquarius rules science and technology, making it chic to be a geek now. If you're sitting on an invention or an idea for a must-have app, start talking to people who can help you bring it to life. (Have them sign an NDA to protect your intellectual property, though!) Learn software or figure out how to use AI to scale your business. If you can visualize it, you can do it.

JAN 21

SUN-PLUTO MEETUP

Once every year, the dazzling Sun makes an appointment with stormy Pluto, an event that can feel as intense as a Queen's Gambit chess match. The Sun reveals, Pluto conceals, which automatically puts them at cross purposes. As they meet up in communal Aquarius for the first time since the late 1700s, the world stage feels like an improv show. Competitive vibes could amplify to a cutthroat level while alliances emerge in the most unexpected places. If you don't have a team that you trust, start taking steps to amend that at once. And even if you do, keep one eyebrow raised at any suggestions that are brought to the collective. What seems like a generous act could be a power play in disguise.

WANING QUARTER MOON IN SCORPIO (3:31PM)

How wisely have you invested? From the way you spend your time to the people you share it with, stop and do an audit. Last week's full moon in Cancer revealed relationships that felt nourishing to your soul. Today's quarter moon in devoted, discerning Scorpio puts everyone under the microscope. Heartwarming exchanges don't tell the whole story—not by a long shot! Dig a little deeper into people's personal history and don't be afraid to probe, should the "facts" not seem to line up. This could be a good thing! You could uncover data that helps you make a more informed choice and build a stronger bond of trust.

JAN 23

MERCURY-MARS OPPOSITION

You know what you want, but as shrewd Mercury in Capricorn opposes combative Mars retrograde in Cancer, your ideas might be diametrically opposed to what other key players have in mind. There's no easy way around this. Trying to convince people to follow your "proven methodology" will make you look stubborn and rebellious. At the same time, giving in to other people's demands can make you feel weak. Accept that you're going to have to compromise somewhere, and hopefully you can choose your battles.

MERCURY-URANUS TRINE

Let your imagination wander off leash today, as mindful Mercury in Capricorn trines mad scientist Uranus in Taurus. With both planets in practical earth signs, you probably won't stray too far from reality, but nudge yourself a bit further from your comfort zone than usual. Slide into the DMs of a professional prospect. Put feelers out to see who might want to join you for a crypto conference or self-development seminar. Don't shy away from the oft-taboo topic of money because these conversations could spawn all sorts of income-generating ideas.

JAN 25 VENUS-MARS TRINE #1 OF 2

If you catch yourself doodling someone's name in a heart, there's no need to blush. Blame it on today's flowing trine between the love planets Venus and Mars. If you want to cop to your crush, you're in luck. This passionate pair is canoodling in water signs— Venus is in Pisces and Mars is in Cancer—setting the stage for a tender exchange of feelings. But with reactive Mars still retrograde, defenses may be higher than usual, too.

Try not to read into your person's every twitch and tick. There's a good chance those bodily responses have nothing to do with you. Coupled? Study your partner's nuances now and, instead of criticizing them, celebrate these unique traits.

JAN 27–FEB 14 MERCURY IN AQUARIUS

Slip off the blazer and slide into your lab coat. As mentalist Mercury shifts out of conventional Capricorn and into mad scientist Aquarius, everything is up for experimentation. New ideas and inventions flood in. Over the next few weeks, you could become obsessed with learning everything there is to know about an offbeat topic. Dive down the rabbit hole! Just make sure the research you find is credible and not funded by someone with a hidden agenda. (Mercury in Aquarius can spin up conspiracy theories.) Under the influence of team-spirited Aquarius, Mercury helps you forge new bonds both IRL and virtually. Community is healing and uplifting, especially during tense times; in fact, "tending and befriending" is a known stress response. Don't isolate!

JAN 29

MERCURY-PLUTO MEETUP

Forget about settling for status quo! As inquisitive Mercury unites with investigative Pluto, you want deeper answers. What's really going on here, and what else might be possible? This once-a-year meetup cranks open the discovery vault. Since both planets are touring "anything goes" Aquarius, you might be drawn to subject matter that is dark, mystical and revolutionary. Just be warned that Pluto can pull you into some shadowy places. If you start to feel creeped out or pessimistic, close those browser tabs and go do something   to lift your mood!

AQUARIUS NEW MOON (7:36AM; 9°51') AND LUNAR NEW YEAR'S EVE – WOOD SNAKE

Let's get together and feel alright! The new moon in "one love" Aquarius sends out a strong reminder that we are all connected. And thanks to a globally expansive trine to Jupiter in Gemini, this is a powerful moment for reaching across borders and diversifying your dream team. Each year, the Aquarius new moon dovetails with the Chinese Lunar New Year's Eve. Tonight, the enchanting Wood Dragon disappears in a puff of smoke, handing the magic stick to 2025's reigning creature, the seductive Wood Snake. This is the second of the two-year wood element cycle, which puts the emphasis on growth and cultivating our natural gifts between now and February 17, 2026. Add romantic and artistic gifts to that list! The Snake is ruled by luscious, beauty-loving Venus, a far tamer vibe than the warring Mars energy that the Dragon brought. Send up the prayers for peace!

JAN 30

URANUS RETROGRADE ENDS

Train your sites on that wild hare and get ready for a hot pursuit! After a five month retrograde that began last September 1, shock-jock Uranus wakes up and jolts us all into action. As the planetary innovator makes a U-Turn in money-minded Taurus, opportunities to improve your economic status could crop up everywhere. Don't get stuck on projects that aren't clicking into place. Business opportunities could arise when you're out doing mundane tasks like picking up your coffee or chatting up another parent at a PTA meeting. No matter what you do for a living, keep your mind open to boundary-pushing and edgy possibilities. Pursuing one of them could lead to quite the bounty in the days ahead. Let's go!

SUN-JUPITER TRINE

Exactly how wide can you open your mind? Today's free-flowing exchange between the idealistic Aquarius Sun and philosophical Jupiter in Gemini could pull you out of any mental ruts you've been stuck in. Novelty is the antidote to a pedantic mindset so if you need to trigger your own ingenuity, step away from the usual places. If you can't get past a sticking point, could you adopt an attitude of curiosity? Go for a walk (or drive) off your beaten path. Peruse a site that's not in your usual feed. Under the mentally agile influence of this air trine, thinking outside the box can lead to a breakthrough.

February

FEBRUARY
Moon Phase Calendar

SUN	MON	TUE	WED	THU	FRI	SAT
						1 ♓ ♈ 8:10PM
2 ♈	**3** ♈ ♉ 10:33PM	**4** ♉	**5** ♉ 2nd Quarter	**6** ♉ ♊ 1:44AM	**7** ♊	**8** ♊ ♋ 6:04AM
9 ♋	**10** ♋ ♌ 12:01PM	**11** ♌	**12** ♌ Full Moon 8:53AM ♍ 8:07PM	**13** ♍	**14** ♍	**15** ♍ ♎ 6:45AM
16 ♎	**17** ♎ ♏ 7:19PM	**18** ♏	**19** ♏	**20** ♏ → ♐ 7:55AM ♐ 4th Quarter	**21** ♐	**22** ♐ ♑ 6:09PM
23 ♑	**24** ♑	**25** ♑ ♒ 12:40AM	**26** ♒	**27** ♒ → ♓ 3:46AM ♓ New Moon 7:45PM	**28** ♓	

Times listed are Eastern US Time Zone

KEY

♈ ARIES	♌ LEO	♐ SAGITTARIUS	**FM** FULL MOON
♉ TAURUS	♍ VIRGO	♑ CAPRICORN	**NM** NEW MOON
♊ GEMINI	♎ LIBRA	♒ AQUARIUS	**LE** LUNAR ECLIPSE
♋ CANCER	♏ SCORPIO	♓ PISCES	**SE** SOLAR ECLIPSE

FEB 12, 8:53AM

full moon in LEO (24°06')

LEO FULL MOON CRYSTAL

TIGER'S EYE

This confidence-boosting stone contains the power of the mid-day Sun, the ruler of Leo. Use Tiger's Eye to enhance creativity and connect to personal agency. With its swirling hues of amber and brown, this talisman directs your attention to what's truly important in your life.

LEO FULL MOON = CELEBRATE

The unique way that you shine

The people who make your heart sing

Your romantic nature

Your fashion sense

Your childlike wonder

The places where you feel like a natural leader

Your fiercely competitive streak that won't let you quit on yourself

FEB 27, 7:45PM

new moon in
Pisces (9°41′)

PISCES NEW MOON CRYSTAL

AMETHYST

This relaxing purple crystal increases inner peace and tunes you in to your Pisces-ruled intuition. Keep amethyst by your bedside to sanctify sleep and invite powerful messages from your dreams.

PISCES NEW MOON = FOCUS

Connect to your dreams, spiritual exploration

Find creative outlets

Give back

Inspire others

Form supportive alliances

Express empathy so people feel seen and understood

February 2025

Longitude & Retrograde Ephemeris [00:00 UT]

Day	Sid.time	☉	☽	+12h☽	☿	♀	♂	♃	♄	♅	♆	♇	☊	☊	⚸	⚷	Day
1 Sa	08:45:49	♒12°22′15	♓14°57′39	♓22°07′46	♒06°22	♓27°26	℞ 20°27	℞ 11°17	♓17°25	♉23°15	♓27°58	♒02°03	℞ 29°51	℞ 28°10	♎24°00	♈19°30	1 Sa
2 Su	08:49:46	♒13°23′10	♓29°18′19	♈06°28′25	♒08°03	♓28°13	♋20°10	♊11°17	♓17°31	♉23°15	♓27°59	♒02°05	♓29°48	D 28°09	♎24°06	♈19°31	2 Su
3 Mo	08:53:42	♒14°24′03	♈13°38′04	♈20°46′29	♒09°44	♓29°00	♋19°53	♊11°16	♓17°38	♉23°15	♓28°01	♒02°07	♓29°45	♓28°10	♎24°13	♈19°33	3 Mo
4 Tu	08:57:39	♒15°24′55	♈27°53′48	♉04°59′21	♒11°25	♓29°45	♋19°37	♊11°16	♓17°45	♉23°16	♓28°03	♒02°08	♓29°41	♓28°11	♎24°20	♈19°35	4 Tu
5 We	09:01:35	♒16°25′46	♉12°03′24	♉19°05′20	♒13°08	♈00°29	♋19°22	D 11°16	♓17°51	♉23°16	♓28°05	♒02°10	♓29°38	♓28°12	♎24°26	♈19°37	5 We
6 Th	09:05:32	♒17°26′35	♉26°05′30	♊03°03′19	♒14°51	♈01°12	♋19°07	♊11°16	♓17°58	♉23°16	♓28°06	♒02°12	♓29°35	℞ 28°12	♎24°33	♈19°39	6 Th
7 Fr	09:09:29	♒18°27′23	♊09°59′07	♊16°52′22	♒16°35	♈01°54	♋18°54	♊11°17	♓18°05	♉23°17	♓28°08	♒02°14	♓29°32	♓28°10	♎24°40	♈19°41	7 Fr
8 Sa	09:13:25	♒19°28′09	♊23°43′22	♋00°31′32	♒18°20	♈02°35	♋18°41	♊11°18	♓18°12	♉23°17	♓28°10	♒02°16	♓29°29	♓28°06	♎24°46	♈19°43	8 Sa
9 Su	09:17:22	♒20°28′53	♋07°17′10	♋13°59′40	♒20°05	♈03°15	♋18°29	♊11°18	♓18°18	♉23°18	♓28°12	♒02°18	♓29°25	♓28°00	♎24°53	♈19°45	9 Su
10 Mo	09:21:18	♒21°29′36	♋20°39′20	♋27°15′33	♒21°52	♈03°53	♋18°17	♊11°19	♓18°25	♉23°18	♓28°14	♒02°20	♓29°22	♓27°54	♎25°00	♈19°48	10 Mo
11 Tu	09:25:15	♒22°30′18	♌03°48′37	♌10°18′00	♒23°39	♈04°30	♋18°07	♊11°21	♓18°32	♉23°19	♓28°16	♒02°22	♓29°19	♓27°48	♎25°06	♈19°50	11 Tu
12 We	09:29:11	♒23°30′59	♌16°44′00	♌23°06′12	♒25°27	♈05°06	♋17°57	♊11°22	♓18°39	♉23°19	♓28°18	♒02°23	♓29°16	♓27°42	♎25°13	♈19°52	12 We
13 Th	09:33:08	♒24°31′37	♌29°24′58	♍05°39′58	♒27°15	♈05°40	♋17°48	♊11°24	♓18°46	♉23°20	♓28°20	♒02°25	♓29°13	♓27°38	♎25°19	♈19°54	13 Th
14 Fr	09:37:04	♒25°32′15	♍11°51′42	♍17°59′55	♒29°04	♈06°13	♋17°39	♊11°26	♓18°53	♉23°21	♓28°22	♒02°27	♓29°10	♓27°35	♎25°26	♈19°57	14 Fr
15 Sa	09:41:01	♒26°32′51	♍24°05′14	♎00°07′33	♓00°54	♈06°44	♋17°32	♊11°28	♓19°00	♉23°21	♓28°24	♒02°29	♓29°06	♓27°34	♎25°33	♈19°59	15 Sa
16 Su	09:44:58	♒27°33′25	♎06°07′34	♎12°05′18	♓02°44	♈07°14	♋17°25	♊11°30	♓19°07	♉23°22	♓28°26	♒02°31	♓29°03	D 27°34	♎25°39	♈20°01	16 Su
17 Mo	09:48:54	♒28°33′59	♎18°01′33	♎23°56′26	♓04°35	♈07°42	♋17°20	♊11°32	♓19°14	♉23°23	♓28°28	♒02°32	♓29°00	♓27°35	♎25°46	♈20°04	17 Mo
18 Tu	09:52:51	♒29°34′31	♎29°50′51	♏05°44′57	♓06°26	♈08°08	♋17°14	♊11°35	♓19°21	♉23°24	♓28°30	♒02°34	♓28°57	♓27°37	♎25°53	♈20°06	18 Tu
19 We	09:56:47	♓00°35′01	♏11°39′43	♏17°35′22	♓08°18	♈08°33	♋17°10	♊11°38	♓19°28	♉23°25	♓28°32	♒02°36	♓28°54	♓27°39	♎25°59	♈20°09	19 We
20 Th	10:00:44	♓01°35′31	♏23°32′55	♏29°32′36	♓10°09	♈08°55	♋17°07	♊11°41	♓19°35	♉23°26	♓28°34	♒02°38	♓28°51	♓27°40	♎26°06	♈20°11	20 Th
21 Fr	10:04:40	♓02°35′59	♐05°35′24	♐11°41′35	♓12°01	♈09°16	♋17°04	♊11°44	♓19°43	♉23°27	♓28°36	♒02°39	♓28°47	℞ 27°40	♎26°13	♈20°14	21 Fr
22 Sa	10:08:37	♓03°36′26	♐17°52′05	♐24°07′04	♓13°52	♈09°35	♋17°02	♊11°47	♓19°50	♉23°28	♓28°38	♒02°41	♓28°44	♓27°39	♎26°19	♈20°17	22 Sa
23 Su	10:12:33	♓04°36′52	♑00°27′26	♑06°53′11	♓15°43	♈09°52	♋17°01	♊11°51	♓19°57	♉23°30	♓28°40	♒02°43	♓28°41	♓27°37	♎26°26	♈20°19	23 Su
24 Mo	10:16:30	♓05°37′16	♑13°25′03	♑20°02′52	♓17°33	♈10°07	♋17°00	♊11°54	♓20°04	♉23°31	♓28°42	♒02°44	♓28°38	♓27°35	♎26°33	♈20°22	24 Mo
25 Tu	10:20:27	♓06°37′39	♑26°47′11	♒03°37′32	♓19°21	♈10°20	D 17°01	♊11°58	♓20°12	♉23°32	♓28°44	♒02°46	♓28°35	♓27°32	♎26°39	♈20°25	25 Tu
26 We	10:24:23	♓07°38′00	♒10°34′12	♒17°36′27	♓21°08	♈10°30	♋17°02	♊12°03	♓20°19	♉23°33	♓28°47	♒02°48	♓28°31	♓27°29	♎26°46	♈20°28	26 We
27 Th	10:28:20	♓08°38′20	♒24°44′16	♓01°56′39	♓22°54	♈10°39	♋17°04	♊12°07	♓20°26	♉23°35	♓28°49	♒02°49	♓28°28	♓27°26	♎26°53	♈20°30	27 Th
28 Fr	10:32:16	♓09°38′38	♓09°13′20	♓16°33′03	♓24°37	♈10°45	♋17°06	♊12°11	♓20°34	♉23°36	♓28°51	♒02°51	♓28°25	♓27°24	♎26°59	♈20°33	28 Fr
Δ Delta	01:46:27	27°16′22″	-354°15′40″	-354°25′17″	48°14′	-13°18′	-3°21′	0°53′	3°08′	0°20′	0°53′	0°48′	-1°25′	-0°45′	2°59′	1°03′	Delta

Ephemeris tables and data provided by **Astro-Seek.com.** All times in UTC.

FEBRUARY
MONTHLY HOTSPOTS

FEB 1 VENUS-NEPTUNE MEETUP #1 OF 3

Shall we dance? Venus in Pisces falls under Neptune's spellbinding sway as the two meet for their first of three conjunctions in 2025. Romance takes on a magical glow as the universe sprinkles stardust on all your encounters. But before you dive headfirst into the fantasy, hit pause. Make sure to look beyond the fairytale sheen to see what's real and what might be an illusion. If you've been caught in a tangled web with a friend or loved one, today's compassionate vibes offer the perfect chance to mend fences and heal those wounds. Let the cosmic currents guide you toward love and forgiveness.

FEB 3 MERCURY-JUPITER TRINE

It won't be hard to sway the masses today as articulate Mercury in Aquarius and grandiose Jupiter in Gemini sync up in verbose air signs. A dollop of charm and a few pumps of enthusiasm may be enough to turn a "no" to a "yes" for now. But don't rest on any laurels. Big talk needs to be followed up by solid action, the kind that yields results. To avoid getting a reputation as a demagogue, lay out next steps and be sure to make good on them in the coming days. The air-sign trine of Mercury and Jupiter can inflate your reputation. If you're not shining the way you long to be, work on polishing up your personal brand.

FEB 4

VENUS IN ARIES (FEB 4-MAR 27)

H-O-T-T-O-G-O! Seductive Venus fire-spins into the bold and brash sign of Aries, heating things up in the Ram's realm for nearly two whole months. Love will be lit during this longer-than-usual cycle, but it also comes with a flame-orange warning flag. On March 1, Venus spins into a six-week retrograde, which could tamp down some of the bold, impulsive energy that her tour through Aries brings. Fortunately, there's a solid month ahead to relish Venus in direct motion. Love may spark quickly and extinguish just as fast in this rapid-fire sign. But don't shy away from the thrill. If your romantic life has slowed to a standstill, Venus in fearless Aries reignites your courage. Note: In the impetuous sign of Aries, Venus finds herself in "detriment," making it tough for the planet of slow seduction to keep a semblance of cool. Unexpected (and intense!) attractions might catch you off-guard. If you're already spoken for, there's no need to act on these impulses. Try to channel that vibrant energy back to your S.O.

JUPITER RETROGRADE ENDS

Enough with the double talk! After five months of frustrating detours and mental chess games, the road to truth is in sight again. Maximizer Jupiter powers forward in clever, communicative Gemini, where it's been retrograde since last October 9. In the wake of months of introspective rewiring, you may find that you have copious wisdom to share. Plug into articulate Jupiter-in-Gemini to write an article, record a podcast or revive a once-lively group chat. Curiosity may have led you astray since last October, but starting now, it could pave the way to a vibrant social life or a new hobby that you've always wanted to try. Don't be shy about striking up conversations! Tag-team efforts will be blessed with the mighty planet's powers. This is your cosmic cue to think big and assert yourself boldly (well, once you have all the facts). Jupiter in Gemini can amplify your voice and help you reach a global crowd.

FEB 5 WAXING QUARTER MOON IN TAURUS (3:02AM)

Time for a cosmic check-in! Today's waxing quarter moon in sensible Taurus invites you to fine-tune your goals. Instead of barreling towards the finish line, ease off the accelerator and give all projects a thorough evaluation. Are you clear about the value you're offering? Do you know where you ultimately want to land this plane? Now's the time to fortify your strategies to avoid wasting time and energy. While you may feel like scaling back, don't do minimalism for minimalism's sake. Infuse simplicity with sophistication. Toss out the worn and welcome in the elegant.

FEB 9

SUN-MERCURY MEETUP

There is no "I" in "team" as the Sun unites with social Mercury in Aquarius. But that doesn't mean you can't bring your original vibe to a group effort. Under these inclusive skies, band together with a diverse crew and see what you can cook up together. Keep your eyes open for people's hidden potential. The missing link for a project or plan might be someone you've casually interacted with for months. Go ahead and ask the not-so-obvious questions. You could discover mind blowing synergies that you had no clue existed.

MARS-SATURN TRINE

Gas or brakes? You won't be sure which pedal to ride today as speed-demon Mars in Cancer unites with take-it-slow Saturn in Pisces. Because Mars is retrograde and both planets are in water signs, home and family matters demand attention. Ignore a leaky faucet or a relative's eye rolls at your own peril today. These could quickly snowball into much bigger problems if you don't address them now. It's possible trouble's been brewing unbeknownst to you for a while. Solution-minded Saturn can help you get to the source of the issue and hammer out long-lasting fixes. Keep your temper in check.

FEB 10 MERCURY-URANUS SQUARE

Pause before you post! Your radical ideas might stir up more chaos than change, as unruly Uranus in bullheaded Taurus clashes with Mercury in rebellious Aquarius. Challenging the norm is one thing, but this feisty energy could drag you into a troll fight that zaps hours of your time. Instead of firing off impulsive rants, take time to refine your message. Being the maverick could backfire spectacularly if you wind up spreading disinformation. If you're pitching a new concept, make sure your arguments are well-structured and backed by solid data. Innovation is valued, but clarity is crucial. Today, aim to be understood, not just heard.

FEB 11 SUN-URANUS SQUARE

Stay sharp and tread carefully! Today's cosmic climate is extra heated as the Aquarius Sun squares off with abrasive Uranus in Taurus, sparking potential flare-ups and ego battles. This biannual clash tends to magnify power struggles and impulsive reactions. With both celestial bodies in unyielding fixed signs, expect a lot of stubborn "my way or the highway" standoffs. People are likely to react first and think later, making it easy for small disagreements to escalate. Be the calm in the storm. Aim to diffuse tensions and contribute to solutions, not conflicts. Keep your cool and steer clear of unnecessary drama!

FEB 12 FULL MOON IN LEO (8:53AM; 24°06')

Courage unleashed! Today marks the annual full moon in wholehearted Leo, which emboldens you to live—and love—out loud. Be audacious with your style choices and shameless with the PDA. If you and a certain someone have been coyly circling each other, this could be the day where you bite the bullet and cop to your attraction. The playful, theatrical energy of the day can be fun, but don't be performative at the expense of forging a deeper, emotional connection. With the full moon forming a tense square to unpredictable Uranus and opposing loose-lipped Mercury, be strategic about what you share. If you're divulging personal details to a new friend or unveiling a work project, hold a few details back as you build trust.

FEB 14–APR 16 MERCURY IN PISCES

Let yourself get swept away this V-Day! Flirty Mercury sets sail in fantasy-fueled Pisces, drifting through this imaginative sign's waters for a solid month. As the messenger planet cranks up the volume on your intuition, you could download all sorts of divine inspiration, from song lyrics to the vision of an installation art piece. Your subconscious will be buzzing, especially after dark. Make time for candlelight meditations, sound baths and any activities that relax your mind so you can receive messages and insights. Don't rush to share them all though! Mercury in Pisces can drive up ambiguity. Since the messenger planet is spinning retrograde (in Pisces and Aries) from March 15 to April 7, you'll need to navigate through some foggy communications. Pay close attention to the unsaid. Body language and subtle signals might reveal more than words ever could!

FEB 18-MAR 20
SUN IN PISCES (5:07AM)

Pisces season begins today as the Sun casts its line in the watery realm of the Fish, awakening waves of empathy, creativity, and intuition. Compassion reigns supreme for the coming four weeks, a welcome shift after the coolly detached energy of Aquarius season. Forget what the algorithms are serving and tune in to your own soul wisdom.

This is a time for dreaming, dancing and flowing with the natural current of the universe— and that requires deep surrender to the unknown. Faith may be tested while the Sun tours this elusive sign since things may not be as they initially appear. During this time, work to cultivate substantial connections rather than fleeting, surface-level interactions. Boundaries can get blurry, so take time to feel your way into situations, making sure that they really do work for you before saying "yes."

FEB 20

MERCURY-JUPITER SQUARE

Watch out for a rising tide of know-it-all attitudes today, as fickle Mercury in Pisces clashes with overconfident Jupiter in Gemini. Everywhere you turn, people seem to be making snap judgments and drawing hasty conclusions. The first solution that pops up isn't necessarily the right one, so do your research. Even if you're absolutely sure you're on the money or you're feeling a strong gut instinct, it pays to double-check your facts. Under this mashup, people could be overstating their cases and it's easy to be swayed by an appealing pitch. Challenge for the day: Allow yourself to deeply desire something (or someone) without following the urge to immediately possess it.

WANING QUARTER MOON IN SAGITTARIUS (12:33PM)

Today's waning quarter moon in straightforward Sagittarius ushers in a wave of clarity and sets the stage for open dialogues. If you've been mulling over an issue since last week's full moon, you may finally see the situation in a new light and discover a silver lining. Ready to wrap up an ideological debate? Focus less on winning or losing and more on understanding different perspectives. Open up the conversation to various viewpoints and strive to see the bigger picture. This broader approach can help resolve conflicts and bring about the peace of mind you've been seeking.

FEB 23

MERCURY-MARS TRINE

What have you been stuffing down or keeping inside? Hours before wrapping up its eleven-week retrograde, forthright Mars gets a nudge from communicator Mercury, prompting you to spill. With both planets in emotional water signs, words could rush out like an undammed river. If you feel that swell of energy rising, make sure you're in front of an empathic (and appropriate!) audience. Prickly Mars is retrograde in sensitive Cancer while Mercury in Pisces can make your feelings as clear as a swirling eddy. While it's important to unload, you don't want to pull anyone into an emotional riptide. Best to sort through the emotions that come up before staging any direct confrontations.

MARS RETROGRADE ENDS

If your 2025 hygge season's been hectic, blame it on aggravating Mars. Since last December 6, the energizer planet has been buried in a frustrating retrograde—in homespun Cancer, no less. Tonight, the red planet resumes forward motion, dialing down that frenetic energy. For the final stretch of winter, set up the craft table and mix up some craft cocktails, as you get into the spirit of cold-weather communing. Vanquish the tension under your roof by decluttering, redecorating and making sure everyone has enough space to do their thing. The red planet's motivational influence may inspire a home-based business or a pre-spring fitness challenge with roommates and relatives. If cabin fever has fanned the flames of conflict, here's your cue to escape to the slopes for a weekend, or maybe the beach!

FEB 25 MERCURY-SATURN MEETUP

Every word counts today as mouthy Mercury connects the dots with sober Saturn. But with both planets in dreamy, ethereal Pisces, it's almost too easy to make a slip of the tongue. Do your best to pause and think before delivering any sort of judgment—or simply musing aloud. If you're ready to make a serious statement, you can speak with gravitas. To come across as polished and prepared, go easy on the upspeak and vocal fry. This is also a powerful day for consulting experts whose empirical processes can help you turn a lofty vision into a reality.

FEB 27 NEW MOON IN PISCES (7:45PM; 9°41')

The year's only new moon in Pisces opens up a portal to the divine, marking one of 2025's most potent days for tapping into your own mystical energy. Find at least a few moments during the day to settle into a serene spot, tune out the 3D world and connect to your inner voice. Since new moons make excellent starting blocks, up the ante and begin a 21-day meditation series or sign up for a poetry or Tarot workshop. A sacred healing session or plant medicine ceremony may also be calling your name under these numinous moonbeams. Whatever bubbles up in your imagination is worth taking note of. Guard your nascent dreams from people who are disconnected from their spiritual sides. With Jupiter in Gemini squaring this new moon, one teasing comment could discourage you from pursuing a worthwhile thread.

March

MARCH
Moon Phase Calendar

KEY

♈ ARIES	♌ LEO	♐ SAGITTARIUS	**FM** FULL MOON
♉ TAURUS	♍ VIRGO	♑ CAPRICORN	**NM** NEW MOON
♊ GEMINI	♎ LIBRA	♒ AQUARIUS	**LE** LUNAR ECLIPSE
♋ CANCER	♏ SCORPIO	♓ PISCES	**SE** SOLAR ECLIPSE

SUN	MON	TUE	WED	THU	FRI	SAT
						1 ♓ ♈ 4:52AM
2 ♈	**3** ♈ ♉ 5:37AM	**4** ♉	**5** ♉ ♊ 7:29AM	**6** ♊ 2nd Quarter	**7** ♊ ♋ 11:29AM	**8** ♋
9 ♋ ♌ 6:59PM	**10** ♌	**11** ♌	**12** ♌ ♍ 3:56AM	**13** ♍	**14** ♍ Full Moon & Lunar Eclipse 2:55AM ♎ Full Moon	**15** ♎
16 ♎	**17** ♎ ♏ 3:30AM	**18** ♏	**19** ♏ ♐ 4:17PM	**20** ♐	**21** ♐	**22** ♐→♑ 3:29AM ♑ 4th Quarter
23 ♑	**24** ♑ ♒ 11:25AM	**25** ♒	**26** ♒ ♓ 3:31PM	**27** ♓	**28** ♓ ♈ 4:36PM	**29** ♈ New Moon & Solar Eclipse 6:58AM
30 ♈ ♉ 4:16PM	**31** ♉					

Times listed are Eastern US Time Zone

Total Lunar Eclipse

MARCH 14, 2:55AM
full moon in
Virgo (23°57')

VIRGO FULL MOON CRYSTAL

MOSS AGATE

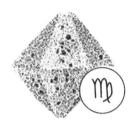

With its swirls of green, this stone connects you to the healing powers of nature. Moss Agate is known to ease anxiety and reduce people-pleasing and judgment that can creep in under Virgo's watch.

VIRGO FULL MOON = CELEBRATE!

The serenity of a freshly cleaned space

Streamlined systems

Your helpful spirit

Being of service to those in need

Taking great care of your body by eating clean and exercising

The magic of nature and organic beauty

MARCH 29, 6:58AM

new moon in Aries (9°00')

ARIES NEW MOON CRYSTAL

CARNELIAN

This vibrant orange stone wakes up the sacral chakra to connect you to your instinctual truth. Use carnelian to enhance confidence and creativity as you step into your Aries-inspired power. This crystal also supports with new beginnings.

ARIES NEW MOON = FOCUS

Sharpen your competitive edge

Blaze your own trail

Take the initiative with people and activities that matter to you

Try new things

March 2025

Longitude & Retrograde Ephemeris [00:00 UT]

Day	Sid.time	☉	☽	+12h☽	☿	♀	♂	♃	♄	♅	♆	♇	☊	☊	⚸	⚷	Day
1 Sa	10:36:13	♓10°38′54	♓23°55′25	♈01°19′02	♓26°17	♈10°48	♋17°09	♊12°16	♓20°41	♉23°38	♓28°53	♒02°53	℞ 28°22	℞ 27°24	♎27°06	♈20°36	1 Sa
2 Su	10:40:09	♓11°39′08	♈08°43′26	♈16°07′17	℞s 27°53	♈10°50	♋17°13	♊12°21	♓20°48	♉23°39	♓28°55	♒02°54	♓28°19	D 27°24	♎27°13	♈20°39	2 Su
3 Mo	10:44:06	♓12°39′21	♈23°30′11	♉00°50′53	♓29°26	℞ 10°48	♋17°18	♊12°26	♓20°56	♉23°41	♓28°57	♒02°56	♓28°16	♓27°25	♎27°19	♈20°42	3 Mo
4 Tu	10:48:02	♓13°39′31	♉08°09′11	♉15°24′04	♈00°54	♈10°45	♋17°23	♊12°31	♓21°03	♉23°42	♓29°00	♒02°57	♓28°12	♓27°26	♎27°26	♈20°45	4 Tu
5 We	10:51:59	♓14°39′39	♉22°35′30	♉29°42′42	♈02°17	♈10°39	♋17°29	♊12°36	♓21°10	♉23°44	♓29°02	♒02°59	♓28°09	♓27°27	♎27°33	♈20°48	5 We
6 Th	10:55:56	♓15°39′46	♊06°45′51	♊13°44′22	♈03°34	♈10°30	♋17°36	♊12°42	♓21°18	♉23°46	♓29°04	♒03°01	♓28°06	♓27°27	♎27°39	♈20°51	6 Th
7 Fr	10:59:52	♓16°39′50	♊20°38′38	♊27°28′12	♈04°45	♈10°19	♋17°43	♊12°48	♓21°25	♉23°48	♓29°06	♒03°02	♓28°03	℞ 27°28	♎27°46	♈20°54	7 Fr
8 Sa	11:03:49	♓17°39′52	♋04°13′33	♋10°54′24	♈05°49	♈10°05	♋17°51	♊12°53	♓21°32	♉23°49	♓29°09	♒03°04	♓28°00	♓27°27	♎27°53	♈20°57	8 Sa
9 Su	11:07:45	♓18°39′52	♋17°31′16	♋24°03′55	♈06°46	♈09°49	♋17°59	♊12°59	♓21°40	♉23°51	♓29°11	♒03°05	♓27°56	♓27°26	♎27°59	♈21°00	9 Su
10 Mo	11:11:42	♓19°39′50	♌00°32′56	♌06°58′04	♈07°35	♈09°30	♋18°08	♊13°06	♓21°47	♉23°53	♓29°13	♒03°06	♓27°53	♓27°25	♎28°06	♈21°03	10 Mo
11 Tu	11:15:38	♓20°39′45	♌13°19′56	♌19°38′18	♈08°16	♈09°09	♋18°18	♊13°12	♓21°55	♉23°55	♓29°15	♒03°08	♓27°50	♓27°24	♎28°13	♈21°07	11 Tu
12 We	11:19:35	♓21°39′39	♌25°53′45	♍02°06′04	♈08°48	♈08°46	♋18°28	♊13°18	♓22°02	♉23°57	♓29°18	♒03°09	♓27°47	♓27°24	♎28°19	♈21°10	12 We
13 Th	11:23:31	♓22°39′30	♍08°15′49	♍14°22′48	♈09°12	♈08°20	♋18°39	♊13°25	♓22°09	♉23°59	♓29°20	♒03°11	♓27°44	♓27°23	♎28°26	♈21°13	13 Th
14 Fr	11:27:28	♓23°39′19	♍20°27′36	♍26°30′02	♈09°28	♈07°53	♋18°50	♊13°32	♓22°17	♉24°01	♓29°22	♒03°12	♓27°41	♓27°23	♎28°33	♈21°16	14 Fr
15 Sa	11:31:25	♓24°39′06	♎02°30′41	♎08°29′25	♈09°34	♈07°23	♋19°02	♊13°39	♓22°24	♉24°03	♓29°24	♒03°13	♓27°37	D 27°23	♎28°39	♈21°19	15 Sa
16 Su	11:35:21	♓25°38′52	♎14°26′50	♎20°22′52	℞ 09°33	♈06°52	♋19°14	♊13°46	♓22°32	♉24°05	♓29°27	♒03°15	♓27°34	♓27°23	♎28°46	♈21°23	16 Su
17 Mo	11:39:18	♓26°38′35	♎26°18′11	♏02°12′44	♈09°22	♈06°19	♋19°27	♊13°53	♓22°39	♉24°08	♓29°29	♒03°16	♓27°31	♓27°23	♎28°53	♈21°26	17 Mo
18 Tu	11:43:14	♓27°38′17	♏08°07′15	♏14°01′46	♈09°04	♈05°45	♋19°41	♊14°00	♓22°46	♉24°10	♓29°31	♒03°17	♓27°28	℞ 27°23	♎28°59	♈21°29	18 Tu
19 We	11:47:11	♓28°37′57	♏19°57′04	♏25°53′14	♈08°39	♈05°09	♋19°55	♊14°08	♓22°54	♉24°12	♓29°33	♒03°19	♓27°25	♓27°23	♎29°06	♈21°33	19 We
20 Th	11:51:07	♓29°37′35	♐01°51′07	♐07°50′51	♈08°07	♈04°33	♋20°09	♊14°16	♓23°01	♉24°14	♓29°36	♒03°20	♓27°22	♓27°23	♎29°13	♈21°36	20 Th
21 Fr	11:55:04	♈00°37′12	♐13°53′21	♐19°58′45	♈07°28	♈03°56	♋20°24	♊14°24	♓23°09	♉24°17	♓29°38	♒03°21	♓27°18	♓27°22	♎29°19	♈21°39	21 Fr
22 Sa	11:59:00	♈01°36′46	♐26°07′59	♑02°21′14	♈06°45	♈03°18	♋20°39	♊14°31	♓23°16	♉24°19	♓29°40	♒03°22	♓27°15	♓27°22	♎29°26	♈21°43	22 Sa
23 Su	12:02:57	♈02°36′19	♑08°39′23	♑15°02′34	♈05°58	♈02°40	♋20°55	♊14°40	♓23°23	♉24°22	♓29°43	♒03°23	♓27°12	D 27°22	♎29°33	♈21°46	23 Su
24 Mo	12:06:53	♈03°35′50	♑21°31′37	♑28°06′33	♈05°07	♈02°03	♋21°11	♊14°48	♓23°31	♉24°24	♓29°45	♒03°24	♓27°09	♓27°23	♎29°39	♈21°50	24 Mo
25 Tu	12:10:50	♈04°35′20	♒04°48′06	♒11°36′04	♈04°15	♈01°25	♋21°28	♊14°56	♓23°38	♉24°26	♓29°47	♒03°26	♓27°06	♓27°23	♎29°46	♈21°53	25 Tu
26 We	12:14:47	♈05°34′48	♒18°30′57	♒25°32′20	♈03°22	♈00°48	♋21°45	♊15°05	♓23°45	♉24°29	♓29°49	♒03°27	♓27°02	♓27°24	♎29°53	♈21°57	26 We
27 Th	12:18:43	♈06°34′13	♓02°40′25	♓09°54′25	♈02°30	♈00°12	♋22°02	♊15°13	♓23°53	♉24°32	♓29°52	♒03°28	♓26°59	♓27°25	♎29°59	♈22°00	27 Th
28 Fr	12:22:40	♈07°33′37	♓17°14′16	♓24°38′47	♈01°38	♓29°37	♋22°20	♊15°22	♓24°00	♉24°34	♓29°54	♒03°29	♓26°56	♓27°25	♏00°06	♈22°03	28 Fr
29 Sa	12:26:36	♈08°32′59	♈02°07′35	♈09°39′12	♈00°49	♓29°03	♋22°38	♊15°31	♓24°07	♉24°37	♓29°56	♒03°30	♓26°53	℞ 27°25	♏00°13	♈22°07	29 Sa
30 Su	12:30:33	♈09°32′19	♈17°12′59	♈24°47′18	♈00°04	♓28°31	♋22°57	♊15°40	♓24°14	♉24°39	♓29°58	♒03°31	♓26°50	♓27°25	♏00°19	♈22°10	30 Su
31 Mo	12:34:29	♈10°31′37	♉02°21′25	♉09°53′43	♓29°22	♓28°00	♋23°16	♊15°49	♓24°22	♉24°42	♈00°01	♒03°32	♓26°47	♓27°24	♏00°26	♈22°14	31 Mo
Δ Delta	01:58:16	-29°52′42″	-398°26′00″	398°34′41″	3°05′	12°48′	6°06′	3°32′	3°40′	1°04′	-1°07′	0°39′	-1°35′	-0°00′	3°19′	1°37′	Delta

Ephemeris tables and data provided by **Astro-Seek.com.** All times in UTC.

MARCH
MONTHLY HOTSPOTS

MAR 1–APR 12 VENUS TURNS RETROGRADE IN ARIES AND PISCES

Romance hits a six-week speedbump as Venus turns retrograde, first in passionate Aries (until March 27), then, backwards through fantasy-fueled Pisces until April 12. As the planet of love shifts from being an "evening star" (appearing at dusk) to a "morning star" (glimmering in the sky just before dawn) get ready to put old love stories, limiting beliefs and toxic relationships to bed. Arguments can flare between lovers and friends while Venus backs up through combative Aries. As the gloves come off, do your best to not burn an important bridge to the ground. Thankfully, Venus only turns retrograde every 18 months, but this one may be especially feisty. Nostalgia is the magic elixir. Do things that revive a bygone era, like revisiting a place you haven't been to since the honeymoon phase. In autonomous Aries and solitary Pisces, taking time for independent activities that fuel self-love can also restore equilibrium in relationships.

MAR 2

MERCURY-NEPTUNE MEETUP

Fog descending! Esoteric Neptune aligns with Mercury in the dreamy realm of Pisces, making it challenging to distinguish between what's real and what's merely an illusion. Conversations seem enveloped in confusion, and you might find your focus slipping. Don't swim against the current. Instead, lean into your intuition and let your imagination take the lead. Have you been overly critical of others or yourself lately? The empathetic energy of today's skies encourages a more compassionate approach. Buried emotions may surface, so don't be surprised if you find yourself feeling teary. If you've been grappling with a recurring issue, stay open to potentially transformative insights that could lead to healing.

SUN-JUPITER SQUARE

The magnetic pull of other people's demands can be hard to ignore when the Sun is in Pisces, the sign of sacrifice. But as el Sol squares off with indie-spirited Jupiter for the day, your heart—and the rest of you—could use a break from playing caretaker to everyone around you. That's not to say you should screen out the world. Jupiter is in playful, convivial Gemini, pointing you toward lighthearted engagements with people whose wit you deeply appreciate. While you're out having fun, guard against gullibility. People will be talking a good game—with no real plan for how they'll actually carry it out. Make sure you're not overpromising, either.

MARCH 3–29 MERCURY IN ARIES

Goodbye, groupthink. Hello, independent thought. Intellectual Mercury charges into bold, fiery Aries today, igniting a spark of daring and outspoken energy. Ready to voice your opinions without hesitation? Aries encourages direct communication. Say exactly what you mean and ensure your words match your intentions. Get those fiery words out fast though! On March 15, Mercury will follow in Venus' footsteps, turning retrograde in both Aries (until March 29), then Pisces (until April 7). Even before the backspin, the line between helpful and harsh can become practically invisible. Have a key point to make? Keep your message crisp and clear. Skip the lengthy explanations and drive home your points with sharp one-liners.

MAR 6 WAXING QUARTER MOON IN GEMINI (11:32AM)

Embrace the intellectual buzz as today's waxing quarter moon builds momentum in communicative Gemini. Forget about sitting still. It's an optimal day for brainstorming and networking. Gemini's airy influence encourages lively exchanges but beware of scattering your focus. As you get swept up in the flurry of ideas and dialogues, you could lose track of your ultimate goal. To avoid information overload, write up an outline or create a meeting agenda. Inject a bit of Gemini's clever banter to keep your communications fresh.

MAR 8 SUN-MARS TRINE

Sensitivity is a superpower today as the Pisces Sun trines guardian Mars in Cancer. You may feel an intuitive drive to protect your loved ones or stick up for a random stranger who's in need of an ally. With family front and center, this is the perfect day to heal old wounds. Forthright Mars gives you the courage to approach a long-standing conflict while also leaning into empathy. In some cases, the brave thing may be putting up an iron-clad boundary with someone who consistently takes advantage of your kindness. No guilt! This is best for everyone involved since resentment can poison even the most soulful relationships.

MAR 11 MERCURY-VENUS MEETUP

Today's spicy sync-up of Mercury and Venus in Aries is like a clarion call for "love warriors." (No surprise Aries Glennon Doyle wrote a book with that title.) Situations could push you to fight for your romantic ideals, or to push past fears of rejection to let your desires be known. Even the usually reserved might find themselves emboldened, ready to engage in some heart-racing flirting. Whether you're typically shy or naturally audacious, today's the day to take the lead in love. For long-term couples, healthy competition can spark up a feisty, sexy dynamic. Meet on the racquetball court, break out a board game, or challenge your partner to a bake-off. Make sure you play with the intention to win!

MAR 12 SUN-SATURN MEETUP

The effusive Sun holds its once-per-year meetup with sobering Saturn today, teaming up in watery, mystical Pisces. This "Day of Challenges" can feel like an annual inspection as you run your bright ideas through a series of stress tests. While this may turn up some harsh realities, try to adopt a "better safe than sorry" approach. Knowing where your weak points lie can be useful data. Now you can avert a future crisis and know where you should redirect your energy so you aren't wasting valuable time and resources.

MAR 14 FULL MOON IN VIRGO (2:55AM) (TOTAL LUNAR ECLIPSE; 23°57')

Embrace the clean girl aesthetic today, as the year's only full moon in Virgo—a total lunar eclipse—scrubs away any resistance to taking great care of yourself. This is the first eclipse in discerning Virgo since September 2016, so get ready for an unflinching life edit. If you've been slipping on healthy habits over the winter or slacking at work, you could get a stern wakeup call over the next two weeks. Since eclipses tend to reveal things that are hiding in the shadows, you may be surprised to mildly shocked by what you discover. Before things spiral out any further, lean into these meticulous moonbeams and straighten up your act. General rule: As you implement new routines, try to keep them simple and manageable. Because this eclipse is opposed by minimalist Saturn and hazy Neptune, the last thing you want to do is set yourself up for failure by over-complexifying your goals. Lean into technology for support with anything that truly is complicated. Is there an app for that? With wizardly Uranus trading friendly fire with the eclipse, an AI companion could lend an incredible assist, especially with Virgoan duties like progress-tracking and scheduling.

MAR 15–APR 7 MERCURY RETROGRADE IN ARIES AND PISCES

Brace for impact! Mercury darts into its first retrograde of 2025, muddling communication and throwing a wrench into neatly ordered plans. From March 15 to 29, the messenger planet reverses course in the fiery sign of the Ram, sparking a period of heated communications and hasty decisions. Tempers will flare as words fly without thought. Go easy on the smack-talking and careful not to start any needless rivalries. Aries inspires quick action, but retrograde demands caution. It may be necessary to pump the brakes on projects that require a more aggressive approach. Fine-tune personal goals and actions, ensuring they truly align with your ambitions. When Mercury reverses into Pisces on March 29, you can access a deep level of creativity and divine inspiration that supports rapid growth once the retrograde ends on April 7. Patience and precision are your allies now, so adjust your sails accordingly.

MAR 19 SUN-NEPTUNE MEETUP

The Sun and Neptune come together in ethereal Pisces, turning the world into an enchanted forest for the day. Under this once-per-year spell, you can readily access—and manifest—dreams that have been buried in your psyche. Find time to step back from the noise and do some creative visualization along with some spiritual reflection. Wherever possible, reshuffle your schedule to prioritize projects that can be done while in "flow state." This is a day to lead with vision and let practicalities take a backseat.

MAR 20–APR 19 SUN IN ARIES (5:01AM; SPRING EQUINOX)

Happy Astrological New Year! The spring equinox marks the start of Aries season each year, refreshing our cosmic calendar in Tropical (Western) astrology. As the Sun catapults into this passionate, adventurous zodiac sign, it's no wonder we all feel too restless to be cooped up indoors. Don't think twice. Grab a jacket, then get outside for springtime bike rides and pickleball dates. Dial up the excitement in your life and love affairs by pushing the envelope a little. 'Tis the season for artfully mismatched patterns and shameless PDA. But keep a steady hand: Aries' fiery spirit can ignite people's competitive and self-centered sides. Set your sights on your ambitions, but make sure to share the glory with the people who help you rise to the top. With both Mercury and Venus retrograde  in Aries this cycle, navigating this season comes with its challenges. Keep selfish tendencies in check and curb your impatience, ensuring you don't burn out before you achieve your fullest shine.

MAR 22

WANING QUARTER MOON IN SAGITTARIUS (7:29AM)

Enough deliberating, it's time to take charge. Today's waning quarter moon in commanding Capricorn sharpens your focus on long-term goals and ushers in a refreshing wave of prodcutivity. Last week's total lunar eclipse in Virgo performed a "life audit" on us all and may have illuminated a few tough, but unavoidable, facts. If you haven't quite gotten around to dealing with matters yet, consider this quarter moon your cue to take the reins. In wise, pragmatic Capricorn, this lunar lift advises you to move beyond the binary of right versus wrong. Focus on solutions and figure out what you can improve going forward. A solid plan could emerge today, perhaps one that involves hiring experts or reaching out to a mentor figure.

SUN-VENUS RETROGRADE MEETUP

It's a pivotal moment for love as the Sun and Venus retrograde converge in Aries, marking an inferior conjunction (and cazimi) that occurs once every 584 days during the mid-phase of every Venus retrograde cycle. Much like a new moon, you can think of this as a 'new Venus'—a time to reset your romantic narratives as if the sky has gone dark and the slate is wiped clean. Consider celebrating this moment by setting up a love altar adorned with symbols of your ideal romance or releasing past grievances through a burning ritual. Starting today, Venus disappears from the evening skies, reemerging as a brilliant morning star within a week, heralding a new dawn for love and beauty. Using this metaphorically, what would you like to put to bed when it comes to love? And, uh, who might you finally want to lure INTO your bed? Reflect and write it down, so your vision of love can rise strong and clear after Venus turns direct again on April 7. Until then, keep your mind wide open to possibilities as you parse through what (and possibly who) should stay and what or who should go.

MAR 24 SUN-MERCURY RETROGRADE MEETUP

Can you verify that data? The Aries Sun syncs up with Mercury retrograde, shining a light on inconsistencies and flawed thinking. If you plan to challenge anyone's assertions, bring the receipts, proof, timelines and screenshots—whatever it takes to make it an open-and-shut case. Without ample evidence, you could set yourself up for backlash. If you're sharing ideas, open the floor for questions. Allow people to voice any objections and if you can't address them immediately, don't attempt to fudge it. Better to say, "Let me get back to you on that" than to risk getting a reputation as an unreliable source of truth.

MAR 27

VENUS RETROGRADE IN PISCES (MAR 27–APR 12)

What are your relationship do's and don'ts? As retrograde Venus slides back from assertive Aries into boundary-challenged Pisces, you might need to tape them to your mirror for a firm, daily reminder. Old, counterproductive habits could creep back in between now and April 12, such as making sacrifices to "earn" love or ignoring a date's glaring red flags. Even in healthy relationships, it's important to know where your limits lie so you can avoid poisoning the vibe with resentment. If the walls around your heart resemble the gates of King's Landing, this retrograde could be your cue to soften a little. At the very least, begin to process unresolved emotions so you can find closure. Now for the good news. While Venus slogged through an unhappy detriment (weakened position) in Aries, the love planet absolutely thrives in Pisces, which is its exalted place in the zodiac. Even while retrograde, a Venus-in-

Pisces cycle elicits empathy among partners and rekindles soul connections. With the right person, you may practically read each other's minds now.

VENUS RETROGRADE-NEPTUNE MEETUP #2 OF 3

Shall we meet again? Die-hard romantics Venus and Neptune unite for the second of three dances this year. This time they unite in Pisces, turning up the dials on fairy-tale romance. This time around there's a plot twist: Venus is retrograde, cast in the role of Sleeping Beauty instead of the eager seductress. Under this spell, it's easy to miss someone's bids for attention or take a generous partner for granted. With boundaries practically invisible today, you could easily overstep someone's limits without realizing it. Take extra precaution and get consent before making any moves, whether they involve physical touch or doling out well-meaning advice to a struggling friend. Under this tender transit, they may be too triggered to hear it.

MAR 29

NEW MOON IN ARIES (6:58AM; SUPERMOON) (PARTIAL SOLAR ECLIPSE; 9°00')

Wipe the slate clean! Today's new moon in Aries, the only one in 2025, is no ordinary fresh start. It's also a supermoon and a partial solar eclipse, pouring rocket fuel into your tanks and charging up your ventures with unexpected momentum. That's not all! This new moon sits at a friendly angle to expansive Jupiter and powerhouse Pluto. Efforts you initiate today could send you soaring onto the global stage and attract VIP-level support. Even though Mercury and Venus are retrograde, you may have to leap into a groundbreaking project with both feet. (Just make sure you set up a safety net.) Get ready for rapid developments and surprising twists along the way, some that may propel you to leave behind parts of your former self. Over the next six months, leading up to the Aries full moon, ask yourself: How can I transform my passions into tangible outcomes? This is a rare opportunity to harness this fiery energy and shape your future. Make it count!

MERCURY RETROGRADE IN PISCES (MAR 29–APR 7)

Mercury retrograde slips back from in-your-face Aries to elusive Pisces, throwing interactions into deeper confusion. Take nothing at face value for the next ten days, not even people's expressions of delight or approval. No matter how much you want situations to work out, you can't force them now. One thing spiritual Pisces understands is that "what's meant to be, will be." In the meanwhile, observe what's going on inside of you. How do you deal with waiting for an answer: Are you anxious? Do you start making up disempowering stories about what people are thinking? Do you want to quit and move on rather than face the possibility of "rejection"? Let all feelings arise without interacting with them. They are not wrong or right; they simply "are." There is true power in being able to hold the space of the unknown. In that mystical, in-between state, miraculous solutions can arise. Just plan on taking a lot of long, deep breaths.

MERCURY RETROGRADE-NEPTUNE MEETUP

Today, Mercury do-si-do's with another planet. This time it's spiritual, numinous Neptune that's connecting to the cosmic messenger for the second of three confabs. With Mercury retrograde for this round, the fog is thick and facts may be imperceptible. Rather than swim upstream, go with the flow! It's an ideal day to color outside the lines or maybe just forget the lines altogether. As you suspend your judgment (and maybe your grip on what is rational), you could dream up the sorts of ideas that, as Pisces Steve Jobs said, "Put a ding in the universe."

MAR 27-DEC 20 BLACK MOON LILITH IN SCORPIO

Passion, power, erotic liberation! Get ready to plunge into an explicit (and potentially NSFW) exploration of your sexuality as Black Moon Lilith moves out of justice-oriented Libra and into Scorpio's seductive cauldron. Lilith is not a planet, but a point in the sky—a void between the Earth and moon that astrologers have come to associate with the scorned, then empowered, feminine aspect of our personalities. This nine-month transit sparks new conversations around sexual liberation and intimacy, encouraging society to break down stigmas and own the full spectrum of our emotions. Since Scorpio rules the reproductive organs, Lilith could evoke a rage-fueled uprising against restrictive laws around abortion, IVF and reproductive freedom for women.

MAR 30-OCT 22 NEPTUNE IN ARIES

Realm shift! Fantasy agent Neptune is switching signs, leaving its home sign of Pisces for the first time since April 4, 2011. From plant medicine ceremonies to astrology and manifestation practices to the lightning-fast transfer of data, the past fourteen years have melted our boundaries between the visible and invisible universe. What on earth could be next? Buckle up as the boundary-dissolving planet takes a wild, hoverboard ride through pioneering Aries for the next seven months—a preview of a longer tour that picks back up again from January 26, 2026-March 23, 2039. This is a huge deal! To put a finer point on it, the last time Neptune trekked through Aries was 1862 to 1875, a time that brought a newly industrialized economy (hello, city life) and the U.S. Civil War. Neptune is the planet of compassion while Aries is on a nonstop combat mission. We may all have to toughen up and develop some grit to make it through this tenuous transition.

April

4

APRIL
Moon Phase Calendar

SUN	MON	TUE	WED	THU	FRI	SAT
		1 ♉ ♊ 4:26PM	**2** ♊	**3** ♊ ♋ 6:50PM	**4** ♋ 2nd Quarter	**5** ♋
6 ♋ ♌ 12:34AM	**7** ♌	**8** ♌ ♍ 9:40AM	**9** ♍	**10** ♍ ♎ 9:12PM	**11** ♎	**12** ♎ Full Moon 8:22PM
13 ♎ ♏ 9:54AM	**14** ♏	**15** ♏ ♐ 10:37PM	**16** ♐	**17** ♐	**18** ♐ ♑ 10:12AM	**19** ♑
20 ♑ → ♒ 7:22PM ♒ 4th Quarter	**21** ♒	**22** ♒	**23** ♒ ♓ 1:07AM	**24** ♓	**25** ♓ ♈ 3:24AM	**26** ♈
27 ♈ → ♉ 3:17AM ♉ New Moon 3:31PM	**28** ♉	**29** ♉ ♊ 2:34AM	**30** ♊			

Times listed are Eastern US Time Zone

KEY

♈	ARIES	♌	LEO	♐	SAGITTARIUS
♉	TAURUS	♍	VIRGO	♑	CAPRICORN
♊	GEMINI	♎	LIBRA	♒	AQUARIUS
♋	CANCER	♏	SCORPIO	♓	PISCES

FM FULL MOON
NM NEW MOON
LE LUNAR ECLIPSE
SE SOLAR ECLIPSE

APRIL 12, 8:22PM

full moon in
Libra (23°20')

LIBRA FULL MOON CRYSTAL

ROSE QUARTZ

This pale pink crystal is the stone of pure love, radiating the compassion and romance of Libra. Said to be beneficial for heart healing and fertility, Rose Quartz carries goddess energy and can be used for inspiration and protection.

LIBRA FULL MOON = CELEBRATE!

The power of partnerships and synergistic connections

Dressing up and socializing

Transcendent music and the arts

Peaceful moments of serenity

The parts of your life that are in beautiful balance

new moon in Taurus (7°47′)

TAURUS NEW MOON CRYSTAL

BLUE LACE AGATE

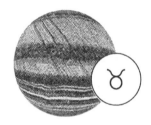

This soothing, soft blue stone helps you relax and tap into a deep inner calm. Blue Lace Agate unblocks the Taurus-ruled throat chakra so you can speak your truth and share what's valuable to you.

TAURUS NEW MOON = FOCUS

Define your values

Set up healthy and rewarding routines

Enjoy arts and culture

Simplify complexities

Budget

Get out in nature

April 2025

Longitude & Retrograde Ephemeris [00:00 UT]

Day	Sid.time	☉	☽	+12h☽	☿	♀	♂	♃	♄	♅	♆	♇	☊	☊	⚸	⚷	Day
1 Tu	12:38:26	♈11°30'52	♉17°23'33	♉24°49'28	℞ 28°44	℞ 27°31	♋23°36	♊15°58	♓24°29	♉24°45	♈00°03	♒03°33	℞ 26°43	℞ 27°22	♏00°33	♈22°17	**1** Tu
2 We	12:42:22	♈12°30'06	♊02°11'05	♊09°27'14	♓28°12	♓27°04	♋23°55	♊16°08	♓24°36	♉24°48	♈00°05	♒03°34	♓26°40	♓27°20	♏00°39	♈22°21	**2** We
3 Th	12:46:19	♈13°29'18	♊16°37'53	♊23°42'12	♓27°44	♓26°39	♋24°15	♊16°17	♓24°43	♉24°50	♈00°07	♒03°35	♓26°37	♓27°18	♏00°46	♈22°25	**3** Th
4 Fr	12:50:16	♈14°28'27	♋00°40'29	♋07°32'14	♓27°22	♓26°16	♋24°36	♊16°27	♓24°50	♉24°53	♈00°10	♒03°35	♓26°34	♓27°17	♏00°53	♈22°28	**4** Fr
5 Sa	12:54:12	♈15°27'33	♋14°17'59	♋20°57'31	♓27°06	♓25°56	♋24°57	♊16°36	♓24°57	♉24°56	♈00°12	♒03°36	♓26°31	♓27°17	♏00°59	♈22°32	**5** Sa
6 Su	12:58:09	♈16°26'38	♋27°31'32	♌03°59'59	♓26°55	♓25°37	♋25°18	♊16°46	♓25°05	♉24°59	♈00°14	♒03°37	♓26°28	D 27°17	♏01°06	♈22°35	**6** Su
7 Mo	13:02:05	♈17°25'40	♌10°23'39	♌16°42'35	♓26°50	♓25°21	♋25°40	♊16°56	♓25°12	♉25°02	♈00°16	♒03°38	♓26°24	♓27°18	♏01°13	♈22°39	**7** Mo
8 Tu	13:06:02	♈18°24'39	♌22°57'36	♌29°08'44	Ds 26°50	♓25°08	♋26°01	♊17°06	♓25°19	♉25°05	♈00°18	♒03°39	♓26°21	♓27°20	♏01°19	♈22°42	**8** Tu
9 We	13:09:58	♈19°23'37	♍05°16'50	♍11°21'55	♓26°55	♓24°57	♋26°23	♊17°16	♓25°26	♉25°08	♈00°21	♒03°39	♓26°18	♓27°21	♏01°26	♈22°46	**9** We
10 Th	13:13:55	♈20°22'32	♍17°24'45	♍23°25'19	♓27°06	♓24°48	♋26°46	♊17°26	♓25°33	♉25°11	♈00°23	♒03°40	♓26°15	♓27°22	♏01°33	♈22°49	**10** Th
11 Fr	13:17:51	♈21°21'25	♍29°24'22	♎05°21'50	♓27°22	♓24°42	♋27°09	♊17°37	♓25°40	♉25°14	♈00°25	♒03°41	♓26°12	℞ 27°23	♏01°39	♈22°53	**11** Fr
12 Sa	13:21:48	♈22°20'16	♎11°18'23	♎17°13'56	♓27°42	♓24°38	♋27°32	♊17°47	♓25°47	♉25°17	♈00°27	♒03°41	♓26°08	♓27°22	♏01°46	♈22°57	**12** Sa
13 Su	13:25:45	♈23°19'05	♎23°09'07	♎29°03'48	♓28°08	♓24°37	♋27°55	♊17°58	♓25°53	♉25°20	♈00°29	♒03°42	♓26°05	♓27°20	♏01°53	♈23°00	**13** Su
14 Mo	13:29:41	♈24°17'52	♏04°58'38	♏10°53'27	♓28°37	D 24°38	♋28°18	♊18°08	♓26°00	♉25°23	♈00°31	♒03°43	♓26°02	♓27°16	♏01°59	♈23°04	**14** Mo
15 Tu	13:33:38	♈25°16'37	♏16°48'54	♏22°44'52	♓29°11	♓24°42	♋28°42	♊18°19	♓26°07	♉25°26	♈00°33	♒03°43	♓25°59	♓27°12	♏02°06	♈23°07	**15** Tu
16 We	13:37:34	♈26°15'20	♏28°41'58	♐04°40'09	♓29°49	♓24°47	♋29°06	♊18°30	♓26°14	♉25°29	♈00°36	♒03°44	♓25°56	♓27°07	♏02°13	♈23°11	**16** We
17 Th	13:41:31	♈27°14'02	♐10°40'05	♐16°41'44	♈00°30	♓24°55	♋29°30	♊18°41	♓26°21	♉25°32	♈00°38	♒03°44	♓25°53	♓27°02	♏02°19	♈23°14	**17** Th
18 Fr	13:45:27	♈28°12'41	♐22°45'51	♐28°52'26	♈01°16	♓25°05	♋29°55	♊18°52	♓26°27	♉25°36	♈00°40	♒03°45	♓25°49	♓26°57	♏02°26	♈23°18	**18** Fr
19 Sa	13:49:24	♈29°11'20	♑05°02'16	♑11°15'25	♈02°04	♓25°18	♌00°20	♊19°03	♓26°34	♉25°39	♈00°42	♒03°45	♓25°46	♓26°53	♏02°33	♈23°22	**19** Sa
20 Su	13:53:20	♉00°09'56	♑17°32'43	♑23°54'14	♈02°56	♓25°32	♌00°45	♊19°14	♓26°41	♉25°42	♈00°44	♒03°46	♓25°43	♓26°51	♏02°39	♈23°25	**20** Su
21 Mo	13:57:17	♉01°08'30	♒00°20'49	♒06°52'29	♈03°51	♓25°49	♌01°10	♊19°25	♓26°47	♉25°45	♈00°46	♒03°46	♓25°40	♓26°50	♏02°46	♈23°29	**21** Mo
22 Tu	14:01:14	♉02°07'03	♒13°30'05	♒20°13'32	♈04°50	♓26°07	♌01°36	♊19°36	♓26°54	♉25°49	♈00°48	♒03°46	♓25°37	D 26°51	♏02°53	♈23°32	**22** Tu
23 We	14:05:10	♉03°05'35	♒27°03'32	♓03°59'52	♈05°51	♓26°27	♌02°01	♊19°48	♓27°00	♉25°52	♈00°50	♒03°47	♓25°33	♓26°52	♏02°59	♈23°36	**23** We
24 Th	14:09:07	♉04°04'04	♓11°03'01	♓18°12'28	♈06°54	♓26°49	♌02°27	♊19°59	♓27°07	♉25°55	♈00°52	♒03°47	♓25°30	♓26°53	♏03°06	♈23°39	**24** Th
25 Fr	14:13:03	♉05°02'33	♓25°28'25	♈02°50'00	♈08°01	♓27°13	♌02°54	♊20°11	♓27°13	♉25°58	♈00°54	♒03°47	♓25°27	♓26°54	♏03°13	♈23°43	**25** Fr
26 Sa	14:16:60	♉06°00'59	♈10°17'02	♈17°48'15	♈09°10	♓27°38	♌03°20	♊20°22	♓27°19	♉26°02	♈00°56	♒03°48	♓25°24	℞ 26°53	♏03°19	♈23°46	**26** Sa
27 Su	14:20:56	♉06°59'24	♈25°23'06	♉02°59'57	D 10°21	♓28°06	♌03°47	♊20°34	♓27°26	♉26°05	♈00°58	♒03°48	♓25°21	♓26°51	♏03°26	♈23°50	**27** Su
28 Mo	14:24:53	♉07°57'47	♉10°38'02	♉18°15'32	♈11°35	♓28°34	♌04°13	♊20°46	♓27°32	♉26°08	♈01°00	♒03°48	♓25°18	♓26°47	♏03°33	♈23°53	**28** Mo
29 Tu	14:28:49	♉08°56'08	♉25°51'34	♊03°24'23	♈12°51	♓29°04	♌04°40	♊20°58	♓27°38	♉26°12	♈01°02	♒03°48	♓25°14	♓26°41	♏03°40	♈23°57	**29** Tu
30 We	14:32:46	♉09°54'27	♊10°53'16	♊18°16'44	♈14°10	♓29°36	♌05°08	♊21°10	♓27°44	♉26°15	♈01°03	♒03°48	♓25°11	♓26°34	♏03°46	♈24°00	**30** We
Δ Delta	01:54:20	28°23'34"	383°29'42"	383°27'15"	-15°25'	2°04'	11°32'	5°11'	3°15'	1°30'	1°00'	0°15'	-1°32'	-0°47'	3°13'	1°42'	**Delta**

Ephemeris tables and data provided by **Astro-Seek.com.** All times in UTC.

APRIL
MONTHLY HOTSPOTS

APR 4

MARS-SATURN TRINE

With Mars in Cancer joining forces with Saturn in Pisces, your intuition and emotional depth are your secret weapons. Mars in Cancer encourages you to protect what you cherish and advance with care, while Saturn in Pisces adds a layer of spiritual wisdom, urging you to trust your instincts. This cosmic combo allows you to tap into the subtle undercurrents of any situation. Instead of rushing forward, feel your way through the pros and cons, letting your intuition guide your next steps. Take a calculated risk that aligns with your emotional truth—you'll know when the timing feels just right.

WAXING QUARTER MOON IN CANCER (10:14PM)

Feeling like your bedroom is more of a snore than a sanctuary? Tired of cooking up the same old soups and roasted root veggies? It's time to add some zest to your nest! The waxing quarter moon in cozy Cancer is here to awaken your inner Nate Berkus and inspire a mini home makeover. But before you start knocking down walls, remember that this lunar phase is too brief for major renovations. Instead, think small but impactful—like a fresh coat of paint, rearranging your living room, or tackling that overdue closet clean-out. If you're on the hunt for a new home, start scouring Zillow or exploring neighborhoods that catch your eye. Pay attention to the amenities and attractions that align with your optimal lifestyle. With la luna lighting the way, you might just stumble upon a listing that ticks all your boxes.

APR 6 VENUS-MARS TRINE #2 OF 2

Set aside those attachment fears and open yourself up to deeper intimacy today, as the love planets canoodle in sensual water signs. This is their second of three nostalgic trines while Mars is in Cancer and Venus is in Pisces, but there's a twist. When they last met this way on January 25, Mars was retrograde, which could have churned up some self-protective defenses. This time around it's Venus who's on a reverse commute, which may obscure the clear signals that you're attempting to send out. A surefire recipe for romantic success? Lean into nostalgia. Scroll through old photos, get tickets to see a band you've both always loved. If time permits, slip off for a couple nights to a place where you can both let your hair down and relax. If you're single and looking, you might feel brave enough to shoot your shot with a crush that never got off the ground.

APR 7

VENUS-SATURN MEETUP #2 OF 3

For the second time this year, Venus falls under Saturn's stern command which could turn love into serious business. With the planet of romance in reverse, you may need to review agreements before you can launch ahead with any dating strategies or relationship goals. Under this strained alignment, old wounds may be scratched, especially since both planets are in sacrificial Pisces. You could find yourself hashing out that same old argument that was never fully resolved. Before you trot out a laundry list of complaints (including who's done more of the laundry), take a moment to find gratitude for the things that are actually going right between you. We're not suggesting you overlook your grievances. Just remember that the person standing in front of you, whether a lover or a friend, is someone you generally adore, not a monster trying to dump their responsibilities on you.

MERCURY RETROGRADE ENDS

After a choppy three weeks, messenger Mercury wakes up from its befuddling three-week retrograde and powers forward through intuitive Pisces until April 16. With the messenger planet backstroking through the Fish's murky waters since March 29, emotions may have overtaken everyone's better senses—and let's not even talk about the rage cleaning you did while it was backing up through Aries from March 15 to 29. If you found yourself ugly crying, whether "inexplicably" or for a damn good reason, hopefully those tears were healing. But enough of this three-hanky drama! With Mercury back on track, the chronic misunderstandings that disrupted your early spring can pave the way to healing reconciliations. Contracts that were held up in red tape could finally move into the negotiation (and signing!) phase. But don't lose the important message Mercury retrograde taught about the pitfalls of skimming the surface instead of finding out what lies beneath. Even if you learned this in a tough love kind of way, you can spring forward with a new resolve to slow down, get every question answered and read the fine print.

APR 12

FULL MOON IN LIBRA (8:22PM; 23°20')

Birds of a feather might just stay together forever under the light of today's full moon in Libra, the sign of partnerships. If you're still searching for your perfect plus-one, cast a wider net. This full moon gets a buddy pass from global Jupiter (in Gemini), which could magnetize interest from a far-flung locale. Since Jupiter is the galactic gambler, you might as well make "nothing ventured, nothing gained" your mantra. Slide into the DMs of that deejay in Berlin who you've been following for months or invite your "will they, won't they" crush out on a proper Saturday night date. If you've been at odds with your person, these diplomatic moonbeams set the stage for a productive dialogue. The only catch? Feisty Mars in Cancer is squaring la luna, so go in softly to avoid riling up anyone's defense mechanisms or accidentally triggering their inner eight-year-old brat. Need to rebalance the load with a collaborator? Fair-minded Libra reminds us that an "even split" is different for everyone. Divvy up duties in a way that feels manageable for both of you and consider outsourcing things that you both hate doing.

VENUS RETROGRADE ENDS

Cupid is back on the scene, bearing a freshly sharpened quiver of arrows. And after six weeks of misfires and mojo-dulling vibes, it's about damn time. Blame the delayed spring fever on romantic Venus who went retrograde on March 1. Here's hoping you made it out relatively unscathed, free from bad romances, bad haircuts and any other bad decisions in the interpersonal realm. As Venus corrects course today—and powers forward through poetic Pisces until April 30—get ready for a romantic uprising. Pull your most theatrical pieces to the front of your closet, especially those amazing shoes you tucked away for the winter. All the world's a fantasy novel while Venus floats through the sign of the spring-fevered Fish. While you're at it, spice up your social life with a spiritual element. A little woo goes a long way when it comes to forming lasting bonds.

APRIL 16-MAY 10 MERCURY IN ARIES

Fear not, you haven't lost your edge! Today, spitfire Mercury swings back into Aries for its second pass, making up for the time it lost during its recent retrograde. While Mercury backtracked through fiery Aries from March 15 to 29, it prompted deep self-reflection and sparked some seriously stormy misunderstandings. Did you snap at someone close or worse, drag them to mutual friends? It's time to drop the excuses. Even if they did push all your buttons, the retrograde may have intensified your reactions. But with Mercury now moving direct, the fog lifts, and clarity returns. Capitalize on the next few weeks to smooth things over and try your absolute hardest to make amends. It's time to clear the air and move forward, one way or another.

APR 17 MERCURY-NEPTUNE MEETUP

Okay, so this is awkward. For the first time since the late 1800s, intellectual Mercury teams up with subliminal Neptune in the abrasive field of Aries. Problems can be solved with both logic and intuition today, so don't ignore either input stream. Still, you may be hard-pressed to access the levels of sensitivity and compassion that you tapped so easily last month, when these planets teamed up in Pisces. A desire to experiment with new methodologies could overrun your ability to read the room. Slow down so you don't steamroll people who aren't up to speed on the latest and greatest technology. You may have to explain (and re-explain) those novel concepts before you get anyone on board for a test run.

APRIL 18-JUNE 17 MARS IN LEO

Palace intrigue heats up again, as red-hot Mars struts back into Leo, escalating drama and elevating luxury. What's the fun of having all the toys unless you have people to play with? With Mars in this magnanimous realm, sharing is caring and spoiling the ones you love is even better. Life feels like a giant talent show now, with everyone vying for the trophy. Warning! Competition can get fierce during this transit, and if you aren't careful, it could devolve into a full-on game of thrones. Rather than go "House of Lannister" on potential allies, make an effort to recognize and uplift others. Even simple acts like remixing someone's post on social media can work wonders, making them feel valued and visible. No matter your relationship status, invite in a romantic renaissance by developing a more playful spirit. How can you pump up the passion with your love interest or get more direct results from digital dating? Doing the same thing over and over will only yield expected results. Daring Mars wants you to color outside those lines and give a new tactic a try.

APR 19

MARS-NEPTUNE TRINE

Mind blown! Another groundbreaking transit shakes up the month. For the first time since the 1800s, flamboyant Mars in Leo fistbumps dreamweaver Neptune in Aries, turning the world into an episode of Drag Race. "To thine own self be true" is the world's mantra while these boundary bashing and blurring planets link arms. There may be some highly entertaining ideas bandied about, coupled with stunning displays of ego. (Wow. Just. Wow.) Be mindful about who you hoist onto a pedestal. Loudmouthed "leaders" could be vaulted into power, creating chaos with their charismatic sideshows. While you may feel like pushing the envelope, think carefully before you post anything agitating under this celestial starmap. Is the controversy worth it? One impulsive rant or offensive photo could get you canceled or start a war in your personal life.

SUN IN TAURUS (3:56PM) (APR 19-MAY 20)

IWelcome to Taurus season! After four dynamic weeks of Aries' fiery energy, it's time to transition from fire to earth, focusing on stability and productivity. The passionate Aries spark has ignited your drive, and now Taurus, the steadfast Bull, is here to help you channel that energy into achieving your goals. It's time to refine those raw ideas and set the wheels in motion. Reminder! Taurus isn't all work and no play; this sign also has a taste for the finer things. So, while you're busy moving the needle, don't forget to sprinkle some luxury into your routine. The beauty of Taurus season is finding that balance between indulgence and practicality. Enjoying life's luxuries doesn't have to lead to extravagant spending. Take pleasure in nature, museum hop, or rediscover treasures in your own wardrobe. And if you're feeling inclined to splurge on a special treat, shop around and find the best deal you can.

APR 20

WANING QUARTER MOON IN AQUARIUS (9:35PM)

Last week's full moon in Libra got us all passionately fired up about partnerships. But in your eagerness to claim "two" as your magic number, did you get a little too zealous, even obsessive? Today's quarter moon in coolly objective Aquarius redirects your tunnel vision and helps you see things from a more levelheaded perspective. Take a 30,000-foot view of this connection and honestly weigh the potential pros and cons. You might have a surprising realization: You're trying to fit the relationship (or potential relationship) into the wrong box. Don't impose limits on the future by trying to force things to go a certain way. When you let go of control, you allow unexpected magic to flow in.

SUN-MARS SQUARE

Watch for power struggles today as the stalwart Taurus Sun clashes with headstrong Mars in Leo. A snarky retort could accidentally come across as a confrontation or insult. Big egos are at play, but beware the temptation to match someone's bloviating with your own simulated swagger. It's crucial to keep a level head and choose diplomacy over drama. Remember, asserting your viewpoint doesn't require overpowering the conversation. Finding common ground might be challenging, but it's the key to maintaining peace and making progress.

APR 23 SUN-PLUTO SQUARE

Who's on top? During this intense biannual face-off between domineering Pluto and the ego-driven Sun, emotions can run high. It's natural to feel upset if you sense a power struggle brewing, but beware of knee-jerk reactions. Today, they're likely to do more harm than good. If standing up to a bully, demonstrate strength by maintaining your composure. But heed this caution: With both planets anchored in stubborn fixed signs (Pluto's in Aquarius and the Sun is in Taurus), no one will be in the mood to compromise. If a stalemate ensues and no one's willing to give even an inch, it might be wise to call a time-out and revisit the issue on another day.

APR 24 VENUS-SATURN MEETUP #3 OF 3

Quit playing games with their hearts! Harmonizer Venus duets with no-nonsense Saturn for the third and final time this year. As they merge in gullible Pisces, it's time to stop making excuses and blow the whistle on the breadcrumbers, ghosters and garden variety players. Because Venus was retrograde on their last conjunction (April 7), a few deceptive types may have slid past your radar. Today, it becomes glaringly obvious who is worthy of your precious time and who needs to be kicked off the island. Creative compromises could emerge for couples who've been struggling to find equanimity. Don't soft-pedal issues that need to be brought out into the open. Time is precious, and you don't want to waste your life pining for someone who "isn't ready" to move in your desired direction, and may never be!

APR 26 MARS-PLUTO OPPOSITION

Tempers, egos, and mind games, oh my! When fiery Mars in regal Leo opposes power-hungry Pluto in revolutionary Aquarius, the atmosphere could crackle with tension, teetering on the edge of a full-blown showdown. You might unwittingly wander into a psychological battlefield, where it's all too easy to snap and lose your cool. Staying composed won't just be your greatest asset today—it'll also be your biggest challenge. Keep your wits about you and don't take the bait, no matter how tempting it may be to react.

APR 27 NEW MOON IN TAURUS (3:31PM; 7°47'; SUPERMOON)

Practical magic is in the air—no wand needed! Thanks to a potent supermoon in Taurus, you'll easily strike a balance between the sensual and the sensible. If life has felt unstable, this is your opportunity to reground yourself. Start by simplifying: Break down complex plans back to basics, draft blueprints, and streamline systems. To make sure all new developments are welcome, minimize uncertainties in crucial areas like time, money, and relationships. Taurus encourages a slow, steady approach to achieving your goals without sacrificing beauty or quality. Embrace eco-friendly and upcycled choices, supporting brands that respect our planet. Keeping a level head may take a little effort today, since the new moon gets caught in a three-way tug-of-war (a T-square) with stormy Pluto in Aquarius and feisty Mars in Leo. As you map out your trajectory, don't get caught up in the "compare and despair" trap with the cool kids. The only approval ratings that matter today are your own.

APR 30-JUN 6 VENUS IN ARIES

Let's see some swag! As magnetic Venus zips back into fiery and self-determined Aries for the second time this year, you'll have ample opportunities to right any wrongs that disrupted your love life during the spring Venus retrograde. The first step might be this: reclaiming your self-sovereignty in relationships that have grown too close for comfort. While Venus was melting into a puddle of goo in Pisces, codependence may have crept into the healthiest bonds. Or maybe the cozy vibes have dulled the once-sexy sparks. Harness the autonomous energy of Aries and declare the next four weeks a personal reclamation. Get obsessed with a hobby and guard your "me time" like a hawk. The person who's been taking you for granted could swiftly wake up and realize your value.

May

MAY
Moon Phase Calendar

SUN	MON	TUE	WED	THU	FRI	SAT
				1 ♊ 3:23AM	**2** ♋	**3** ♋ ♌ 7:29AM
4 ♌ 2nd Quarter	**5** ♌ ♍ 3:40PM	**6** ♍	**7** ♍	**8** ♍ ♎ 3:06AM	**9** ♎	**10** ♎ ♏ 3:58PM
11 ♏	**12** ♏ Full Moon 12:56PM	**13** ♏ ♐ 4:35AM	**14** ♐	**15** ♐ ♑ 3:58PM	**16** ♑	**17** ♑
18 ♑ ♒ 1:29AM	**19** ♒	**20** ♒ 4th Quarter ♓ 8:28AM	**21** ♓	**22** ♓ ♈ 12:26PM	**23** ♈	**24** ♈ ♉ 1:38PM
25 ♉	**26** ♉→♊ 1:21PM ♊ New Moon 11:02PM	**27** ♊	**28** ♊ ♋ 1:33PM	**29** ♋	**30** ♋ ♌ 4:17PM	**31** ♌

Times listed are Eastern US Time Zone

KEY

♈ ARIES	♌ LEO	♐ SAGITTARIUS	**FM**	FULL MOON
♉ TAURUS	♍ VIRGO	♑ CAPRICORN	**NM**	NEW MOON
♊ GEMINI	♎ LIBRA	♒ AQUARIUS	**LE**	LUNAR ECLIPSE
♋ CANCER	♏ SCORPIO	♓ PISCES	**SE**	SOLAR ECLIPSE

MAY 12, 12:56PM
full moon in
Scorpio (22°13')

SCORPIO FULL MOON CRYSTAL

HEMATITE

This silvery stone is a great protection while under the spell of empathic, intuitive Scorpio. Hematite reflects and deflects any negative energy so you don't absorb it. With its high iron content, it also helps circulate Scorpio-ruled blood and wake you up for springtime.

SCORPIO FULL MOON = CELEBRATE!

Your loyal and caring spirit

Intense exchanges

The sexiest parts of yourself

The ways you've transformed your struggles into gold

True friendship

Resourcefulness and raw creative expression

Supermoon

MAY 26, 11:02PM

new moon in Gemini (6°06')

GEMINI NEW MOON CRYSTAL

PHANTOM QUARTZ

Shift your Gemini-ruled mindset with this protective, empowering stone. Phantom Quartz facilitates unexpected breakthroughs and promotes personal growth.

GEMINI NEW MOON = FOCUS

Sharpen your communication style

Write and make media

Become active in your local community

Socialize with new people

Flirt and joke!

Pair up on short-term collaborations

May 2025

Day	Sid.time	☉	☽	+12h☽	☿	♀	♂	♃	♄	♅	♆	♇	☊	☊	⚸	⚷	Day
1 Th	14:36:43	♉10°52′45	♊25°34′24	♋02°45′12	♈15°30	♈00°09	♌05°35	♊21°22	♓27°50	♉26°19	♈01°05	♒03°48	℞ 25°08	℞ 26°28	♏03°53	♈24°04	**1** Th
2 Fr	14:40:39	♉11°51′01	♋09°49′09	♋16°45′37	♈16°53	♈00°43	♌06°03	♊21°34	♓27°56	♉26°22	♈01°07	♒03°49	♓25°05	♓26°23	♏04°00	♈24°07	**2** Fr
3 Sa	14:44:36	♉12°49′14	♋23°35′01	♌00°17′03	♈18°18	♈01°19	♌06°31	♊21°46	♓28°02	♉26°25	♈01°09	♒03°49	♓25°02	♓26°19	♏04°06	♈24°11	**3** Sa
4 Su	14:48:32	♉13°47′25	♌06°52′28	♌13°21′13	♈19°45	♈01°56	♌06°58	♊21°58	♓28°08	♉26°29	♈01°11	♒03°49	♓24°59	♓26°18	♏04°13	♈24°14	**4** Su
5 Mo	14:52:29	♉14°45′35	♌19°44′12	♌26°01′35	♈21°14	♈02°33	♌07°27	♊22°10	♓28°14	♉26°32	♈01°12	℞03°49	♓24°55	D 26°17	♏04°20	♈24°18	**5** Mo
6 Tu	14:56:25	♉15°43′42	♍02°14′18	♍08°22′36	♈22°45	♈03°13	♌07°55	♊22°23	♓28°20	♉26°36	♈01°14	♒03°49	♓24°52	♓26°18	♏04°26	♈24°21	**6** Tu
7 We	15:00:22	♉16°41′48	♍14°27′27	♍20°29′03	♈24°18	♈03°53	♌08°23	♊22°35	♓28°26	♉26°39	♈01°16	♒03°49	♓24°49	♓26°20	♏04°33	♈24°24	**7** We
8 Th	15:04:18	♉17°39′51	♍26°28′21	♎02°25′32	♈25°52	♈04°34	♌08°52	♊22°47	♓28°32	♉26°43	♈01°18	♒03°48	♓24°46	℞ 26°20	♏04°40	♈24°28	**8** Th
9 Fr	15:08:15	♉18°37′53	♎08°21′28	♎14°16′14	♈27°29	♈05°16	♌09°21	♊23°00	♓28°37	♉26°46	♈01°19	♒03°48	♓24°43	♓26°19	♏04°46	♈24°31	**9** Fr
10 Sa	15:12:12	♉19°35′53	♎20°10′37	♎26°04′40	♈29°08	♈05°59	♌09°50	♊23°12	♓28°43	♉26°50	♈01°21	♒03°48	♓24°39	♓26°16	♏04°53	♈24°34	**10** Sa
11 Su	15:16:08	♉20°33′51	♏01°59′05	♏07°53′46	♉00°49	♈06°44	♌10°19	♊23°25	♓28°48	♉26°53	♈01°23	♒03°48	♓24°36	♓26°11	♏05°00	♈24°38	**11** Su
12 Mo	15:20:05	♉21°31′48	♏13°49′23	♏19°45′48	♉02°32	♈07°29	♌10°48	♊23°38	♓28°54	♉26°56	♈01°24	♒03°48	♓24°33	♓26°04	♏05°06	♈24°41	**12** Mo
13 Tu	15:24:01	♉22°29′43	♏25°43′34	♐01°42′32	♉04°17	♈08°15	♌11°18	♊23°50	♓28°59	♉27°00	♈01°26	♒03°48	♓24°30	♓25°54	♏05°13	♈24°44	**13** Tu
14 We	15:27:58	♉23°27′36	♐07°43′13	♐13°45′25	♉06°04	♈09°01	♌11°47	♊24°03	♓29°05	♉27°03	♈01°28	♒03°47	♓24°27	♓25°44	♏05°20	♈24°47	**14** We
15 Th	15:31:54	♉24°25′28	♐19°49′41	♐25°55′49	♉07°52	♈09°49	♌12°17	♊24°16	♓29°10	♉27°07	♈01°29	♒03°47	♓24°24	♓25°33	♏05°26	♈24°51	**15** Th
16 Fr	15:35:51	♉25°23′19	♑02°04′23	♑08°15′12	♉09°43	♈10°37	♌12°47	♊24°29	♓29°15	♉27°10	♈01°31	♒03°47	♓24°20	♓25°23	♏05°33	♈24°54	**16** Fr
17 Sa	15:39:47	♉26°21′09	♑14°28′54	♑20°45′20	♉11°36	♈11°26	♌13°17	♊24°42	♓29°20	♉27°14	♈01°32	♒03°47	♓24°17	♓25°14	♏05°40	♈24°57	**17** Sa
18 Su	15:43:44	♉27°18′57	♑27°05′13	♒03°28′26	♉13°31	♈12°16	♌13°47	♊24°55	♓29°25	♉27°17	♈01°34	♒03°46	♓24°14	♓25°08	♏05°46	♈25°00	**18** Su
19 Mo	15:47:41	♉28°16′44	♒09°55′45	♒16°27′04	♉15°28	♈13°07	♌14°17	♊25°07	♓29°30	♉27°21	♈01°35	♒03°46	♓24°11	♓25°04	♏05°53	♈25°03	**19** Mo
20 Tu	15:51:37	♉29°14′30	♒23°03′11	♒29°44′01	♉17°26	♈13°58	♌14°48	♊25°20	♓29°35	♉27°24	♈01°36	♒03°45	♓24°08	♓25°02	♏06°00	♈25°06	**20** Tu
21 We	15:55:34	♊00°12′15	♓06°30′18	♓13°21′52	♉19°27	♈14°50	♌15°18	♊25°34	♓29°40	♉27°28	♈01°38	♒03°45	♓24°05	D 25°02	♏06°06	♈25°09	**21** We
22 Th	15:59:30	♊01°09′59	♓20°19′21	♓27°22′24	♉21°29	♈15°42	♌15°49	♊25°47	♓29°45	♉27°31	♈01°39	♒03°44	♓24°01	♓25°03	♏06°13	♈25°12	**22** Th
23 Fr	16:03:27	♊02°07′41	♈04°31′26	♈11°45′48	♉23°33	♈16°35	♌16°20	♊26°00	♓29°50	♉27°35	♈01°41	♒03°44	♓23°58	℞ 25°03	♏06°20	♈25°16	**23** Fr
24 Sa	16:07:23	♊03°05′23	♈19°05′39	♈26°29′57	♉25°39	♈17°29	♌16°51	♊26°13	♓29°54	♉27°38	♈01°42	♒03°43	♓23°55	♓25°01	♏06°26	♈25°19	**24** Sa
25 Su	16:11:20	♊04°03′03	♉03°58′26	♉11°29′45	♉27°46	♈18°23	♌17°22	♊26°26	♓29°59	♉27°42	♈01°43	♒03°43	♓23°52	♓24°56	♏06°33	♈25°21	**25** Su
26 Mo	16:15:16	♊05°00′43	♉19°03′16	♉26°37′19	♉29°54	♈19°17	♌17°53	♊26°39	♈00°03	♉27°45	♈01°44	♒03°42	♓23°49	♓24°49	♏06°40	♈25°24	**26** Mo
27 Tu	16:19:13	♊05°58′22	♊04°11′07	♊11°42′53	♊02°04	♈20°13	♌18°25	♊26°53	♈00°08	♉27°49	♈01°46	♒03°42	♓23°45	♓24°40	♏06°47	♈25°27	**27** Tu
28 We	16:23:10	♊06°55′59	♊19°11′49	♊26°36′18	♊04°14	♈21°08	♌18°56	♊27°06	♈00°12	♉27°52	♈01°47	♒03°41	♓23°42	♓24°30	♏06°53	♈25°30	**28** We
29 Th	16:27:06	♊07°53′36	♋03°55′46	♋11°08′56	♊06°26	♈22°04	♌19°28	♊27°19	♈00°16	♉27°56	♈01°48	♒03°41	♓23°39	♓24°19	♏07°00	♈25°33	**29** Th
30 Fr	16:31:03	♊08°51′11	♋18°15′37	♋25°14′58	♊08°38	♈23°01	♌19°59	♊27°33	♈00°21	♉27°59	♈01°49	♒03°40	♓23°36	♓24°10	♏07°07	♈25°36	**30** Fr
31 Sa	16:34:59	♊09°48′44	♌02°07′14	♌08°51′56	♊10°50	♈23°58	♌20°31	♊27°46	♈00°25	♉28°03	♈01°50	♒03°39	♓23°33	♓24°03	♏07°13	♈25°39	**31** Sa
Δ Delta	01:58:16	28°55′59″	396°32′49″	396°06′44″	55°19′	23°48′	14°55′	6°24′	-2°34′	1°44′	0°45′	-0°09′	-1°35′	-2°24′	3°20′	1°34′	**Delta**

Ephemeris tables and data provided by **Astro-Seek.com.** All times in UTC.

5

MAY 2 VENUS-NEPTUNE MEETUP #3 OF 3

For the third and final time this year, Venus and Neptune co-star in a fairy-tale romance, uniting overhead in an exact conjunction. Their first two love scenes took place while both planets were in Pisces—on February 1 and again on March 27, while Venus was retrograde. No doubt those moments stirred up all sorts of feelings, from hope to desire to intense longing; yet, with both planets in passive Pisces, you may have been hesitant to act upon your urges. Now, as Venus and Neptune complete their trilogy in fearless Aries, the stage is set for you to shoot your shot. No vision of love is too idealistic today, whether you're sharing it aloud with friends or inviting someone to join you in a full-color fantasy.

MAY 4

WAXING QUARTER MOON IN LEO (9:52AM)

A pinch of passion can go a long way, as long as you sprinkle it mindfully. With today's waxing quarter moon in vibrant Leo, it's time to add some flair to your routine, especially if things have gotten a bit monotonous. Elevate presentations with artsy photos and plug your text into colorful templates. (Hello, Canva.) When inviting people to hang out, make it sound like the event of the season ("You won't believe the tickets I scored for Friday night!") instead of underselling it ("I'm going to a show, but I'm not sure this is your thing...""). While you don't have to go full Chappell Roan with your outfit choices, the Leo quarter moon loves a sequin and anything that falls into the "tasteful flair" camp. Today is about turning heads and leaving people wanting more.

PLUTO RETROGRADE IN AQUARIUS (MAY 4-OCT 13)

Power struggles disrupt peaceful team efforts, as Pluto begins its annual five-month retrograde in Aquarius, the sign of collaborations. As this calculating planet goes into snooze mode, you might notice stagnation in the way your squad operates or how your goals are progressing. If you're feeling stuck or unable to gain traction, consider it a sign to pump the brakes, then, pop the hood. Is everyone aligned around the end game and the strategy for achieving it? This frustrating, five-month cycle can be a hidden blessing if you use it to strengthen your internal processes. In your zeal to change the world, did you bite off more than you can chew? Pluto is solidly in Aquarius until 2044, so release that pressure valve and try a phased approach. What could you achieve by the end of 2025 without tearing yourself (and your team) apart with stress in the process? Remember: One win builds upon the next.

MAY 10-25 MERCURY IN TAURUS

Mental Mercury shifts into sensible Taurus, helping you think in a tactical way. No doubt some, "Wouldn't it be crazy if…" ideas got floated while Mercury was in Aries for the last few weeks. But do these concepts have legs? Run them through stress tests and see which ones have potential to go the distance—and ideally, be profitable. Then, get down to brass tacks. Crunch the numbers, plot a few action steps and carve out dedicated hours to methodically work through the details. This granular effort can feel agonizing in moments, but stick with it. You could save yourself hours of time, not to mention precious resources, by doing advance planning. With Mother's Day happening on May 11, lean into this traditional energy to plan a celebration that's both meaningful and luxe.

MAY 12

FULL MOON IN SCORPIO (12:56PM; 22°13')

Intense attractions could become all-consuming as the year's only full moon in Scorpio charges the air with mystery and seduction. With experimental Uranus opposing la luna, peak erotic experiences await if you're willing to explore flavors beyond vanilla. Choose a safe word because trust and lust are mutually exclusive under these sensitive moonbeams. Watch out for jealousy and possessiveness, too, which could flare up under the slightest provocation. Maybe you're overreacting, maybe you're not, but either way, nothing gets resolved in the heat of anger. Do your best to deescalate, even if that means taking a timeout when emotions get hot. All sorts of joint ventures could be inked in the two weeks following this lunation, but make sure everyone's role is spelled out clearly to avoid power struggles. Financial abundance could flow your way in the form of royalties, inheritances or investment dollars from a funding source. Make sure you know the tax liabilities for anything you bring in.

MERCURY-PLUTO SQUARE

Is someone secretly eyeing your spotlight? With Mercury in determined Taurus locking horns with secretive Pluto in Aquarius, it's wise to keep your big ideas under wraps for now. If you've been pouring your heart into a project, resist the urge to share it too soon. Not only might your hard work receive a lukewarm response, but there could also be opportunists lurking, ready to swipe your brilliance for themselves. However, there's a silver lining to these mixed signals; if a key stakeholder gives you a firm "no," you'll gain clarity on where to refine and strengthen your concept for a more compelling pitch. And if a promising offer comes your way, dig deep and do your homework before committing to anything.

MAY 17 SUN-URANUS MEETUP

Change is the only constant today, as the Sun and revolutionary Uranus host their once-per-year summit in the skies. Even if there are no outside catalysts, you'll feel a strong urge to shake up any stagnant area of your life. Easy, though. With wrench-throwing Uranus in the mix, an unexpected plot twist could catch you off guard, and the Sun can give you a case of extreme overconfidence. Fortunately, both celestial bodies are in rock-steady Taurus, which can offset some of the chaos this yearly conjunction brings. Focus on finding a solution that's not only innovative but also sustainable in the long run. And as you do, don't let your mouth write a check that your a$$ can't cash.

MAY 18 MERCURY-MARS SQUARE

Let your word be your bond today and make sure you're prepared to back up your claims with legit credentials. Grandstanding Mars is in Leo, making everyone prone to exaggeration. Nothing wrong with adding a few colorful details! But if you're bedazzling the truth with too many questionable assumptions, you could get called out, even canceled. Avoid the backlash and lean into no-nonsense Mercury in Taurus who is busy regulating every statement. On the other hand, are you flying too low under the radar? Stop wearing struggle like a merit badge. Support is all around you, but you have to ask for it!

MAY 20

WANING QUARTER MOON IN AQUARIUS (7:59AM)

About a week ago, the Scorpio full moon ignited your passion for a particular goal or desire, possibly pushing you into overdrive. But did that intensity spawn an obsession? Today's quarter moon in clear-sighted Aquarius is here to help you step back and gain a more balanced perspective. Nothing wrong with wanting to have creative control, but in the process, you may be alienating potential supporters and limiting your own expansion. Certain aspects of this mission could benefit from some outside input. Consider a team-oriented approach. The trick is to delegate to savvy, capable people, even if you have to train them on your specifications.

SUN IN GEMINI (2:55PM) (MAY 20-JUN 20)

Unleash your journalistic curiosity as the Sun sashays into inquisitive Gemini for the next month. This buzzy, intellectual solar cycle makes us want to interact and know all the details about one another. Ask the questions, yes, even the nosy ones, in the name of getting to the bottom of who you're dealing with. The only catch? If you plan to pry, be prepared to have other people "in your business," too. Gemini, the sign of the Twins, unites kindred spirits. The best place to start searching for them is right in your own backyard. During Gemini season, the local scene usually buzzes with life. But if your neighborhood feels a little too placid, it might be time to stir things up. Collaborate with local venues to inject some fun into the community vibe. From mural painting to karaoke nights to outdoor concerts, it won't be hard to find willing playmates to help you bring events to life.

MAY 22 VENUS-MARS TRINE

Cosmic lovebirds Venus and Mars dance a passionate tango as they flow into a "fire trine," which is a pulse-quickening 120-degree angle. Planning a date? Detour away from the usual places! Single? Steer clear of the usual suspects. With Venus in adventurous Aries and firecracker Mars in playful Leo, the new and unexplored will be a total turn-on. Need to have an honest chat about the state of your union? In these outspoken fire signs, Venus and Mars pull no punches. We'll all be a lot more unrestrained, which will certainly be exhilarating, but maybe not the best when it comes to setting boundaries. Couples can harness this energy to get started on a co-created project. From renovating the kitchen to starting a YouTube channel to planning a summer vacation with your friend group, put your heads together and start scheming.

MAY 24

SUN-PLUTO TRINE

Seduction is an art form today as the head-turning Gemini Sun and sultry Pluto in Aquarius make eyes at each other in the sky. There's never a good reason to hide your light, but you don't need to turn it up to full wattage to grab attention. Play up your mystique in small ways. In love, a flash of skin, a suggestive comment, a quick glance—these are all things that can leave people wondering and wanting more. There are plenty of ways to be powerful without using force. With both planets in heady air signs, use your wit and intellect to get to the top.

MERCURY-URANUS MEETUP

With clever Mercury and disruptor Uranus syncing up in Taurus, today could bring a breakthrough in your work or finances—if you're willing to think outside the box. Embrace a growth mindset and explore innovative ways to make your daily tasks more efficient, perhaps by experimenting with new technology or fresh strategies. This cosmic duo might also ignite a desire for a stylish refresh, whether it's revamping your home décor or updating your spring wardrobe. If you've been feeling stuck creatively, go on a sourcing mission. Window shopping, a walk through a gallery district, perhaps?

SATURN IN ARIES (MAY 24-SEP 1)

Break new ground! Taskmaster Saturn starts fresh today, moving into Aries for the first time since 1998. This cycle supplies a powerful blend of discipline and drive, pushing you to take bold action while keeping a steady eye on long-term goals. Alas, this won't be a cake walk. Saturn is in "fall" in Aries, one of its least comfortable positions in the zodiac since its measured approach clashes with the restless impatience of Aries. For the next few months, you may struggle—but ultimately succeed—with channeling your passion into a productive effort. Step up as a leader, take responsibility for your actions, and lay the foundation for future achievements. This short-but-impactful cycle may end on September 1, but it picks up again next year, when Saturn begins its unbroken lap through Aries from February 13, 2026 to April 12, 2028.

MAY 25-JUN 8 MERCURY IN GEMINI

Mic drops: incoming! Voluble Mercury throws a homecoming rager as it zooms into Gemini and pours a double shot of articulation! There's no time like the present to work on your memoir, record a podcast episode, or build your following with daily Instagram Lives. While Mercury hangs out in the sign of the Twins, it's dynamic duos for the win! Wordplay is foreplay during this cycle and you could woo some fascinating people by adding colorful adjectives and flowery metaphors to your everyday chatter. If you've hit a creative wall, gather your smartest friends. Brainstorms could turn into full-blown mental monsoons—but good luck staying focused for long during this distractible cycle!

MAY 26 NEW MOON IN GEMINI (11:02PM; 6°06'; SUPERMOON)

Kindred spirits unite! The year's only new moon in Gemini—a potent supermoon—sparks exciting synergies with friends old and new. Cooperative, communicative vibes are in the air, so ride the wave! When you join forces with people who share your enthusiasm, it feels like 1+1=3. Even better? Neptune and Saturn are at a friendly angle to la luna, guiding you toward collaborators who bring the rare mix of imagination and stability. And you'll have no trouble magnetizing them, thanks to supportive beams from seductive Pluto and friendly Mercury. Whatever words are rattling around in your head need to be articulated. Find a sounding board who will listen without judgment. This cathartic conversation could seed a meaningful media project that blossoms into something bigger over the coming six months.

MAY 27 MERCURY-PLUTO TRINE

Stay on your tippy toes today. With clever Mercury in Gemini and perceptive Pluto in Aquarius teaming up in sharp-minded air signs, the atmosphere is buzzing with quick wit and even quicker opinions. Someone could lob a question your way that requires an immediate, strategic response. Keep your answer concise and don't reveal too much. With furtive Pluto in the mix, a touch of mystery can work to your advantage. Drop a hint, and let people ask if they want to know more. If you're trying to uncover someone's true intentions, focus on their body language just as much as their words. Sometimes, what's left unsaid speaks louder than anything.

MAY 30 MERCURY-SUN MEETUP

Trust your instincts and speak your truth! There's zero room for hesitation today. With the bold Sun and articulate Mercury joining forces in chatty Gemini, your words carry extra weight, making others sit up and take notice. This is your moment to communicate with confidence and charisma, but here's a tip: Steer clear of overpromising or simply telling people what they want to hear. Instead, be genuine and straightforward, delivering your message with conviction. Remember, the best conversations are a two-way street, so be sure to listen as much as you talk to keep the dialogue flowing smoothly.

June

JUNE
Moon Phase Calendar

SUN	MON	TUE	WED	THU	FRI	SAT
1 ♌ ♍ 11:00PM	**2** ♍ 2nd Quarter	**3** ♍	**4** ♍ ♎ 9:38AM	**5** ♎	**6** ♎ ♏ 10:23PM	**7** ♏
8 ♏	**9** ♏ ♐ 10:56AM	**10** ♐	**11** ♐ Full Moon 3:44AM ♐→♑ 9:55PM	**12** ♑	**13** ♑	**14** ♑ ♒ 7:00AM
15 ♒	**16** ♒ ♓ 2:09PM	**17** ♓	**18** ♓ 4th Quarter ♓→♈ 7:08PM	**19** ♈	**20** ♈ ♉ 9:53PM	**21** ♉
22 ♉ ♊ 10:57PM	**23** ♊	**24** ♊ ♋ 11:44PM	**25** ♋ New Moon 6:32AM	**26** ♋	**27** ♋ ♌ 2:05AM	**28** ♌
29 ♌ ♍ 7:44AM	**30** ♍					

Times listed are Eastern US Time Zone

KEY

♈ ARIES	♌ LEO	♐ SAGITTARIUS	**FM** FULL MOON		
♉ TAURUS	♍ VIRGO	♑ CAPRICORN	**NM** NEW MOON		
♊ GEMINI	♎ LIBRA	♒ AQUARIUS	**LE** LUNAR ECLIPSE		
♋ CANCER	♏ SCORPIO	♓ PISCES	**SE** SOLAR ECLIPSE		

JUNE 11, 3:44AM
full moon in
Sagittarius (20°39')

SAGITTARIUS FULL MOON CRYSTAL

BLUE APATITE

This turquoise-hued crystal represents Sagittarian optimism and restores a positive, proactive approach to life. Blue Apatite activates the throat chakra and can help you speak your truth under this live-out-loud full moon.

SAGITTARIUS FULL MOON = CELEBRATE!

The spirit of wanderlust

Your unvarnished truths

Loved ones who live far away

The passport stamps you've collected or hope to one day

Visionary ideas that you're bringing to life

Diversity, inclusivity and cross-cultural connections

JUNE 25, 6:32AM

new moon in Cancer (4°08′)

CANCER NEW MOON CRYSTAL

MOONSTONE

Like the moon-ruled sign of Cancer, this iridescent bluish-white stone is associated with the divine feminine and fertility. Moonstone supports with birthing new ideas and tuning in to your destiny.

6

CANCER NEW MOON = FOCUS

Spend time near water

Connect to family

Get in touch with your emotions

Nourish yourself with good food and close friends

Spruce up your spaces so you feel at home everywhere

June 2025

Longitude & Retrograde Ephemeris [00:00 UT]

Day	Sid.time	☉	☽	+12h☽	☿	♀	♂	♃	♄	♅	♆	♇	☊	☊	⚸	⚷	Day
1 Su	16:38:56	♊10°46′17	♌15°29′42	♌22°00′24	♊13°02	♈24°55	♌21°03	♊27°59	♈00°29	♉28°06	♈01°51	℞ 03°39	℞ 23°30	℞ 23°59	♏07°20	♈25°41	**1** Su
2 Mo	16:42:52	♊11°43′48	♌28°24′54	♍04°43′19	♊15°13	♈25°53	♌21°35	♊28°13	♈00°33	♉28°09	♈01°52	♒03°38	♓23°26	♓23°57	♏07°27	♈25°44	**2** Mo
3 Tu	16:46:49	♊12°41′17	♍10°56′38	♍17°05′06	♊17°24	♈26°51	♌22°07	♊28°26	♈00°36	♉28°13	♈01°54	♒03°37	♓23°23	♓23°56	♏07°33	♈25°47	**3** Tu
4 We	16:50:46	♊13°38′45	♍23°09′46	♍29°10′55	♊19°35	♈27°50	♌22°39	♊28°40	♈00°40	♉28°16	♈01°55	♒03°36	♓23°20	D 23°56	♏07°40	♈25°49	**4** We
5 Th	16:54:42	♊14°36′12	♎05°09′36	♎11°06′06	♊21°44	♈28°49	♌23°12	♊28°53	♈00°44	♉28°20	♈01°55	♒03°35	♓23°17	℞ 23°56	♏07°47	♈25°52	**5** Th
6 Fr	16:58:39	♊15°33′38	♎17°01′23	♎22°55′41	♊23°51	♈29°48	♌23°44	♊29°07	♈00°48	♉28°23	♈01°56	♒03°35	♓23°14	♓23°54	♏07°53	♈25°55	**6** Fr
7 Sa	17:02:35	♊16°31′03	♎28°49′54	♏04°44′10	♊25°58	♉00°47	♌24°17	♊29°20	♈00°51	♉28°26	♈01°57	♒03°34	♓23°11	♓23°50	♏08°00	♈25°57	**7** Sa
8 Su	17:06:32	♊17°28′27	♏10°39′19	♏16°35′20	♊28°02	♉01°47	♌24°49	♊29°34	♈00°54	♉28°30	♈01°58	♒03°33	♓23°07	♓23°43	♏08°07	♈26°00	**8** Su
9 Mo	17:10:28	♊18°25′50	♏22°32′58	♏28°32′07	♋00°05	♉02°48	♌25°22	♊29°48	♈00°58	♉28°33	♈01°59	♒03°32	♓23°04	♓23°34	♏08°13	♈26°02	**9** Mo
10 Tu	17:14:25	♊19°23′12	♐04°33′24	♐10°36′37	♋02°05	♉03°48	♌25°55	♋00°01	♈01°01	♉28°36	♈02°00	♒03°31	♓23°01	♓23°22	♏08°20	♈26°05	**10** Tu
11 We	17:18:21	♊20°20′33	♐16°42′19	♐22°50′13	♋04°04	♉04°49	♌26°28	♋00°15	♈01°04	♉28°40	♈02°01	♒03°30	♓22°58	♓23°09	♏08°27	♈26°07	**11** We
12 Th	17:22:18	♊21°17′53	♐29°00′47	♑05°13′41	♋06°00	♉05°50	♌27°01	♋00°28	♈01°07	♉28°43	♈02°01	♒03°29	♓22°55	♓22°55	♏08°33	♈26°09	**12** Th
13 Fr	17:26:15	♊22°15′12	♑11°29′22	♑17°47′29	♋07°54	♉06°52	♌27°34	♋00°42	♈01°10	♉28°46	♈02°02	♒03°28	♓22°51	♓22°43	♏08°40	♈26°12	**13** Fr
14 Sa	17:30:11	♊23°12′32	♑24°08′28	♒00°32′00	♋09°46	♉07°54	♌28°07	♋00°56	♈01°13	♉28°50	♈02°03	♒03°27	♓22°48	♓22°32	♏08°47	♈26°14	**14** Sa
15 Su	17:34:08	♊24°09′50	♒06°58′34	♒13°27′52	♋11°35	♉08°56	♌28°41	♋01°09	♈01°16	♉28°53	♈02°04	♒03°26	♓22°45	♓22°24	♏08°54	♈26°16	**15** Su
16 Mo	17:38:04	♊25°07′08	♒20°00′28	♒26°36′05	♋13°22	♉09°58	♌29°14	♋01°23	♈01°19	♉28°56	♈02°04	♒03°25	♓22°42	♓22°19	♏09°00	♈26°18	**16** Mo
17 Tu	17:42:01	♊26°04′26	♓03°15′22	♓09°58′04	♋15°07	♉11°01	♌29°47	♋01°37	♈01°21	♉28°59	♈02°05	♒03°24	♓22°39	♓22°16	♏09°07	♈26°21	**17** Tu
18 We	17:45:57	♊27°01′42	♓16°44′48	♓23°35′20	♋16°49	♉12°03	♍00°21	♋01°50	♈01°24	♉29°03	♈02°05	♒03°23	♓22°36	♓22°15	♏09°14	♈26°23	**18** We
19 Th	17:49:54	♊27°58′59	♈00°30′16	♈07°29′16	♋18°28	♉13°06	♍00°55	♋02°04	♈01°26	♉29°06	♈02°06	♒03°22	♓22°32	♓22°15	♏09°20	♈26°25	**19** Th
20 Fr	17:53:50	♊28°56′16	♈14°32′48	♈21°40′20	♋20°05	♉14°10	♍01°29	♋02°18	♈01°29	♉29°09	♈02°06	♒03°21	♓22°29	♓22°15	♏09°27	♈26°27	**20** Fr
21 Sa	17:57:47	♊29°53′33	♈28°52′09	♉06°07′29	♋21°40	♉15°13	♍02°02	♋02°31	♈01°31	♉29°12	♈02°07	♒03°20	♓22°26	♓22°12	♏09°34	♈26°29	**21** Sa
22 Su	18:01:44	♋00°50′49	♉13°26′18	♉20°47′31	♋23°12	♉16°17	♍02°36	♋02°45	♈01°33	♉29°15	♈02°07	♒03°19	♓22°23	♓22°08	♏09°40	♈26°31	**22** Su
23 Mo	18:05:40	♋01°48′06	♉28°10′51	♊05°34′57	♋24°42	♉17°21	♍03°10	♋02°59	♈01°35	♉29°18	♈02°08	♒03°18	♓22°20	♓22°01	♏09°47	♈26°33	**23** Mo
24 Tu	18:09:37	♋02°45′22	♊12°59′16	♊20°22′19	♋26°09	♉18°25	♍03°44	♋03°13	♈01°37	♉29°21	♈02°08	♒03°16	♓22°17	♓21°51	♏09°54	♈26°35	**24** Tu
25 We	18:13:33	♋03°42′38	♊27°43′30	♋05°01′19	♋27°34	♉19°29	♍04°19	♋03°26	♈01°39	♉29°24	♈02°08	♒03°15	♓22°13	♓21°40	♏10°00	♈26°36	**25** We
26 Th	18:17:30	♋04°39′54	♋12°15′17	♋19°24′07	♋28°56	♉20°34	♍04°53	♋03°40	♈01°41	♉29°27	♈02°09	♒03°14	♓22°10	♓21°29	♏10°07	♈26°38	**26** Th
27 Fr	18:21:26	♋05°37′09	♋26°27′37	♌03°24′47	♌00°15	♉21°39	♍05°27	♋03°54	♈01°42	♉29°30	♈02°09	♒03°13	♓22°07	♓21°20	♏10°14	♈26°40	**27** Fr
28 Sa	18:25:23	♋06°34′24	♌10°15′45	♌16°59′55	♌01°32	♉22°44	♍06°02	♋04°07	♈01°44	♉29°33	♈02°09	♒03°12	♓22°04	♓21°12	♏10°20	♈26°42	**28** Sa
29 Su	18:29:19	♋07°31′38	♌23°37′43	♍00°08′53	♌02°46	♉23°49	♍06°36	♋04°21	♈01°45	♉29°36	♈02°09	♒03°10	♓22°01	♓21°07	♏10°27	♈26°43	**29** Su
30 Mo	18:33:16	♋08°28′52	♍06°34′09	♍12°53′29	♌03°57	♉24°54	♍07°11	♋04°35	♈01°47	♉29°39	♈02°10	♒03°09	♓21°57	♓21°04	♏10°34	♈26°45	**30** Mo
Δ Delta	01:54:20	27°42′35″	381°04′27″	380°53′04″	50°55′	29°58′	16°07′	6°35′	1°18′	1°33′	0°18′	-0°29′	-1°32′	-2°54′	3°13′	1°03′	**Delta**

Ephemeris tables and data provided by **Astro-Seek.com.** All times in UTC.

JUNE
MONTHLY HOTSPOTS

JUN 2 WAXING QUARTER MOON IN VIRGO (11:40PM)

Grab the magnifying glass and take a closer look. With the waxing quarter moon in discerning Virgo, every flaw and imperfection that might have slipped past you earlier is now coming into focus. Last week's Gemini new moon may have sparked a flurry of new ideas, but now it's time to back them up with a practical plan. Fine-tune your strategy and put a step-by-step strategy in place. Before you finalize anything, take the time to carefully review your work and ensure it's polished to perfection. Since Virgo also rules health and wellness, it's the perfect moment to start integrating clean and green habits into your pre-summer routine. Let this cosmic energy support your journey to a healthier, more organized lifestyle.

JUN 6-JUL 4 VENUS IN TAURUS

Sweet sensuality is in the air! Affectionate Venus returns to her cozy home in tactile Taurus, awakening our senses and whetting our appetites for all things luxurious. This is the time to indulge in life's earthy pleasures, from a plant-based meal to the vivid hues of seasonal flowers. Pamper yourself and spoil those you love, because "too much of a good thing" feels just right under Taurus's influence. Relationships can also deepen and become more serious during this stabilizing transit, as Taurus's traditional energy encourages lasting connections and grounded commitments.

JUN 8

MERCURY-JUPITER MEETUP

The cosmic muse is coming through the loudspeaker today as communicator Mercury teams up with expansive Jupiter in curious Gemini. With these two effervescent planets joining forces, your words will flow effortlessly, making it a breeze to get conversations started. Ask plenty of thoughtful questions and be sure to open up and share what's on your mind. You never know where a kindred spirit connection might lead. Skip the small talk and dive into broad, intellectual conversations. You're in for a meeting of the minds that could spark something truly special.

MERCURY IN CANCER (JUN 8-26)

Clarify your boundaries and keep personal intel under wraps. With communicator Mercury nesting in sentimental Cancer for the next few weeks, extreme privacy is the best policy. Take time to create a solid emotional bond with people before revealing your innermost thoughts. If you've been pondering a social media break, consider taking the month of June off from scrolling and posting. (Your meals will still be memorable even if you don't share them with the world!) Channel your energy into zhushing your space to make it both streamlined and cozy. Make a gallery wall of cherished family photos, update to smart gadgets, liven up rooms with verdant houseplants and colorful textiles.

JUN 9

MERCURY-SATURN SQUARE

Defensive much? You could lash out at the slightest provocation under today's thin-skinned square between Mercury in Cancer and Saturn in prickly Aries. Don't jump to conclusions about other people's motives. Even if their actions appear inconsiderate, there could be more to the story than you initially realize. Knee-jerk reactions could come back to bite you. When you find yourself resisting something "on principle," take a look at what that might really be about. Are you afraid of losing control or being exposed as not having all the answers? Keep the imposter syndrome in check but do make sure you've done all your homework.

VENUS-PLUTO SQUARE

Watch out for power struggles and emotional battles as seductive Venus in Taurus squares off with intense Pluto in Aquarius for a one-day clash. While it's tempting to push back against someone's domineering behavior, think twice. Matching their aggression will only add fuel to the fire, deepening any rifts. Instead, try to uncover the root issue driving this friction. Spoiler alert: It might just trace back to an old childhood wound (doesn't it always?). You might find yourself obsessing over someone who's wronged you, which could lead to impulsive behavior like firing off a heated text or trolling their social media. If you're in a solid relationship, you might feel the urge to push bae's buttons just to keep things "exciting." Be sure you know what you're getting into before you awaken any sleeping giants.

JUPITER IN CANCER (JUN 9-JUN 30, 2026)

Surf's up! Big-hearted, philosophical Jupiter sets sail on nurturing Cancer's emotion ocean—its first visit to this sign since 2014! As the red-spotted planet sounds a global call for empathy, kindness and compassion are en vogue again. Home and family ties take center stage during this yearlong transit. Now's the time to create a sanctuary that nurtures your soul, but that doesn't mean you'll be stuck inside the same four walls. Reconnect to long-distance relatives or take a life-changing trip to your ancestral homeland. Jupiter is "exalted" in Cancer, making this its most powerful position in the zodiac. Jupiter in domestic Cancer can heat up the residential real estate market while also creating greater opportunities for first-time home buyers. Fiscal security is also highlighted, so start tucking away more funds in your investment accounts. Need to make more bank? Home-based businesses are blessed by enterprising Jupiter in Cancer.

MERCURY-NEPTUNE SQUARE

Your logical left brain battles your intuitive right brain as analytical Mercury in Aries also squares off with subliminal Neptune in Pisces. This cosmic clash could leave you feeling torn between following standard operating procedures or scrapping the safe route to go follow your gut instincts. And with both planets in take-charge cardinal signs, your ego might be having too loud of a say. To cut through the confusion, think about how your choice will impact your life in ten minutes, ten months, and ten years. You might be surprised by the clarity it brings!

JUN 11
FULL MOON IN SAGITTARIUS (3:44AM; 20°39')

Modesty, schmodesty. There's almost no way to be "too much" under the supersizing influence of the year's only full moon in Sagittarius. Stretch beyond the limits of what's safe and familiar. With daredevil Mars fistbumping the full moon, this could bring untold rewards over the coming two weeks. (Just make sure you know the difference between a "savvy risk" and a "foolish gamble.") If you have the time and means, pack your bags for an epic getaway. Otherwise, broaden your horizons through summer classes, personal growth work and diverse experiences that push you into inspiring new terrain. Nothing ventured, nothing gained!

JUN 15

MARS-URANUS SQUARE

Negotiate? Not today! As unruly Uranus in stubborn Taurus battles fiery Mars in proud Leo, tensions are bound to escalate. The battle lines are drawn, and neither side seems eager to wave the white flag. Do your best to stay mindful and avoid burning any bridges you might need to cross later. Patience will be your saving grace today!

JUPITER-SATURN SQUARE

Your ego is not your amigo, but good luck remembering that today! As hypersensitive Jupiter in Cancer combats authoritative Saturn in Aries, pride steers the ship and people can be downright petty. Don't waste time trying to reason with narcissists, especially when adulting is a distant dream. Better to let everyone sulk (or fume!) in their corners. You can approach the topic again—or not!—once the storm clears. While you wait for molehills to stop looking like mountains, see if you can find a common cause. While you may have very different approaches for achieving an end goal, do you actually want the same thing? Focusing on that may be the saving grace today—especially with someone you consider "family."

JUN 17-AUG 6 MARS IN VIRGO

Order in the court! As action-oriented Mars charges into detail-driven Virgo, the next month and a half is optimized for efficiency. Turn your lofty ideas into actionable plans, complete with budgets and schedules. This health-focused, fix-it-fast transit motivates you to improve every aspect of your life, from your eating habits to your workflow. There's no better time to push a wellness routine in place as Mars supplies the motivation and Virgo helps you track results and stick to a regimen. Expect a surge in productive energy, but be mindful of how you come across when doling out advice. You might sound more critical than you mean to, especially since Mars in Virgo can make us all especially judgmental. Keep this in mind: You'll attract more flies with honey than with your "helpful hints."

JUN 18

WANING QUARTER MOON IN PISCES (3:19PM)

Stuck in a creative logjam? Today's imaginative quarter moon in Pisces gets inspiration flowing. Before you start sourcing ideas from art and fashion feeds, put down your phone and fully immerse yourself in every sensation around you. Under this meditative transit, you need less input and more quiet time. If you're looking to turn dreams into reality, Pisces' manifesting energy is on your side. A supportive person may be just a text (or a thought!) away. Don't be surprised if someone crosses your mind and then you bump into them shortly after—this is a day made for serendipity. If burnout is creeping in, book a healing treatment or head home early to recharge.

JUPITER-NEPTUNE SQUARE

What's the big idea? As visionary Jupiter in Cancer plays tug-of-war with spiritual Neptune in Aries, it breaks our thinking out of the box. Fresh possibilities could become tangible realities at an accelerated pace. But tap the sensitivity of Neptune and weigh it against the gung-ho momentum of Jupiter. It's great to blaze trails, but how will new developments affect the ecosystem of your life? If you forgot to consider feelings or ask for consent, you may need to revise plans. But that's not the same as people-pleasing! If you're hiding your truth because you don't want to make people "feel bad," play with being self-authorized and making a bold move.

JUN 20-JUL 22 SUN IN CANCER (10:42PM)

Happy Solstice! The Sun reaches its highest point in the northern hemisphere, signaling the start of Cancer season each year. For the next month, we'll all radiate feelings of warmth, connection and nourishment that are hallmarks of this water sign. Home is where the heart is now, so get your space set up for both nesting and guesting. Has it been a while since you've visited beloved relatives and your oldest, dearest friends? Tap the nostalgic vibes of Cancer season and meet up for picnics, beach days or longer visits to your hometown. Tender emotions may surface regularly but don't keep them in. Cathartic Marco Polos with your besties can keep you sane when everyone else is spiraling.

JUN 22 SUN-SATURN SQUARE

If your stomach is in knots, don't reflexively reach for the probiotics. It's Cancer season and your symptoms may be a reflection of what's happening in your emotional life. But as Saturn in Aries challenges el Sol, tune in to your needs. Have you been biting your tongue and keeping your opinions to yourself? Perhaps you've been swallowing your feelings when the going gets tough. Today's remedy: Stop and listen to your own internal dialogue, the way a nurturing parent would soothe a child. Something needs to change here, but first, give yourself permission to be (privately) annoyed, frustrated or irritated without feeling guilty. Once you acknowledge those feelings, you can get proactive. The goal is to implement changes in a wise, mature and measured way.

JUN 23 SUN-NEPTUNE SQUARE

Martyr alert! As the Sun in compassionate Cancer gets snared by sacrificial Neptune in Aries, everyone's doing the most. Do your best to NOT get sucked in. This "competitive caretaking" could leave you feeling put upon, exhausted and unappreciated for all your genuine efforts. Do an internal audit: Are you asking too much of people? (Even if they "owe" you.) Keeping score? Perhaps it's time to slow down a little, take a break, and stop trying to accomplish everything at warp speed. If you start operating at a more human pace, you might find that others are happy to get on board and help.

JUN 24 SUN-JUPITER MEETUP, THE DAY OF MIRACLES

Energy and optimism reign as the magnanimous Sun and generous Jupiter align for their once-per-year meetup—also known as a cazimi. For the first time in over a decade, they're joining forces in nurturing Cancer, shining lucky rays on home, family and personal finances. If you've been searching for a new place to call home, the perfect listing could appear or maybe you'll finally bury the hatchet with a beloved relative. On this "Day of Miracles," the Sun and Jupiter cast a rosy, can-do glow over all endeavors. Embrace this positive momentum and find new ways to uplift others and share your light with the world.

JUN 25 NEW MOON IN CANCER (6:31AM; 4°07')

Serve it up, family-style! The year's only new moon in Cancer sets the stage for close-knit bonding. If you're the type who's "never met a stranger," you may want to tighten up the radius of your inner circle so you can devote quality attention to the unwavering supporters in your life. Over the next two weeks, find ways to sing their praises and make sure they get the VIP treatment from you. Spending time near water will be especially rejuvenating now, so reply "yes" to those pool parties and beach weekends! On the home front, this nurturing new moon might reveal a dreamy real estate opportunity or inspire an interior design makeover. Whether you're cleaning out your storage spaces or doing a soul-soothing house-blessing ritual, now's the perfect time for a midyear energy cleanse to refresh your most sacred spaces. Just be careful not to bite off more than you can chew! This new moon aligns with maximizer Jupiter and clashes with Saturn and Neptune in impulsive Aries, which can give your projects "scope creep" or set the stage for unrealistic expectations.

JUN 26-SEP 2 MERCURY IN LEO

Curtains up! Social Mercury struts into playful and passionate Leo, turning up the heat on your summer fun. If your calendar suddenly fills with beach parties and your creativity skyrockets, you can thank Mercury's lively jaunt through this colorful sign's terrain. For the first part of this cycle, express yourself with warmth, excitement, and maybe even a touch of theatrical flair. But here's a head's up: From July 18 to August 11, Mercury will spin into a summer retrograde through Leo, marking three weeks where dialing DOWN the drama will be imperative. Try to resolve any brewing tension before then. If you're pitching an idea or giving a presentation, lean into storytelling and bold visuals to drive your message home.

JUN 27 MERCURY-SATURN TRINE

Speak with conviction and you'll be unstoppable! As communicator Mercury in Leo dances into a potent fire trine with disciplined Saturn in Aries, present yourself with authority and confidence. This is your chance to back up your words with action and prove to your peers that you're someone who delivers. By coming through with the complete package, you could secure a sought-after opportunity, or at the very least, earn the respect of the MVPs.

JUN 28 MERCURY-NEPTUNE TRINE

Mercury in Leo and Neptune in Aries form a powerful fire trine today, fueling your creativity and intuition with bold, assertive energy. This dynamic alignment pushes you to step up and take charge, using both confidence and insight to make an impact. While setting boundaries might feel secondary, harness this strong-willed energy to be both a commanding presence and a supportive listener. Rather than jumping in with solutions, let others speak their truth, showing them that you're fully engaged. To sharpen your own divine connection, try a moving meditation like yoga or a quiet hike. As you do, ask your guides for unmistakable signs that will propel you toward your highest path.

6

JUN 29 MERCURY-PLUTO OPPOSITION

What's really going on here? Today's triggering cosmic energy could push all your buttons, as people attempt to play mental chess and veil their true intentions. With calculating Pluto in Aquarius opposing communicator Mercury in Leo, it's best to keep things close to the vest and avoid making assumptions. Even if your observational skills are sharp, the full story might be more complicated than it appears. Even the most basic exchanges could be riddled with suggestive tones and innuendoes. Instead of trying to decode what someone's really saying, just ask, "What do you mean?" and let them do the explaining. If a power struggle starts to simmer, bow out gracefully before things get heated.

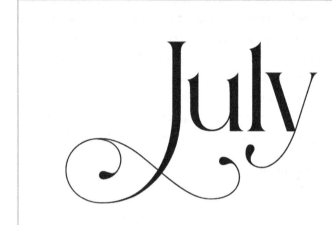

July

7

JULY
Moon Phase Calendar

SUN	MON	TUE	WED	THU	FRI	SAT
		1 ♍ ♎ 5:16PM	**2** ♎ 2nd Quarter	**3** ♎	**4** ♎ ♏ 5:33AM	**5** ♏
6 ♏ ♐ 6:06PM	**7** ♐	**8** ♐	**9** ♐ ♑ 4:55AM	**10** ♑ Full Moon 4:37PM	**11** ♑ ♒ 1:21PM	**12** ♒
13 ♒ ♓ 7:45PM	**14** ♓	**15** ♓	**16** ♓ ♈ 12:32AM	**17** ♈ 4th Quarter	**18** ♈ ♉ 3:59AM	**19** ♉
20 ♉ ♊ 6:22AM	**21** ♊	**22** ♊ ♋ 8:26AM	**23** ♋	**24** ♋→♌ 11:28AM ♌ New Moon 3:11PM	**25** ♌	**26** ♌ ♍ 4:55PM
27 ♍	**28** ♍	**29** ♍ ♎ 1:43AM	**30** ♎	**31** ♎ ♏ 1:25PM		

Times listed are Eastern US Time Zone

KEY

♈	ARIES	♌	LEO	♐	SAGITTARIUS	**FM**	FULL MOON
♉	TAURUS	♍	VIRGO	♑	CAPRICORN	**NM**	NEW MOON
♊	GEMINI	♎	LIBRA	♒	AQUARIUS	**LE**	LUNAR ECLIPSE
♋	CANCER	♏	SCORPIO	♓	PISCES	**SE**	SOLAR ECLIPSE

JULY 10, 4:37PM

full moon in Capricorn (18°50')

CAPRICORN FULL MOON CRYSTAL

AZURITE

This pebbled blue and green stone is excellent for supporting concentration and getting you motivated for those Capricorn-fueled missions. Azurite clears your mind of distractions, sharpens mental powers and increases access to your innate wisdom.

CAPRICORN FULL MOON = CELEBRATE!

Your current milestones and wins

Your competitive edge

Perseverance

Time outdoors and in nature

The people who champion you and help you grow

The places where you feel confident taking charge and leading the troops

JULY 24, 3:11 PM

new moon in Leo (2°08')

LEO NEW MOON CRYSTAL

CITRINE

Golden Citrine glows with the regal, joy-inducing hue of Leo! This stone boosts ambition and self-esteem while helping you attract abundance during one of the most creative seasons of the year.

7

LEO NEW MOON = FOCUS

Find your place to shine

Spend time with kids

Take a leadership role

Host and attend glamorous parties

Enjoy romance and playtime

July 2025

Longitude & Retrograde Ephemeris [00:00 UT]

Day	Sid.time	☉	☽	+12h☽	☿	♀	♂	♃	♄	♅	♆	♇	☊	☊	⚸	⚷	Day
1 Tu	18:37:13	♋09°26′06	♍19°07′48	♍25°17′15	℞s 05°06	♉26°00	♍07°46	♋04°48	♈01°48	♉29°42	♈02°10	℞ 03°08	℞ 21°54	℞ 21°03	♏10°41	♈26°46	**1** Tu
2 We	18:41:09	♋10°23′19	♎01°22′50	♎07°24′50	♌06°11	♉27°05	♍08°20	♋05°02	♈01°49	♉29°45	♈02°10	♒03°07	♓21°51	D 21°03	♏10°47	♈26°48	**2** We
3 Th	18:45:06	♋11°20′32	♎13°24′18	♎19°21′29	♌07°14	♉28°11	♍08°55	♋05°16	♈01°50	♉29°48	♈02°10	♒03°05	♓21°48	℞ 21°04	♏10°54	♈26°49	**3** Th
4 Fr	18:49:02	♋12°17′44	♎25°17′27	♏01°12′29	♌08°13	♉29°17	♍09°30	♋05°29	♈01°51	♉29°50	♈02°10	♒03°04	♓21°45	♓21°03	♏11°01	♈26°51	**4** Fr
5 Sa	18:52:59	♋13°14′56	♏07°07′33	♏13°02′53	♌09°09	♊00°23	♍10°05	♋05°43	♈01°52	♉29°53	℞ 02°10	♒03°03	♓21°42	♓21°00	♏11°07	♈26°52	**5** Sa
6 Su	18:56:55	♋14°12′08	♏18°59′24	♏24°57′12	♌10°02	♊01°29	♍10°40	♋05°57	♈01°53	♉29°56	♈02°10	♒03°02	♓21°38	♓20°55	♏11°14	♈26°53	**6** Su
7 Mo	19:00:52	♋15°09′20	♐00°57′07	♐06°59′11	♌10°52	♊02°36	♍11°15	♋06°10	♈01°54	♉29°59	♈02°10	♒03°00	♓21°35	♓20°48	♏11°21	♈26°55	**7** Mo
8 Tu	19:04:48	♋16°06′32	♐13°04′04	♐19°11′41	♌11°38	♊03°42	♍11°51	♋06°24	♈01°54	♊00°01	♈02°10	♒02°59	♓21°32	♓20°38	♏11°27	♈26°56	**8** Tu
9 We	19:08:45	♋17°03′44	♐25°22′36	♑01°36′34	♌12°20	♊04°49	♍12°26	♋06°37	♈01°55	♊00°04	♈02°10	♒02°58	♓21°29	♓20°28	♏11°34	♈26°57	**9** We
10 Th	19:12:42	♋18°00′55	♑07°54′03	♑14°14′43	♌12°59	♊05°56	♍13°01	♋06°51	♈01°55	♊00°07	♈02°10	♒02°56	♓21°26	♓20°17	♏11°41	♈26°58	**10** Th
11 Fr	19:16:38	♋18°58′07	♑20°38′53	♑27°06′09	♌13°33	♊07°03	♍13°37	♋07°05	♈01°55	♊00°09	♈02°09	♒02°55	♓21°23	♓20°06	♏11°47	♈26°59	**11** Fr
12 Sa	19:20:35	♋19°55′19	♒03°36′47	♒10°10′18	♌14°04	♊08°10	♍14°12	♋07°18	♈01°55	♊00°12	♈02°09	♒02°53	♓21°19	♓19°57	♏11°54	♈27°00	**12** Sa
13 Su	19:24:31	♋20°52′32	♒16°46′59	♒23°26′19	♌14°30	♊09°17	♍14°48	♋07°32	♈01°56	♊00°14	♈02°09	♒02°52	♓21°16	♓19°51	♏12°01	♈27°01	**13** Su
14 Mo	19:28:28	♋21°49′44	♓00°08′37	♓06°53′21	♌14°52	♊10°24	♍15°24	♋07°45	℞ 01°56	♊00°17	♈02°09	♒02°51	♓21°13	♓19°47	♏12°08	♈27°02	**14** Mo
15 Tu	19:32:24	♋22°46′57	♓13°40′55	♓20°30′48	♌15°09	♊11°32	♍15°59	♋07°58	♈01°55	♊00°19	♈02°08	♒02°49	♓21°10	♓19°45	♏12°14	♈27°03	**15** Tu
16 We	19:36:21	♋23°44′11	♓27°23′26	♈04°18′20	♌15°22	♊12°39	♍16°35	♋08°12	♈01°55	♊00°22	♈02°08	♒02°48	♓21°07	D 19°45	♏12°21	♈27°04	**16** We
17 Th	19:40:18	♋24°41′25	♈11°15′56	♈18°15′44	♌15°31	♊13°47	♍17°11	♋08°25	♈01°55	♊00°24	♈02°08	♒02°47	♓21°03	♓19°46	♏12°28	♈27°04	**17** Th
18 Fr	19:44:14	♋25°38′40	♈25°18′07	♉02°22′33	♌15°34	♊14°55	♍17°47	♋08°39	♈01°54	♊00°26	♈02°07	♒02°45	♓21°00	♓19°47	♏12°34	♈27°05	**18** Fr
19 Sa	19:48:11	♋26°35′55	♉09°29′18	♉16°37′41	℞ 15°32	♊16°03	♍18°23	♋08°52	♈01°54	♊00°29	♈02°07	♒02°44	♓20°57	℞ 19°46	♏12°41	♈27°06	**19** Sa
20 Su	19:52:07	♋27°33′12	♉23°47′50	♊00°58′54	♌15°26	♊17°11	♍18°59	♋09°05	♈01°53	♊00°31	♈02°06	♒02°42	♓20°54	♓19°43	♏12°48	♈27°06	**20** Su
21 Mo	19:56:04	♋28°30′29	♊08°10′52	♊15°22′42	♌15°15	♊18°20	♍19°35	♋09°19	♈01°52	♊00°33	♈02°06	♒02°41	♓20°51	♓19°39	♏12°54	♈27°07	**21** Mo
22 Tu	20:00:00	♋29°27′47	♊22°34′15	♊29°44′22	♌14°59	♊19°28	♍20°11	♋09°32	♈01°52	♊00°35	♈02°05	♒02°40	♓20°48	♓19°32	♏13°01	♈27°07	**22** Tu
23 We	20:03:57	♌00°25′06	♋06°52′49	♋13°58′27	♌14°38	♊20°36	♍20°48	♋09°45	♈01°51	♊00°37	♈02°05	♒02°38	♓20°44	♓19°25	♏13°08	♈27°08	**23** We
24 Th	20:07:53	♌01°22′26	♋21°01′04	♋27°59′36	♌14°13	♊21°45	♍21°24	♋09°58	♈01°50	♊00°39	♈02°04	♒02°37	♓20°41	♓19°17	♏13°14	♈27°08	**24** Th
25 Fr	20:11:50	♌02°19′45	♌04°53′59	♌11°43′21	♌13°44	♊22°54	♍22°00	♋10°11	♈01°49	♊00°42	♈02°04	♒02°35	♓20°38	♓19°10	♏13°21	♈27°08	**25** Fr
26 Sa	20:15:47	♌03°17′06	♌18°27′48	♌25°06′44	♌13°10	♊24°03	♍22°37	♋10°24	♈01°47	♊00°44	♈02°03	♒02°34	♓20°35	♓19°05	♏13°28	♈27°09	**26** Sa
27 Su	20:19:43	♌04°14′27	♍01°40′29	♍08°08′41	♌12°34	♊25°11	♍23°14	♋10°38	♈01°46	♊00°46	♈02°02	♒02°32	♓20°32	♓19°01	♏13°35	♈27°09	**27** Su
28 Mo	20:23:40	♌05°11′49	♍14°31′53	♍20°49′57	♌11°54	♊26°20	♍23°50	♋10°51	♈01°45	♊00°47	♈02°02	♒02°31	♓20°29	♓19°00	♏13°41	♈27°09	**28** Mo
29 Tu	20:27:36	♌06°09′11	♍27°03′37	♎03°12′54	♌11°12	♊27°30	♍24°27	♋11°04	♈01°43	♊00°49	♈02°01	♒02°30	♓20°25	D 19°00	♏13°48	♈27°09	**29** Tu
30 We	20:31:33	♌07°06′34	♎09°18′40	♎15°21′05	♌10°29	♊28°39	♍25°04	♋11°16	♈01°41	♊00°51	♈02°00	♒02°28	♓20°22	♓19°01	♏13°55	♈27°09	**30** We
31 Th	20:35:29	♌08°03′57	♎21°21′05	♎27°18′55	♌09°44	♊29°48	♍25°41	♋11°29	♈01°40	♊00°53	♈01°59	♒02°27	♓20°19	♓19°03	♏14°01	℞ 27°09	**31** Th
Δ Delta	01:58:15	28°37′51″	392°13′17″	392°01′40″	4°38′	33°48′	17°55′	6°40′	-0°08′	1°11′	-0°10′	-0°41′	-1°35′	-2°00′	3°20′	0°22′	**Delta**

Ephemeris tables and data provided by **Astro-Seek.com.** All times in UTC.

7

JULY
MONTHLY HOTSPOTS

JUL 2 WAXING QUARTER MOON IN LIBRA (3:30PM)

No more sweeping that conflict under the rug. It's time to face the music and hopefully drum up a harmonious solution for all. Today's waxing quarter moon is in Libra, the most balanced and strategic of the signs. This can help you navigate any speedbumps on the path to peace. Take a deep breath, because you may have to weather some unpleasant conversations before you can make strides forward. Try not to let your feelings cloud the facts. Be open to other perspectives and don't be afraid to apologize if the fault lies with you. Without shaming or blaming, hold people accountable for their part in the matter. Creative solutions can emerge if you stay focused on finding win-wins.

JUL 4

VENUS-URANUS MEETUP

This Independence Day comes with an extra round of fireworks as seductive Venus sets off sparks with renegade Uranus in Taurus. This randy, rowdy mashup could inspire you to do something wildly unexpected, especially when it comes to your love life. It's all fun and games until someone crosses a line, so get consent before making any moves. Single and looking? Sparks could ignite with someone who might not normally turn your head. With both planets in sensual earth signs, the attraction might begin with a physical attraction that enraptures you both.

VENUS IN GEMINI (11:31AM) (JUL 4-30)

Wordplay is foreplay, as Venus logs into articulate Gemini. Clever conversations and tantalizing text threads can get pulses racing, but don't get stuck in the superficial, flirty zone. During this sapiosexual spell, deep and intellectual exchanges might feel better than (or at least as good as) sex. Feel like pushing boundaries? Go ahead—dive into taboo topics or challenge outdated norms that don't resonate with you. With Venus in this curious sign, the desire to explore new territory is irresistible. Just be mindful of mixed signals, as they're bound to surface during this silver-tongued transit.

NEPTUNE RETROGRADE (JUL 4-DEC 10)

Peel back the layers of your psyche, as Neptune slips into its annual, five-month retrograde. For the first time since 1875, Neptune spins back through fiery Aries, creating an added sense of urgency around self-care and soul-searching. During this part of the retrograde, which lasts until October 22, confront issues around identity, self-assertion, and how you wield your personal power. You may address impulsive behaviors or reactions that have been masking deeper wounds. When Neptune shifts back into Pisces on October 22—it's last retrograde lap through this sign in our lifetimes—lingering emotional wounds could demand attention. Keep an eye out for energy vampires and codependent dynamics during this boundary-blurring phase through Pisces, which lasts until December 10.

JULY 7

URANUS IN GEMINI (JUL 7-NOV 7)

Welcome to the innovation station! For the first time since 1941-49, zany Uranus plugs into Gemini's grid, bringing a thrilling mix of excitement and unpredictability to our lives. During this dynamic transit, everything's up for grabs. Uranus in Gemini shakes up daily routines and supercharges minds with groundbreaking ideas. Expect the unexpected—whether it's through a radical shift in how you communicate, a sudden change in your social circles, or an intense fascination with cutting-edge technology. Life may feel like a sci-fi movie some days, with the costumes and gadgets to match. This four-month period is a preview of a longer cycle that begins again from April 25, 2026 to May 22, 2033. Collectively, we are breaking free from a static, singular way of doing things and embracing a "both/and" mindset rather than one focused on "either/ or." This game-changing planet's purpose is to disrupt the status quo. Stay flexible and ready to pivot at a moment's notice. Uranus in Gemini is here to revolutionize the way you think, connect, and engage with the world. The more open you are to change, the more exciting and rewarding this transit will be!

VENUS-PLUTO TRINE

Charisma is an aphrodisiac today as seductive Venus in Gemini aligns with smoldering Pluto in communicative air signs. Watching someone move confidently and command a room will send your pulse racing. You might find yourself drawn to a well-connected VIP or meet someone intriguing through a mutual acquaintance. Say "yes" to that exclusive invite or ticketed event where you can mingle with the who's who—or team up with a partner to make a powerful impact for a cause close to your heart. This is the perfect day to work your influence and connect with others who share your ambitious drive!

JUL 10 FULL MOON IN CAPRICORN (4:37PM; 18°50')

Time for a mid-year assessment. What have you accomplished since the beginning of 2025? Do you even remember your New Year's resolutions? Consider how relevant they still are as the year's unfolded. Today's full moon in goal-getter Capricorn is here to shine a light on your progress—or lack thereof. With an energizing trine to motivator Mars in Virgo, it's the perfect moment to review, revamp, and recalibrate your plans. Capricorn is all about ambition and high achievement, but don't forget to celebrate the wins you've already scored. Remember, there's no gold star for burning out in the name of productivity. Take a moment to acknowledge your progress and show gratitude to those who've supported your journey. It's all about balancing the hustle with a little self-love!

JUL 13-NOV 27 SATURN RETROGRADE

Are you pushing forward with purpose or charging ahead without a clear plan? Cosmic inspector Saturn begins its annual four-and-a-half-month retrograde today. For the first time since the late 90s, it's backing up through "me first" Aries, prompting you to take a closer look at how you assert your ambitions, personal power, and leadership. While the ringed taskmaster reverses through this sign until September 1, you might reevaluate your personal brand. A solo project could hit a speedbump, or you could intentionally slow down your timeline for quality's sake. From September 1 until November 27, Saturn backspins into imaginative Pisces, where the lines between reality and dreams can blur. If you've been swept up in a pipe dream, Saturn's reversal will deliver the reality check you need. But don't dismiss your dreams entirely—this is also a time to cultivate any spiritual or artistic talents you've been exploring. Use this retrograde to master the basics, refine your skills, and lay a solid foundation before taking things to the next level.

JULY 17 WANING QUARTER MOON IN ARIES (8:37PM)

It's not enough to simply speak up for yourself under today's waning quarter moon in assertive Aries. If you're looking for support, you'll need to capture people's interest without overwhelming them or applying too much pressure. Even if there's a bit of tension brewing, make sure to present your requests with confidence and composure. Approach every conversation with a can-do attitude, because when enthusiastic Aries is in the spotlight, people are eager to be part of the winning team! Keep things positive, and you'll rally the troops in no time.

JUL 18-AUG 11 MERCURY RETROGRADE IN LEO

Roll up the red carpet! As Mercury pivots into a three-week retrograde in glamorous, flamboyant Leo, it's better to fly under the radar than risk getting overexposed. Scrambled romantic signals, celebrity breakups and flagrant fashion faux pas will interrupt your summer program. Hold off on bold style choices and save any risky cosmetic procedures until after August 11. Exes might resurface, and lovers' quarrels could ignite out of nowhere. With Mercury's backspin in Leo, however, there's a risk of being too lowkey. Don't let opportunities slip by out of fear or insecurity. Conflict resolution will be challenging, and blame-shifting could backfire. The best way to navigate this turbulent phase is to stay humble and keep your heart open—without being overly trusting, too soon. Leo rules our "kings and queens," and this retrograde could reveal some fascinating (and perhaps disturbing) information about those in power. Before stepping into a leadership role, make sure you know what you're getting into. Heavy is the head that wears the crown—at least until August 11.

JUL 22-AUG 22 SUN IN LEO

Passion, playtime and power couples—oh my! The Sun struts into regal, romantic Leo for its annual four-week run, bringing out the exhibitionists in us all. This solar cycle turns up the volume on our actions, but here's the twist—Mercury is retrograde for the first few weeks of Leo season, adding a reflective layer to the mix until August 11. Dust off those neglected talents and start rehearsing your act. The retrograde period is perfect for fine-tuning your vision and positioning your personal "brand" for its ascent. If you've got a product to promote, give it one last high-gloss polish during the retrograde and plan your big reveal once Mercury goes direct. Confidence is your best accessory now, as long as you aren't faking it 'til you make it.

JUL 23 VENUS-MARS SQUARE

Communications could hit a rough patch today, under a challenging dust-up between cosmic lovebirds Venus as Mars. Venus is tossing up a word salad in Gemini, turning even the simplest conversations into mind boggling debates. With Mars in critical, detail-oriented Virgo, it's crucial to focus on solutions rather than zeroing in on your other people's "flaws." This could be tricky with these planets at odds. If you've hit a romantic plateau, this Mars-Venus square is your cue to shake things up. Single? Spark up a conversation with someone new. With both planets in mutable signs, it's the perfect moment to step outside your comfort zone and reignite that spark!

JUL 24

SUN-SATURN TRINE

Turn your passion into action! For the first time since the late 1800s, the courageous Leo Sun forms a royal flush with can-do Saturn in Aries, pumping you up with purposeful intention. With both of these authoritative planets in fire signs, there's an opportunity to dream big. If you've been scattering your focus, rein it in. Take time to visualize what the business world calls your BHAG—your "big, hairy, audacious goal." Picture yourself at the finish line of an accomplishment that feels challenging, even out of reach. Then, start thinking about the first step you can take in that direction. Micro moves can catalyze major results over time. Leaders and decision-makers, this transit reminds you that with great power comes great responsibility. Use this energy wisely to build something that lasts, and don't shy away from putting in the effort. The universe is giving you the green light to make a lasting impact. Don't hide your shine!

SUN-NEPTUNE TRINE

Declare your boldest dreams—the universe is ready to respond with fiery enthusiasm! Today, the radiant Sun in Leo teams up with visionary Neptune in Aries, urging you to speak your desires into existence with confidence and passion. Miracles could arrive in the form of sudden flashes of inspiration or spontaneous opportunities that ignite your spirit. Don't reflexively pass on invitations that feel out of your comfort zone, especially if they involve travel or adrenaline-pumping activities. They might be the sparks that light your way to a new, fulfilling path. For example, joining a new friend for whitewater rafting or going camping at a music festival could lead to a thrilling and perfectly-timed breakthrough. As you call on the universe for support, ask for these blessings to arrive with a motivating surge of energy, fueling your drive to conquer whatever comes your way.

NEW MOON IN LEO (3:11PM; 2°08')

Cupid fires off a fresh quiver of arrows today, as the new moon in Leo marks an annual romantic reset. This proactive lunar lift wants you back in the driver's seat (and on the throne) in your love life. If you've stopped articulating your desires or sharing your feelings, that ends today. With Mercury retrograde in Leo—and the new moon connecting to serious Saturn and mysterious Neptune and Pluto—it's ultra-important to send out clear signals to the people who matter in your life. Speak up when you have something to contribute to the conversation—and ask questions when you want to know more. This new moon is a powerful starting block for creative projects. How can you develop your talents over the next six months? Block off time and search out the support you need, whether a coach, teacher or art supplies.

JUL 25 SUN-PLUTO OPPOSITION

Power plays could disrupt your normally smooth interactions today as the commanding Sun clashes with intense Pluto. Stay alert for subtle intimidation tactics and be wary of people who attempt to ply you with charm and flattery. With Pluto in persuasive Aquarius and the Sun in proud Leo, someone might try to slip past your defenses by appealing to your vanity. Don't give people access to your inner sanctum—of your intellectual property—until you're sure of their true intentions. (Even then, you might have them sign an NDA.) At the same time, consider whether you're being too guarded with someone who actually HAS earned your trust. Are old fears clouding your judgment? It might be hard to see clearly today. If your instincts are raising red flags, don't brush it off. Stall on decision-making and conduct an independent investigation to get the full story.

JUL 30-AUG 25 VENUS IN CANCER

The nostalgic is romantic starting today, as love planet Venus sails out of Gemini's cerebral port and into Cancer's sentimental waters. After three weeks of overthinking every move, surrender and let your emotions take the wheel. During this warm-fuzzy phase, you may find yourself craving nurturing and comfort. Stay in rather than booking every spare moment with social activities. Private, relaxed moments allow you to connect to friends, lovers or your S.O. in the intimate style that Cancer prefers. Couples could find a shared focus turning to domestic matters, whether you're exchanging keys, pondering a renovation or shopping for an apartment (all things best done after Mercury turns direct on August 11). Be mindful not to bring too much caretaking into your romantic connections if you don't want to go from "hot mama" to "mother hen" in your partner's eyes.

JUL 30 CHIRON RETROGRADE

Wounded healer Chiron slips into its annual retrograde today, backing up through self-aware Aries until January 2. During its journey through the Ram's realm (2018–2027), the transformative asteroid is teaching us all lessons in self- empowerment and the constructive use of anger. If you've been feeling silenced, thwarted or resentful, this period provides an important window for introspection. Are you using the power of your voice to dominate others? If you've been playing a game of "the person who speaks the loudest wins," switch your strategy to active listening, where the goal is to understand rather than respond. For those who feel perpetually talked over, this retrograde gets you closer to the core of any confidence issues that may be standing in the way of your self-expression.

JUL 31 SUN-MERCURY RETROGRADE MEETUP

Say what? As the Leo Sun bangs into Mercury retrograde in Leo, pride and egos are on full display, which could turn even the most basic communication into an epic power struggle. ("Did that junior exec seriously just ask me to get him a coffee?") Hold off on making any pitches if you can, but if that's not an option, run a thorough LinkedIn and Google search on the people you're presenting to, noting who's in charge of what. Green lights could turn red fast if you threaten people's authority or make them feel "less than" in any way.

August

8

AUGUST
Moon Phase Calendar

SUN	MON	TUE	WED	THU	FRI	SAT
					1 ♏︎ 2nd Quarter	**2** ♏︎
3 ♏︎ ♐︎ 2:00AM	**4** ♐︎	**5** ♐︎ ♑︎ 1:04PM	**6** ♑︎	**7** ♑︎ ♒︎ 9:18PM	**8** ♒︎	**9** ♒︎ Full Moon 3:55AM
10 ♒︎ ♓︎ 2:50AM	**11** ♓︎	**12** ♓︎ ♈︎ 6:33AM	**13** ♈︎	**14** ♈︎ ♉︎ 9:22AM	**15** ♉︎	**16** ♉︎ 4th Quarter ♉︎→♊︎ 12:01PM
17 ♊︎	**18** ♊︎ ♋︎ 3:05PM	**19** ♋︎	**20** ♋︎ ♌︎ 7:17PM	**21** ♌︎	**22** ♌︎	**23** ♌︎→♍︎ 1:24AM ♍︎ New Moon 2:07AM
24 ♍︎	**25** ♍︎ ♎︎ 10:08AM	**26** ♎︎	**27** ♎︎ ♏︎ 9:27PM	**28** ♏︎	**29** ♏︎	**30** ♏︎ ♐︎ 10:04AM
31 ♐︎ 2nd Quarter						

Times listed are Eastern US Time Zone

KEY

♈︎ ARIES	♌︎ LEO	♐︎ SAGITTARIUS	**FM** FULL MOON
♉︎ TAURUS	♍︎ VIRGO	♑︎ CAPRICORN	**NM** NEW MOON
♊︎ GEMINI	♎︎ LIBRA	♒︎ AQUARIUS	**LE** LUNAR ECLIPSE
♋︎ CANCER	♏︎ SCORPIO	♓︎ PISCES	**SE** SOLAR ECLIPSE

AUGUST 9, 3:55AM
full moon in
Aquarius (17°00')

AQUARIUS FULL MOON CRYSTAL

LABRADORITE

Rainbow-hued labradorite looks different from every angle, reflecting the diversity and originality that Aquarius celebrates. An "illusion-buster," this stone protects us from over-serving others. Labradorite enables big-picture thinking and is powerful for meditation and insight.

AQUARIUS FULL MOON = CELEBRATE!

Your weirdest ideas

Teams and communities where you feel seen and embraced

Your sharing and accepting spirit

Technology that keeps you connected

Hopes and dreams for the future

Your idealistic nature that refuses to give up on humanity

8

AUGUST 23, 2:07AM

new moon in
Virgo (0°23')

VIRGO NEW MOON CRYSTAL

LEPIDOLITE

This soothing stone is also called the "grandmother stone" or "peace stone." Use it to calm your nerves and ease the worrying tendency that Virgo can stir up. Lepidolite encourages us to quiet inner criticism and embrace self-love and compassion.

VIRGO NEW MOON = FOCUS

Adopt (or cuddle) a pet

Work out and eat clean

Hire service providers and assistants

Practice random acts of kindness

Embrace healthy routines

Implement efficient systems

Break projects into actionable steps

August 2025

Longitude & Retrograde Ephemeris [00:00 UT]

Day	Sid.time	☉	☽	+12h☽	☿	♀	♂	♃	♄	♅	♆	♇	☊	☊	⚸	⚷	Day
1 Fr	20:39:26	♌ 09°01'21	♏ 03°15'34	♏ 09°11'17	℞ 09°00	♋ 00°57	♍ 26°18	♋ 11°42	℞ 01°38	♊ 00°55	℞ 01°58	℞ 02°25	℞ 20°16	♓ 19°04	♏ 14°08	℞ 27°09	**1** Fr
2 Sa	20:43:22	♌ 09°58'45	♏ 15°07'05	♏ 21°03'11	♌ 08°16	♋ 02°07	♍ 26°55	♋ 11°55	♈ 01°36	♊ 00°57	♈ 01°58	♒ 02°24	♓ 20°13	℞ 19°04	♏ 14°15	♈ 27°09	**2** Sa
3 Su	20:47:19	♌ 10°56'11	♏ 27°00'36	♐ 02°59'29	♌ 07°33	♋ 03°17	♍ 27°32	♋ 12°08	♈ 01°34	♊ 00°58	♈ 01°57	♒ 02°23	♓ 20°09	♓ 19°02	♏ 14°21	♈ 27°09	**3** Su
4 Mo	20:51:16	♌ 11°53'36	♐ 09°00'47	♐ 15°04'36	♌ 06°53	♋ 04°26	♍ 28°09	♋ 12°21	♈ 01°32	♊ 01°00	♈ 01°56	♒ 02°21	♓ 20°06	♓ 18°59	♏ 14°28	♈ 27°09	**4** Mo
5 Tu	20:55:12	♌ 12°51'03	♐ 21°11'47	♐ 27°22'18	♌ 06°16	♋ 05°36	♍ 28°46	♋ 12°33	♈ 01°30	♊ 01°01	♈ 01°55	♒ 02°20	♓ 20°03	♓ 18°55	♏ 14°35	♈ 27°09	**5** Tu
6 We	20:59:09	♌ 13°48'30	♑ 03°36'53	♑ 09°55'23	♌ 05°43	♋ 06°46	♍ 29°23	♋ 12°46	♈ 01°27	♊ 01°03	♈ 01°54	♒ 02°18	♓ 20°00	♓ 18°50	♏ 14°42	♈ 27°08	**6** We
7 Th	21:03:05	♌ 14°45'58	♑ 16°18'24	♑ 22°45'35	♌ 05°14	♋ 07°56	♎ 00°00	♋ 12°58	♈ 01°25	♊ 01°04	♈ 01°53	♒ 02°17	♓ 19°57	♓ 18°44	♏ 14°48	♈ 27°08	**7** Th
8 Fr	21:07:02	♌ 15°43'27	♑ 29°17'24	♒ 05°53'20	♌ 04°50	♋ 09°06	♎ 00°38	♋ 13°11	♈ 01°23	♊ 01°06	♈ 01°52	♒ 02°16	♓ 19°54	♓ 18°39	♏ 14°55	♈ 27°07	**8** Fr
9 Sa	21:10:58	♌ 16°40'57	♒ 12°33'43	♒ 19°17'53	♌ 04°32	♋ 10°16	♎ 01°15	♋ 13°23	♈ 01°20	♊ 01°07	♈ 01°51	♒ 02°14	♓ 19°50	♓ 18°34	♏ 15°02	♈ 27°07	**9** Sa
10 Su	21:14:55	♌ 17°38'28	♒ 26°06'03	♓ 02°57'27	♌ 04°20	♋ 11°26	♎ 01°53	♋ 13°36	♈ 01°17	♊ 01°09	♈ 01°50	♒ 02°13	♓ 19°47	♓ 18°31	♏ 15°08	♈ 27°06	**10** Su
11 Mo	21:18:51	♌ 18°36'00	♓ 09°52'12	♓ 16°49'29	♌ 04°15	♋ 12°37	♎ 02°30	♋ 13°48	♈ 01°15	♊ 01°10	♈ 01°49	♒ 02°12	♓ 19°44	♓ 18°29	♏ 15°15	♈ 27°06	**11** Mo
12 Tu	21:22:48	♌ 19°33'33	♓ 23°49'23	♈ 00°51'05	Ds 04°16	♋ 13°47	♎ 03°08	♋ 14°00	♈ 01°12	♊ 01°11	♈ 01°48	♒ 02°10	♓ 19°41	D 18°29	♏ 15°22	♈ 27°05	**12** Tu
13 We	21:26:45	♌ 20°31'07	♈ 07°54'40	♈ 14°59'19	♌ 04°24	♋ 14°58	♎ 03°46	♋ 14°13	♈ 01°09	♊ 01°13	♈ 01°47	♒ 02°09	♓ 19°38	♓ 18°30	♏ 15°28	♈ 27°05	**13** We
14 Th	21:30:41	♌ 21°28'43	♈ 22°05'10	♈ 29°11'27	♌ 04°40	♋ 16°08	♎ 04°23	♋ 14°25	♈ 01°06	♊ 01°14	♈ 01°45	♒ 02°08	♓ 19°35	♓ 18°32	♏ 15°35	♈ 27°04	**14** Th
15 Fr	21:34:38	♌ 22°26'21	♉ 06°18'19	♉ 13°25'01	♌ 05°02	♋ 17°19	♎ 05°01	♋ 14°37	♈ 01°03	♊ 01°15	♈ 01°44	♒ 02°06	♓ 19°31	♓ 18°33	♏ 15°42	♈ 27°03	**15** Fr
16 Sa	21:38:34	♌ 23°24'00	♉ 20°31'45	♉ 27°37'46	♌ 05°32	♋ 18°30	♎ 05°39	♋ 14°49	♈ 01°00	♊ 01°16	♈ 01°43	♒ 02°05	♓ 19°28	♓ 18°34	♏ 15°49	♈ 27°02	**16** Sa
17 Su	21:42:31	♌ 24°21'40	♊ 04°43'17	♊ 11°47'31	♌ 06°09	♋ 19°41	♎ 06°17	♋ 15°01	♈ 00°57	♊ 01°17	♈ 01°42	♒ 02°04	♓ 19°25	℞ 18°33	♏ 15°55	♈ 27°01	**17** Su
18 Mo	21:46:27	♌ 25°19'22	♊ 18°50'42	♊ 25°52'02	♌ 06°53	♋ 20°52	♎ 06°55	♋ 15°13	♈ 00°54	♊ 01°18	♈ 01°41	♒ 02°02	♓ 19°22	♓ 18°32	♏ 16°02	♈ 27°00	**18** Mo
19 Tu	21:50:24	♌ 26°17'06	♋ 02°51'41	♋ 09°48'54	♌ 07°44	♋ 22°03	♎ 07°33	♋ 15°25	♈ 00°50	♊ 01°19	♈ 01°39	♒ 02°01	♓ 19°19	♓ 18°30	♏ 16°09	♈ 26°59	**19** Tu
20 We	21:54:20	♌ 27°14'52	♋ 16°43'48	♋ 23°35'40	♌ 08°41	♋ 23°14	♎ 08°11	♋ 15°37	♈ 00°47	♊ 01°20	♈ 01°38	♒ 02°00	♓ 19°15	♓ 18°27	♏ 16°15	♈ 26°58	**20** We
21 Th	21:58:17	♌ 28°12'39	♌ 00°24'37	♌ 07°09'59	♌ 09°45	♋ 24°25	♎ 08°50	♋ 15°48	♈ 00°43	♊ 01°21	♈ 01°37	♒ 01°59	♓ 19°12	♓ 18°24	♏ 16°22	♈ 26°57	**21** Th
22 Fr	22:02:14	♌ 29°10'27	♌ 13°51'56	♌ 20°29'52	♌ 10°56	♋ 25°36	♎ 09°28	♋ 16°00	♈ 00°40	♊ 01°21	♈ 01°35	♒ 01°58	♓ 19°09	♓ 18°21	♏ 16°29	♈ 26°56	**22** Fr
23 Sa	22:06:10	♍ 00°08'17	♌ 27°04'03	♍ 03°33'58	♌ 12°12	♋ 26°48	♎ 10°06	♋ 16°11	♈ 00°36	♊ 01°22	♈ 01°34	♒ 01°56	♓ 19°06	♓ 18°19	♏ 16°35	♈ 26°55	**23** Sa
24 Su	22:10:07	♍ 01°06'08	♍ 10°00'00	♍ 16°21'47	♌ 13°34	♋ 27°59	♎ 10°45	♋ 16°23	♈ 00°32	♊ 01°23	♈ 01°33	♒ 01°55	♓ 19°03	♓ 18°18	♏ 16°42	♈ 26°54	**24** Su
25 Mo	22:14:03	♍ 02°04'01	♍ 22°39'47	♍ 28°53'47	♌ 15°02	♋ 29°10	♎ 11°23	♋ 16°34	♈ 00°29	♊ 01°24	♈ 01°31	♒ 01°54	♓ 19°00	D 18°18	♏ 16°49	♈ 26°53	**25** Mo
26 Tu	22:17:60	♍ 03°01'55	♎ 05°04'23	♎ 11°11'27	16°34	♌ 00°22	♎ 12°02	♋ 16°46	♈ 00°25	♊ 01°24	♈ 01°30	♒ 01°53	♓ 18°56	♓ 18°19	♏ 16°56	♈ 26°51	**26** Tu
27 We	22:21:56	♍ 03°59'50	♎ 17°15'44	♎ 23°17'12	♌ 18°10	♌ 01°34	♎ 12°40	♋ 16°57	♈ 00°21	♊ 01°25	♈ 01°29	♒ 01°52	♓ 18°53	♓ 18°20	♏ 17°02	♈ 26°50	**27** We
28 Th	22:25:53	♍ 04°57'47	♎ 29°16'41	♏ 05°14'16	♌ 19°51	♌ 02°45	♎ 13°19	♋ 17°08	♈ 00°17	♊ 01°25	♈ 01°27	♒ 01°50	♓ 18°50	♓ 18°21	♏ 17°09	♈ 26°48	**28** Th
29 Fr	22:29:49	♍ 05°55'45	♏ 11°10'50	♏ 17°06'32	♌ 21°35	♌ 03°57	♎ 13°58	♋ 17°19	♈ 00°13	♊ 01°26	♈ 01°26	♒ 01°49	♓ 18°47	♓ 18°22	♏ 17°16	♈ 26°47	**29** Fr
30 Sa	22:33:46	♍ 06°53'44	♏ 23°02'19	♏ 28°58'22	♌ 23°21	♌ 05°09	♎ 14°37	♋ 17°30	♈ 00°09	♊ 01°26	♈ 01°24	♒ 01°48	♓ 18°44	♓ 18°23	♏ 17°22	♈ 26°45	**30** Sa
31 Su	22:37:43	♍ 07°51'45	♐ 04°55'39	♐ 10°54'22	♌ 25°11	♌ 06°21	♎ 15°15	♋ 17°41	♈ 00°05	♊ 01°26	♈ 01°23	♒ 01°47	♓ 18°41	♓ 18°23	♏ 17°29	♈ 26°44	**31** Su
Δ Delta	01:58:17	28°50'24"	391°40'04"	391°43'04"	16°11'	35°23'	18°57'	5°58'	-1°32'	0°31'	-0°35'	-0°38'	-1°35'	-0°40'	3°20'	-0°25'	**Delta**

Ephemeris tables and data provided by **Astro-Seek.com.** All times in UTC.

8

AUGUST
MONTHLY HOTSPOTS

8

AUG 1

WAXING QUARTER MOON IN SCORPIO (8:41AM)

To share or not to share? Today's balancing Scorpio quarter moon helps you figure out what's worth revealing and what's better left unsaid. If you're too cryptic, it might frustrate people who are trying to get a clear read on you—and that, in turn, can make you seem harder to trust. On the flip side, you don't want to flood people by oversharing. Try to strike a balance between coming across as approachable and discerning. Let people earn your confidence gradually, but don't be so guarded that it feels like they need to jump through hoops to get close!

VENUS-SATURN SQUARE

Avoid riding on assumptions today. As Venus in sensitive Cancer clashes with authoritative Saturn in feisty Aries, any attempts to read between the lines will only leave you feeling confused and upset. Whether it's romantic or business-related, take stock: Are you both on the same page about where you're heading together? If one of you feels burdened with doing all the emotional (or literal) heavy lifting, don't move forward without addressing it first. It's crucial that both parties feel heard and supported but ease into any tense discussions. The frustration you've been carrying could be breaking news to the other person who thought everything was "fine." If you want to clear the air, make sure to extend the benefit of the doubt.

VENUS-NEPTUNE SQUARE

Mixed signals and muddled messages could also be part of today's already-complex forecast. Venus in nurturing Cancer forms her second square of the day, this time with hazy Neptune in headstrong Aries. Attempts to launch a charm offensive could backfire, causing people to feel like you're giving them a hard sell. If you're seeking advice, make sure you're asking opinions from people with actual experience. The cacophony of hot takes could be downright overwhelming. Here's a thought: Keep some things to yourself and let them marinate. Remember, feelings are fleeting and usually aren't the whole story.

AUG 6-SEP 22 MARS IN LIBRA

Summer flings could turn serious over the next seven weeks, as lusty Mars blazes into Libra and amps up everyone's urge to merge for the rest of the season. Easy though! It's tempting to romanticize when Mars blasts into this "love and marriage" sign every other year. As the impatient red planet accelerates the action, you could get locked into a serious situation before you REALLY know what (and who) you're dealing with. If it's longevity you're after, what's the rush? That goes for all sorts of partnerships, from pleasure to business. Lean into Libra's languorous vibes and make the courtship process the exciting part. For couples, Mars in Libra adds a dash of spice, but it can also stir up passive-aggressive bickering, especially if one  of you is pulling an unequal share of the load. Mars is in "detriment" in Libra, meaning it's an uncomfortable place. And it makes sense: Mars is the god of war, while Libra is all about peace, love and harmony. It will take extra effort to maintain your emotional equilibrium now.

AUG 8

MARS-URANUS TRINE

It's all about who you know! Networking efforts shift into fifth gear as driven Mars in Libra connects the dots with team-spirited Uranus in Gemini. With these overachieving planets in social air signs, this is one of the best days of the year for assembling a supergroup. If you've already formed your soul squad, put your heads together. Genius ideas could sprout promising (and profitable!) wings under this air-sign trine. Struggling to find a meeting time that works for everyone? Start a group on Marco Polo or Slack to get the ball rolling in the meanwhile.

MARS-SATURN OPPOSITION

We'd never tell you to give up on a dream, but if you're hitting roadblocks, pull over and recalibrate your plan. Today, assertive Mars locks horns with restrictive Saturn, but here's where things get wonky. With Mars in patient Libra and Saturn in impulsive Aries, everything could feel wildly out of balance. Hitting the gas when the direction is confusing could take you on a senseless detour. So, chill. This speedbump could be a blessing in disguise. Bake in time to test your ideas, gather crucial feedback and make sure your actions are aligned with your core values. Once you've fine-tuned the details, you'll be primed for a powerful comeback!

8

AUG 9

FULL MOON IN AQUARIUS (3:55AM; 17°00')

There's strength in numbers today, as the year's only full moon in collaborative, forward-thinking Aquarius lights up the skies. If you've been struggling to get ahead, here's your cue to reach out to community. Surround yourself with people who fuel your mission and give you the courage to speak out. Just remember to give credit where it's due. What goes around, comes around. Feeling too blessed to be stressed? Share your good fortune with people who could use a leg up. Aquarius is the sign of activism, so dive in and make a difference! Rally behind a cause you're passionate about or raise your voice against injustice. While teamwork is the theme, here's a cosmic reminder: Blending in doesn't mean losing yourself. This full moon wants you to let individuality shine.

MARS-NEPTUNE OPPOSITION

Know thy limits! With relentless Mars in Libra facing off against boundary-blurring Neptune in Aries, finding the "stop" button could feel impossible. It's easy to lose track of how much might be considered "overboard" under this exhausting cosmic clash. But if you push too hard, burnout is practically guaranteed. Mars in genial Libra wants to keep everyone happy, while Neptune in dreamy Aries urges you to give it your all—even when you're running on fumes. Generosity may surge, but be mindful of your energy reserves. Instead of soldiering through, build in essential breaks to avoid crashing.

AUG 10 MARS-PLUTO TRINE

Forget brainstorms. Today's intellectual air trine between potent Mars and Pluto could deliver mental monsoons! Everyone's genius will be firing on all cylinders. See what happens when you team up with other great minds. Mars fuels your boldness while Pluto gives you the strategic savvy to unpack a problem that's been vexing you. If you hit on a groundbreaking solution, let the decision-makers in on it. But first, make sure you've adequately stamped your name on any ideas you want credit for. Both Mars and Pluto are known for being cutthroat, and even while in sociable air signs (Mars in Libra, Pluto in Aquarius), they still caution against being overly trusting.

AUG 11 MERCURY RETROGRADE ENDS

If a feral cat got hold of your tongue over the past few weeks, you might be shy about letting out so much as a "mew." Blame it on mouthy Mercury, who's been on a retrograde stalk through Leo's jungle since July 18. There's nothing healthy about holding in emotions forever, and fortunately, you won't have to. This dramatic arc takes a turn for the positive as Mercury shifts back into direct motion today. Better still? The silver-tongued celestial flirt roams happily through Leo's jungle until September 2. What felt like a Greek tragedy earlier this month might not become a comedy overnight (or ever). But maybe you'll finally be able to laugh about it...a little...or glean the golden lesson from the experience. Have you noticed any glaring gaps in leadership since July 18? Don't ignore the call of the crown if you're supposed to take charge around here. And if you're trying to get a clear read on a love interest, signals become way more obvious starting today.

AUG 12 VENUS-JUPITER MEETUP

Naughty by nurture? As bawdy Jupiter aligns with loving Venus in the tender sign of Cancer, the stage is set for a love story steeped in TLC and devotion. It's been more than a decade since Venus and Jupiter met in the Crab's compassionate realm making this a banner day for sweet, soulful affection. Focus on relationships that are truly reciprocal. If that means casting your net into new waters, so be it. Worldly, adventurous Jupiter invites you to expand your romantic boundaries. As you do, let superficial flings dissolve and half-hearted entanglements fade away. Even if no one good is on your radar today, start making space for authentic, heartfelt connections in your life. Couples could benefit from a change of scenery over the coming week, ideally in a cozy, intimate setting. Even if you're tucked away at home, try to find minutes to screen out the rest of the world and relax in each other's company.

AUG 16 WANING QUARTER MOON IN TAURUS (1:12AM)

Stop, drop and reprioritize. Today's grounding quarter moon in sensible yet sensual Taurus reconnects you with your deepest values. Assess your priorities and principles, ensuring you're firmly anchored in them before making any significant choices. If you feel your focus drifting, trip back to the essentials and eliminate the excess. Less is more as long as you don't veer into extreme austerity. Trim back on areas where you might be overindulging, and consider how you can reintroduce little luxuries in more sustainable ways. Taurus energy loves to splurge but also respects resourcefulness, allowing you to enjoy the best of both worlds. If your spending is starting to exceed your budget or if a project is expanding beyond its initial scope, plan a "money date." Choose a cozy cafe, bring your budgets, and review them in a setting that makes the task feel like a treat rather than a chore.

8

AUG 22-SEP 22 SUN IN VIRGO (4:34PM)

Back to basics! As the Sun waves goodbye to the high-drama of Leo and enters meticulous Virgo, it casts a healthy glow on our late-summer affairs. Clean living is the new flex, especially after a month of Leo's indulgent hedonism. In preparation for September's back-to-everything bustle, lean into this earth sign's efficiency to get life organized and systematized. Whether it's decluttering your space or fine-tuning your digital tools, give every corner of your life a thorough once-over. Don't spend ALL your time folding laundry and wiping down surfaces. Outdoorsy Virgo season beckons you into sunshine for bike rides to the beach, yoga in the park and sunset pickleball tournaments. Virgo's green ethos inspires conscious consumerism. Look for brands that are environmentally focused, sustainably sourced and have fair labor practices. Savor the harvest of fresh, locally sourced produce, each bite packed with vitality-boosting nutrients.

AUG 23 NEW MOON IN VIRGO (2:07AM; 0°23') #1 OF 2

Bless this mess? Absolutely not. Today's new moon in Virgo—the first of a rare, back-to-back pair in 2025—sends us into efficiency overload. It's time to sort, file, organize, systematize—and energize. Reduce space by decluttering both your physical and virtual environments. Those distracting piles and unchecked messages take up a lot of psychic energy, even when you're worrying about when to get them done. Chip away at them by devoting a daily block of time for clearing the slate. With this new moon squaring Gemini, you may need to pull back from distractions in order to get the job done. If that means temporarily hiding a few apps and muting threads, so be it. Since wellness is Virgo's domain, use this lunar launch to get a fitness routine in motion. Could your meals be healthier, your sleep more sanctified? Feather your nest with everything you need to keep your body humming like a well-oiled machine—from a fridge full of fresh produce, snacks like raw almonds in the pantry and an essential oil diffuser on your nightstand.

AUG 24 SUN-URANUS SQUARE

Do your very best to remain solution-oriented today. As the Sun in meticulous Virgo squares off with wrench-throwing Uranus in Gemini, control issues may flare while rebellious actions could escalate tensions. This biannual clash tends to heighten ego battles and power struggles, prompting quick, unconsidered reactions. With Uranus playing devil's advocate in Gemini, contrarian attitudes can make it impossible to align around anything. Thanks to the flaw-finding Virgo Sun, nitpicking can intensify, leading to standoffs. Aim to be a problem solver in the face of any discord. If that's not possible, call a timeout until tomorrow when the skies are more agreeable.

AUG 25

VENUS IN LEO (AUG 25-SEP 19)

Romantic Venus restores her sultry roar as she shimmies into the lion's den until September 19. If you've had trouble tapping into your fierceness over the past few weeks, the tide turns now. This glamorous, amorous cycle calls for high-fashion 'fits, eight-course dinners and full-on PDA. This is a powerful time to initiate creative projects, dive back into the dating pool, or rev up romance, either with a new interest or long-term love. Work on your personal branding to make sure your front-facing presentation is a proper reflection of the genius within. With Mercury fully out of retrograde, the coast is clear to hire a stylist, set up a photo shoot or work with a professional designer. When it comes to love, this Venus cycle holds nothing back. Hire the skywriter, gush like a hopeful on The Bachelor ("I am so ready to take this journey with you..."), swipe right like it was your second job. But don't forget legendary Leo Whitney Houston's words: Learning to love yourself is the greatest love of all.

VENUS-SATURN TRINE

Love goals take a more solid shape today as romantic Venus in Leo swings into a harmonizing fire trine with structured Saturn in Aries. With both planets in outspoken fire signs, it won't be hard to bring up the subject of "us" or to simply start a conversation (with anyone, anywhere) about your ideal vision for your romantic life. With future-focused Saturn involved, couples can discuss ways to support each other's ambitions. You may have to find creative ways to make time for the relationship while also cheering on one another's independent growth. Stuck in a situationship? If you're ready for more than the other person has to give, thank them for the experience and gracefully move forward. Consider it a blessing that you didn't invest more time in the wrong match. And if you're the one who doesn't see a long-term future, be mature and set them free instead of keeping them hanging on.

AUG 26 VENUS-NEPTUNE TRINE

Take the guardrails off your imagination as passionate Venus in Leo fist-bumps inspirational Neptune in Aries. This energizing fire trine turns up the heat on emotions, melting barriers and fostering deep connections. However, that surge of openness and warmth could also leave you vulnerable to a charming raconteur. Sharpen your discernment to ensure that only the truly deserving gain access to your inner circle. If you're typically reserved or tend to keep a stiff upper lip, today offers a beautiful opportunity to soften those defenses. Embrace the courage to connect authentically and allow your heart to lead the way. It's an optimal day for heartfelt exchanges. Embrace the spirit of boldness and spontaneity in your relationships.

AUG 27 VENUS-PLUTO OPPOSITION

Trust issues could flare up today as Venus in dramatic Leo locks horns with calculating Pluto in cool Aquarius. If you experience yourself having a knee-jerk reaction to a perceived betrayal—or even the slightest feeling of neglect—try to remember that appearances can be deceiving. While it's wise to flag suspicious behavior, do your detective work before flinging accusations. Even if you find evidence, you're not likely to get any answers by intensely grilling the "suspect." If you're just getting to know someone, pay attention to red flags and leave any situation where you feel unsafe or uncomfortable. Did someone's profile raise suspicion on an app? Don't ignore your intuition. Report and block anyone who seems outright inappropriate.

AUG 31 WAXING QUARTER MOON IN SAGITTARIUS (2:25AM)

Feeling bogged down by the minutiae and missing your spark? Today's balancing quarter moon in expansive Sagittarius reignites your visionary zeal. While a detailed plan supported by data is essential, it's the thrill of potential and purpose that truly drives us. Take time to evaluate areas where you've become inflexible and open up to alternative viewpoints. Remember, exploring new ideas doesn't commit you to them—it simply broadens your horizons. If you've hit a wall, step away from the competitive fray today and reconnect with what brings you joy. Sagittarius, the philosopher of the zodiac, encourages you to consider broader implications. Are your efforts inclusive enough? How do your plans affect the community, your environment, and your loved ones? Scrutinize your approach and make a few adjustments. **Results may already manifest with next week's full moon!**

8

September

SEPTEMBER
Moon Phase Calendar

SUN	MON	TUE	WED	THU	FRI	SAT
	1 ♐ 9:45PM	**2** ♑	**3** ♑	**4** ♒ 6:32AM	**5** ♒	**6** ♓ 11:54AM
7 ♓ Full Moon & Lunar Eclipse 2:09PM	**8** ♓ 2:37PM	**9** ♈	**10** ♈ ♉ 4:03PM	**11** ♉	**12** ♊ 5:38PM	**13** ♊
14 ♊ 4th Quarter ♊→♋ 8:30PM	**15** ♋	**16** ♋	**17** ♋ ♌ 1:02AM	**18** ♌	**19** ♌ ♍ 8:23AM	**20** ♍
21 ♍ New Moon & Solar Eclipse 3:54PM ♍→♎ 5:41PM	**22** ♎	**23** ♎	**24** ♎ ♏ 5:00AM	**25** ♏	**26** ♏ ♐ 5:37PM	**27** ♐
28 ♐	**29** ♐→♑ 5:55AM ♑ 2nd Quarter	**30** ♑				

Times listed are Eastern US Time Zone

KEY

♈ ARIES	♌ LEO	♐ SAGITTARIUS	**FM**	FULL MOON
♉ TAURUS	♍ VIRGO	♑ CAPRICORN	**NM**	NEW MOON
♊ GEMINI	♎ LIBRA	♒ AQUARIUS	**LE**	LUNAR ECLIPSE
♋ CANCER	♏ SCORPIO	♓ PISCES	**SE**	SOLAR ECLIPSE

9

SEPTEMBER 7, 2:09PM

full moon in Pisces (15°23')

PISCES FULL MOON CRYSTAL

ANGELITE

This pale blue stone activates the Pisces-ruled upper chakras (throat, third-eye and crown), allowing your mind to download messages from your angels, guides and your higher self. Angelite can dissolve emotional or energetic boundaries that may be holding you back from progress.

PISCES FULL MOON = CELEBRATE!

Your secret fantasies

Your creative spirit

Messages from your dreams

People who inspire you to think beyond current limitations

Compassion and empathy

Blurry lines that don't need to be sharpened

The beauty in "ugly" things

9

Partial Solar Eclipse

SEPTEMBER 21, 3:54PM

new moon in
Virgo (29°05')

VIRGO NEW MOON CRYSTAL

LEPIDOLITE

This soothing stone is also called the "grandmother stone" or "peace stone." Use it to calm your nerves and ease the worrying tendency that Virgo can stir up. Lepidolite encourages us to quiet inner criticism and embrace self-love and compassion.

VIRGO NEW MOON = FOCUS

Adopt (or cuddle) a pet

Work out and eat clean

Hire service providers and assistants

Practice random acts of kindness

Embrace healthy routines

Implement efficient systems

Break projects into actionable steps

9

September 2025

Longitude & Retrograde Ephemeris [00:00 UT]

Day	Sid.time	☉	☽	+12h☽	☿	♀	♂	♃	♄	♅	♆	♇	☊	☊	⚸	⚷	Day
1 Mo	22:41:39	♍08°49'47	♐16°55'30	♐22°59'13	♌27°03	♌07°33	♎15°54	♋17°52	℞ 00°01	♊01°27	℞ 01°21	℞ 01°46	℞ 18°37	℞ 18°23	♏17°36	℞ 26°42	**1** Mo
2 Tu	22:45:36	♍09°47'51	♐29°06'28	♑05°17'20	♌28°56	♌08°45	♎16°33	♋18°03	♓29°57	♊01°27	♈01°20	♒01°45	♓18°34	♓18°23	♏17°42	♈26°41	**2** Tu
3 We	22:49:32	♍10°45'56	♑11°32'43	♑17°52'37	♍00°50	♌09°57	♎17°12	♋18°13	♓29°52	♊01°27	♈01°18	♒01°44	♓18°31	♓18°22	♏17°49	♈26°39	**3** We
4 Th	22:53:29	♍11°44'02	♑24°17'46	♒00°48'02	♍02°46	♌11°09	♎17°51	♋18°24	♓29°48	♊01°27	♈01°17	♒01°43	♓18°28	♓18°21	♏17°56	♈26°37	**4** Th
5 Fr	22:57:25	♍12°42'10	♒07°24'01	♒14°05'21	♍04°42	♌12°22	♎18°31	♋18°34	♓29°44	♊01°27	♈01°15	♒01°42	♓18°25	♓18°20	♏18°03	♈26°35	**5** Fr
6 Sa	23:01:22	♍13°40'19	♒20°52'26	♒27°44'42	♍06°38	♌13°34	♎19°10	♋18°45	♓29°40	♊01°27	♈01°14	♒01°41	♓18°21	♓18°20	♏18°09	♈26°34	**6** Sa
7 Su	23:05:18	♍14°38'30	♓04°42'19	♓11°44'29	♍08°34	♌14°47	♎19°49	♋18°55	♓29°35	℞ 01°27	♈01°12	♒01°40	♓18°18	♓18°20	♏18°16	♈26°32	**7** Su
8 Mo	23:09:15	♍15°36'43	♓18°51'09	♓26°01'18	♍10°31	♌15°59	♎20°29	♋19°05	♓29°31	♊01°27	♈01°10	♒01°39	♓18°15	D 18°19	♏18°23	♈26°30	**8** Mo
9 Tu	23:13:12	♍16°34'57	♈03°14'44	♈10°30'18	♍12°26	♌17°12	♎21°08	♋19°15	♓29°26	♊01°27	♈01°09	♒01°38	♓18°12	♓18°20	♏18°29	♈26°28	**9** Tu
10 We	23:17:08	♍17°33'13	♈17°47'43	♈25°05'45	♍14°22	♌18°24	♎21°47	♋19°25	♓29°22	♊01°27	♈01°07	♒01°37	♓18°09	♓18°20	♏18°36	♈26°26	**10** We
11 Th	23:21:05	♍18°31'31	♉02°24'09	♉09°41'42	♍16°16	♌19°37	♎22°27	♋19°35	♓29°17	♊01°27	♈01°06	♒01°36	♓18°06	℞ 18°20	♏18°43	♈26°24	**11** Th
12 Fr	23:25:01	♍19°29'51	♉16°58'13	♉24°12'39	♍18°10	♌20°50	♎23°07	♋19°45	♓29°13	♊01°26	♈01°04	♒01°36	♓18°02	♓18°20	♏18°49	♈26°22	**12** Fr
13 Sa	23:28:58	♍20°28'14	♊01°24'57	♊08°34'13	♍20°03	♌22°03	♎23°46	♋19°54	♓29°08	♊01°26	♈01°02	♒01°35	♓17°59	♓18°19	♏18°56	♈26°20	**13** Sa
14 Su	23:32:54	♍21°26'38	♊15°40'33	♊22°43'15	♍21°55	♌23°15	♎24°26	♋20°04	♓29°04	♊01°26	♈01°01	♒01°34	♓17°56	♓18°19	♏19°03	♈26°18	**14** Su
15 Mo	23:36:51	♍22°25'05	♊29°42'35	♋06°37'58	♍23°47	♌24°28	♎25°06	♋20°13	♓28°59	♊01°25	♈00°59	♒01°33	♓17°53	D 18°19	♏19°10	♈26°16	**15** Mo
16 Tu	23:40:47	♍23°23'34	♋13°29'46	♋20°17'33	♍25°37	♌25°41	♎25°46	♋20°22	♓28°54	♊01°25	♈00°57	♒01°32	♓17°50	♓18°20	♏19°16	♈26°13	**16** Tu
17 We	23:44:44	♍24°22'05	♋27°01'45	♌03°42'01	♍27°26	♌26°55	♎26°26	♋20°32	♓28°50	♊01°24	♈00°56	♒01°32	♓17°47	♓18°20	♏19°23	♈26°11	**17** We
18 Th	23:48:41	♍25°20'38	♌10°18'49	♌16°51'49	♍29°14	♌28°08	♎27°06	♋20°41	♓28°45	♊01°24	♈00°54	♒01°31	♓17°43	♓18°21	♏19°30	♈26°09	**18** Th
19 Fr	23:52:37	♍26°19'13	♌23°21'32	♌29°47'39	♎01°01	♌29°21	♎27°46	♋20°50	♓28°41	♊01°23	♈00°52	♒01°30	♓17°40	♓18°21	♏19°36	♈26°07	**19** Fr
20 Sa	23:56:34	♍27°17'50	♍06°10'40	♍12°30'18	♎02°48	♍00°34	♎28°26	♋20°59	♓28°36	♊01°23	♈00°51	♒01°30	♓17°37	♓18°22	♏19°43	♈26°04	**20** Sa
21 Su	00:00:30	♍28°16'30	♍18°47'02	♍25°00'38	♎04°33	♍01°47	♎29°06	♋21°07	♓28°31	♊01°22	♈00°49	♒01°29	♓17°34	℞ 18°22	♏19°50	♈26°02	**21** Su
22 Mo	00:04:27	♍29°15'11	♎01°11'36	♎07°19'42	♎06°17	♍03°01	♎29°46	♋21°16	♓28°27	♊01°21	♈00°48	♒01°28	♓17°31	♓18°22	♏19°57	♈26°00	**22** Mo
23 Tu	00:08:23	♎00°13'54	♎13°25'29	♎19°28'47	♎08°00	♍04°14	♏00°27	♋21°24	♓28°22	♊01°20	♈00°46	♒01°28	♓17°27	♓18°21	♏20°03	♈25°57	**23** Tu
24 We	00:12:20	♎01°12'39	♎25°30'11	♏01°29'33	♎09°42	♍05°28	♏01°07	♋21°33	♓28°17	♊01°19	♈00°44	♒01°27	♓17°24	♓18°19	♏20°10	♈25°55	**24** We
25 Th	00:16:16	♎02°11'26	♏07°27'33	♏13°24'09	♎11°23	♍06°41	♏01°47	♋21°41	♓28°13	♊01°18	♈00°43	♒01°27	♓17°21	♓18°17	♏20°17	♈25°52	**25** Th
26 Fr	00:20:13	♎03°10'14	♏19°20'03	♏25°15'16	♎13°03	♍07°55	♏02°28	♋21°49	♓28°08	♊01°18	♈00°41	♒01°26	♓17°18	♓18°15	♏20°23	♈25°50	**26** Fr
27 Sa	00:24:09	♎04°09'05	♐01°10'39	♐07°06'13	♎14°43	♍09°09	♏03°08	♋21°57	♓28°03	♊01°17	♈00°39	♒01°26	♓17°15	♓18°13	♏20°30	♈25°47	**27** Sa
28 Su	00:28:06	♎05°07'57	♐13°02'53	♐19°00'46	♎16°21	♍10°22	♏03°49	♋22°05	♓27°59	♊01°15	♈00°38	♒01°25	♓17°12	♓18°11	♏20°37	♈25°45	**28** Su
29 Mo	00:32:03	♎06°06'52	♐25°00'48	♑01°03'09	♎17°58	♍11°36	♏04°30	♋22°12	♓27°54	♊01°14	♈00°36	♒01°25	♓17°08	♓18°10	♏20°43	♈25°42	**29** Mo
30 Tu	00:35:59	♎07°05'48	♑07°08'47	♑13°17'53	♎19°35	♍12°50	♏05°11	♋22°20	♓27°50	♊01°13	♈00°34	♒01°24	♓17°05	D 18°09	♏20°50	♈25°40	**30** Tu
Δ Delta	01:54:19	28°16'00"	380°13'17"	380°18'40"	52°32'	35°16'	19°16'	4°28'	2°11'	-0°13'	-0°46'	-0°21'	-1°32'	-0°13'	3°14'	-1°02'	**Delta**

Ephemeris tables and data provided by **Astro-Seek.com.** All times in UTC.

SEPTEMBER
MONTHLY HOTSPOTS

SEP 1–NOV 27 SATURN RETROGRADE IN PISCES

Inspect to protect! Cosmic auditor Saturn, who's been retrograde in Aries since July 13, slips back into Pisces, the sign of soulful and subconscious healing. For the remaining three months of its backspin (until November 27), the taskmaster planet puts the kibosh on escapism and brings a healthy dose of reality checks to match your fantasies. If you put the cart before the horse while Saturn was in Aries, you may need to backtrack and make sure you have proper support for your mission. During this part of the retrograde, take time to master the basics or polish your core skills before hanging your shingle.

SEP 2-18 MERCURY IN VIRGO

Embrace the minimalist ethos as strategic Mercury buzzes into its home sign of Virgo and directs you to streamline and simplify. Fling open cupboards, closets and storage spaces and give the contents an unflinching review. Donate, swap and say farewell to things that are no longer your vibe. More importantly, don't race to replace them. Having fewer, but more treasured, objects can be preferable to stuffing every square inch of your home with "stuff." Wellness is earthy Virgo's domain. Since Mercury loves to monitor data, a fitness tracker could become your ultimate fall accessory. Speaking of monitoring, watch a tendency to be nosy and critical over the next few weeks. This opinionated Mercury cycle turns everyone into a life coach, but if your advice wasn't asked for, think twice before offering it. Instead, turn the focus to making your own life better.

SEP 3 MERCURY-URANUS SQUARE

Can you put your money where your mouth is? Mercury in detail-oriented Virgo spins into a testy square with Uranus in quick-witted Gemini. This could serve up a stark reality check, prompting a necessary shift in your game plan. While "faking it till you make it" has its moments, that approach won't cut it now. Your brilliant ideas risk remaining unrealized if you're caught overpromising and underdelivering. This misstep could chip away at your credibility, painting you more as an unreliable dreamer than the pioneering innovator you aim to be. To avoid this pitfall, streamline your master plan into manageable phases. Celebrate a small milestone rather than rushing toward a premature victory lap. Remember, those incremental achievements are what actually build substantial success.

SEPT 4 MARS-JUPITER SQUARE

Familiarity can breed contempt today, so look out! As Mars in Libra locks into a tense square with maximizer Jupiter in Cancer, you may feel pressured, manipulated or otherwise guilt-tripped by the people closest to you. (And all they did was ask you how you wanted them to prepare your coffee!) It's not about a lack of appreciation, but rather a growing sense of obligation that is making it hard for you—or the other person involved—to say "no." If you're the egregious over-functioner, take this as your cue to pause and pull back. With a little time and space, the other person is bound to pick up the reins. First, they might need to miss you a little—excruciating as that pause in the action can be. Maybe it's you who needs a longer lapse in between heartfelt huddles. Be honest but kind, making sure to reassure loved ones that you're not abandoning them—and that yes, you WILL be back. Is a romantic relationship wilting from neglect as you tend to family and close friends? Unless it's truly an emergency, don't cancel your coffee date (or ignore your buzzing app) to go dry a sister's tears. Send an empowering "You've got this" text, then follow Cupid's arrows to your bliss.

SEP 6, 2025–FEB 3, 2026 URANUS RETROGRADE

Did someone hit the mute button on your rebel yell? Renegade Uranus spins into its annual, five-month retrograde, and for the first time since the 1940s, its backspin begins in motormouthed Gemini. On November 7, the side-spinning planet paddles back through money-minded Taurus for the remainder of its retrograde, until February 3, 2026. Starting today, begin a period of reevaluation and innovation in how you communicate, think, and connect. Question old beliefs and explore new ideas, especially in the Gemini-ruled realms of technology, education, and media. As Uranus retraces its steps, be prepared for unexpected revelations that challenge conventional thinking. When Uranus reverses into Taurus on November 7, it takes its final trip through the Bull's pen in our lifetimes. This will be a chance to crystallize all the hard-won economic lessons you've learned since this cycle began in 2018. Values—and what you consider valuable—may have evolved in ways you never expected. Take stock.

SEP 7 FULL MOON IN PISCES (2:09PM; 15°23') (TOTAL LUNAR ECLIPSE IN PISCES)

Surrender to a soulful, spiritual groove—you might not have any other choice as the annual full moon in Pisces arrives as a total lunar eclipse. At its best, this full moon can be enchanted and poetic, helping you voice your dreams and deeply held desires. Let down your walls and boundaries a bit. A willingness to be open—and to just try new experiences—could bring major life shifts as the full moon trines worldly, adventurous

9

Jupiter. But that's no excuse for casting good sense aside. Because this full moon is also a shadowy lunar eclipse, you may romanticize to the point of delusion. Careful not to put a rose-tinted filter over your eclipse glasses. There's good and bad to everything (and everyone) but it's essential to look at the full picture, especially since analytical Mercury opposes the full moon. A snake who's been lurking in the grass could be exposed within 2-4 weeks of this full moon. No more excuses! As the twelfth and final sign of the zodiac, Pisces helps us let it go. Farewell, toxic frenemies and energy vampires! Hello, to all that is good, true and beautiful—traits that go WAY beyond surface appearances.

SEP 13 SUN-MERCURY MEETUP IN VIRGO

As the Sun and congenial Mercury sync up in service-oriented Virgo, look for ways to contribute, no matter how small. Show up with an extra coffee in hand, help a friend make a few last-minute Canva graphics for a presentation, offer a relative a ride to a doctor's appointment. And if you find yourself at your desk (which is likely), don't just plow ahead on the most stressful task. Instead, make "working smarter not harder" your operating principle. Use apps and trackers to keep organized, and if the load gets too heavy, ask for support. Got some advice to offer? Don't mince words, but follow persnickety Virgo's directive to be clear and make every syllable count.

SEP 14 WANING QUARTER MOON IN GEMINI (6:33AM)

Feeling out of sorts or just not quite connected? It's time to open up and talk it out! Today's waning quarter moon in communicative Gemini is perfect for dissecting, digesting, and discussing recent developments, especially any revelations sparked by last week's Pisces full moon. If concepts or situations seem too vague, this lunar phase helps you articulate them clearly and straightforwardly. A creative idea is always stimulating, but it truly begins to sparkle when paired with a concrete plan. If your enthusiasm for a recent passion has cooled, give yourself permission to shift directions. It's all part of the process of finding what truly resonates with you.

SEP 17 MERCURY-SATURN OPPOSITION

Analysis paralysis alert! Today could have you stuck in a cycle of overthinking as detail-oriented Mercury in meticulous Virgo opposes exacting Saturn in dreamy Pisces. Nothing wrong with using your imagination, but if you've ventured too far from the tried and true, this cosmic matchup urges you to check your work and ensure all details are in order. Master the rules before you attempt to break them. You may discover that certain guidelines are there for a reason, and only a few need tweaking. See how much work you just saved yourself? Whew.

SEP 18

MERCURY IN LIBRA (SEP 18-OCT 6)

Stop clutching your pearls and start pricing out diamonds. Messenger Mercury swaps signs, ending a tour through critical, analytical Virgo. The messenger planet's next stop is in lighthearted Libra, the sign of peaceful cooperation, diplomacy and decadent romance. Petty squabbles could dissolve, paving the way for long-overdue compromises. But giving an inch doesn't mean letting people take a mile. Libra is governed by the symbol of the scales, reminding us to retain a healthy balance of give and take. In this partnership-oriented sign, communicative Mercury helps us negotiate healthy agreements in our relationships. Culture vultures, come out to play! Now's the time to appreciate art, get tickets for live music and mingle with the cognoscenti. Fete the fall with fashionable gatherings: signature cocktails, curated playlists AND guest lists.

SEP 18 MERCURY-NEPTUNE OPPOSITION

Decision-making could get tricky as precise Mercury in harmony-seeking Libra faces off against elusive Neptune in assertive Aries. If you're giving instructions, go over them multiple times to ensure clarity—miscommunication is likely with this planetary tussle. Finding it hard to focus? Libra's need for balance and Aries' impulsivity can make concentrating a challenge, so it's essential to take regular mental breaks. To keep track of all the details in a complex project, lean on the structured beauty of a digital spreadsheet or embrace the simplicity of a traditional notebook. This will help you navigate the confusion with a bit more grace.

SEP 19

MERCURY-URANUS TRINE

Eureka! The two most clever planets sync in sweet harmony today. Mercury in diplomatic Libra trines Uranus in witty Gemini, sparking a meeting of the minds. As they merge their energies in genius air signs, entire industries can be disrupted— or maybe you'll just pull yourself out of a longstanding rut. Planning to make a pitch? Remember, you can only prep so much in advance. Stay present while avoiding the hard sell. You'll win people over with your relatable approach.

MERCURY-PLUTO TRINE

Make your move! Today's cosmic alignment between Mercury in savvy Libra and Pluto in forward-thinking Aquarius supercharges your persuasive skills. This potent trine infuses you with a winning combination of charm and intelligence, making you nearly irresistible in negotiations. Trust in your ability to nail the perfect pitch or steer any conversation with grace. For an extra boost of confidence, keep a few key points handy in your Notes app or scribble them on a slip of paper. With this stellar support, you're set to sway any audience in your favor!

VENUS IN VIRGO (SEP 19-OCT 13)

Romantic Venus tucks into virtuous Virgo, returning us all to modesty for a few weeks. Hang on to your corset strings! Love (and fashion) might get downright Regency Era for the next four weeks as fans go a-fluttering. Anything NSFW should be kept strictly private during this three-week cycle, which favors subtlety and stability. This downshift may feel sudden after Venus in Leo's hair-flipping excess. The highs and lows, the dramatic arcs—we could all use a break from Cupid's reality shows. Tone down the pyrotechnics and opt for earthy sensuality. There's so much to enjoy when you slow down and savor the simple things, from the warmth of someone's touch to the radiance of a fresh-faced glow. With beauty queen Venus in au natural Virgo, apply product with a lighter touch or skip it and slay with a no-makeup look. From decor to wardrobe, the classics win, especially if they are sustainably sourced and eco-chic.

SEP 20 VENUS-URANUS SQUARE

Need some breathing room? Even the smoothest relationships may experience turbulence as Venus in fastidious Virgo squares rebellious Uranus in duplicitous Gemini. Minor discrepancies can feel like major chasms. Compromise might seem like a foreign concept today. It's easy to fault-find or feel like nothing that either of you do is right. However, remember that today's fussy energy will dissipate as quickly as it arrived. Opt for a time-out rather than make any knee-jerk decisions that can't be undone. There's a fine line between offering helpful advice and unfairly judging people. Under these reckless skies, a fleeting romantic adventure might seem enticing, but don't lose sight of your core values in the rush of excitement.

SEP 21

SUN-SATURN OPPOSITION

Reality check or total buzzkill? Today's opposition between the Virgo Sun and cautious Saturn in Pisces might feel like a harsh splash of cold water on your dreams. But don't let this dampen your spirit or water down your convictions. Use this moment to glean valuable insights from any criticism or obstacles that come your way. Perhaps it's time to pare down, wrap up lingering projects, or solidify your schedule and budget. Slow down, but don't come to a complete halt. This is just a bump in the road, not the end of your journey!

NEW MOON IN VIRGO #2 (3:54PM; 29°05') (PARTIAL SOLAR ECLIPSE)

Eclipse season comes to a masterful finale with today's solar eclipse in vigilant Virgo. This one's doubly special, since it's also the second of a rare, back-to-back pair of Virgo new moons. Productivity has been in high gear since August 23, when the first Virgo new moon set the stage for disciplined developments. The pace could accelerate today, but that's not all. Since eclipses are known for bringing plot twists, your projects can move in unexpected directions. Brace yourself for potential changes with support staff and suppliers. While you may discover ways to improve your efforts, don't rush to tear up all the hard work you've put in. Watch out for perfectionism, Virgo's pitfall. New moons are starting blocks, so trust the process and embrace the lessons that come from acquiring new skills. If you want to add cachet to your resume, look for growth opportunities within your company. It may be time to sign up for specialized training that can bump you to a new paygrade. Want to make a difference in the world, or at least your corner of it? Virgo is the sign of selfless service. Seek volunteer opportunities where you can earn your earth angel halo. But whatever you do, make sure you have a solid plan in place for how to accomplish it. The eclipse will oppose structure-obsessed Saturn, underscoring the need to project-manage any pipe dreams if you want them to become tangible realities.

SEP 22

MARS IN SCORPIO (SEP 22-NOV 4)

Prepare for a season of deep dives and intense emotions as fiery Mars plunges into the enigmatic depths of Scorpio. This potent transit may stir up competitive urges or spark flares of jealousy. As power plays become more pronounced, you also have a golden opportunity to climb the ladder in any hierarchy. Just be careful not to come off as ruthless or too self-centered. As lusty Mars heats up sultry Scorpio over the coming six weeks, expect your romantic life to sizzle like never before. A smoldering connection could suddenly ignite, transforming into a passionate conflagration. However, this transit can also fan the flames of jealousy and possessiveness, so keep your cool. If you sense a genuine betrayal, Mars gives you the courage to address it head-on or even walk away. But a word of caution: Intense emotions might lead to paranoia. Before you point fingers, make sure your suspicions are based on facts, not fears. Remember, true investigation respects privacy—no snooping allowed!

SUN IN LIBRA (2:19PM) (SEP 22-OCT 22)

Collaborate, cooperate, co-create! Dynamic duos are all the rage for the next month as Libra season begins with the autumnal equinox. Pair up for the win, but not necessarily with someone who is basically your twin. Libra is the sign of the scales, encouraging you to achieve a happy equilibrium by finding a complementary force who can balance you out. Is it time to make a peace offering? Libra's harmonious vibes smooth over rough patches in our most important unions. It's rarely too late to at least TRY to make amends. The gracious diplomacy of Libra season will make others more amenable to accepting apologies. The spirit of justice is in the air! On a personal level, make sure you're playing fair in all your dealings. Legal matters come into focus under this sign's watch. Make agreements official, hire an attorney to review contracts or help you pursue an outstanding case.

SEP 23

SUN-NEPTUNE OPPOSITION

Lost in a vortex of indecision? As the vacillating Libra Sun opposes elusive Neptune in Aries, the mental fog thickens. With logic on hiatus, it's virtually impossible to figure out next steps. The second the "right" choice appears, someone discovers another option, which MIGHT be better, but then again... No matter how hard you try to find qualified people to advise you, this transit can obscure the clearest of intentions. Don't even bother poking the bear. Whatever is hidden behind Neptune's smoke screens won't be revealed today. Focus your energy on what you can directly influence and lean into Libra's diplomatic approach when dealing with difficult people.

SUN-URANUS TRINE

If you've reached a plateau, you may get the urge to shake things up today, but don't throw all common sense out the window. As the balanced Libra Sun gets swayed by rebellious Uranus in Gemini, you won't have the best gauge of what's "too much" versus what's "not quite enough." This dynamic cosmic connection brings a flash of "Eureka!" to your endeavors, inspiring bold leaps into uncharted territories. If your intuition nudges you toward a risky move, you may be tempted to act on impulse. However, temper your spontaneity with a bit of caution—make sure to do your homework before diving

9

headfirst into unexplored waters. Experimenting could blow up in your face if you haven't considered the impact it will have on other areas of your life.

SEP 24

SUN-PLUTO TRINE

Your charisma is electrifying today as the Libra Sun sings a dynamic duet with magnetic Pluto in Aquarius. Harness this potent energy wisely! A witty quip can pack a powerful punch, but if there's too much truth or taunting, it could come across as a backhanded compliment. Keep an eye on your intensity level and give people a chance to respond to your questions before flooding them with more information. Looking to amplify your influence? Don't reveal your entire hand. Keeping an air of mystery about your intentions can work wonders to bring people back for more (and more!).

MARS-PLUTO SQUARE

All is NOT fair in love, lust or war, as cutthroat Mars in Scorpio squares off with domineering Pluto in Aquarius. This intense astrological combat stirs up a cauldron of emotions like resentment, jealousy, and possessiveness. Everyone will be easily triggered, making this one of 2025's worst days for attempting to negotiate a compromise. Keep your cards close to your vest when around anyone who might be considered future competition. Feeling tension in a relationship? Now is not the time to demand a deep, revealing conversation. You won't get a straight answer out of anyone under these tight-lipped skies. Erotic innuendos may be both titillating and insanely difficult to read. To avoid sending out mixed signals yourself, wait a couple days before pursuing anything (or anyone) that's questionable.

SEP 29 WAXING QUARTER MOON IN CAPRICORN (7:54PM)

Struggling with the elusive "work-life" balance? It might be time for a rapid realignment, courtesy of today's waxing quarter moon in goal-oriented Capricorn. It's fulfilling to chase achievements, but how you get to the finish line matters. Are you overextending yourself instead of handing off tasks? Trying to juggle everything solo could stall crucial projects. If your professional ambitions are hiking up your stress, consider making strategic adjustments. Instead of cramming in "just one more task," what if you logged off and hit an exercise class to rejuvenate? And if your career progress has been more of a crawl lately, the illuminating energy of this moon phase might spotlight a valuable work opportunity that helps enhance your skills. Whether it's picking up an extra shift or enrolling in a webinar, small steps could soon restore your momentum and your finances!

9

October

OCTOBER
Moon Phase Calendar

SUN	MON	TUE	WED	THU	FRI	SAT
			1 ♑ ♒ 3:52PM	**2** ♒	**3** ♒ ♓ 10:07PM	**4** ♓
5 ♓	**6** ♓→♈ 12:48AM ♈ Full Moon 11:48PM	**7** ♈	**8** ♈ ♉ 1:12AM	**9** ♉	**10** ♉ ♊ 1:12AM	**11** ♊
12 ♊ ♋ 2:37AM	**13** ♋ 4th Quarter	**14** ♋ ♌ 6:47AM	**15** ♌	**16** ♌ ♍ 2:06PM	**17** ♍	**18** ♍
19 ♍ ♎ 12:01AM	**20** ♎	**21** ♎ New Moon 8:25AM ♎→♏ 11:42AM	**22** ♏	**23** ♏	**24** ♏ ♐ 12:19AM	**25** ♐
26 ♐ ♑ 12:53PM	**27** ♑	**28** ♑ ♒ 11:55PM	**29** ♒ 2nd Quarter	**30** ♒	**31** ♒ ♓ 7:46AM	

Times listed are Eastern US Time Zone

10

KEY

♈ ARIES	♌ LEO	♐ SAGITTARIUS	**FM** FULL MOON		
♉ TAURUS	♍ VIRGO	♑ CAPRICORN	**NM** NEW MOON		
♊ GEMINI	♎ LIBRA	♒ AQUARIUS	**LE** LUNAR ECLIPSE		
♋ CANCER	♏ SCORPIO	♓ PISCES	**SE** SOLAR ECLIPSE		

OCTOBER 6, 11:48PM
full moon in
Aries (14°08′)

ARIES FULL MOON CRYSTAL

BLOODSTONE
A dramatic dark-green with flecks of red, this stone is historically given to brave warriors. Use bloodstone to build resilience and pump up self-confidence as you step out as an individual. This circulation-boosting crystal enhances vitality and makes you feel alive.

ARIES FULL MOON = CELEBRATE!

Your inner (and outer) baddie

New experiences you're brave enough to try

Your competitive nature

Every unique feature that makes you a rare individual

Your fighting spirit that won't give up

10

OCTOBER 21, 8:25AM

new moon in
Libra (28°22')

LIBRA NEW MOON CRYSTAL

MALACHITE
Green like the heart chakra, this stone supports
the profound emotional transformations we
can make during Libra season. Malachite also
invites wealth and prosperity into your home,
perfect for this time of beauty and abundance.

LIBRA NEW MOON = FOCUS

Find synergies

Nurture romantic relationships

Enjoy art, music and fashion

Beautify everything

Network to build your contact list

10

October 2025

Longitude & Retrograde Ephemeris [00:00 UT]

Day	Sid.time	☉	☽	+12h☽	☿	♀	♂	♃	♄	♅	♆	♇	☊	☊	⚸	⚷	Day
1 We	00:39:56	♎08°04'45	♑19°31'24	♑25°49'29	♎21°11	♍14°04	♏05°51	♋22°27	℞ 27°45	℞ 01°12	℞ 00°33	℞ 01°24	℞ 17°02	♓18°10	♏20°57	℞ 25°37	1 We
2 Th	00:43:52	♎09°03'45	♒02°13'02	♒08°42'05	♎22°46	♍15°18	♏06°32	♋22°35	♓27°40	♊01°11	♈00°31	♒01°24	♓16°59	♓18°11	♏21°04	♈25°34	2 Th
3 Fr	00:47:49	♎10°02'46	♒15°17'27	♒21°59'01	♎24°19	♍16°32	♏07°13	♋22°42	♓27°36	♊01°10	♈00°29	♒01°23	♓16°56	♓18°12	♏21°10	♈25°32	3 Fr
4 Sa	00:51:45	♎11°01'49	♒28°47'23	♓05°42'10	♎25°53	♍17°46	♏07°54	♋22°49	♓27°31	♊01°08	♈00°28	♒01°23	♓16°52	♓18°14	♏21°17	♈25°29	4 Sa
5 Su	00:55:42	♎12°00'53	♓12°43'44	♓19°51'24	♎27°25	♍19°00	♏08°35	♋22°55	♓27°27	♊01°07	♈00°26	♒01°23	♓16°49	♓18°15	♏21°24	♈25°26	5 Su
6 Mo	00:59:38	♎13°00'00	♓27°05'10	♈04°24'00	♎28°56	♍20°14	♏09°16	♋23°02	♓27°23	♊01°05	♈00°24	♒01°22	♓16°46	℞ 18°15	♏21°30	♈25°24	6 Mo
7 Tu	01:03:35	♎13°59'08	♈11°47'37	♈19°14'36	♏00°27	♍21°28	♏09°58	♋23°09	♓27°18	♊01°04	♈00°23	♒01°22	♓16°43	♓18°13	♏21°37	♈25°21	7 Tu
8 We	01:07:32	♎14°58'18	♈26°44'26	♉04°15'30	♏01°57	♍22°42	♏10°39	♋23°15	♓27°14	♊01°03	♈00°21	♒01°22	♓16°40	♓18°11	♏21°44	♈25°18	8 We
9 Th	01:11:28	♎15°57'31	♉11°47'08	♉19°17'42	♏03°26	♍23°56	♏11°20	♋23°21	♓27°10	♊01°01	♈00°20	♒01°22	♓16°37	♓18°07	♏21°51	♈25°16	9 Th
10 Fr	01:15:25	♎16°56'46	♉26°46'33	♊04°12'13	♏04°54	♍25°10	♏12°01	♋23°27	♓27°05	♊00°59	♈00°18	♒01°22	♓16°33	♓18°03	♏21°57	♈25°13	10 Fr
11 Sa	01:19:21	♎17°56'03	♊11°34'18	♊18°51'36	♏06°22	♍26°25	♏12°43	♋23°33	♓27°01	♊00°58	♈00°16	♒01°22	♓16°30	♓17°59	♏22°04	♈25°10	11 Sa
12 Su	01:23:18	♎18°55'23	♊26°04'01	♋03°10'44	♏07°48	♍27°39	♏13°24	♋23°39	♓26°57	♊00°56	♈00°15	♒01°22	♓16°27	♓17°56	♏22°11	♈25°07	12 Su
13 Mo	01:27:14	♎19°54'45	♋10°11'56	♋17°07'07	♏09°14	♍28°53	♏14°06	♋23°44	♓26°53	♊00°55	♈00°13	♒01°22	♓16°24	♓17°54	♏22°17	♈25°05	13 Mo
14 Tu	01:31:11	♎20°54'09	♋23°56'47	♌00°40'38	♏10°39	♎00°08	♏14°48	♋23°50	♓26°49	♊00°53	♈00°12	♒01°22	♓16°21	D 17°54	♏22°24	♈25°02	14 Tu
15 We	01:35:07	♎21°53'35	♌07°19'21	♌13°52'49	♏12°03	♎01°22	♏15°29	♋23°55	♓26°45	♊00°51	♈00°10	D 01°22	♓16°18	♓17°55	♏22°31	♈24°59	15 We
16 Th	01:39:04	♎22°53'04	♌20°21'48	♌26°46'15	♏13°26	♎02°37	♏16°11	♋24°00	♓26°41	♊00°49	♈00°09	♒01°22	♓16°14	♓17°56	♏22°38	♈24°56	16 Th
17 Fr	01:43:01	♎23°52'35	♍03°06'58	♍09°23'53	♏14°48	♎03°51	♏16°53	♋24°05	♓26°37	♊00°47	♈00°07	♒01°22	♓16°11	♓17°58	♏22°44	♈24°54	17 Fr
18 Sa	01:46:57	♎24°52'08	♍15°37'48	♍21°48'37	♏16°09	♎05°06	♏17°35	♋24°10	♓26°33	♊00°46	♈00°06	♒01°22	♓16°08	♓17°59	♏22°51	♈24°51	18 Sa
19 Su	01:50:54	♎25°51'43	♍27°57'04	♎04°03'02	♏17°29	♎06°21	♏18°17	♋24°14	♓26°30	♊00°44	♈00°04	♒01°22	♓16°05	℞ 17°58	♏22°58	♈24°48	19 Su
20 Mo	01:54:50	♎26°51'20	♎10°07'11	♎16°09'20	♏18°48	♎07°35	♏18°59	♋24°19	♓26°26	♊00°42	♈00°03	♒01°22	♓16°02	♓17°56	♏23°04	♈24°45	20 Mo
21 Tu	01:58:47	♎27°51'00	♎22°10'08	♎28°09'21	♏20°06	♎08°50	♏19°41	♋24°23	♓26°22	♊00°40	♈00°01	♒01°22	♓15°58	♓17°52	♏23°11	♈24°42	21 Tu
22 We	02:02:43	♎28°50'42	♏04°07'36	♏10°04'40	℞s 21°23	♎10°05	♏20°23	♋24°27	♓26°19	♊00°38	♈00°00	♒01°22	♓15°55	♓17°45	♏23°18	♈24°40	22 We
23 Th	02:06:40	♎29°50'25	♏16°01'08	♏21°56'49	♏22°38	♎11°19	♏21°05	♋24°31	♓26°15	♊00°36	♓29°59	♒01°23	♓15°52	♓17°38	♏23°25	♈24°37	23 Th
24 Fr	02:10:36	♏00°50'11	♏27°52'21	♐03°47'34	♏23°51	♎12°34	♏21°47	♋24°35	♓26°12	♊00°34	♓29°57	♒01°23	♓15°49	♓17°29	♏23°31	♈24°34	24 Fr
25 Sa	02:14:33	♏01°49'58	♐09°43'09	♐15°39'01	♏25°03	♎13°49	♏22°30	♋24°38	♓26°08	♊00°32	♓29°56	♒01°23	♓15°46	♓17°21	♏23°38	♈24°31	25 Sa
26 Su	02:18:30	♏02°49'48	♐21°35'53	♐27°33'46	♏26°13	♎15°04	♏23°12	♋24°41	♓26°05	♊00°29	♓29°55	♒01°24	♓15°43	♓17°13	♏23°45	♈24°29	26 Su
27 Mo	02:22:26	♏03°49'39	♑03°33'29	♑09°35'05	♏27°22	♎16°19	♏23°55	♋24°45	♓26°02	♊00°27	♓29°53	♒01°24	♓15°39	♓17°07	♏23°51	♈24°26	27 Mo
28 Tu	02:26:23	♏04°49'31	♑15°39'28	♑21°46'46	♏28°28	♎17°34	♏24°37	♋24°47	♓25°59	♊00°25	♓29°52	♒01°24	♓15°36	♓17°02	♏23°58	♈24°23	28 Tu
29 We	02:30:19	♏05°49'26	♑27°57'57	♒04°13'09	♏29°31	♎18°48	♏25°20	♋24°50	♓25°56	♊00°23	♓29°51	♒01°25	♓15°33	♓17°00	♏24°05	♈24°21	29 We
30 Th	02:34:16	♏06°49'22	♒10°33'21	♒16°58'43	♐00°32	♎20°03	♏26°02	♋24°53	♓25°53	♊00°21	♓29°49	♒01°25	♓15°30	D 17°00	♏24°12	♈24°18	30 Th
31 Fr	02:38:12	♏07°49'19	♒23°30'10	♓00°07'48	♐01°30	♎21°18	♏26°45	♋24°55	♓25°50	♊00°18	♓29°48	♒01°26	♓15°27	♓17°01	♏24°18	♈24°15	31 Fr
Δ Delta	01:58:15	29°44'33"	393°58'45"	394°18'18"	40°19'	37°14'	20°53'	2°27'	-1°54'	-0°53'	0°44'	0°01'	-1°35'	-1°08'	3°21'	-1°21'	Delta

Ephemeris tables and data provided by **Astro-Seek.com.** All times in UTC.

OCTOBER
MONTHLY HOTSPOTS

OCT 1 MERCURY-JUPITER SQUARE

As Mercury in diplomatic Libra squares off against expansive Jupiter in nurturing Cancer, your words carry weight—perhaps more than you intend. This expressive cosmic duo amplifies communication, but watch out! It's easy to promise more than you can humanly deliver. You're likely coming from a good place. You want to be helpful or shore up someone's mood. Remember: You can't solve the world's problems in a single conversation. Be mindful of overstepping emotional boundaries or getting overly involved in problems that aren't yours to solve. Think big, but speak judiciously to ensure that your intentions align with your impact.

OCT 6

MERCURY IN SCORPIO (OCT 6-29)

Messenger Mercury slides into secretive Scorpio, urging you to strengthen your filters and adopt an air of mystery. Maintain a measure of control to build intrigue by keeping them guessing. If you're not ready for a big announcement, it's wise to hold off on the grand reveals and press statements for now. The upcoming weeks are perfect for behind-the-scenes work—researching, editing, and crafting your magnum opus. Secure any confidential information and bolster your passwords. During this transit, expect a loyalty test or two, as suspicion tends to increase. If you find your trust alarms sounding, be mindful not to question others too intensely. Avoid the temptation to conduct an FBI-level interrogation—instead, allow trust to develop or repair slowly and naturally.

FULL MOON IN ARIES (11:48PM; 14°08')

Work the room! Steal the spotlight! And don't you dare apologize for being over the top. The annual full moon in Aries unleashes a tsunami of boldness, cueing you to let your most flamboyant self shine. Who cares if tongues wag? Take the focus off of audience approval and make the day about unleashing a daring round of raw self-expression. The Aries drive to be #1 may spike the competitive energy. Nothing wrong with a healthy desire to be the best. But if the vibe begins to verge on cutthroat, diffuse the tension before a fight breaks out. One savvy way to do that? Share the glory and signal boost some of the other deserving talents in your midst. The full moon touches base with deep-feeling

Neptune, which could unlock a floodgate of bottled-up emotions, especially anger. Channel any rage constructively. A vigorous workout or karaoke power ballads—whatever it takes to deescalate drama and metabolize those feels!

OCT 7 MERCURY-PLUTO SQUARE

Dialogues may turn into diatribes as Mercury in secretive Scorpio battles Pluto in renegade Aquarius. Speaking truth to power is one thing. But if someone attempts to draw you into an ideological wrestling match, get out of the ring before egos get bruised. This investigative energy can help you uncover hidden truths and renew your mindset once you do. Guard against the darker undertones that might lead to paranoid thinking or manipulative tactics. You may have no choice but to face tough issues head-on, but maintain integrity and strive for clarity and fairness in all exchanges.

OCT 11 VENUS-SATURN OPPOSITION

Have your relationship boundaries been too porous? If you've been setting aside your own instincts for the sake of harmony, today's opposition of Venus in Virgo and Neptune in PIsces blows the whistle. You know you need clearly defined limits; yet in the heat of a certain connection, you could have lost your steely determination. Today's cosmic climate offers a chance to step back and reassess. Feeling uncertain about someone in particular? Hold off on making any hasty decisions while the stars cast a somewhat gloomy shadow over your judgment. While it's crucial to heed any warning signs, recognize that your current ability to differentiate a minor issue from a crisis might be a bit clouded. Take this time to reflect and ensure you're not overreacting or underreacting—balance is key.

OCT 13

WANING QUARTER MOON IN CANCER (2:13PM)

Cozy season vibes are calling today as the waning Cancer moon brings visions of chunky knit sweaters and pumpkin spice everything into your field. Where could you bring more homey touches to your daily life? Tuck slippers under your desk, frame a few family photos, splurge on that espresso maker for your kitchen. (If you're a regular coffeeshop-goer, it will pay for itself in a few months!) Pause between professional duties to connect with coworkers. Call a relative you've lost touch with. When you're back at base camp, set up your living room for movie, craft and game nights. On the lookout for a new space? Set up alerts from Zillow and Redfin. A lucky listing could pop up while you're organizing your office supplies or folding laundry.

VENUS IN LIBRA (OCT 13–NOV 6)

Elevate, luxuriate, decorate! Beauty queen Venus dons a tiara and floats into Libra for her annual homecoming parade. Willpower is fairly nonexistent while Venus is in Libra, which can make us go weak in the face of bespoke, luxury treasures: cashmere sweaters from a capsule collection, reserve Pinots aged in oak barrels. Lovers, rejoice! The next few weeks are peak cuffing season as Venus unites kindred souls. Situationships may evolve into exclusive relationships or simply fade away, clearing space for the real deal. In a relationship? Spoil your S.O. mercilessly and speak up about your own desires. If you don't ask, you don't get! With Venus in gentle Libra, slow and steady devotion wins the race in all realms. Dial down the pressure, dial up the sweet gestures and charm. Pay attention to visuals, too. Taking care of your body and looking your personal best doesn't make you vain. It's called valuing yourself and it can help you attract people who will do the same!

VENUS-NEPTUNE OPPOSITION

The line between fantasy and reality may become imperceptible today. Shortly after Venus takes its first step in Libra, it gets into standoff with quixotic Neptune in Aries. You may be swept up in a whirlwind attraction or put someone on a pedestal, only to realize later that you completely misread their character. While it's tempting to lose yourself in the allure of idealized love, remember that true connection is built on authenticity, not illusions. Stay grounded and keep your heart open, but don't ignore red flags. This cosmic combo can inspire creative passion, but be mindful of seeing what you want to see rather than what's really there.

PLUTO DIRECT IN AQUARIUS

Viva la revolución! After five months spent simmering in a low-power retrograde, alchemical Pluto wakes up and turns direct in humanitarian Aquarius. Pluto's backspin, which began on May 4, inspired deep reflection—especially around the systems, structures, and social circles that needed a serious transformation. Now that the metamorphic planet is back in forward motion, you have the green light to start acting on those game-changing visions. But no need to rush! Pluto is in the early stages of its long transit through the Water Bearer's realm, which lasts until January 19, 2044! Over the next two decades, it will bring radical shifts in technology, social justice, and how we connect with our communities. Look for ways to improve your corner of the not-so-lonely planet. Whether you're syncing up with family, starting an organization or joining an existing one, you'll find strength in numbers.

10

VENUS-URANUS TRINE

Relationships could take an unexpected but exhilarating turn today as Venus in Libra flows into a harmonious trine with change-agent Uranus in Gemini. Couples who've been at odds for the past few days could suddenly tap into a creative (and potentially hilarious) solution. Don't walk around in a tech trance when you're waiting for your coffee or picking up dry cleaning. You could miss the chance to exchange witty banter—and contact 'deets—with a charming person the universe places in your path. This cosmic connection favors unconventional attractions and out-of-the-box thinking. The person who stimulates your intellect wins!

VENUS-PLUTO TRINE

Deep, transformative vibes will also permeate today's interactions as Venus in Libra forms her second trine of the day, this time with intense Pluto, who's just wrapped up its retrograde in Aquarius. This cosmic combo invites you to connect on a soul level. Cut through surface-level interactions and reveal something that you don't share often—with the caveat that this won't give you a vulnerability hangover tomorrow. (General rule: Share your partially healed scars instead of the trauma of fresh wounds.) Pluto's influence can bring powerful breakthroughs and healing. Under these sultry skies, a magnetic attraction could take your breath away. Relationships formed today may feel fated, as if destiny is pulling the strings!

OCT 17 SUN-JUPITER SQUARE

Emotional attachments make it hard to play fair under today's cosmic clash. You can see the path to compromise, thanks to the diplomatic Libra Sun. But Jupiter in sensitive Cancer cranks up your personal bias, making it hard to be impartial, even when you're playing peacemaker. Think twice about getting in the middle of complex family dynamics. In your efforts to assuage someone who is moody and difficult, you might wind up taking on more than you can honestly handle. Is this actually your cross to bear? Be helpful from a distance rather than jumping into the line of other people's fire. Be supportive without sacrificing yourself. The deeper emotional needs that surface today may require multiple conversations—and the support of a professional like a therapist or mediator—to be resolved.

10

OCT 20 MERCURY-MARS MEETUP

Retract those claws...or maybe just sharpen them first. With Mercury and Mars entwined in fierce, calculating Scorpio, conversations could cut deep today. Power struggles, hidden agendas, and under-the-table tactics might surface, so keep your guard up. Don't fan the flames with biting, venomous remarks. Scorpio's sting can leave lasting wounds, and once those words are out, there's no taking them back. Instead, embrace Scorpio's strategic side. Know your limits and what you're willing to settle for before you even enter the ring. This is a day to negotiate with precision, staying laser-focused on your ultimate goal. If things start to get too intense, don't be afraid to step back, cool down, and strike when the moment is right. Scorpio's energy favors those who play the long game, so use this passionate surge to speak your truth...but with the right amount of stealth and control.

OCT 21 NEW MOON IN LIBRA (8:25AM; 28°22')

The year's only new moon in Libra revs up romance today, serving important lessons in chemistry. Under this pink-hued glow, it's easy to fall in love with people's potential but we won't be so gifted at spotting red flags. Even the greatest person on the planet is still prone to human flaws. This new moon encourages a balanced perspective in all realms. With Jupiter in Cancer squaring la luna, your inner circle may have some pretty strong opinions about your partnership choices. Similarly, you could find yourself getting overly involved in other people's love lives. Keep the focus on your own desires and close the opinion polls. Your heart wants what it wants and unless they are personally affected by your choices, you don't owe the bystanders an explanation. Couples may have those important talks about supporting each other's independence without feeling threatened. Autonomy and togetherness can coexist beautifully, but it takes some finesse!

OCT 22

NEPTUNE RETROGRADE IN PISCES (OCT 22–DEC 10)

Numinous Neptune, who's been retrograde in Aries since July 4, backstrokes into its home sign of Pisces. Deeper waters beckon as the celestial mystic amplifies the introspective, dreamlike energy of this transit. Since Neptune first entered Aries on March 30, you may have felt called to redefine your entire identity. A burst of pioneering energy sparked trailblazing visions and idealistic pursuits. Once the retrograde began on July 4, Neptune's fog may have clouded the path forward, creating tension between your desire for action and the haziness of what comes next. Now, as Neptune slips back into Pisces, the focus shifts to surrender and spiritual reflection, allowing you to gracefully integrate the lessons of these past months. If you've been on the fence about travel plans, think "escape"—but with intention. This is prime time for a soulful retreat, whether that's a weekend of yoga and sound baths or a painting workshop

10

in Positano. Just watch out for Neptune's tendency to blur reality and fantasy. While you may feel drawn to mystical or healing experiences, choose your guides carefully. Boundless Neptune in reverse drops our defenses, making us more impressionable and open to suggestion. Shield your psychic space with salt baths, crystal jewelry and protective rituals. Hydrate well—Neptune rules the seas, so a refillable water bottle might just be your best travel companion.

SUN IN SCORPIO (11:51PM) (OCT 22–NOV 21)

Money, power, success! With the Sun blazing into magnetic Scorpio, you've got a month to tap into hidden financial opportunities and rev up your earning potential. Instead of dwelling on what's missing from your bank account, get strategic. A deep dive into your closet could unearth treasures to flip on Depop or Poshmark. Maybe a local business could use your freelance Canva skills for social media graphics. During this magnetic Scorpio solar cycle, energy flows where your attention goes, so make sure you're radaring in on people, places and things that stoke your inner fire. Scorpio also rules long-term investments and joint ventures. Curious about cryptocurrency or real estate? Now's the time to learn! Thinking about partnering up for a big venture? Schedule that chemistry meeting with a potential business partner. If you need startup capital, this zodiac season's magic could connect you with the perfect investor. And don't limit yourself to the 9-5 grind—Scorpio turns us into night owls. A passive revenue stream, like a downloadable product or rental equipment, could earn you money while you sleep.

OCT 24

10

SUN-PLUTO SQUARE

Buried tensions are bubbling below the surface, but with the secretive Scorpio Sun squaring surreptitious Pluto, no one is in a rush to bring them out into the open. While you don't want an active emotional volcano to erupt, consider the cost of avoidance. The anticipation of conflict may be more stressful than the conflict itself. Nevertheless, this will not be an easy situation to navigate. Scorpio's probing energy wants to uncover the truth, while rebellious Pluto in Aquarius demands radical change and independence. You may feel caught between holding on to what feels safe and diving into the unknown. Use this cosmic friction to break through old patterns but be mindful of not forcing things. Power struggles could arise, but with awareness, this aspect can help you transform and evolve—on your own terms!

MERCURY-JUPITER TRINE #1 OF 3

Your inner world may be far more alluring than anything that's happening "out there" today. As Mercury in sultry Scorpio forms a provocative trine with limitless Jupiter in Cancer, there's no telling what fantasies you'll spin up. This cosmic combo could spark spicy pillow talk and inspire seductive moves to match. The only imperative is that you and your partner are both into it. Whether with a love interest or trusted bestie, you may be motivated to initiate a conversation about your private thoughts and emotions. Since Jupiter can create big energy, stay aware. You don't want to flood people with your revelations. Gauge their moods before you start pulling skeletons out of the closet.

OCT 25 MERCURY-SATURN TRINE #1 OF 3

Every detail counts today as analytical Mercury in Scorpio gets swept into Saturn's grind. Whether you're putting the final touches on a project for work or making a weighty decision about your personal life, stay hypervigilant through every aspect of the process. With both planets in sensitive water signs, intuitive hits will be strong. If your Spidey senses start to tingle, investigate! Your curiosity could lead you to a growth opportunity that helps you create lasting security for yourself. A well-connected or experienced person could help you get to the next level. Be prepared to follow through if you ask them to make an introduction. Remember: Your work will reflect on the person who vouched for you.

OCT 28 MARS-JUPITER TRINE

Today's energy is outright alchemical thanks to a free-flowing trine between Mars in Scorpio and Jupiter in Cancer. This dynamic duet brings penetrating insights, extreme willpower and the energy to act upon your deepest convictions. Supersized ideas spring to life, and you'll be inspired to give them your all. The wholehearted devotion of these two planets can help you move mountains in a remarkably short period of time. The pitfall would be playing too small or underestimating your impact. While empathy is favored, this is not the time for modesty or extreme caution. Jupiter the gambler and Mars the warrior call for epic leaps—or plunges! With both planets in deep-feeling water signs, mine the magic that's hidden below the surface. Don't overlook the obvious!

10

MERCURY-NEPTUNE TRINE #1 OF 3

Ask, believe, receive! Today, as mental Mercury in Scorpio tunes in to mystical Neptune's Piscean frequency, use the Law of Attraction to your advantage and visualize what you desire. Manifestation doesn't require a laborious effort to pull off. With these planets in intuitive, magnetic water signs, try holding a vision of what it would feel like to already have what you want. That alone will send a powerful message to the universe. Instead of swimming upstream, float WITH the current. Under this flowing mashup, your intuition may be borderline psychic. Read the reports and check the data, but also follow your gut.

MERCURY IN SAGITTARIUS (OCT 29-NOV 18)

After weeks of mind games and hidden agendas, clarity is finally on the horizon. Mercury shifts out of secretive Scorpio and into straightforward Sagittarius for its annual tour through this philosophical, outspoken fire sign. With the messenger planet firing arrows into Sagittarius' domain, authenticity is back in vogue. But with so many truth arrows flying around, no one is keen to listen. Go easy on the opinionated rants and zealous preaching over the next few weeks. Sagittarius is the sign of global expansion and cross-cultural connections. You may discover surprising common ground by reaching across the proverbial aisle. Mediamakers and entrepreneurs will have no shortage of big ideas. Capture them all for consideration! Just don't rush to pull the trigger on any venture until you've thoroughly mapped it out, especially if doing so means taking a gamble on your essential resources.

WAXING QUARTER MOON IN AQUARIUS (12:21PM)

Today's quarter moon in forward-thinking Aquarius urges you to scrutinize your digital footprint. Whether it's turning off location services, beefing up your privacy settings, or blocking cookies, reclaim control over the relentless data-tracking from the apps and websites you frequent. In the analog world, assess the dynamics of your social circle. Are trust and discretion upheld among your colleagues? Distance yourself from the gossips or people whose questionable activities could sully your good name. Need to get your squad back on the same page? Propose a team-building session or an offsite retreat to reenergize and refocus. If it's been too long since you've connected with your core crew, this is also an ideal time to organize a seasonal get-together. Keep it lighthearted and casual, like pub trivia or costumed karaoke to fete Halloween!

10

MARS-SATURN TRINE

Hit your cruising altitude and let the tailwind guide you! Speedy Mars in Scorpio plays nice with cautious Saturn in Pisces today, helping you advance at a pace that won't throw you into an anxiety spiral. Be excited but not desperate, direct but diplomatic. You can even make a strongly worded statement about your competitive advantage and why you're the best person for a job. Just be prepared to back up your claims with action and evidence. Radar in on people's emotions, pain points and deepest desires. With Mars and Pluto both in sensitive water signs, you'll need to make people FEEL something if you want to spur them to action.

MERCURY-URANUS OPPOSITION

Brace yourself for a whirlwind of ideas and sudden insights! No subject is too out there today as Mercury in philosophical Sagittarius opposes Uranus in whimsical Gemini. Together, they'll whip up your curiosity, which could lead you down a research rabbit hole or pull you into hours of scrolling for quick, catchy information. Conversations may shift directions unexpectedly, sparking brilliant, if fleeting, revelations. Fast friendships may form under these skies, but don't bank on most of them being permanent. Enjoy the day's exchanges for what they are—dynamic bursts of inspiration that can help you break through any creative blocks.

November

NOVEMBER
Moon Phase Calendar

SUN	MON	TUE	WED	THU	FRI	SAT
						1 ☾ ♓
2 ♓ ♈ 10:39AM	**3** ♈	**4** ♈ ♉ 11:16AM	**5** ♉ Full Moon 8:19AM	**6** ♉ ♊ 10:20AM	**7** ♊	**8** ♊ ♋ 10:06AM
9 ♋	**10** ♋ ♌ 12:34PM	**11** ♌	**12** ♌ 4th Quarter ♌→♍ 6:52PM	**13** ♍	**14** ♍	**15** ♍ ♎ 4:44AM
16 ♎	**17** ♎ ♏ 4:44PM	**18** ♏	**19** ♏	**20** ♍ New Moon 1:47AM ♍→♐ 5:26AM	**21** ♐	**22** ♐ ♑ 5:53PM
23 ♑	**24** ♑	**25** ♑ ♒ 5:16AM	**26** ♒	**27** ♒ ♓ 2:24PM	**28** ♓ 2nd Quarter	**29** ♓ ♈ 8:07PM
30 ♈						

Times listed are Eastern US Time Zone

KEY

♈	ARIES	♌	LEO	♐	SAGITTARIUS
♉	TAURUS	♍	VIRGO	♑	CAPRICORN
♊	GEMINI	♎	LIBRA	♒	AQUARIUS
♋	CANCER	♏	SCORPIO	♓	PISCES

FM	FULL MOON
NM	NEW MOON
LE	LUNAR ECLIPSE
SE	SOLAR ECLIPSE

11

Supermoon

NOVEMBER 5, 8:19AM

full moon in Taurus (13°23')

TAURUS FULL MOON CRYSTAL

COPPER

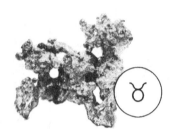

One of the Earth's most healing materials, copper brings the signature stability of earth-sign Taurus. This gem balances the chakras and shifts stagnant energy, charging you up to connect with loved ones during holiday celebrations. The weight of copper grounds you as you to tap into the quantum field—the place of limitless ideas and possibilities.

TAURUS FULL MOON = CELEBRATE!

The simple things that bring you joy

The beauty of nature

Your favorite music and artists

Finding holiday gifts that are sustainable and earth-friendly

Creating a comfortable home environment

Food that you love

11

NOVEMBER 20, 1:47AM

new moon in Scorpio (28°12')

SCORPIO NEW MOON CRYSTAL

SERPENTINE

With its dramatic swirls of pale yellow and ash grey, this crystal activates the Scorpio kundalini energy, helping you transcend your ego and detoxify your body. Serpentine creates a bridge between the physical and spiritual realms so you can access ancient wisdom and messages from your guides.

SCORPIO NEW MOON = FOCUS

Build trusted bonds

Share secrets

Form strategic partnerships

Explore your erotic nature

Join forces (and finances)

Give everything you do more sizzle and spice

11

November 2025

Longitude & Retrograde Ephemeris [00:00 UT]

Day	Sid.time	☉	☽	+12h☽	☿	♀	♂	♃	♄	♅	♆	♇	☊	☋	⚸	⚷	Day
1 Sa	02:42:09	♏08°49′18	♓06°52′24	♓13°43′51	℞s 02°25	♎22°33	♏27°28	♋24°57	℞ 25°47	℞ 00°16	℞ 29°47	♒01°26	℞ 15°24	♓17°02	♏24°25	℞ 24°12	**1** Sa
2 Su	02:46:05	♏09°49′19	♓20°42′47	♓27°48′44	♐03°16	♎23°48	♏28°10	♋24°59	♓25°45	♊00°14	♓29°46	♒01°27	♓15°20	℞ 17°02	♏24°32	♈24°10	**2** Su
3 Mo	02:50:02	♏10°49′21	♈05°01′59	♈12°21′42	♐04°03	♎25°03	♏28°53	♋25°01	♓25°42	♊00°12	♓29°45	♒01°27	♓15°17	♓17°01	♏24°38	♈24°07	**3** Mo
4 Tu	02:53:59	♏11°49′25	♈19°47′43	♈27°18′43	♐04°45	♎26°18	♏29°36	♋25°03	♓25°39	♊00°09	♓29°44	♒01°28	♓15°14	♓16°57	♏24°45	♈24°05	**4** Tu
5 We	02:57:55	♏12°49′31	♉04°54′10	♉12°32′18	♐05°22	♎27°34	♐00°19	♋25°04	♓25°37	♊00°07	♓29°42	♒01°28	♓15°11	♓16°51	♏24°52	♈24°02	**5** We
6 Th	03:01:52	♏13°49′39	♉20°12′16	♉27°52′07	♐05°54	♎28°49	♐01°02	♋25°05	♓25°35	♊00°05	♓29°41	♒01°29	♓15°08	♓16°43	♏24°59	♈23°59	**6** Th
7 Fr	03:05:48	♏14°49′48	♊05°30′54	♊13°06′42	♐06°19	♏00°04	♐01°45	♋25°06	♓25°33	♊00°02	♓29°40	♒01°30	♓15°04	♓16°34	♏25°05	♈23°57	**7** Fr
8 Sa	03:09:45	♏15°50′00	♊20°38′46	♊28°05′31	♐06°38	♏01°19	♐02°28	♋25°07	♓25°30	♊00°00	♓29°39	♒01°30	♓15°01	♓16°25	♏25°12	♈23°54	**8** Sa
9 Su	03:13:41	♏16°50′13	♋05°26′31	♋12°40′41	♐06°48	♏02°34	♐03°12	♋25°08	♓25°28	♉29°57	♓29°38	♒01°31	♓14°58	♓16°18	♏25°19	♈23°52	**9** Su
10 Mo	03:17:38	♏17°50′29	♋19°48′02	♋26°47′54	℞ 06°51	♏03°49	♐03°55	♋25°08	♓25°26	♉29°55	♓29°37	♒01°32	♓14°55	♓16°12	♏25°25	♈23°49	**10** Mo
11 Tu	03:21:34	♏18°50′46	♌03°40′45	♌10°26′18	♐06°45	♏05°04	♐04°38	♋25°09	♓25°25	♉29°52	♓29°36	♒01°33	♓14°52	♓16°09	♏25°32	♈23°47	**11** Tu
12 We	03:25:31	♏19°51′05	♌17°05′18	♌23°37′43	♐06°29	♏06°20	♐05°22	℞ 25°09	♓25°23	♉29°50	♓29°35	♒01°33	♓14°49	♓16°08	♏25°39	♈23°44	**12** We
13 Th	03:29:28	♏20°51′27	♍00°04′28	♍06°25′42	♐06°03	♏07°35	♐06°05	♋25°08	♓25°21	♉29°48	♓29°34	♒01°34	♓14°45	D 16°08	♏25°46	♈23°42	**13** Th
14 Fr	03:33:24	♏21°51′50	♍12°42′22	♍18°54′38	♐05°27	♏08°50	♐06°49	♋25°08	♓25°20	♉29°45	♓29°34	♒01°35	♓14°42	♓16°08	♏25°52	♈23°40	**14** Fr
15 Sa	03:37:21	♏22°52′14	♍25°03′28	♎01°09′01	♐04°41	♏10°05	♐07°32	♋25°08	♓25°18	♉29°43	♓29°33	♒01°36	♓14°39	℞ 16°08	♏25°59	♈23°37	**15** Sa
16 Su	03:41:17	♏23°52′41	♎07°12′10	♎13°13′01	♐03°45	♏11°21	♐08°16	♋25°07	♓25°17	♉29°40	♓29°32	♒01°37	♓14°36	♓16°06	♏26°06	♈23°35	**16** Su
17 Mo	03:45:14	♏24°53′10	♎19°12′22	♎25°10′13	♐02°40	♏12°36	♐09°00	♋25°06	♓25°16	♉29°38	♓29°31	♒01°38	♓14°33	♓16°01	♏26°12	♈23°33	**17** Mo
18 Tu	03:49:10	♏25°53′40	♏01°07′17	♏07°03′29	♐01°28	♏13°51	♐09°43	♋25°05	♓25°14	♉29°35	♓29°30	♒01°39	♓14°30	♓15°53	♏26°19	♈23°30	**18** Tu
19 We	03:53:07	♏26°54′13	♏12°59′27	♏18°55′01	♐00°11	♏15°07	♐10°27	♋25°03	♓25°13	♉29°33	♓29°30	♒01°40	♓14°26	♓15°43	♏26°26	♈23°28	**19** We
20 Th	03:57:03	♏27°54′46	♏24°50′47	♐00°46′30	♏28°50	♏16°22	♐11°11	♋25°02	♓25°13	♉29°30	♓29°29	♒01°41	♓14°23	♓15°30	♏26°33	♈23°26	**20** Th
21 Fr	04:01:00	♏28°55′22	♐06°42′43	♐12°39′15	♏27°29	♏17°37	♐11°55	♋25°00	♓25°12	♉29°28	♓29°28	♒01°42	♓14°20	♓15°16	♏26°39	♈23°24	**21** Fr
22 Sa	04:04:57	♏29°55′59	♐18°36′36	♐24°34′34	♏26°09	♏18°53	♐12°39	♋24°58	♓25°11	♉29°25	♓29°28	♒01°43	♓14°17	♓15°01	♏26°46	♈23°22	**22** Sa
23 Su	04:08:53	♐00°56′37	♑00°33′45	♑06°33′59	♏24°55	♏20°08	♐13°23	♋24°56	♓25°10	♉29°23	♓29°27	♒01°44	♓14°14	♓14°48	♏26°53	♈23°20	**23** Su
24 Mo	04:12:50	♐01°57′16	♑12°35′55	♑18°39′28	♏23°47	♏21°23	♐14°07	♋24°53	♓25°10	♉29°20	♓29°26	♒01°45	♓14°10	♓14°37	♏26°59	♈23°18	**24** Mo
25 Tu	04:16:46	♐02°57′57	♑24°45′22	♒00°53′36	♏22°49	♏22°39	♐14°51	♋24°51	♓25°09	♉29°18	♓29°26	♒01°46	♓14°07	♓14°29	♏27°06	♈23°16	**25** Tu
26 We	04:20:43	♐03°58′39	♒07°05′00	♒13°19′39	♏22°01	♏23°54	♐15°35	♋24°48	♓25°09	♉29°15	♓29°25	♒01°47	♓14°04	♓14°23	♏27°13	♈23°14	**26** We
27 Th	04:24:39	♐04°59′22	♒19°38′26	♒26°01′27	♏21°24	♏25°10	♐16°20	♋24°45	♓25°09	♉29°12	♓29°25	♒01°49	♓14°01	♓14°21	♏27°20	♈23°12	**27** Th
28 Fr	04:28:36	♐06°00′06	♓02°29′39	♓09°03′07	♏20°59	♏26°25	♐17°04	♋24°42	♓25°09	♉29°10	♓29°25	♒01°50	♓13°58	♓14°20	♏27°26	♈23°10	**28** Fr
29 Sa	04:32:33	♐07°00′51	♓15°42′46	♓22°28′36	♏20°45	♏27°41	♐17°48	♋24°39	D 25°09	♉29°08	♓29°24	♒01°51	♓13°55	♓14°20	♏27°33	♈23°08	**29** Sa
30 Su	04:36:29	♐08°01′36	♓29°21′22	♈06°20′51	Ds 20°42	♏28°56	♐18°33	♋24°35	♓25°09	♉29°05	♓29°24	♒01°52	♓13°51	♓14°19	♏27°40	♈23°06	**30** Su
Δ Delta	01:54:19	29°12′18″	382°28′58″	-382°37′00″	-11°42′	36°22′	21°05′	-0°22′	-0°38′	-1°11′	-0°23′	0°26′	-1°32′	-2°42′	3°14′	-1°06′	**Delta**

Ephemeris tables and data provided by **Astro-Seek.com.** All times in UTC.

NOVEMBER
MONTHLY HOTSPOTS

NOV 2 VENUS-JUPITER SQUARE

Feeling torn between head and heart? With Jupiter in Cancer squaring off against Venus in Libra, you're craving deep emotional connections, but also trying to keep things smooth and balanced. Jupiter's all about big feelings and nurturing vibes, while Venus wants harmony and beauty in your relationships. It's a cosmic tug-of-war between going all-in on love and making sure everything stays just right. The sweet spot? Let your heart lead, but don't overdo it—keep those emotions in check while still honoring your deeper desires. Balance is key, so find your flow without tipping the scales too far!

NOV 3 MARS-NEPTUNE TRINE

Trust your gut, because today the universe is practically trolling you with hints. With insistent Mars in psychic Scorpio vibing with Neptune in intuitive Pisces, the signs and serendipities are impossible to miss. Don't brush them off—these cosmic nudges are guiding you to exactly where you need to be. Couples will feel a perfect balance between passion and deep trust, as Neptune's compassion cools Mars' fiery intensity. Single? You'll be drawn to someone with spiritual depth, not just raw chemistry. Forget the sparkly unicorns. Soulful connection will captivate your heart today.

NOV 4

MARS IN SAGITTARIUS (NOV 4–DEC 15)

Your visionary dreams are set to soar as Mars charges into entrepreneurial Sagittarius, lighting a fire under your feet. Got a bucket-list adventure in mind? Thinking about launching a world-changing project or business? This transit fills your tank with unstoppable go-for-it energy. Skip the holiday comfort comas and endless social media scrolling. Instead, fuel up with an inspiring workshop or dive into a metaphysical book to keep the momentum going. In love, Mars dares you to venture into uncharted territory. Single? Give someone totally out of your usual orbit a shot. Coupled up? Plan an adventurous trip or sneak away from family gatherings for a romantic escape. Whether it's a sun-soaked beach or city lights, a change of scenery could seriously reignite the spark. With Mars in Sagittarius, your end-of-year vibe is all about bold moves and passionate amour.

MARS-URANUS OPPOSITION

Hold on tight! Mars in Sagittarius is firing up your ambitions, but with Uranus in Gemini hurling curveballs into the mix, it's going to be a wild ride! This cosmic clash brings spontaneous plot twists, pushing you to think fast and adapt on the fly. Got big plans? Be flexible because Uranus loves to shake things up when you least expect it. But here's the thing—chaos can be your secret weapon. Lean into the unpredictability, and you might stumble upon a breakthrough idea or an unexpected opportunity that blows your mind. Relationships could get a jolt, too! You or your partner may crave more freedom, leading to some intense "let's change things up" moments. Single? You might meet someone totally out of the blue, who challenges everything you thought you wanted. This isn't the time to play it safe—Mars and Uranus are daring you to take bold risks and embrace the unexpected. Buckle up, because this opposition will take you places you never saw coming!

NOV 5
FULL MOON IN TAURUS (8:19AM; 13°23'; SUPERMOON)

The earth moves under your feet as the full supermoon rises in grounded Taurus! This lunation shines a light on your values, security, and everything you've been building since the spring. Anchor your visionary ideas into reality. With some thoughtful planning you can make them tangible, even profitable, over the coming weeks. Taurus loves luxury, and this supermoon invites you to indulge in sensual pleasures, like a decadent dinner reservation, booking spa treatments for the upcoming weekend (seaweed mud wraps and collagen-stimulating facials, please!) or an evening of visual stimulation at an art exhibit. This moon also brings emotional clarity around your values, helping you sort through what really matters. If you've been feeling off balance, this is your moment to slow down, regroup, and focus on creating more stability.

NOV 6–30 VENUS IN SCORPIO

Venus shimmies into smoldering Scorpio, cranking up the sex appeal. Just talking about what turns you on could get pulses racing, and chemistry heats up fast behind closed doors. Channel your erotic energy through dance, sensual movement, or spicy adventures between the sheets. With Venus here, secrecy and mystery are irresistibly hot, but be careful—temptations could take you into taboo territory. Trust and lust are equally important under Scorpio's watch. The green-eyed monster could rear its head during this cycle. Karma might be your kink, but vengeance? Don't get caught up in that. Let this Venus cycle take you to new levels of passion, without losing sight of honor and respect.

URANUS RETROGRADE IN TAURUS (NOV 7–FEB 3, 2026)

Uranus, who's been retrograde in duplicitous Gemini since September 6, slips back into Taurus for the final retrograde, of our lifetime, in this sign. Until February 3, it channels its rebellious energy toward our money, routines and personal values. This chaotic cycle may bring a few shakeups in your financial life or even your self-worth. Old money issues or unexpected expenses could pop up, pushing you to rethink how you handle your resources. But don't panic! This is your cosmic cue to get creative and find new ways to build lasting security. Uranus loves change, and though it can feel destabilizing, this transit is about finding freedom in places you've been stuck. Stay open to breaking out of old patterns—you might discover an unconventional path to financial freedom!

VENUS-PLUTO SQUARE

Feel the heat, but watch out for power struggles! As Venus in seductive Scorpio squares off with intense Pluto in Aquarius, love and relationships take on a biting edge. This transit brings deep emotional currents to the surface. Expect a surge of passion, attraction, and even obsession. But with Pluto in the mix, things can get a little intense, and control issues may creep in. Be mindful of any hidden agendas or jealousy. While the chemistry is off the charts, this square can push you to confront deep fears around trust and vulnerability. Secrets could emerge, revealing the truth beneath the surface. In love, you'll be craving more depth, intimacy, and raw connection—but be careful not to let power dynamics take over. This is a time for emotional honesty while avoiding manipulative moves.

NOV 9–18 MERCURY RETROGRADE IN SAGITTARIUS

Please DON'T say the quiet part out loud. Today, big-mouthed Mercury spins retrograde in tactless Sagittarius, flashing a code red blurt alert. This three-week cycle lasts until November 29, but before Mercury moves back into Scorpio on the 18th, honesty can be particularly brutal, smashing relationships to smithereens. If you don't want to spend the holidays estranged from your nearest and dearest, think twice about going on any attacks, even if you're "just trying to be helpful." Equally disruptive are off-color remarks and X-rated humor which could fall flat with a general audience. Visiting loved ones might require extra precautions during this argumentative time. If you need to cut a trip short or stay at a hotel to preserve the peace, err on the side of "personal space." Leave early for the airport and triple check all reservations since this retrograde can be particularly disruptive of travel.

11

NOV 11–MAR 10, 2026
JUPITER RETROGRADE IN CANCER

How sturdy is your emotional foundation? As Jupiter pulls the brakes in nurturing Cancer, inward reflection is called for. Have you been chasing success at the expense of personal fulfillment? This four-month cycle can help you true up your outer ambitions with your longing for inner peace. Opportunities for growth may not come as fast during this period, but that's okay! Jupiter retrograde encourages you to redefine what abundance means on a more holistic level. Revisit your long-term goals with a nurturing touch, focusing on what brings you comfort and joy. Check in with your loved ones to make sure everyone is feeling safe and supported. With knowledge-seeking Jupiter in this family-friendly sign, dig in and discover more about your roots. Get a genetic test from 23andMe or reach out to relatives overseas. A pilgrimage might be in order!

NOV 12

WANING QUARTER MOON IN LEO (12:28AM)

When does "just a little more" cross the line into "hella extra"? The answer could reveal itself during today's moderating quarter moon in Leo. Have you fallen into a rut of basic-ness? Add a few glamorous, theatrical bells and whistles to your presentations. Already creeping into "Liberace Museum" terrain? This lunar leveling wags a bejeweled finger at anything too ostentatious. Leo style maven Coco Chanel advised people to remove one accessory before walking out the door. Apply this principle broadly today. If stress has been rising, book a massage (Leo rules the back) or stream an upbeat dance class. Pampering yourself pays off in productivity and pleasure!

MERCURY-MARS MEETUP

Contentious much? With fiery Mars merging with retrograde Mercury in outspoken Sagittarius, you might fire off a zinger before your brain has a chance to catch up. Quick comebacks feel almost irresistible under this transit, but watch out—you may not have all the facts straight. With Mercury retrograde in the mix, misunderstandings are bound to pop up, and the truth could look very different from the drama unfolding in your head. Before you let those fiery words fly, take a moment to cool off, think it through, and separate fact from fiction. Sometimes silence really is golden!

11

NOV 17

SUN-JUPITER TRINE

The divine feminine is rising and alchemizing! Jupiter in woman-powered Cancer dances into an ultra-rare trine with the Scorpio Sun, bringing a welcome reminder of the powerful role women play in shaping our world. With both heavenly bodies in water signs, emotions will be passionate and palpable. Don't hold back if you have feelings to express. Candid Jupiter can pull our deepest confessions out of Scorpio's vault. There's freedom in owning your truth and being witnessed. Start the sharing with people you know and trust before you unleash on TikTok and wind up on a million strangers' FYPs.

SUN-SATURN TRINE

As the Scorpio Sun and disciplined Saturn in Pisces unite in compassionate water signs, a calm but comforting approach will win the day. Know the difference between reacting and responding. Instead of flying into action at every provocation, step back and assess the best course of action. Smart solutions are best when backed by wisdom. If someone is pushing you to do something that feels out of alignment, opt for passive resistance rather than confronting them head on.

NOV 18-29 MERCURY RETROGRADE IN SCORPIO

Cat and mouse games could go awry as Mercury slips back into manipulative Scorpio to complete its retrograde, which ends on November 29. On the one hand, this brings relief from fiery feuds that have been going on since the messenger planet pulled a U-turn in Sagittarius on November 9. But for the next eleven days, life could feel like an extended game of Clue. Prepared to pass those loyalty tests? Trust is a must with Mercury reversing through this suspicious sign, and don't expect anyone to extend the benefit of the doubt. Show and prove, AND pledge your allegiance, if you want the keys to anyone's kingdom.

NOV 19

MERCURY-URANUS OPPOSITION

Your mind and mouth are moving at two totally different speeds under today's cosmic collision between irreverent Mercury, who's retrograde in Scorpio, and erratic Uranus in Taurus. With Mercury in sharp-tongued Scorpio, your zingers come with stingers. Just because you've thought of the prizewinning comeback, doesn't mean you should say it out loud. But hold your tongue before rebellious Uranus seizes the mic. Polarizing discussions can flame up fast today, and rabble-rouser Uranus won't want to back down from a debate.

11

Consider whether you're sowing chaos and contention rather than actually promoting progress. You don't have to force everyone to agree (that's not happening today) but at least reach a place of common decency and respect.

MERCURY-NEPTUNE TRINE #2 OF 3

Pay attention to what's bubbling beneath the surface today. With Mercury retrograde in investigative Scorpio dreamweaving with mystical Neptune in Pisces, you're being nudged to tap into your subconscious. This cosmic alignment may uncover hidden truths or forgotten visions buried deep in your imagination. Instead of getting caught up in overanalyzing, embrace a flow state through meditation, music, or creativity. Even with Mercury in reverse, your intuition is extra sharp now. Double-check your facts, but don't ignore that inner voice.

NOV 20

NEW MOON IN SCORPIO (1:47AM; 28°12')

Want to turn a leaden aspect of your life into pure, shimmering gold? Get the ball rolling on those transformational efforts. Real change takes work—it never just happens overnight. But this is a NEW moon, so it's all about jumping off the starting block. Scorpio works in the shadows, so don't try to force the positive vibes—not without paying attention to the full range of feelings involved with making change. It can be scary to let go! The fear of the unknown is what keeps most people stuck in a cycle. With both curious Mercury and esoteric Neptune trine the new moon, you could just as easily channel the information you need as you could discover it on a deep Google search. Acknowledge where you're blocked, then search for savvy mentors and guides who can help you untangle the mysterious machinations of your mind. With Uranus opposite the new moon, you might even find some of them in the virtual realm.

SUN-MERCURY RETROGRADE MEETUP

Get ready for some deep introspection as the Sun merges with Mercury retrograde in the intense sign of Scorpio. This cosmic meetup shines a spotlight on buried truths and unfinished business, especially in relationships or personal goals. Mercury retrograde's influence slows things down, inviting you to revisit past decisions and rethink your next steps. Old secrets may resurface, or a former flame could reappear, demanding closure. Don't rush the process! This is a powerful time for reflection and recalibration. Tune in to your gut instincts and dig deep—you're on the verge of a major breakthrough.

11

SUN-URANUS OPPOSITION

Everyone's skin is especially thin today as the sensitive Scorpio Sun faces down button-pushing Uranus in Taurus. Steer clear of trolls who are always spoiling for a fight. And don't go playing devil's advocate yourself. You can try to smooth things over by focusing on common ground, but easy does it. Attempts to break the tension with humor may go over like a lead balloon. Although you might feel anxious about a pending event, this isn't the day to demand a firm answer or make a binding decision. Plans could change at a moment's notice. If you must pivot quickly, adopt a flexible attitude instead of digging in your heels. (Tough, given that the Sun and Uranus are at loggerheads in tenacious fixed signs.) Stay nimble! A completely unexpected approach could actually lead to a breakthrough.

SUN-NEPTUNE TRINE

Let your intuition take the wheel today as the soulful Scorpio Sun forms a harmonious trine with dreamy Neptune in Pisces. This cosmic connection heightens your empathy and creativity, making it easier to tap into the subtle energies around you. Loosen up a little control. Instead of forcing outcomes, trust your inner wisdom and let things unfold organically. In the end, you'll be grateful for the extra integration time that comes from a slower pace. Conversations could take on a spiritual or emotional tone. You could lose track of time creating art, playing music or daydreaming. The more you surrender to the flow, the more magic you'll manifest. Just stay grounded so you don't drift too far into fantasy.

SUN IN SAGITTARIUS (8:36PM) (NOV 21–DEC 21)

Inclusivity is the name of the game as the Sun bursts into diversifying Sagittarius for a month. After huddling with your inner circle during Scorpio season, break out! Celebrate the differences that make us all dynamic. Play ambassador for people who haven't learned how to access the "one love" vibes. The spirit of transparency is in the air, so if you need to have an honest chat with someone before the holidays kick in, hash it out after Mercury turns direct on November 29. "Anywhere but home" always seems like the ideal destination for Sagittarius season; yes, even while Mercury is retrograde. With careful planning your holiday travel can go off without a hitch. This sporty solar cycle could get you bundled up and onto the slopes—or onto your yoga mat to warm your body from the inside out.

11

MERCURY-SATURN TRINE #2 OF 3

Slow your roll and think things through today as detail-oriented Mercury in Scorpio teams up with taskmaster Saturn in Pisces. Whether you're sealing the deal or putting the finishing touches on a project, Saturn rewards thorough, no-nonsense work. With both planets in emotional water signs, don't be shy about leaning on your inner circle for support. A savvy mentor or well-connected friend might hold the key to leveling up, but if you ask for an intro, be ready to follow through. Remember, your actions reflect on the person who's vouching for you, so bring your A-game once that door swings open!

MERCURY-JUPITER TRINE #2 OF 3

Big ideas are bubbling to the surface today as investigative Mercury, currently retrograde in Scorpio, forms a flowing trine to optimistic Jupiter in nurturing Cancer. With these security-loving signs at the helm, you'll be in the mood to research and brainstorm the particulars around your long-term plans. Conversations today could lead to major breakthroughs if you're willing to look underneath certain rocks. This watery cosmic combo amps up your intuition, making it easy to pick up on what's unsaid. But with Mercury retrograde, don't ride on assumptions. Someone's silence does not necessarily mean they are ghosting you. A close friend or relative might offer a golden opportunity or priceless advice—listen closely! Just be mindful not to bite off more than you can chew. Dream big but keep it manageable.

NOV 24 MERCURY-VENUS MEETUP

Some secrets aren't meant to be kept in the vault forever. If you've been agonizing over the right time to reveal your feelings, this day might greenlight the dialogue, as messenger Mercury (retrograde) meets up with heart-centered Venus at the same degree of Scorpio. A "coeur-a-coeur" could spontaneously erupt! Should you bump into a person-of-interest on the street—and dive right into a deep conversation—you may decide to move your sidewalk talk to a coffee shop...or a more private location. One caveat: While Venus loves to be swept away, this CAN be a slippery slope, given Mercury's backspin. With both planets tangoing through erotically charged (and vengeful) Scorpio, it might be better to cut things short if you encounter someone surreptitious, like a shady client who owes you money or someone you slept with who suddenly stopped texting you back. Power struggles may arise, or you might get swept right back into an old dynamic that leaves you feeling frustrated and out of control. But if you're dealing with a beautiful soul, this could be the day to lay it all on the line and see what emerges!

NOV 26

VENUS-JUPITER TRINE

"Warm and fuzzy" could be surprisingly seductive today, so give the nice ones a chance. Venus, gliding through passionate Scorpio, forms a harmonious trine to generous Jupiter in nurturing Cancer, which turns up the heat on all things heartfelt. Whether you're strengthening the bond with your significant other or forging meaningful connections with close friends, today serves a buffet of soul-stirring moments. Jupiter's expansive energy could bring game-changing surprises, like a friend date blossoming into something romantic or a creative collaboration taking off with an artist you've stanned for years. Open your channels wide and let the magic unfold!

VENUS-SATURN TRINE

Fantasy mingles with reality for a highly seductive cocktail. As romantic Venus in Scorpio connects with mature Saturn in Pisces, love could take a turn for the serious. Single? Don't rule out a slightly older prospect or a stable person you might have written off as "boring." (Those secure attachments have their benefits!) For couples, it's a great day to talk about the future and to make concrete plans for some holiday activities you can enjoy as a duo. Nostalgic activities may be on the menu, especially if you want to rev up romance.

NOV 27 SATURN RETROGRADE ENDS

Taskmaster Saturn straightens out after a five-month retrograde period that began in fiery Aries on July 13, and moved into healing, watery Pisces on September 1. Saturn's backspin brought plenty of soul-searching and personal growth—along with a few harsh but necessary lessons. You may have learned a lot about the pitfalls of being both aggressive and passive. No one would call a transit like this fun, but the growth and maturity that it can bring is priceless. Got an artistic or spiritual gift to contribute to the world? While Saturn takes one more lap through Pisces, until February 13, 2026, practice the skills that lead to mastery. If you're already an expert, contribute to someone else's inner growth by sharing the wisdom of your own experience.

11

NOV 28 WAXING QUARTER MOON IN PISCES (1:58AM)

Subtle energies speak volumes today as the quarter moon in intuitive Pisces amplifies your sixth sense. What aren't people saying out loud? Pay attention to prolonged silences, facial expressions and body language that don't match the mood. While it's still important to get the facts, these are reliable guides for assessing the temperature of your environment. If you've been an open book (and who hasn't during Sagittarius season?), keep a little more mystery to yourself. It's an alluring trait today, one that leaves people hungry to know more. And since Pisces is the master of illusion, it's a wise security measure. Establishing trust takes time. Pace yourself and let things flow organically. Don't be surprised if this "tuned in" approach leads you to a miraculous discovery! Serendipities are probably not mere coincidences today. If something seems like a sign, follow that thread.

NOV 29

MERCURY RETROGRADE ENDS

All those dodgy, befuddling interactions should clear up a lot today as Mercury pivots out of a mind-bending three-week retrograde that began in Sagittarius on November 9. With the silver-tongued messenger casting spells in Scorpio since November 18, nothing has been quite as it seems. Starting today, wires will slowly but surely uncross. Cutthroat dynamics could soften into healthy competition, but don't drop ALL self-protective shields. Mercury's backspin may have revealed some shady characters who don't deserve a second (third or fourth) chance. As Mercury continues its undercover crawl through Scorpio until December 11, continue to vet your engagements carefully and keep reading the fine print with a massive magnifying glass.

VENUS-URANUS OPPOSITION

Assume nothing today...but expect anything! Controlling Venus in Scorpio is at loggerheads with bombastic Uranus in Taurus. Strong emotions might erupt like an active volcano under this explosive and unpredictable face-off. If people signal a need for "space," give it to them instead of frantically texting or pushing for a talk. Feeling the urge for more freedom? You don't have to throw out the baby with the bathwater. It's totally possible to create more space in a relationship without calling the whole thing off. Rule for the day? Assume nothing. And avoid making any unilateral decisions. Check in and get consensus (and consent) before taking action.

VENUS-NEPTUNE TRINE

Ooh la la! Venus in Scorpio gets in a flowing formation with enchanting Neptune in Pisces, spicing up the day. Their dynamic dance, which generally happens twice a year, sends seductive undercurrents rippling through the ether. Cast a spell with nonverbal cues, dab on a titillating fragrance; let a flash of colorful lingerie peek through your clothing. A little cat-and-mouse game can be arousing in affairs de coeur. Wait a little longer to reply to a new love interest's text—but not so long that they think you're uninterested. Uncertainty builds anticipation...and attraction. The only risk of a Venus-Neptune trine is that it can make boundaries a little hazy. Don't lose sight of all propriety in the heat of the moment. There's a time and a place for everything.

VENUS IN SAGITTARIUS (NOV 30-DEC 24)

Ardent Venus swings into worldly Sagittarius, stirring up attractions across every aisle. After a bout of "Should I or shouldn't I?" you may feel ready to take a Vegas-sized gamble in the game of love. One way or another, candid confessions could come spilling out, blowing covers off of shady lovers everywhere. During this happy go lucky circuit it will be easier to brush off a "rejection" and keep on swiping...then probably laugh about it all and become BFFs with your now not-so-secret crush. Cross-cultural connections simmer with extra masala. If you can squeeze in a pre-Christmas baecation, even for a night or two, it promises to be epic. Close to home, you can find your romantic and artistic stimulation...anywhere BUT "the usual places."

11

December

12

DECEMBER
Moon Phase Calendar

SUN	MON	TUE	WED	THU	FRI	SAT
	1 ♈ ♉ 10:13PM	**2** ♉	**3** ♉ ♊ 9:48PM	**4** ♊ Full Moon 6:14PM	**5** ♊ ♋ 8:54PM	**6** ♋
7 ♋ ♌ 9:48PM	**8** ♌	**9** ♌	**10** ♌ ♍ 2:20AM	**11** ♍ 4th Quarter	**12** ♍ ♎ 11:04AM	**13** ♎
14 ♎ ♏ 10:51PM	**15** ♏	**16** ♏	**17** ♏ ♐ 11:38AM	**18** ♐	**19** ♐ New Moon 8:43PM ♐→♑ 11:53PM	**20** ♑
21 ♑	**22** ♑ ♒ 10:52AM	**23** ♒	**24** ♒ ♓ 8:09PM	**25** ♓	**26** ♓	**27** ♓→♈ 3:02AM ♈ 2nd Quarter
28 ♈	**29** ♈ ♉ 6:57AM	**30** ♉	**31** ♉ ♊ 8:13AM			

Times listed are Eastern US Time Zone

KEY

♈ ARIES	♌ LEO	♐ SAGITTARIUS	**FM**	FULL MOON	
♉ TAURUS	♍ VIRGO	♑ CAPRICORN	**NM**	NEW MOON	
♊ GEMINI	♎ LIBRA	♒ AQUARIUS	**LE**	LUNAR ECLIPSE	
♋ CANCER	♏ SCORPIO	♓ PISCES	**SE**	SOLAR ECLIPSE	

12

DECEMBER 4, 6:14PM
full moon in Gemini (13°04')

GEMINI FULL MOON CRYSTAL

DALMATIAN JASPER

This black-and-white-flecked stone helps balance the yin and yang of dualistic Gemini. Dalmatian Jasper can evoke a sense of childlike wonder along with bursts of hope and joy—all while supporting the release of anger and resentment.

GEMINI FULL MOON = CELEBRATE!

Friends who are always up for a hangout

The silly things that make you laugh

Your favorite local haunts

People who are easy to flirt with (no strings attached)

Inside jokes

Books, movies and experiences that stimulate your mind

DECEMBER 19, 8:43PM
new moon in
Sagittarius (28°25′)

SAGITTARIUS NEW MOON CRYSTAL

LAPIS LAZULI
This bright blue, high-vibrational stone helps you tap into your inner wisdom and gain confidence with self-expression. Lapis Lazuli connects you to the Sagittarian values of integrity, clarity and intuition.

SAGITTARIUS NEW MOON = FOCUS

Turn each day into an adventure

Travel to new places—locally and globally

Broaden your social horizons

Speak your truth while hearing new perspectives

Study and invest in self-development

Make media and share your message

12

December 2025

Longitude & Retrograde Ephemeris [00:00 UT]

Day	Sid.time	☉	☽	+12h☽	☿	♀	♂	♃	♄	♅	♆	♇	☊	☊	⚸	⚷	Day
1 Mo	04:40:26	♐09°02'23	♈13°27'36	♈20°40'59	DS 20°50	♐00°11	♐19°17	℞ 24°32	♓25°09	℞ 29°03	℞ 29°23	♒01°54	℞ 13°48	℞ 14°17	♏27°46	℞ 23°05	**1** Mo
2 Tu	04:44:22	♐10°03'11	♈28°01'13	♉05°27'12	♏21°08	♐01°27	♐20°02	♋24°28	♓25°10	♉29°00	♓29°23	♒01°55	♓13°45	♓14°12	♏27°53	♈23°03	**2** Tu
3 We	04:48:19	♐11°04'00	♉12°58'41	♉20°34'07	♏21°35	♐02°42	♐20°46	♋24°24	♓25°10	♉28°58	♓29°23	♒01°56	♓13°42	♓14°04	♏28°00	♈23°01	**3** We
4 Th	04:52:15	♐12°04'49	♉28°12'47	♊05°52'48	♏22°09	♐03°58	♐21°31	♋24°19	♓25°11	♉28°55	♓29°23	♒01°58	♓13°39	♓13°54	♏28°07	♈23°00	**4** Th
5 Fr	04:56:12	♐13°05'40	♊13°33'12	♊21°11'57	♏22°51	♐05°13	♐22°16	♋24°15	♓25°11	♉28°53	♓29°22	♒01°59	♓13°36	♓13°43	♏28°13	♈22°58	**5** Fr
6 Sa	05:00:08	♐14°06'32	♊28°48'08	♋06°19'53	♏23°39	♐06°29	♐23°00	♋24°10	♓25°12	♉28°50	♓29°22	♒02°00	♓13°32	♓13°31	♏28°20	♈22°57	**6** Sa
7 Su	05:04:05	♐15°07'25	♋13°46'32	♋21°06'39	♏24°33	♐07°44	♐23°45	♋24°06	♓25°13	♉28°48	♓29°22	♒02°02	♓13°29	♓13°21	♏28°27	♈22°55	**7** Su
8 Mo	05:08:02	♐16°08'20	♋28°20'02	♌05°25'42	♏25°32	♐09°00	♐24°30	♋24°01	♓25°14	♉28°46	♓29°22	♒02°03	♓13°26	♓13°13	♏28°33	♈22°54	**8** Mo
9 Tu	05:11:58	♐17°09'15	♌12°23'57	♌19°14'18	♏26°34	♐10°15	♐25°15	♋23°56	♓25°15	♉28°43	♓29°22	♒02°05	♓13°23	♓13°07	♏28°40	♈22°52	**9** Tu
10 We	05:15:55	♐18°10'11	♌25°57'21	♍02°33'02	♏27°41	♐11°31	♐26°00	♋23°50	♓25°17	♉28°41	♓29°22	♒02°06	♓13°20	♓13°05	♏28°47	♈22°51	**10** We
11 Th	05:19:51	♐19°11'09	♍09°02'13	♍15°25'00	♏28°51	♐12°46	♐26°45	♋23°45	♓25°18	♉28°39	D 29°22	♒02°08	♓13°16	♓13°04	♏28°54	♈22°50	**11** Th
12 Fr	05:23:48	♐20°12'07	♍21°42'27	♍27°54'45	♐00°04	♐14°02	♐27°30	♋23°39	♓25°19	♉28°36	♓29°22	♒02°09	♓13°13	♓13°04	♏29°00	♈22°49	**12** Fr
13 Sa	05:27:44	♐21°13'07	♎04°03'00	♎10°07'25	♐01°19	♐15°17	♐28°15	♋23°34	♓25°21	♉28°34	♓29°22	♒02°11	♓13°10	♓13°03	♏29°07	♈22°47	**13** Sa
14 Su	05:31:41	♐22°14'08	♎16°09'04	♎22°08'09	♐02°36	♐16°33	♐29°00	♋23°28	♓25°22	♉28°32	♓29°22	♒02°12	♓13°07	♓13°01	♏29°14	♈22°46	**14** Su
15 Mo	05:35:37	♐23°15'10	♎28°05'38	♏04°01'39	♐03°55	♐17°48	♐29°45	♋23°22	♓25°24	♉28°30	♓29°22	♒02°14	♓13°04	♓12°57	♏29°21	♈22°45	**15** Mo
16 Tu	05:39:34	♐24°16'13	♏09°57'05	♏15°51'58	♐05°16	♐19°04	♑00°31	♋23°15	♓25°26	♉28°27	♓29°22	♒02°15	♓13°01	♓12°49	♏29°27	♈22°44	**16** Tu
17 We	05:43:31	♐25°17'17	♏21°47'05	♏27°42'22	♐06°38	♐20°19	♑01°16	♋23°09	♓25°28	♉28°25	♓29°23	♒02°17	♓12°57	♓12°38	♏29°34	♈22°43	**17** We
18 Th	05:47:27	♐26°18'22	♐03°38'29	♐09°35'17	D 08°01	♐21°35	♑02°01	♋23°03	♓25°30	♉28°23	♓29°23	♒02°19	♓12°54	♓12°26	♏29°41	♈22°42	**18** Th
19 Fr	05:51:24	♐27°19'27	♐15°33'22	♐21°32'29	♐09°25	♐22°50	♑02°47	♋22°56	♓25°32	♉28°21	♓29°23	♒02°20	♓12°51	♓12°11	♏29°47	♈22°41	**19** Fr
20 Sa	05:55:20	♐28°20'34	♐27°33'10	♑03°35'09	♐10°50	♐24°06	♑03°32	♋22°49	♓25°35	♉28°19	♓29°23	♒02°22	♓12°48	♓11°57	♏29°54	♈22°41	**20** Sa
21 Su	05:59:17	♐29°21'40	♑09°38'56	♑15°44'14	♐12°16	♐25°21	♑04°18	♋22°43	♓25°37	♉28°17	♓29°24	♒02°23	♓12°45	♓11°43	♐00°01	♈22°40	**21** Su
22 Mo	06:03:13	♑00°22'48	♑21°51'34	♑28°00'41	♐13°43	♐26°37	♑05°03	♋22°36	♓25°39	♉28°15	♓29°24	♒02°25	♓12°42	♓11°32	♐00°08	♈22°39	**22** Mo
23 Tu	06:07:10	♑01°23'55	♒04°12'07	♒10°25'42	♐15°11	♐27°52	♑05°49	♋22°29	♓25°42	♉28°13	♓29°25	♒02°27	♓12°38	♓11°23	♐00°14	♈22°39	**23** Tu
24 We	06:11:06	♑02°25'03	♒16°42'04	♒23°01'03	♐16°39	♐29°08	♑06°34	♋22°21	♓25°45	♉28°11	♓29°25	♒02°29	♓12°35	♓11°18	♐00°21	♈22°38	**24** We
25 Th	06:15:03	♑03°26'11	♒29°23'24	♓05°49'01	♐18°07	♑00°23	♑07°20	♋22°14	♓25°47	♉28°09	♓29°26	♒02°30	♓12°32	♓11°15	♐00°28	♈22°38	**25** Th
26 Fr	06:18:60	♑04°27'19	♓12°18'41	♓18°52'21	♐19°36	♑01°39	♑08°06	♋22°07	♓25°50	♉28°07	♓29°26	♒02°32	♓12°29	D 11°14	♐00°34	♈22°37	**26** Fr
27 Sa	06:22:56	♑05°28'27	♓25°30'50	♈02°14'01	♐21°06	♑02°54	♑08°51	♋21°59	♓25°53	♉28°05	♓29°27	♒02°34	♓12°26	♓11°15	♐00°41	♈22°37	**27** Sa
28 Su	06:26:53	♑06°29'35	♈09°02'40	♈15°56'35	♐22°35	♑04°10	♑09°37	♋21°52	♓25°56	♉28°03	♓29°27	♒02°35	♓12°22	℞ 11°15	♐00°48	♈22°36	**28** Su
29 Mo	06:30:49	♑07°30'43	♈22°56'23	♉00°01'36	♐24°06	♑05°25	♑10°23	♋21°44	♓25°59	♉28°02	♓29°28	♒02°37	♓12°19	♓11°14	♐00°55	♈22°36	**29** Mo
30 Tu	06:34:46	♑08°31'51	♉07°12'37	♉14°28'38	♐25°36	♑06°41	♑11°09	♋21°37	♓26°03	♉28°00	♓29°28	♒02°39	♓12°16	♓11°11	♐01°01	♈22°36	**30** Tu
31 We	06:38:42	♑09°32'59	♉21°49'42	♉29°14'38	♐27°07	♑07°56	♑11°55	♋21°29	♓26°06	♉27°58	♓29°29	♒02°41	♓12°13	♓11°05	♐01°08	♈22°36	**31** We
Δ Delta	01:58:15	30°30'36"	398°22'06"	398°33'38"	36°17'	37°45'	22°37'	-3°02'	0°56'	-1°04'	0°05'	0°47'	-1°35'	-3°11'	3°21'	-0°28'	**Delta**

Ephemeris tables and data provided by **Astro-Seek.com.** All times in UTC.

DECEMBER
MONTHLY HOTSPOTS

DEC 4 FULL MOON IN GEMINI (6:14PM; 13°04'; SUPERMOON)

Wordplay, wit and wisdom! Everyone's got a story to tell under the loquacious full supermoon in Gemini. Articulate your dreams, desires and wishes aloud. Post about them on social media and see who wants to help you manifest your vision. Gemini rules peers and platonic partnerships and under this lunation, a creative partnership could turn into an official dynamic duo. Plan a drop or debut or just get the buzz going! Need a new set of wheels? This full moon may light the way to the perfect car or mobile accessory for commutes. Surround yourself with uplifting people today because vibes are contagious. With nefarious Pluto and people-pleasing Venus influencing the supermoon, use your charm selectively. It's easy to tell people what they want to hear and even easier to lead them on. Stay on the side of good karma and be transparent.

DEC 6 MERCURY-JUPITER TRINE #3 OF 3

Third time's the charm! With Mercury now direct in intense Scorpio, it's forming its third harmonious trine to expansive Jupiter in nurturing Cancer. You've had a chance to revisit and refine your ideas during Mercury's retrograde phase last month, and now everything's clicking into place. This celestial alignment opens the floodgates for big breakthroughs and aha moments. Dive deep into those meaningful conversations and brainstorming sessions—you've laid the groundwork, and now it's time to act. Opportunities that felt just out of reach might suddenly land in your lap. Just remember to pace yourself; while enthusiasm is high, steady steps will turn your grand visions into lasting realities. Embrace this momentum—you've earned it!

DEC 7 MERCURY-SATURN TRINE #3 OF 3

Break out the fine-toothed comb. As analytical Mercury in Scorpio and mature Saturn in Pisces form their third in a trio of alliances since late October, you may have a final draft that's ready to review. Both planets are now in direct motion, giving you the green light for action. Whether you're making a big decision or finishing a project, make sure you've turned over every detail before you proceed. In emotional water signs, these planets prompt you to reach out to your inner circle for support. Has a close friend or wise relative been through something similar? Don't let pride stand in the way. Get their advice and opinion, even if it only winds up being food for thought.

12

DEC 10

NEPTUNE DIRECT IN PISCES

Wake up, Sleeping Beauty. Dreamy Neptune rises from its annual, five-month retrograde, which will change the current from downstream to upstream. Certain areas of life that have been mired in illusion or uncertainty begin slowly moving in a proactive direction. This year's U-turn is particularly poignant as it marks Neptune's final lap through its home sign of Pisces—the seas it's been paddling through since 2011! The world has become a lot more spiritual and psychedelic since this transit began raising the collective vibration fourteen years ago. What mystical adventures await you now? Is there a spiritual experience you want to have? An artistic milestone you'd like to achieve? Neptune in Pisces is your muse until January 26, 2026, when the compassionate planet heads back into Aries for thirteen years. Add some soul to your goals. Tap into your creative right brain (and the divine flow) with journaling, meditation or visualization exercises.

MERCURY-URANUS OPPOSITION

Get ready for a mental shake-up! When Mercury in deep-diving Scorpio faces off with wildcard Uranus in stubborn Taurus, surprises are bound to pop up. Expect intense, no-BS conversations that could turn into power struggles—especially if you're clinging to the old while craving change. Shocking news or revelations might rock your world, but they can also free you from stuck situations. Stay grounded before making any impulsive moves, especially with money. While this transit might feel like a cosmic curveball, it's clearing space for breakthroughs and fresh perspectives. Embrace the disruption—it's leading you to transformation!

DEC 11

MERCURY-NEPTUNE TRINE #3

Ask, believe, receive! As Mercury in Scorpio forms its third trine to mystical Neptune (now direct in Pisces) since late October it's time to harness that dreamy, intuitive energy and turn it into something tangible. You don't need to grind away to get what you want—instead, go with the flow and use the Law of Attraction to manifest your desires. Visualize your goals clearly and let the universe handle the details. With Mercury and Neptune in sync, your intuition is next-level psychic, so trust your gut. Sure, check the facts, but don't overthink it. Your inner guidance knows the way better than any data report!

WANING QUARTER MOON IN VIRGO (3:51PM)

Don't sweat the small stuff, but don't ignore it either. Fine lines and wrinkles can interfere with plans as the quarter moon in Virgo plays inspector for the day. Proof your work before sending it off, making sure everything's spellchecked, accurate and up to date. Ask an eagle-eyed friend to read your text before you impulsively fire it off. Falling prey to perfectionism? Adjust your expectations instead of comparing and despairing. Are you asking more of people than they can humanly provide? Today's moonbeams may guide you to more qualified service providers who can help you get the job done to code. But even then, get real. Timelines and budgets may also need adjusting unless you're willing to simplify your strategy.

MERCURY IN SAGITTARIUS (DEC 11–JAN 1, 2026)
Dream it, do it! The messenger planet jets back into Sagittarius, picking up plans that got sidelined when Mercury turned retrograde in this sign back on November 9. Go big and bold with your 2026 resolutions! Between now and New Year's Day, you'll be able to articulate some of your grandest dreams in colorful detail. But don't waste your best material on people who don't get it. Wait until you find the perfect audience to share your genius. With worldly Sagittarius energy flowing, they might be located 50, 500 or 5,000 miles from your front door!

DEC 14 MARS-NEPTUNE SQUARE
It may seem thrilling to take a gamble today, but that's a slippery slope. Unless you have all the facts in front of you, hedge your bets! With the most active planet (Mars) at loggerheads with the most passive one (Neptune), you could take yourself on a wild ride of impulsivity and skewed intuition. Go back to the drawing board and do some quality research. With both planets in mutable signs—Mars in Sagittarius and Neptune in Pisces—plans may fluctuate wildly. Don't assume that a "maybe" is a "yes" until you've 100 percent confirmed it. Moreover, don't let anyone sweet talk you into making decisions, especially if they involve a financial transaction.

DEC 15–JAN 23, 2026 MARS IN CAPRICORN
How obsessed are you with success? You're about to find out as goal-getter Mars leaps into ambitious Capricorn and brings out your desire to do, be, and have, the best. Mars is exalted in Capricorn, meaning it's one of its most powerful positions on the zodiac wheel. Harness the red planet's power to finish the year strong—and start 2026 even stronger. The cream always rises to the top! Remember: Grabbing the brass ring isn't just about laser focus and tireless hustle. The endorsement of prestigious people may be your golden ticket into the big leagues. Use the holiday season to mingle with the influencers or begin next year joining an industry group where you can casually rub shoulders with the VIPs. Already in the VIP lounge?

12

DEC 16 SUN-SATURN SQUARE

Too much too soon? This twice-a-year battle between the optimistic Sagittarius Sun and speed-checking Saturn in Pisces can make you feel a little stressed about the future. It's also an important reality check. You might not be able to realistically deliver what you're promising within the budget and timeline—so better to speak up now. Instead of getting discouraged, go back to the drawing board or tighten up your blueprint. Consider this brief pause a blessing in disguise. You could spot an error or a flaw in your plans just in the nick of time.

DEC 19
NEW MOON IN SAGITTARIUS (8:43PM; 28°25')

Borders become bridges as today's new moon in Sagittarius sets the stage for multicultural mingling and cross-cultural collabs. Better yet? Harmonious, loving Venus is co-piloting the mission, helping patch over any conflicts that may have flared during last month's Mercury retrograde. With healing Neptune and serious Saturn squaring the new moon, don't gloss over any structures that need to be put in place moving forward. Sagittarius rules travel. Switch to a wide-angle lens and zoom in on other parts of the world, from Perth to Portugal. Searches could turn up virtual connections or the perfect Airbnb to book for your winter vacation. Even though it's almost time for a holiday break, this new moon brings a burst of "cosmic capital" for start-up initiatives. Entrepreneurs, give your vision some thought today. What benchmarks would you love to achieve over the coming six months? Even taking one small action to move the needle today can send a strong signal to the universe that says, "I'm ready for this journey!"

DEC 20 SUN-NEPTUNE SQUARE

Hit pause and take stock of how realistic your ambitious ideas are. As the holiday timeline kicks in, people are just not eager to take on a big project. While you don't want to limit yourself, hazy Neptune in Pisces clashing with the confident Sun in Sagittarius can obscure facts or draw in people who over-promise under the twinkling lights. Err on the side of caution and scale down anything that's become overly complex. Stressing people out with elaborate party instructions or over-the-top dress codes, for example, can cause a ripple of tension that kills the fun of getting together. This cosmic clash can create a foggy atmosphere, making it hard to see the full picture. Get clear about other people's boundaries and time limits—and be up front about your own.

DEC 21

VENUS-SATURN SQUARE

If you've been cruising along with your holiday season indulging, today's Grinchlike aspect between hedonistic Venus and disciplined Saturn could turn on the "slow down" warning light. Even at this "most wonderful time of the year," it's possible to have too much of a good thing. Go easy on the sugary treats, boozy libations and sloppy mistletoe moments. Self-control is sexy, at least according to Saturn. Smart too, since this transit may reveal how close you've gone to being over budget. Think twice before going overboard with the hand-blown ornaments and stocking stuffers that will only wind up in people's junk drawers. Find your "enough" button and hit it fast!

DEC 21–JAN 19, 2026
SUN IN CAPRICORN (10:03AM)

It's beginning to look a lot like solstice! The Sun enters Capricorn today, marking the shortest day of the year for those living in the northern hemisphere. Carve out space to meditate, reflect and find gratitude for the high points of your 2025. Then, clarify what you'd like to leave behind as you enter 2026. What golden lessons are you excited to bring with you into the New Year? The winter solstice always coincides with the Sun's move into grounding, elegant Capricorn. And since the celestial Sea Goat is the governor of goalsetting, how perfect is it that we get to make our resolutions under these rays every year? Get a running list going in your Notes app for now, so you can enjoy the holidays pressure-free. Capricorn season rallies on until January 19, 2026, so fear not! You're not going to lose your momentum (or your "high pro glow") if you start building your supersized visions after NYD.

DEC 24

VENUS-NEPTUNE SQUARE

Christmas Eve is meant for relaxing in the spirit of joy and togetherness. Try not to blow the assignment as people-pleasing Venus squares boundary-challenged Neptune. In your desire to play Santa for everyone you love, you could exhaust yourself wrapping presents instead of putting them in bags or sacrificing your family time to pick a friend up from the airport who is perfectly capable of taking a Lyft. With Venus in maximizer Sagittarius and Neptune in sacrificial Pisces, it will be hard to know where your limits lie. No one will be mad if you pick up a pie from the bakery instead of trying to play pastry chef in the eleventh hour! Create space to be with your favorite people.

VENUS IN CAPRICORN (DEC 24–JAN 17, 2026)

12

Nothing wrong with a little strategic placement of the mistletoe this Christmas Eve. With amorous Venus settling into Capricorn's VIP lounge until January 17, your tastes could elevate as sky-high as the Star of Bethlehem. Defining nebulous situationships could be a fun game of "You show me your bucket list, I'll show you mine!" Or, if you're the type who doesn't even think about bucket lists, well, maybe it's time to write one up along with your New Year's resolutions. With driven Capricorn ruling romance for the next few weeks, couples could achieve something memorable—and profitable—as a pair. No apologies for being attracted to status now. Couples can align around your shared future, discussing your 2026 dreams by the fireplace. If you're single and looking, search for someone who is ready for meaningful co-creation, like now.

DEC 27 WAXING QUARTER MOON IN ARIES (2:09PM)

Chasing after shiny objects is not recommended under today's moderating quarter moon in Aries. It's fine to be attracted to the sparkliest person in the room or the most expensive item on the shelf. But weigh that impulse against your long-range plans. Rushing can backfire, so ease slowly into any new arrangements. Test the waters with a trial run. It's a lot less expensive than buying a season pass, especially if you've never tried an activity before. If you've been scattering your energy this month, take a pause to assess what's really in alignment with YOU. Devote more time to a few key interests instead of attempting to learn everything all at once!

DEC 30 MERCURY-SATURN SQUARE

Reality check! With Mercury in adventurous Sagittarius squaring off against Saturn in dreamy Pisces, those grand New Year's Eve plans might need a little fine-tuning. Sure, the idea of a big celebration sounds great, but have you thought about the practical details? Last-minute complications could pop up, so double-check your reservations, confirm the guest list, and set realistic expectations. This transit urges you to end the year with a mix of optimism and realism. It's not about canceling the fun—just making sure it's grounded in what's actually doable. Start 2026 on solid ground, not drifting off in a cloud of wishful thinking.

12

The AstroTwins'

TREND REPORT

THE YEAR OF THE DIVINE PENDULUM

How will the trends swing in this year of transition?
Here are The AstroTwins' predictions for some of
2025's biggest global shifts.

2025 COLORS OF THE YEAR

As we leave behind the past and step into a still-unclear future, burnt and smoky hues blend perfectly with the transitional qualities of 2025. This year favors a palette that's both mysterious and energizing, evoking images of sacred embers, volcanic landscapes and mist-laden dawns.

SMOKY AMETHYST

Tone: A deep, muted purple with gray undertones
Energy: Transformation, intuition, tranquility

DUSKY ROSEWOOD

Tone: A deep, smoked rose with a slightly ashen quality
Energy: Compassion, mystery, refinement

BURNISHED TERRACOTTA

Tone: A warm, earthy red-brown with burnt undertones
Energy: Grounding, warmth and stability

JADE FOREST

Tone: A saturated and darkened forest green
Energy: Nourishing, esoteric, restorative

WORKPLACE

At a glance: *The workplace shifts toward flexibility, lifelong learning, and wellness-focused culture. Savvy companies will prioritize training in both hard skills and emotional intelligence, creating an office environment that feels more like home.*

OFFICE CULTURE & LEADERSHIP

HYBRID, FRACTIONAL, REMOTE: THE NEW ROLE PLAYING

Jupiter and Uranus in dualistic Gemini accelerate the trend toward the part-time model of hybrid workplaces and fractional executives. Offices may become more flexible, with fewer employees working full-time onsite.

DIVERSE SKILLSETS BECOME AN ASSET

Portfolio-based work—a career that combines multiple titles or roles across disparate sectors—is another exciting trend that speaks to the diversity of skills many workers bring. Why yes, you can be an accountant and a food photographer or part of both the marketing and the business development teams. If you've got range, there's no need to shoehorn yourself into a box this year.

MENTAL HEALTH AND WELLNESS BENEFITS

With the lunar nodes in the compassionate and health-conscious signs of Pisces and Virgo, workplaces may go to new lengths to encourage wellness. More offices may include on-site meditation spaces, mental health days and employee access to therapy, yoga and gyms. Companies may also adopt policies that encourage regular breaks and time off to reduce burnout, creating a supportive culture that reflects the Pisces-Virgo influence on care and well-being.

NEW WAYS TO CREATE "CULTURE" ADD STEAM TO THE TEAM

Workers floating in and out of roles or coming into the office can present challenges around teamwork. As transformational Pluto moves through communal Aquarius, new strategies will emerge to help companies unify their staff and create camaraderie, while also respecting that the office is no longer the source of social bonding that it was during the early Google and startup era.

Periodic offsites and team-building retreats could become essential ingredients to creating culture where the Zoom square fails (add a line item to your department budget for travel!). Beyond basic bonding experiences, these perks can foster a desirable corporate culture and inspire workers to be part of the company's mission—especially if hosted in locations like a boutique hotel's idyllic property or in a city's buzziest neighborhood.

HOW ABOUT SOME OUTDOOR SPACE TOO?

Confinement, begone! As we progress into the second half of the decade, the air element prevails (Jupiter, Uranus and Pluto visit air signs in 2025 alone). Offices with terraces, rooftops and outdoor meeting spaces will become must-have amenities for recruiting and retaining top talent. Forget about the flatscreens and foosball machines of yore. Greenspaces, air-purifying plants and natural light are the new luxury perks. The new "corner office" could be open-air access with wifi, a barista and even a pool! And with Pluto in communal Aquarius, we can expect to see food trucks, fitness classes and other "experiences" become part of the modern worker's lifestyle. Biophilic design, where architecture and nature intertwine, will increase in popularity with the lunar nodes in Virgo and Pisces.

WANTED: EMOTIONALLY INTELLIGENT LEADERS Hard

skills won't be the only key assets to bring to the table in the Age of Aquarius. A high emotional IQ will also be a marker for success and leadership in 2025

and beyond. Companies may increase investments in interpersonal training for their teams. There are now five generations sharing office space. Gen Alpha, first born in 2010, is not far behind. The vastly divergent communication styles, comfort level with technology and values are already creating clashes. Executives may lean into personality tests, gamified icebreakers and other common-interest activities to mitigate volatility and create cohesion.

NEW DEVELOPMENTS FOR ETHICAL AI AND TRANSPARENT DATA PRACTICES: Privacy policies? Check.

Pluto in Aquarius emphasizes transparency and ethics, particularly surrounding data and technology. In the workplace, this could lead to innovative practices around ethical AI use and data privacy, with companies hammering out clear policies on data collection, employee surveillance and AI usage for the team. This will become crucial while Uranus visits Gemini from July 7 to November 7.

ENTREPRENEURSHIP

At a glance: As the independent workforce continues to rise, discovering ways to stand out and create security shift alongside technology.

STAND OUT WITH PERSONAL BRANDING

With professional Saturn and enchanting Neptune heading into individualistic Aries, employees will need to stand out with added starpower. Creating a personal brand or an enhanced, personality-driven presence will be a plus. Not simply as a means to outshine the competition, but rather to make a clear-cut statement about what unique skills you bring to the table. For the indie-spirited workers out there, becoming a creator and building a community can lead to brand deals and paid endorsements. The trick? Positioning yourself as an asset to the company you work for rather than a threat of competition. Unless, of course, you're building your own brand to break free from the employee grind. But even then, it may be smarter to keep relationships intact. Perhaps you can turn your former employer into a client in the process.

INDEPENDENT CONTRACTORS, UNITE?

Remote and gig work will continue to gain popularity with Saturn and Uranus in indie-spirited Aries. But what about those security measures like health insurance and paid time off—not to mention policies and protocols around ethics, hourly rates and so on? There are currently 64 million independent contractors in the United States workforce, and half of them are women. Independent contractors may become more vocal about protecting the freedom and flexibility of their work arrangements while still negotiating benefits, health insurance, unemployment

and basic protections against dangers like non-payment, on-the-job injuries and workplace abuse. With rule-making Saturn in autonomous Aries from May 24 to September 1, there could be backlash if policy-makers and government organizations become too involved, especially from companies that find it cost-prohibitive to classify short-term and gig workers as employees. (We saw a preview of this during Pluto's short dip into Aquarius in early 2024.)

RESKILLING, UPSKILLING AND CONTINUING EDUCATION

TREND With technology and AI rapidly advancing, people must continually update their tools to stay competitive in fast-changing industries. Saturn in Aries, which encourages individual growth and self-sufficiency, drives a trend toward continuous skill-building and refreshing. Savvy companies will invest in ongoing training of workers, funding their continued learning via micro-certifications, short courses, tuition matching and digital boot camps. Paid education may become a benefit that bigger companies use to entice staff to stay long-term.

HOME SWEET OFFICE

Once Jupiter moves into Cancer on June 9, workplaces may reimagine their physical spaces to create a sense of belonging and comfort. Offices will feature communal spaces that feel like home, with comfortable furniture, wellness rooms, and even family-friendly zones. This trend could foster a more nurturing atmosphere, making the workplace feel like an extension of your WFH sanctuary. Companies may also organize more "family days" and community service activities, nurturing a workplace culture rooted in compassion and shared values. We could see more kid-friendly offices that offer on-site care, education and experiences, especially during holidays.

CO-WORKING FOR FOCUS AND PRODUCTIVITY

The ADHD technique of "body doubling" could become a popular strategy for remote workers to adopt in 2025—especially in this era of distraction! Body doubling involves working alongside another person to support each other with staying focused and productive, even if your tasks are independent. Whether IRL or virtually, this can stave off isolation and replace the built-in accountability of an office environment. Remote teams might even set up an office in the metaverse, using dashboard and app-based programs like Teamflow HQ which allow customized decor that looks and feels like home.

THE ECONOMY

At a glance: *The economy is primed for groundbreaking shifts, from real estate innovation to digital finance and renewable energy markets. Here's what the stars have in store for our wallets and investments this year.*

RESIDENTIAL REAL ESTATE VALUES CREEP SKYWARD

While interest prices may be going down at a glacial pace, Jupiter in Cancer is set to increase existing home prices after June 9. Property investment may see a surge, particularly in suburban and rural areas, as remote work becomes more entrenched. Global Jupiter could inspire international house hunting. A savvy portfolio addition? Yes, but this trend will be tricky on a worldwide scale as gentrification drives up prices in once-affordable locations, amplifying class divisions.

REAL ESTATE AND CO-LIVING SPACES GET REIMAGINED

As the remote work trend persists—and housing becomes increasingly expensive—urban adaptation could be the new real estate trend. The spate of empty commercial buildings in cities across the U.S. may soon be transformed into co-living and multi-use hubs. In 2024, Brownstone Shared Housing repurposed a San Francisco bank into bunkbed-style "sleeping pods" that rent for $700 a month. Dorm-like living (with a stylish upgrade) could become an appealing Age of Aquarius housing solution, offering private rooms with shared amenities, such as a kitchen, laundry, cafeteria and a built-in community to stave off isolation. The basic roommate situation just got rebranded (sorry, Monica and Phoebe).

GAS PRICES AND INTEREST RATES REMAIN HIGH

Despite campaign trail promises, the Republicans are unlikely to cause any massive, overnight shifts to consumer prices. Same for interest rates, which are controlled by the Federal Reserve along with (vastly international) supply chains. The cost of living will remain high with respect to income for many Americans, causing the true Pluto-in-Aquarius grassroots shift toward collectivism. Shared resources won't just be the domain of Rent The Runway and Zipcar. Co-op grocery stores won't just be the realm of wellness-obsessed Brooklynites. Get ready for some new models of economic pooling to emerge, ones that may run on the barter system or alternate forms of currency like trading time and labor to cover a portion of costs.

NEW DEVELOPMENTS IN ELECTRIC VEHICLE BATTERIES

Solid-state batteries, projected to transform energy storage in the next five to ten years, are gaining momentum for their safety, longevity and higher energy density compared to today's lithium-ion batteries. By replacing liquid electrolytes with solid materials, this technology offers solutions to key limitations in EVs and renewable energy storage, such as driving range and battery lifespan. While mass-market adoption may still be some years away, major automakers and tech companies are heavily invested in development. For investors, this creates a strategic window to monitor breakthroughs that could accelerate adoption. Solid-state batteries align with the shift toward sustainability and renewable energy, making them an exciting trend to follow closely.

URANIUM AND NUCLEAR ENERGY A (TRICKY) FOSSIL FUEL ANTIDOTE? Is it time to nuke

your portfolio—literally? In 2025, uranium is heating up as a major player in the energy market, especially as the world looks for sustainable, low-carbon power sources. Nuclear energy is back in the spotlight, with advancements making it safer and more efficient than ever. This could spark a boom in uranium mining as countries aim to cut fossil fuel dependence and invest in cleaner, high-output options. With nuclear power's massive potential to generate energy with minimal emissions, uranium might just be the "it" commodity in the resource market. But it's not all smooth sailing—volatile prices, environmental concerns and tight regulations around mining mean there's a lot to watch as we venture into this nuclear-powered future.

SHROOM BOOM: THE PSILOCYBIN WAVE RISES So,

is it time to invest in that fungi farm? For the past decade-plus, Neptune in Pisces has popularized the use of "plant medicine." Psychedelics have been used to treat everything from depression to PTSD. Studies are underway to prove the positive impact of controlled psychedelics on mental and psychological health, conducted by the likes of Johns Hopkins and Brown University. States began to decriminalize psilocybin in 2019. Ever since corporate Saturn entered Pisces in 2023, investors are eyeing Big Psychedelics as a promising category, even though legalization was thwarted in 2024 ballot measures. Nevertheless, market research site Fact.MR predicts that the psychedelic market is projected to hit $1.18 billion by the end of 2034.

DIGITAL AND DECENTRALIZED FINANCE

Pluto's transit through "power to the people" Aquarius, which has already been previewed on and off since March 2023, shifts away from traditional banking and toward digital finance and decentralized currencies. Prior Pluto-in-Aquarius periods brought major economic reforms and new financial systems emerged, like the Coinage Act of 1792, which established the U.S. dollar and the national mint. In 2025, we anticipate continued disruption in financial markets as cryptocurrencies, blockchain and alternative assets gain further legitimacy. Time to add Bitcoin

to your portfolio? With some forecasters even projecting a "Bitcoin arms race" with Russia and China, what seemed farfetched a couple years ago could become a new investing norm.

THE FEDERAL RESERVE UNDER FIRE

As decentralized banking gains momentum, the regulatory powers of the Federal Reserve are likely to weaken, throwing the economy into uncharted waters for our modern times. With Musk, Trump and other billionaires on the cryptocurrency wagon, this threat to the Fed is more than likely. A period of turbulence and potential crashes could lie ahead. While this may potentially make way for a Pluto-in-Aquarius "new economy," the transition period will be anything but smooth. The Federal Reserve has the cosmos on its side as much as crypto does in 2025. Fun fact: The Federal Reserve was established by Woodrow Wilson in 1913—when the lunar nodes were similarly in Pisces and Virgo—as a means of stabilizing the banking system. Similarly, the first central bank was birthed by founding father Alexander Hamilton in 1781 when Pluto last spun through Aquarius.

INNOVATION

At a glance: *From renewable energy to machine learning, AI and 3D printing, this year's innovations are set to reshape daily life and pave the way for a more sustainable world.*

THE FOURTH INDUSTRIAL REVOLUTION IS HERE

Neptune's 1862-75 transit through Aries dovetailed with the Second Industrial Revolution, which pushed innovation in manufacturing and energy systems. Coal and steam redefined industry then, but as Neptune circles back to the Ram's realm for the first time since the 19th century, it's clear we need to pivot from fossil fuels to renewable sources. Geothermal energy, battery storage, and even fusion advancements could be key players in this transition. With mysterious, evolutionary Pluto in Aquarius, the sign that rules electricity and energy, we may tap into a totally new source of power in the coming years. As innovative Uranus and transformational Pluto meet in several 120-degree trines spanning 2024-30,

we'll see this develop. Interestingly, the 1770-71 Uranus-Pluto earth trines featured a peak moment in the First Industrial Revolution with the advent of a machine called the Spinning Jenny. This development moved textile production from the home to factory manufacturing. (This earth trine repeated again for the first time in September 2024 between Uranus in Taurus and Pluto in Capricorn.) From August 21 to September 15, 2025, Uranus and Pluto will form air trines in Gemini and Aquarius, a peak opportunity for the Fourth Industrial Revolution that could accelerate innovations in such fields as AI, technology, neuroscience, quantum computing, wind-powered industries, robotics, aeronautics and space development.

ARTIFICIAL SUPERINTELLIGENCE—ARE WE HEADED FOR DINOSAUR STATUS?

Claude, you're so basic! The next era of AI is being created to match, then surpass, our human cognitive capacities. Our homo sapiens brains may not be built for actual multitasking, but they might not need to once Artificial General Intelligence (AGI) and, next, Artificial Superintelligence (ASI) are developed. While top researchers have declared these decades away, OpenAI's Sam Altman (a triple Taurus) boldly asserted that AGI could be engineered and deployed as early as 2025. Will this empower us as citizens or will it hand corporations control over our data, rights and sovereignty? It's a debate that's certain to shape the Pluto in Aquarius era to 2044 and beyond.

PUBLIC TRANSPORTATION, AUTONOMOUS VEHICLES AND...FLYING CARS?

How we get around could evolve as two of the most future-forward planets, Jupiter and Uranus, spend time in Gemini, the sign that governs transportation. Expect more cities to offer e-bike and e-car

sharing programs that help citizens get around with a lower footprint. Public transportation in cities like LA and Seattle, arguably underutilized, could get a friendly facelift with increased safety measures and amenities at stations that woo the professional commuter. Driverless cars, or "autonomous vehicles" as they're being called, are projected to populate

more roads in 2025, with Uber rolling them out in Atlanta and Tesla's recently-debuted cybercab. But perhaps the most jaw-dropping of them all will be the Alef "Model A," a flying car that can rise vertically above traffic to beat congestion, while otherwise functioning as an eye-catching road vehicle. With a projected price tag of nearly $300K, these won't solve gridlock overnight. But much like Henry Ford's Model T, released in October 1908 during a prior Saturn in Aries period, this will just be the beginning as we move into the air sign-heavy second half of the 2020s.

SMARTPHONES GET SMARTER

Smartphones could get a jaw-dropping upgrade, as revolutionary Uranus spins into Gemini, the sign that rules telecommunication. During this seven-year cycle, mobile devices may morph into hyper-intelligent companions: advanced AI-driven personal assistants capable of anticipating needs, real-time language translation and enhanced AR capabilities. The prior Uranus-in-Gemini cycle brought TVs into homes and the prototype of the first computer. This time around, that phone in your pocket could become an even-more-indispensable hub for work, social life and everything in between.

BIG BROTHER RECOGNIZES YOUR FACE

With Saturn and Neptune moving into Aries, the sign ruling the face, 2025 is primed for major advancements in facial recognition technology, especially as it intersects with Uranus in Gemini's machine learning and AI innovations. Saturn spawns next-level precision and structure, making software accurate and reliable. Meanwhile, Neptune adds an element of subtlety that could help devices detect minute facial expressions and identify emotional states. New debates about privacy and data ethics will be sparked as the technology becomes more widely (mis)used and refined.

3D-PRINT ME A SANDWICH, PLEASE?
Move over, air fryers and Instant Pots! With Jupiter in culinary Cancer starting June 2025, innovation in food production is set to accelerate. Get ready to 3D print your kids' lunches into fun shapes and stackables. Breakthroughs in lab-grown proteins can also help address food scarcity while easing environmental pressures on traditional farming. These developments may help to alleviate food insecurity in underserved areas. However, as alternative foods gain momentum, wellness advocates could raise legitimate concerns about the long-term health and environmental impacts of synthetic food sources.

EVS KEEP ON ROLLING
With both expansive Jupiter and sci-fi Uranus in mobile Gemini, the electric vehicle market will remain on the road to progress. 2025 will bring advancements in sustainable transportation around electric and hydrogen-powered vehicles. As governments push for greener initiatives, expect EV infrastructure to expand rapidly, including widespread installation of charging stations and advancements in battery technology, making eco-friendly travel more accessible and efficient. Opportunities to offer services and accessories for electric vehicles could open up new pathways to prosperity.

AGRICULTURAL INNOVATIONS AND SUSTAINABILITY
The South Node's tour through Virgo could sound the alarm around the need to support the world's agricultural providers and the landscape itself. Regenerative farming techniques that reverse the harm done will become more important than ever, ensuring that soil continues to be fertile for longer periods of time. As climate change, war and economic scarcity ramp up food insecurity for wide swaths of the world, agricultural technology may offer more interesting (and sometimes eyebrow-raising) solutions such as lab-grown meat and vertical farming.

WELLNESS

At a glance: Tech and innovation keep surging into the wellness world, fueling longevity and a customized approach to medicine.

BREAKTHROUGHS IN THE ADDICTION CRISIS

Saturn and the North Node in Pisces, the sign that rules mental health and addiction, is making 2025 ripe for major advancements in treatments. A groundbreaking clinical trial of a fentanyl vaccine, set for mid-2025, could shift the landscape of opioid treatment, blocking the drug's access to the brain and providing a powerful tool against relapse. Alcoholics Anonymous was established during the 1935 Saturn-in-Pisces transit. Eerily, Pisces musician Kurt Cobain—whose struggles with addiction defined much of his music—was both born and died during Saturn transits through Pisces.

INJECTABLES: THE NEW CURE-ALLS?

Sharp metal objects, like needles, are ruled by Aries. As business-savvy Saturn and healing Neptune are in this sign for part of 2025, injectable treatments could see another popularity spike. Semiglutides, like Ozempic and Tirzepetide, have been touted by celebrities from Oprah to Kelly Clarkson. Medi-spas have added these items to their roster, along with cosmetic injectables like Daxi, a Botox alternative which boasts a longer duration of wrinkle-busting results. Watch for IV clinics that offer care and prevention through Vitamin C drips and other energy boosters in that, er, vein.

OUTDOOR HOSPITALS?

With the lunar nodes in earthy Virgo and watery Pisces, hospitals and healthcare buildings will trend toward better use of their outdoor space. Medical centers will continue the trend of incorporating "healthscapes" (think: physical therapy on an outdoor bridge) and interiors that incorporate biophilic design elements such as natural lighting, trees and solariums.

THE HRT AND MENOPAUSE GOLD RUSH BUILDS

O give me a hormone? As Jupiter in Cancer amplifies our focus on female wellness, hormone replacement therapy (HRT) is set to become widely accessible and covered by more insurance policies. Formerly stigmatized by an erroneous study, HRT is fast becoming a proactive choice for managing symptoms of perimenopause and menopause, such as mood swings and cardiovascular health. For biological males and females alike, testosterone may also become tapped as a helper hormone to support cognitive function, bone density and sexual health.

AGING WITH DIGNITY, PURPOSE AND COMMUNITY

As the population lives longer, quality of life will become ever more important

for seniors. While Saturn, which rules elders, is in youthful Aries from March 24 to September 1, and compassionate Neptune dips into Aries from March 30 to October 22, society could make more efforts to restructure and accommodate its oldest residents. In Japan, there are currently over 8,000 "dementia cafes." The first one, The Restaurant of Mistaken Orders, was created by a Japanese

television director who wanted to change perceptions around aging and cognitive changes. People with dementia work as servers for a couple hours a day. And when a wrong or mixed-up order arrives tableside, as it frequently does, the server is treated with patience and kindness. These spaces were inspired by the original Alzheimer's Cafe movement that sprang up in The Netherlands in 1997, the last time Saturn was in Aries! Meanwhile, AI firms will continue to develop technology that allows loved ones to "live forever" with voice duplication and avatars to stay connected after they've passed away.

NEW AND AFFORDABLE HEALTH INSURANCE ALTERNATIVES

Struggling to afford those monthly health insurance premiums? With Pluto in Aquarius, the trend is moving toward flexible, patient-centered healthcare that keeps costs down and puts people first. Expect fresh alternatives to pop up in 2025 and beyond. Direct Primary Care (DPC) memberships are gaining popularity, offering unlimited access to your doc for a monthly fee. Micro-insurance options and pay-as-you-go telehealth services could emerge to offer coverage on an as-needed basis. Amazon is already experimenting with its One Medical services, which offers Prime members affordable healthcare at $9/ month membership, virtual visits from $29, along with prescriptions and in-person care in select areas. Next up: an AI "nurse" to take your pulse and vitals?

GENE KEYS: THE PERSONALIZED WELLNESS WAVE

Thanks to the pioneering energy of 2025's planets, biotech companies could roll out newly effective treatments for chronic diseases, alongside preventive vaccines for emerging global health threats. Uranus in Gemini could accelerate the accessibility of genetic engineering and personalized medicine. Over this seven-year cycle, gene editing technologies like CRISPR will become more refined and available to the public, enabling personalized treatment plans based on your genetic profiles. This level of precision could bring tailored therapies for everything from cancer to rare genetic disorders.

DATING

At a glance: A date with destiny—or a digital dupe? Commingling enters the quantum field opening up a brand new set of security issues.

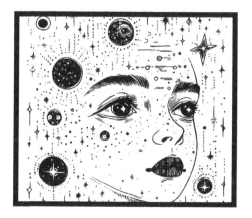

ROMANTIC REIGNS LOOSEN

Don't hate, individuate! The portmanteau has become passé, especially in the wake of last year's Bennifer 2.0 breakup. As Saturn and Neptune swing into self-sovereign Aries for part of the year, the trend toward individualism will rise. Boundary-hound Saturn could find us fiercely guarding the perimeters of our selfhood. Meanwhile, boundary-dissolving Neptune reveals where we might be stubbornly guarding our turf at the expense of love and connection.

AI CHANGES THE ROMANTIC PLAYING FIELD

As chatbots become more emotionally responsive, AI interactions could fill in loneliness gaps for people struggling with sentient seduction. Life could soon imitate the 2013 movie Her (which premiered the last time Jupiter was in Cancer) in which an isolated writer becomes obsessed with "Samantha," his AI assistant, voiced by Scarlett Johansson. (Seduce me, Siri!) Need some love advice but already exhausted your besties talking about that f-boy? Start a fresh thread with an AI-powered dating coach. Based on surveys and personal assessments, we may soon be getting real-time direction from a savvy chatbot who understands everything from our attachment styles to our romantic preferences.

DATE MY DUPE?

Romance will get a high-tech integration with AR and VR dating experiences becoming increasingly commonplace. Couples may meet for coffee in the metaverse, enjoying immersive virtual dates and holographic interactions. Having a bad hair day? Style your avatar and send that digital double onscreen as your iridescent understudy. But beware: As facial recognition software and AI-generated personas become more advanced, get ready for a new catfishing conundrum and widespread debate about the use of technology in our personal interactions.

SAPIOSEXUAL STIMULATION: SMART IS SEXY

Sorry, but those thirst trap gym selfies aren't gonna close the deal in 2025. As outer planets move from the sensual signs of Taurus and Pisces into

heady, intellectual ones (Aries, Gemini, Aquarius), brains become as important as brawn. Sapiosexual attractions, which arise from intellectual and conversational repartee, will spice up the boring dating landscape.

THE DANCE OF THE DEMISEXUAL: EMOTIONAL INTELLIGENCE

Once Jupiter moves into Cancer in June, demisexual relationships—in which attraction arises from a deep emotional connection—will be in the spotlight. If you've "done the work" with therapists, healers and your own damn journal while Saturn and Neptune have been in Pisces, this emotional intelligence will be a solid asset.

SEX AS A "WEAPON" A foreboding future for women's reproductive rights hovers like a cloud of fear over U.S. women, which could sharply impact hetero relationships in 2025. Some American women may follow in the footsteps of the South Korean 4B movement, which was born in 2019 when intimate-partner violence rates soared to 41 percent. In Korean, "bihon, bichulsan, biyeonae and bisekseu" translates into "no sex, no childbirth, no dating and no marriage with men." If federal protections are not returned to women's reproductive rights, this trend could ride the wave of the #MeToo or #ShoutYourAbortion movements of recent years.

RELATIONSHIPS

At a glance: Humans are wired to connect, but our mating patterns have changed since we moved from the Agrarian Age to the Aquarian Age. In 2025, relationships get a major remix as planets move into the playful, independent and renegade signs of Aries, Gemini and Aquarius.

RELATIONSHIPS BREAK FROM TRADITIONAL "I need space" was once the death knell of a relationship, but not in 2025. With Saturn and Neptune heading into self-sovereign Aries, carving out autonomy zones can be the saving grace for monogamous couples. Self-development work and individual healing will be required as the foundation for healthy relationships. The catch? This kind of exploration can trigger a host of emotions that need to be processed with a therapist instead of projected onto a partner. That might be optimized by embracing the "together apart" model. Think: separate homes, bedrooms, friend groups, even travel experiences as an antidote to the ennui that can set in from compulsory relational bonding. Monogamy doesn't have to mean monotony, as the saying goes.

VERY MINDFUL, VERY SECURE

Anxious meet avoidant? Not in the meet-cutes of 2025! With the South Node anchoring in sensible Virgo, having a "secure attacher" on your arm could become the romantic status symbol for another set of the population. A trusted, stable relationship will be #couplegoals, especially once Jupiter nestles into Cancer on June 9. Relationship retreats could spring up from Bali to Costa Rica, designed to teach mindful communication, healthy conflict resolution and overall relationship wellness.

PLANT MEDICINE AS A CURE FOR THE INSECURE

Longing for deeper connection but scared to drop your defenses? Couples struggling to get to the "next level" of intimacy may turn to psychedelics for support. As the North Node joins Saturn and Neptune in subconscious Pisces on January 11, it amplifies the desire for boundless connection. Guided therapeutic sessions using MDMA and psilocybin can help couples tap into deeper empathy and communicate without fear and ego. Although the FDA refused to approve MDMA-assisted therapy in 2024, esoteric Neptune's move into trailblazing Aries is certain to keep the fight for controlled legalization going strong.

THE NEW OLD-FASHIONED ROMANTICS—TRAD WIVES STICK AROUND

Next stop: Ballerina Farm? The #tradwife takeover isn't going away anytime soon. Emboldened by fall 2024's conservative election results and Mars spending the first quarter of the year in Cancer, we may see a new crop of "traditional wives" playing dress-up in the kitchen like Libra content creators Nara Smith and Cancer Hannah Neeleman. Home time and shared domestic bliss could become the new special occasion in 2025, especially as restaurant prices continue to soar. Instead of the polarizing #tradwife and #traddad, the influence of Jupiter and Uranus in equalizing Gemini may serve up a #domesticdreamteam in more moderate circles.

BEYOND THE COUPLE—NEW ARRANGEMENTS AND ROLES

In more progressive circles, devoted couples may opt to open their relationships in 2025, allowing for other sexual or romantic partners who meet a need that falls outside what the primary relationship can provide. Quads, closed Vs and throuples may become more common labels, lifting the veil of secrecy and shame off of non-monogamy. Polyfidelity, a lifestyle that coach Martha Beck has recently begun to share her experience with, could also gain popularity—an exclusive arrangement within an intimate group of three or more.

BEYOND THE BREAKUP Even breakups become fluid in 2025, which means "conscious uncoupling" could replace the messy divorce starting this year. This mindful methodology created by therapist Katherine Woodward Thomas helps people close out relationships with forgiveness, love and respect. It was famously used by Gwyneth Paltrow and Chris Martin in their amicable 2014 breakup, which took place the last time Jupiter was in Cancer.

FASHION

At a glance: A style revolution is in store as 2025's fashion blends retro rebellion, eco-conscious upcycling, and wearable tech.

PUTTING THE "APP" IN "APPAREL" Fashion and tech continue to merge with both pioneering Jupiter and innovative Uranus in Gemini. In 2025, we could see a rise in wearable technology, like garments embedded with wellness-tracking sensors. Smart fabrics that adapt to temperature, weather and other environmental conditions could find their way into everything from jackets to shoes. As the decade wages on, app integrations may give us control of everything from color to lighting effects of our clothes and accessories.

RETURN OF THE 1940S Calling all hepcats and kittens! "Youth culture" fashion sprang up in the 1940s, the last time Uranus rebelled in spritely Gemini. From two-piece bikinis to the word "teenager," this transit turned our halcyon days into an expressive era. (Bye, school uniforms!) In 2025, we could see a revival of this iconic period, when "hipsters" and "hepcats" rocked billowing Zoot Suits and Taurus Katherine-Hepburn made jaws drop with her gender-fluid penchant for tuxedos and tailored blazers. Destiny's Child alum Kelly Rowland welcomed Kamala Harris to the stage in Houston rocking a Zoot Suit in October 2024, giving us a preview of what's in store.

PROTEST FASHION It's important to note that Zoot Suits had already been popularized by African Americans in the jazz scene in the 1930s. And in the Forties, they became an emblem of resistance. Despite wartime fabric rationing, Mexican Americans in California adopted the generously-cut garb in protest of systemic racism and classism. Racial tension in 1943 led to the Zoot Suit Riots (not just the name of a big band swing song), a series of violent clashes between white U.S. servicemen and Latinos in Los Angeles. With rebellious Uranus back in Gemini this year, protest fashion such as flags, scarves (like the keffiyeh) and other symbology will continue to emerge as icons of social movements.

UPCYCLING AND CIRCULARITY—SUSTAINABLE FASHION SURGE
Speaking of fabric rations, it's no secret that the fashion industry is one of the world's biggest waste creators. Literal mountains of textiles have washed ashore in Ghana, tossed out to sea as retailers debut the next season's trends in rapid succession. In 2025, we will see moves to reduce this trend, partially from legislative restrictions and also from major fashion houses and brands looking to align their ethics with sustainability—and woo Gen Z and Gen Alpha consumers. Retailers looking to be associated with climate consciousness could offer in-store credits to customers who turn in gently-used garments to upcycling programs.

ECO-FRIENDLY MATERIALS
With the South Node in Virgo, the use of eco-friendly materials, such as organic cotton, recycled fabrics and biodegradable textiles (cactus leather!), could become mainstream, driven by consumer demand for environmental responsibility. Interestingly, Levi Strauss & Co. began manufacturing the first jeans when Neptune was last in Aries in 1873.

MILITARY FASHION With Saturn and Neptune in Aries, the sign that rules the military, get ready for a comeback of Spartan, war-era uniforms. Street style may soon look like a sea of pea coats and trenches, sailor-inspired styles (navy piping and bow ties), brass buttons, combat boots and pins. Couture prices, not necessary. Head to the secondhand bins at your local Army & Navy store.

SERPENTINE STYLE The Year of the Wood Snake could bring a round of snake-inspired fashion. 3D-printed "skins," made on vegan materials like Piñatex, a "leather" made from pineapple leaf fiber, could become the ethical version of this iconic texture. Accessories that rattle, strandlike earrings that dangle and rings and bracelets that wind around our limbs could appear as a paean to the python.

FAMILY LIFE

At a glance: From flexible love models to soul-deep emotional bonds, and a fresh take on "family" that goes beyond shared DNA, this year will expand the way we connect, nest, and foster intimacy.

LIVING THAT GOLDEN GIRLS LIFE Thank you for being a friend! As Gen X ages and "gray divorce" becomes more common (couples splitting after 50), being alone in an empty nest is not an appealing option for many. With Uranus moving into peer-based Gemini this year, savvy singles can make like Dorothy Zbornak, Blanche Devereaux and Rose Nylund, and form co-living arrangements to support each other through the golden years. The modern spin involves something more creative than the foursome's Miami home, however. How about converting a commercial building into multiple lofts, setting up tiny homes on a plot of land or investing in a vacation villa that will one day be your primary residence?

LEGAL RECOGNITION OF THE MODERN FAMILY

Historically, Jupiter in Cancer cycles have brought notable shifts in family recognition. Some were marked by milestone Supreme Court decisions, including The United States v. Windsor which granted federal recognition to same-sex marriage in 2013, and Loving v. Virginia, which lifted the ban on interracial marriage in 1967. In 2025, we may see some nations boasting policies reflecting expanded definitions around families—ones that are more inclusive of diverse relationships. (The United States will not be the leader here.) Multi-parent or co-parenting arrangements could gain traction, allowing extended families or even friends to legally share child-rearing responsibilities.

DEPOPULATION OR REPOPULATION?

With Pluto in Aquarius shaking up social structures, there's a push to reimagine "family" beyond the nuclear template. Inflation has made childrearing increasingly unaffordable, while the threat of climate change has many adults opting out of parenthood. Humanity has definitely reached a crossroads. Lower birth rates are already having an impact in places like Taiwan, Spain and Puerto Rico. This trend is reshaping the economic and social landscape. In 2025, expect to see more governments offering reproductive incentives for families, while also restricting birth control and abortion access. In 2024, China was already actively working to revive a "positive view of marriage and childbearing," according to the New York Times. Along with political propaganda, universities are developing courses on the topic while officials are going door-to-door to discuss pregnancy plans with women.

MINI BABY BOOM

With lusty Mars retrograde as we start the year—in fertile Leo and nurturing Cancer—we may see a crush of Mommy marketing targeted at twentysomethings. Once Uranus returns to Gemini midyear, where it last transited during the actual baby boom in the

POST-MARRIAGE FAMILIES—EXES COLLABORATE

Friendly exes may choose to remain in each other's lives, forming a supportive brand of platonic partnership that includes sharing expenses and raising kids. Expect new terminology (such as "parenting marriage") to spread, describing former duos who continue to coexist for a shared mission.

HOME SCHOOLING PODS

With the threat of gun violence and the rise of anti-trans sentiment, bullying and political divisiveness have turned schools into danger zones for many kids. In 2025, home schooling could hold appeal, especially while educational Jupiter is in domestic Cancer. No need for it to fall on the shoulders of a parent, either. Families may form education pods to create what our friend Danita refers to as a "micro-school," where kids learn together and socialize in small groups with a dedicated teacher.

1940s, there could be an unanticipated spike in birth rates. In June, Jupiter's move into homey Cancer could bring another fertility wave as people feel drawn to create their own cozy clans. The difference this time? The new boom of babies could be raised in a non-nuclear family structure.

SHALL WE NEST? MEET YOUR "NESTING PARTNER"

Expect to crave more TLC and companionship after Jupiter's midyear move into Cancer. A "nesting partner" is the roommate with benefits, someone who shares in the responsibility of making the house feel like a home. This might involve an exchange, for example, where one person cooks all the meals or remodels the second bathroom for reduced rent. With real estate prices skyrocketing and housing demand outpacing the inventory of homes, there's sound economic logic here, even if separate rooms are part of the game plan.

FOOD

At a glance: In 2025, food focuses on inside-out nourishment with biohacking diets and a fresh spin on fast food.

BIOHACK THE CLOCK

With outer planets moving into youthful signs like Aries and Gemini, expect to hear more about foods like bone broth and hemp seeds that boost cellular repair, reduce inflammation and sustain vitality. Collagen, popular for its skin-firming and joint-support benefits, may see increased use. Muscle-building supplements like creatine could become a more widespread ingredient in bars and powdered drinks for maintaining strength and resilience.

IS THAT VEGAN?

With the lunar nodes in compassionate Pisces and environmentally aware Virgo, the popularity of organic, sustainable and eco-conscious foods will continue to swell. Consumer demand may bring a fresh crop of farmers' markets and community food gardens as well as "small batch" productions of perishable foods.

AND HOW ABOUT THAT PACKAGING?

Brands that promote zero-waste packaging, vegan options and are transparent about sourcing from environmentally responsible producers through the supply chain will thrive as people align their personal health choices with a commitment to the planet. While we may see higher prices for these options, we anticipate larger manufacturers testing green packaging and prominently labeling that products are cruelty-free or vegan.

FOOD SHORTAGES AND FAMINES

Are those eggs gonna get cheaper? Unlikely, at least for the time being, as Uranus continues to destabilize economic trends until April 2026. As climate chaos ensues and supply chains continue to be impacted by geopolitical alliances, grocery bills will remain high. Food banks and discount grocers that sell overstock will see longer lines. Globally, Jupiter's move into Cancer on June 9 will force the world to deal with famines created by war and climate in places like Gaza, Yemen and Sudan.

DATA-DRIVEN DIETS Uranus in Gemini, historically linked to breakthroughs in communication and technology, will drive advancements in personalized wellness. In 2025, wearable tech, AI-powered health apps,

and genetic testing will offer data-driven solutions, allowing us to monitor health in real-time. But that's not where the data capture ends. With the Aries influence of individualization, we anticipate a new wave of apps that turn this information into highly customized eating and supplement plans, fitness regimens and lifestyle recommendations for preventative care and vitality.

A FRESH SPIN ON FAST FOOD

As enterprising Jupiter lands in Cancer, the food and restaurant industries will see both growth and innovation. Interestingly, both McDonalds and Burger King opened their doors during a prior Jupiter-in-Cancer transit from 1954-55. As we peer beyond the golden arches, we see a broadened expansion of fast food. The self-described "plant forward" chain Sweetgreen, which serves salads, grain bowls and lean proteins, plans to expand by 15% in 2025 and 20% in 2026. Next up: a bone broth bar? Or maybe a self-serve smoothie machine with programmable "toppings" like collagen shots, chia seeds and electrolytes. A wellness junkie can dream!

THE CULTURE OF CUISINE

Sharing meals is a common bond on every continent. With worldly Jupiter in Cancer, movements centered on protecting or reviving traditional cuisines could spring up. Culinary fusion could also hit big, a nod to bicultural identities. Once Uranus lands in Gemini on July 7, look for more experimental food combinations and the blending of global dishes with cutting-edge cooking technologies.

POLITICS

At a glance: *These trends suggest that 2025 will bring a mix of assertive leadership, increased nationalism, global diplomacy, technological regulation, and youth-led movements—all shaped by the transformative energy of Neptune in Aries and Uranus in Gemini.*

REPRODUCTIVE RIGHTS: FIGHT OR FLIGHT?

Combative Mars begins 2025 retrograde in Leo and Cancer, the signs of fertility and motherhood, fomenting anger around reproductive injustice—which may intensify with the March 14 and 29 eclipses, and Neptune's move into Aries on March 30. In 1873, during Neptune's prior Aries transit, the U.S. passed the Comstock Act, which criminalized the distribution of contraceptive information. The overturn of Roe v. Wade in 2022 has reignited similar debates, and this transit may evoke a fresh wave of protests and advocacy efforts, as activists and state lawmakers alike fight for policies that align with their beliefs. Telemedicine may become crucial for access and advocacy in states where abortion rights are restricted or under threat. As protective Jupiter moves into Cancer on June 9, we are likely to see more attempts to codify reproductive rights in progressive states, while more conservative ones may seek to strengthen restrictions. This ideological civil war could shift populations and spur migrations.

BILLIONAIRE TECH BROS: THE NEW THIRD PARTY?

If 2024 showed us anything, it's that Silicon Valley billionaires are shamelessly pulling political strings. From Elon Musk's frenzied endorsement of Donald Trump (including the illegal million-dollar sweepstakes) to Peter Thiel's backing of JD Vance and Jeff Bezos' endorsement snub of VP Harris in The Washington Post, tech bros are exerting influence. Not that it ends at the ballot: Musk, who's been trading phone calls with Putin since 2022, also owns the Starlink satellite network, which has been instrumental in Ukraine's ability to operate drones (or not) during the ongoing war. With Pluto in Aquarius for the next two decades, these tech oligarchs could bypass international law and move into an era of unchecked power.

SURGE IN NATIONALISM AND IDEOLOGICAL DIVIDES Leaders

will continue to lean heavily into national pride to rally support, which could mean heightened political polarization and a rise in debates over sovereignty, immigration and what it truly means to "belong." Expect (more) fiery rhetoric and campaigns that draw stark lines between "us" and "them," sparking fierce debates on national identity. Saturn in combative Aries could reinforce border wars, both literal and ideological, creating a high-stakes atmosphere where competing views on freedom, independence and belonging dominate global conversations. Celestial silver lining? The Berlin Wall fell when Jupiter was in Cancer in 1989, bringing hope for signs of unity.

IMMIGRATION UNDER FIRE

Immigrants have been the target of increased conservative ire since worldly Jupiter moved into a weakened "detriment" position in Gemini on May 25, 2024. As the transit continues through June 9, 2025, xenophobia could ramp up further. Uranus heads into Gemini on July 7 for the first time since the 1940s, a phase that coincided with part of the Holocaust and the heightened divisions that led to World War II.

XENOPHOBIA INTENSIFIES, ASYLUM ZONES FORM By June

9, when Jupiter moves into Cancer, the sign of family and safety, dogma around "homeland security" and "border control" will intensify. Race- and class-based nationalism will create deeper divisions among neighbors in certain regions. Uranus in Gemini will bring a radical shift in local government. Sanctuary cities with progressive policies may serve as asylum zones for immigrants and families with an immigrant parent in threat of deportation.

TECHNOLOGICAL REGULATION AND CYBERSECURITY CONCERNS

With Uranus in Gemini—a transit linked to technology breakthroughs of the 1940s such as the development of computers and radar—2025 will be a year where governments are racing to keep up with rapid change. Political leaders may turn their focus toward regulating emerging tech, from AI and quantum computing to cryptocurrencies, as these innovations reshape industries and economies. Cybersecurity will be a top priority, with new laws and international alliances aimed at guarding against cyber warfare and digital threats. (Sorry TikTok, the clock may be ticking for you.) As Uranus in Gemini drives tech to new heights, expect intensified efforts to protect data, privacy and national security in an increasingly connected world.

WHOSE FREEDOM OF SPEECH IS IT ANYWAY?

In 2025, free speech and expression are likely to become key battlegrounds, as planets create a charged atmosphere around personal liberties, censorship and societal control. The last time Pluto transited Aquarius (1778–98), societies witnessed radical changes with the rise of democratic ideals, revolutions and declarations of rights, as well as responses that aimed to suppress dissenting voices. Get ready for a similar cycle, where free speech reform and resistance to censorship—along with fierce hate speech and rhetoric—could intensify.

RISE OF BOLD, REFORMIST LEADERS

In response to the "red wave" of the U.S. elections, a grassroots movement of reformist leaders will emerge with plans to tackle today's biggest issues head-on. The last time Neptune was in Aries, figures like U.S. Presidents Abraham Lincoln and Ulysses S. Grant reshaped post-Civil War America, enacting sweeping Reconstruction reforms aimed at building a more just society. Fast forward to the 1930s and 40s, when FDR's New Deal programs transformed American life to combat the Great Depression, while global icons like Mahatma Gandhi sparked anti-colonial movements. Notably, Gandhi began his anti-violence fast in 1919 while Jupiter was in Cancer, emphasizing justice and compassion for all.

YOUTH-LED MOVEMENTS AND REVOLTS

With Pluto and Uranus making waves in expressive air signs, 2025 is poised to be a banner year for youth-led political movements and reform. Just as new communication methods and youth activism in the 1940s helped drive early civil rights movements and post-WWII cultural shifts, today's

young leaders are organizing around climate change, economic reform and social justice. Jupiter, which rules universities, in communicative Gemini since May 2024 (and until June 2025), has stirred intense campus clashes and global, student-led demonstrations around the Mideast conflict. Much like the Paris Student Riots that occurred when Saturn was in Aries in 1968, along with the U.S. riots that occurred after the assassination of MLK, we may see tension over social injustices boil into mass civil revolts.

GLOBAL ALLIANCES EMERGE

Global cooperation and domestic protection will be high priority, as leaders come together to tackle continued cross-border challenges. Past Uranus in Gemini cycles brought major alliance-building moments like NATO's founding in 1949, setting the stage for powerful partnerships. Now, as the high-minded planet returns to this position, expect a renewed focus on diplomacy and collective security,

with world leaders working overtime to stabilize volatile regions, address climate change and strengthen cybersecurity. This cosmic energy could bring a wave of international summits, with leaders signing agreements on everything from renewable energy initiatives to humanitarian relief for refugees in conflict zones.

A RETURN TO DIPLOMACY?

Midyear, Jupiter's nurturing vibe in Cancer brings a softer touch to diplomacy, inspiring humanitarian efforts that uplift vulnerable communities, foster global goodwill and protect women and children who were overwhelmingly victimized in the wars of 2024. Global leaders on the right side of history may join forces, creating a safer, more interconnected world through shared action.

WAR

At a glance: *Ongoing war seems unavoidable, as planets return to positions they were in during the French Revolution, U.S. Civil War and WWII, but in 2025, the tactics may change.*

INTENSE, REGIONAL CONFLICTS

Uranus in Gemini has historically coincided with intense, regional wars, some longer than others. The Arab-Israeli War and the Indo-Pakistani War both occurred during this transit in the 1940s. As we enter 2025, conflicts like these are raging around the globe and are likely to draw in major superpowers.

WATER WARS

With Neptune, the god of the seas, pirating its way through Aries, the sign of war, the crux of conflicts may revolve around fresh water resources and control over transboundary waters, which are shared by two or more nations. In the Middle East, disputes over the Tigris and Euphrates Rivers, as well as the Jordan River have erupted into outright wars. In Sudan, battles for the Nile River's resources are a key factor of social strife. In 2025, more water wars could erupt— or be resolved in ways that give new autocrats power over this increasingly valuable natural resource.

CIVIL WARS

Both Neptune in Aries and Uranus in Gemini are transits that have dovetailed with civil wars, such as the American Civil War, which began shortly before Neptune moved into Aries in 1862. As liberal and conservative factions continue to divide, we may see a rise in internal conflicts within nations, fueled by ideological divides and calls for independence or systemic reform. Groups will continue to mobilize on Signal, Telegram and Reddit. On the ground (and on your screen), battles may wage between the #tradwives and "childless cat ladies" who have very different definitions of a "femininomenon."

TECHNOLOGICAL WARFARE AND DRONES

Advancements in military technology could bring even more precision to weapons, which aligns with the warring energy of Saturn and Neptune in Aries. Previous transits introduced the Gatling gun in 1862. Firearms were used on the battlefield for the first time in Japan while Neptune was in Aries way back in 1548. In 2025, warfare will increasingly involve drones, AI and cyber attacks, allowing for more remote and precise combat. While this reduces the need for large troop deployments, it heightens the risk of civilian casualties. Simultaneously, gun control continues to be a fraught issue, dividing people politically for the rest of the decade.

CELEBRITIES

At a glance: Celebrities come in all formats in 2025, from the enviable off-duty It Couple, strolling arm-in-arm through LA, to the new crop of AI influencers who are real enough to turn the masses into superfans.

COZY COUPLES IN THE SPOTLIGHT

Met Gala moments are always fun, but Jupiter's move through casual Gemini and homey Cancer could bring a fascination with watching celeb couples in their off-duty downtime. Cozy duos who will lead this charge? We nominate Gemini Tom Holland, who is the ultimate bestie and champion for Virgo GF Zendaya. Marriage and babies could be in the cards for these two in 2025. Cancer Selena Gomez and Pisces Benny Blanco could turn us all into homebodies with glimpses into Benny's self-described "kooky" pad, complete with plush oversized couches, a custom-built pizza oven and a kitchen full of cookbooks. Cancer singer Kali Uchis and Gemini Don Toliver, who became parents last year, are solid candidates for a reality show about Gen Z family life.

MOVE OVER, MADAME TUSSAUD...YOUR BOT HAS ARRIVED

AI celebrities could walk the virtual red carpet in 2025, becoming movie stars in their own right (though we're not betting on any Oscar nods quite yet). These hyper-realistic, interactive avatars will respond, evolve and even "perform," in real-time. They may become for today's kids what YouTube celebrities are for Gen Z and Gen Alpha. Soon enough, these virtual influencers could secure brand deals, film roles and ad campaigns. Start crafting your avatar now, because you might be its future momager!

ARTISTS AND ARTIFICIAL INTELLIGENCE SETTLE THEIR DIFFERENCES?

Can actors and artists fight the tide of AI—or are we headed into an "if you can't beat the bots, join 'em" era? In February 2025, the first AI-enhanced single will be up for a Grammy.. "Now and Then," the Beatles' final song, uses technologically remastered original vocals by John Lennon and guitar recordings by George Harrison, with new contributions by the two surviving band members, (Gemini)

Paul McCartney and (Cancer) Ringo Starr, who both have Jupiter in their signs in 2025.

COLLECT MY NFTS

Celebrity NFTs could go through a second, AI-assisted wave, giving fans exclusive access to their favorite stars in collectible, limited-edition form. Drops could feature everything from a Cowboy Carter virtual tour with Beyoncé to Taylor Swift's iconic Eras to Rihanna and A$AP Rocky's capsule collection of best looks. Sports NFTs could also have a second wave in ways far more interesting (and interactive) than the NBA Top Shot cards of 2021 with simple highlight moments selling for fees more jaw-dropping than LeBron's famous dunk. Think: augmented reality with VIP experiences and limited-edition digital memorabilia. A recent partnership between Disney Music Group and Audioshake will unlock new listening experiences from Disney's vast catalog. Get ready for a unique wave of pop culture marketing, as everything old becomes futuristically new again.

A NEW WAVE OF POLITICAL AND PATRIOTIC MUSIC

Rage against the machine? As a conservative wave unleashes on the United States in 2025, music will be the outlet it's always been for expressing anti-government beliefs, fighting oppression and providing cathartic release for marginalized groups. With the North Node joining Neptune and Saturn in Pisces, the sign of resistance and poetry, this genre will go beyond

TikTok dance memes. Get ready for a new crop of albums like Public Enemy's It Takes a Nation of Millions to Hold Us Back, which dropped during this same nodal transit in 1988. Simultaneously, musicians across the globe could record patriotic anthems, underscoring the growing trend toward nationalism, which intensifies while Jupiter is in Gemini and Cancer.

CELEBRITY ACTIVISM

Bold, outspoken celebrity activism sweeps in with 2025's transits that are all about breaking norms and pushing for social reform. Just as stars in the 1940s and 1960s rallied against war and fought for civil rights, today's celebrities will continue to champion climate action, racial justice and gender equality. Music festivals could evolve into awareness events and fundraisers, with a blend of

high-visibility headliners (Miley! Charli!) to indie breakouts like the openly bisexual Gemini Steve Lacy and Capricorn Dominic Fike with his unique perspective on recovery, prison reform and second chances.

FIGHT SONGS, RAP BATTLES AND DIVA DUELS

They're not like us? With warrior Aries and catty Gemini energy flowing around, the (Scorpio-Gemini) Drake-Kendrick era of rap battles is certain to get beefier. While these back-and-forths may be part of hip hop's tradition, tea-spilling song titles and lyrics may continue to seep across genres and genders.

ANTI-HEROES IN THE LIMELIGHT

Guerilla-style activism, recorded for TikTok and YouTube, could turn renegade anti-heroes into a new kind of celebrity for the Age of Aquarius. With Neptune in Aries, social justice work could turn into its own form of performance art, in the spirit of Aquarius Banksy. Artists like Chappell Roan and Tyler the Creator, both Pisces, could provide the mood and soundtrack for this renegade, politically awakened genre.

THE ARTS

At a glance: *Arts and entertainment blend tech-driven, immersive experiences with raw, unfiltered realism. Expect everything from VR exhibitions and interactive stories to politically charged art that tackles contemporary issues—along with a burst of nostalgic family TV.*

ESCAPISM AND SPECIAL EFFECTS

Forget about a simple stroll through a gallery this year. The North Node's tour through Pisces pumps up the collective desire for escapism. In 2025, VR art and interactive exhibitions bring a new dimension to modern art. Expect multi-sensory installations that invite audiences to step right into the piece itself and engage in ways we've only imagined. We may see a resurgence of rom-coms and romance novels that play out idealized representations of love—as well as sci-fi movies like 2024's The Substance with next-gen special effects that sweep us into an alternate universe.

LET'S WRITE THIS SCRIPT TOGETHER, SHALL WE?

The audience becomes the creator! With Uranus in partner-powered Gemini, TV shows and some movies may have multiple plot twists and endings, based on the viewer's input. As AR and AI technology develops, interactive control of narratives may turn us into characters in the stories themselves, much like a next-level video game. This trend will make the storytelling experience more personalized and participatory.

ART ALSO GETS REAL

Across the board, a movement AWAY from romanticism will slowly unspool. As surreal Neptune lands in unabashed Aries, a defiant artistic movement may arise that embraces raw, in-your-face stories. Neptune's last transit from ethereal Pisces to aggressive Aries marked a shift in the arts from Romanticism to Realism, and the birth of what we consider "modern art." As the first movement to openly challenge institutional norms, Realism pushed back against the elite Academy of Art, staging independent exhibitions and focusing on subjects formerly not deemed worthy of representation, such as working class people and urban scenes. Today's anti-establishment wave could surface through stripped-down, acoustic "live sessions," lo-fi graphics (think: 'zines put together on a Xerox machine), and films in the spirit of the 1990s Dogme 95 movement, whose manifesto pledged to focus on traditional stories and action sans special effects.

RAW POLITICAL COMMENTARY

In the late 1960s, Saturn in Aries fueled music, art and literature that captured the spirit of protests and civil rights movements. When the ringed planet toured the Ram's realm in the late 1930s, the Social Realism movement portrayed the pain of the Depression era, using art to depict the socioeconomic inequities of the time. Now, in 2025, we're in for a new wave of ideological art that tackles today's biggest issues like climate change, racial justice and political divides. Artists will use their voices, canvases and lyrics as both commentary and calls to action, creating work that doesn't just reflect the times but inspires change.

A RETURN TO RAUNCHINESS

Raunchy humor makes a comeback as Saturn and Neptune move into unga-bunga Aries. In 2024, Billie Eilish and Charli XCX tried to "guess the color of my underwear" and Chappell Roan got graphic about her "knee deep in the passenger seat" moments. But will the rules of the game become lopsided, with female-identified performers taking on the swagger once reserved for sexist men? The line could get blurry. Simultaneously,

there could be a bro backlash from male entertainers who feel "restricted" by the global move toward inclusivity. Comedians may buck against cultural sensitivity, pushing the offensiveness to new lows.

FAMILY-ORIENTED AND NOSTALGIC CONTENT

With Jupiter in cozy Cancer, family-friendly content will be in the spotlight, highlighting the current state of domestic life. Modern Family debuted during the last Jupiter-in-Cancer cycle of 2013-14, as well as Transparent, the series centering around a family's experience with their father's gender transition. Jupiter's 1978 swing through Cancer evolved to Diff'rent Strokes, which tackled issues of race, class and adoption. The 1954-55 Jupiter in Cancer cycle brought pillars of the era's "family television," like Lassie and Father Knows Best. Nostalgic series from the early days of TV could gain popularity and even be turned into modern-day reboots.

TRAVEL

At a glance: Have local guide, will travel. In 2025, journey will be more immersive—and less disruptive—of the native environments. Restorative, health-based travel will also be popular, so start scoping out retreats.

LOW-IMPACT TOURISM With

the South Node moving through eco-conscious Virgo, and Uranus finishing up the last parts of its seven-year journey through Taurus, opt for low-impact travel that leaves a smaller footprint. Look for a rise in eco-friendly accommodations, carbon-offset options and destinations dedicated to conservation and sustainability. Conscious explorers will be drawn to lush eco-lodges, renewable energy-powered stays and guided trips that respect local ecosystems and support the indigenous people and residential businesses. Cultural awareness orientation may be integrated into the registration and welcome process for retreats and visits to off-the-beaten-path destinations.

WELLNESS AND RETREAT

TRAVEL With the North Node joining Saturn and Neptune in healing Pisces, wellness travel continues to have a heydey. Yoga and meditation will be huge draws, along with holistic spa services and customized menus that involve a "detox" or "reset." Retreats may offer plant medicine ceremonies, sound baths and other soul work. With the 9 Universal Year's emphasis on rest and renewal, travelers will flock to serene locations to unwind and connect to their spiritual intelligence

LIVE LIKE A LOCAL Take a hard

pass on those well-worn tourist traps. As nomadic Jupiter nestles into intimate Cancer on June 9, travelers will crave authentic connections, with experiences that bring them closer to local traditions, flavors and hidden gems—ones that are increasingly hard to find as social media turns every "best-kept secret" into a crowded hotspot. Vacationers may adopt a cameras-off policy, opting to NOT share every moment (or even the fact that they're off the grid) on Insta, but rather, to cherish the memories privately, staying present to experience them fully.

Made in United States
North Haven, CT
03 January 2025

63898961R00343